Gilbert Stuart

Gilbert Stuart

Carrie Rebora Barratt and Ellen G. Miles

The Metropolitan Museum of Art, New York

Yale University Press, New Haven and London

This catalogue is published in conjunction with the exhibition "Gilbert Stuart," which has been organized by The Metropolitan Museum of Art, New York, and the National Portrait Gallery, Smithsonian Institution, Washington, D.C. The exhibition is on view at The Metropolitan Museum of Art, October 21, 2004–January 16, 2005; and, for the National Portrait Gallery, at the National Gallery of Art, Washington, March 27–July 31, 2005.

The exhibition is made possible by The Henry Luce Foundation, The Peter Jay Sharp Foundation, and the Donald W. Reynolds Foundation.

The George Washington Gallery at The Metropolitan Museum of Art is made possible by First American Funds and U.S. Bank.

The catalogue is made possible by The Henry Luce Foundation.

Additional support for the catalogue has been provided by the William Cullen Bryant Fellows of The Metropolitan Museum of Art.

Published by The Metropolitan Museum of Art, New York
John P. O'Neill, Editor in Chief
Margaret Aspinwall, Senior Editor
Bruce Campbell, Designer
Sally Van Devanter, Production Manager, with the assistance of Zoya Feldman
Minjee Cho, Desktop Publishing

Unless otherwise specified, all photographs were supplied by the owners of the works of art, who hold the copyright thereto, and are reproduced with permission. Photographs of works in the Metropolitan Museum's collection are by the Photograph Studio, The Metropolitan Museum of Art; new photography is by Bruce Schwarz. Additional photograph credits: cat. 8, Sotheby's, New York; cat. 20, Jamison Miller; cat. 21, Jackson Smith; cat. 36, Malcolm Varon, N.Y.C. ©2003; cat. 43, Cathy Carver; cat. 55, Lorene Emerson; cat. 62, Collection of Judith and Steaven Jones ©2004 Museum Associates/LACMA.

Typeset in Caslon
Separations by Professional Graphics, Rockford, Illinois
Printed and bound by CS Graphics PTE Ltd., Singapore

Jacket / cover illustration: Detail of cat. 45, *George Washington* (the Lansdowne portrait), 1796. National Portrait Gallery, Smithsonian Institution, Washington, D.C.; acquired as a gift to the nation through the generosity of the Donald W. Reynolds Foundation (NPG.2001.13)

Frontispiece: Detail of cat. 6, *The Skater (William Grant)*, 1782. National Gallery of Art, Washington, D.C.; Andrew Mellon Collection (1950.18.1)

Cataloging in Publication Data is available from the Library of Congress.
    ISBN 1-58839-122-1 (hc)
    ISBN 1-58839-124-8 (pbk)
    ISBN 0-300-10495-2 (Yale University Press)

Contents

Sponsors' Statements

DONALD W. REYNOLDS FOUNDATION

In 2001, the Donald W. Reynolds Foundation provided a gift of $30 million to the Smithsonian's National Portrait Gallery to purchase and fund a national tour of Gilbert Stuart's Lansdowne portrait of George Washington. Our intent was to reintroduce our first president to children across the country and to assure that one of our nation's most recognizable and well-known portraits would be available for future generations of Americans to enjoy forever.

The trustees of the Donald W. Reynolds Foundation are pleased to support the organization of the exhibition *Gilbert Stuart* and its presentation in Washington, D.C., and to provide additional audiences the opportunity to view Gilbert Stuart's Lansdowne portrait of George Washington.

Steven L. Anderson
President
Donald W. Reynolds Foundation

FIRST AMERICAN FUNDS AND U.S. BANK

First American Funds and U.S. Bank Corporate Trust Services are pleased to sponsor the George Washington Gallery in the exhibition *Gilbert Stuart* at The Metropolitan Museum of Art. The gallery is an unprecedented display of fourteen paintings of the first president of the United States (and one of Martha Washington) painted by Gilbert Stuart.

The First American Funds mutual fund family is the fifth-largest bank-proprietary fund family in the United States as of June 30, 2004. The funds originated in 1981 and are advised by U.S. Bancorp Asset Management, a national investment firm that also provides customized portfolio management to private clients, corporations, public entities, nonprofit organizations, and other institutions. U.S. Bank Corporate Trust Services is the leading provider of municipal trust services and a top provider of corporate, escrow,

and structured finance services. The parent company of U.S. Bancorp Asset Management and U.S. Bank Corporate Trust Services is U.S. Bancorp, which is headquartered in Minneapolis.

Our sponsorship of the George Washington Gallery reflects our great admiration for George Washington, who represents First American Funds' corporate identity. His integrity, determination, and stability of leadership symbolize the attributes that we strive for in our business. Please enjoy the gallery with our best wishes.

Thomas Schreier
President, First American Funds
CEO, U.S. Bancorp
Asset Management

Diane Thormodsgard
President, U.S. Bank
Corporate Trust and
Institutional Trust & Custody

THE HENRY LUCE FOUNDATION

The Henry Luce Foundation is honored to support the exhibition *Gilbert Stuart* and its accompanyig catalogue. Organized by The Metropolitan Museum of Art and the National Portrait Gallery, this first retrospective of Stuart's portraits since 1967 will go beyond the familiar images of George Washington to introduce to a new generation one of America's best-known but perhaps little-understood artists.

The foundation is pleased that the Stuart exhibition joins the roster of 200 exhibitions it has supported that explore American art and creativity. Established in 1982, the foundation's American art program is dedicated to scholarship in American art history and to raising awareness of it both in the United States and overseas. Since the program's inception, the Luce Foundation has distributed more than $100 million to some 250 museums, universities, and service organizations in 47 states, the District of Columbia, and the United Kingdom.

Established in 1936 by the late Henry R. Luce, co-founder and editor-in-chief of Time Inc., the Luce Foundation also supports higher education, Asian affairs, theology, women in science and engineering, and public policy and the environment. The foundation's support of the Metropolitan Museum over the years includes several major exhibitions, funds for the two-volume catalogue *American Sculpture in The Metropolitan Museum of Art*, and, most notably, the establishment in 1988 of the Henry R. Luce Center for the Study of American Art—the pioneer of visible art-storage centers for permanent collections.

The Luce Foundation congratulates the Metropolitan Museum's talented staff for its continued devotion to American arts, as evidenced by this beautiful and compelling exhibition of the works of one of America's art-historical forefathers, Gilbert Stuart.

Michael Gilligan
President
The Henry Luce Foundation

THE PETER JAY SHARP FOUNDATION

The Peter Jay Sharp Foundation is honored to support the exhibition *Gilbert Stuart* at The Metropolitan Museum of Art. This presentation expresses our continuing interest in encouraging the public's exposure to the richness of American artistic production.

While the foundation's main focus is to improve the quality of life in the New York metropolitan area, we have supported schools and institutions ranging in scope from the Princeton University Art Museum and cancer research at Johns Hopkins Medical School to the Washington-based Conservation Fund.

We thank Philippe de Montebello and his remarkable staff at The Metropolitan Museum of Art for organizing this wonderful insight into the early days of our Republic. Gilbert Stuart recorded a cross section of this country's early residents. We are pleased to help expose his special view of our nation's beginning.

Norman L. Peck
President and Director
The Peter Jay Sharp Foundation

Directors' Foreword

The most successful and resourceful portraitist of America's early national period, Gilbert Stuart (1755–1828) possessed enormous natural talent, which he devoted to the representation of human likeness and character, bringing his witty and irascible manner to bear on each of his works, including his incisive portraits of George Washington. This retrospective exhibition presents new art-historical ideas and research about Stuart's paintings, working methods, and relationships with his patrons. It highlights his achievement by showing a carefully chosen group of portraits of exceptional quality, ranging in date from the early works he produced in Newport, Rhode Island, in the early 1770s to those executed in Boston just before his death. The sites of Stuart's production provide the logical framework for the organization of the exhibition.

Stuart developed and maintained a distinctive portrait style, tailoring his work to suit his subjects. He began his career in his hometown of Newport, where he showed the first signs of genius, not merely precocious talent but adept technique controlled by his rather quirky and appealing take on contemporary portraiture. He mastered the techniques of the English late-eighteenth-century grand manner during his years in London (1775–87) and Dublin (1787–93). From Dublin, Stuart went to New York, where he filled a large number of commissions in a short period with remarkable skill, making his reintroduction to America a huge success. There he also secured an introduction that enabled him to paint President George Washington.

In 1794 Stuart moved to Philadelphia, where he arranged for sittings with Washington. A special section of this exhibition is devoted to Stuart's portraits of the first president of the United States, with key examples of each type: the so-called Vaughan, Athenaeum, and Lansdowne portraits. Accustomed to putting his clients at ease by engaging them in conversation, even joking with then, Stuart was at a loss with Washington, writing to a colleague, "An apathy seemed to seize [Washington] and a vacuity spread over his countenance, most appalling to paint." The artist, of course, prevailed, and the exhibition explores these famous and popular works by addressing issues of patronage, image, technique, chronology, and interpretation. From Philadelphia, Stuart followed the federal government to Washington, D.C. (1803–5), where his experiments with images of statesmen and diplomats, including Thomas Jefferson and James Madison, were an unqualified success. In Boston, where Stuart lived out his life, he painted richly nuanced portraits, retaining his technical and perceptive talents to the end.

The exhibition and catalogue result from the collaboration of Carrie Rebora Barratt, Curator of American Paintings and Sculpture and Manager of The Henry R. Luce Center for the Study of American Art at The Metropolitan Museum of Art, and Ellen G. Miles, Curator of Painting and Sculpture at the National Portrait Gallery, Smithsonian Institution, Washington, D.C. Colleagues at both institutions, and at the National Gallery of Art, which kindly offered to be the Washington venue since the National Portrait Gallery is closed for renovation, have worked to bring this splendid exhibition to fruition.

We express our great appreciation to the lenders to this exhibition and hope that they will share in the pleasure that comes from presenting a display that so richly represents Stuart's career.

We are grateful to The Henry Luce Foundation, which pledged support for this project at the Metropolitan Museum when the publication and exhibition were in their nascent stages. The Donald W. Reynolds Foundation enabled the acquisition, as a gift to the nation, of Gilbert Stuart's greatest American painting, the Lansdowne portrait of George Washington, and has supported the organization of the exhibition and its presentation in Washington, D.C. The Metropolitan also acknowledges the generosity of The Peter Jay Sharp Foundation for its grant toward the exhibition in New York. The George Washington Gallery at the New York venue is made possible by First American Funds and U.S. Bank. Additional funding for the catalogue has been provided by the Metropolitan Museum's William Cullen Bryant Fellows.

Philippe de Montebello
Director
The Metropolitan Museum of Art

Marc Pachter
Director
National Portrait Gallery, Smithsonian Institution

Lenders to the Exhibition

Acknowledgments

An exhibition is manifested as a museum installation, in a publication, and in its contribution to scholarship and museum studies. And thus it is that we avail ourselves, in these acknowledgments, of the opportunity to thank our colleagues in all aspects of the project. Over the past four years we have worked with scores of individuals who have enriched our presentation of Gilbert Stuart's work.

We begin with thanks to those within our own institutions, The Metropolitan Museum of Art and the National Portrait Gallery, recognizing the spirit of teamwork and collaboration that must exist for any major exhibition to reach fruition. At the Metropolitan Museum, we are grateful, as always, for the wisdom and guidance of Philippe de Montebello, Director, whose enlightened leadership makes all things possible at the Museum. In partnership with him, associate directors Mahrukh Tarapor and Doralynn Pines resolved myriad complexities. We also thank Martha Deese, Sian Wetherill, Suzanne Rubin Schein, Tanya Maggos, Betsy Wilford, and Amanda Maloney in their offices. Linda Sylling expertly managed the team responsible for the installation. Emily Kernan Rafferty and members of the Development Department, particularly Nina McN. Diefenbach, Andrea Kann, and Kerstin M. Larsen, helped us with logistics and fund-raising. Sharon H. Cott and Rebecca Noonan drew up the exhibition contracts. We also thank Kathleen Arffman and Suzanne Shenton of Visitor Services, and Nicholas W. Apps of Special Events.

This Metropolitan Museum publication is one of many overseen this year by John P. O'Neill, and we are in awe of his ability to continually make beautiful books that elegantly suit their subject matter. We thank him and his highly skilled staff in the Editorial Department for giving a lasting vehicle to our notions about Stuart and his work. The editor for this project was our perceptive colleague Margaret Aspinwall, with expert assistance from Kathleen Howard, Nancy Cohen, Jacolyn A. Mott, Alarik Skarstrom, Fronia W. Simpson, and others. Peter Antony guided the book through production with Gwen Roginsky, Sally Van Devanter, Minjee Cho, and Paula Torres. Connie Harper-Castle aided us in the ordering of photographs. The book was promoted and distributed by Yale University Press.

Our colleagues in the American Wing offered unflagging support and brought diverse expertise to bear on our researches on Stuart. We particularly thank Morrison H. Heckscher, H. Barbara Weinberg, Alice Cooney Frelinghuysen, Kevin J. Avery, Thayer Tolles, Amelia Peck, Peter M. Kenny, and Beth Carver Wees. On a daily basis, the exhibition was handled by Catherine Scandalis, who graciously applied her aptitude for details, forethought, and problem-solving skills to so many aspects of this project. She was enabled in her work by Kathryn Sill, Katie Banser, Karen Zimmerman, Jeanne Ko, Elaine Bradson, and Rachel Bean. We were extremely fortunate that Karen Sherry came at a crucial time to help us meet deadlines. Over the past four years, a crew of talented assistants came our way through the Museum's internship program. Their work in the trenches—photocopying, collating, filing—often delivered gratifying results, including the discovery of locations for paintings, new archival sources, and more. For their help we thank Suzanne Bailey, Elizabeth Clark, Kimberly Curtiss, Daniel R. Koch, Isabel S. Lowell, Shayna McConville, Victoria McGrath, Nanette Scofield, and Xiao Situ. We are also very fortunate to have had several sharp researchers from Sotheby's American Arts Course, including Josephine Patton, Franklin Perkins, and Therese Sathue.

We received expert help on dress in Stuart's portraits from Stéphane Houy-Towner in the Costume Institute Library and assistance on furniture portrayed from William Rieder in European Sculpture and Decorative Arts. Conservators assisted our research in significant ways, teaching us so much about what we often cannot see with the naked eye. We extend special thanks to Dorothy Mahon for examining many pictures with us and for tending to several paintings; to George Bisacca for his advice on Stuart's wood supports; to Pascale Patris for her help with picture frames; and to Hubert von Sonnenburg for his words of wisdom regarding the portraits of George Washington.

In the Metropolitan Museum's Photograph Studio, we relied upon Barbara Bridgers and Bruce Schwarz to make beautiful photographs, and in the Photograph and Slide Library we worked with Carol E. Lekarew and Sandra Wiskari-Lukowski. Kenneth Soehner and his staff availed us of every resource in the Thomas J. Watson Library. The Metropolitan's Registrar adjudicated loans and made the shipping arrangements for the exhibition. We thank Lisa Cain for her extraordinary efforts and extend gratitude to her entire department, especially Herbert M. Moskowitz, Aileen K. Chuk, Willa M. Cox, William Hickman, Gerald P. Lunney, John McCormack, Wayne Morales, and Jorge Roldan.

At the Metropolitan Museum, Daniel Kershaw designed the exhibition in partnership with Emil Micah as graphic designer. The show was installed by Donald Templeton, Gary Burnett, Sean Farrell, and Rob Davis. Egle Žygas, along with Harold Holzer, Elyse Topalian, Jennifer Oetting, and Diana Pitt, expertly communicated news of the exhibition to the press. Alice Schwarz and Elizabeth Hammer organized the myriad exhibition programs with advice from Kent Lydecker, Stella Paul, Teresa Russo, and Nicholas Ruocco. For features on the Museum's Web site, we thank Terri Constant and Liz Block.

At the National Portrait Gallery, Marc Pachter's leadership was indispensable to the project. As the man most responsible for acquiring Stuart's Lansdowne portrait for his museum, and hence the nation, in 2001, his efforts on behalf of this artist's legacy precisely coincided with ours. His support for the exhibition and the amount of staff effort, time, and energy that have gone into it are much appreciated. Even as the National Portrait Gallery was moved from its elegant building to new offices and, as of this writing, still awaits the reopening of its galleries, the staff infused this exhibition and publication project with vital energy and dedication. We thank Carolyn Carr for her special help, a blend of administrative abilities with an art historian's understanding of the material and a curiosity about eighteenth-century portraiture. Brandon Brame Fortune and Margaret Christman contributed a constant flow of answers to questions large and small, while Jessica Hoffman deserves extra credit not only for gathering photographs, but also for following up on countless details cheerfully and efficiently. Beverly Cox coordinated virtually every aspect of logistical arrangements with the assistance of Cindy Zarate of the Smithsonian Office of Contracts, while Pie Friendly and Maria Elena Gutierrez assisted with fund-raising. Linda

Thrift in the Catalog of American Portraits generously provided assistance with photographs, and Deborah Sisum and Susan Foster Garton contributed their knowledge and expertise. Cecilia Chin, Patricia Lynagh, Alice Clarke, Stephanie Moye, and Jesse Foley at the National Portrait Gallery/Smithsonian American Art Museum library were very helpful, as always. Molly Grimsley coordinated the arrangements for the transfer of the exhibition to and from Washington. We also thank Cindy Lou Molnar, Eloise Baden, Wendy Wick Reaves, Sidney Hart, David Ward, Frederick Voss, Andy Klafter, Dru Dowdy, Marianne Gurley, Jennifer Robertson, Eileen Kim, and Yvette Stickell. At the Archives of American Art, Richard Wattenmaker and Liza Kirwin offered research support at critical moments.

We express great appreciation to Earl A. Powell III, director of the National Gallery of Art, and his staff not only for their significant loans, but also for providing galleries for the exhibition when it became apparent that renovations to the National Portrait Gallery would not be completed in time for the show. In addition to Franklin Kelly, senior curator of American and British paintings, many other friends at the National Gallery became implicated in the process: Jamé Anderson, Gordon Anson, Faya Causey, Deborah Chotner, Ruth Anderson Coggeshall, Philip Conisbee, Elizabeth A. Croog, Rio DeNaro, Sally Freitag, Jason Herrick, Peter Huestis, Barbara Keyes, Donna Kirk, Mark Leithauser, Susan McCullough, Ross Merrill, Judy Metro, Christine Myers, John Olson, Isabelle Raval, Naomi Remes, Alan Shestack, Abbie Sprague, Melissa Stegeman, Michael Swicklick, D. Dodge Thompson, Tamara Wilson, Barbara Goldstein Wood, and Deborah Ziska.

Research for the exhibition and catalogue was carried out by a splendid team, to whom we express appreciation and debt. In New York, Lois Stainman lived and breathed Gilbert Stuart, pursuing research with the sort of passion and diligence we have come to expect from her. She paid special attention to Stuart's English portraits, and her discoveries contribute mightily to this project. Laura Mills filled the files on our Boston and Newport sitters until they bulged with material so rich that it became a challenge to write up the evidence within the allotted page count. In Ireland, Desmond Fitz-Gerald, the Knight of Glin, was in frequent contact with us throughout the project and very kindly introduced us to Aidan O'Boyle, an intrepid and intelligent doctoral candidate at Trinity College, Dublin, who was able to conduct research for us even while pursuing his own advanced studies. It is owing to his trips to the Public Record Office in Belfast that we are able to present so much new information on Stuart's Irish work.

A Curatorial Research Fellowship for 2002/2003 awarded to Ellen Miles by the Getty Grant Program enabled research on Stuart and his Philadelphia sitters. Funding from the Donald W. Reynolds Foundation for the tour of the Lansdowne portrait of George Washington made possible additional research at the William L. Clements Library in Ann Arbor, Michigan, and the Huntington Library in San Marino, California, while a lecture provided opportunity for study at the American Antiquarian Society in Worcester, Massachusetts. At the National Portrait Gallery, Emily C. Burns, who began work on Gilbert Stuart during a summer internship at the Metropolitan Museum and then moved to Washington, continued her research on his portrait subjects. Other members of an outstanding team of interns and volunteers who contributed to the research and writing of catalogue entries were Christopher H. Jones, Themis Chryssostomides, Edurne Poggi-Aranda, Virginia K. Burden, Kyra M. Swanson, and Sarah Efird Stephens. Special thanks go to Patricia Svoboda, who, with assistance of volunteers Cheryl Tennille, Nicole Becker, and Susan Cohen, translated for our use several French letters in the papers of Elizabeth Patterson Bonaparte at the Maryland Historical Society.

We owe thanks to our resourceful and generous colleagues who welcomed our visits, shared their knowledge of their collections, and otherwise helped us with everything from interpretations of the portraits or manuscripts in their care to the challenge of obtaining good photographs: David Chase, Allison Kemmerer, and Ruth Quattlebaum, Addison Gallery of American Art, Phillips Academy, Andover, Massachusetts; Georgia Barnhill, American Antiquarian Society; Robert S. Cox, American Philosophical Society, Philadelphia; Judith Barter, Denise Mahoney, Sarah E. Kelly, and Caroline Nutley, Art Institute of Chicago; Jeffrey Ray, Susan Drinan, and Randee Dutton, Atwater Kent Museum of Philadelphia; Sona Johnston and Beth Ryan, Baltimore Museum of Art; Fred Hill, James Hill, David Hill, Daisy Hill, and Bruce Weber, Berry-Hill Galleries, New York; Hina Hirayama, Boston Athenaeum; Katy Kline, Laura J. Latman, Linda J. Docherty, and Scott Dimond, Bowdoin College, Brunswick, Maine; Sheena Stoddard, D. J. Clark, and Stephen Price, Bristol Museums and Art Gallery; Richard Lapham and Gregory J. Godon, The Brook (Club), New York; Teresa Carbone and Ruth Janson, Brooklyn Museum; James Crawford, Canajoharie Library and Art Gallery, Canajoharie, New York; Louise Lippincott and Elizabeth T. Brown, Carnegie Museum of Art, Pittsburgh; Melina LaMarche, Christie's Images, Inc.; Richard Hampton Jenrette and Margize Howell, Classical American Homes Preservation Trust, New York; Bruce Naramore, Travis Bowman, and Anne Ricard Cassidy, Clermont State Historic Site, Germantown, New York; Kathleen E. McKeever, Henry Adams, and Monica Wolf, The Cleveland Museum of Art; Gina Woodward, College of William and Mary, Williamsburg, Virgina; Barbara Luck, Catherine H. Grosfils, and George H. Yetter, Colonial Williamsburg Foundation; Lynne Bassett, Connecticut Historical Society, Hartford; Sarah Cash, Nancy Swallow, and Kelly O'Neil Baker, The Corcoran Gallery of Art, Washington, D.C.; Jack Eckert and Tom Horrocks, Francis A. Countway Library of Medicine, Harvard Medical School, Boston; Melanie Blake, Courtauld Institute of Art, London; Theodore E. Stebbins Jr., Sandra Grindlay, Kimberly Orcutt, and David Carpenter, Fogg Art Museum, Harvard University Art Museums, Cambridge, Massachusetts; Susan Grace Galassi, Katherine M. Gerlough, and Diane Farynyk, Frick Collection, New York; Donna Kovalenko, Frye Art Museum, Seattle; LuLen Walker, Georgetown University, Washington, D.C.; Angela Mack and Joyce N. Baker, Gibbes Museum of Art, Charleston, South Carolina; Susanne Olson, Gore Place House Museum, Waltham, Massachusetts; Claudine Dixon, UCLA Hammer Museum, Los Angeles; Stuart P. Feld, Hirschl and Adler Galleries, New York; Kristen Froelich and Randee Dutton, Historical Society of Pennsylvania, Philadelphia; Jeanne Stalker and Sharon Longest, Homeland Foundation; Barbara J. MacAdam and Mark Mitchell, Hood Museum of Art, Dartmouth College, Hanover, New Hampshire; Alexandra Kappler, Jessica Smith, and Jacqueline Dugas, Huntington Library, Art Collections, and Botanical Gardens, San Marino, California; John Orbell, Moira Lovegrove, and Jane Waller, The Baring Archive, ING Bank NV, London; Robert Hitchings, Kirn Memorial Library, Norfolk, Virginia; Cindy Altman, Kykuit, Sleepy Hollow, New York; James A. Manninen, Legg Mason Wood

Walker, Boston; James Green, Library Company of Philadelphia; Saundra Taylor, Lilly Library, Indiana University, Bloomington; Alex Kidson, Liverpool Art Gallery; Bruce Robertson, Ilene Susan Fort, Giselle Arteaga-Johnson, Michele Brady, and Cheryle T. Robertson, Los Angeles County Museum of Art; Donna-Jean Metta, Town Office, Machias, Maine; Nancy Davis, Mary E. Herbert, Lance Humphries, and Helen Jean Burn, Maryland Historical Society, Baltimore; Jeffrey Mifflin, Massachusetts General Hospital, Boston; Mary T. Claffey and Kimberly Nusco, Massachusetts Historical Society, Boston; Trinkett Clark and Karen Cardinal, Mead Art Museum, Amherst College, Amherst, Massachusetts; Patrick Noon and DeAnn M. Dankowski, The Minneapolis Institute of Arts; Joan W. Kaufman, Mount Auburn Cemetery, Cambridge, Massachusetts; Linda Ayres, Barbara McMillan, Carol Cadou, Mary V. Thompson, and Dawn Bonner, Mount Vernon Ladies' Association; Faye Haur, Museum of the City of New York; Carol Troyen, Erica Hirshler, Sue Reed, Irene Konefal, and Lizabeth Dion, Museum of Fine Arts, Boston; Adrian Le Harivel, Aoife Lyons, and Marie McFeely, National Gallery of Ireland, Dublin; Karie Diethorn, National Park Service, Philadelphia; Jacob Simon, Lucy Peltz, Tim Moreton, and Emma Butterfield, National Portrait Gallery, London; Margaret Conrads and Stacey Sherman, The Nelson-Atkins Museum of Art, Kansas City, Missouri; Timothy L. Decker, The New Jersey Historical Society, Newark; Bert Lippincott, Newport Historical Society, Newport, Rhode Island; Lee Vedder, New-York Historical Society; Stefan Saks, Thomas Lisanti, Robert Rainwater, Clayton C. Kirking, and Roseanne Panebianco, New York Public Library; Lisa Little and Clare Baxter, The Northumberland Estates; Ron Hoffman and Rebecca Wrenn, Omohundro Institute of Early American History and Culture, Williamsburg; Brian Allen and Emma Floyd, Paul Mellon Centre for Studies in British Art, London; Patrick Leehey, Paul Revere House, Boston; Kim Sajet, Aella C. Diamantopoulos, Barbara Katus, Sylvia Yount, and Judy Hayman, Pennsylvania Academy of the Fine Arts, Philadelphia; Kathleen A. Foster and Stacy Bomento, Philadelphia Museum of Art; Matthew Schultz, Philadelphia Society for the Preservation of Landmarks; Ed Desrochers, Phillips Exeter Academy, Exeter, New Hampshire; Sherrie Goodhue, Pickering House, Salem, Massachusetts; Susan Danly, Portland Museum of Art, Portland, Maine; Maureen McCormick, John Wilmerding, Alexia Hughes, Barbara Oberg, and Martha J. King, Princeton University, Princeton, New Jersey; Cheryl V. Helms, Lisa Long, Maris Humphries, and Laurel DeStefano, Redwood Library and Athenaeum, Newport, Rhode Island; Edward F. Sanderson, Rhode Island Historical Preservation and Heritage Commission; Rick Stattler, Rhode Island Historical Society Library, Providence; Maureen O'Brien, Tom Michie, and Melody Ennis, Museum of Art, Rhode Island School of Design, Providence; Bertha Saunders, Rockefeller Collection, New York; Judith M. Guston, Karen Schoenewaldt, Rosenbach Museum and Library, Philadelphia; Stella Mason, Royal College of Surgeons, London; Robert Schwarz, Robert Schwarz Jr., Marie Schwarz, and David Cassidy, Schwarz Gallery, Philadelphia; Stephen Lloyd, James Holloway, and Susanna Kerr, Scottish National Portrait Gallery, Edinburgh; Michael Goodison, Smith College Museum of Art, Northampton, Massachusetts; Susan Palmer, Sir John Soane Museum, London; Melinda Talbot, Society for the Preservation of New England Antiquities, Boston; Lucy Fenwick, Sotheby's, London; Hopewell Norwood, Sotheby's, New York; Marc Simpson, Brian Allen, and Monique Le Blanc, Sterling and Francine Clark Art Institute, Williamstown, Massachusetts; Anna Sheppard, Tate, London; Susan R. Stein, T. Jefferson Looney, Lisa Francavilla, and Jessica Tyree, Thomas Jefferson Memorial Foundation, Monticello, Virginia; Anne Crookshank and Philip McEvansoneya, Trinity College, Dublin; Barbara Wolanin, United States Capitol, Washington, D.C.; John C. Dann, Barbara De Wolfe, and Arlene Phillips Shy, William L. Clements Library, University of Michigan, Ann Arbor; Kevin Cawley and Sara Weber, University of Notre Dame, South Bend, Indiana; Jacqueline Jacovini and Albert Porter, University of Pennsylvania Art Collection, Philadelphia; Frank Futral, Roosevelt-Vanderbilt National Historic Sites, U.S. Department of the Interior, National Park Service, Hyde Park, New York; William R. Johnston, The Walters Art Museum, Baltimore; Eleanor P. DeLorme, Jewett Art Center, Wellesley College, Wellesley, Massachusetts; William C. Allman, Lydia Tederick, and Harmony Haskins, The White House, Washington, D.C.; Leslie Greene Bowman, Wendy Cooper, and Anne Verplanck, Winterthur Museum, Winterthur, Delaware; Rita Albertson, Philip Klausmeyer, Kate Lau, David Brigham, and Selina Bartlett, Worcester Art Museum, Worcester, Massachusetts; Robin Jaffee Frank and Suzanne Warner, Yale University Art Gallery, New Haven, Connecticut.

We are also grateful to staff members at the following organizations: Albany Institute of History and Art; Allentown Art Museum; American Embassy, Dublin; American Irish Historical Society Library, New York; American Kennel Club, New York; American Tract Society, Boston; Phillips Academy, Andover, Massachusetts; Archdiocese of Boston; Archdiocese of Baltimore; The Archives of American Art, Washington, D.C., and New York; The Bostonian Society, Boston; The Boston Public Library; Catholic University of America, Department of Archives, Manuscripts and Museum Collections; City of Boston, Office of the City Clerk, Archives and Records Management Division; Christie's, London and New York; Miller Library, Colby College, Waterville, Maine; Witt Library, Courtauld Institute of Art, London; Friends of Montpelier; Frick Art Reference Library, New York; Gilbert Stuart Birthplace and Museum, North Kingston, Rhode Island; Henry Ford Museum and Greenfield Village, Dearborn, Michigan; Joseph Brant Museum, Burlington, Ontario, Canada; Knox's Headquarters State Historic Site, Vails Gate, New York; Library Company of Philadelphia; Library of Congress, Washington, D.C.; Maine Historical Society, Portland; Milwaukee Art Museum; National Library of Medicine, Bethesda, Maryland; National Library of Scotland, Edinburgh; National Museum of the American Indian Library, Washington, D.C.; Heinz Archive, National Portrait Gallery, London; New Britain Museum of American Art, New Britain, Connecticut; Newburyport Public Library, Newburyport, Massachusetts; New Orleans Museum of Art; Peabody Essex Museum; Pilgrim Society, Plymouth, Massachusetts; Rhode Island State Archives and Department of Administration, Providence; Royal Academy of Arts Library, London; Royal Horticultural Society, London; Schuyler Mansion State Historic Site, Albany, New York; Sotheby's, London and New York; Supreme Judicial Court, Boston; University of Pennsylvania Archives, Philadelphia; Vose Galleries, Boston; Winterthur Library, Winterthur, Delaware.

In our travels seeking out paintings by Stuart far and wide, we encountered many people who helped us immeasurably by leading us to pictures or otherwise abetting our research. For their kindness and for discussions about Stuart's work and life over the years, we thank Edwin Ahlstrom, Michael Barratt, Wendy Bellion, Mr. and Mrs. Francis M. Blodget, Nathaniel R. Bowditch, Sargent Bradlee Jr., Paul Caffrey, Samuel Codman, Francis Coolidge, Alford Warriner Cooley, Susan Detweiler, Davida Deutsch, Julia and Jonathan Goldstein, Adam Greenhalgh, Helen Kessler, William Kloss, Malcolm Lindsay, Ellie Macartney-Filgate, John Macartney-Filgate, Terence Macartney-Filgate, Marion Mecklenburg, Sarah Meschutt, Donald W. Moore, Philip Mould, the Earl of Normanton, William Oedel, Alan Parrish and Paula Chadis, Robert Price, Jules Prown, Mr. and Mrs. Francis F. Randolph, Tudor and Barbara Richards, Isadora Rose-de Viejo, Marvin Sadik, David Saltonstall, Anthony M. Sammarco, Adrien Sassoon, Elle Shushan, Danny D. Smith, Paul Staiti, Louise Strandberg, Ann Sturgis, Tim Sturgis, Lady Ethel Sykes, and Lois and Anthony Winston.

We are indebted to those Stuart scholars without whom a catalogue and exhibition of this magnitude would be unthinkable. George C. Mason, John Hill Morgan, and Lawrence Park did the grueling early documentary digging on the artist's oeuvre, and we are eternally grateful for their books. Many have worked on the artist in the intervening years, but it was Dorinda Evans who brought Stuart's work and career into focus with her recent biography, an exceptional volume filled with new assessments, primary source documentation, and just enough speculation to inspire continued work on the artist. We learned much from her work and took from it our cue for how to augment and expand the scholarship on Stuart. We reserve our final words of thanks for David M. Meschutt, whose profound and detailed knowledge of Stuart's sitters and the time and places in which they lived helped us beyond measure. A most generous scholar, he shared his catalogue raisonné notes with us, undertook research on our behalf, and read this entire manuscript.

This catalogue is dedicated to family and friends.

Carrie Rebora Barratt
Curator, American Paintings and Sculpture
Manager, The Henry R. Luce Center for the Study of American Art
The Metropolitan Museum of Art

Ellen G. Miles
Curator of Painting and Sculpture
National Portrait Gallery, Smithsonian Institution

Gilbert Stuart

Making Faces: Gilbert Stuart and His Portraits

CARRIE REBORA BARRATT AND ELLEN G. MILES

To the round-about question, to find out his calling or profession, Mr. Stuart answered with a grave face, and serious tone, that he sometimes dressed gentlemen's and ladies' hair. . . . —"You are a hair-dresser then?" "What!" said he, "do you take me for a barber?" "I beg your pardon sir, but I inferred it from what you said. If I mistook you, may I take the liberty to ask what you are then?" "Why I sometimes brush a gentleman's coat, or hat, and sometimes adjust a cravat." "O, you are a valet then, to some nobleman?" "A valet! Indeed, sir, I am not. I am not a servant—to be sure I make coats and waistcoats for gentlemen." "Oh! You are a tailor!" "Tailor! do I look like a tailor?" "I'll assure you, I never handled a goose, other than a roasted one." . . . "What the devil are you then?" . . . After checking his laughter, and pumping up a fresh flow of spirits by a large pinch of snuff, he said to them very gravely, "Now gentlemen, I will not play the fool with you any longer, but will tell you, upon my honour as a gentleman, my bona fide *profession. I get my bread by making faces." He then screwed up his countenance, and twisted the lineaments of his visage.*[1]

For Gilbert Stuart, painting portraits and telling tales were inextricably linked activities. According to one who knew him, he developed "the habit of talking to endeavour to call forth the character of his sitters," to capture unguarded appearance, gesture, and expression.[2] As his stories circulated and he repeated anecdotes told to him, the exchange of yarns came to define the painter and his process. The painter Henry Sargent recalled that Stuart had even retold to him a story he once told to Stuart.[3] These accounts have come to form the core of the historical understanding of Gilbert Stuart's personality and artistic methods, as well as his attitude toward sitters and his practice of the profession of portrait painting.

To early biographers, these narratives provided a way to convey his personality. The writers fashioned Stuart's life story out of a series of anecdotes. The American artist and critic William Dunlap acquired a fund of information through interviews and letters with Stuart's acquaintances; Stuart's friend the Irish painter John Dowling Herbert told of Stuart's life in Dublin; and his daughter Jane Stuart refuted many stories by telling her own.[4] As time passed writers increasingly had to depend on these stories because of the dearth of documentation. While twentieth-century historians William T. Whitley, James Thomas Flexner, and Charles Merrill Mount published new information gleaned from newspapers and journals contemporary with Stuart's life and work in their captivating biographies of the artist, they also relied on stories retold until the sources were blurred and the information became further spun and elaborated.[5] Stuart is, indeed, a painter for whom there are as many tales as pictures.

1. Benjamin Waterhouse, as told in Dunlap 1834, vol. 1, pp. 189–90.
2. Dunlap 1834, vol. 1, p. 210.
3. Sargent's account is given ibid., p. 219.
4. Ibid., pp. 162–223; Herbert 1836, pp. 226–48; J. Stuart 1876; J. Stuart 1877.
5. Whitley 1932; James Thomas Flexner, *America's Old Masters: First Artists of the New World* (New York: Viking Press, 1939); Flexner 1947; Flexner 1955; Mount 1964.

Detail of cat. 16, *Self-Portrait*, 1786

Fig. 1. Charles Willson Peale and Rembrandt Peale, *Gilbert Stuart*, 1805. Oil on canvas, 23½ x 19½ in. (59.7 x 49.5 cm). The New-York Historical Society (1867.302)

6. Herbert 1836, p. 226.
7. Eliza Susan Quincy, journal entry of March 13, 1816, Eliza Susan Quincy Papers, Rhode Island Historical Society, Providence.
8. John Neal, "Our Painters I," *Atlantic Monthly* 22 (December 1868), p. 641.

The material is compelling and seems to bring the painter to life. However, it allows for interpretive misdirection, especially when the artist's motives are presumed. Stuart's legacy, as defined by his work, by this anecdotal material, and by secondary sources, is full of contradictory evidence. He was extremely prolific and may have painted over a thousand portraits, but quite often he failed to finish works especially if the sitters annoyed or bored him. He commanded high prices for his work but constantly teetered on the verge of bankruptcy. He was charming and cantankerous, tolerant and opinionated, curious and dogmatic, easily offended but resilient, articulate, and verbose. He is ranked among the most important American portrait painters, but his father was a Scot and he lived under British rule for more than half his life, including his youth in colonial Newport and almost twenty years in the British Isles. Characterizations of him are in equal contrast, describing someone at once noble, charming, and dreadful. Herbert said that Stuart's manner of speech was captivating and somewhat affected, "like an imitation of [the actor] John Kemble, to whom he bore a great resemblance," a comparison that Stuart himself enjoyed.[6] In 1816 Eliza Susan Quincy described him as

Fig. 2. Gilbert Stuart's snuff box. Silver, H. 1½ in., diam. 4½ in. (3.8, 10.5 cm). Historical Society of Pennsylvania Collection, Atwater Kent Museum of Philadelphia; Gift of Garret C. Neagle (HSP.T.9.147)

"one of, if not the most frightful looking man I ever saw, but his small grey eye is sharp & so acute that his glance seems to cut into the individual before him."[7] The next year, *Atlantic Monthly* writer John Neal found him "a man of noble type, robust and hearty, with a large frame and the bearing of a man who might stand before kings, . . . fresh-looking, old fashioned, reminding you constantly of Washington himself, or General Knox or Greene."[8]

First-hand accounts of Stuart by his clients confirms his erratic manner and demeanor, which more often beguiled than offended. Sitters sought out his company and anticipated the skillful portrait that would result. As Dunlap explained, "his colloquial powers were of the first order, and made him the delight of all who were thrown in his way; whether exercised to draw forth character and expression from his sitters, or in the quiet of a *tete-a-tete*, or to 'set the table in a roar,' while the wine circulated, as was but too much the custom of the time and the man."[9] John Adams (see cats. 59, 90) told Josiah Quincy (see cat. 91), "I should like to sit to Stuart from the first of January to the last of December, for he lets me do just as I please and keeps me constantly amused by his conversation."[10] Lord Chancellor of Ireland John FitzGibbon (see cat. 19) invited him to dinner; General Horatio Gates (see cat. 26) drank Madeira with him; the painter John Neagle painted his portrait (fig. 4) and took snuff with him; and scores of others visited his studio or invited him to their homes for portraits, for entertainment, and, by the end of his life, just to meet this amazing individual. After Stuart's death in 1828, his treasured silver snuff box (fig. 2) was given by Isaac P. Davis, his Boston friend and patron, to the painter Thomas Sully.

Through the plethora of stories, we learn of a man who was reluctant to change his work to suit his client and who invariably had a cunning rebuff for one who asked him to do so. To a sitter who returned his portrait, complaining that the muslin of the cravat was too coarse, Stuart responded that he would buy a piece of the finest texture cloth and have it glued on the offending part of the painting.[11] When Philadelphia lawyer Horace Binney (fig. 77) pointed out that Stuart had painted the buttons on the wrong side of his jacket, Stuart said, "Well, thank God, I am no tailor," and according to Binney, "immediately took his pencil and with a stroke drew the *lapelle* to the collar of the coat," making it double-breasted.[12] When John Fowler, the archbishop of Dublin, demanded an alteration to his portrait, Stuart explained, "That's not to be done; . . . a dressmaker may alter a dress; a milliner a cap; a tailor a coat; but a painter may give up his art, if he attempts to alter to please."[13] Stuart later delivered the offending portrait with an invoice.

Stuart was often accused of lacking any sense of professionalism. Said John Quincy Adams, when he was trying to get Stuart to finish a portrait of his father, John Adams, "Mr. Stuart thinks it is the prerogative of genius to disdain the performance of his engagements."[14] The Earl of Clonmell, Lord Chief Justice of the King's Bench in Ireland, argued with Stuart over portraits of himself and his children and came to blows with the artist. He wrote in his diary, "I have had a picture painted by Stuart, and lost a front tooth. It is time I should learn to keep my mouth shut and learn gravity and discretion of speech."[15] Another gentleman called on the painter to sit for his portrait but left when he found out that Stuart's price

9. Dunlap 1834, vol. 1, p. 162.
10. Josiah Quincy, *Figures of the Past from the Leaves of Old Journals* (Boston: Roberts Brothers, 1883), p. 83.
11. Dunlap 1834, vol. 1, p. 218.
12. Mason 1879, pp. 139–41; the original has not been located. The entry recounts additional anecdotes about Stuart and comments on other portraits.
13. Herbert 1836, p. 234.
14. John Quincy Adams, letter to John Singleton Copley, April 29, 1811, quoted in Oliver 1967, p. 135.
15. Clonmell's diary for September 14, 1790, quoted in Whitley 1932, p. 84.

Fig. 3. John Henri Isaac Browere, *Gilbert Stuart*, 1825. Plaster, H. 28⅛ in. (71.5 cm). Redwood Library and Athenaeum, Newport, R.I.

Fig. 4. John Neagle, *Gilbert Stuart*, 1825. Oil on canvas, 27⅛ x 22⅛ (68.9 x 56.2 cm). Museum of Fine Arts, Boston; Robert Edwards Fund (1975.807)

was 5 guineas for a head, half payable in advance. Two years later, having received an unsatisfactory portrait from another artist, the client returned to Stuart only to find that his price was by then 30 guineas a head. The fellow insisted that the painter was obliged to charge the original amount, but eventually agreed to Stuart's terms as well as "to the mortification of paying for two sets of portraits."[16] Stuart could be blunt and offensive to some sitters. A husband and wife visited Stuart, he a handsome figure, she less so. Stuart did his best with the woman but could never make her as lovely as the husband wished. He worked and reworked, at one point in the long process explaining to the man that spouses were rarely pleased with each other's portraits. Eventually the client snapped and his wife burst into tears, causing the painter to lose all composure, take a pinch of snuff and exclaim, "What a —— business is this of a portrait painter—you bring him a *potatoe*, and expect he will paint you a peach."[17]

The antidote to the retelling of these tales came in documentary work conducted in the late nineteenth and early twentieth centuries, when catalogues raisonnés were researched for many of America's earliest master painters. George Champlin Mason and Lawrence Park organized Stuart's known work into checklists. Mason corresponded with the children or grandchildren of Stuart's sitters about the portraits they had inherited, and Park's entries are replete with biogra-

16. Dunlap 1834, vol. 1, p. 188.

17. Ibid., pp. 220–21.

18. Mason 1879; Park 1926. Mason's work was done at the request of Jane Stuart, who disliked Dunlap's biography. Park's catalogue, compiled in the 1920s, was completed after his death by William Sawitzky and published by Helen Clay Frick. Their papers survive, Mason's at the Rhode Island Historical Society, Providence, and Park's in the Joseph Downs Collection of Manuscripts and Printed Ephemera, Winterthur Library, Winterthur Del.

19. See Jouett 1816. This manuscript, with invaluable comments on Stuart's approach to portraiture, belonged to dealer Harry MacNeill Bland in 1939. It was published again in William Barrow Floyd, *Jouett, Bush, Fraser: An Historical and Stylistic Analysis* (Lexington, Ky.: s.n., 1967), pp. 169–77, and is now unlocated.

20. DeLorme 1979a; DeLorme 1979b.

21. Pressly 1986; Rather 1993; Davis 2001.

phical information on the sitters and formal descriptions of the portraits.[18] John Hill Morgan, whose biography of Stuart is found in the first volume of Park's work, published a record of Stuart's painting methods: conversations with Stuart that the young artist Matthew Harris Jouett jotted down when studying with him for four months in 1816.[19] Jouett recorded Stuart's "rude hints and observations" in a stream-of-consciousness manner, one lucid comment after another without transitional phrasing or specific context, thus providing tantalizing clues to Stuart's thought processes and working methods. Jouett described the organization of Stuart's palette, his preferred brushstrokes, the use of shadow, the means of capturing expression, and the lessons he learned by studying works by Sir Joshua Reynolds and Benjamin West, as well as by earlier painters, among them Titian and Correggio. And Stuart gossiped and told tales throughout, affirming that he talked incessantly while painting.

The publications of Mason and Park have fueled many scholarly projects because their documentary evidence provided the means for others to assess, analyze, judge, and reorganize Stuart's oeuvre. Surprisingly, however, it was not until 1967 that the first exhibition to show the full range of Stuart's work since the retrospective put together by the Museum of Fine Arts, Boston, in 1880, was organized by Edgar P. Richardson for the National Gallery of Art, Washington, and the Museum of Art, Rhode Island School of Design, Providence, to celebrate Stuart's Rhode Island roots. Since that time a number of art historians have concentrated on specific areas. Eleanor DeLorme wrote two extensive articles on the artist, seeking out new documentation especially on his late career in Boston.[20] Others have focused on single works: William Pressly, John Davis, and Susan Rather have grappled with Stuart's complex imagery, interrogating the paintings themselves, connecting them to the age-old tales, and finding new evidence of Stuart's methods.[21] Dorinda Evans, in her recent biography of the artist, *The Genius of Gilbert Stuart*, has synthesized the voluminous bibliography and added more documentary

Fig. 5. Sarah Goodridge, *Gilbert Stuart*, ca. 1825. Watercolor on ivory, 3⅝ x 2¾ in. (9.2 x 7 cm). The Metropolitan Museum of Art, New York; The Moses Lazarus Collection, Gift of Josephine and Sarah Lazarus, in memory of their father, 1888–95 (95.14.123)

Fig. 6. Anson Dickinson, *Gilbert Stuart*, ca. 1825. Watercolor on ivory, 3 x 2½ in. (7.6 x 5 cm). The New-York Historical Society (X.25)

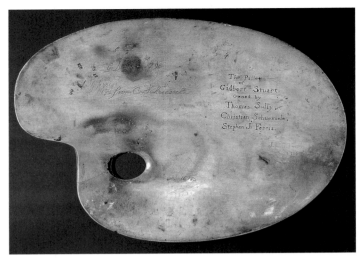

Fig. 7. Gilbert Stuart's palette (reverse). Wood, 11¾ x 16½ in. (29.7 x 41.9 cm). National Portrait Gallery, Smithsonian Institution, Washington, D.C.; Gift of Mrs. J. L. G. Ferris (AD/NPG.74.21)

Fig. 8. George Adams Jr., drawing instruments owned by Gilbert Stuart, ca. 1780. Brass, steel, ivory, ebony, in a velvet-lined mahogany case, closed 11⅜ x 17⅛ x 4⅛ in. (29 x 43.5 x 10.5 cm). National Portrait Gallery, Smithsonian Institution, Washington, D.C.; Gift of the Family of the late Lester Hoadley Sellers (AD/NPG.96.5)

tary material, notably Stuart's conversations with Salem resident Henry Pickering, as well as observations of Stuart's work by Unitarian minister Horace Holley and the reminiscences of his childhood friend Dr. Benjamin Waterhouse. Her close work on Stuart has led her to attribute to Stuart an extraordinary aptitude for conveying sentience and the "presence of a soul" in his portraits. In a separate study, she has focused on what she defines as an affliction of bipolarity and has brought this psychology to bear on questions of attribution in Stuart's work.[22]

This exhibition and catalogue take the position that study of Stuart's sitters adds an important dimension to knowledge of the artist's practice of portraiture. His clients were not merely the people he portrayed but also the facilitators of his progress, the monitors of his mood, and the very recorders of the anecdotes on which we have come to rely. Information about his sitters is crucial to viewing and interpreting the portraits and the artist's unique talents. They lead to increased comprehension of the formal qualities of the paintings. The catalogue entries on ninety-two paintings that follow—a select but generously representative sampling of the artist's work—diverge from the tradition of discussing Stuart's biography in favor of an approach that offers rich and vast evidence of the artist's working methods and relationship to his patrons. Revelations about Stuart become apparent because any careful study of portraiture reveals as much about the painter as about the portrayed, if not more. Care has been taken to identify the sitters, provide biographical information, and define their position in the circle of Stuart's patrons. Archival manuscript material, some previously unidentified or unpublished, revealing the personality of a sitter or the link between sitter and artist, has made it possible to further interpret Stuart's compositional inventiveness.

Our organizational system follows Stuart through the eight cities in which he worked: Newport, Edinburgh, London, Dublin, New York, Philadelphia, Washington, D.C., and Boston. A short essay about the artist's experience in each city precedes the pertinent catalogue entries. A special section within the Philadelphia chapter is devoted to fourteen of Stuart's celebrated portraits of George Washington, with particular attention to his three life portraits of the first president of the United States. In each place, the circumstances for being a portrait painter differed, and Stuart faced varying expectations and demands conditioned by his own growing reputation, his ambitions, competing portraitists, and his health. In Newport, he was trained by an itinerant Scottish painter, and his identity and talent attracted him to the local elite, many of them business associates of his Scottish father. In London, he became an integral part of the highly codified system of British portraiture as upheld by the Royal Academy of Arts. There, he studied with the American painter Benjamin West (see cat. 12) and then set himself up independently in his own studio, acquiring the tools of his trade. From English painter Nathaniel Dance, he obtained his palette (fig. 7), which had once belonged to English portrait painter Thomas Hudson, and from artist Ozias Humphry he obtained a boxed set of drawing instruments (fig. 8).[23] He found favor with Sir Joshua Reynolds (see cat. 14), who recognized his gifts and helped him claim still greater success in the relatively small city of Dublin. There, the residents received him as a British painter and commissioned works on the grand scale they expected from one trained in London. The Irish may have been surprised to learn of Stuart's American roots when he spoke of returning "to my native soil" to paint the president.[24]

When Stuart returned home and obtained sittings with George Washington (see cats. 35–49) and many others, he worked not in some distinctively American idiom but used skills honed in the British Isles in his work. In so doing, he satisfied the demand in the United States for lasting images of the nation's early leaders created in an international language of portraiture. His work garnered him a steady stream of sitters, including the next four presidents, as well as a tremendous following among contemporary painters. In the twelve years he spent in New York, Philadelphia, and Washington, his demanding patrons required a high level of accomplishment, almost to the point of exhausting the artist. He spent his last two decades in Boston, where patrons were more admiring and less impatient, although still puzzled over his crankiness and unpredictable delays, which increased in his old age. But the work never decreased in expression or skill. At a time when portraits were used in the United States to celebrate national achievements and public heroes as well as the self-aware experiences of private individuals, Stuart set higher standards in portrait painting for his sitters, his colleagues, and his students. By examining his work city by city and portrait by portrait, we hope to reengage an interest in the interconnection between artist and sitter, between sitter and society, and between artist and politics, connections that characterize the first decades of the new nation.

22. Evans 1999; Evans 2004.
23. On the early provenance of the palette, which later belonged to painters Thomas Sully, Christian Schussele, Stephen J. Ferris, and John Leon Gerome Ferris, see Dunlap 1834, vol. 1, p. 192. For the history of the drawing instruments and their use in making copies of portraits, see Evans 1999, pp. 85, 148 n. 17.
24. Herbert 1836, p. 248.

Stuart in Newport and Scotland (1755–75)

In the years before the American Revolution—the time of Gilbert Stuart's youth—Newport, Rhode Island, was a heady place. The Gulf Stream climate that prevailed year-round on the fertile seaport island suited a local culture of religious and commercial tolerance extraordinary in the British North American colonies. The town deserved to be called a resort: a place where Anglicans maintained friendships with Sephardic Jews and Quakers, where small-time retailers could rise to big-time merchant status and where dire poverty was virtually nonexistent. The strong economy easily absorbed the influx of new residents from northern and southern colonies and from Europe, many of whom made good livings through speculative commerce of venture cargo both overseas and along the coast. In an exercise that balanced business acumen with savvy ingenuity, the mercantile giants of Newport developed a system of economic leverage: by the 1760s, more than thirty distilleries made West Indian molasses into rum to be bartered in Africa for slaves, who were exchanged primarily in the southern colonies for goods and by-products that could, in turn, be deployed in the acquisition of silver, textiles, and other luxury goods from England. Vast numbers of privateers supported by equally vast numbers of carpenters, shipbuilders, and retailers, as well as some of the country's most ostentatious consumers, sailed the Indian Ocean, the Red Sea, to Europe, and along North American routes. They enhanced their triangle trade by carrying sugar and indigo, along with prized Narragansett pacers, spermaceti candles, barrel staves, cheese, and—thanks to such fine cabinetmakers as John Cahoone, John Goddard, and John Townsend—some of the highest-quality furniture made anywhere in the world.[1]

In 1729 Bishop George Berkeley settled in Newport to make arrangements for the college he would set up in Bermuda, and even he, a learned, worldly, and ambitious man, was shocked by the resplendence of Newport. The architecture, music, and theater were surprising, but the sight of men dressed "in flaming scarlet coats and waistcoats, laced and fringed with brightest glaring yellow" redoubled the effect. Not to be left out, "the sly Quakers," he wrote in his memoirs, "not venturing on these charming coats and waistcoats, yet loving finery, figured a way with plate on their sideboards"[2] Indeed, most of the choice goods acquired in trade remained in Newport, filling the magnificent homes built along the wharves. The names Redwood, Banister, Malbone, Hunter, and Rodriguez, among others, became synonymous with high style, and the far-reaching reputations of members of those families conveyed the message that Newport was an entrepreneur's paradise.

1. On Newport's economy, see Elaine Forman Crane, *A Dependent People: Newport, Rhode Island in the Revolutionary Era* (New York: Fordham University Press, 1992); Carl E. Swanson, *Predators and Prizes: American Privateering and Imperial Warfare, 1739–1748* (Columbia: University of South Carolina Press, 1991); Jay Coughtry, *The Notorious Triangle: Rhode Island and the African Slave Trade, 1700–1807* (Philadelphia: Temple University Press, 1981); Margaretta M. Lovell, "Such Furniture as Will be Most Profitable': The Business of Cabinetmaking in Eighteenth-Century Newport," *Winterthur Portfolio* 26 (April 1991), pp. 27–62.

2. Quoted in Stanley C. Hughes, "Very Rev. Dean George Berkeley, D.D.," in *Early Religious Leaders of Newport: Eight Addresses Delivered before the Newport Historical Society, 1917* (Newport: The Society, Mercury Pub. Co., 1918), p. 90.

Detail of cat. 4, *Benjamin Waterhouse*

Fig. 9. *The Hunter Dogs*, ca. 1769. Oil on canvas, 25 x 30 in. (63.5 x 76 cm). The Preservation Society of Newport County, Newport, R.I.

When Dr. John Moffatt, one of a considerable number of Scots who fled to Newport after the Battle of Culloden Moor in 1746, arrived from Edinburgh in the late 1740s, he not only pursued his medical career but also determined the economic benefits to be derived from locally produced snuff. In 1751 he persuaded the millwright Gilbert Stuart Sr. to come from Perth, Scotland, and set up a snuff mill just outside Newport, in Kingston, where the Mattatuxet River reaches the head of Pettaquamscutt River. Gilbert Stuart was born in the millhouse on December 3, 1755, and was raised there until 1761, when his mother, Elizabeth Anthony, inherited a small property in Newport. By that time Dr. Moffatt's financial prognostications had been foiled by Newport's extraordinary trade relationships, and it became more profitable to import snuff than to produce it. The Stuarts moved up to the retail business with a shop on Banister's Wharf, selling and trading snuff, mustard flour, and a variety of dry goods including ribbons, sewing implements, linen, silk, shoe buckles, writing paper, hats, and earthenware cups.[3] Both senior Stuarts were pewholders at Trinity Church, members of the congregation who tithed for seats, and they sent their son to the grammar school run by the clergy.

Unlike John Singleton Copley, son of Irish tobacconists, who absorbed into his artistic practice the mechanisms of Boston's commercial trade, Gilbert Stuart would not emerge from Newport's global emporium with a head for business.[4] Portraiture did not have as clear a connection to Newport's marketplace as it did to Boston's. Stuart's predecessors in Newport came and went quickly: John Smibert remained in town for just a few months, Joseph Blackburn stayed for less than a

3. See Gilbert Stuart's advertisement in the *Newport Mercury*, November 16–24, 1766.
4. On Copley's mercantile upbringing, see Paul Staiti, "Accounting for Copley," in Carrie Rebora and Paul Staiti et al., *John Singleton Copley in America*, exh. cat. (New York: Metropolitan Museum of Art, 1995), pp. 25–29.

5. On Hunter, see *ANB*, vol. 11, pp. 526–57; E. B. Krumbhaar, "Doctor William Hunter of Newport," *Annals of Surgery*, January 1935, pp. 506–28.

6. On Alexander, see Saunders and Miles 1987, pp. 298–300; Pam McLellan Geddy, "Cosmo Alexander's Travels and Patrons in America," *Antiques* 112 (November 1977), pp. 972–77; G. L. M. Goodfellow, "Cosmo Alexander in America," *Art Quarterly* 26 (autumn 1963), pp. 309–22.

7. See Hunter, letter to Charles C. Bogart, July 22, 1811, American Academy of the Fine Arts Papers, New-York Historical Society.

8. See Margaret Hall Hunter and Una Pope-Hennessy, eds., *The Aristocratic Journey; being the outspoken letters of Mrs. Basil Hall written during a fourteen months' sojourn in America, 1827–28* (New York: G. P. Putnam's Sons, 1931), p. 94.

Fig. 10. *Mrs. Aaron Lopez and Her Son*, ca. 1773. Oil on canvas, 26 x 21½ in. (66 x 54.6 cm). The Detroit Institute of Arts; Gift of Dexter M. Ferry, Jr. (48.146)

year. Robert Feke moved to Newport after his marriage to a local girl in 1742 but persuaded her to move to Philadelphia with him after six years. Only the less ambitious Samuel King stayed, despite commissions few and far between.

These painters were long gone by the time Stuart came of age. He learned to sketch faces and caricatures from an African slave, Neptune Thurston, and had in common with his best friend, Benjamin Waterhouse (see cat. 4), a talent for drawing. He was better known in his youth as a superbly talented organist, the prize pupil of Trinity Church organist John Knoechel. Indeed, whenever and wherever in need, Stuart would seek employment at a local church before he would solicit commissions for portraits.

Stuart's earliest known painting dates from about 1769 and portrays two spaniels belonging to Dr. William Hunter, nestling under a Townsend-Goddard side table (fig. 9).[5] That year, Hunter had two painters in his employ: the thirteen-year-old Stuart and the recently arrived Aberdeen artist Cosmo Alexander (1724–1772), who was executing portraits of Hunter and his wife.[6] Quite plausibly Alexander introduced Stuart to Hunter, perhaps having already met the boy and taken him as an apprentice. Stuart copied some of Alexander's portraits, a mutually satisfactory situation between a notably charismatic and genteel artist and his protégé.[7] Alexander was the son and grandson of portraitists and was named for Cosimo III de' Medici, patron of his father, John. He trained in Italy and also served as a purchasing agent for Scottish art collectors. Such were his connections and friendships that in 1754 the architect James Gibbs bequeathed to Alexander his London townhouse and its contents. Apparently this did not come with the requisite affluence, for within about ten years Alexander left it all behind for an itinerant career on North America's eastern seaboard. He went between Philadelphia, New York, and Boston seeking commissions from émigré Scots for a few years before landing in Newport in 1769. When he had exhausted the possibilities of painting his compatriots there, he decided to return to Edinburgh and took Stuart with him.

The portraitist and his apprentice traveled first in the fall of 1770 to Philadelphia, presumably to paint portraits but also perhaps because Stuart's family connections there secured their passage abroad. Stuart's uncle Joseph Anthony ran a merchant shipping business based in Philadelphia, which made it possible for Alexander and Stuart to visit Williamsburg, Norfolk, and Charleston en route to Edinburgh, where they arrived sometime in 1771 or 1772. Stuart's apprenticeship was cut short when Alexander died unexpectedly in August 1772. He learned more of contemporary Scottish portraiture from Alexander's brother-in-law, Sir George Chalmers, who likely took some care to continue the younger artist's training, although he is usually charged with abandoning Stuart in financial straits at the University of Glasgow.[8] The portraits Stuart produced on his return to Newport in the fall of 1773 are a departure from Alexander's work but show the influence of Chalmers, an artist whose role in Stuart's artistic education

9. Waterhouse "Autobiography," p. 22.

should be recognized if only because it is arguably the high point of his scant artistic legacy.

Alexander's and Chalmers's short courses on provincial Scottish portraiture served Stuart well in Newport, where he quickly developed a following of Scots attracted to his intimate likenesses. He quickly received commissions from John Banister, his father's landlord and one of the savviest merchants in town (see cats. 1, 2); Banister's business associate Francis Malbone (see cat. 3); William Redwood, director of the Redwood Library and Athenaeum, founded in 1747 and maintained as the city's intellectual and social hub; and Aaron Lopez (see fig. 10) and Jacob Rodriguez Rivera, Portuguese Jews who developed the local manufacturing of spermaceti candles and controlled rum exports. Stuart's unexplained refusal to paint a full-length portrait of Abraham Redwood, founder of the Redwood Library, was an early demonstration of the willful manner in which he would conduct his art practice and his life thereafter.

Stuart never clearly articulated his politics, but certain brash comments such as "Hang the King . . . he lives too far off to do us any good" give an idea of his views.[9] Yet the departure of his friend Waterhouse for medical school abroad followed by the evacuation of his family to Nova Scotia, where his father had purchased land in 1761, left Stuart alone in Newport by the summer of 1775. Restless and lonely, Stuart sailed for London on September 8, 1775.

CRB

1. John Banister

ca. 1773
Oil on canvas, 36 x 30 in. (91.4 x 76.2 cm)
Redwood Library and Athenaeum, Newport,
Rhode Island; Gift of David Melville
(RLC.PA.110)

2. Christian Stelle Banister and Her Son, John

ca. 1773
Oil on canvas, 35 ½ x 30 in. (90.2 x 76.2 cm)
Redwood Library and Athenaeum, Newport,
Rhode Island; Gift of David Melville
(RLC.PA.109)

1. Recorded by Pierre Eugene du Simitiere, who visited Newport in 1769, as quoted in "The Fine Arts in Newport," *Magazine of American History* 3 (1879), p. 452.

2. Antoinette F. Downing and Vincent J. Scully Jr., *The Architectural Heritage of Newport, Rhode Island, 1640–1915* (Cambridge, Mass.: Harvard University Press, 1952), p. 181.

3. On Banister, see Darius Baker, "The Newport Banisters," *Bulletin of the Newport Historical Society*, January 1923, pp. 1–20; "John Banister," in Clifford K. Shipton and John L. Sibley, *Biographical Sketches of Those Who Attended Harvard College in Classes 1764–1767*, Sibley's Harvard Graduates, vol. 16 (Boston: Massachusetts Historical Society, 1972), pp. 13–14. On Banister's business, see Jay Coughtry, *The Notorious Triangle: Rhode Island and the African Slave Trade, 1700–1807* (Philadelphia: Temple University Press, 1981), p. 169; Carl E. Swanson, *Predators and Prizes: American Privateering and Imperial Warfare, 1739–1748* (Columbia: University of South Carolina Press, 1991), pp. 52, 109, 124.

4. The portraits are listed in Mason 1897, p. 132 (both); Park 1926, pp. 126–27, nos. 46 (Banister), 47 (Mrs. Banister and son). Gilbert Stuart Sr. moved to "the North Part of Banister's Row, in Thames Street" in September 1765; see advertisement, *Newport Mercury*, September 30, 1765, p. 4. See also records of rent payments from Stuart to Banister in John Banister's "Cash Book" and Banister's letter of October 1765 introducing Stuart to a colleague in Boston and putting up security for his purchases, Newport Historical Society.

5. "Inventory of the personal estate of John Banister Esqr late of Newport deceased taken and appraised by the undersigned as the same was shewn and set

Lord Hugh Percy, later second Duke of Northumberland and one of Stuart's most important patrons in London (see cats. 17, 18; fig. 18), wrote that Mr. and Mrs. John Banister "would grace the Court of St. James."[1] Percy may have been taken with Banister's intelligence, honed at Harvard, and his art collection, which included a supposed Van Dyck self-portrait as well as portraits of Cromwell, Charles I and his queen, the queen of Charles II, William and Mary, and others. Percy and his fellow British commanders made the Banisters' elegant house (which still stands) their headquarters as of December 7, 1777.

To others, John Banister (1744–1831) was an irascible, autocratic, self-admiring, stiff fellow, the son of a ruthless and "inveterate smuggler" who perpetuated his father's shady trading methods for maximum capital gain.[2] Banister's involvement in real estate and international trade earned him possibly the largest fortune in town, including vast tracks of town and wharf property inherited from his father, John Banister Sr., and from his mother, Hermione Pelham, the great-granddaughter of Benedict Arnold, the first charter governor of Rhode Island.[3] He increased his assets through marriage in 1768 to Christian Stelle (1747–1830), daughter of Captain Isaac Stelle, one of Newport's most successful merchants in the sugar, molasses, rum, and slave trades. Their only child, John Banister III (1769–1831), was baptized in Trinity Church on October 17, 1769.

The Banisters sat for Stuart soon after he returned from Scotland in 1773; presumably Stuart's father, a tenant on Banister's Wharf who had known John Banister's father, made the introductions.[4] The Banister family's history of commissioning portraits set them apart from their peers in Newport, who filled their homes with the best of everything from local and foreign sources but did not regularly order paintings as did residents in other major colonial cities.[5] John Banister's parents and his parents-in-law had all sat for Robert Feke in the late 1740s, and by the late 1760s these four portraits hung in his own home.[6] He took a chance in hiring Stuart, whose local reputation, if he had any, was based on a single work, the portrait of Dr. Hunter's spaniels painted about four years earlier (fig. 9). But Banister had little choice, for although he knew Samuel King, Newport's only resident portraitist, there were few competent painters in town.[7] Stuart provided his patrons with more modern images than the rococo portraits hanging in their home. The Banisters wear lavish costumes and compelling facial expressions, and Stuart included a spaniel as an afterthought to complete the portrayal of elegant domesticity.[8]

Stuart's portrait of Mrs. Banister and her son is regularly compared with Cosmo Alexander's portrait of Deborah Malbone Hunter and her daughter Eliza

I

forth to us by David Melville Administrator," March 11, 1808, Index of Wills, Newport City Hall, lists furniture, carpets, textiles, luxury implements, along with nine pictures.

6. These portraits by Feke are of John Banister, 1748 (Toledo Museum of Art); Mrs. John Banister, 1748 (Detroit Institute of Arts); Isaac Stelle, ca. 1749 (Newport Historical Society); Penelope Goodson Stelle, ca. 1749 (Newport Historical Society).

7. Banister sat for a miniature (unlocated) as recorded in the will of Christian Banister, May 19, 1828, Index of Wills, Newport City Hall.

(Preservation Society of Newport County).[9] Yet, where Alexander's work is subtle and scumbled, Stuart's is crisp and polished, and where Alexander's palette is restrained, nearly monochromatic, Stuart's is vibrant, even garish in passages. His portrait of John Banister is formally similar to Alexander's portrait of Alexander Grant (fig. 11), except that Stuart's work, even at this early state, is imaginative and brings his sitter to life, while Alexander's client is relatively vacant. Mrs. Banister's ermine-trimmed figure suggests Stuart's acquaintance with Alexander's double portrait of Lady Barbara and Lady Margaret Stuart, daughters of Charles, fourth Earl of Traquair (private collection), the ambitious composition of which resonates in Stuart's portrait of the Malbone brothers

2

8. According to the report filed at the Center for
Conservation and Technical Studies, Harvard
University Art Museums, Cambridge, Mass., the
boy's left arm originally folded across his chest in a
hand-in-coat pose; this was changed when the
dog was placed on top of the boy. Shipton and
Sibley (*Biographical Sketches*, pp. 13–14) record that
the directors ordered a bouquet painted on
Christian's bosom in 1859, but this seems not to
have been done.
9. For the comparison of Stuart's portrait of Mrs.
Banister and her son with Alexander's portrait of

(cat. 3). And yet Stuart's faces are livelier, his figures slightly less stiff than those of his mentor. A formative year had passed since Alexander's death, and Stuart was beginning to cast off the technical methods learned from his master. Stuart's approach was not a trait of American primitivism, as some have thought, but rather a hallmark of contemporary Scottish portraiture.[10] The conspicuous linearity in the Banister portraits—the finicky costume details, sharp garment edges, and crisply defined facial features—indicates familiarity with the works of George Chalmers, Alexander's brother-in-law. While early paintings by Cosmo's father, John Alexander, would not have been particularly impressive to Stuart, contemporary works by Chalmers stuck with him. Stuart's portrait

Fig. 11. Cosmo Alexander, *Alexander Grant*, 1770. Oil on canvas, 50¼ x 40 in. (127.7 x 101.6 cm). The Art Institute of Chicago; Ada Turnbull Hertle Fund (1977.2)

Fig. 12. Sir George Chalmers, *Gideon Loudown*, 1764. Oil on canvas, 26 x 21 in. (66 x 53.3 cm). Location unknown (photo: Scottish National Portrait Gallery, Edinburgh)

Mrs. Hunter and her daughter, see, most recently, Evans 1999, pp. 6–7.

10. See Flexner 1955b, p. 234; see also Barbara Novak, *American Painting of the Nineteenth Century*, 2nd ed. (New York: Harper and Row, 1979), p. 32.

of Banister is strikingly like Chalmers's portraits of Field Marshal Gideon Loudown (fig. 12) and Oliver Colt of Auldhame and Inveresk (private collection).

Banister remained in Newport during the British occupation, sustaining property damage considerable enough to warrant a trip to England in 1781 to try to get compensation. He received some satisfaction in the British courts and returned to Newport, where he served as justice of the peace and became more involved with the Redwood Library. The Stuart portraits remained in the Banister home; they passed to John Banister III upon the death of his mother and then to his wife, Elizabeth Thurston Banister. She died in 1838, leaving substantial property to David and Patience Melville. David Melville presented the pair of portraits to the Redwood Library in 1859.

CRB

3. FRANCIS MALBONE AND HIS BROTHER SAUNDERS

ca. 1774
Oil on canvas, 36 x 44 in. (91.4 x 111.8 cm)
Museum of Fine Arts, Boston; Gift of Francis Malbone Blodget Jr. and Gift of a Friend of the Department of American Decorative Arts and Sculpture and Emily L. Ainsley Fund (1991.436)

1. The portrait is not listed in Mason 1879; it is listed in Park 1926, pp. 500–501, no. 520.
2. For Copley's portraits, see Carrie Rebora and Paul Staiti et al., *John Singleton Copley in America*, exh. cat. (New York: Metropolitan Museum of Art, 1995).

Stuart's portrayal of the two young sons of the Newport distiller and trader Francis Malbone provides visual evidence that Stuart studied the work of John Singleton Copley.[1] This double portrait is a veritable collage of passages from Copley portraits: the reflective tabletop; the inscription on the letter—"Newport"—defining the site; the wood, metal, and glass inkstand—an occasion for the demonstration of talent in rendering texture and material differences; the detailed costumes; the ornate chair splat; the elaborate gestures—one boy rests his right elbow on a closed book and places a finger of that hand to his temple while the other holds a letter with the fingertips of his left hand and crosses over his right hand holding a quill; and the glowing orblike faces. If appropriating Copley's vocabulary of props and gestures were not enough, Stuart also mimicked Copley's tendency to balance plasticity of form with severe outline. Just how he saw Copley's portraits remains part of the enigma of Gilbert Stuart, for he left no documents, notes, or sketches from a trip to Boston.[2]

3

Fig. 13. John Singleton Copley, *Thomas and Sarah Morris Mifflin*, 1773. Oil on canvas, 60½ x 48 in. (153.7 x 121.9cm). Philadelphia Museum of Art

Stuart could have seen a few portraits by Copley in Newport, chief among them the one of John Bours (Worcester Art Museum). Bours owned a retail shop, served on the board of the Redwood Library, and held a pew at Trinity Church, quite close to those of Stuart's parents.[3] Copley portrayed Bours in a languid pose and with a faraway look,[4] and in Newport, in the company of relatively mundane works by Samuel King, Cosmo Alexander, and others, such a picture could well have struck Stuart with the expressive possibilities of the medium. Yet the portrait of Bours does not explain how Stuart arrived at his idea for the Malbone brothers.

According to Benjamin Waterhouse, Stuart was in Boston "when the first blood was spilt at Lexington," in other words about April 19, 1775, and he left on June 7, before the Battle of Bunker Hill.[5] Such a specific account can hardly be erroneous, but Stuart may also have been to Boston the year before. In June 1774 Copley had sailed for England and the Continent, leaving his studio empty. Many of his sitters had fled town at the outbreak of the revolution, taking their portraits with them. Even if Stuart had introduced himself to Copley's half brother the artist Henry Pelham, as has been suggested, he would not have seen much.[6] Stuart must have gone to Boston in late 1773 or early 1774, when he could have seen many Copley portraits, including the one of Mr. and Mrs. Thomas Mifflin (fig. 13). Stuart's composition for the Malbone portrait is similar to Copley's in

3. There are numerous mentions of the Stuarts, the Malbones, and the Bourses in George C. Mason, *Annals of Trinity Church, Newport, Rhode Island: 1698–1821* (Newport: G. C. Mason, 1890).

4. See Staiti, in Rebora and Staiti, *Copley in America*, pp. 264–66, no. 56.

5. Waterhouse, in Dunlap 1834, vol. 1, p. 169. The artist Mather Brown confirmed this information, although not specific to dates, in saying that Stuart taught him when he was twelve years old, i.e., before October 1775. See Evans 1999, p. 10; Mather Brown, letter to Catherine and Mary Byles, March 2, 1817, Mather Brown Correspondence, Massachusetts Historical Society, Boston.

6. Evans (1999, p. 10) suggests that Stuart visited Pelham and saw Copley's studio.

7. *Newport Mercury*, January 8, 1785.

8. In Park 1926, p. 500, Francis Malbone Jr. is mistaken for Francis Sr. as a founder of the firm of Evan and Francis Malbone.

9. The daughters were Elizabeth (ca. 1756–1832), Margaret (1761–1809), Catherine (1766–1847), and Mary (d. 1852). The Malbones also had two children who died young, Margaret (1754–1757) and Reodolphus (1765–1767).

10. Francis continued the firm of Evan and Francis Malbone with Daniel Mason (1755–1797). By 1784 the firm's name was Malbone and Mason; see advertisement, *Newport Mercury*, July 3, 1784, p. 1. Saunders's dates are gleaned from the record of his christening on May 31, 1764, at Trinity Church, Newport, and his obituaries in the *Newport Mercury*, May 28, 1836, and the *Rhode Island Republican*, May 25, 1836, both of which give his age at death as seventy-two.

11. Francis and Freelove Malbone had eight children: Margaret (1781–1782), William T. (Bill) (1783–1827), Reodolphus (1784–1825), Catherine, Freelove Sophia (1788–1823), Saunders (b. 1790), Elizabeth (b. 1801), Francis (d. 1817).

12. Saunders Malbone, letter to Peter Ayualt, October 11, 1791, Ms. 9001-A, Rhode Island Historical Society, Newport (RLC.PA.114).

many ways, especially the situation of figures on opposite sides of a table and the expressive spotlighted faces and complicated arrangement of hands. Stuart quotes Copley's eerie shadowing around fingers that are functioning according to task. This ambitious work reveals Stuart's emerging approach to portraiture. He would retain some compositional details seen here—Francis Malbone's tented hand on top of a letter appears later in the full-length portrait of George Washington (cat. 49)—and abandon others, such as the emphasis on glossy hardwood furniture, which was important in the furniture towns of Boston and Newport but superfluous in portraiture in London and Dublin, Stuart's next cities of residence.

The circumstances of this commission, as of all Stuart's Newport commissions, are unknown. Francis Malbone (1727–1785), a man of "uprightness, impartiality, [and] candour," had arrived in Newport from Princess Anne County, Virginia, about 1758, following Godfrey Malbone, probably his cousin.[7] Godfrey Malbone's youngest daughter, Deborah, was married to Dr. Hunter, Stuart's first client (see fig. 9). Francis Malbone and his brother, Evan, supplied rum and cordage to Aaron Lopez, another Stuart patron (see fig. 10).[8] In a town with few portraitists, it makes sense that Francis Malbone engaged Stuart for a portrait of his sons, for the artist had begun to attract attention.

Stuart portrayed Francis Jr. (1759–1809) and his brother Saunders (1764–1836) alone, without their parents or their sisters, as scions of this prosperous family.[9] Francis Jr. and Saunders, who was named for his mother, Margaret Saunders (1730–1775), went into business with their father, with Francis becoming the more prominent of the two.[10] Little is known of Saunders. Francis, on the other hand, enhanced his mercantile fortune by his marriage to Freelove Sophia Tweedy (1763–1829), daughter of William Tweedy, who ran with his brother John the largest drug-importing operation in the American colonies.[11] After the war, Francis and Saunders opened a retail store in Newport where, as Saunders put it in 1791, they intended "to begin the world again."[12] Francis also served as a captain in the Artillery Company in Newport for seventeen years, resigning when he was elected to Congress as a Federalist in 1793. He was elected to the Rhode Island House of Representatives in 1807 and in 1809 was elected to the Unites States Senate, an office he held for just a few months before taking a mortal fall down the steps of the Capitol.

CRB

4. BENJAMIN WATERHOUSE

1775
Oil on canvas, 22 x 18 in. (55.9 x 45.7 cm)
Redwood Library and Athenaeum, Newport,
Rhode Island; Bequest of Louisa Lee Waterhouse
(Mrs. Benjamin Waterhouse) of Cambridge,
Massachusetts (RLC.PA.114)

Benjamin Waterhouse (1754–1846) was born in Newport, the son of Timothy Waterhouse, formerly of New Hampshire, a judge in the Newport court of common pleas, and Hannah Proud, whose family had emigrated from Yorkshire, England.[1] Her brother was the cabinetmaker, Joseph Proud. Nearly two years older than Stuart, Waterhouse may have met him at the parish school, but their friendship developed from a mutual talent for drawing that they pursued until Waterhouse, on seeing Stuart's portrait of Dr. Hunter's dogs (fig. 9), "gave up the contest in despair."[2] At almost the same time that Cosmo Alexander took Stuart as an apprentice, the Scottish surgeon John Halliburton took Waterhouse as his protégé, offering him lessons and practical experience with his patients. By his own account, Waterhouse consumed every book on philosophy,

4

1. The bibliography on Waterhouse is voluminous and, in addition to the forthcoming biography by Philip Cash, includes Josiah Charles Trent, "The London Years of Benjamin Waterhouse," *Journal of the History of Medicine and Allied Sciences* 1 (January 1946), pp. 25–40; Josiah Charles Trent, "Benjamin Waterhouse," *Journal of the History of Medicine and Allied Sciences* 1 (July 1946), pp. 357–64; Philip Cash, "The Well-Placed and the Misplaced Philosophers: Benjamin Rush of Philadelphia and Benjamin Waterhouse of Boston," *Transactions and Studies of the College of Physicians of Philadelphia* 9 (1987), pp. 25–44; Yoshio

chemistry, and medicine in the Redwood Library.[3] In time, he designed a plan to continue his studies in London. Abraham Redwood, who had introduced Waterhouse to Halliburton, supported Waterhouse's proposed program of education, rationalizing that he had "founded a library in Newport, and will now give them a Physician, . . . an American one."[4] He wrote an introduction for Waterhouse to take to his own uncle Dr. John Fothergill in London and provided passage for him on Captain Folger's ship *Thomas* in March 1775.[5]

Waterhouse's trip to London was already planned by the time he sat for Stuart in January 1775.[6] He is shown in what was undoubtedly his habitual costume: drab brown jacket and waistcoat with fabric buttons, a simple pleated shirt with high collar and

Fig. 14. John Singleton Copley, *Paul Revere*, 1769. Oil on canvas, 35 x 28 ½ in. (88.9 x 72.3 cm). Museum of Fine Arts, Boston; Gift of Joseph W. Revere, William B. Revere, and Edward H. R. Revere (30.781)

Higomoto, "The Democratization of American Medicine: Benjamin Waterhouse and Medical Men in Massachusetts" (Ph.D. diss., Brown University, 1997). We are grateful to Philip Cash for sharing the manuscript of his biography with us.

2. Waterhouse "Autobiography," p. 10.

3. Ibid., pp. 12–14.

4. Ibid., p. 24. On Redwood's help to Waterhouse, see also George Herbert Waterhouse, *Descendants of Richard Waterhouse of Portsmouth, N.H.* (Wakefield, Mass., 1934; typescript on deposit at the New England Genealogical Society, Boston, Ms. 549), p. 197.

5. The precise relationship between Fothergill and Waterhouse is open to debate. Waterhouse referred to Fothergill as his "great uncle on my mother's side," while the family genealogy records that Fothergill was a first cousin to Hannah Proud, which would make her son a first cousin once removed to Fothergill.

6. The portrait is listed in Mason 1879, p. 275; Park 1926, pp. 790–91, no. 884. It has been erroneously dated to 1776, when the friends were both in London, or to 1780, the date of a later, now lost, portrait of Waterhouse; the misdating is described in Evans 1999, p. 127 n. 12.

sleeves with a small red and gold button at the cuff. The student looks up from his reading; the words are illegible but the format of the page with marginal notes indicates a scholarly text. The two volumes next in line for his attention are leather bound, one with a metal clasp attached to the gold-embossed black binding, the spine of the other showing the partially legible name of the author, ———*oerhaave*, referring to Hermann Boerhaave, the renowned Dutch physician, teacher, and author.

Waterhouse did not take the picture with him to London but probably left it with his family for he had it in his possession for his long life, and his widow gave it to the Redwood Library. How the sitting came about is a matter of speculation. Did Waterhouse ask to sit for a portrait for his family; did Stuart ask him to sit as a gesture of friendship; did the two of them seize upon the idea of an experimental portrait in which the painter could study his subject as he had never done before? The result was that the friendship of Stuart and Waterhouse allowed Stuart to paint his most accomplished portrait to date.

Stuart studied his friend's face to a degree unprecedented in his previous work. He achieved a variety of flesh tones, glossy and matte areas on the complexion, and modeling of the head and adjacent hand, replete with folds and sinew, so convincing that Waterhouse's cheek convincingly rests on his knuckles. Stuart once again mimicked Copley, giving authentic plasticity to the face and hands, accurately portrayed but vaguely rendered clothing, and piercing eyes that, for the first time in his work, suggest vitality. Scholars regularly compare Stuart's portrait of Waterhouse to Copley's of Paul Revere (fig. 14). Yet, for the progress of Stuart's eye and hand, the more remarkable juxtaposition is between *Waterhouse* and Stuart's own portrait of the Malbone brothers (cat. 3) from just months earlier.

As Stuart pursued his artistic career in London and Waterhouse his medical studies, their lives overlapped but less than might be expected. By the time Stuart arrived in London in the fall of 1775, Waterhouse had left for Edinburgh. When he returned to London in the summer of 1776, they resumed their conversations about art, inspired by the museums and galleries of London. Waterhouse may have given up drawing in favor

7. See his letter to his son-in-law, William Ware, August 25, 1831, in which he discusses "throwing into the papers a few remarks on certain portraits in the Athenaeum exhibition," Ware Family Papers, Massachusetts Historical Society, Boston.

8. See William H. Gerdts and Theodore E. Stebbins Jr., "A Man of Genius": The Art of Washington Allston (1779–1843), exh. cat. (Boston: Museum of Fine Arts, 1979), p. 16; Nathalia Wright, ed., The Correspondence of Washington Allston (Lexington: University Press of Kentucky, 1993), p. 580.

9. [Benjamin Waterhouse], "Sketch of the Life of Benjamin Waterhouse, M.D.," Polyanthos 2 (May 1806), p. 75. This essay is attributed to Waterhouse by Philip Cash in the manuscript for his forthcoming biography of Waterhouse.

10. Diary of John Quincy Adams, July 16, 1831, Adams Papers, Massachusetts Historical Society, Boston. Quotations from the Adams Papers are from the microfilm edition, by permission of the Massachusetts Historical Society.

11. Waterhouse "Autobiography."

of medicine, but he remained opinionated, articulate, and learned about drawing, painting, and sculpture. Waterhouse soon left again, this time for a three-year period of study (1777–80) at the University of Leiden, where he resided in the home of John Adams (see cats. 59, 90), then American minister to the Netherlands. His studies finished, Waterhouse joined Fothergill's practice in London for a short time but soon returned to Newport to honor his obligation to Redwood. He practiced in Newport for three years, until 1783, when he became involved in the founding of the Harvard Medical School in Cambridge (it moved to Boston in 1810). He brought there the collection of minerals of Dr. John Coakley Lettsom of Leiden, established a botanic garden, and taught under the title Professor of the Theory and Practice of Physic, all the while maintaining a private practice and lecturing on natural history at Brown University in Providence.

By far, Waterhouse's greatest legacy was the introduction of smallpox vaccine to America in 1800, a monumental advance in the history of American medicine. In 1813 President Madison appointed him medical supervisor for several institutions along New England coast, a position he held until 1820. He spent the last decade of his life writing An Essay on Junius and his Letters, embracing a sketch of the life and character of William Pitt, earl of Chatham (Boston, 1831), while also writing the essay "Statuary and Painting" and sending anonymous art criticism to the local papers.[7] He maintained an avid interest in the arts, in part through his rather paternalistic friendship with Washington Allston (see cat. 88), whom Waterhouse had taken as a boarder in 1796.[8]

Waterhouse and Stuart did not rekindle the closeness of their childhood friendship when both were in Boston, but about 1806, Waterhouse praised Stuart as a "man of transcendant talents in almost every department of ordinary knowledge."[9] Indeed, Waterhouse might have published a biography of Stuart but for the artist's wife who "with tears in her eyes intreated him not to do it."[10] He had been asked to do so by William Ellery Channing, the Unitarian clergyman who, like Waterhouse, came from Newport and spent his adult life in Boston and whom Stuart painted in 1805 (Fine Arts Museums of San Francisco). Waterhouse instead respected both Charlotte Coates Stuart's wishes and his own by preserving his acute reminiscences of Stuart in his autobiography, material on which much study of Stuart is based.[11]

CRB

Stuart in London (1775–87)

A nineteen-year-old Stuart disembarked in London in November 1775 with virtually no plans: no arrangements for study, no ingrained political views to affiliate him with compatriots or particular clients, little if any ambition in one direction or another. Unlike those colonial artists who arrived with the appropriate letters of introduction to potential patrons and set to work, this artist had nothing. He did not seek out Benjamin West, the esteemed artist from Pennsylvania who by the time of Stuart's arrival was history painter to King George III and regularly and generously took in young Americans as studio assistants. Stuart's friend Waterhouse (see cat. 4), who had preceded him to London, had gone to Edinburgh. Rather than seek portrait commissions, Stuart supported himself on a salary of 150 pounds a year by playing the organ at Saint Catherine's Church in Foster Lane, near Saint Paul's Cathedral, a job he got when, serendipitously hearing music coming from the church, he found auditions for the post of organist being conducted and put himself up for the position. He also took flute lessons. When Waterhouse returned to London in the summer of 1776, he found Stuart in rooms rented from a tailor named John Palmer in York Buildings, a narrow street of boardinghouses on the River Thames just below the Strand at the end of Buckingham Street. He had on his easel a group portrait, the family of Alexander Grant, perhaps the same Scottish gentleman who had patronized Stuart's teacher Cosmo Alexander. Stuart probably did not finish the portrait for it was never seen again.[1]

The methodical Waterhouse enjoyed Stuart's conviviality, even as Stuart's unreliability tested his patience. Waterhouse took it upon himself to make Stuart focus on his painting, and more than once, he paid Stuart's debts. He persuaded Stuart to move in with his medical student friends on Gracechurch Street, a better neighborhood and near his own home. During the summer and fall Waterhouse and Stuart spent at least one day each week viewing sites and pictures, using William Maitland's *History and Survey of London*, a tome for scholars rather than tourists.[2] They walked the narrow streets lined with red brick buildings, becoming familiar with the highly commercial and stratified city, and they favored the Royal Collection above all else.

Stuart took some commissions that fall, all linked to Waterhouse's scientific colleagues, the first of which came from William Curtis, a botanist who worked at the Apothecaries Company in Gracechurch Street, near Stuart's and Waterhouse's rooms. Stuart made a keen character study of the affable but serious young man (fig. 15) posed with plates showing his illustration of foxglove (*Digitalis purpurea*) from the first fascicle of what would become his life's work, *Flora Londinensis: or Plates and Descriptions of Such Plants as Grow Wild in the Environs of London* (1775–98). Waterhouse's uncle Dr. John Fothergill paid Stuart ten guineas to paint a

1. See Evans 1999, p. 128 n. 16, regarding Stuart's delivering letters from Newport to Alexander Grant on arriving in London and the speculation that he may have begun a portrait of Grant. Nothing else is known about Alexander Grant, including any connection between him and William Grant, *The Skater* (cat. 6).
2. William Maitland, *The History and Survey of London from Its Foundation to the Present Time* (London: T. Osborne, 1760).

Detail of cat. 17, *Joseph Brant*

Fig. 15. *William Curtis*, 1776–77. Oil on canvas, 33¾ x 28 in. (85.7 x 71 cm). The Royal Horticultural Society, Lindley Library, London

portrait of Waterhouse (unlocated), and Waterhouse used his influence to get Stuart the distinguished commission to paint a full-length exhibition piece of the medical philanthropist Dr. John Coakley Lettsom (unlocated). That Stuart finished neither of these pictures did not deter Waterhouse from convincing a group of his fellow students to pool their money for a portrait of their lecturer Dr. George Fordyce, a Scottish physician. Stuart took the assignment and the payment but never began the work, compelling Waterhouse to return his friends' contributions out of his own pocket.[3]

There are at least three versions of how Stuart went to Benjamin West's studio at 14 Newman Street, some part of each of which may be accurate. Waterhouse claimed to have sought out West, hoping to find a place as a studio assistant for his talented but wayward friend in anticipation of his own return to medical school.[4] Another rendition has Stuart knocking on West's door at the very moment that Joseph Wharton, a friend from Philadelphia, and a party of Americans were at dinner.[5] Wharton vouched for Stuart on learning that he was a nephew of his friend Joseph Anthony. Finally there is the story of Stuart's appeal directly to West, a request not for artistic instruction but for salvation from pitiable circumstances. About mid-December 1776, Stuart drafted a letter from Waterhouse's rooms at 30 Gracechurch Street. Stuart explained to West that "poverty and ignorance are my only excuse" and described his plight: "Pitty me Good Sir I've just arriv'd at the age of 21 an age when most young men have done something worthy of notice & find myself Ignorant without Business or Friends, without the necessarys of life so far that for some time I have been reduced to one miserable meal a day & frequently not even that, destitute of the means of acquiring knowledge, my hopes from home Blasted & incapable of returning thither, pitching headlong into misery I have this only hope I pray that it may not be too great, to live & learn without being a Burthen."[6] When Waterhouse left for medical school early in 1777, Stuart moved to 27 Villiers Street, in his old neighborhood near the river. Soon, however, West took him in as a resident assistant to work finishing draperies and backgrounds on what Stuart would later refer to as his master's "ten-acre pictures."[7]

As a central member of West's coterie over the next decade, Stuart was drawn into the mix of the public commerce of art and its private display, the competition for exhibition venues, and the nascent critical press that described every episode contributing to the dynamism of the British art scene. The center of the London art world, the ten-year-old Royal Academy of Arts, would soon be relocated in the freshly renovated Somerset House on the Strand, with space for a school, a library, and the so-called Great Room for the annual exhibition of contemporary painting. The academy's first president, Sir Joshua Reynolds, in his prime as a portraitist, teacher, and administrator, faced stiff competition from Thomas Gainsborough, who returned to London from Bath in 1774, and perhaps also rivalry with the fashionable George Romney, who, back in London in 1775 after travels on the Continent, cultivated a strong private clientele. Myriad other painters, including John Hoppner, John Opie, Joseph Wright of Derby, and foreigners such as John Singleton Copley and West, invigorated the increasingly competitive market for portraits, driven by clients from diverse segments of society. Stuart stayed

3. There is evidence of at least two other pictures painted at this time, now missing: Admiral Peter Ranier (Evans 1999, p. 128 n. 17) and a double portrait of sisters, one dark haired, the other a redhead, posed as tragic and comic muses.
4. Dunlap 1834, vol. 1, p. 173.
5. Ibid., p. 174.
6. Stuart, letter to West, [December 1776], Miscellaneous Manuscripts, New-York Historical Society.
7. Dunlap 1834, vol. 1, p. 178.

Fig. 16. *Caleb Whitefoord*, 1782. Oil on canvas, 30 x 25 in. (76.2 x 63.5 cm). Montclair Art Museum, Montclair, N.J.; Museum Purchase, Clayton E. Freeman Fund (1945.110)

on the margins of the academy, never enrolling in the school nor promoting himself for membership, but he attended Reynolds's discourses and submitted portraits to several of the annual exhibitions over the course of a decade. Nonetheless, West did what he could for Stuart: as a member of the hanging committee for the 1777 academy exhibition, West surely helped get Stuart's portrait of a woman (unidentified) into the show.

Stuart repaid West's help and encouragement with gratitude and respect tempered by his desire to follow his own views as an artist. He studied the works of Reynolds, Gainsborough, and Romney, and quickly diverged from West's style. West, meanwhile, may have tolerated Stuart's increasing allegiance to other painters, in part because the student never failed to follow his teacher's example when called upon to work on or copy his canvases. And Stuart was saved from the responsibility of being West's prize student by the arrival in 1780 of the young American history painter John Trumbull. Trumbull and Stuart, both headstrong, smart, and extremely talented, got on very well, but it was Trumbull who worked steadily and gratefully on West's various historical tableaux, even while in prison for treason between November 1780 and June 1781. Stuart painted Trumbull's portrait during his time in jail (fig. 169). After West and Copley paid his release bond, Trumbull was deported, but he returned to West's studio as soon as he could in June 1784. By that time, Stuart had left the studio.

Just how fully Stuart assimilated the fashionable, painterly English idiom— and thereby strayed from West's linear technique—became clear in his portrait of the Scottish diplomat and connoisseur Caleb Whitefoord (fig. 16) and his full-length painting of the barrister William Grant, better known as *The Skater* (cat. 6), both displayed at the 1782 Royal Academy exhibition. Stuart's pictures suggested the inextricable link between student and teacher, if not in matters of technique then certainly in personal connections. For example, Whitefoord, a friend of West, would serve as secretary of the British commission at the signing of the preliminary treaty of peace between the American colonies and England in November 1782. He was meant to sit for West for the conversation piece that West would paint of that momentous occasion, but before his departure for Paris in April 1782, Whitefoord sat for Stuart rather than West, perhaps so West would have a good image of the secretary from which to work later on.[8] *The Skater* refers obliquely to West's and Stuart's shared expertise on the ice. A reviewer of the academy exhibition jested about their mutual admiration: "Mr. Stuart is in Partnership with Mr. West; where it is not uncommon for Wits to divert themselves with Applications for Things they do not immediately want; because they are told by Mr. West that Mr. Stuart is the only Portrait Painter in the World; and by Mr. Stuart that no Man has any Pretensions in History Painting but Mr. West."[9]

Just after the 1782 academy exhibition, the portraitist Nathaniel Dance encouraged Stuart to strike out on his own: "You are strong enough to stand alone; take rooms; those who would be unwilling to sit to Mr. West's pupil will be glad to sit to Mr. Stuart."[10] Shrewd advice, for after Stuart moved to 7 Newman Street, down the block from West's, his patronage grew appreciably, beginning with a commission from the successful printseller John Boydell for portraits of fifteen contemporary British artists. While some artists, especially Reynolds, deemed such

8. *Signing of the Preliminary Treaty of Peace in 1782*, 1783–84 (Henry Francis du Pont Winterthur Museum, Winterthur, Del.); see Von Erffa and Staley 1986, pp. 218–19, no. 105.

9. "Postscript Account of the Exhibition of Paintings, &c. at the Royal Academy," *St. James's Chronicle*, May 2, 1782, p. 4.

10. Mason 1879, p. 277.

Fig. 17. *Isaac Barré*, 1785. Oil on canvas, 35⅞ x 27¾ in. (91 x 70.5 cm). Brooklyn Museum, New York; Carll H. de Silver Fund (16.25)

Fig. 18. *Hugh Percy, Second Duke of North- umberland*, 1785. Oil on canvas, 28 x 22¼ in. (71.1 x 57.8 cm). The Northumberland Estates, Alnwick Castle, Collection of the Duke of Northumberland

commercial work degrading, Stuart had no problem with it and seized the oppor- tunity to paint many of his more established colleagues, including West (cat. 12), Copley (cat. 13), and even Reynolds (cat. 14), as well as the noted engravers James Heath (fig. 35), William Woollett (cat. 10), and John Hall (cat. 11). Stuart showed two of these pictures along with seven other portraits at the 1783 exhibition of the Incorporated Society of Artists, a group founded in 1761 by the most prominent artists of the day but abandoned by most of them in favor of the Royal Academy. Stuart's participation in this organization served him well, as a reviewer singled him out as one of the "ablest artists" in the show, one whose "portraits promise great future increase of merit."[11]

Stuart continued work on the Boydell portraits for the next two years, even as he accepted many other orders. Despite the volume of commissions, Stuart was in financial straights. In April 1785, Stuart received a visit from Isaac Barré; John Jervis, the Earl of St. Vincent; and Hugh Percy. According to Stuart, who recounted the visit to others, they "came unexpectedly one morning into my room, locked the door and then explained the intention of their visit. . . . They under- stood . . . that I was under pecuniary embarrassments, and offered me assistance, which I declined. They then said they would sit for their portraits. Of course I was ready to serve them. They then advised that I should make it a rule that half-price must be paid at the first sitting. They insisted on setting the example, and I fol- lowed the practice ever after this delicate mode of showing their friendship."[12] The pictures ordered seem to have been tokens exchanged among friends to provide financial aid to their artist-friend. That day, Isaac Barré commissioned three bust- length portraits of himself: one for himself (National Portrait Gallery, London); one for John Parker, Baron Boringdon (Yale Center for British Art, New Haven); and one for the Earl of St. Vincent (fig. 17).[13] Lord Hugh Percy, soon to be the second Duke of Northumberland, recorded payment to Stuart on April 22 and

11. "Society of Artists," *Morning Chronicle and London Advertiser*, May 1, 1783, p. 3.

12. Dunlap 1834, vol. 1, p. 188, as told to him by Charles Fraser; also in Mason 1879, pp. 17–18, as told by Stuart to Thomas Sully.

13. See draft entry on the portrait of Barré by Teresa A. Carbone, *American Paintings in the Brooklyn Museum: Artists Born by 1876* (forthcoming, 2005).

Fig. 19. *Samuel Barrington*, 1785. Oil on canvas, 30 x 25 in. (76.2 x 63.5 cm). Saltram Park (Morley Collection), The National Trust, England (photo: National Portrait Gallery, London)

Fig. 20. *John Henderson as Iago*, 1785. Oil on canvas, 20¼ x 16½ in. (51.4 x 41.9 cm). Victoria and Albert Museum, London (photo: V&A Images)

Fig. 21. *Alexander Pope as Posthumus*, 1786. Oil on canvas, 16⅜ x 11½ in. (41.5 x 29 cm). Garrick Club, London

June 29, 1785, for two portraits of himself (both, collection of the Duke of Northumberland; see fig. 18).[14] The Earl of St. Vincent commissioned a portrait of himself (National Maritime Museum, Greenwich) and then apparently sent more than 2,000 pounds of business to Stuart only to be so dissatisfied that he would later publicly call Stuart an ingrate.[15]

While St. Vincent held Stuart in contempt, Percy retained Stuart's services with a series of commissions, and Barré's connections paid off. In 1785 Stuart undertook a commission for twenty-four portraits for Baron Boringdon, who was working with Robert Adam on renovations to his family home, Saltram, in Devonshire.[16] There, Stuart's work would complete a cycle of portraits begun many years before by Boringdon's childhood friend Reynolds, who recommended Stuart for the work. For Boringdon's friends in the naval service, including Admiral Samuel Barrington (fig. 19), Stuart adapted the conventional practice for head-and-shoulders-with-uniform portraits to his own skill for capturing likeness and character, a successful venture that led to still more commissions from military officers such as Captain John Gell (cat. 15). That year the publisher John Bell, a colleague of Boydell's, involved Stuart in the production of a book of full-length portraits of the finest actors of the day. Stuart painted the heads only—emotive, richly described heads—with other artists providing the theatrical settings and costumes—of John Henderson as Iago (fig. 20); Alexander Pope as Posthumus (fig. 21); John Philip Kemble as Richard III, Macbeth, and Orestes; Joseph Holman as Philip Faulconbridge; and others.[17]

With the Boydell, Boringdon, and Bell commissions simultaneously under way, in addition to other work, Stuart reached what must be considered the apogee of his productivity in London. In 1785, he moved into a new home and studio at 3 New Burlington Street, and he exhibited at the Royal Academy his full-length portrait of Gell, an obvious homage to Reynolds. That year he helped Reynolds

14. The Duke of Northumberland's Ledger Book, 1783–85, Alnwick Castle, Northumberland.

15. Kathryn Cave, ed., *The Diary of Joseph Farington* (New Haven: Yale University Press, 1982), vol. 7, p. 2544.

16. The twenty-four pictures remain at Saltram House and have been catalogued for the National Trust by F. St. John Gore with revisions by Alastair Laing and the assistance of Derek Holdaway. On the Adam renovation, see Eileen Harris, *The Genius of Robert Adam: His Interiors* (New Haven: Yale University Press, 2001), pp. 232–41.

17. The painting of Kemble as Richard III is in a private collection. The other portraits of him plus those of Holman and others are unlocated; see Evans 1999, pp. 134–35 n. 25.

solve his dilemma over what to paint for Empress Catherine the Great of Russia, who in 1785 asked for a history painting of any subject Reynolds desired. According to Stuart, Reynolds feared that whatever he chose would invoke "some latent satyre" about his client, and Stuart "relieved him by proposing Hercules. I met Sir J. soon after he had finished it, and he requested me to go and see it."[18] Despite the urging of Horace Walpole and others that Reynolds paint a more appropriate subject, Reynolds painted *The Infant Hercules Strangling the Serpents* (State Hermitage, Saint Petersburg). No doubt due in part to Reynolds's attentions, Stuart's pictures hung in the main salon of the academy, adjacent to the president's own works, a circumstance that moved him from the margins to the center of the annual competition among portraitists.

By 1786, Stuart was reportedly earning 1,500 pounds a year, ten times what he made as an organist a decade before. That year he married Charlotte Coates, a contralto who shared his love of music, the sister of Dr. William Coates, whom he met while attending anatomy lectures by Dr. William Cruikshank. His best client at the time was Lord Percy, by then the second Duke of Northumberland, who, having received his own portrait from Stuart, next commissioned a portrait of the Mohawk chief Joseph Brant (cat. 17) then visiting England, a nearly lifesize group portrait of his children (cat. 18), and full-length portraits of himself and his wife.[19] Stuart lived at the duke's country home, Syon, an arrangement that may also have aided Stuart with debts incurred on his New Burlington Street house. Stuart's facility as a painter carried him through the first two commissions, but circumstances, such as his financial troubles and separation from his wife who moved to her parents' home in Reading when he moved to Syon, seem to have made it difficult for him to work. He did not finish the portraits of Northumberland and his wife, perhaps never even starting them, and he failed to keep up with his other orders. It is hard to imagine that Stuart did not have studio assistants, but there is no proof that he had help and his increasing inability to fulfill his commissions lends to the notion that he worked alone. He finished all fifteen of the Boydell pictures but only seven of the twenty-four for Boringdon.

The London newspaper the *World* for April 1787 acclaimed Stuart "the Vandyke of the Time." This was indeed high praise connecting as it did a virtually self-taught artist from the colonies to England's most revered portraitist. "In the most arduous and valuable achievements of portrait painting, *identity* and *duration*, Stuart takes the lead of every competitor. . . . Stuart dives deep," the writer declared, "less deep than Sir Joshua, more deep than every other pencil— Stuart dives deep into mind, and brings up with him a conspicuous draught of character and characteristic thought—all as sensible to feeling and to sight as the most palpable projection of any feature of a face."[20] Such praise could not help Stuart with the problems that arose from having taken on too many ambitious commissions and by having the bills associated with a large house and a growing family. Stuart and his wife would have twelve children—five sons and seven daughters—of whom little is known.[21] Money is always given as the reason for Stuart's departure from London, rather than any sort of problem of competing portraitists, but it amounted to the same thing. As Stuart failed to keep up with his commissions and attract new ones, his fortunes fell as his expenses rose. One

18. Pickering 1810, in which Stuart refers to the empress of Austria. On the picture, see David Mannings and Martin Postle, *Sir Joshua Reynolds: A Complete Catalogue of His Paintings* (New Haven: Yale University Press, 2000), p. 539, no. 2094.

19. The only primary-source mention of the full-length portrait of the duke is in Oliver Oldschool, "His Grace, the Duke of Northumberland, Stuart Pinxit," *The Port Folio* 5 (1805), pp. 156–57. See also Park 1926, p. 556, no. 587.

20. "Stuart—the Vandyke of the Time," *The World*, April 18, 1787, p. 3.

21. Evans 1999, pp. 97–98, 152 n. 11.

22. Quoted from an unidentified source in Whitley 1932, p. 67.

23. Quoted and described in ibid., pp. 66–67.

story of Stuart's financial troubles and forced departure from England comes through a conversation between Sir Thomas Lawrence and Henry Hope, Lord Holland. Lawrence explained: "'I knew Stuart well, and I believe the real cause of his leaving England was his having become tired of the inside of some of our prisons.' 'Well then,' said Lord Holland, 'after all, it was his love of freedom that took him to America.'"[22] There is no record of Stuart ever having been incarcerated in London, but rumors of his predicament must have reached a point that such a notion was believable. By August 1787, newspapers reported variously that Stuart had offers of commissions in France and that he had been called home by his father.[23] In fact, the painter and his wife had gone to Dublin.

CRB

5. SELF-PORTRAIT

1778

Oil on canvas, 16¾ x 12¾ in. (42.5 x 32.4 cm)
Redwood Library and Athenaeum, Newport,
Rhode Island; Bequest of Louisa Lee Waterhouse
(Mrs. Benjamin Waterhouse) of Cambridge,
Massachusetts (RLC.PA.113)

Dorinda Evans has assessed the artist's self-portrait of 1778 as "the greatest leap in his artistic career."[1] In it he abandoned his usually meticulous composition made up of solid forms in favor of a more fluid approach, perhaps paying heed to Sir Joshua Reynolds's advice in the published version of his annual discourse of December 14, 1770, that a fine painter should leave "minute discriminations" to "the lower painter, like the florist or collector of shells."[2] It is unlikely that Stuart read the Royal Academy lectures with a definite plan for improving his work. Instead, his work progressed and changed gradually according to circumstance and challenge rather than as the result of a systematic effort.

Stuart recalled the execution of this portrait as "rather of accident than premeditation."[3] One day, he purchased, with 12 borrowed guineas, a portrait by the seventeenth-century English painter William Dobson. His teacher Benjamin West was so struck by it that he tried to buy it from him. West first offered 15 guineas and went up to 50, but Stuart would not sell. Then he softened: "I know your candour & goodness—I ask no equivalent for the picture, but when you tell me I can paint a portrait as good as this of Dobson's, the picture shall be yours." To this West agreed. Stuart decided to emulate Dobson's work in a self-portrait. He pleased West with the result and made good on the bet by giving West the old picture. As with most of Stuart's recollections, this one is both plausible and subject to interpretation. He was perpetually in need of cash, and there are no other recorded instances of his being so taken with a painting. Yet in his memory of the incident he valued the approval of his master over the money. For West's part, might he have risked his reputation as a teacher of high moral standards and ethical principles just to get the portrait? In Stuart's self-portrait the palette is dark and the figure is in shadow but otherwise it hardly looks like a Dobson portrait.[4] It may have been "as good" without being the same, thus making the entire gambit a ploy on West's part to goad his student to buckle down and paint. In fact, Stuart painted a version of West's most recent self-portrait (fig. 22), a three-quarter pose, bust-length portrait of the artist facing right and wearing a wide-brimmed black hat cocked to his left and opening his face to the light. West derived his image from Peter Paul Rubens's self-portrait of 1623 (fig. 23), which both he and Stuart would have seen in the Royal Collection at Buckingham House. Stuart may have won his master's praise by painting a picture that paid him homage. As for the Dobson portrait, there is no trace of it in the inventories of West's collection taken at his death.

1. See Evans 1999, p. 15. The painting is listed in Mason 1879, p. 261; Park 1926, p. 718, no. 796.
2. Sir Joshua Reynolds, *Discourses on Art*, ed. Robert Wark (1959; reprint, New Haven: Yale University Press for the Paul Mellon Centre for Studies in British Art, 1975), p. 50.
3. Pickering 1817 (October 29).
4. See Malcolm Rogers, *William Dobson, 1611–46*, exh. cat. (London: National Portrait Gallery, 1983).

5. The inscription was covered by a relining to the canvas. The Latin "aetatis suae 24" means "in his 24th year." Stuart turned twenty-three, entering his twenty-fourth year, on December 3, 1778.

6. Charles Willson Peale, letter to Rembrandt Peale, September 11, 1808, Peale Family Papers, Letterbook 9, American Philosophical Society, Philadelphia.

7. Dunlap 1834, vol. 1, p. 208.

8. Thomas Sully, "Journal," August 11, 1829, Historical Society of Pennsylvania, Philadelphia.

9. "Stuart's Gallery of Paintings," *Columbian Centinel*, August 16, 1828.

Stuart gave his self-portrait to Benjamin Waterhouse, who had been at the University of Leiden since 1777 and in 1780 was in London en route home to Newport. According to Waterhouse, Stuart had painted the picture especially for him. Waterhouse described it as an unfinished likeness with an inscription on the back of the canvas: *G. Stuart Pictor / se ipso pinxit. A.D. 1778. Ætatis Suae 24.*[5]

Waterhouse had the portrait in his home in Cambridge, Massachusetts, when he described it to Charles Willson Peale in 1808, proclaiming it Stuart's only self-portrait, "a wonderfull fine piece, painted in broad shadow."[6] He also told Peale that the picture was unfinished and that he feared it would remain so, a touching sentiment considering that Waterhouse and Stuart had been out of touch for many years although by then both lived in the Boston area. Waterhouse described a visit by Stuart to his home: "After spending the night at my house, he got up early in the morning, and went into the room where hung this head . . . when I heard him talking to it thus: 'Gibby, you needn't be ashamed of that—there is the perfection of the art or I know nothing of the matter.' And after I made my appearance, he said to me, 'I should like to see A. B. or C. attempt to copy it.' I remarked that most people took it for a very old picture. He replied, 'Yes, I suppose so; I *olified* it on purpose that they should think so,'—punning on the Latin word *oleum*—oil."[7] Stuart's description of giving his painting the look of an "old picture" recalls its supposed relationship with a Dobson portrait, although Waterhouse seems not to have known the story.

Waterhouse submitted the picture to the memorial exhibition of Stuart's work held at the Boston Athenaeum just after his death in 1828, where among the viewers was the painter Thomas Sully, who had studied with Stuart in Boston and regarded it as very strong likeness.[8] According to another viewer, "[It is] the head of the painter himself. . . . He is represented as looking in a mirror, intently copying his own face. . . . It is executed in a technical manner, a manner that better pleases the artist than ordinary setters. People who sit for their pictures always shut their mouths, and are apt to think

Fig. 22. Benjamin West, *Self-Portrait*, ca. 1776. Oil on canvas, 30¼ x 25⅛ in. (76.8 x 63.8 cm). The Baltimore Museum of Art; Gift of Dr. Morton K. Blaustein, Barbara B. Hirschhorn, and Elizabeth B. Roswell, in memory of Jacob and Hilda K. Blaustein (BMA 1981.73)

Fig. 23. Peter Paul Rubens, *Self-Portrait*, 1623. Oil on panel, 33½ x 24¼ (85.9 x 62.2 cm). The Royal Collection © 2004, Her Majesty Queen Elizabeth II

5

of their own looks, but here the mouth is relaxed, making it a picture of *intense attention* in copying his own features and mind. He intentionally gave the whole, in the colouring, and in the indistinct marks of the Rubens-hat, shirt-collar, and hair, the cast of an old picture. As he painted this to please himself and his friend, he could pursue his own taste."[9]

CRB

6. THE SKATER (WILLIAM GRANT)

1782
Oil on canvas, 96¼ x 58 in. (244.5 x 147.4 cm)
National Gallery of Art, Washington, D.C.;
Andrew W. Mellon Collection (1950.18.1)

1. *Exhibition of Works by the Old Masters, and by Deceased Masters of the British School*, exh. cat. (London: Royal Academy of Arts, 1878), no. 190; "The Old Masters at the Royal Academy," *Saturday Review*, January 12, 1878, p. 50; "The Old Masters at Burlington House: Second Notice," *London Illustrated News*, January 19, 1878, p. 66; "The Old Masters at Burlington House: Third Notice," *London Illustrated News*, January 26, 1878, p. 91; Whitley 1932, p. 34; Mulgrave Phipps Jackson, letter to George Champlin Mason, August 14, 1878, George Champlin Mason Papers, Manuscript Division, Rhode Island Historical Society, Providence. The painting is listed in Mason 1879, pp. 187–90; Park 1926, pp. 358–59, no. 343.

In 1878, Lord Charles Pelham-Clinton lent this portrait of his wife's grandfather to a Royal Academy exhibition as a work by Thomas Gainsborough. Countering this misattribution, the press offered such wildly diverse suggestions of artist as Henry Raeburn, George Romney, John Hoppner, or Martin Archer Shee.[1] More information was sought about the sitter, thought to be the key missing piece of the puzzle. By the close of the exhibition, the work had been assigned to Gilbert Stuart, but still nothing was known of the subject, despite the painting's having descended in his family.[2] *The Skater* got its narrative title at an exhibition at the Tate Gallery in 1946, shortly before Andrew Mellon acquired the picture from a descendant of the subject, by which time the subject's biography had been entirely subsumed in the analysis of what was going on in the picture.[3] The story of Stuart's "well-made and graceful" client, William Grant, who arrived at the Newman Street studio of Benjamin West, where Stuart was working, with the remark "that the day was better suited for skating than sitting for one's portrait," thus provoking an excursion, has become art-historical legend.[4]

Grant's elegant athleticism has long eclipsed his background: his father was the obscure landholder Ludovick Grant of Edinburgh and Congalton, descended from King Alpin, first king of the Picts and Scots. The clan of Grant came with the Normans to England, first appeared in Scotland during the mid-thirteenth century, and later came to notoriety for supporting the House of Hanover during the uprisings of 1715 and 1745.[5] In 1782, William Grant (1750–1821) was a thirty-two-year-old barrister practicing in London. He and Stuart may have been linked in fundamental ways, through their Scottish heritage and the network of Scottish nationals in London. Stuart and Grant could have met through Romney, for whom Grant sat in 1781 (fig. 24) and again in 1787.[6] Grant also sat to the miniaturist George Engleheart for a tiny, jolly likeness (fig. 25) and would later go to John Opie, an artist perpetually on the fringes of the portrait scene, for a painting of his children (LaSalle University Art Museum, Philadelphia).

Fig. 24. George Romney, *William Grant*, 1781. Oil on canvas, 29½ x 25 in. (73.7 x 63.5 cm). Private collection (photo: National Portrait Gallery, London)

Fig. 25. George Engleheart, *William Grant*, ca. 1776. Watercolor on ivory, H. 1⅜ in. (3.4 cm). Private collection (photo: Christie's, London)

2. Mulgrave Phipps Jackson, letter to Jane Stuart, March 22, 1878, Mason Papers, Rhode Island Historical Society.

3. *American Painting from the Eighteenth Century to the Present Day*, exh. cat. (London: Tate Gallery, 1946), checklist no. 206. On the painting's provenance, see Miles 1995, pp. 162–63.

4. Dunlap 1834, vol. I, p. 183.

5. George Way of Plean and Romilly Squire, *Collins Scottish Clan and Family Encyclopedia* (New York: Harper Collins, 1994), pp. 29–30.

6. Romney later painted a portrait of Grant's wife, Dorothea Dalrymple, in 1794, the year of their marriage; see Thomas Humfrey Ward and W. Roberts, *Romney: A Biographical and Critical Essay, with a Catalogue Raisonné of His Works* (London: T. Agnew and Sons; New York: Charles Scribner's Sons, 1904), pp. 63–64. The portraits mentioned here, including the pictures by Opie and Engleheart, were sold at Christie's, London, November 13, 1973, and March 22, 1974, the property of Mrs. Georgiana Bordewich, the Grant descendant from whom Andrew Mellon acquired *The Skater*.

7. Dunlap 1834, vol. I, p. 184.

8. Ibid., p. 183.

9. Quoted in Whitley 1932, p. 32.

10. "Account of the Exhibition of Paintings &c at the Royal Academy," *St. James Chronicle, and London Advertiser*, May 2–4, 1782, p. 2; letter signed "Candid," *Morning Chronicle and London Advertiser*, May 9, 1782; *London Courant*, quoted in Whitley 1932, p. 33.

11. Dunlap 1834, vol. I, p. 184.

12. See John Murdoch, "Architecture and Experience: The Visitor and the Spaces of Somerset House, 1780-1796," in David H. Solkin, ed., *Art on the Line: The Royal Academy Exhibitions at Somerset House 1780-1836*, exh. cat. (New Haven, London: Yale University Press for the Paul Mellon Centre for Studies in British Art and the Courtauld Institute Gallery, 2001), pp. 9–22.

13. Dunlap 1834, vol. I, p. 183.

14. Miles 1995, p. 168.

15. Pressly 1986, p. 46.

In the 1782 Royal Academy annual exhibition, Stuart's picture was number 190—*Portrait of a gentleman skating*. The display turned the subject into a momentary sensation. Grant "was compelled to make a retreat" from the gallery to escape the crowd that followed him around, exclaiming, "That is he, there is the gentleman."[7] Few would have known his name since the academy's standards of discretion forbade the listing of sitters' names in the catalogue. Indeed, Grant disappeared from sight and record after that, while his picture has been discussed in the literature ever since.

The Italian lexicographer Giuseppe Baretti first noticed the painting in West's studio: "What a charming picture! Who but that great artist, West, could have painted such a one!" Even if Baretti had been astute enough to see that the portrait of the man skating bore no resemblance to West's work, he might have assumed, in accordance with London studio tradition, that if West had anything to do with the picture, it would be attributed to him. On a return visit to the studio, Baretti saw Stuart painting on the canvas: "What, young man, does Mr. West permit you to touch his pictures?" When Stuart told him the picture was his own work, Baretti responded, "Why . . . it is almost as good as Mr. West can paint."[8]

Horace Walpole regularly scribbled notes in his Royal Academy catalogues as he walked through the exhibitions. In 1782, next to the entry for number 190, he wrote "very good," which was high praise from this terse connoisseur.[9] One critic commented that the picture was "reposed, animated, and well drawn"; another was struck by "the neatness of the execution"; and a third found Stuart's work lacking "Freedom of Pencil, and Elegance of Taste."[10] In the academy's politicized and competitive forum, the review of one artist's work often implied an affront to another's, so that the phrases about the painting being well drawn and neat would have been understood by the cognoscenti as a slight against Sir Joshua Reynolds, the academy president, who was then being criticized for the messy manner of his brushwork. The Duke of Rutland, who would become one of Stuart's major supporters, raved to Reynolds about Stuart's picture: "I wish you to go to the exhibition with me, for there is a portrait there which you must see, every body is enchanted with it."[11]

During the 1780s, full-length portraits—known as exhibition pieces—were the test of an artist's abilities. Hundreds of head-and-shoulders images appeared at the academy each year, most of them hung below the so-called line, a permanent hanging rail slightly lower than midway between the floor and the cornice devised by the architect William Chambers for the Great Room at Somerset House. This innovation, meant to allow eye-level viewing of the smaller pictures and unobstructed sight lines up to the larger ones, soon became less a matter of arranging pictures and more a matter of prestige: the coveted exhibition spots were on top.[12] As he had done in previous years, Stuart prepared bust-length portraits for the 1782 show, one of the diplomat Caleb Whitefoord (fig. 16) and another of the artist Dominic Serres (unlocated), but he needed to submit a large painting to be noticed in the room. He had previously turned down offers for or failed to finish at least three full-length canvases, but he conceded that "there must be a beginning" and started work on his portrait of Grant.[13]

Technical examination at the National Gallery of Art, Washington, reveals significant pentimenti in the hat, shoulders, coattail, and right leg, demonstrating that he struggled with the picture.[14] Its conceptual brilliance, however, has inspired a number of theoretical interpretations. William Pressly argues that the somber tonalities of the scene do not merely describe winter but create a setting for the melancholy hero, "the man whose superior endowments elevate him above the rest of humanity."[15] This type pervaded English eighteenth-century society, as young men feigned glum dispositions in

Fig. 26. Thomas Gainsborough, *Giovanna Baccelli*, 1782. Oil on canvas, 88½ x 57 in. (226.7 x 148.6 cm). Tate, London

order to been seen as poetic, sensitive, and of genius-level intelligence. In painting, the exemplary picture was Joseph Wright of Derby's recumbent, pastoral portrait of Sir Brooke Boothby (Tate Britain), which was shown at the academy in 1781. The connection between the paintings of Grant and Boothby notwithstanding—dark clothing, wide-awake hats, wry smiles, outdoor settings—Pressly pushes beyond formal inspection and brings the picture back around to Stuart, who suffered from "debilitating states of mind" and may have painted the picture as a projection of his own psychological maladies, a melancholic scene by a melancholic painter. Dorinda Evans's acceptance of Stuart's manic-depressive tendencies is woven throughout her interpretations of his work, except for *The Skater*, which she relates to his passion for music. The suggestion is that he designed his palette according to a theory of harmony, equating the spectrum of color to a musical scale.[16] And in the most recent study, Gwendolyn Allday invokes hermetic philosophy and ascribes the look of the painting to Stuart's dabblings in alchemy and the creation of a work with links to "the mystical tradition of signs and symbols."[17]

Stuart, indeed, thought carefully and strategically to create a work that would get hung in the optimal position at the Royal Academy and resonate among viewers. One of the strategies artists used to get good placement in the Royal Academy galleries was to figure out what other artists were submitting. Newspaper critics conducted informal previews at the studios, anticipating what might be in the exhibition, and artists carried out their own investigations. Stuart may have learned that the 1782 show would include two other portraits with subjects in poses of physical exertion, counter to prevailing modes of polite comportment. Joseph Wright's painting *Two Young Gentlemen in the Characters of Archers* (fig. 29), which hung next to Stuart's portrait of Serres, was the least provocative since the active subjects were young men. Young women were held to the strictest rules of posture, and Gainsborough's portrait of Giovanna Baccelli (fig. 26), principal ballerina at the King's Theatre, Haymarket, brushed the outside boundaries of decorum. The very act of dancing on stage, even in classical ballet, encouraged voyeurism of "a threatening feminine sexuality that had no right to be seen in respectable society."[18] Gainsborough heightened the controversy by showing Madame Baccelli, already in the press for her liaison with the Duke of Dorset, dancing *Les amans surpris*, her triumph of the current season, in a pastoral setting, thus emphasizing her nymphlike character. The similarity of William Grant's pose to Giovanna Baccelli's suggests that Stuart knew of Gainsborough's portrait and planned his own to attract some of the attention that made the difference between simply a good portrait and a sensation.

The story that Stuart turned his client's small talk about the weather into an idea for the picture belies the artistic brilliance of the conception for it was a shockingly modern picture of a gentleman in motion. A reviewer wrote, "One would have thought that almost every attitude of a single figure had long been exhausted in this land of portrait painting, but one is now exhibited which . . . produces the most powerful effect."[19] Such a response would have been just what Stuart wanted: a reaction to his picture strong enough to attract attention and talk without giving him a naughty reputation. Although Stuart did not go so far as to paint a dancer, he came fairly close, for England's doyen of skating, Robert Jones, a lieutenant in the Royal Artillery, in his popular treatise *The Art of Skating*, compared skating to dancing in similarity of motion

16. Evans 1999, pp. 25–26.
17. Gwendolyn Leigh Allday, "Gilbert Stuart's *The Skater* (1782) and the Hermetic Tradition in Anglo-American Painting" (master's thesis, College of Santa Fe, N.M., 2003), p. 4.
18. Gill Perry, "The Spectacle of the Muse: Exhibiting the Actress at the Royal Academy," in *Art on the Line*, p. 115; see also Michael Rosenthal and Martin Myrone, eds., *Gainsborough*, exh. cat. (London: Tate Publishing, 2002), no. 57. Reynolds held out from the 1782 exhibition a similar picture, *Miss Emily Pott as Thais*. Pressly (1986, p. 44) suggests that Gainsborough's portrait of Giovanna Baccelli was possibly a source of inspiration for Stuart's portrait of Grant.
19. Sir John Cullum, letter to Frederick Hervey, bishop of Derry and Earl of Bristol, May 1, 1782, quoted in Whitley 1932, p. 33.

20. Robert Jones, *The Art of Skating; Founded on Certain Principles Deduced from Many Years' Experience; by which That noble, healthy, and agreeable exercise is reduced to an Art and may be taught and learned by a regular method, with ease and safety.* (London: Y. G. Smeeton, 1772), p. v.

21. Nigel Brown, *Ice-Skating: A History* (New York: A. S. Barnes and Co., 1959), p. 33.

22. According to Evans (1999, p. 27), "The self-control, upright posture, and graceful movement indicate dignity; and dignity combined with intellect and serenity were taken at the time to be unmistakable signs of the noble or virtuous person."

23. Morgan 1939, p. 86; Jones, *Art of Skating*, p. 18.

24. Aileen Ribeiro, *The Art of Dress: Fashion in England and France 1750–1820* (New Haven: Yale University Press, 1995), p. 49; *Collins Scottish Clan and Family Encyclopedia*, pp. 29–30.

25. See also Phillis Emily Cunnington and Alan Mansfield, *English Costume for Sports and Outdoor Recreation from the Sixteenth to the Nineteenth Centuries* (London: Adam and Charles Beck, 1969), p. 302–3.

26. John Galt, *The Life, Studies, and Works of Benjamin West, Esq., President of the Royal Academy of London* (London: Printed for T. Cadell and W. Davies, 1820), p. 28.

27. Dick Button, "The Art of Skating," *Antiques* 105 (February 1973), pp. 351–62.

28. Galt, *Life, Studies, and Works of West*, p. 29.

29. Dunlap 1834, vol. 1, p. 183.

30. Marcia Pointon, "Portrait! Portrait! Portrait!" in *Art on the Line*, p. 95. See also Andrea Pearson, "Gilbert Stuart's *The Skater (Portrait of William Grant)* and Henry Raeburn's *The Reverend Robert Walker D.D., Skating on Duddingston Loch:* A Study of Sources," *Rutgers Art Review* 8 (1987), p. 65, for the suggestion that West's interest in skating may have inspired Stuart's subject.

31. Miles 1995, p. 167.

32. Dunlap 1834, vol. 1, p. 183.

and in artfulness of execution and the sense of amusement.[20] Grant's tight roll recorded in a pattern etched on the ice made a stunning contrast to Madame Baccelli's uninhibited leap. English pleasure skating, or rolling, was made fashionable in the 1660s by the Stuart monarchs, and its proper practice was codified to meet standards of correct behavior.[21] Stuart carefully composed his picture so that, even if Grant were perceived as the counterpart to Madame Baccelli, no one would question the morality of the scene.

Grant was less suspect than the dancer because he was male, of elite status, and thus not subject to the same scrutiny for lascivious tendencies. His body is composed and contained, unmistakably dignified, whereas Madame Baccelli's is expressive and open, her right arm tucked behind her and her left arm swept out to the side, showing her curvaceous bodice.[22] Stuart recognized, as he said later, "the importance of keeping the figure in its circle of motion," and he depicted Grant's skating technique as according to method: "incline the body forwards, and the head to the left, directing the eyes that way; let the arms be easily crossed over the breast."[23] Those who would question the propriety of Englishmen skating would have been relieved to find that Grant was Scottish. Edinburgh was the capital of skating in Britain, the city that had set up the first ice club in the world as early as 1742 to monitor the rules of the discipline.

Stuart provided key information in the lower quarter of his composition, the part that hung closest to the viewer's line of vision at the academy. Grant's state-of-the-art iron-bladed runners with curled fenders have crossed toe straps of black leather so thin that they were barely noticeable on his fine shoes. His clothing defined him as the perfect gentleman. Observed an aristocratic traveler on his visit to London in 1782, "If you wish to be full drest you wear black." Grant's black silk velvet suit with short waistcoat and knee-length frock coat was up to the moment in style; the turned-down collar and fur lapels would be taken as a sign of nobility, not merely a feature of winter garb. He wears a small circular badge on his hat indicative of his distinguished Scottish heritage. And the beaver hat itself, round with a broad flat brim, sometimes called a wide-awake, put him in fashion's advance guard.[24] Stuart placed men in varicolored outfits and cocked hats in the background, setting off Grant as the best-dressed man on the pond. There was no special costume for skating, only the notion that garments be sensibly close-fitting and neat; long coats that could get caught on skate blades or blow into the path of another skater were to be avoided.[25]

Skating threw Londoners of various social ranks together, and those wary of encountering the wrong sort on the ice would carefully choose their ponds. The long canal in Saint James Park leading from Buckingham House to Whitehall Palace was the most popular spot and therefore the most crowded and socially suspect. Benjamin West, a fine skater himself, might have passed on to Stuart the advice he got when he arrived: in Saint James Park "only the populace assemble; on the Serpentine [in Hyde Park], the company, although better, is also promiscuous; but the persons who frequent the basin in the [Kensington] Gardens are generally of the rank of gentlemen."[26] For Grant's picture, Stuart chose the Serpentine and provided architectural markers so that there could be no misunderstanding of the location: in the distance are the northwest side of Buckingham House and, rising from behind the curve of the hill, the towers of Westminster Abbey. Stuart's Hyde Park scene includes only gentlemen skating according to code. Behind Grant to the left, two skaters with legs akimbo face one another and doff their caps in the so-called Serpentine Salutation.[27] Stuart may have learned this skating figure from West, who was given some credit for introducing it in London.[28]

Stuart, too, could skate, and "[h]is celerity and activity accordingly attracted crowds on the Serpentine river" when he and Grant were on the ice.[29] If both Stuart and West got attention while skating in London, it is likely that Stuart's submission of a skating picture to the Royal Academy would have been recognized as a homage to his teacher or as mildly self-referential. Intimates of West at the exhibition might have known that Stuart's painting quoted directly from a sketch West had made as the genesis of a skating picture, in which figures complete the Serpentine Salutation (British Museum, London). Art historian Marcia Pointon explains that artists often internalized themselves in their work for display at the academy, contributing to "the convivial activity of identification, recognition, self-recognition, emulation, and self-projection."[30] It has been noted, indeed, that the gentleman leaning on the tree at the far right of the picture looks like Stuart.[31] In this analysis William Grant is lost under a stylish wide-awake hat that finds its retrospective prototype in the same flat-brimmed design worn by West in his self-portrait of about 1776 and by Stuart in his of 1778 (fig. 22, cat. 5). Stuart admitted that during his and Grant's outing on the Serpentine, Grant hit a crack in the ice and held onto the hem of Stuart's coat to be guided off the ice.[32] Stuart endowed his client with qualities of dexterity and athleticism he found in himself and his teacher.

CRB

7. HENRIETTA ELIZABETH FREDERICA VANE

1782–83

Oil on canvas, 65 ⅞ x 38 ⅜ in. (167.3 x 97.5 cm)
Smith College Museum of Art, Northampton,
Massachusetts; Given in memory of Jessie Rand
Goldthwait, class of 1890, by her husband, Dr. Joel E.
Goldthwait, and daughter, Mrs. Roger W. Bennett
(Margaret Rand Goldthwait, class of 1921), 1957

Having succeeded at the Royal Academy annual exhibition of 1782, Stuart followed Thomas Gainsborough's lead and abandoned that venue the following year, when he sent nine pictures, including this one (No. 266 *Portrait of Young Lady—whole length*) to the Incorporated Society of Artists.[1] His choice of the out-of-fashion and ramshackle society over the academy, in its newly renovated rooms in Somerset House on the Strand, baffled audiences then and has confused scholars ever since. William Whitley attributed Stuart's move to "simply good nature, the desire to assist a struggling body of men of his own craft, now in distress."[2] Charles Merrill Mount portrayed the decision as strategic rather than generous: Stuart was the most talented member and leader, in effect, of a dissident movement away from the academy, who seized upon an "enormous" opportunity to "cast his net wide to solicit patronage and to demonstrate the full scope of his talents."[3] Dorinda Evans avoided the question of why the artist showed at the "rival and much inferior exhibition" with the explanation that he had rejected the academy.[4] These three opinions essentially provide an inventory of aspects of Stuart's conflicted personality: good natured, opportunistic, and indifferent.

Similarly, the nine portraits of the 1783 showing constitute a catalogue of what the artist had to offer at the time.[5] The group was made up of six men, two women, and a child and within that configuration was represented a social cross section of portrait commissions: a nobleman, a clergyman, two artists, one lady, one actress, two gentlemen, and an heiress. In format, the canvases included four bust lengths, two kit-cats, one three-quarter length, one full length, and an oval. By any standard, the outstanding work was the portrait of Henrietta Vane, the child-heiress in full length with a landscape setting. This enchanting ten-year-old, with her curly blond hair and open, slightly come-hither gaze, wears a billowy white dress with fitted bodice and sleeves set off by a

1. The painting is not listed in Mason 1879 or Park 1926.
2. Whitley 1932, p. 37.
3. Mount 1964, p. 84.
4. Evans 1999, p. 27.
5. *The Exhibition of the Royal Academy, M.DCC.LXXXIII: The Fifteenth* (London: T. Cadell, 1783), nos. 260–68.

6. "Royal Academy," *Gazetteer and New Daily Advertiser*, May 3, 1782, p. 3. The comment concerns Stuart's portrait of Caleb Whitefoord (fig. 16).

7. See Marcia Pointon, "Portrait! Portrait! Portrait!" in David H. Solkin, ed., *Art on the Line: The Royal Academy Exhibitions at Somerset House 1780-1836*, exh. cat. (New Haven, London: Yale University Press for the Paul Mellon Centre for Studies in British Art and the Courtauld Institute Gallery, 2001), p. 105, for a discussion of the meaning of likeness at exhibitions of the 1780s.

8. De Lorme 1979a, p. 345, compares *Henrietta Vane* with Gainsborough's *Mr. and Mrs. Andrews*, ca. 1748 (National Gallery, London), and his *Honourable Mrs. Graham*, 1777 (National Gallery of Scotland, Edinburgh).

9. Emily Ballew Neff, no. 33, in Neff and William L. Pressly, *John Singleton Copley in England*, exh. cat. (Houston: Museum of Fine Arts, 1995), pp. 155–56.

sash, cuffs, and neckline bow of apricot-hue *changeant* silk that matches the floral embellishment on her straw hat and her dainty slippers. The mass of creamy ruffle-edged fabric flowing behind her and over her right shoulder has nothing to do with costume but protects her literally and figuratively from the rough-hewn boulder on which she leans and situates her luxuriously in the foreground of a pastoral scene. The gratuitous cloth answers the critic who in 1782 disparaged one of Stuart's portraits for "a want of fullness of drapery."[6]

If Henrietta's lavish clothing sets her apart from her surroundings, her gestures draw her back into the site: she gently tugs at a flowering vine, pulling it down toward the flowers gathered in a basket at her feet. The portrait follows Reynolds's prescriptions for eliding the boundaries among portraiture, fancy painting, and history: a picture of a pretty girl in a frothy costume against an unspecified outdoor setting could delight those looking for likeness just as it pleased viewers who did not know the girl herself.[7] The picture nods to Gainsborough, who more regularly than Reynolds incorporated his sitters into the landscape, but the entwined trees at left are so thinly painted as to be transparent—indeed they were an afterthought, outlined and sketchily brushed in over the initially painted horizon line. The sitter's thumb-and-forefinger grasp of the vine physically connects her to the natural setting, but she remains a Reynoldsian type, as seen in Reynolds's portrait of Lady Catherine Pelham-Clinton (fig. 27), a small child tossing chicken feed, wearing a costume similar in palette and some details to Henrietta's. The picture is pastoral, romantic, contrived, and full of frivolous details, just like the one by Stuart.[8]

Stuart's depiction of the little girl followed the contemporary notion that the most successful portraits of the day achieved likeness and ideality, a mix of the real and the fairy tale, perhaps especially appropriate for a female child. In this way, in style and nuance, his portrait of Henrietta anticipates Copley's 1785 conversation piece of the youngest daughters of George III (fig. 28), an image recently interpreted as evoking the "exuberance of childhood" and the contemporary vogue for raising children according to the developmental recommendations of John Locke and Jean-Jacques Rousseau.[9] Stuart's and Copley's compositions feature elegant children and ornamental plant life, evoking the metaphorical—children and plants both grow according to the degree and type of nurturing—and the actual—they are better off if they spend time outdoors.

Fig. 27. Sir Joshua Reynolds, *Lady Catherine Pelham-Clinton*, 1781. Oil on canvas, 55 x 44.8 in. (139.7 x 114 cm). Private collection (photo: Photographic Survey, Courtauld Institute of Art)

Fig. 28. John Singleton Copley, *Three Youngest Daughters of George III*, 1785. Oil on canvas, 104½ x 73 in. (265.4 x 185.4 cm). The Royal Collection © 2004, Her Majesty Queen Elizabeth II

7

Henrietta Elizabeth Frederica Vane (ca. 1773–1807), cousin to Henry, second Earl of Darlington, was the only daughter and heiress of the Honourable Charles Vane of Mount Ida, Norfolk, he the sixth son of Gilbert Vane, second Baron Barnard of Barnard Castle in the County Palatine of Durham, a peerage created in 1698 for his father, Christopher. The Vanes descended from Sir Henry Vane the younger, who served as governor of colonial Massachusetts 1636–37 and was beheaded on suspicion of high treason against King Charles II in 1662. In the summer of 1795, Miss Vane married Sir William Langham (1771–1812), eighth baronet and sheriff of Northampton County, and they had three children, William Henry, Henrietta, and Charlotte.

CRB

8. MASTER CLARKE

1783–84
Oil on canvas, 50 x 40 in. (127 x 101.6 cm)
Collection of Mr. and Mrs. Massimo Ferragamo

About the same time Stuart wrote to West pleading for assistance, he probably attended Sir Joshua Reynolds's seventh annual discourse, on December 10, 1776, before the students of the Royal Academy of Arts. At this lecture, Reynolds extolled the work of Anthony van Dyck, the Dutch painter who enriched the whole of British painting with his magnificent portraits for Charles I, even while he criticized modern painters' understanding of it: "The great variety of excellent portraits with which Van Dyck has enriched this nation, we are not content to admire for their real excellence, but extend our approbation even to the dress which happened to be the fashion of that age. We all

Fig. 29. Joseph Wright of Derby, *Two Young Gentlemen in the Characters of Archers*, ca. 1781–82. Oil on canvas, 71½ x 54 in. (181.6 x 137.2 cm). Location unknown (photo: Sotheby's, London)

Fig. 30. Sir Joshua Reynolds, *Dudley Alexander Sydney Cosby and John Dyke Acland (The Archers)*, 1769. Oil on canvas, 92⅞ x 70⅞ in. (236 x 180 cm). Private collection (photo: Christie's Images)

8

1. Sir Joshua Reynolds, *Discourses on Art*, ed. Robert Wark (1959; reprint, New Haven: Yale University Press for the Paul Mellon Centre for Studies in British Art, 1975), p. 138.

2. The painting is not listed in Mason 1879 or Park 1926.

3. Clare Rose, *Children's Clothes since 1750* (London: B. T. Batsford, 1989), pp. 48–53; Phillis Emily Cunnington and Anne Buck, *Children's Costume in England, from the Fourteenth to the End of the Nineteenth Century* (London: Adam and Charles Black, 1965), p. 124; Karen Baclawski, *The Guide to Historic Costume* (New York: Drama Book Publishers, 1995), pp. 65–66.

4. See Aileen Ribeiro, *The Dress Worn at Masquerades in England, 1730–1790, and Its Relation to Fancy Dress in Portraiture* (New York: Garland Publishing, 1984), pp. 205–16.

5. Quoted in T. Roberts, *The English Bowman, or Tracts on Archery* (London: C. Roworth, 1801), pp. 80–81.

6. George Agar Hansard, *The Book of Archery* (London: Henry G. Bohn, 1841), p. 69.

very well remember how common it was a few years ago for portraits to be drawn in this fantastick dress; and this custom is not yet entirely laid aside."[1] Stuart might have thought himself indifferent to this trend, for slit sleeves, an old-style doublet, and a wide lace collar were never seen in any of his works. He came fairly close, though, in his portrait of Master Clarke, a picture filled with all of the hallmarks of contemporary fashionable British portraiture.[2]

The boy was the son of Richard Hall Clarke of Bridwell, Halberton, a village near Tiverton, and Agnes Were, a celebrated beauty and heiress of a local Devonshire family. They married in 1774, same year fire destroyed the family's seventeenth-century ancestral home, which they soon rebuilt as a Georgian house on an improved site with extensive parks and a lake. The Clarkes had two sons, Richard and John, one of whom is the subject of Stuart's portrait. The boy has on a cherry red double-breasted skeleton suit, a one-piece garment with lower front and back flaps worn by boys between about the ages of six, when they were breeched from dresses, and twelve, when they were outfitted in proper versions of adult clothing with jackets, waistcoats, and trousers.[3] His wide, layered, and ruffled collar was a transitional embellishment, recalling the flounces of his earlier gowns even after he was dressed to allow such activities as archery. The outfit follows the actual fashion for clothing derived from Van Dyck portraits for use in real life.[4] His long curly locks are part of the same nostalgic fashion for a boy younger than twelve.

Nearly every contemporary portraitist of note made use of a pose with a long bow and arrow against a rural landscape—Reynolds, Nathaniel Dance, Joseph Wright of Derby, Henry Raeburn, among others—and they followed the prior generation—Thomas Hudson, Allan Ramsay, and other midcentury painters who originally popularized it at the time when training in archery was mandatory for upper-class boys. Roger Ascham, a sixteenth-century English humanist and scholar, in his treatise *Toxophilus* (1545), advocated archery as a form of physical education for young scholars "on account of the manliness of the diversion" and as "an exercise most wholesome, and also a pastime most honest; wherein labor prepareth the body to hardness, and the mind to courageousness."[5] In the seventeenth century, with endorsements from Charles II, archery became a required course of study and exercise at Westminster, Harrow, Eton, and other superior schools. Some schools dropped the requirement during the mid-eighteenth century, only to reconsider its value in the 1780s.

In composing this portrait, Stuart may have had in mind Wright's portrait entitled *Two Young Gentlemen in the Characters of Archers* (fig. 29), which hung next to Stuart's portrait of the artist Dominic Serres at the Royal Academy exhibition of 1782. Wright's boys are somewhat older than Master Clarke, and they shoot their bows and arrows; Stuart's child merely holds the gear without any indication that he knows what to do with it. Both pictures feature boys standing against a patch of trees in full green of summer, a mode of theatrical presentation—sharply drawn figures against a fluid landscape—derived from Reynolds. Wright was probably inspired by Reynolds's double portrait of Dudley Alexander Sydney Cosby and John Dyke Acland as archers, exhibited at the Royal Academy in 1770 (fig. 30). The portrait remained in Reynolds's studio until 1779, refused by the subjects, which would have given Stuart ample occasion to see it. If they were seen together, Stuart's, Wright's, and Reynolds's archers would seem to be a series portraying the development of a British archer, from the learning stages in childhood, to the first athletic trials of youth, to the vigorous physicality and determination of manhood. Stuart's commission from Richard Clarke for a small boy's portrait did not afford the opportunity for the portrayal of dynamic athleticism, although Stuart's *Skater* of 1782 (cat. 6) demonstrated that he was able to capture such vitality.

Master Clarke stands in the park of his family home, Bridwell, near the butt-field, an earthen mound against which rested the targets for archers, common at schools and in the grandest home parks. Stuart's portrait of this young archer can be seen as promoting "a love for the robust amusements in which our martial ancestors delighted, . . . [and keeping] alive that spirit of fortitude and patriotism which they bequeathed to us as a heirloom."[6]

CRB

9. ELEANOR GORDON

ca. 1783–84
Oil on canvas, 49 x 39¾ in. (124.5 x 101 cm)
Berry-Hill Galleries, Inc., New York

1. Sir Samuel Gordon was a Scot raised in Ireland who settled in England in 1760, became sheriff of Newark, and was created a baronet in 1764. He had one son and three daughters, the youngest of whom was named Eleanor. See "Collectors' Questions: Who was Eleanor Gordon?" *Country Life* 128 (December 1, 1960), p. 133, as Miss Eleanor Gordon. The painting is not listed in Mason 1879 or Park 1926.

2. *One Hundred Paintings by Old Masters* (Paris: Galerie Sedelmeyer, 1896), p. 96, as *Eleanor Gordon*, by George Romney; T. Humphry Ward and William Roberts, *Romney: A Biographical and Critical Essay, with a Catalogue Raisonné of His Works* (London: T. Agnew and Sons, 1904), vol. 2, p. 62.

3. Parke-Bernet, New York, May 24, 1944, lot 85, as *Miss Eleanor Gordon*, by George Romney.

4. Mount 1964, p. 359, as *Eleanor Gordon*, by Gilbert Stuart, owned by Hirschl and Adler Gallery, New York.

5. Hirschl and Adler advertised the picture in *Art Quarterly*, spring 1967. Sotheby's, London, June 26, 1968, lot 40, as *Eleanor Gordon*, by Gilbert Stuart, property of a New York collector. The complete provenance is as follows: Galerie Sedelmeyer, Paris, by 1896 (*Miss Eleanor Gordon*, by Romney); Parke-Bernet, New York, May 24, 1944, lot 85 (*Miss Eleanor Gordon*, by George Romney); Mr. and Mrs. Alvin M. Owsley, Dallas, 1959; K. Bernard-Smith, Alexandria, New South Wales, Australia, 1960; to M. Knoedler and Co., New York; to Hirschl and Adler Gallery, New York, by 1967; sold, Sotheby's, London, June 26, 1968, lot 40

In December 1960, the owner of this painting, K. Bernard-Smith, asked the editors of *Country Life*, "Who was Eleanor Gordon?" He knew her name because it is inscribed on the canvas at lower right, probably by her descendants in the nineteenth century. He submitted his query with a photograph of the portrait and the information that George Romney was the artist. *Country Life*'s answer was that she might have been the daughter of Sir Samuel Gordon of Newark-on-Trent, Nottinghamshire.[1]

During the late nineteenth century, the portrait was owned by the Galerie Sedelmeyer in Paris, where it was noted by the Romney scholars T. Humphry Ward and William Roberts and included in their catalogue raisonné.[2] The picture changed hands at least once during the early twentieth century and was brought to auction in New York in May 1944.[3] During the next twenty years, the picture went from New York to Dallas to Australia and back to New York, which has led to speculation that there may be more than one picture. During these years, the attribution changed definitively from Romney to Stuart, due to Charles Merrill Mount, who was scrutinizing Stuart's work for a biography and oeuvre checklist. The picture, though close to Romney, lacks that painter's precision, his near geometrical approach to mapping out the composition, and his clearly bound areas of pigment, especially in the figures. Mount published the work as a Stuart in 1964, and the change in attribution to an American artist seems to have brought the picture to New York for sale, first at M. Knoedler and Company and then at Hirschl and Adler Gallery.[4] After the portrait failed to sell in New York, it was sent in June 1968 to auction in London, where it sold to American collectors.[5]

From the mid-1780s, the apparent date of this portrait, Stuart's work is a tricky blend of influences as he shifted from mode to mode, attempting either to settle into a style he could call his own or, more likely, trying out the methods of various artists for the challenge. As with *The Skater* (cat. 6), which by the late nineteenth century had become disassociated with Stuart and which conjured for connoisseurs bits of the work of several different artists, this portrait is a pastiche of techniques, more from Gainsborough than from Reynolds with a strong dose of Romneyish restraint. In her brief discussion of *Eleanor Gordon*, Dorinda Evans invokes all three of these big names not in conjunction with the style of the painting, but as the source of Stuart's knowledge about "gender-based portrait stereotypes" by which a woman would be set outdoors, thereby "associated with nature in her procreative role," and given some prop—in this case the sheet music—redolent of her "refined sensibilities."[6] *Eleanor Gordon* is, indeed, true to stereotype and

Fig. 31. George Romney, *Charlotte Clive*, ca. 1783–85. Oil on canvas, 50 x 40 in. (127 x 101.6 cm). Powis Castle, The Powis Collection (The National Trust), England (photo: Photographic Survey, Courtauld Institute of Art)

(*Eleanor Gordon*, by Gilbert Stuart, property of a New York collector); purchased at that sale by a private collector; consigned to Berry-Hill Galleries, New York, 2003.

6. Evans 1999, p. 30.

7. Oliver Oldschool, "His Grace, the Duke of Northumberland, Stuart Pinxit," *The Port Folio* 5 (1805), p. 156–57.

8. "The Arts," *Morning Post and Daily Advertiser*, April 28, 1786, and May 27, 1786.

9. J. Stuart 1877a, p. 644. She also explained that Benjamin West had been employed to make six copies of Stuart's portrait of Lady Charlotte Clive.

10. I am extremely grateful to Alex Kidson of the Walker Art Gallery, Liverpool, for providing me with this information and other significant help in understanding the possible relationship between Stuart and Romney.

11. Jouett 1816, p. 86.

12. Evans 1999, p. 30.

13. Notes from Richard Burke, Department of Music, Hunter College, New York, to Bruce Weber, Berry-Hill Galleries, New York, June 2003.

hardly a stretch for an artist who was capable of much greater expression of character, but perhaps not unexpected from one who painted women infrequently in England. As the critic Oliver Oldschool wrote in the early nineteenth century, Stuart "was so exact in delineating his lineaments, that one may almost say of him what Hogarth said of another artist, 'that he never deviates into grace:' from all which we may fairly infer that he never was a favourite portrait painter with the ladies."[7]

There are but a handful of female portraits recorded from Stuart's years in London and Ireland, of which few are located. Various inventories of his work include contemporary hearsay about commissions received or contemplated but perhaps not even begun. The *Morning Post and Daily Advertiser*, for example, reported in April 1786 its hope to see "a charming picture" of the actress Elizabeth Billington emerge from his studio.[8] Many years later, Stuart's daughter Jane described her father's portrait of Lady Charlotte Clive, daughter of Robert Clive, Baron Clive of Plassey, as "a beautiful picture of a very lovely woman."[9] Jane Stuart's reference to Charlotte Clive may provide a key to understanding *Eleanor Gordon*, for that painting bears many similarities to Romney's portrait of Miss Clive (fig. 31). She sat for Romney seven times between April 1783 and April 1784, after which the picture, in some state of finish, remained in his studio until September 1785 when it was paid for and collected.[10] Stuart would have had ample opportunity to see the portrait in Romney's Cavendish Square painting room and to work from it. Stuart's painting includes obvious pentimenti, particularly in the background, in the arms, and in the dress, recording his struggles to make his picture right. The women wear the same Grecian-style white dress, but where the crimson sash on Romney's young lady disappears behind her, Stuart's billows up in soft folds, a captivating detail that recurs frequently in his work from then on. Stuart's sitter is erect and nearly full face toward the spectator, while Romney's is slightly languid with her face in near profile, illustrating a tenet Stuart articulated years later: "Never suffer a sitter to lean against the back of the chair. It constrains the attitude, and the gen[l] air of the person to be particularly attended."[11]

Romney's reductive tendencies by the mid-1780s led him to eliminate pictorial attributes: by his hand, Miss Clive's fingers seem grasping, ready to receive. Stuart more conventionally gave his sitter a piece of music, which turns out to be not sheet music, as has been suggested,[12] but a manuscript in which the staves in the middle are blank. The system inscribed at top and bottom is a ritornello that works as both the introductory and closing passages, marked with the Italian notation "fine" at the bottom of the sheet. While crucial information is missing on the page—the clefs, meter, and key signatures— enough is given to surmise that the piece is a jig or more properly a gigue, among the most popular dances at the time. The musicologist Richard Burke has surmised from this that the piece was composed by the sitter for her own delight in playing. "If she were a singer," Burke reasons, "Stuart, who is clearly meticulous in his painting of musical notation, would probably have depicted a piece with words."[13]

There is no reason to suspect that the inscription of Eleanor Gordon's name on the canvas is erroneous—the handwriting is authentic to the period. Yet the idea that she may be someone else remains tantalizing. The facial similarity to Charlotte Clive as portrayed by Romney is compelling, but nothing is known of Miss Clive's musical abilities. The music alone warrants the suggestion that the young lady could be Charlotte Coates, the accomplished instrumentalist and contralto whom Stuart met in 1782 and married in 1786. There is no record that Stuart painted his wife, but in the absence of many female clients, this experimental portrait might have required just such a friendly subject.

CRB

9

THE BOYDELL PICTURES, 1783–86

Fairly soon after his success at the Royal Academy exhibition of 1782, Stuart accepted a major commission from the politician, print publisher, entrepreneur, and patron of the arts John Boydell (1719–1804), dubbed by the Prince of Wales "the Commercial Maecenas" of the day.[1] Stuart would paint a series of fifteen waist-length portraits of painters and engravers, each of whom was involved in Boydell's business in one way or another. In a brilliant stroke of marketing strategy, Boydell decided to renovate his shop at 90 Cheapside, at the corner of Ironmonger Lane, in the city's finest retail neighborhood, to accommodate a display of the paintings after which some of his best-selling prints had been made. In this way, he turned his operation into an exhibition gallery filled with large canvases, which, in effect, promoted print sales. That he represented the work of London's most esteemed artists could scarcely be lost on visitors who also saw, thanks to Stuart's portraits, the faces of the artists shown with their works. Through these portraits, Boydell publicized his stable of painters—John Singleton Copley (cat. 13), Ozias Humphry (fig. 32), William Miller, Richard Paton (fig. 33), Sir Joshua Reynolds (cat. 14), and Benjamin West (cat. 12)—as well as the engravers who worked with him—John Browne, Richard Earlom, Georg Sigmund Facius, Johann Gottlieb Facius (fig. 34), John Hall (cat. 11), James Heath (fig. 35), William Sharp, and William Woollett (cat. 10). Stuart also painted portraits of Boydell himself and his nephew Josiah Boydell, a draftsman and engraver.[2]

The son of a Shropshire land surveyor, Boydell moved to London at about age twenty-one and became an apprentice to the engraver W. H. Toms, who helped him enroll in drawing classes at Saint Martin's Lane Academy.[3] In 1745 Boydell struck out on his own as an engraver, and by the early 1760s he had begun importing prints for sale in his shop. Within a decade, he had further enhanced his business by broaching publishing agreements with artists, with profitable terms for both parties, and became England's largest exporter of prints. He commissioned paintings and arranged liaisons among the artists, engravers, and draftsmen, an enterprise that took maximum advantage of the British

1. Richard Altick, *The Shows of London* (Cambridge, Mass.: Harvard University Press, 1978), p. 108.
2. The portraits of Miller, Browne, Earlom, G. S. Facius, Sharp, and John Boydell are unlocated. The portrait of Josiah Boydell may be the one of an unidentified man at the Museum of Art, Rhode Island School of Design, Providence. On Heath and Humphry, see Elizabeth Mankin Kornhauser, *American Paintings before 1945 in the Wadsworth Atheneum* (New Haven: Yale University Press, 1996), vol. 2, pp. 687–92.
3. The best source of information on Boydell is Hermann Arnold Bruntjen, *John Boydell (1719–1804): A Study of Art Patronage and Publishing in Georgian London* (New York: Garland Publishing, 1985).

Fig. 32. *Ozias Humphry*, 1784. Oil on canvas, 27½ x 23¼ in. (69.9 x 59.1 cm). Wadsworth Atheneum, Hartford; Gift of Samuel P. Avery (1920.1026)

Fig. 33. *Richard Paton*, ca. 1785. Oil on canvas, 36 x 28 in. (91.4 x 71.1 cm). Private collection

Fig. 34. *Johann Gottlieb Facius*, ca. 1785. Oil on canvas, 36⅛ x 28⅛ in. (91.7 x 71.4 cm). Frye Art Museum, Seattle (photo: Susan Dirk / Under the Light)

Fig. 35. *James Heath*, 1784. Oil on canvas, oval 23⅝ x 22⅜ in. (60 x 56.8 cm). Wadsworth Atheneum, Hartford

4. On Copley's *Death of Major Peirson,* see Jules David Prown, *John Singleton Copley* (Cambridge, Mass.: Harvard University Press, 1966), vol. 2, pp. 302–10; Emily Ballew Neff and William L. Pressly, *John Singleton Copley in England,* exh. cat. (Houston: Museum of Fine Arts, 1995), pp. 60–90, 140–54.

5. Pickering 1810 (November 17).

Copyright Act of 1735, a law sponsored by the artist William Hogarth to protect the rights of artists against the sale of unauthorized reproductions of their work. Boydell produced a highly commercial product, advertised his stock in handsomely printed catalogues, and, at the same time, acted as patron—sometimes purchasing work outright and other times splitting profits. The business was fraught with delays and disappointments but nonetheless reaped good profits and publicity. He catered to the people who would visit the Royal Academy exhibitions and admired the paintings of Reynolds and West but were more inclined to buy a print after their work than to purchase an actual painting.

Boydell's next step was to bridge the gap between art and commerce by exhibiting paintings and prints together. He maintained his sales rooms on the ground floor and converted the second floor into a gallery, approximately 80 by 17 feet. The cornerstone of his first installation would be Copley's *Death of Major Peirson* (Tate Britain), a grand scene of the British victory over the French at Saint Helier, Guernsey, on January 5, 1781.[4] Boydell extended the commission and paid Copley 800 pounds in 1782, probably about the same time he began conversations with Stuart. He may have given Stuart the commission on the basis of his expressive likeness of Caleb Whiteford (fig. 16), which received praise at the Royal Academy in 1782. But West, Stuart's mentor who is connected with several of the portraits and had such a strong business relationship with Boydell, must have played a role in Stuart's getting the job.

Many years later, Stuart would recall that he began his series of portraits with those of Reynolds and West, a flawed recollection that probably invokes the spirit of the project rather that the actual order of its completion.[5] He almost certainly first painted the portraits of Woollett and Paton, the two that he submitted to the exhibition of Incorporated Society of Artists in the spring of 1783. At some point early on, he had a sitting with the painter James Barry, who quit the project when he learned that he had not been painted first. Then Stuart worked on the portraits of Copley, Heath, and Josiah Boydell, pictures integral to Boydell's plan to make a spectacular display in late summer 1784 of Copley's large history painting surmounted by the portraits of the painter, engraver, and draftsman on the publishing project. Boydell engaged the architect Robert Adam to

Fig. 36. Robert Adam, *Design of an Ornament for the Top of a Picture Frame for Mr. Alderman Boydell, April 3, 1784.* Sir John Soane's Museum, London

design the installation.[6] In April 1784, Adam came up with three proposals: the first shows a unornamented ogee-cove frame surmounted by trophies of war and two circular portraits flanking an oval one (fig. 36). Adam's sketches of the portraits, presumably just for placement, are cursory with no definite relationship to Stuart's actual compositions, except for the shape and size of the canvases: of the fifteen portraits in the group, Copley's is the only oval. Adam's second design has fewer trophies and swags, the circular portraits hang on either side of the large history painting, and only Copley's portrait is on top. The third design, featuring a careful fitting of pictures of various sizes—portraits, paintings, and prints—was for an adjacent wall in the eventual full display.

Stuart's portraits of Copley, Heath, and Boydell went on display during the summer of 1784 at 28 Haymarket in Copley's one-man show of *Peirson*, the *Death of the Earl of Chatham*, and *Watson and the Shark*. Copley was not the only major artist to boycott the Royal Academy annual that summer: Thomas Gainsborough mounted twenty-five of his paintings in his house in Pall Mall. At the close of Copley's show, Boydell moved *Peirson* and the first of Stuart's portraits to Cheapside, where more portraits, paintings, and prints gradually joined the installation.[7] The keen observer Sophie von la Roche praised the display in the fall of 1786,[8] and in November 1786 the critic signing his name "Fabius" gave a detailed description of the installation. He referred to Stuart's portraits as "strong likenesses."[9]

Stuart's portraits of the artists and engravers reveal his increasing talent for bust-length portraits, a traditional format at which he excelled. He kept to a set format: most of the artists are portrayed seated in the same upholstered armchair next to a draped table and working on a painting or engraving for Boydell. As a group, the portraits might be described as having less finesse and finish than Stuart's more elegantly conceived portraits for London's elite. According to a contemporary critic who looked to Van Dyck's series of refined portraits of seventeenth-century artists as the obvious prototype that Stuart had clearly ignored: "They were all strong resemblances, but a set of more uninteresting, vapid countenances it is not easy to imagine; neither dignity, elevation nor grace, appear in any one of them; and had not the catalogue given their names, they might have passed for a company of cheesemongers and grocers . . . and many others were delineated as smug upon the mart as so many mercers or haberdashers of small wares."[10] Placing the blame for shabby appearance on the subjects themselves took some of the onus off Stuart, who may, in fact, have conceived the series for just this effect: these were his colleagues, not his patrons, a rare opportunity to paint a great number of his fellows in a manner commensurate with his perception of their status and aspect in London society. The project also marked the beginnings of what would become the artist's forte: the interpretation of personality in portraiture.

As for Boydell, hailed in 1785 as "the Medicis of his time and place," his business thrived.[11] He incorporated Stuart's portraits into his next project, the so-called Shakespeare Gallery, a display of paintings and prints he commissioned for an illustrated edition of the plays. With the imprimatur of Romney—who had been left out of the initial gallery venture and seems to have wanted to participate in the next—he announced the scheme in December 1786 and opened it three years later, the biggest and most profitable venture of his career.[12]

CRB

6. Eileen Harris, "Robert Adam's Ornaments for Alderman Boydell's Picture Frames," *Furniture History* 26 (1990), pp. 93–96.

7. The display was advertised in the *Morning Herald*, August 6, 1784: "Three ovals are placed on top of the frame, in the center of which is Mr Copley's portrait, painted by that able artist Mr. Stuart. The portrait of Mr. Heath, who is to engrave the subject, is on one side, and that of Mr. Josiah Boydell, who is to make the drawing on the other."

8. Sophie von la Roche, *Sophie in London, 1786*, translated from German by Clare Williams (London: J. Cape, 1933), pp. 237–39, September 18, 1786.

9. Fabius, "The Arts: No. II. Alderman Boydell's Gallery," *Morning Post and Daily Advertiser*, November 14, 1786, p. 2.

10. *Monthly Magazine; or British Register*, July 1804, quoted in Whitley 1932, p. 54.

11. "The Arts," unidentified clipping dated October 1785, "Press Cuttings from English Newspapers on Matters of Artistic Interest, 1686–1835," Victoria and Albert Museum Library, London.

12. See Winifred H. Friedman, *Boydell's Shakespeare Gallery* (New York: Garland Publishing, 1976), p. 214; *A Collection of Prints and Pictures Painted for the Purpose of Illustrating the Dramatic Works of Shakespeare by the Artists of Great Britain* (London: Shakespeare Gallery, 1796); *A Catalogue of the Pictures &c in the Shakespeare Gallery, Pall-Mall* (London: Printed for the proprietors, 1796); Richard W. Hutton and Laura Nelke, *Alderman Boydell's Shakespeare Gallery* (Chicago: Smart Gallery, 1978). On Romney, see Alex Kidson, *George Romney, 1734–1802*, exh. cat. (Princeton, N.J.: Princeton University Press, 2002), p. 25.

10. WILLIAM WOOLLETT

1783
Oil on canvas, 35 ½ x 27 ¾ in. (90.2 x 70.5 cm)
Tate, London; Presented by Henry Farrer, 1849

An "odd little figure" who fired a cannon from his rooftop upon finishing an important plate, William Woollett (1735–1785) was the most talented engraver of landscapes and history paintings of his day.[1] The son of a flax weaver in Maidstone, Kent, Woollett discovered his talent in engraving early on, moved to London, and apprenticed to John Tinney. By the late 1750s Woollett saw his career swiftly improved by John Boydell, who hired him to produce a plate after a painting by Claude Lorraine. The good sales of this

1. Whitley 1932, p. 39. The painting is listed in Mason 1879, p. 282; Park 1926, p. 833, no. 939.

2. Hermann Arnold Bruntjen, *John Boydell (1719–1804): A Study of Art Patronage and Publishing in Georgian London* (New York: Garland Publishing, 1985), p. 18

3. Richard Altick, *The Shows of London* (Cambridge, Mass.: Harvard University Press, 1978), p. 106; Bruntjen, *John Boydell*, p. 36.

4. See Von Erffa and Staley 1986, pp. 205–6, no. 83, *Cromwell Dissolving the Long Parliament* (RA 1783; Woollett print 1789); p. 206, no. 84, *General Monk Receiving Charles II on the Beach at Dover*, 1782 (RA 1783; Woollett print 1789); pp. 208–9, no. 88, *The Battle of the Boyne*, 1778 (RA 1780; Hall engraving 1781, published by West, Hall, and Woollett); pp. 209–10, no. 90, *The Battle of La Hogue*, 1775–80 (RA 1780; Woollett engraving 1781, published by West, Hall, and Woollett); pp. 211–12, no. 93, *The Death of General Wolfe*, 1770 (RA 1771; Woollett engraving 1776, published by Woollett, Boydell, and Ryland).

5. On the banyan and turban as worn by artists, see Carrie Rebora Barratt, "Oriental Undress and the Artist," *Porticus: Journal of the Memorial Art Gallery of the University of Rochester* 20 (2001), pp. 18–26; Brandon Brame Fortune, "Banyans and the Scholarly Image," in *Franklin and His Friends: Portraying the Man of Science in Eighteenth-Century America*, exh. cat. (Washington, D.C.: Smithsonian National Portrait Gallery, 1999), pp. 51–65.

6. "The National Gallery: Portrait of Woollett, the Engraver," *Illustrated London News*, September 1, 1849, p. 60.

7. Woollett wears the same working clothes in his self-portrait (Bentlif Art Gallery, Maidstone, Eng.) and in an engraving made by J. K. Sherwin, engraver to the Prince of Wales, published August 12, 1784. Both images can be seen in the Heinz Archive, National Portrait Gallery, London.

8. Staley, no. 100, in Von Erffa and Staley 1986, p. 216.

9. Whitley 1932, p. 39.

10. *St. James Chronicle*, May 25–27, 1783, quoted in Whitley 1932, p. 38.

11. "The Arts," *Public Advertiser*, June 7, 1785, p. 2; F. L——T, "Extempore on the Death of Mr. William Woollett, Engraver to His Majesty," *Public Advertiser*, June 3, 1785, p. 2. See also *Morning Post and Daily Advertiser*, May 27, 1785, p. 3.

image compelled Boydell to hire Woollett again in 1761, this time for nine engravings after landscapes by Richard Wilson, the first of which, *The Destruction of the Children of Niobe* (ca. 1759–60; Yale Center for British Art, New Haven), had sold eight thousand copies by late 1764.[2] They continued their lucrative collaboration with engravings after works by George Stubbs, Jacob van Ruisdael, and others. When Boydell and Woollett joined forces with Benjamin West to issue a mezzotint after his phenomenally popular history painting *The Death of General Wolfe* (1770; National Gallery of Canada, Ottawa), the partnership allotted percentages of the profits to all. Distribution and sale of the print began shortly after publication on January 1, 1776, and by the time sales waned about 1790, the print had accrued approximately 15,000 pounds, making it "one of the most commercially successful prints ever published."[3] Along with the nearly as profitable companion image of West's *William Penn's Treaty with the Indians*, engraved by John Hall (see cat. 11), the *Wolfe* enterprise not only secured Boydell's operation, but created sustaining business relationships: West, Woollett, and Hall collaborated on a series of no fewer than five highly profitable scenes from the history of Britain.[4] Partly as a result of Woollett's work with West, he was appointed historical engraver to King George III.

Stuart's portrait of Woollett, a swiftly executed effort in a vibrant palette of reds and greens, memorializes the relationship between the engraver, West, and Boydell, and re-creates Woollett's process of engraving *Wolfe* some twelve years before. Woollett is swathed in a banyan, a vast T-shaped gentleman's robe, and velvet turban covering his shaved head, typical working dress for many artists of the time.[5] He looks up from his labor, an attitude that inspired a rumor that the image was intended to portray the engraver as he confronted the difficulty of making a change to the plate requested by West: "Woollett consenting, without a murmur, to make a trifling alteration . . . though it cost him three or four months labor."[6] He sits at a cloth-covered table atop which is a draped slant board to facilitate the engraving process and holds a sharp tool in his right hand against the metal plate.[7] West's painting is just next to him; it shows a figure of a grenadier, the same that appears in the drawing West holds in his self-portrait of about 1776 (fig. 22). According to Allan Staley, West's engravers usually worked, as shown here, with the full-scale canvases rather than reduced copies, suggesting that Stuart's re-creation of Woollett's process is correct. Staley also says, however, that in 1773 Boydell owned and exhibited a small oil-on-panel version of the picture (private collection), which must have been made to facilitate the engraving.[8]

Stuart's spaniel Dash barked uncontrollably at Woollett when he visited the studio, and the dog "seemed anxious to chew apart the finished picture when it stood glistening on the easel."[9] Stuart finished the portrait in time for the exhibition of the Incorporated Society of Artists in the spring of 1783, where it was shown, as "Portrait of an Artist," alongside Stuart's portrait of the marine painter Richard Paton (fig. 33). It received praise as "the man himself," and the reviewer suggested that the portrait should be engraved.[10] Woollett died shortly after the painting went on view with the others at Boydell's Cheapside gallery, and Boydell did publish a print, engraved by Caroline Watson, in September 1785.

Woollett was eulogized as "Poor Woollett [who] died just as his professional situation had begun to grow very lucrative to him," but he was also lauded for his talents and fame.[11] He was buried at Old Saint Pancras, and in 1791 a monument by Thomas Banks was erected in Westminster Abbey, paid for in part by West and Boydell.

CRB

11. JOHN HALL

ca. 1783–84
Oil on canvas, 36 x 28 in. (91.4 x 71.1 cm)
National Portrait Gallery, London (NPG 693)

John Hall (1739–1797) moved from his hometown of Colchester to London quite early and worked as a china painter in the porcelain works in Chelsea and an enameler at Battersea before training with the French engraver Simon François Ravenet the elder. Hall's expertise as an engraver got him commissions from publisher John Bell for theatrical prints, and in time, his portfolio included engravings after works by Sir Joshua Reynolds, Thomas Gainsborough, Benjamin West, Nathaniel Dance, Francis Cotes, and

1. Von Erffa and Staley 1986, pp. 208–10, nos. 85–87.
2. The portrait of Hall is listed in Mason 1879, p. 193; Park 1926, p. 377, no. 367.

others, some of these through John Boydell's influence. Hall succeeded his colleague and sometime business partner William Woollett as historical engraver to the king upon Woollett's death in 1785.

Hall collaborated with West and Boydell on the publication of prints after West's *William Penn's Treaty with the Indians* (1771; Pennsylvania Academy of the Fine Arts, Philadelphia). His mezzotint engraving of *Penn's Treaty* was issued June 12, 1775, about six months before Woollett's of *The Death of General Wolfe* (see cat. 10). Like Woollett, Hall probably worked from both large and small versions of West's composition in the engraving process. Although West's engravers usually worked from the original paintings, his *Wolfe* and *Penn's Treaty* warranted extraordinary measures not only because of the potential for commercial success but also because West demanded special attention to these particular works.[1] Hall also meticulously executed a drawing in graphite and ink, squared in red chalk for transfer for his engraving plate (Historical Society of Pennsylvania, Philadelphia).

The engraving of *Penn's Treaty* was Hall's most successful plate and among the most lucrative Boydell had published, making it the obvious choice for inclusion in Stuart's portrait of the engraver. Stuart took care to show the entire scene of *Penn's Treaty*, so that the story as told by West is legible. In honor of his teacher and in light of contemporary politics, Stuart probably liked the resonance between the situation shown in this image, the treaty between William Penn, the founder of the Pennsylvania colony, and the Lenape Indians about 1682, and the one just coming to a close between Britain and the American colonies.

Hall is more formally dressed than his colleague Woollett, with his powdered wig tied in a queue and a jacket, waistcoat, and softly ruffled shirt defining him as a gentleman artist.[2] The other crucial difference between the two portraits, which would likely have been hung together in Boydell's shop along with West's small paintings of *Wolfe* and *Penn's Treaty,* is that this engraver holds a proof copy of the print. Thus, Woollett personifies the engraver at work, in his studio costume with his tools and source material at hand, while Hall takes on the role of the engraver as businessman, having just completed his work and preparing for distribution and sale. The completed print in Hall's hands, in fact, makes the tools on the table redundant, except that the cutters and burnishers declare his profession.

CRB

12. BENJAMIN WEST

1783–84
Oil on canvas, 35 ½ x 27 ½ in. (90.2 x 69.9 cm)
National Portrait Gallery, London (NPG 349)

In John Boydell's gallery, Benjamin West's presence in the display rivaled that of John Singleton Copley. Copley's image was beyond compare for sheer grandeur of representation, but West was everywhere the visitor looked. Stuart's portrait of William Woollett (cat. 10) reminded viewers of West's initial claim to fame at the Royal Academy exhibition of 1771 with his painting *The Death of General Wolfe* (National Gallery of Canada, Ottawa), which was hailed as revolutionary and clever for its portrayal of recent history as it was rather than through classical costumes and setting, and which was purchased by Lord Grosvenor and praised by the king, who commissioned a replica. Stuart's portrait of John Hall (cat. 11) took West's story further, referring to *William Penn's Treaty with the Indians* of 1771 (Pennsylvania Academy of the Fine Arts, Philadelphia), another much-admired picture and a strong reminder of West's American heritage.

West (1738–1820) came from Springfield, Pennsylvania, and after working in Philadelphia and New York, sailed for Italy in 1760, with support from a group of gentlemen including William Smith (see cat. 61), provost of the College of Philadelphia (now the University of Pennsylvania).[1] He lived and toured in Italy for three years before settling in London, where he succeeded immediately with paintings on view at the Society of Artists of Great Britain and the newly established Royal Academy, including *Agrippina Landing at Brundisium with the Ashes of Germanicus* (1768; Yale University Art Gallery, New Haven) and *The Departure of Regulus from Rome* (1769; Collection of Her Majesty Queen Elizabeth II). These sober portrayals of ancient subjects, inspired by the work of Anton Raphael Mengs and grounded in the classical tradition of history painting then popular in London, brought him respect. His achievement with *Wolfe* and *Penn's Treaty* led to his appointment as history painter to King George III in 1772 and to a brilliant career as an educator and painter, culminating in his election to succeed Sir Joshua Reynolds as president of the Royal Academy upon the latter's death in 1792.

West first sat for Stuart about 1780, three years after Stuart had entered his studio, in an exercise that would give Stuart a picture for submission to the 1781 Royal Academy annual exhibition. Stuart produced a shimmering image of West (fig. 37) with sharply drawn features, a faraway look in the eyes, a slight smile on the lips, and coiffed and powdered hair; wearing a rich olive coat with white satin lining over a gold-trimmed iridescent pale green waistcoat and a sheer shirt with delicately dotted frill; and sitting in a languid pose suited to a poet or a prince. At the Royal Academy, the portrait won for Stuart his first published review: "An excellent portrait of Mr. West, indeed I do not know a better one in the room."[2] This was high praise indeed since Reynolds's masterful triple portrait *The Ladies Waldegrave* (National Gallery of Scotland, Edinburgh) was also exhibited that year.

Stuart's second portrait of West was commissioned by Boydell. It can be dated by West's drawing of the occasion (fig. 38), featuring a rather grouchy-looking Stuart sitting with legs crossed and dabbing a long brush at a large palette with a pot of snuff on the seat edge of his upholstered side chair. The drawing is inscribed in West's handwriting, *Mr. Stewart, painting Mr. West's portrait. 1783.* Stuart's image of West this time is less sleek but more compelling.[3] West sits in the stock Boydell portrait chair and holds a porte crayon in his right hand and with his left supports the calf-bound second volume of Boydell's illustrated Bible, for which he had drawn illustrations. His powdered hair is slightly mussed; he wears a green coat with white shirt and unruffled frill so simple that

1. On West, see Von Erffa and Staley 1986, the definitive biography and catalogue raisonné.
2. Quoted from *St. James Chronicle* in Whitley 1932, p. 27.
3. The painting is listed in Mason 1879, p. 277; Park 1926, pp. 800–801, no. 894.

12

Fig. 37. *Benjamin West*, 1781. Oil on canvas, 36 x 28 in. (91.4 x 71.1 cm). Tate, London

Fig. 38. Benjamin West, *Mr. Stewart, Painting Mr. West's Portrait*, 1783. Graphite on paper, 6⅞ x 4⅞ in. (17.6 x 12.6 cm). The British Museum, London

a reviewer of the picture charged that its mundane aspect "originated in the bad taste of the sitter."[4] These two portraits may pose the question of West's personal style, but they more readily betray Stuart's use of costume for effect. The dazzling suit in the early portrait is just that: an effect meant to dazzle as Stuart boasted of his painting skills and drew attention to his teacher in the Royal Academy arena. The less flamboyant suit in the second picture gives way to a more important accoutrement, namely the Bible, which complemented the painting in the background and alluded to West's identity as a religious painter.

About the same time West sat for Stuart in 1783, he was at work on *Moses Receiving the Laws* (Palace of Westminster, London), which he would submit to the 1784 Royal Academy exhibition as a triptych with two other biblical subjects.[5] This 18-by-12-foot painting was one of thirty-six pictures commissioned by the king in 1779 for a royal chapel at Windsor Castle, the so-called Chapel of Revealed Religion, a lavish but doomed project. West finished the *Moses* by the spring of 1784, a huge undertaking accomplished with the help of Stuart and John Trumbull, both of whom are in the composition, Trumbull on the left side and Stuart at lower right.

Stuart's inclusion of the central figure of Moses in his portrait of West is extremely clever, for in broadcasting West's major undertakings for the king and publicizing the picture on view at the Royal Academy, it depicts West in a situation similar to Moses'— receiving orders from on high (for West, the king). However, Stuart used his own painting of *Moses Receiving the Laws* (Saint Pancras Parish Church, London) as the painting behind West in his portrait. It was the first picture entrusted to him by West. West rarely painted single religious figures, but that was called for in designs for stained-glass windows in the Fitzroy Chapel, the church West attended. For this commission, in 1777, West asked Stuart to paint an image West had conceived for an unrealized project for Saint Paul's Cathedral.[6] The aspect of West with a student painting on his easel refers either to his generosity as a teacher or to his passing off student work as his own. Stuart's unfailing respect for West argues for the former, even though by 1783 Stuart had struck out on his own and may have wished to make known just how much the student had done for the teacher. CRB

4. *Monthly Magazine; or British Register*, July 1804.
5. See Von Erffa and Staley 1986, pp. 299–300, no. 258. The other two paintings in the triptych were *Call of the Prophet Isaiah* and *Call of the Prophet Jeremiah*.
6. Von Erffa and Staley 1986, pp. 302–3, no. 260.

13. JOHN SINGLETON COPLEY

ca. 1784
Oil on canvas, oval 26½ x 22¼ in. (67.3 x 56.5 cm)
National Portrait Gallery, London (NPG 2143)

Fig. 39. John Singleton Copley, *Self-Portrait*, 1780–84. Oil on canvas, image diam. 17¾ in. (45.1 cm). National Portrait Gallery, Smithsonian Institution, Washington, D.C.; Gift of The Morris and Gwendolyn Cafritz Foundation with matching funds from the Smithsonian Institution

1. See *Proposals for Publishing, by Subscription, an Engraved Print, from the Original Picture, now painting by John Singleton Copley, R.A. Elect, representing the Death of the Late Earl of Chatham, to be engraved by Mr. John Keyse Sherwin* (London, 1780). On Copley, see Jules David Prown, *John Singleton Copley* (Cambridge, Mass.: Harvard University Press, 1966), the definitive biography and catalogue raisonné.
2. The painting is listed in Mason 1879, p. 164; Park 1926, pp. 240–41, no. 190.
3. Allan Cunningham, *The Lives of the Most Eminent British Painters and Sculptors* (New York: J. and J. Harper, 1831), vol. 4, p. 144.

The first business John Singleton Copley (1738–1815) had with John Boydell was an arrangement for the sale by subscription of prints after Copley's *Death of the Earl of Chatham* (1779–81; Tate Britain).[1] The success of this venture led to discussions about creating a picture of the recent victory of the British at Guernsey. In 1782, Boydell paid Copley 800 pounds to paint *The Death of Major Peirson* (Tate Britain) and again agreed to split the proceeds from the print. In the spring of 1784, Stuart began the portrait of Copley that would accompany *Peirson* just as Copley was finishing his work.[2] About the same time Robert Adam was asked to design a frame for *Peirson* (see fig. 36). Stuart's task was thus to make a portrait that fit into this frame festooned with carved embellishments and that could be seen from a height of more than twelve feet. In the summer of 1784, the project came to fruition with two exhibitions, one organized by Copley in the Haymarket and the other by Boydell in his gallery in Cheapside.

Stuart surely knew the self-portrait that Copley had completed by 1784 (fig. 39). This painting, a rare foray by Copley into this genre, is an experimental piece, all swift strokes, scumbly dry brushwork, and exaggerated highlights, lending an impression of moody haphazardness that was at odds with both his usual sharp-focus manner and his cool, self-absorbed personal behavior. He was described by a friend, George Carter, as "very thin, pale, a little pock-marked, prominent eyebrows, small eyes, which, after fatigue, seemed a day's march in his head."[3] Contemporaries and modern scholars alike stress Copley's lavish mode of dress and love of finery, the splendid aspect so impressive as to eclipse an accurate physical description of the man.

Stuart concentrated more on the man and less on his clothing. He slightly blurred Copley's deep-set dark brown eyes, making them look bigger to catch the gaze of the viewer below. The naturalism in the portrayal, more so here than in any of the other portraits Stuart painted for Boydell, would have been a striking complement to the crisply painted scene of war. In fact, for Copley's portrait as well as for the other two in the frame above *Peirson*, of Josiah Boydell and James Heath, Stuart worked with a recognizable compositional prototype: the highly fashionable Georgian portrait miniature, an object of reverence and power that belies its tiny size. In the manner of Richard Cosway, the reigning painter of miniatures of the day, Copley's picture is oval with the sitter at three-quarter pose, head high in the composition, with fluffy pink-edged clouds in a pale blue sky at left and a darker area of the heavens at right, at the sitter's back. The conventional background worked well for Stuart, as the smoky blue sky above the buildings of the town of Saint Helier in *Peirson* would seem to continue up, out of the rectangular picture plane and into the oval portrait above. Moreover, the sky set off Copley's red velvet coat—nearly the same color as those on the British soldiers below—crisp white ruffled shirt, coiffed and powdered hair pulled back in a ribboned queue, delicate complexion, and fine features. Copley's image exudes vigor and authority. Sitting tall and erect, Copley confronts his viewers with a strong jaw and serious demeanor. It was an image that pleased those who knew Copley best. His granddaughter Martha Babcock Amory recalled that her father, Lord Lyndhurst, had told her, "it was the best and most agreeable likeness ever executed of his father."[4]

Stuart's contact with Copley is difficult to document, but Stuart knew Copley's work well enough to comment on it and to employ some of his techniques. Stuart

13

4. Martha Babcock Amory, *Domestic and Artistic Life of John Singleton Copley* (Boston: Houghton, Mifflin, and Co., 1882), p. 195.

5. Henry Sargent, Charles Robert Leslie, and John Neagle, quoted in Dunlap 1834, vol. 1, pp. 125–26, 217.

6. Pickering 1817 (October 4).

7. Pickering 1810.

seems to have alternately admired and disapproved of his work, reportedly exclaiming on one occasion that "the industry of Copley was marvelous," on another that Copley so labored over his work that the flesh resembled "tanned leather," and on another that he was an expert at "managing paint" but quite tedious in his methods.[5] He told Henry Pickering, years later in Boston, that Copley should never have changed his style in London: "Copley had first a manner of his own; & a very good manner . . . but [he] wished afterwards to adopt a more perfect one, & totally failed."[6] Stuart compared Copley's ambitions to those of "a cow dancing a hornpipe" and decided early on to leave Copley "to himself . . . [for] Copley was of a jealous disposition, tho' a great painter."[7]

Copley was born in Boston and achieved astounding success there, painting more than 350 portraits before leaving in 1774 for a tour of the Continent. He settled in London in 1776, where he continued to paint portraits while striking out as a history painter. His grand narrative painting *Watson and the Shark* (National Gallery of Art, Washington) was acclaimed at the Royal Academy of 1778, and he was invited to membership there the following year. His next great picture, *The Death of the Earl of Chatham*, was composed of more than fifty life portraits. His success with *Peirson* followed soon thereafter and earned him permission to paint the youngest daughters of King George III (fig. 28) and a commission to paint an enormous scene of the recent British victory over the Spanish, *The Siege of Gibraltar* (Guildhall Art Gallery, London), for the Corporation of the City of London. During his final years, he painted many portraits, some of them grand, allegorical works.

CRB

14. JOSHUA REYNOLDS

1784
Oil on canvas, 36⅛ x 30⅛ (91.8 x 76.5 cm)
National Gallery of Art, Washington, D.C.;
Andrew W. Mellon Collection (1942.8.21)

The master of his own image, as regulated by myriad self-portraits and dutifully copied by his many students, Sir Joshua Reynolds (1723–1792) sat for a select number of fellow painters.[1] Stuart's portrait is exceedingly rare, for he was neither Reynolds's student nor his peer. Although the portrait overall is characterized by Stuart's increasingly accomplished delicate, shorthand strokes, in the manner of Gainsborough, his use of loose hatch work of pigment in the wig and deployment of thick paint for the face imitate Reynolds's technique.[2] Reynolds's good friend Samuel Felton thought it was a self-portrait, "undoubtedly the best painted Head of Sir Joshua."[3]

The sixty-one-year-old Royal Academy president and recently appointed principal painter to King George III sat for Stuart during July of 1784. Reynolds recorded his appointments with Stuart in a pocket diary free of other commitments on July 23, 28, and 30 at 9:30 AM.[4] With this three-sitting schedule, Stuart might have been following Reynolds's own proscription on not bothering a sitter with more sittings than three, but they had a fourth, on August 27 at 9 AM. Stuart had met Reynolds at least once before these sittings when in 1783 he delivered some supplies from Benjamin West at the time Reynolds was working on his dramatic portrait of Sarah Siddons as the Tragic Muse (Huntington Art Collections, San Marino). Stuart would later call the painting overworked: it was much better when he had first seen it than it was the following spring on exhibition.[5]

Stuart imitated Reynolds's technique in many of his portraits and attended some of his lectures, enough so Stuart could later describe Reynolds to Washington Allston as "a good painter, . . . [who] has done incalculable mischief to the rising generation by many of his remarks." Stuart continued, "You may elevate your mind as much as you can; but, while you have nature before you as a model, paint what you see, and look with your own eyes."[6] He also recalled the Royal Academy president as "an admirable man in every respect," an opinion that seems contrary to his unsympathetic portrayal of the man.[7] In his portraits, Stuart flattered Copley (cat. 13) and manipulated West's image (cat. 12), but neither of those portraits is as candid as the one of Reynolds: he is aged, weak in the jaw, obviously deaf, and shown without allusion to his profession. Instead of a palette or brush, he holds a shiny gold box of snuff. Sir Joshua rejected the image,

Fig. 40. Angelica Kauffman, *Joshua Reynolds*, 1767. Oil on canvas, 50 x 40 in. (127 x 101.6 cm). Saltram Park (Morley Collection), The National Trust, England

14

1. See David Mannings and Martin Postle, *Sir Joshua Reynolds: A Complete Catalogue of His Paintings* (New Haven: Yale University Press, 2000), pp. 46–63.

2. The painting is listed in Mason 1879, p. 248; Park 1926, pp. 641–42, no. 702.

3. Samuel Felton, *Testimonies to the Genius and Memory of Sir Joshua Reynolds* (London, 1792), p. 67.

4. Sir Joshua Reynolds's pocket ledger, Royal Academy of Arts, London.

5. J. Stuart 1877a, p. 643.

6. Dunlap 1834, vol. 1, p. 184.

7. Pickering 1810.

8. Charles Fraser, quoted in Dunlap 1834, vol. 1, p. 184.

9. Charles Robert Leslie and Tom Taylor, *Life and Times of Sir Joshua Reynolds: With Notices of Some of His Contemporaries* (London: J. Murray, 1865), vol. 2, p. 501.

10. See Anne Robinson, letter to her brother Thomas Robinson, second Lord Grantham, December 31, 1784, Morley Papers, Bedfordshire Record Office, Bedford, Eng., vol. 1, fol. 67v: "I dare say you will like his Pictures very much, as they are very strong and good likeness's, Sir Joshua recommends him, & has set to him."

11. *Monthly Magazine; or British Register*, July 1804, quoted in Whitley 1932, p. 54.

12. Whitley 1932, pp. 46–47.

13. Susan Rather, "Stuart and Reynolds: A Portrait of Challenge," *Eighteenth Century Studies* 27 (fall 1993), pp. 61–84.

14. Dunlap 1834, vol. 1, p. 193.

15. Miles 1995, p. 174.

16. Richard Wendorf, *Sir Joshua Reynolds: Painter in Society* (Cambridge, Mass.: Harvard University Press, 1996), p. 40.

17. Evans 1999, pp. 33–34.

protesting that "if [Stuart's portrait] was like him, he did not know his own appearance."[8] Yet the man who looked at himself in the mirror so often in order to execute his own self-portraits seems to have objected to the image and to Boydell's commercial project, not to the painter or his methods. Reynolds told his student James Northcote that it would be "degrading himself to paint for a print-seller," yet he obliged Stuart by sitting.[9] Just a few months later, he recommended Stuart to John Parker, Baron Boringdon, for a series of bust-length portraits that would hang alongside his own works at Boringdon's country home, Saltram.[10]

From the beginning, when the critic of the *Monthly Magazine; or British Register* wondered why the Royal Academy president "was depicted with a wig that was as tight and close as a hackney coachman's caxon, and in the act of taking a pinch of snuff," the portrait has been branded as derogatory.[11] Stuart's early biographers agreed that the likeness was irreverent but excused the resourceful and loquacious Stuart and blamed the icy and deaf Reynolds. William Whitley said the sessions "must have been exceedingly interesting, though no doubt trying" for Stuart since Reynolds could not hear his entertaining stories.[12] More recently, Susan Rather proposed that Stuart painted an autobiographically charged, subversive image that "pits Stuart, the American, against Reynolds, the sophisticated leader of the English school of painting," in a portrayal that features the subject as deaf, cranky, and addicted to snuff, all of which was true.[13] The sniffing of the powdery narcotic was common and legal, but neither elegant nor polite, and Stuart himself called his own addiction "a pernicious, vile, dirty habit, and, like all bad habits, to be carefully avoided."[14] Rather describes Stuart's approach to painting Reynolds as tantamount to insubordination as he employed precisely the sort of grim naturalism that Reynolds deplored in contemporary portraiture. Ellen Miles has cautioned that Stuart's tactic for Reynolds's portrait, especially the snuff element, while daring, exemplifies his "exceptional gift of interpreting personality through the choice of a characteristic pose, in this case, one with which he was very familiar."[15] Stuart courageously characterized on canvas a man at once so esteemed as not to be criticized but so well known that a bitingly accurate portrait could not do much harm. On the contrary, the picture endeared Stuart to Reynolds.

Compared to the flattering image of Reynolds by Angelica Kauffman (fig. 40), Stuart's portrait is, according to Reynolds scholar Richard Wendorf, "formal, reticent, reserved."[16] The inclusion of a box of snuff in a portrait of so lofty a figure described "an audacious strategy" made all the more provocative by the situation of Reynolds's painting hand, his right, as not just idle, but limply holding a pinch of snuff between thumb and forefinger. In Stuart's favor, however, Wendorf explains that he captured Reynolds quite accurately as the "very cool man" so many others described. Dorinda Evans reads in it a "dual emphasis on office and humility," which led to a conflicted portrayal of a man of high position and "self-deprecat[ing] manner."[17]

Reynolds came from a humble upbringing in Plympton, Devonshire, and studied painting with Thomas Hudson in London during the early 1740s. His brilliant career as a professional portraitist followed a two-year sojourn in Rome. A founding member of the Royal Academy in 1768, he accepted its presidency and a knighthood that year and ruled the organization until his death.

CRB

15. JOHN GELL

1785
Oil on canvas, 94 ½ x 58 ½ in. (240 x 148.6 cm)
The Metropolitan Museum of Art, New York;
Purchase, Dorothy Schwartz Gift, Joseph Pulitzer
Bequest, and 2000 Benefit Fund, 2000 (2000.450)

Known for his exceptional ability to convey character in a face, Stuart expertly varied the component parts of his compositions as suited to his clients. For his portrait of John Gell (1738/40–1806), Stuart adapted his talents to the tried-and-true English approach to military officers, a distinguished tradition epitomized in the works of Allan Ramsay and Thomas Hudson earlier in the century that made every man in uniform the apparent descendant of the Apollo Belvedere.[1] In contemporary London, the prototype, Sir Joshua Reynolds's *Commodore Augustus Keppel* (National Maritime Museum, Greenwich), was more than thirty years old but still pervasive. Stuart paid homage to this successful picture, posing Gell with precision according to type: he stands in contrapposto with one foot in front of the other in nearly perpendicular arrangement, twists his body toward the back leg, and points in the direction opposite to his head, which is slightly turned in shadow. The background of rocky shoreline, ominous sky, and storm-tossed sea complete the dramatic effect appropriate for this sort of picture, setting a nonspecific stage for the figure, which is described in detail. Gell wears the meticulously observed full-dress uniform of a naval captain with over three years seniority: cream-lined, gold-trimmed navy-blue coat with gold buttons embossed with anchors over cream trousers and waistcoat, white shirt with black stock, and a sword with tasseled hilt. The finely rendered figure of the officer set against the dramatic background achieved the desired aspect of heroism. Stuart, following Reynolds, enhanced the effect with relatively fine brushwork on the body of the sitter as a foil to the painterly handling of the background. At exhibition, those looking for allegiances between painters would have seen the picture as an indication that Stuart, the artist so closely aligned with West, was associating himself with Reynolds, the Royal Academy president.

Reynolds may have secured for Stuart the commission to paint Gell, which would contribute to Stuart's decision to approach the portrait in a Reynoldsian manner. In the early 1760s, Reynolds had painted a portrait of Gell's older brother Philip, an outdoor hunting portrait derived from a Van Dyck prototype.[2] The Gells' ancestral seat was Hopton Hall in Derbyshire, and while Philip Gell managed the estate, his younger brother saw active naval duty in Nova Scotia, the American colonies, the East Indies, Portugal, Toulouse, and Genoa. He began his career as a lieutenant in the British Navy in 1760, became commander in 1762, and rose to Admiral of the White in 1799. During the American Revolution, Gell commanded the 32-gun frigate *Thetis*, which captured the American brigs *Triton* out of New York and *Active* out of Newburyport. He was then called to the East Indies and served the squadron as captain on the 70-gun *Monarca*, which took part in five victorious actions, after which Gell returned to England in early 1785. He must have sat for Stuart almost immediately for the picture to have been completed in time for the Royal Academy exhibition that spring. The question is whether he went to Reynolds first only to be recommended to the younger painter. The following January and February, Gell had seven sittings with Reynolds for a portrait commissioned by Sir Edward Hughes, his commander in recent battles. The result was a three-quarter-length picture (fig. 41) that is quite similar to Stuart's exhibition piece—indeed, Reynolds originally painted Gell's right arm outstretched with pointing finger, a pose now lost to conservation treatment—and shares even greater affinity with a recently discovered bust-length portrait of Gell by Stuart (private collection).[3]

Whatever the arrangement between the painters, there can be no doubt that Reynolds aided Stuart at the time. He sat for him, sent patrons to him, and helped him

1. *Gell* is not listed in Mason 1879 but is in Park 1926, pp. 343–44, no. 320. See also Stuart's full-length portrait of Rear Admiral John Jervis, the Earl of St. Vincent (National Maritime Museum, Greenwich).

2. See David Mannings and Martin Postle, *Sir Joshua Reynolds: A Complete Catalogue of His Paintings* (New Haven: Yale University Press, 2000), p. 213, no. 713; Nicholas Penny, ed., *Reynolds*, exh. cat. (London: Royal Academy of Arts in association with Weidenfeld and Nicolson, 1986), p. 215, no. 50.

3. See Mannings and Postle, *Reynolds*, p. 213.

Fig. 41. Sir Joshua Reynolds, *John Gell*, 1780.
Oil on canvas, 50 x 40 in. (127 x 101.5 cm).
National Maritime Museum, Greenwich

make a good showing at the academy. The three pictures Stuart submitted in 1785, *Gell* and bust portraits of Admiral Barrington (part of the commission for Saltram House that Reynolds had helped secure for Stuart; fig. 19) and Thomas Dawson, Baron Dartrey and Viscount Cremorne (unlocated), were hung in the academy's Great Room, where William Dunlap saw them in "the best lights, and most conspicuous places."[4] The portrait of Gell hung on the same wall as five portraits by Reynolds, including the acclaimed full-length of the Prince of Wales. But some saw disadvantage in this placement: "in any other part of the room, this piece would have appeared excellent, but it is unfortunately placed in a situation among the very finest pieces of the president."[5] The reviews of *Gell*, in fact, say little about the picture itself, instead describing its place in the academy's competition. One critic deemed Stuart one of the "ingenious American artists," thus grouping him with West and his new student Mather Brown.[6] The artist and critic John Hoppner wrote of *Gell* in specific contrast to John Singleton Copley's *Three Youngest Daughters of King George III* (fig. 28) in an effort to promote his own entries, a full-length portrait of a gentleman and portraits of the three princesses:

Before the merits of this picture can be fairly estimated, it is necessary to enquire in what the excellence of a portrait consists. If in figures floundering from the midst of a quantity of fluttering back-ground, this picture is deficient. If in a back-ground decorated with red trees, green clouds and yellow water, this picture is deficient. If in covering the parts of the canvas not occupied by the figure with garlands of roses and lilies, and tulips, and parrots feathers, to prevent the eye from resting upon the principal figure, this picture is deficient. For it is only a plain and admirably well painted portrait of Capt. Gell, without any trickery to dazzle the eye, or mislead the judgment. The likeness is very strong, which we understand to be almost invariably the case with the portraits of this artist. The water does not seem painted from the same pallet as the figure, nor is it sufficiently limpid. If the air and posture of the figure may be thought stiff, it should be considered that it is characteristic in a veteran officer; and if it should be thought coldly correct, that correctness, perhaps, was all the painter had in view. We confess a partiality for young artists, who aim at something; tho' those are likewise entitled to their share of praise, who commit either few or trivial errors. Upon the whole, we think this picture not entirely undeserving of being placed as a companion to Hoppner's *whole-length of Mr.* Norton.[7]

Stuart may have attempted to navigate the complicated politics of competition at the academy by honoring its president with a work painted in homage to his style, but he saw this work founder in antagonisms and rivalries that were of little interest or use to him.

CRB

4. Dunlap 1834, vol. 1, p. 193. A portrait of Dartrey, of disputed attribution to Stuart, is at the Montclair Art Museum, Montclair, N.J.
5. "Exhibition of the Royal Academy," *Universal Daily Register*, May 7, 1785.
6. "Exhibition of the Royal Academy," *Universal Daily Register*, April 23, 1785, p. 2.
7. [John Hoppner], "Royal Academy Exhibition," *Morning Post and Daily Advertiser*, May 9, 1785, p. 3. See also Emily Ballew Neff and William L. Pressly, *John Singleton Copley in England*, exh. cat. (Houston: Museum of Fine Arts, 1995), pp. 155–58.

16. Self-Portrait

1786

Oil on canvas, 10⅝ x 8⅞ in. (27 x 22.5 cm)

The Metropolitan Museum of Art, New York;

Fletcher Fund, 1926 (26.16)

This, Stuart's smallest painting, captures the full breadth of his expressive powers and technical brilliance. Executed on a rectangular scrap of canvas, the piercing self-image in three-quarter view is just a head, a collar, and a suggestion of a shirt that dissolve into a pale green background.[1] With expert swiftness, Stuart brushed in his strong red-tipped nose, thin lips, and deep eye sockets—his eyes are but slits, squinting at his viewer. Several strokes of deep brown describe his unruly hair and sideburns. It is a work of intensity that has contributed to more than one historian's suggesting that Stuart had mental maladies—debilitating melancholia or manic depression.[2] His daughter Jane described him as "a pale-looking man, . . . of a sad expression and with dark brown hair, which curled slightly about his neck. It was often said that he looked like Charles I." He was about "five feet ten with powerful frame and graceful manners, and was exceedingly well-bred; but with an expression so searching that it amounted to severity. . . . On one occasion, a lady, who was sitting to him, said . . . 'I am frightened to death; he looks as if he knew everything I had ever done in my life.'"[3] According to Jane, Stuart painted it for his wife about the time of their marriage in 1786.[4] This information makes it a work of extraordinary intimacy, a token of affection rather in the vein of a portrait miniature meant to be cherished by one person, the very person who would presumably have known best the traits of this complicated man.

Compared to the crisply delineated, character-filled portraits Stuart painted in the 1780s, this visually ominous one seems an anomaly, a rakish work in a state inappropriate for exhibition or presentation. This quality may accord with its being intended for his wife, in which case it should be considered a conceptually finished work. Stuart once said that "the true and perfect image of man is seen in a mist of hazy atmosphere," a statement of his artistic vision and which implied that his reading of his sitter's character came at this preliminary stage of composition.[5] Strokes and touches after that would bring the image to a level of finish commensurate with contemporary ideals in portraiture; indeed, during this period Stuart's fame for his portrayal of character in a sitter's face came from his habit of judicious rather than absolute finish. His self-portrait, even in its thinly painted state, defines precisely the features the artist deemed crucial to the portrayal of likeness and character: the nose and the brow. He felt that a likeness depended on the nose, a theory he demonstrated "by putting his thumb under his large and flexible proboscis, and turning it up, so as to display the ample nostrils, [and then] he would exclaim, 'Who would know my portrait with such a nose as this?'"[6]

This work, whether finished as far as the artist meant it to be or unfinished—abandoned—provides crucial information about Stuart's working method. He blocked in the head with opaque pigment and then worked in transparent hues, building to his desired level of finish. He later told the artist John S. Cogdell that he used a small, blunt brush to form the head and its angles "to come at the masses of light and shadow."[7] Rejecting Benjamin West's teachings, which yielded heavily outlined results in paint, Stuart shunned drawing as a "loss of time," preferring to work like a sculptor "where the great corners & rude masses are blockd off first."[8] According to William Dunlap, who saw Stuart at work in the mid-1780s, "He commenced his pictures faint, like the reflexions in a dull glass, and strengthened as the work progressed, making the parts all more determined, with colour, light, and shade."[9] Even in his most considered, formal portraits, Stuart's application of pigment remains thin.

1. The painting is listed in Mason 1879, p. 261; Park 1926, pp. 718–19, no. 797.

2. See Pressly 1986, pp. 48–50; Evans 2004.

3. J. Stuart 1877a, pp. 643–44.

4. Jane Stuart's letter, dated December 16, 1885, is now lost but is quoted in Park 1926, pp. 718–19, no. 797: "He painted a small picture in oil of himself for my mother (in London after great persuasion), but could not be induced to finish it. Some years since I gave this head to the late Mrs. H. G. Otis, which she left to her son Harry, who died quite recently in some part of Europe."

5. Stuart, quoted by Matthew Jouett in Mason 1879, p. 67.

6. Dunlap 1834, vol. 1, p. 218. See also Pickering 1817 (November 10).

7. John S. Cogdell's diary, vol. 3, entry for September 13, 1816, Joseph Downs Collection of Manuscripts and Printed Ephemera, Winterthur Library, Winterthur, Del.

8. Jouett 1816, p. 85.

9. Dunlap 1834, vol. 1, p. 216.

16

10. Park lists a pen-and-ink self-portrait by Stuart that is now lost. A portrait of a gentleman (Tate Britain) often reproduced as a self-portrait is not him.

Stuart painted just two self-portraits: this one and the earlier portrait in homage of West (cat. 5). West's drawing of Stuart (fig. 38), taken as the student painted his teacher for John Boydell (see cat. 12), is closer in date to this image and indeed shows the same small eyes, narrow jawline, large nose, and disheveled hair.[10]   CRB

17. JOSEPH BRANT

1786
Oil on canvas, 23½ x 24 in. (59.7 x 61 cm)
The Northumberland Estates, Alnwick Castle,
Collection of the Duke of Northumberland (SY.11)

Of the three patrons, Isaac Barré, John Jervis, and Hugh Percy, who visited Stuart in the spring of 1785 with offers of assistance, Percy was the only one to stick with him. His commissions and support helped Stuart with his debts, while Stuart offered Percy, at the very moment of his elevation in the peerage, a variation of a court painter, an extremely talented artist without prior political commitment devoted to the proper memorialization of his family and friends.

Percy was the eldest son of Hugh Smithson Percy, the first Duke of Northumberland, who by act of Parliament took the surname of his wife, the heiress Elizabeth Seymour Percy, in order to inherit her family's fortune and the earldom of Northumberland. The younger Hugh Percy had a distinguished military career: he fought in the Seven Years War and in 1764 was aide-de-camp to George III, concurrently serving in Parliament as the member for Westminster (1763–76). Percy opposed the king's policies toward the American colonies but in 1774 went to Boston under General Thomas Gage. By 1777, now a lieutenant general, Percy's disputes with General Sir William Howe led him to request recall from service in America. He succeeded to the Percy peerage through his mother in 1776, and at his father's death in 1786, he became duke, lord lieutenant, and vice-admiral of Northumberland.

The second duke carried on renovations the family's properties with the help of Robert Adam: the Gothic-style Alnwick Castle in Northumberland; Northumberland House near Charing Cross, London, built in the seventeenth century; and Syon House and Gardens in Kew, which had been built in 1547 from the ruins of Bridgettine Monastery of Sion.[1] To the corridor of portraits of family ancestors at Syon, the first

1. On these architectural projects, see Eileen Harris, *The Genius of Robert Adam: His Interiors* (New Haven: Yale University Press, 2001), pp. 64–103.

Fig. 43. George Romney, *Joseph Brant*, 1776. Oil on canvas, 50 x 39 in. (127 x 99 cm). The National Gallery of Canada, Ottawa (8005)

Fig. 44. *Joseph Brant*, 1786. Oil on canvas, 30 x 25 in. (76.2 x 63.5 cm). Fenimore Art Museum, Cooperstown, N.Y.

17

duke had added portraits of himself and his wife by Sir Joshua Reynolds (collection of the Duke of Northumberland), a tradition continued by his son when he sat for Stuart. The portraits Percy paid for in the spring and summer of 1785 were probably of himself, one showing him as commander of the second troop of horse grenadier guards (fig. 18) and the other in a uniform that was overpainted by another artist some time after April 1788 when he received the Order of the Garter (both, collection of the Duke of Northumberland). In 1786 he asked Stuart to paint a visiting dignitary from North America, Joseph Brant, and in 1787, full-length portraits of himself and the Duchess of Northumberland and a large conversation-piece painting of their children (cat. 18).

Brant (1743–1807), whose given Mohawk name was Thayendanegea, and Percy met when both commanded allied British troops near Boston during the American Revolution. They formed a bond that led to Percy's Mohawk adoption under the name Thorighwegeri, or the Evergreen Brake, "a titled house never dies."[2] After Percy returned to England, he kept up a lifelong correspondence and exchange of ceremonial gifts with Brant.[3] Born in the Ohio country to a prominent Native North American family, Brant was raised after the death of his father by a succession of stepfathers, each of whom linked his family to another tribe; he assumed the name of one of these, Brant Canagaraduncka. He fought in the French and Indian War under the command of his sister's common-law husband, Sir William Johnson, and he rose in rank to lead Native Americans allied with the British in the Six Nations Confederacy during the revolution. Esteemed for his fine language skills, he worked as an interpreter for the British Indian Department. He sailed for London in November 1775 to lobby for the protection of Mohawk lands in North America. The limits of royal favor gained by the commission would be tested in the ensuing war, but the charismatic Brant, with his keen comprehension of cultural difference, created a sensation as he smoothly navigated the system by adopting English-style politesse for his negotiations. The Earl of Warwick commissioned his portrait from George Romney (fig. 43), the Freemasons initiated him as a member, and he was presented at court. George III bestowed him with a small silver gorget, modeled on an armor's protection for the throat,[4] emblazoned with the royal crest and inscribed "The Gift of a Friend to Capt. Brant."[5]

With reassurances of protection for his people and their land, Brant returned to North America in June 1776, only to see the gradual devastation of the Iroquois Confederacy and the Native Americans' ultimate betrayal when the Treaty of Paris of 1783 made no provision for the welfare of the allied Native Americans. Loss of lands and concern for the economic viability of the Six Nations took Brant back to London in December 1785 to request compensation for service and assistance in future territorial disputes. By focusing on concessions for loyalty rather than recrimination for damage done, Brant succeeded in getting the king's pledge on Iroquois land and his promise of a pension for Brant's service to the British Indian Department.

Brant, hailed as the king of the Mohawks upon arrival in London in 1785, held a place of honor, title, and respect in English society that made him the acquaintance of aristocrats and royals, including the teenage Prince of Wales. Frederica Charlotte Louise, Baroness von Riedesel, effused, "His countenance is manly and intelligent, his disposition very mild. His manners are polished and he expresses himself with fluency."[6] Brant conducted himself in a manner that made the occasional irreverence endearingly peculiar rather than offensive. In his role as ambassador for his nation at court, Brant presented a seductive public image that merged diplomat and warrior, gentleman and brute, "creatively adapt[ing] Iroquois customs in order to take advantage of whatever few

2. J. Ross Robertson, ed., *The Diary of Mrs. John Graves Simcoe, Wife of the First Lieutenant-Governor of the Province of Upper Canada, 1792–6* (Toronto: W. Briggs, 1911), p. 141. On Brant, see, for example, *ANB*, vol. 3, pp. 430–32; Isabel Thompson Kelsay, *Joseph Brant, 1743–1807: Man of Two Worlds* (Syracuse, N.Y.: Syracuse University Press, 1984); William L. Stone, *Life of Joseph Brant* (1838; Albany: J. Munsell, 1865); Marc Jack Smith, "Joseph Brant: Mohawk Statesman" (Ph.D. diss., University of Wisconsin, 1946). See also Charles M. Johnston, ed., *The Valley of the Six Nations: A Collection of Documents on the Indian Lands of the Grand River* (Toronto: Champlain Society for the Government of Ontario, University of Toronto, 1964); Barbara Graymont, *The Iroquois in the American Revolution* (Syracuse, N.Y.: Syracuse University Press, 1972); James Paxton, "The Myth of the Loyalist Iroquois: Joseph Brant and the Invention of a Canadian Tradition," paper delivered at the Conference on Iroquois Research, Rensselaerville Institute, Rensselaerville, N.Y., October 6, 2002, published at http://www.wampumchronicles.com/josephbrant.html.

3. In 1805, Northumberland gave Brant a ceremonial tomahawk with a silver plaque inscribed "Given to my friend Joseph Brant from the Duke of Northumberland 1805"; *Realm of the Iroquois* (Alexandria, Va.: Time-Life Books, 1993), illus. p. 138.

4. Daniel Christian Fueter made ceremonial badges on royal command in 1760 and 1764 for presentation to Native American chiefs who had signed treaties with Britain, the so-called gorget captains; Arthur Woodward, "Highlights on Indian Trade Silver," *Antiques* 47 (June 1945), p. 330. See also Charlotte Wilcoxen, "Indian-Trade Silver of the New York Colonial Frontier," *Antiques* 106 (December 1979), pp. 1356–61.

5. Brant's gorget is in the Rochester Museum and Science Center, Rochester, N.Y.

6. Quoted in L. A. Wood, *War Chief of the Six Nations* (Toronto: Glasgow, Brook, 1920), p. 109.

7. See Paxton, "The Myth of the Loyalist Iroquois," p. 6.

8. There is a copy of the print in the National Portrait Gallery, London. See also J. Fawcett Thompson, "Thayendanegea the Mohawk and His Several Portraits," *Connoisseur* 170 (January 1969), pp. 49–53.

9. Clipping dated 1786 from Royal Academy Reviews, Paul Mellon Centre for Studies in British Art, London. See Milton W. Hamilton, "Joseph Brant Painted by Rigaud," *New York History* 40 (July 1959), pp. 257–54, which illustrates the picture in black and white and says it was probably destroyed by fire. See also *Portraits of Thayendanegea, Joseph Brant*, exh. cat. (Ontario: Burlington Cultural Center, 1993).

10. The painting, not in Mason 1879, is listed in Park 1926, p. 747, no. 831.

11. The same medallion appears in the portrait of Brant by William von Moll Berczy of 1807 (National Gallery of Canada, Ottawa). A similar medal, though unframed, is illustrated in Harrold E. Gillingham, "Early American Indian Medals," *Antiques* 6 (December 1924), p. 314, fig. 8.

12. Evans (1999, p. 135 n. 3) rejects the attribution of these pictures to Stuart.

13. Kelsay, *Joseph Brant*, p. 389.

opportunities colonialism presented."[7] He played his role through costume, as he donned English suits for some occasions, full Iroquois chieftain garb for others, and even a combination when it suited.

Portraits magnified his desired appearance. In 1776 Romney depicted the thirty-three-year-old Brant as a stern-faced warrior in billowing shirtsleeves, with colorful sashes at his waist and across his chest and crimson feathers shooting like flames from his black headband. He wears the emblems marking his service to England—the king's ceremonial gorget and a silver Masonic pendant—and holds a tomahawk. The picture appeared in the *London Magazine* and in 1779 John Raphael Smith's mezzotint engraving, inscribed "Joseph Tayandaneega called the Brant, the Great Captain of the Six Nations," further disseminated Romney's compelling portrait.[8] In 1786, for sittings with John Francis Rigaud, Brant wore his dark green British Indian Department coat with a surfeit of Iroquois regalia (unlocated). The full-length exhibition piece appeared at the Royal Academy that year with the title "A Mohawk," and it received a sharp review: "This is indeed a *savage* looking picture, unharmonious, cold, and dry, and characteristical of the scalp-stealing tribe."[9] Although seeming to describe the painting rather than the subject, the writer expressed the typically hostile attitude toward the Native Americans in England. And the painting was a detriment to Rigaud's further advancement in the highly politicized arena of the academy and among those who kept track of the predilections of artists and patrons.

Like Romney's portrait of Brant, Stuart's was a personal commission rather than an intended exhibition piece. Stuart gave Brant a fully modeled visage projecting the strong characterization for which he had become so well known.[10] The limpid eyes, strong nose, resolute mouth, and slightly flaccid jawline describe a man of intelligent determination capable of conciliatory debate. The clothing maintains his nationality and his dignity: over his open-collar shirt a cape of small joined silver rings encircles his shoulders, a wide silver armband is on his right biceps, and four silver bracelets are on his exposed right wrist. A black shawl with silver-thread fringe covers his left shoulder and arm, and on his head, with dark hair pulled back in a queue, is a close-fitting black and red cap embellished with more silver rings and with a tuft of yellow, orange, and black feathers fixed to the band. The silver ornamentation conveys his high rank; some of it was costume embellishment, but most pieces would have been ceremonial gifts. Tied around his neck he wears the gorget from George III on a blue satin ribbon, and hanging below that, a medallion portrait of the king in an imposing brass locket.[11] He is, by Stuart's brush, the exemplification of the savage and noble, an Iroquois statesman ornamented by the British. He entertains the royal encomiums, even as his poignant facial expression seems to acknowledge the equivocation in the king's promises of assistance.

The soldier and statesman Francis Rawdon-Hastings, who like Northumberland saw distinguished military service in America during the revolution, also commissioned a portrait of Brant from Stuart (fig. 44), a replica of which was discovered at the British Museum in the 1930s.[12] This image of Brant looking to the left and wrapped in a red blanket with a large shell hanging from his neck was engraved in 1786 (National Portrait Gallery, London) and was copied by the enameler Henry Bone as a gift to Brant's third wife, Catherine (Joseph Brant Museum, Burlington, Ontario). One of Brant's daughters later said that it was the most accurate likeness of her father she had ever seen.[13]

CRB

1787
Oil on canvas, 71 ½ x 94 in. (181.6 x 238.8 cm)
The Northumberland Estates, Alnwick Castle,
Collection of the Duke of Northumberland
(04317/T198)

1. *World*, June 14, 1787, p. 3. See also the Duke of
Northumberland's Ledger Book, July 29, 1787, "To
Sundries for a Picture of the Children—£129.9.0,"
Alnwick Castle, Northumberland. The painting is
not listed in Mason 1879 or Park 1926.

Fig. 45. Sir Joshua Reynolds, *The Marlborough Family*, 1777–78. Oil on canvas, 125¼ x 113¾ in. (318 x 289 cm). Collection of the Duke of Marlborough, Blenheim Palace, Oxfordshire

Fig. 46. George Romney, *The Leveson-Gower Children*, 1776. Oil on canvas, 79½ x 91¼ in. (202 x 232 cm). Abbot Hall Art Gallery, Kendal, Cumbria, England

In June 1787, the *World* reported that "Stuart has nearly finished the Duke of Northumberland's family picture. The children, Lady Elizabeth, Lady Agnes, Lady Julia, and Lord Percy, with a distant view of Syon in the background, form this agreeable work."[1] The duke married twice: in July 1764 to Lady Anne Stuart, whom he divorced in 1779, and in May 1779 to his sister-in-law Frances Julia Burrell (1752–1820), by whom he had three daughters and three sons. In the group portrait, the girls surround their little brother Hugh (1785–1847), who would become the third duke.[2] In the lore surrounding the picture, the children posed for Stuart outdoors near the river, tiny Lord Percy threw stones in the water to ripple his sisters' reflections, and the eldest girl was teased by her siblings for her vanity.[3] More likely, according to customary portrait practice and the improbability of getting four children to stay posed for long, they would have sat for the painter individually, and indoors. The keen resemblance among the three youngest children suggests either a striking family resemblance or the likelihood that Stuart had very little time with each one. The eldest girl is more particularized, yet her face, tight-bodiced robe *à l'anglaise*, and pose are borrowed from the eldest girl in Reynolds's portrait of the Marlborough family (fig. 45), which Stuart could have seen at the Royal Academy in 1778.

In the Marlborough picture, reciprocal gestures by the sitters provide control and order for the riot of costume, accoutrement, and background detail, making it successful at the academy in precisely the way that Copley's 1785 portrait of the three youngest daughters of George III (fig. 28) was not. Stuart was aware of the Copley painting since the most scathing criticism of it was embedded in a review by John Hoppner of Stuart's portrait of John Gell (cat. 15).[4] With his picture of the Percy children, Stuart used similar elements as those in Copley's ebullient tableau—a dog, a phaeton, a landscape setting—but he simplified the composition considerably. The toddler heir and the middle sister are seated on iridescent gold drapery in a pony cart, while the eldest girl, in a large-brimmed hat with wide blue satin ribbons that match the one at her waist, stands at right and reaches toward the boy. He points down at his youngest sister, who kneels to caress the greyhound, her hat behind her. It is a picture of such austere elegance, the effect of translucent paint and broadly applied strokes untempered by fussy detail, that when William Whitley inquired about the portrait, the Duke of Northumberland told him it was by John Hoppner,[5] although these characteristics make a stronger comparison to the work of George Romney.

Contact between Stuart and Romney is impossible to trace, but they must have known one another.[6] Both largely self-taught, they came to London—Romney in 1762 and Stuart in 1775—near destitution and without friends or patrons, and they took residence in garretlike rooms in seedy neighborhoods. Eight years after arrival in the city, each threw in his lot with the Incorporated Society of Artists—Romney in 1770, Stuart in 1783—as an alternative to the Royal Academy. When each made enough money to move to fine quarters, both chose homes and studios not in the neighborhoods where established painters settled, but in a nouveau riche section of town, Cavendish Square for Romney and New Burlington Street for Stuart. Throughout their careers in London, both aligned themselves from time to time with Reynolds, whether by mimicking his style or emulating his practice, a strategy that had no lasting effect on the canvases of either but helped promote both to fame. The principal difference between them may

18

2. Northumberland and his wife would have two more sons, Henry (1787–1794) and Algernon (1792–1865), who would become the fourth duke.

3. Whitley 1932, p. 63; Mount 1964, p. 119.

4. [John Hoppner], "Royal Academy Exhibition," *Morning Post and Daily Advertiser*, May 9, 1785, p. 3.

5. Whitley 1932, p. 63.

6. J. Stuart (1877a, p. 643) wrote that her father had recommended Romney's heads to her "as being exceedingly beautiful and more true to nature than any others he had ever seen, not even excepting those of Sir Joshua." On Romney, see Alex Kidson, *George Romney, 1734–1802*, exh. cat. (Princeton, N.J.: Princeton University Press, 2002), p. 28, who made an extensive study of patronage in London during this period. See also Kidson, review of Dorinda Evans's *The Genius of Gilbert Stuart* (*Burlington Magazine* 142 [November 2000], p. 710), p. 10, in which he discovers "a deep instinctual bond" between Romney and Stuart. For all references to Romney, I am indebted to Kidson's excellent reading of Romney's career.

7. Kidson, *George Romney*, p. 117.

have been in their personalities: Romney was shy, aloof, and methodical; Stuart was gregarious, talkative, and disorganized. The result was the same. Both attracted a select clientele who shunned publicity and fanfare, did not care about the academy's annual exhibitions, and appreciated the exclusivity inherent in the practice of one so covert (Romney) or so obviously unambitious (Stuart) in his practice.

Stuart must have known Romney's portrait of the Leveson-Gower children, painted in 1776 for Granville Leveson-Gower, second Earl Gower (fig. 46). Alex Kidson described Romney's achievement in this picture as having created for the children "a world of their own that the adult viewer is hard-pressed to invade . . . [and] the way that each child occupies his or her place in a rigorously ordered pattern, an analogue for the child's vision of the world rather than the messy construct of adults."[7] Stuart's picture, too, has this conceptual clarity, suggesting a deliberate description not of the children themselves, but of their milieu. Indeed, the vacancy in their faces may be the result of Stuart's frustration at working with children, with their undeveloped personalities, limited experiences, and fleeting attention spans. They appear angelic, which is, after all, the way their father would have wanted it.

CRB

Stuart in Dublin (1787–93)

S tuart was first recorded in Dublin at a dinner of the Artists of Dublin, a group that had gathered for their annual Saint Luke's Day event on October 18, 1787. One of their number monopolized the table with boasts of an intimate friendship with Sir Joshua Reynolds. Stuart became outraged and, on learning that the man's name was Pack, shouted, "Well, I have often heard of a Pack of nonsense, but I never saw it before."[1] The party exploded with hilarity, and when it subsided attention turned to Stuart, who proceeded with an account of his life without revealing his reason for being in their company. Stuart might have mentioned that, like Christopher Pack, he too was an acquaintance of the president of London's Royal Academy of Arts, but he never mentioned Reynolds, speaking instead of his compatriot-mentor Benjamin West, albeit with an episode that gave Stuart the upper hand in matters of the brush. Beginning in Dublin, he would admit to being no man's student, was accepting of word-of-mouth commissions and recommendations from reliable sources, but claimed independence and a place at the top of his profession. He made as much clear to his colleagues, none of whom, including Pack, could touch his success over the next five years.

Reynolds had arranged for Stuart to take a commission in his stead. Reynolds had been invited to Dublin several times by his patron Charles Manners, fourth Duke of Rutland and Lord Lieutenant of Ireland, but while he executed five portraits of Rutland and three of his wife, Mary Isabella Somerset, Lady Granby, in London, he rarely traveled, declining invitations year after year, as in June 1786: "I am very much flattered by your Grace's kind invitation to Ireland, and very much mortified that it is not in my power to accept of it this year."[2] He wrote the same the following summer, but sent Stuart and Pack in his stead, not only for portraits but to help him with his pet project, a national gallery. Rutland and Stuart would have worked well together. The September 19, 1787, issue of the *Dublin Evening Post* described Rutland in words that would just as well apply to Stuart: "His Grace is a philosopher by habit, rather than principle; and naturally enjoys that exemption from care, which in others is the effect of resolution."[3] But Rutland died on October 24, 1787.[4] His body was shipped to England for burial on November 17, about a month after Stuart's arrival. The death was a blow for Stuart, and he would later collapse time in his version of the event, telling his daughter Jane that he had entered Dublin just as the duke's cortege was leaving.[5]

Stuart may have foundered for a while, but not for long. By the 1780s, Dublin had reached a historic apogee as a thriving industrial metropolis, with a strong market for trade and other business, and was a beautiful Georgian city with splen-

1. Herbert 1836, p. 228; details of the party, pp. 230–31. On Stuart's career in Ireland, see Crean 1990.
2. Whitley 1932, p. 69. On Reynolds's portraits of Rutland, see David Mannings and Martin Postle, *Sir Joshua Reynolds: A Complete Catalogue of His Paintings* (New Haven: Yale University Press, 2000), pp. 319–20.
3. Quoted in Crean 1990, p. 182.
4. See ibid., pp. 106–8.
5. J. Stuart 1877a, p. 645.

Detail of cat. 23, *Catherine Lane Barker*

Fig. 47. *Luke White*, ca. 1790. Oil on canvas, 30 x 25 in. (76.2 x 63.5 cm). National Gallery of Art, Washington, D.C.; Andrew W. Mellon Collection (1942.8.28)

did modern architecture, flourishing cultural institutions for dance, music, and theater, and sophisticated craftsmen in furniture, silver, glass, and textiles. Stuart found little competition among portraitists in Dublin. Hugh Douglas Hamilton had moved to London in 1764. The English portraitist Francis Wheatley, who had been in Dublin from 1779 to 1783, was now back in London. The painter Henry Pelham, John Singleton Copley's half brother, had lived in Ireland since the early 1780s, but in County Kerry, far enough from Dublin that he catered to a different clientele. Robert Home suited some among the elite, but within about a decade of his arrival in Dublin in 1779 he had exhausted the market; he may have left for India in 1789 because Stuart took away any possibilities of work. Home's studio assistant, John Dowling Herbert, quickly latched onto Stuart. Whether or not Herbert worked for Stuart, there can be no question of his close relationship with him, as his witty chronicle of Stuart's life in Dublin proves.[6] Stuart encountered a number of aspiring portraitists who sought him out because they were eager for a role model so long absent in the city. In 1788, Stuart advised Martin Archer Shee not to waste his youth in Ireland and to go to the Royal Academy. Shee followed Stuart's advice to acclaim, in 1830 becoming its president.[7] The Irish miniature painters George Place, William Cuming, and Walter Robertson gained much from studying Stuart's oils, and John Comerford later recalled that "he owed more to [Stuart] for what he now is than to all the rest of the artists in the world."[8]

Within a month of Stuart's arrival, the Dublin *Evening Herald* announced that "Mr. Stewart, an English gentleman lately arrived in the metropolis, excels in his delicacy of colouring and graceful attitudes . . . and has a happy method of disposing his figures and at the same time preserving a strong resemblance."[9] The writer got the nationality wrong, either a mistake based on the fact that Stuart had come from London or an assumption that a fine portraitist must be English. Such public notices plus his connection to Rutland gave him vast opportunities from among the Anglo-Irish ascendancy, the ruling elite in Dublin.

Commissions kept Stuart in Dublin for nearly six years, although initially he may not have intended to stay any longer than it would have taken him to paint the Duke of Rutland's portrait. He returned to London for several weeks in early 1788, causing speculation that he had merely been trying out the Irish capital: "Stuart's last trip to Ireland so far answered perfectly, as to establish for his portraits in that kingdom, as in this, a preeminent fame for identity."[10] Whose portraits he painted during the fall of 1787 are a mystery. Herbert named Luke White (fig. 47), Jonathan Fisher, and Henry Grattan, perhaps the most influential man in the Irish Parliament, as Stuart's first sitters.[11] But Herbert's dates may not be right, for by the following fall, the papers were still anticipating what he might produce:

6. Herbert 1836, pp. 226–48.

7. Martin Archer Shee, *The Life of Sir Martin Archer Shee: President of the Royal Academy, F.R.S., D.C.L.* (London: Longman, Green, Longman, and Roberts, 1860), p. 67.

8. "A Review of the Professors of the Fine Arts in this Kingdom," *Evening Herald*, 1789, Press Cuttings from English Newspapers on Matters of Artistic Interest, 1688–1825, Victoria and Albert Museum, London. See Chester Harding, letter to Stuart, January 6, 1825, transcribed in Mason 1879, p. 73.

9. Quoted in Crean 1990, p. 102.

10. *London World*, April 1, 1788, Press Cuttings from English Newspapers on Matters of Artistic Interest, 1688–1825, Victoria and Albert Museum, London.

11. Herbert 1836, pp. 235–37. On White, see Miles 1995, pp. 177–79, where it is stated that Stuart also painted White's wife and son.

Fig. 48. *Hugh Hamilton, Dean of Armagh*,
ca. 1790. Oil on canvas, 30 x 25 in. (76.2 x 63.5 cm).
Private collection

"Stuart, a portrait painter fit to be mentioned even with Sir Joshua, must wait this account of his works . . . as for the works themselves all Dublin is waiting."[12] As in London in 1775–76, Stuart took time to find his way in Dublin in 1787–88. Many of his most prominent clients in London had attachments to the Irish Parliament, including Isaac Barré, Lord Dartrey, Viscount Percy, John Beresford, and Francis Rawdon-Hastings, for whom Stuart had painted a portrait of Joseph Brant (fig. 44) and who would later succeed to peerage in Ireland as the Earl of Moira and sit for the painter (unlocated). Rawdon was, by late 1788, poised to head the war ministry, and the Duke of Northumberland, Stuart's last great patron in London, was ready to assume the position of Lord Lieutenant of Ireland, if George III's diagnosed insanity caused a regency government. With the king's recovery, the Tory party remained in power for the time being.

Either Rawdon or Northumberland could have introduced Stuart to Grattan, whose efforts to maintain Ireland's independence from England would have been enhanced during a regency. Stuart apparently began a full-length portrait of Grattan, posed in the House of Commons and holding the Irish Bill of Rights, but the work was never finished.[13] Stuart did finish portraits of Grattan's most vehement opponents in Parliament, John FitzGibbon, Lord Chancellor of Ireland (cat. 19), and John Foster, Speaker of the Irish House of Commons (cat. 20). Stuart's failure to finish Grattan's portrait may be attributable to his accepting too much work. Herbert remembered that Stuart's "portraits were so well reported by the cognoscenti, that a rage to possess some specimen of his pencil took place, and a difficulty of obtaining a finished picture became universal, so fond was he of touching the half-price,"[14] that is, taking half of his fee in advance, a business strategy learned in London.

Yet, for all of the pictures Stuart was said to have started but failed to finish in Ireland, there are many more that define this period as one of prolific work. He was able to balance the divided interests of the Anglo-Irish political elite and keep his own position uncomplicated. An index of his sitters in Dublin reveals an intricate network of relationships and alliances, from the parvenu FitzGibbon to the country squire William Barker (cat. 24) to the aristocrat and bibliophile William Conyngham (cat. 25). Even after his death, the Duke of Rutland loomed over Stuart's Irish career as his early sanction of the painter continued to be influential. In addition, Charles Agar, archbishop of Dublin and first Earl of Normanton, may have been Stuart's most important conduit to work in Dublin. In the interconnections of kinship, the basis for any portraitist's strategy for commissions, Agar would have known of Stuart through his wife's cousin, Sir George Macartney, Earl Macartney, who sat for Stuart in London on the recommendation of his brother-in-law, the Duke of Northumberland. Agar's wife, Jane, Countess of

12. *London World*, December 27, 1788, Press Cuttings from English Newspapers on Matters of Artistic Interest, 1688–1825, Victoria and Albert Museum, London.

13. There are bust-length portraits of Grattan with problematic attributions to Stuart at the Wadsworth Atheneum, Hartford, and the National Gallery of Ireland, Dublin.

14. Herbert 1836, p. 226.

15. See Jane, Countess of Normanton, letter to her cousin Lord Macartney, June 16, 1787, Macartney Papers, Public Record Office of Northern Ireland, Belfast, D.572/9/9, asking him to sit for his portrait. On Agar and Stuart, see A. P. W. Malcomson, *Archbishop Charles Agar: Churchman and Politics in Ireland, 1760–1810* (Dublin: Four Courts Press, 2002), pp. 62–64.

16. The date associated with this group of pictures comes in the diary of Lord Clonmell, the entry for October 19, 1789, where he says he had finished the last sitting for his portrait. See Whitley 1932, p. 84. The pictures remain at Somerly; see James Digman Wingfield and Joseph Rubens Powell, *The Picture Gallery of Somerly Looking South*, 1866 (Somerly, Ringwood, Hampshire), which shows the nineteenth-century installation of the gallery at Somerly, the English seat of the Agars, including the Stuart portraits on the far wall.

17. For a complete list with locations, see Crean 1990, pp. 392–406, and chap. 6, "Organized Religion in Eighteenth-Century Ireland: Stuart's Portraits of Irish Bishops in Context," pp. 192–226.

18. See ibid., pp. 151–53; Evans 1999, p. 138 n. 20.

19. See Evans 1999, p. 138 n. 20; Crean 1990, pp. 407–13.

20. Herbert 1832, p. 247.

21. Ibid., p. 246.

22. Ibid., p. 248.

23. Ibid.

24. *Dublin Chronicle*, March 19, 1793, quoted in Whitley 1932, p. 87.

Normanton, had asked Macartney to have his picture painted for her and, indeed, he gave her the picture.[15] By about 1790, Stuart had completed no fewer than four portraits for the Agars, including pictures of Agar himself and his wife and portraits of their friends John Scott, first Earl of Clonmell, and Hugh Carleton, Viscount Carleton.[16] Clonmell, Lord Chief Justice of the King's Bench in Ireland, commissioned a double portrait of his children, Thomas and Charlotte (private collection). Stuart's work for Agar had the effect of making him the choice for ecclesiastical portraiture, and over the next few years he made a good living by painting bishops and deans of the Church of England. Among others, he painted John Fowler, archbishop of Dublin; William Bennett, bishop of Cork and Ross; Euseby Cleaver, bishop of Cort; William Preston, bishop of Kildare; Hugh Hamilton, dean of Armagh (fig. 48); and perhaps most importantly William Beresford, Lord Bishop of Ossory, a chief adviser to FitzGibbon and brother of John Beresford, said to be the third in a triumvirate—FitzGibbon, Foster, and Beresford—who were the leading reactionary politicians in 1790s Ireland.[17] Stuart made certain that his work became known beyond the confines of Parliament and the Anglican rectories by arranging with Charles Howard Hodges to engrave mezzotints of the portraits. Similar to the collaboration with John Boydell in London, Hodges and Stuart assembled a handsome portfolio of prints of the leading figures in the Irish church and state, which turned out to be an extremely profitable venture.

Stuart's way of life in Dublin is hard to pin down. He seems to have lived in the neighborhood of the aging painter Robert West and then moved to Stillorgan, a village on the outskirts of Dublin. There, he may have lived in a house owned by the Earl of Carysfort, an arrangement about which nothing is known.[18] As for the provocative speculations on Stuart's frequent visits to the Dublin jails, there is only one documented incident of incarceration, at Marshalsea Prison during the summer of 1789, probably for debt.[19] Stuart tells a tale that he gained his freedom from that place by his keen knowledge of governmental affairs and the fact that FitzGibbon had assumed his high office just when Stuart was in prison. He seized the moment between "the abdication of one [official], [and] the investiture of the other" to demand his liberty.[20] On another occasion, Stuart told Herbert that he got out of prison by painting portraits of his jailors, embellishing the tale with stories of being chased in the streets by wardens and paying them off to the extent that "it has cost me more to bailiffs for my liberty than would pay the debt for which they were to arrest me."[21]

Stuart left Dublin just as abruptly as he had arrived, leaving unfinished business, half-begun portraits, and disappointed clients. Herbert reported that when asked what would become of the canvases left in his studio, Stuart replied, "the artists of Dublin will get employed in finishing them. . . . The likeness is there, and the finishing may be better than I should have made it."[22] The notion that Stuart had conducted a scam to attract half-payments, never intending to finish the works, lends credence to characterizations of the artist as a conniving opportunist, always looking ahead rather than behind and, in this case, seeing far beyond Dublin to across the ocean. To Herbert, he had confided a much more honorable plan: "When I can nett a sum sufficient to take me to America, I shall be off to my native soil. There I expect to make a fortune by Washington alone. I calculate upon making a plurality of his portraits, whole lengths, that will enable me to realize; and if I should be fortunate, I will repay my English and Irish creditors. To Ireland and England I shall bid adieu."[23]

Yet, the speculative notion of painting the new American president cannot have been the only reason Stuart left Great Britain after eighteen years there. In Ireland the rise in revolutionary tensions increased about 1791 as anti-Catholic factions organized and the governmental debates over union with England, which came to pass in 1800, became heated. The upheaval of the long-standing religious and social order threatened all artistic patronage in Ireland, as did Britain's declaration of war against France in February 1793. Stuart had intended to sail directly to Philadelphia but changed his plans: he sailed for New York on the ship of Captain John Shaw, a New Yorker who sat for Stuart, if not on board, then soon after arrival. The *Dublin Chronicle* reported on March 19, 1793: "Mr. Stewart's quitting this kingdom for America gives a fair opening to the abilities of Mr. Pack, who now stands unrivalled as a portrait painter."[24]

CRB

19. John FitzGibbon

1789–90
Oil on canvas, 96½ x 60⅝ in. (254 x 154 cm)
The Cleveland Museum of Art, Cleveland, Ohio;
General Income Fund (1919.910)

Of Stuart's ill-fated prospective patron the fourth Duke of Rutland, John FitzGibbon said: "I love the man. He stood by me and I must stand by him."[1] Within a year of making this statement of feigned loyalty (FitzGibbon was rumored to have been in an affair with the Duchess of Rutland), Rutland's sudden death elevated FitzGibbon to extraordinary prominence. In December 1787, FitzGibbon commissioned from Sir Joshua Reynolds a posthumous portrait of his political ally, a job Reynolds accepted immediately, perhaps aware of the irony that he had turned down the duke's invitation to paint him from life just months before.[2] In 1788 Reynolds made FitzGibbon a replica of his 1784 full-length image of the duke in Garter robes (private collection), a stunning work that surely informed FitzGibbon's next commission: an equally grand portrait of himself by Stuart, the painter Reynolds had dispatched to Dublin in his stead.[3]

The occasion may have been a celebration of FitzGibbon's rise in the summer of 1789 as Lord Chancellor of Ireland, a position of supremacy that FitzGibbon took to mean the deployment of high intelligence, vitriolic arrogance, and a reinvigorated desire to accumulate the lavish trappings of status. Through the generosity of King George III, who granted 1,000 pounds toward the equipage and preparation for "the Employment of Chancellor," FitzGibbon ordered new robes of office and then spent an additional 7,000 pounds on a new state coach, the most opulent vehicle yet owned in Ireland by a parliamentary official.[4] For his house at 6 Ely Place, where he hosted sumptuous banquets and elegant soirées, he imported French Louis Quatorze furniture and Italian paintings and added to his exceptional wine cellar. His enormous appetite for fine things, cultivated in childhood and perfected in his maturity, enhanced a life already well lived, a personality in continual flux according to circumstance. Stuart's portrait captures all of this.

1. Ann C. Kavanaugh, *John FitzGibbon, Earl of Clare: Protestant Reaction and English Authority in Late Eighteenth-Century Ireland* (Dublin; Portland, Ore.: Irish Academic Press, 1997), p. 124.

2. Whitley 1932, p. 69. On Reynolds's portraits of Rutland, see David Mannings and Martin Postle, *Sir Joshua Reynolds: A Complete Catalogue of His Paintings* (New Haven: Yale University Press, 2000), pp. 319–20.

3. The painting is listed in Mason 1879, p. 180; Park 1926, pp. 324–25, no. 297. Three other versions of Stuart's portrait of FitzGibbon are known, none of which has a firm attribution to the artist. A bust-length image in civilian dress was sold at Sotheby's, New York, April 23, 1982, lot 13. A small full-length portrait was at Christie's, London, May 20, 1999, lot 137 (unsold). Another small full-length is recorded in Mount 1964, p. 159, as in a private collection San Francisco in 1963, and deemed to be the engraver's version.

4. Grant to FitzGibbon recorded in the *Journal of the Irish House of Commons* 66 (February 1, 1790), appendix 3, p. ccxci. The coach is now in the National Museum of Ireland, on view at

Fig. 49. Charles Hodges after Gilbert Stuart, *John FitzGibbon*, 1790. Mezzotint, 26½ x 16¼ in. (67.4 x 41.2 cm). National Gallery of Ireland, Dublin

Fig. 50. Benjamin West, *George III*, 1779. Oil on canvas, 100½ x 72 in. (255.3 x 182.9 cm). The Royal Collection © 2004, Her Majesty Queen Elizabeth II

Newbridge House, County Dublin; see John Conforth, "Coaching Forth a Masterpiece," *Country Life* 187 (January 21, 1993), pp. 36–37.

5. The definitive biography is Kavanaugh, *John FitzGibbon, Earl of Clare*. See also Edith Mary Johnston-Liik, *History of the Irish Parliament, 1692–1800* (Belfast: Ulster Historical Foundation, 2002), vol. 4, pp. 165–71; William Denis Griffin, "John FitzGibbon, Earl of Clare" (Ph.D. diss, Fordham University, 1962); William D. Griffin, "John FitzGibbon, Earl of Clare," *History Today* 16 (July 1966), pp. 484–93; and an obituary, Dr. William Magee, "Character of John, Earl of Clare, Late Lord High Chancellor of Ireland," *Annual Register* 23 (1802), pp. 705–11.

6. *Dublin Evening Post*, April 10 and May 29, 1784, quoted in Kavanaugh, *John FitzGibbon, Earl of Clare*, pp. 64–65.

7. Kavanaugh, *John FitzGibbon, Earl of Clare*, pp. 156–59; "Memoirs of His Excellency John Fitzgibbon, Lord High Chancellor," *Walker's Hibernian Magazine*, August–September 1789, pp. 394, 449–51.

The son of a prominent and wealthy barrister, FitzGibbon was born in 1749 at Mount Shannon near Donnybrook, Dublin.[5] He attended Trinity College, graduated with distinction from Christ Church, Oxford, and was called to the Irish bar in 1772. He sat in Parliament for the University of Dublin from 1778 to 1783 and then for Kilmallock, during which time he also served as sheriff for County Limerick and attorney general, and developed a reputation as a hard drinker, a ladies' man, and worse. In 1784 the papers nicknamed him "Jack Fitzpetulant," charged him with "bestial sexual excess," and detailed his involvement in a lurid underworld of sexual scandal and dissolute behavior.[6] Not wont to reform or succumb to public pressure, he was nonetheless compelled to leave public politics. This disgrace notwithstanding, he developed a lucrative legal practice and countered his unsavory habits by marrying Anna Whalley, a great beauty with impeccable social skills. His appointment to the Lord Chancellorship of Ireland was criticized by those fearful of naming an Irishman to the office, but the king and his advisers prevailed. FitzGibbon became the first Irish national since 1725 to hold this ancient and venerable English title. He subsequently served as chair of the Irish House of Lords, supreme judge in the Court of Chancery, and keeper of the Great Seal of Ireland.

FitzGibbon's transformation, during which "the lewd, arrogant, effeminate coxcomb" turned into a gentleman suited to rule the country, was undertaken by the Dublin papers, which focused on such positive attributes as his clear voice, his profound legal knowledge, his quickness in debate, and the solidity of his determination.[7] FitzGibbon studiously distanced himself from governmental corruption, but his authority knew no bounds, and he destroyed the careers of others to effect the act of union between Ireland and England, a battle he fought until victorious in 1800. In retirement after the Irish Parliament was dissolved, FitzGibbon languished as one of the most hated men of the age; his funeral procession in 1802 was trailed by a jeering, pelting mob. His most recent

biographer found much to fault him for: "Even when every allowance is made for his intelligence, and his many virtues and abilities, FitzGibbon's character remains disturbing, violent, and repulsive. . . . He alternated between gracious kindness and sadistic bullying . . . [and] self-contempt drove him to a perpetual quest to remake himself in a more satisfactory image and likeness."[8]

Before 1789 FitzGibbon had seized only one opportunity, and a tiny one at that, to deploy portraiture in the service of his self-image. He sat to the miniaturist Richard Cosway in 1781 (private collection). He engaged several painters during his term of office as Lord Chancellor, Stuart being the first and Hugh Douglas Hamilton (National Gallery of Ireland, Dublin) and John Hoppner (unlocated) the near simultaneous last two in 1799. His interest in his image extended to prints after the portraits, a process that seems to have frustrated him. In 1799 he asked John Boydell to produce a mezzotint from the Hoppner portrait, since Charles Hodges's after the Stuart, published September 29, 1790, was "a vile bad one" (fig. 49).[9] FitzGibbon's aversion to the print does not necessarily translate into disappointment in the oil portrait, for there is every reason to suspect that the picture successfully captured the Lord Chancellor, a slender man with delicate features and "the haughty air, the imperious glance, and despotic will of a Roman emperor."[10] He seems to have commissioned a copy of Stuart's portrait, which he gave to Trinity College about December 1795 rather than sit for a new picture, a sure sign that it pleased him.[11]

Stuart meticulously transcribed the array of accoutrements associated with FitzGibbon's office, perhaps knowing the pleasure his patron took in lavish stuff. The Lord Chancellor's black gown with gold bullion lace trim and toggles was of standard, if luxuriant, design, meant to match the robe worn by the Speaker in the House of Commons (see cat. 20), but it could be embellished by a creative tailor and an inspired owner. Stuart recorded the figured black silk damask, the most expensive of all fabrics, and articulated the minute fittings and pattern in the lace embellishments.[12] Under the robe, FitzGibbon wears a black satin suit with low-heeled dress pumps; only the Lord Chancellor and the Speaker of the House wore the formal full-bottom wig, as accurately portrayed by Stuart. Stuart was also aware of the regalia pertinent to his patron's role, which was nearly identical to that of the Lord Chancellor of England. At FitzGibbon's right is the ornate harped crown of the silver-gilt mace, a staff decorated with seated figures of Britannia and Hibernia, flora, putti, and the royal arms, signifying augmented power that is carried before the chancellor when he processes into the House of Lords. Stuart's bravura treatment of the Lord Chancellor's purse, the square satin and velvet bag at FitzGibbon's right foot embroidered and appliquéd with the royal arms and which would hold the official's speech, suggests that he had special access to this item. FitzGibbon's purse bearer and nephew, John Beresford, who would have worn the purse around his neck like an apron in processions, may have given Stuart, whom he knew from sittings for his own portrait in London, a close look at the item.

Stuart also studied FitzGibbon. He told the artist John Dowling Herbert that he visited the Lord Chancellor at Ely Place and, on one occasion, was invited to dinner and seated next to him for "some private chat." Just after the meal commenced, a latecomer arrived, took a place off to the side, and was scrutinized by FitzGibbon and Stuart together: "Now, Stuart, you are so accustomed to look all men that come before you in the face, you must be a good judge of character, do you know that gentleman at the side-table?' 'No, my lord, I never saw him before.' 'Well, now tell me what sort of man he is in his disposition.' 'Is he a friend?' 'No.' 'Then I may speak freely.' 'Yes.' 'Why, then, my

8. Kavanaugh, *John FitzGibbon, Earl of Clare*, p. 17.

9. FitzGibbon, letter to Lord Auckland, June 1799, Public Record Office of Northern Ireland, Belfast, T.3229/1. Stuart's painting was also engraved at bust length by W. Sedgwick.

10. J. Roderick O'Flanagan, *The Lives of the Lord Chancellors and Keepers of the Great Seal of Ireland* (London: Longmans, Green and Co., 1870), vol. 2, p. 164.

11. The copy was once thought to have been started by Stuart and finished by another artist, then it bore an attribution to Robert Home, and now it is unattributed. Chester Harding, on a visit to Dublin, thought the picture was by Stuart and wrote to him, January 6, 1825: "I saw several of your pictures, one a full-length of the Lord Chancellor of Ireland, Fitz Gibbon (I think that is the name), and a very fine picture it is, in a good state of preservation"; quoted in Mason 1879, p. 73.

12. Patricia McCabe, "Trappings of Sovereignty: The Accoutrements of the Lords Chancellor of Ireland," *Irish Architectural and Decorative Studies: The Journal of the Irish Georgian Society* 5 (2002), pp. 48–73; Aileen Ribeiro, Courtauld Institute of Art, London, letter to Margaret Stenz, Nelson-Atkins Museum of Art, April 29, 1993.

13. Herbert 1836, pp. 245–46.

14. Crean 1990, pp. 257, 260.

lord, I think if G-d A—y ever wrote a legible hand, he is the greatest rascal that ever disgraced society.' His lordship was so tickled with my true development of character, he laughed immoderately. It was a hit."[13]

Yet Stuart did not exercise such freedom of expression when it came to portraying his host. The portrait is stiff and uneven, with a range of technique—from the extraordinary facility employed in the purse to the tight, linear technique used for FitzGibbon's judicial wig and lean face—that has led to a suggestion that Stuart had an assistant on the picture or adopted a newly controlled style to suit his Irish patrons.[14] There can be no question in general of Stuart's savvy approach to his clientele, and for FitzGibbon, a man as approachable as he was ruthless, as generous as he was mean, Stuart invoked a tried and true compositional format, harking back to Van Dyck and looking to Reynolds to give his demanding and flamboyant, but perhaps relatively unsophisticated, client a work appropriate to his cosmopolitan interior decor. In his few previous attempts at full-length portraiture, Stuart proved he could paint to suit: an athletic conceit for a young Scottish lawyer (cat. 6), a perfectly contemporary and light image of a ten-year-old girl (cat. 7), and a highly conventional naval portrait (cat. 15). What was called for in this instance was a version of royal portraiture, a picture that would match Reynolds's replica image of Rutland and evoke the stiff formality of Benjamin West's portraits of George III (see fig. 50). Even if FitzGibbon did not know West's royal portraits, Stuart figured him for a patron who would appreciate dazzling effects of costume over an insightful portrayal of character. Or it may be that Stuart found a perfect solution for such a slippery character. As FitzGibbon was in the midst of transforming himself to suit his newly elevated public status, Stuart may have thought best to leave his face blank.

CRB

20. JOHN FOSTER

1790—91
Oil on canvas, 83 ¼ x 59 in. (211.5 x 149.9 cm)
The Nelson-Atkins Museum of Art, Kansas City, Missouri; Purchase: Nelson Trust (30-20)

1. See Crean 1990, pp. 262–63; Anthony P. W. Malcomson, letter to Margaret Stenz, May 24, 1993, Nelson-Atkins Museum of Art, Kansas City, Mo. The author expresses thanks to Ms. Stenz for sharing her research with us. The painting is not listed in Mason 1879; it is listed in Park 1926, pp. 328–29, no. 303.
2. Foster's robe is preserved in the Museum of Science and Art, Dublin. Aileen Ribeiro, Courtauld Institute of Art, London, in a letter to Margaret Stenz, Nelson-Atkins Museum of Art, April 29, 1993, describes the costume for the

Historians have strained to find evidence that Stuart's portraits of John FitzGibbon (cat. 19), the Lord Chancellor of Ireland, and John Foster, the Speaker of the House, were commissioned as a pair, along with a full-length portrait of Henry Grattan, to grace the halls of the edifice that was the locus of their authority.[1] The Grattan portrait does not exist, but the other two pictures are the same size, the men wear their similar ornate robes and full-bottom wigs denoting their lofty office, both have the silver-gilt mace that gave symbolic power to their office, and they face each other, as is usual in pendant portraits.[2] The settings, however, are disparate: the pro-Union FitzGibbon is posed on a typically English grand-manner stage with column, drapery, and brilliant sky backdrop, while the opposition leader Foster is ensconced in a highly particularized rendition of the Irish House of Commons. But pendant colleagues, as opposed to pendant spouses, were not meant to create a seamless environ of joined compositions.

Yet other than the formal connections, there is absolutely no proof that Parliament wanted these pictures: there is nothing in governmental archives or in the newspapers, where reporters would have been eager for a story that connected these two reactionary politicians who despised each other only slightly more than the public hated them both. They were painted as much as two years apart; FitzGibbon's done and engraved by

Charles Hodges by September 1790 and Foster's undertaken probably in late 1790 or early 1791 and published in mezzotint (fig. 51) in January 1792. Stuart's enterprise in taking so many of his portraits of distinguished Irish politicians to Hodges for engraving may have compelled the painter to seek out the most celebrated men in town. Mezzotints of FitzGibbon and Foster would make known his talents, attract sitters to his studio, and increase his income from painting and the commercial venture of print publishing. In fact, he had made arrangements for the print of Foster's portrait before he had finished painting it.[3]

A receipt dated September 1790 (private collection) showing Foster's payment of 60 guineas to Stuart for a group of family portraits may prove that Foster's portrait was a private commission.[4] He itemized pictures of himself, his two sons, John and Thomas, and his daughter, Anna Dorothea. The amounts suggest that these were half-payments taken in advance, as was Stuart's normal practice. Stuart's portrait of Thomas Foster (private collection) is bust-length, warranting speculation that Foster negotiated a total price of 30 pounds based on the stingy precedent of his having paid precisely that much to Angelica Kauffman in 1775–76 for bust portraits of himself and his wife.[5] The 20 pounds for his daughter's portrait is crossed out and marked as paid, perhaps by Stuart who may have been only slightly more proficient at keeping books than was Foster, a man eager to bargain but notoriously inept in his accounts. The painting connected with this payment may be the double portrait of Anna Dorothea with her cousin Charlotte Anna Dick (see cat. 21), a distinct possibility since, in the tabulation of Stuart's pricing for Foster, if a 30-pound picture is a bust, a 40-pound picture must be bigger and more complicated. It would then follow that 60 pounds would have gotten Foster a still bigger canvas for the one marked "My own." There is, indeed, no other painting by Stuart of Foster to connect to this charge, nor is there conflicting evidence to suggest that Stuart should have been paid more than this for a full-length.[6]

Foster was the chief advocate of the Duke of Rutland's proposed national gallery. Foster updated his portrait collection every fifteen years or so, beginning with the Kauffman and moving to the Stuart and from there to Sir Thomas Lawrence in 1809 (private collection) and William Beechey in 1810 (private collection).[7] In 1786, following his unanimous election to the office of Speaker of the House on September 5, 1785, he commissioned a conversation piece of his family from the Irish watercolorist John James

speaker. Foster's mace was made by John Swift of London in 1765. At the dissolution of the Irish Parliament in 1800, he refused to relinquish it, bequeathed it to his grandson Lord Massereene, who sold it to the Bank of Ireland in 1937. It is now displayed in Old Parliament House, Dublin.

3. *Saunders Newsletter*, April 1791, quoted in Mount 1964, p. 149, advertised the engraving "from the capital whole-length picture now painting of him by Mr. Stuart."

4. Anthony P. W. Malcomson, letter to the Marchioness of Dufferin and Ava, February 22, 1991, photocopy in the Nelson-Atkins Museum of Art, identifies the handwriting as Foster's, except for Stuart's signature.

5. Angelica Kauffman's bills, July 27, 1775, and April 15, 1776, Foster/Massereene Collection, Public Record Office of Northern Ireland, Belfast, D.562/9194–95.

6. The bust-length portrait of Foster that relates to Stuart's full-length (National Gallery of Ireland, on loan to Malahide Castle) and a reduced version of the full-length (private collection) are copies.

7. Bills for Lawrence and Beechey portraits are in the Massereene papers, Foster/Massereene Collection, Public Record Office of Northern Ireland, Belfast, D.207/75.

Fig. 52. "The Children of Erin Seeking Protection from their FOSTER Father," *Walker's Hibernian Magazine* (March 1799). The New York Public Library, Astor, Lenox and Tilden Foundations, General Research Division

8. A. P. W. Malcomson, *John Foster: The Politics of the Anglo-Irish Ascendancy* (London: Oxford University Press, 1978), p. 30. Other biographical information, unless otherwise noted, is derived from this definitive biography.

9. Anna Dorothea Dufferin, "Recollections of a Beloved Father," n.d., Public Record Office of Northern Ireland, Belfast, T.2519/4/1819.

10. "Right Hon. John Foster: Speaker of the Irish House of Commons," *Walker's Hibernian Magazine,* March 1799, p. 139.

11. Quoted in Edith Mary Johnston-Liik, *History of the Irish Parliament, 1692–1800* (Belfast: Ulster Historical Foundation, 2002), vol. 4, p. 225.

12. See James Gandon and Thomas J. Mulvany, *The Life of James Gandon Esq.* (Dublin: Hodges and Smith, 1846), pp. 112–15.

Barralet, a scene of himself with his wife, Margaretta Amelia Burgh, and their three children posed on the front portico of Oriel Temple, his Greek Revival seat in County Louth (private collection). The watercolor shows an exquisitely dressed, accomplished family—the girl with her obedient puppy, her brothers with their handsome steed—poised for success. This picture glosses over Foster's parvenu status, a liability that not only lowered him in the estimation of his colleagues but made him dependent on his official income, perhaps a unique instance in the English or Irish Parliament.[8] The eldest son of Anthony Foster of Collon, Lord Chief Baron of the Exchequer, and Elizabeth Burgh, whose father sat in the Commons for Dunleer and Louth, Foster (1740–1828) was a country gentleman of public stature but scant lineage, with immense agrarian knowledge but little property, an expert economist who helped found the Bank of Ireland in 1783 but had no money and even less business sense.

The paradoxical nature of Foster's existence, the professional versus the private, is thrown into high relief against the strictures of the aristocratic Anglo-Irish ascendancy. He was both blessed and cursed in his political career: all of the esteem he lost among his constituency, he gained back with his practical experience. In terms of personality, he was assertive and stubborn and lacking in finesse, dodging his own ambiguous place in society by taking a stance of absolute intolerance for incursions on the status quo. A tireless promoter of his proprietary interests, he learned from Rutland the transcendent quality of art and architecture and took on portraits, home improvements including a personal arboretum, and civic projects, and other ventures far grander than his wallet could bear. He spared no expense on the education of his children, an honorable trait that nonetheless contributed to his near bankruptcy by 1792.[9] He borrowed money, perpetuating a seemingly inextricable pattern of debt established by his father. His need to improve and refine was, according to a contemporary source, "insatiable," a near pathological response to his circumstance.[10]

Foster attended Trinity College, Dublin, and entered the Irish Parliament at the age of nineteen as member for the borough of Dunleer, even before being called to the bar in 1766. His passionate eloquence on agricultural reform and linen manufacturing earned him respect in the House of Commons, and in 1784 he was appointed Chancellor of the Exchequer under the Duke of Rutland, a position he resigned within several months to assume the duties of Speaker of the House in the fall of 1785. Said one contemporary, in awe of his professional abilities: "Deeply read in the law and privileges of Parliament, no incident occurs in which he is not able to guide the conduct of the House, while his punctuality, his love of order and good taste, give facility to business and a decorous elegance to legislative arrangements."[11] He augmented his parliamentary post with the offices of Privy Councillor and Lord Justice in 1787 and enhanced Parliament itself with a scheme of architectural improvements.

Stuart's portrait is a visual analogue to Foster's career and such a painstaking and anomalous rendering that it is worth considering whether Stuart employed a studio apprentice, if not in the execution of the work, then in the research it would have required. The papers under the fingers of Foster's right hand are documents for "Extending the Linen Manufacture," a reference to Foster's triumphant actions in 1780 to legalize Irish linen trading with countries other than England, and a "Plan for Establishing Bank of Ireland & reducing the Interest of Money to 5 pr. Cent." The packet of letters, one inscribed "Corn Trade" and another "Agric," allude to Foster's involvement with agriculture, specifically his Corn Law of 1784, which granted government funding for the exportation of Irish corn and imposed duties on importation.

The books on the table are those he studied to propose legislation in 1785 that would secure his reputation as an expert on Irish trade and law, which effectively clinched the speaker's chair for him: *Trade of Ireland*, *History of Commerce*, and *Irish Statutes*.

If the attributes call attention to Foster's past, the setting accentuates his present. Few artists had previously recorded the interior of the House of Commons. Francis Wheatley's painting *Henry Grattan Urging the Claim of Irish Rights in 1780* (private collection) articulates the chamber's second-floor gallery of unfluted Ionic columns. This distinguished Palladian interior, arguably the finest in Ireland, was designed by Sir Edward Lovet Pearce and opened in 1731. In 1786 Foster asked the architect James Gandon to modernize the stairs, passageways, and fireplaces, and to install heating flues in the interior walls.[12] Neither Foster nor Stuart could have anticipated just how timely their choice to use the chamber in Foster's portrait would be.

On February 27, 1792, within months of Stuart's finishing Foster's portrait and only weeks after the print was issued, the chamber was consumed by fire. The speaker organized a corps of members to save the books and papers, and the fire brigade, on his orders, kept the damage to just the Commons chamber. There were no human casualties and the House of Lords was preserved. Yet Foster's progressive ambitions for warming the building implicated him in the blaze. He oversaw the rebuilding of the chamber, a task at once onerous and politically charged. By the time it opened in 1796, with a reduced gallery, a subdivided plan, and myriad logistical concessions to modern government administration, the speaker had increased in national stature, such that if Stuart had still been in Dublin and working for Foster, a less specific setting would have been wanted. As it was, *Walker's Hibernian Magazine* for March 1799 altered Stuart's image as a last cry before the inevitable union for the speaker to save his fellow loyal Irish with "Protection from their FOSTER Father" (fig. 52).

CRB

21. ANNA DOROTHEA FOSTER AND CHARLOTTE ANNA DICK

1790–91
Oil on canvas, 36 x 37 in. (91.4 x 94 cm)
Collection of R. Philip and Charlotte Hanes

In Stuart's perhaps best-known and least understood picture from his Dublin period, two attractive young women work together on a needlework project.[1] They could easily be sisters, nearly twins, with the same coloring—glossy light brown hair, blue eyes, peaches-and-cream complexions—distinctive noses, physical proportions, and long ringlets bouncing on shoulders and a short, neatly trimmed fringe of bangs framing their faces. Their matching short-waisted white silk dresses, with tight bodices and sleeves—one girl with wrist-length sleeves with a small ruffle at the cuff, the other with three-quarter-length sleeves with a round cuff—full skirts over voluminous petticoats, broad pink satin sashes, and sophisticated pleated ruff at the neckline announce them as members of Ireland's affluent and fashionable elite. The combination of simple modesty in overall design with elegant detailing and rich fabric puts these dresses at the height of international fashion. The strict profile pose of the sitter at the left—rare in Stuart's oeuvre—features her long, straight nose and plump, rosy cheek. She sits in a gilded and

1. The painting is not listed in Mason 1879 or Park 1926.

Fig. 53. *Mrs. Samuel Dick and Her Daughter Charlotte Anna*, ca. 1790. Oil on canvas, 36 x 29½ in. (91.5 x 75 cm). Private collection (photo: Christie's Images)

2. Ann Bermingham, "Elegant Females and Gentlemen Connoisseurs: The Commerce in Culture and Self-image in Eighteenth-Century England," in Ann Bermingham and John Brewer, eds., *The Consumption of Culture, 1600-1800: Image, Object, Text* (London: Routledge, 1995), pp. 489–513.

3. Mary Gostelow, *A World of Embroidery* (New York: Charles Scribner's Sons, 1975), p. 81. See also Therle Hughes, *English Domestic Needlework, 1660–1860* (New York: MacMillan, 1961), pp. 16–29.

4. See, for example, Mary Elizabeth Burnet, in Washington, Providence 1967, p. 56; Ross Watson, "Irish Portraits in American Collections," *Quarterly Bulletin of the Irish Georgian Society* 12 (April–June 1969), p. 40.

5. *Annual Register* 25 (1804), p. 454; Bernard Burke, *A Genealogical and Heraldic History of the Landed Gentry of Ireland*, edited by Ashworth P. Burke (London: Harrison and Sons, 1904), p. 149.

6. The Forster part of the inscription was the product of the traditional confusion between Forsters and Fosters, who were the same extended Anglo-Irish family. In the most recent plotting of the family tree, Charlotte Anna Dick's grandfather, is listed as Sir Nicholas Forster; see A. P. W. Malcomson, *John Foster: The Politics of the Anglo-Irish Ascendancy* (London: Oxford University Press, 1978), table 1. See also Angelica Kauffman's bills to Mrs. John Foster, spelled Forster, for two portraits, July 27, 1775, and April 15, 1776, Foster/Massereene Collection, Public Record Office of Northern Ireland, Belfast, D.562/9194–95.

damask-upholstered armchair, a rather poorly drawn Hepplewhite model. Her companion sits, but lightly, buoyed up by the great pouf of her skirt, on a bench or stool covered in the same green damask with brass nails along the edge.

The girls occupy themselves with one of the most venerable feminine pastimes, the useful and refined craft of needlework, perhaps the most common of parlor activities meant not merely to busy idle hands but to display accomplishment and invite observation.[2] The girl who works at the tambour frame, a device introduced to England and Ireland in the 1760s from China, has graduated beyond the mere execution of a girlhood sampler to more decorative projects.[3] She looks out at her admirer, openly soliciting attention to herself and her craft, as she expertly wields the hooking device that pulls and ties a chain stitch of brightly colored silk floss according to her wildflower pattern, which the other girl holds for reference. The pattern—upside down to the spectator—is a concisely realistic line drawing of a sparse spray of leggy blossoms, probably a page torn from a women's journal that allowed young women to study nature through copying rather than direct observation. The finished work might be framed as a picture or appliquéd onto furniture. In this case, as the tightly held fabric is quite sheer and so voluminous that it flows over the girl's forearm, the floral embellishment will surely be sewn into a dress, thus turning the parlor project into something its maker will continue to display conspicuously even after it is disengaged from the frame.

In the pairing of needleworker and accomplice, Stuart sets up a situation in which one sitter is given precedence over the other, recalling his only other, though much earlier, double portrait of the Malbone brothers (cat. 3), in which Francis stars and Saunders assumes the supporting role. The girl at the tambour frame is the beneficiary of the artist's full attention, from the details of her dress and the complete view of her face. She sits a bit higher than her friend, her body a bit larger, and this, in addition to her eye-catching activity and outward gaze, warrants speculation that she is of marriageable age. It has seemed sensible, over the years, to identify this girl as Miss Dick, the name that is privileged on the back of the canvas: *Portraits of Miss Dick daugh / ter of Saml Dick Esqr. & who / married Wm. Hoare Hume Esqr / M.P. Co. of Wicklow: and of / Miss Forster her Cousin.* Stuart scholars have unanimously accepted that the accomplished needleworker must be Miss Dick, assisted by her cousin Miss Forster.[4] Yet the inscription is actually a transcription, copied from the back of the canvas onto the lining canvas from an inscription written not by Stuart but by someone who knew Miss Dick well enough to have followed her life to the point of marriage.

On November 19, 1804, William Hoare Hume of Humewood (d. 1815), a member of Parliament for County Wicklow, married Charlotte Anna Dick (after 1773–1864), the daughter of Samuel Dick, a wholesale merchant of distinguished Scottish descent, who was a member of the Dublin Chamber of Commerce, a director of the Hibernian Insurance Company, and a founding director of the Bank of Ireland in 1784.[5] Dick's profitable business interests allowed him to retire by the early 1790s and to acquire a country house, Violet Hill, near Dublin. His wife was Charlotte, daughter of Sir Nicholas Foster (or Forster) of Tullaghan, and cousin of John Foster (see cat. 20).[6] Samuel and Charlotte Dick had two children: Charlotte Anna, who was born within a few years of their marriage in November 1773, and Quentin (1777–1858), who followed in his father's footsteps as a banker and merchant.

Stuart painted at least four portraits for the extended Dick family, starting with Sir John Dick of Braid, who had remained in Scotland and sat for Stuart in 1782 in London (National Gallery of Art, Washington). Stuart also painted a portrait of a Lady Dick

21

7. Mason (1879, p. 175) lists a portrait of Lady Dick. See also Park 1926, p. 288, no. 247.

8. Ross Watson, "Irish Portraits in American Collections," *Quarterly Bulletin of the Irish Georgian Society* 12 (April–June 1969), p. 40.

(unlocated) and a portrait of Mrs. Samuel Dick and her daughter, Charlotte Anna (fig. 53), who bears certain resemblance to the girl in profile in Stuart's double portrait.[7] Charlotte Anna Dick, prominent in the inscription on the present painting, is the hand-maiden to her cousin.

The search for Miss Dick's cousin has led scholars to the daughters of Sir Thomas Forster, Bart., of Tullaghan, MP, Letitia Anna and Sophia Maria.[8] Nothing is known of these women, except that they were sisters, a self-evident clue that nevertheless makes a difference in the study of portraiture. Unless they were born years apart, it would be unusual for one to be portrayed without the other, and especially odd for one to be paired in portraiture with a cousin when there was a sister at hand. Miss Dick had no sister, and neither did her first cousin once removed, Anna Dorothea Foster (1773/74–1865), the only daughter of Speaker Foster, a gentleman of such eminence that his

9. Her death date of 1865, at the age of ninety-two, is recorded in Peter Townend, ed., *Burke's Genealogical and Heraldic History of the Peerage, Baronetage and Knightage*, 104th ed. (London: Burke's Peerage, 1967), p. 797.

10. Marriage recorded in *Annual Register* 22 (1801), p. 52.

11. The portrait of Dorcas, Lady Blackwood, at the Museum of Fine Arts, Boston, is attributed to Stuart and the subject of current research. See Evans 2004, pp. 24–25.

12. Anna Dorothea Dufferin, "Recollections of a Beloved Mother," 1824, Public Record Office of Northern Ireland, Belfast, T.2519/4/1818.

offspring would have to be the center of attention.[9] This girl, along with her family on the front portico of Oriel Temple, Foster's seat in County Louth, appears in a drawing by John James Barralet (private collection), a watercolorist who would later work with Stuart in Philadelphia. Barralet was an expert profilist, treating two of the five Fosters in this manner, but not Anna Dorothea, whose nearly full face is turned down and shaded by her wide-brimmed beribboned hat. Barralet's manner of working verged on caricature, so that his Anna Dorothea does not exactly match the chain-stitching girl in Stuart's portrait, but the likeness is close.

The connections between John Foster and Samuel Dick went beyond family matters. Both were instrumental in the establishment of the Bank of Ireland, and the speaker called on Dick for support during the County Down election of 1790. Dick's son, Quentin, became a Foster protégé, an anti-Union member of Parliament for County Louth. Their association with Stuart also linked them. A receipt written by Speaker Foster and signed by the artist (private collection) establishes several commissions completed by September 1790. The line inscribed "Miss Foster" may refer to the Foster part of the double portrait or another picture of Anna Dorothea that is now lost.

Anna Dorothea, a young woman of sixteen or seventeen in Stuart's portrait, married Sir James Stevenson Blackwood in 1801, a pro-Union member of Parliament for Killyleagh and Bangor.[10] His support of the English Crown was rewarded with the elevation of his mother, Dorcas Stevenson Blackwood, to Baroness Dufferin and Claneboye of Ballyleidy and Killyleagh, a title carried by his wife after 1807.[11] In her middle age, Anna Dorothea recalled learning needlework at her mother's knee, albeit reluctantly: "Needlework of any sort that required fancy in the execution she was fond of, and for many years she had in hands a set of chairs, and window-curtains made of coloured silk flowers, cut out and laid on grey stuff, which she embroidered to enliven the colours of and added many flowers of her own fancying, always preferring those that were an imitation of nature. . . . Whilst I used to read out and draw, and go thro' other lessons in the same room. She delighted in having me always with her, which used to confine me more than suited my taste, but which often taught me a useful lesson of patience."[12]

CRB

22. George Thomas John Nugent

1789–90
Oil on canvas, 49¾ x 40 in. (126.5 x 101.5 cm)
Signed on the dog's collar: G. STUART
UCLA Hammer Museum, Los Angeles;
The Armand Hammer Collection, Gift of the
Armand Hammer Foundation (AH.90.75)

Stuart painted three pictures for George Frederick Nugent, seventh Earl of Westmeath: his own portrait (UCLA Hammer Museum, Los Angeles), a likeness of his wife, Mary Anne Jeffreyes (unlocated), and a full-length of their son, George Thomas John Nugent.[1] For the boy, Stuart worked hard to produce a striking picture. Judging from the few surviving representative examples, he did not develop a specialty in children's portraiture. But he painted youngsters often enough that he developed a knack for an appropriate vocabulary of clothing, attributes, and gestures. This picture employs a conventional trope: the well-behaved child in idyllic setting with his disciplined but playful

22

1. The painting of George Thomas John Nugent is not listed in Mason 1879 or Park 1926.

2. Desmond Shawe-Taylor, *The Georgians: Eighteenth-Century Portraiture and Society* (London: Barrie and Jenkins, 1990), pp. 203–21.

3. Clare Rose, *Children's Clothes since 1750* (New York: Drama Book Publishers; London: B. T. Batsford, 1989), pp. 48–53; Linda Baumgarten, *What Clothes Reveal* (Williamsburg, Va.: Colonial Williamsburg Foundation, 2002), pp. 171–73.

pet as a portent of promise and future accomplishment, a conceit found in the oeuvre of virtually every European portraitist of note from the sixteenth century onward.[2]

George Thomas John Nugent was born July 17, 1785, and his costume suggests that he was about five when he sat for Stuart. He wears a modified skeleton suit, the outfit designed for a young fellow recently breeched from his petticoats but not yet of age to wear proper gentlemen's clothing.[3] His fall-front knee breeches of cream-colored silk with red topstitching button over the lower edge of his scarlet jacket, making a one-piece suit in reasonable facsimile of adult style. The linen shirt, with knife-pleated frilled

Fig. 54. Sir Joshua Reynolds, *The Masters Gawler*, 1777. Oil on canvas, 35 x 27½ in. (90 x 71.4 cm). Birmingham Museum and Art Gallery, Birmingham, England (P52'83)

Fig. 55. *James Ward*, 1779. Oil on canvas, 29½ x 25 in. (74.9 x 63.5 cm). The Minneapolis Institute of Arts; The William Hood Dunwoody Fund (16.2)

muslin collar was at the height of fashion, worn open and spread wide over the coat. To top it off, Stuart's tiny subject wears an enormous black hat, of the so-called Gainsborough or Marlborough type, with large crown and wide brim made of taffeta or beaver, and trimmed with ostrich plumes. The style derived from French ladies' riding hats of the 1770s and came into vogue for children in England during the 1780s.[4] Lord Nugent's hair is coiffed typically for a boy: worn long with bangs, falling to the shoulders and curled at the ends.

Lord Nugent's canine companion is a perfectly rendered Newfoundland, a breed famous for an even temperament and a copious amount of drool, making a cloth an absolute necessity for its owner. Stuart included the cloth in his portrait of Lord Nugent, as did Sir Joshua Reynolds in his portrait of the Masters Gawler (fig. 54). The Newfoundland, so-called after its assumed Canadian origin, was descended from Pyrenean sheepdogs, first employed by fishermen and ever since associated with their skill in the water: they swim ashore with the line that ties boats to land.[5] A largely uncontaminated breed until the nineteenth century, they sported webbed feet, thick, furry underhair that stayed dry under a long, shaggy coat, a protruding muzzle, a hairy, curved tail, and could weigh seventy to one hundred pounds. Celebrated for their life-saving powers and magnificent companionship, they became well regarded as pets for children. During the eighteenth century, stories circulated about the dogs' extraordinary performances for their masters, whether carrying bundles in their mouths, meeting guests at the door, or saving children from drowning. The writer Sir John Hawkins described the virtues of a Newfoundland: "not very rational, but good for tickling under the ears."[6]

Stuart's signature on the dog's collar—G. STUART—has led to assertions by William Pressly that Stuart "identifies with the fawning spaniel who is wholly dependent on the disdainful, young aristocrat," and by Dorinda Evans, who agreed that the artist's rare signature in that peculiar spot equates him with "the child-subjugated dog." She explained, "The negative connotation is played out in the way the boy, with his ostentatious plumed hat, does not deign to touch the dog with his bare fingers. Rather, he holds the dog's potentially slobbering muzzle with a handkerchief and places a ball, in a

4. R. Turner Wilcox, *The Mode in Hats and Headdress* (New York: Charles Scribner's Sons, 1945), p. 156.

5. The dog is now commonly known as the Landseer Newfoundland because of the frequency with which the painter Edwin Landseer (1802–1873) used the dog in his pictures. Freeman Lloyd, "Dog Breeds of the World: Their Origin, Development, and Uses Throughout the Ages," *American Kennel Club Gazette* 49 (August 1, 1932), pp. 24–28, 110; (September 1, 1932), pp. 15–19, 78. See also Hon. Harold MacPherson, "The Newfoundland Dog," in J. R. Smallwood, ed., *The Book of Newfoundland* (St. John's: Newfoundland Book Publishers, 1937), vol. 1, pp. 133–40; William Secord, *Dog Painting, 1840–1940: A Social History of the Dog in Art* (Woodbridge, Eng.: Antique Collectors' Club, 1992), p. 204. The author expresses gratitude for advice to James P. Crowley, Secretary, and Geraldine T. Hayes, Historian and Archivist, the American Kennel Club, New York.

6. Shawe-Taylor, *The Georgians*, pp. 69–71.

7. Pressly 1986, p. 51 n. 24; Evans 1999, p. 50. Stuart signed a dog's collar in one other picture, *Dogs and Woodcock*, ca. 1794 (private collection).

8. Dunlap 1834, vol. 1, p. 207.

controlling gesture, on the dog's forehead."[7] Both scholars undermine their potentially compelling readings with subjective remarks on the attitude and class of the boy and a misunderstanding of the dog's breed. An argument associating the painter with a New-foundland would necessarily attribute to him qualities of steadfast reliability, loyalty, and skill. In his earlier portrait of James Ward (fig. 55), Stuart put the sitter's name on the collar—J. WARD—a clever linking of pet and master. It is tempting to connect Stuart's use of his own name on the collar to his later declaration, "By-and-by you will not by chance kick your foot against a dog-kennel, but out will start a portrait-painter."[8] Yet he meant this as a snide metaphorical characterization of his colleagues.

Lord Nugent later received his education at Eton and Rugby and afterward served with distinction in the military. He married three times, divorcing twice—the second time on petition of adultery—and succeeded as eighth Earl of Westmeath on his father's death in 1814. He sat in Parliament as Lord Lieutenant of Westmeath and died in 1860.

CRB

23. CATHERINE LANE BARKER

ca. 1791
Oil on canvas, 37 ½ x 47 ¾ in. (95.3 x 121.3 cm)
Private collection

24. WILLIAM BARKER

ca. 1791
Oil on canvas, 37 ½ x 47 ¾ in. (95.3 x 121.3 cm)
Private collection

William Barker's grandfather, the second Baronet of Bocking Hall, Essex, went to Kilcooley, Thurles, County Tipperary, in 1725, intending to build a gentleman's country seat on the grounds of the Cistercian abbey there, built in 1182 and reconstructed after a fire in 1445.[1] A frugal and careful man, he handed down the estate in good shape, but without making much progress on the desired house, to his son, also William, in 1746. Like his father, the third baronet protected the family fortune and built little. He arranged the marriages of his two children with his neighbors, William Lane and the elder Chambre Brabazon Ponsonby, the other two principal landowners in the Kilcooley district. William Barker, the fourth and last Baronet of Bocking Hall and Kilcooley Abbey, married the heiress Catherine Lane in 1760, and William's sister, Mary, wed the son and namesake of C. B. Ponsonby. Land titles were thus merged and an heir was produced, in 1763: Mary's son, C. B. Ponsonby, called Chum. William and Catherine Barker had no children of their own and welcomed Mary and her son and daughter, also Mary, into their home near the abbey after the death of her husband. She soon remarried and left her brother's household, becoming the second wife of Robert Staples, the seventh Baronet of Lissan, County Tyrone; her death in 1772 left the children to be raised at Kilcooley. Sir William sent Chum to boarding school in Geneva in 1778, and soon after his return home, in 1791, he married Henrietta, daughter of Thomas Taylour, the first Earl of Bective, a close friend of Sir William. William Barker's estates, title, and surname devolved on his nephew at his death in 1818.

William, the fourth baronet, inherited Kilcooley in 1757 on his graduation from Middle Temple in London and determined to fulfill his grandfather's dream: he would

1. See W. G. Neely, *Kilcooley: Land and People in Tipperary* (Belfast: Universities Press, 1983); Peter Harbison, *Guide to National and Historic Monuments of Ireland*, 3rd ed. (London: Gill and Macmillan, 1992), p. 306.

23

build a grand Palladian house. After his father's death in 1770, William reclaimed the undeveloped lands near the property, advertised for tenants, and within a short time was the landlord of the most flourishing estate in the county. True to family pattern, William stayed out of politics but formed two companies of volunteers (Protestants ready to defend Ireland against French invasion during the American Revolution), whose numbers were largely filled with the tenant farmers who also attended entertainments offered by the Barkers. Mary's letters to her son away at school describe Kilcooley as a pleasant, if insular, place, defined by the Barkers' good fortune, strong marriage, and delight in polite pastimes. William was unfailingly kind, his wife cheerful and shy, and both were devoted to the continual improvement and beautification of the estate. He brought in English elms to enrich the forests, and in 1789 he enhanced the view by digging out a five-acre lake and stocking it with fish and wildfowl shipped from Canada and Greenland. A Gothic boathouse on the far side of the water completed the vista to be seen from the front windows of the house.

Stuart may have been introduced to the members of this bustling aristocratic family circle by the Earl of Bective, who also sat for the artist (fig. 56), and he seems to have taken up residence about 1791.[2] There are bust portraits of Sir William Barker, his sister, Mary, and her second husband, Sir Robert Staples, and the heir C. B. Ponsonby just

2. Evans (1999, p. 49) argues that Stuart must have visited Kilcooley.

24

returned from school and his wife.[3] Some eight years before, in 1783, Barker had invited the Irish portraitist John Trotter to Kilcooley to paint two conversation pieces, one of the Barkers (private collection) and one of the Stapleses (private collection). Pleased with the compositions but disappointed by Trotter's likenesses, Barker apparently asked Stuart to fix the pictures by repainting the faces.[4] Such a request would logically have come after Barker had seen what Stuart could do for him; in effect, Stuart's large, horizontal portraits of William and Catherine Barker were the most ingeniously conceived pictures of Stuart's Dublin career.[5]

The Barkers must have wanted to have a picture gallery in their new home, with their own portraits at the center. The pendant images are virtual biographies describing two individuals intricately linked through formal and philosophical conceits. Stuart captured their pleasant countenances and set them at ease in compositions that define the interior and exterior circumstances of their lives at Kilcooley. The Barkers took pride in their fine clothing despite their distance from the urban centers of high fashion. His Brussels lace shirt frills surely came from the shopping trip he took with Chum en route home from school abroad, and his soft woolen coat with turned-down English collar and close sleeves with small, round three-button cuffs is perfectly restrained. Lady Catherine wears the color and style of the moment: a white silk polonaise multilayered

3. All of these portraits, as well as a copy of Stuart's portrait of the Earl of Bective, are in a private collection. A bust of William Barker attributed to Stuart was at Sotheby's, London, April 13, 1994, lot 64.
4. Neely, *Kilcooley*, p. 81; Anne Crookshank and the Knight of Glin, *The Painters of Ireland, c. 1660–1920* (London: Barrie and Jenkins, 1978), p. 156.
5. Not listed in Mason 1879; listed in Park 1926, pp. 128–30, nos. 51 (Sir William Barker), 52 (Lady Barker).

Fig. 56. *Thomas Taylour, Earl of Bective*, 1790–91. Oil on canvas, 49⅝ x 38½ in. (126 x 98 cm). Elwes and Hanham, Ltd., London

dress in the classicizing mode, with a high waistband holding closed an open-robe gown, tight sleeves from biceps to wrist and a pouf at the shoulders, a sheer fichu to protect her modesty, and dark red ribbons at choice spots as subtle adornment.[6] He wears a formal bag wig; she has coiffed her own gray hair, perhaps enhanced with powder for an elegant effect.

Their personal aspect complements their diligent preoccupation with pursuits suited to their common goals and their traditional husband-and-wife partnership. Stuart situates Sir William literally in the moment, between the past, embodied in the old abbey, and the future, represented by his architectural drawings. On the plan, his finger touches the very room in which his wife sits in her portrait: the dining room with bow-front picture windows oriented to the Gothic boathouse across the man-made pond. That Stuart's rendering of the fifteenth-century tower is inaccurate and the traceried east chancel window is flawed seems a minor bit of artistic license compared with the fact that Lady Catherine is depicted in a room that did not yet exist in the early 1790s. The portraits record Sir William's fantasy: that his wife live in the splendid home he, his father, and his grandfather before him had hoped to build. The abbey behind him, whether correctly drawn or not, enhances Sir William's hereditary occupation of the estate. Or, as Hugh Crean has written, "The visual argument is that the planned house is but a refurbished and expanded claim to land long occupied in the name of the Crown. The medieval abbey becomes a symbol of first occupancy, and its visual presence in Stuart's portrait is used to give historical sanction to the new venture."[7]

The Barkers are allied in their aesthetic pursuits.[8] He practices the gentlemanly skills of connoisseurship and dilettantism, assuming the role of architect to erect not only a house but a place of social privilege for his heirs. For her part, Lady Catherine works a delicate chain stitch on thick silk on her tambour frame following a design of carnations or pinks. She contributes to her husband's vision of their home with a display of her feminine accomplishments that will adorn the home of their dreams.

CRB

6. See Aileen Ribeiro, *The Art of Dress: Fashion in England and France, 1750–1820* (New Haven: Yale University Press, 1995), p. 70.

7. Crean 1990, p. 279.

8. See Ann Bermingham, "Elegant Females and Gentlemen Connoisseurs: The Commerce in Culture and Self-Image in Eighteenth-Century England," in Ann Bermingham and John Brewer eds., *The Consumption of Culture, 1600–1800: Image, Object, Text* (London: Routledge, 1995), pp. 489–513.

25. WILLIAM BURTON CONYNGHAM

ca. 1791–92
Oil on canvas, 35⅞ x 28 in. (91 x 71 cm)
National Gallery of Ireland, Dublin (NGI 562)

1. Mark Odlum, "Slane Castle, Co. Meath," *Country Life* 168 (July 17, 1980), pp. 198–201; (July 24, 1980), pp. 278–80.

2. For Conyngham's biography, see *Annual Register* 17 (1796), pp. 61–63; "Character of the Late Colonel Conyngham," *Walker's Hibernian Magazine*, June 1796, pp. 483–84; C. E. F. Trench, "William Burton Conyngham (1733–1796)," *Journal of the Royal Society of Antiquaries of Ireland* 115 (1985), pp. 40–63; James Kelly, "William Burton Conyngham and the North-West Fishery of the Eighteenth-Century," *Journal of the Royal Society of Antiquaries of Ireland* 115 (1985), pp. 64–85; C. E. F. Trench, "Lieutenant Colonel the Right Hon. William Burton Conyngham, 1733–1796," *Irish Sword* 16 (summer 1986), pp. 17–20.

3. Maurice Craig, *The Architecture of Ireland from the Earliest Times to 1880* (London: B. T. Batsford, 1982), pp. 234–36, 246–47.

4. William Conyngham, "Observations on the Description of the Theatre of Saguntum, as Given by Emanuel Marti, Dean of Alicant, in a Letter Addressed to D. Antonio Felix Zondadario," *Transactions of the Royal Irish Academy* (Dublin: George Bonham, 1789), pp. 29–49.

5. Arthur Young, *A Tour of Ireland* (Dublin, 1780), quoted in Trench, "Conyngham," *Journal of the RSAI*, p. 61. See a similar opinion in Edith Mary Johnston-Liik, *History of the Irish Parliament, 1692–1800* (Belfast: Ulster Historical Foundation, 2002), vol. 3, p. 329.

6. The painting is not listed in Mason 1879; it is listed in Park 1926, p. 235, no. 183.

7. Richard Twiss, *Travels through Portugal and Spain in 1772 and 1773* (London: G. Robinson, T. Becket, and J. Robson, 1775).

Of William Burton Conyngham (1733–1796) it was written: "he is one of history's unfortunate characters who, though constantly mentioned and described, are never brought to life."[1] The second son of the Right Honourable Francis Burton of Buncraggy, County Clare, and his wife, Mary Conyngham, he sat for at least four portraits, each time for a painter of prominence, a fact that makes his historical obscurity all the more peculiar.[2] He intended to be remembered, in deed and in visage. Within a few years of finishing course work at Queen's College, Cambridge, and Lincoln's Inn in 1753, he took a post-graduation tour of Italy and sat for Anton Raphael Mengs in Rome, the only British sitter to be drawn in pastel by the artist (private collection). On his next trip to Italy, about 1760, he was painted by Nathaniel Dance (unlocated), thus making him typical among tourists who not only desired a portrait record of their travels but sought out a compatriot to paint it. Two decades later, by which time he was a member of Parliament, Teller of the Irish Exchequer, and Commissioner of Wide Streets, Conyngham sat for the Irish painter Hugh Douglas Hamilton (unlocated), and that portrait was engraved by Valentine Green. In 1781 he assumed the Conyngham name and arms on the death of his uncle, the Right Honourable Henry Conyngham, first Earl Conyngham. William inherited the family properties at Mount Charles Coo, Donegal, Slane Castle near Drogheda, County Meath, and Harcourt Place, Dublin, and made architectural and engineering improvements on each.[3] (His elder brother, Francis Pierpoint Burton, got the title and the other half of the estate, including castles in Clare and Limerick.)

Conyngham was devoted to public service—as colonel in the Donegal militia and involvement in charitable organizations, schools, hospitals, and a particular interest in the betterment of working conditions at the County Donegal fisheries—and maintained an abiding interest in art and architecture. In 1783 he visited Portugal on a mission to help preserve the fourteenth-century Dominican monastery of Maria da Victoria at Batalha and donated more than 1,000 guineas to the excavation project. He also sketched the ruins and sent the artist J. C. Murphy to make drawings of the site. From there, he went to Spain to study the ruins at Sagunto, near Valencia; he later delivered a scholarly paper on the subject at the Royal Irish Academy, of which he was treasurer.[4] He led the antiquaries section of the Dublin Society, served on the Committee for Superintending the Society's Drawing School (now the National College of Art and Design), and founded the short-lived Society of Antiquaries. A contemporary described him as "a true friend to the interest of Ireland, and far more enlightened upon it than the greater part of well informed people to be found there."[5]

Stuart's portrait of Conyngham describes the enlightened aristocrat, rather than the member of Parliament.[6] Conyngham wears traveling clothes, a soft woolen jacket with a turned-down velvet collar, and an elegant cadogan, or club wig. A friend of the Duke of Rutland and an acquaintance of Sir Joshua Reynolds, Conyngham first sat for Stuart in London about 1785 (fig. 57). The portrait is similar in attitude and detailing to the series of portraits Stuart painted for John Boydell (see "The Boydell Pictures" and cats. 10–14) and was probably the one painted first, executed soon after Conyngham's trip to Portugal and Spain; the folio volumes in this version are inscribed *Travels through Spain*, a reference to Richard Twiss's popular guide.[7] Conyngham took his portrait home and must have shown it to the reporter for the *Evening Herald* who, on announcing Stuart's arrival in Dublin in November 1787, recommended that "His best productions are the portraits

25

Fig. 57. *William Burton Conyngham*, ca. 1785. Oil on canvas, 36 x 28 in. (91.4 x 71.1 cm). Norton Museum of Art, West Palm Beach, Fla.; Bequest of R. H. Norton (53.189)

Fig. 58. Charles Hodges after Gilbert Stuart, *William Burton Conyngham*, 1792. Mezzotint, 15 x 11 in. (38 x 28 cm). National Gallery of Ireland, Dublin

8. *Evening Herald*, November 11, 1787, quoted in Whitley 1932, p. 83.

9. The reverse of cat. 25 is inscribed *Helen Weldon 10th June 1796*, presumably the same woman as mentioned in the newspaper.

10. There is also a line engraving by L. Schiavonetti after Stuart, published by J. Sewell, London, November 1, 1793. Conyngham subscribed for ten copies of the work, according to the *Annual Register* 17 (1796), p. 62.

11. Francis Grose and Edward Ledwich, *Antiquities of Ireland*, 2 vols. (London: Hooper and Wigstead, 1790–97).

12. Trench, "Conyngham," *Journal of the RSAI*, p. 58.

of Lord Conyngham, Colonel Conyngham and the Hon. Mrs. Weldon."[8] The sitters would have been William himself (the colonel), his elder brother Francis (private collection), and their friend Mrs. Helen Weldon (unlocated).[9]

Stuart painted two portraits of Conyngham in Dublin. In one picture (cat. 25), the spines of the books are blank, as are the sheets of stationery, making this composition the most readily representative of Conyngham's wide-ranging literary interests; it is the picture that was used for engraving by Charles Hodges and published by G. Cowen, Dublin, and T. Macklin's, London, November 15, 1792 (fig. 58).[10] A version now at Slane Castle can be dated by the changed inscriptions on the books; the second volume of Francis Grose's *Antiquities of Ireland* was published in 1791 with a dedication to Conyngham.[11] It is suitable that Stuart's portraits variously record Conyngham's interests through books, for his library became his legacy. He collected tomes and prints on his travels, donating them to his pet institutions in Ireland, all the while assembling for himself a personal library that included works by Winckelmann, Vitruvius, Palladio, Algarotti, and Piranesi. After his death, the sale of his library constituted the largest book auction in the country's history.[12]

CRB

Stuart in New York (1793–94)

Stuart boarded Captain John Shaw's ship for New York in March 1793 with a colleague, the Irish painter Walter Robertson, who was to make miniature watercolor-on-ivory versions of his large oils. With Robertson he would take his lucrative experience with engravings in Ireland a few steps further as part of his plan to execute many portraits of George Washington. The long voyage put their nascent relationship to the test. During supper one evening, Stuart, reportedly "under the influence of the devil who steals men's brains if permitted to enter their mouths," insulted Robertson, who was so volatile or drunk or both that he leapt from the table, went to his quarters, and returned with loaded pistols, demanding an apology or a duel.[1] Captain Shaw intervened, Stuart apologized, and each artist painted the captain's portrait (see fig. 59), pictures that were partial payment for passage but that may be construed as souvenirs of a trip that nearly involved the demise of America's finest painter en route home after eighteen years abroad.[2]

The tale that Stuart sailed from Dublin to New York to avoid the circus with "horses and dancing devils and little devils" that was on the boat to Philadelphia may be a tall one.[3] His trip to New York as a preamble to Philadelphia was no mistake. In New York, he painted brilliantly, prolifically, and efficiently, producing splendid portraits in a timely manner for clients who could gain him entrée to the new president's parlor.

As with all of Stuart's plans, there was in this one more flexibility and chance than organization and precision. But he would have counted on certain things: New York was full of prominent people, some of whom he knew; and it was void of fine portraitists. New York had emerged from the revolution with financial strength, celebrity statesmen, the promotional tactics of partisan politics, and a wealthy immigrant population. Recognized as the provisional national capital since 1785, the city came alive as the center of national government when George Washington was sworn in there as first president of the United States in April 1789.[4] Washington came to town with his vice president, John Adams, and his cabinet, among them Thomas Jefferson, Alexander Hamilton, and Edmund Randolph. The patrician families of upstate New York—the Livingstons, Beekmans, Van Rensselaers, and Stuyvesants—who had evacuated their city dwellings along lower Broadway during the war, returned and spruced up their mansions. New York was becoming a cosmopolitan city with a courtly system of posh entertainments derived from the English slowly but surely supplanting old Dutch ways of life. An influx of crafts- and tradesmen from France during the

1. Dunlap 1834, vol. 1, p. 195.
2. Stuart painted two portraits of Shaw (private collection; National Gallery of Ireland, Dublin); it is not known which is the original and which is the replica. The idea that Stuart painted Shaw in return for passage to New York has descended in the family; letter from a family member to Carrie Rebora Barratt, September 22, 2003, Department of American Paintings and Sculpture files, The Metropolitan Museum of Art. Robertson's miniature is unlocated.
3. Pickering 1817 (October 29).
4. Edwin G. Burrows and Mike Wallace, *Gotham: A History of New York City to 1898* (New York: Oxford University Press, 1999), pp. 299–408, provides a lucid and detailed description of the city at this time.

Detail of cat. 32, *John Jay*

Fig. 59. *John Shaw*, 1793. Oil on canvas, 32 x 26 in. (81.3 x 66 cm). National Gallery of Ireland, Dublin

Fig. 60. *Matthew Clarkson*, ca. 1793–94. Oil on canvas, 36⅛ x 28¼ in. (91.6 x 71.8 cm). The Metropolitan Museum of Art, New York; Bequest of Helen Shelton Clarkson, 1937 (38.61)

early 1790s introduced cuisine, coiffures, a new language, theatrical productions, and other ingredients of culture. In some ways the perplexity of British and French influences mirrored the complex political situation of Federalist versus Republican affairs. The city was, as put by the *Boston Gazette,* "a vortex of folly and dissipation"; in short, it fulfilled all the criteria for a successful portrait practice.[5]

Nonetheless, there were virtually no painters in oil and few other portraitists in competition for work. The Irish miniaturist John Ramage painted superb, tiny watercolor-on-ivory images. The Scottish artist brothers Archibald and Alexander Robertson (no relation to Walter) painted small portraits, drew landscapes, and set up an art school, the Columbian Academy of Painting, in 1794. The Italian sculptor Giuseppe Ceracchi had a good practice in New York executing busts of the same notable statesmen who would go to the French profilist C. B. J. Févret de Saint-Mémin, a clever artist who arrived in New York shortly before Stuart but would not begin making portraits for a few years. John Trumbull, Stuart's friend from a decade before when they were in Benjamin West's studio together, may have described the burgeoning but haphazard art scene for him. He had returned to New York in November 1789 to draw portrait studies for later incorporation into his history paintings of signers of the Declaration of Independence and Revolutionary War heroes, so many of whom had converged on New York for Washington's inauguration, either in support of the new government or to jockey for a cabinet position. Trumbull recorded many faces but despaired when the capital moved to Philadelphia in 1790. He fretted over the prospects of being a painter in a nation divided over the present war between Britain and France: "The whole country seemed to be changed into one vast arena . . . on which the two parties, forgetting their national character, were wasting their time, their thoughts, their energy, on this foreign quarrel. . . . In such a state of things, what hope remained for the arts?"[6]

5. Quoted in ibid., p. 300.
6. John Trumbull, *Autobiography, Reminiscences and Letters of John Trumbull from 1756 to 1841* (New York: Wiley and Putnam, 1841), pp. 168–69.

7. Pickering 1817 (October 29).
8. Stuart, letter to Joseph Anthony, November 2, 1794 (original unlocated), photostat, Massachusetts Historical Society, Boston.

Fig. 61. *Aaron Burr*, ca. 1793–94. Oil on canvas, 30¼ x 25 in. (76.8 x 63.5 cm). New Jersey Historical Society, Newark; Gift of David A. Hays for John Chetwood

Despite these misgivings, Trumbull doggedly worked on his history paintings and unveiled his magnificent full-length portrait of Secretary of State Alexander Hamilton (Credit Suisse First Boston), on July 4, 1792, at City Hall, an image perhaps all the more powerful for having been commissioned by the New York Chamber of Commerce some three years earlier but completed just in time to herald Hamilton's redemptive role in helping the city accelerate out of the financial Panic of 1792. By the time Stuart arrived the following spring, the economy had been restored, with stricter banking and trading regulations to monitor the tremendous flow of capital. Trained to paint and to manage his business in the political hotbeds of London and Dublin, Stuart had no trouble balancing commissions from the old landed aristocracy and the new merchant elite, from Federalists and Republicans alike. He painted New York's heroes of the American Revolution, Horatio Gates (cat. 26) and Matthew Clarkson (fig. 60). New York State's Federalist aristocracy sat for Stuart: Stephen Van Rensselaer (National Gallery of Art, Washington); Chancellor Robert R. Livingston (cat. 31), his mother (fig. 72), and others of their family; General Peter Gansevoort (Munson-Williams-Proctor Institute, Utica, N.Y.); Judge William Cooper of Cooperstown (New York State Historical Association, Cooperstown); and John Jacob Astor (Brook Club, New York), who parlayed his country fortune into city opulence.

Captain Shaw, Irish by birth and a New York resident due to marriage and a thriving wine trade, can be counted as Stuart's first New York client, and Senator William Samuel Johnson (private collection), president of Columbia University, may have been next. Stuart himself later bent the truth in saying that he arrived in New York absolutely destitute of acquaintances with the exception of Chief Justice John Jay, whom he had painted in London in 1784.[7] The white lie betrays the fact that Jay was most important to Stuart's business, not only as a client himself (see cat. 32), but as a conduit to others. He introduced the painter to Senator Aaron Burr (fig. 61) and New York jurist Egbert Benson (John Jay Homestead, Katonah, N.Y.), and, most important, provided the introduction to President Washington that the painter desired. But, in fact, Jay was neither Stuart's only friend nor his exclusive means to other commissions. Nearly forty years old, with a considerable body of work to his credit, Stuart was beyond the point of needing to rely on any single person for his professional advancement. Stuart's New York network expanded mainly on the basis of his own earlier commissions.

He painted the Irish shipping agent George Pollock (fig. 68) and his wife, Catherine (National Gallery of Art, Washington), brother-in-law to Dr. William Hartigan who sat to Stuart in Dublin, and who then referred him to their extended family of Yateses (see cats. 27, 28) and Crugers (see cat. 29)—in all, as many as eight portraits—a kindness that left Stuart in their debt, he wrote, "for more civilities than to the world beside."[8] Stuart reacquainted himself with the well-traveled Charlestonians Gabriel and Margaret Izard Manigault, who were elated to find Stuart in New York. Gabriel Manigault met Stuart briefly fifteen years earlier, when he paid a visit to West's studio, and remembered him particularly because his brother Joseph sat for Stuart in 1785 in London. The Manigaults were surprised to find Stuart in New York. Manigault sat for two portraits—one according

Fig. 62. *Gabriel Manigault*, 1794. Oil on canvas, 30¼ x 25½ in. (76.8 x 64.8 cm). Albright-Knox Art Gallery, Buffalo, N.Y.; James G. Forsyth Fund, 1923

Fig. 63. *Margaret Izard Manigault*, 1794. Oil on canvas, 30¼ x 25½ in. (76.8 x 64.8 cm). Albright-Knox Art Gallery, Buffalo, N.Y.; James G. Forsyth Fund, 1923

9. Gabriel Manigault, letter to the Society of Charleston, April 18, 1794, transcribed in Louis Manigault, comp., Manigault Family Letters, Charleston Museum, Charleston, S.C.
10. J. Stuart 1877a, p. 645.
11. Dunlap 1834, vol. 1, p. 195.

to the sitter's taste (private collection) and then again in a picture of Stuart's liking (fig. 62)—and his wife sat once (fig. 63). Walter Robertson produced miniatures of both of them (his, Gibbes Museum of Art, Charleston, S.C.; hers, The Metropolitan Museum of Art). Manigault applauded Stuart as "certainly the best portrait painter who has ever been in America," even while modestly admitting that this was actually not his own opinion, for he might not be a good judge of such things, but it was that of "Mr. Trumbull the painter."[9] Trumbull probably did word-of-mouth campaigning for Stuart, knowing that his friend's success would only bring greater glory to him in the long run.

Stuart had situated himself in New York in the right place, near the corner of Stone and William Streets in the center of the fashionable section of town, at the right time, and exercised a remarkably measured approach to painting clients, depending on their character, station, and requirements.[10] In New York, he concocted a style of painting that combined, in varying degree, the fluidity of his best English pictures with the specificity of his Irish work, a startlingly brilliant combination. And he flaunted his ability to fluctuate, but judiciously, between conventional format and inspired composition depending on what each client wanted. He allowed his studio to become a resort for sitters, their companions, exercising "his skill," wrote William Dunlap, "for their gratification; and gave present éclat and a *short-lived immortality* in exchange for a portion of their wealth."[11] He painted in New York as a professional who knew his trade and succeeded at it, as no artist had done since John Singleton Copley during the summer and fall of 1771. He established the business of portraiture for this generation in America and cultivated the notion that it was a privilege to sit for an expert painter. And then, in November 1794, he left New York, as swiftly as he had come, for Philadelphia and the commission of a lifetime.

CRB

26. HORATIO GATES

1793–94
Oil on canvas, 44¼ x 35⅞ in. (112.4 x 91.1 cm)
The Metropolitan Museum of Art, New York;
Gift of Lucille S. Pfeffer, 1977 (1977.243)

Stuart could have met General Horatio Gates (1728–1806) through John Trumbull, who had once served as Gates's aide-de-camp and was, during the early 1790s, gathering portraits of military heroes to insert in his series of history paintings of great battles from the American Revolution. As early as 1785, Trumbull had begun planning *The Surrender of General Burgoyne at Saratoga, October 16, 1777* (Yale University Art Gallery, New Haven), in which the British commander tenders his sword to Gates, who refuses it and gestures toward his tent in offer of refreshments. Alternatively, Stuart might have known Gates through Henry Cruger (cat. 29), whose estate of more than ninety acres just northeast of the present Madison Square was the site of Gates's retirement, Rose Hill Farm. In 1790 the sixty-two-year-old professional soldier freed the slaves on his Virginia plantation and moved to New York, after a career in the American colonial wars so valiant that he was favorably compared with George Washington, his friend and comrade-at-arms. In that regard there can be no doubt that the look of this portrait was seminal in Stuart's ultimate conception for Washington (see cats. 35–37). Stuart put all his talent into the portrait of Gates, an idealized, retrospective military likeness befitting a hero and highly recommending its painter.

The commission for the picture came from Gates's intimate friend Ebenezer Stevens, a former military man who ran a prosperous mercantile operation after the war. The process of posing was known to Gates, who had been painted by Charles Willson Peale (fig. 64), and he enjoyed bantering with Stuart, "with glass after glass of the celebrated painter's plentiful Madeira!"[1] Stuart used thin glazes and lush brushstrokes on Gates's aging countenance, achieving, not merely realism, but veracity. Stuart's exquisite technique of pulling individual curls of hair over his background, giving them appropriate gloss and weightlessness, is here in full force. Wisps of white hair complement the soft focus on Gates's distinctive facial features: a strong nose, small, dark eyes, a fold under the chin giving way to jowls that describe a man many years advanced from the time he habitually wore a uniform. The crisp rendering of the clothing and Gates's hands, which would seem to belong to a younger man, betray Stuart's employment of traditional British portrait practice, in which the body is painted in the sitter's absence. Some scholars have conjectured that the look of this portrait proves the influence of Copley's hard-edged American work on Stuart.[2] Yet, this is a distinctively British portrait, combining the painterly mastery of Gainsborough with the tight clarity of Romney in a portrait well suited to an English subject.

Born in Maldon, Essex, England, Gates was the son of an army officer and greengrocer. He entered the British army as a young man and was an experienced warrior by the time he was stationed in America during the Seven Years War. Promoted in 1754 to the rank of captain in the Independent Company of Foot in New York, Gates joined General Edward Braddock's campaign to Fort Duquesne in the Ohio Valley in 1755 and was severely wounded. He next served under General Robert Monckton in New York, and after the peace of 1763, he was appointed adjutant general with the rank of brigadier. In the late 1760s, Gates took respite from service at his home in Devonshire but by 1772 had returned to America, where he enjoyed a relatively leisured existence on his plantation in Berkeley County (now

1. Stuart's painting of Gates is listed in Mason 1879, p. 183; Park 1926, pp. 340–43, no. 317. See Samuel White Patterson, *Horatio Gates: Defender of American Liberties* (New York: Columbia University Press, 1941), p. 373, for quotation. All further biographical information on Gates is taken from this source and *ANB*, vol. 8, pp. 788–91.
2. John Caldwell and Oswaldo Rodriguez Roque, *American Paintings in The Metropolitan Museum of Art*, vol. 1, *A Catalogue of Works by Artists Born by 1815* (New York: Metropolitan Museum of Art, 1994), p. 174.

Fig. 64. Charles Willson Peale, *Horatio Gates*, 1782. Oil on canvas, 21⅞ x 19⅞ in. (55.6 x 50.6 cm). Independence National Historical Park, Philadelphia

Fig. 65. Cornelius Tiebout after Gilbert Stuart, *Horatio Gates*, 1796. Stipple engraving, 13⅜ x 11¼ in. (34 x 28.5 cm). The Metropolitan Museum of Art, New York; Gift of William H. Huntington, 1883 (83.2.2032)

3. The medal bears the inscription, on the obverse: HORATIO GATES DUCI STRENUO / COMITIA AMERICANA (The American Congress to Horatio Gates, the valiant commander); and on the reverse: SALUS PROVINCIATUM SEPTENTRIONALIUM / HOSTE AD SARATOGAM / IN DEDITIONEM ACCEPTO / DIE 17 8BRIE 1777 (The safety of the northern regions secured by the surrender of the enemy received at Saratoga, Oct. 17, 1777). The die was cut in France by Nicolas Marie Gatteaux; see C. Wyllys Betts, *American Colonial History Illustrated by Contemporary Medals*, ed. William T. R. Marvin and Lyman Haynes Low (New York: Scott Stamp and Coin Co., 1894), pp. 252–53; Vladimir and Elvira Clain-Stefanelli, *Medals Commemorating Battles of the American Revolution* (Washington, D.C.: National Museum of History and Technology, Smithsonian Institution, 1973), pp. 9–10. The medal was struck in gold by congressional vote on November 4, 1777.

4. James Orr Denby, *The Society of the Cincinnati and Its Museum* (New York: Society of the Cincinnati, 1967); Charles Martin Jones, *Formation and Organization of the Society of the Cincinnati in the State of New Jersey* (n.p.: Society of the Cincinnati in the State of New Jersey, 1957); Major Edgar Erskine Hume, *The Diplomas of the Society of the Cincinnati* (New York, 1935; reprinted from *Americana* 29 [January 1935]). Gates was national vice president of the society and president of the Virginia chapter.

5. Gates, letter to Stevens, December 22, 1796, box cf, no. 9667, Manuscript Department, University of Virginia Library, Charlottesville.

6. "Review and Register of the Fine Arts," *American Monthly Magazine and Critical Review* 1 (August 1817), p. 293. See also *Catalogue of Paintings, Statues, Busts, Drawings, Models, and Engravings,*

West Virginia). At General Washington's behest, Gates joined the commander's staff and served throughout the Revolutionary War in a career, in some ways typical of military giants, that interspersed triumph with defeat and squabbles over appointments with successful strategic planning. He met the invasion of British troops under General John Burgoyne during the late summer of 1777 and won a decisive victory at Saratoga, New York. The so-called Hero of Saratoga garnered such a following that there was talk of making him commander in chief in place of Washington. The scheme failed and harmed Gates's reputation, although he was, in fact, not actively involved with his cunning promoters. He retired to his plantation until called back into service once more. As commander of the Southern Department at the Battle of Camden, South Carolina, in the summer of 1780, Gates suffered a disastrous and humiliating defeat, as his feeble and starving force abandoned the field to General Lord Charles Cornwallis.

Stuart's portrait captures a heroic aspect with elegance and monumentality. It is a standard format for an officer's portrait: a figure in three-quarter pose in slightly more than bust length, in which the subject's formal regalia becomes the hallmark of character and identity. Gates wears the dark blue and buff uniform of a major general, with brass buttons and gold two-starred epaulettes, not the one he wore at Saratoga but a modern version. He holds the hilt of his sword and his black silk hat with one hand and a document inscribed *Convention / of Saratoga 1777* with the other, a tour de force of compositional arrangement in a stacking of hands that manifests at once the subject's gentility—the well-groomed fingers and partially open palm of the left hand—and his virility—the fist that clutches the weapon. Ceremonial insignia mark his valor, most notably the large medal struck by Congress on the occasion of victory at Saratoga. Stuart must have borrowed the medal from Gates, to get it right. The front of the medal is a low-relief narrative: Burgoyne surrenders his sword to Gates, while vanquished troops in the distance lay down their arms near the base of an olive tree and the victorious American army flies its colors.[3] Gates also wears the eagle-shaped pendant of the Society of the Cincinnati, a fraternal organization formed on May 13, 1783, by officers of the Continental Army before disbanding at the end of the revolution with the aim of maintaining national honor, promoting and cherishing union among the states, and extending substantial acts of beneficence.[4] Despite the outcry from zealous republican adversaries who charged that the society fostered an aristocratic military nobility, it took the name of Lucius Quinctius Cincinnatus, a legendary Roman military leader from the fifth century B.C. who saved Rome from barbarian invasions and then retired to his farm without personal reward. Like Washington—who was deemed the modern Cincinnatus—Gates lived according to this model, a landed gentleman in relative seclusion following a controversial career.

Gates apparently liked his portrait. He borrowed the picture from Stevens in 1796 to have a stipple engraving (fig. 65) made by Cornelius Tiebout so that he could share the

26

exh. cat., American Academy of the Fine Arts
(New York: T. and W. Mercein, 1817), no. 132,
"Portrait of Gen. Horatio Gates—lent by Gen.
Stevens." The portrait was lent to another exhibi-
tion, in 1853; see American Art-Union, *Washington
Exhibition in Aid of the New-York Gallery of the
Fine Arts* (New York: J. F. Trow, 1853), no. 2, lent
by Horatio Gates Stevens.

image with others.[5] After Gates's death, Stevens lent the portrait to the second exhibition of the American Academy of the Fine Arts, an organization founded by Robert
Livingston and presided over by Trumbull. A writer for the *American Monthly Magazine
and Critical Review* eloquently summed up the picture for his audience in a manner that
holds true nearly two centuries later: "Our great portrait painter has here represented the
veteran hero of Saratoga, with such graceful ease, such fidelity to nature, and, at the
same time, in such a historical manner, as to render this picture invaluable to the artist
and to the patriot."[6]

CRB

27. RICHARD YATES

1793‒94
Oil on canvas, 29 3/4 x 24 3/8 in. (75.5 x 61.9 cm)
National Gallery of Art, Washington, D.C.;
Andrew W. Mellon Collection (1942.8.29)

28. CATHERINE BRASS YATES

1793‒94
Oil on canvas, 30 x 25 in. (76.2 x 63.5 cm)
National Gallery of Art, Washington, D.C.;
Andrew W. Mellon Collection (1940.1.4)

1. The paintings are not listed in Mason 1879; they are listed in Park 1926, pp. 836‒37, nos. 942, 943.
2. Royal Cortissoz, "The Field of Art," *Scribner's Magazine* 76 (July 1924), p. 111.
3. John Hill Morgan, "A Sketch of the Life of Gilbert Stuart 1755‒1828," in Park 1926, p. 78.

If Stuart's portrait of Richard Yates (1732‒1808) has attracted scant and prosaic commentary over the years, the one of his wife, Catherine Brass Yates (1736?‒?1797), has inspired rhapsodic review, as writers spin words in an effort to explicate the picture's intensity.[1] For the early-twentieth-century critic Royal Cortissoz, the portrait of Mrs. Yates conjured visions of Velázquez, "because Stuart and he were obviously at one in seeking to make the painted surface exquisite. It combines, as a portrait by him combines, firm and weighty statement of fact with a touch equally sure but so light and flowing that the artist seems to be in absolutely effortless command of his instruments."[2] For the Stuart scholar John Hill Morgan, writing in 1926 after he saw the portrait for the first time, it also summoned up Velázquez, but in an art historical tangle of Whistler, Chardin, and Vermeer: "Whistlerian, almost, it might be called, if it were not for the frank naturalism of the portrait. . . . But what had arrested me in the first place and what still remains vivid in my mind was the magnificent painting in the thing, the beauty of the canvas as so much silvery surface. I thought of Chardin. I thought of Vermeer and other magical manipulators of pigment. Above all, I thought of Velasquez . . . [and] how Stuart, in this glorious piece of technique, entered into the company of the great brushmen, how both dexterity and in taste, how in the very essence of painting, he here demonstrated that he was indeed one of the masters."[3]

Fig. 66. Sir Joshua Reynolds, *Anne, Countess of Albemarle*, 1759. Oil on canvas, 49 3/4 x 39 3/4 in. (126.5 x 101 cm). National Gallery, London

Fig. 67. John Singleton Copley, *Portrait of a Lady* (formerly known as *Mrs. Seymour Fort*), ca. 1780. Oil on canvas, 49 1/2 x 39 5/8 in. (125.7 x 100.6 cm). Wadsworth Atheneum, Hartford; Gallery Fund (1901.34)

Fig. 68. *George Pollock*, 1793–94. Oil on canvas, 36¼ x 28⅜ in. (92.2 x 72.1 cm). National Gallery of Art, Washington, D.C.; Andrew W. Mellon Collection (1942.8.18)

Fig. 69. *Lawrence Reid Yates*, 1793–94. Oil on canvas, 30 x 25 in. (76.2 x 63.5 cm). National Gallery of Art, Washington, D.C.; Andrew W. Mellon Collection (1940.1.5)

Of late, and closer to home in terms of Stuart's likely sources of inspiration and study, scholars have compared the portrait of Mrs. Yates with Reynolds's portraits of Anne, Countess of Albemarle (fig. 66) and Lady Caroline Fox (private collection) and Copley's *Portrait of a Lady* (formerly known as *Mrs. Seymour Fort*; fig. 67). All four feature middle-aged women with nimble fingers.[4] Mrs. Yates's portrait also harks back self-referentially to two of Stuart's most successful Irish portraits, those of Anna Dorothea Foster and Catherine Lane Barker (see cats. 21, 23), not only in the deployment of needlework as an evocation of feminine roles and status but also in his artistic strategies for rendering myriad textures—silk, muslin, skin, hair, velvet—and his ability to articulate what has been called a "cool, assessing gaze" that conveys confidence and grace.[5]

It was not some patriotic epiphany that brought about these stunning pendant portraits for the Yateses. Stuart, rather, deployed the techniques he learned abroad, offering high-style British paintings to a cosmopolitan clientele. Especially now, after a recent surface cleaning, these pictures epitomize the seriously calculated effort made by Stuart in New York, where his discerning patrons could wield tremendous influence on his career. He exquisitely balanced brushy and glossy effects to make the portraits appear at once factual and elusive. He knew the difference between feminine and masculine conceptions of portraiture, not only in iconography but also in attitude. And he knew when he had a sitter who would tolerate his controlling attentions, which could take a picture outside the bounds of merely competent. This is the crucial difference between the portraits of Richard and Catherine Yates. For him, Stuart was compelled to stay within the limits of conventional excellence, but for her, he created an extraordinary painting.

Stuart met the Yateses through their son-in-law George Pollock (fig. 68), brother-in-law of the Dr. William Hartigan who sat for him in Dublin. Indeed, both of the Yateses' daughters, Maria and Anna Sophia, had married Pollocks, and the families, along with the Crugers (see cat. 29), had neighboring country houses on the banks of the Hudson River in northern Manhattan. The network of Pollocks, Yateses, and Crugers accounted for a good percentage of Stuart's business in New York. Richard Yates had immigrated to New York from England to enhance his importing business

4. Elizabeth Mankin Kornhauser, in *American Paintings before 1945 in the Wadsworth Atheneum* (Hartford: Wadsworth Atheneum; New Haven: Yale University Press, 1996), pp. 264–66, has disproved the traditional identification of the sitter as Mrs. Seymour Fort. For further citations for these sources, see Miles 1995, p. 194.

5. Miles 1995, p. 194.

27

28

6. Aileen Ribeiro, *Dress in Eighteenth-Century Europe, 1715–1789* (London: Batsford, 1984), p. 113.

7. The portraits of Mr. and Mrs. Yates (Museum of Fine Arts, Boston, and Fine Arts Museums of San Francisco), long thought to be replicas, are now considered early copies after Stuart; see Miles 1995, p. 184.

sometime before 1757, the year he married Catherine Brass, daughter of a shoemaker. Yates was a member of the New York State Chamber of Commerce and the Committee of One Hundred, which was formed in May 1775 by loyalists to rule the city. He remained in New York during the war and saw his business increase in the immediate aftermath, as the triangle trade of flour, sugar, rum, coffee, ginger, and other staples from Britain and the West Indies flourished. He was a partner in business with his brother, Lawrence Reid Yates, who also was portrayed by Stuart in a highly professional, unembellished mode (fig. 69). Richard Yates is in day dress—a blue wool coat—and, seated in an old-fashioned Windsor chair, looks up from his pile of papers and selection of inks and waxes. He is hunched over his work, fingers intertwined in it, with hair powder shaken over his collar and the buttons of his right cuff carelessly left open indicating that he got to his affairs so quickly that he neglected his proper toilet.

His wife, by contrast, is impeccable: swathed in precious fabrics that sheathe her person, from the long, tight sleeves of her gown to the fichu that covers not merely her décolletage but her entire neck, to the gauze mobcap of the sort that had recently returned to vogue. The height of the bonnet elongates her gaunt, narrow face, and the totality suggests knowing elegance. Her nose is as long and sharp as the needle she holds between her index finger and thumb, the pointy terminus of a taut thread from the stitch she has just pulled. Stuart's deceptively simple concept arranges the composition from nose to needle to thread tucked under her thimbled middle finger, wound over her ring finger and around her unbent pinky, to the sheer fabric held tight by three fingers to her bent left arm and upward again, offering a perpetual circle that holds Mrs. Yates's viewer prey to her assessment. The sewing gesture accomplishes a virtuosic range of emblematic meaning. As at the English court, where women knotted and stitched as a pastime, it gave cause "to show off the graceful attitudes of the hands."[6] It makes Mrs. Yates as industrious as her husband in an exacting manner that complements his slightly rumpled habit. And, perhaps above all, Mrs. Yates's gymnastic hands flaunt Stuart's abilities in a town where no painter had accomplished such a feat in decades, and would not for many years to come.[7]

CRB

29. HENRY CRUGER

1793–94

Oil on canvas, 50 x 40 in. (127 x 101.6 cm)

Bristol Museums and Art Gallery, Bristol, England

(524)

Henry Cruger Jr. (1739–1827) had a career "of irreconcilable loyalties."[1] Son of a wealthy New York City merchant, elected to the British House of Commons, Cruger advocated the cause of the American colonies from various privileged positions in England throughout the American Revolution and culminated his distinguished political career in the New York State Senate. He was born to Henry Cruger and Elizabeth Harris, New Yorkers of considerable prominence. His grandfather John Cruger came to America in 1698 from Bristol, England's principal port for Atlantic trade, served as mayor of New York City in 1739–44, and later became an alderman, and ran a successful trade primarily in logwood, mahogany, rum, and sugar, with shipping routes among England, New York, and the West Indies. He was joined in both trade and local politics by his sons, Henry Sr. and John Jr.; John Jr. was first president of the New York City Chamber of Commerce, mayor (1757–66) and a New York delegate to the Stamp Act Congress in 1765.

Henry Cruger Jr., known for his "ready wit and fine conversational powers," spent three years at Kings College (now Columbia University) and left without a degree in 1757 when his father sent him to Bristol to join the countinghouse of Henry Cruger and Company.[2] In 1765 he became a member of the City Council of Bristol and married Hannah Peach, daughter of a politically influential linen merchant. They had one son, Samuel, before her death in 1767. About the same time, Cruger suffered business losses because the American colonists were boycotting English imports as a result of the Stamp Act. He joined the delegation of Bristol merchants protesting Parliament's disregard for the importance of the American colonies to British business interests, which effectively began his political career. His local reputation as an articulate and passionate spokesman for the radical movement gained him election to the House of Commons as a Whig representing Bristol, with Edmund Burke in the other Bristol seat. Although the antagonism between these two members of Parliament reached such a level that both were unseated in 1780, Cruger is remembered for his passionate attempts to convince the members that aggressive policies against independence for the American colonies were counterproductive to England's business interests. After his defeat, Cruger became mayor of Bristol for one year, 1781, during which he fortified trade relationships, especially with American clients. Ultimately he could not salvage economic prosperity for Bristol as more and more overseas trade was conducted to and from Liverpool. In 1790 he left for New York.

Cruger's son Samuel, by now also a businessman, stayed in Bristol, and Cruger traveled with his second wife, Elizabeth Blair, and their six children. He retired from business and was elected to the New York State Senate in 1792, a post he held until his death in 1827. Throughout his career in England, he had remained devoted to his place of birth, at one point sending glass from Bristol for windows in the first New York Hospital, and in 1788, explaining to his brother, "my heart still cleaves to New York."[3] Once back in New York, Cruger was greatly missed in Bristol. About 1794 he sent his portrait to his son Samuel, the arrival of which caused terrific commotion: "When the vessel having it on board arrived in the harbor of Bristol, it was noised through the town that Mr. Cruger himself had arrived. The bells of the city were immediately made to ring a merry peal to announce the glad tidings. An immense crowd assembled on the quay to receive him. Their indignation at the captain of the vessel for having announced

1. *ANB*, vol. 5, p. 818.
2. Henry C. Van Schaack, *Henry Cruger: The Colleague of Edmund Burke in the British Parliament* (New York: C. B. Richardson, 1859), p. 30.
3. Quoted in *ANB*, vol. 5, p. 818.

Fig. 70. George Romney, *Henry Cruger*, ca. 1780–85. Oil on canvas, 30 x 25 in. (76.2 x 63.5 cm). The New-York Historical Society (1976.68)

that Mr. C. was on board, could scarcely be restrained when it was ascertained that it was only his *picture*. As it was, they insisted on having the case opened, and the portrait exhibited to them, which was accordingly done on the wharf."[4]

The portrait that caused the ruckus as a disappointing surrogate for the man himself was the one painted by Stuart.[5] It has remained in Bristol ever since, in the Cruger family until 1943, when it was sold to the Bristol Museums and Art Gallery and subsequently placed on view at the Mansion House at Clifton Down, the official residence of the Lord Mayor of Bristol. The assumption that Cruger sat for Stuart in England about 1781, when he took office in Bristol, was promoted by art historian John Steegman, who conjectured that Stuart may have stopped in Bristol en route to Dublin in 1787, or that Cruger had sat in London, as he had done for George Romney in London in the early 1780s (fig. 70).[6] The intersection of Stuart's and Cruger's travels is difficult to establish, but the appearance of portrait itself proves without doubt that Stuart painted it in New York for display in Bristol. Cruger wears his mayoral robes, an outfit pertinent to a single year of his varied and distinguished career, but the culmination of his time in Bristol.

Cruger's portrait bears the hallmarks of Stuart's New York work: unlike the fluidly painted dashing works he created in a Reynoldsian idiom during the early 1780s, this portrait is characterized by a Romneyesque geometry in compositional layout and extreme attention to portraying Cruger as a human being. He paid meticulous attention to his sitter's decorative costume, the naturalism in the flesh and facial features, and the tabletop props. His portrayal of Cruger's ruddy face, veined hand with buffed fingernails, carefully observed powdered hair, robe, and gloves, and arrangement of the whole before a dark drapery precisely parallels his portrait of Josef de Jaudenes y Nebot (cat. 34). Stuart's expert rendering of age on his sitter's face, as on that of Horatio Gates (cat. 26), further argues for dating the portrait to 1793–94, when Cruger was about fifty-five. As for Stuart's mastery of the peculiar embellishments of the Lord Mayor's regalia—leather gloves with gold embroidery and long fringe as accompaniment to a scarlet mink-lined robe with crenellated elbow-length sleeves—he would have painted from the actual garments, which Cruger took with him to New York, along with his parliamentary robes and wigs, for donation to costume wardrobe at the Park Theatre.[7]

Stuart may have known Cruger in New York as a member of the extended Yates-Pollock-Cruger family (see cats. 27, 28), perhaps introduced through Lawrence Reid Yates, who sat for Stuart in 1793 or 1794 (fig. 69) and in 1795 married Cruger's daughter Matilda. Matilda may also have been painted by Stuart, but that portrait is lost.[8]

CRB

4. Van Schaack, *Henry Cruger*, p. 41.
5. The painting is not listed in Mason 1879 or Park 1926.
6. John Steegman, ca. 1963, handwritten note in the catalogue record for the painting, Bristol Museums and Art Gallery.
7. Van Schaack, *Henry Cruger*, p. 35.
8. A portrait of Matilda Cruger Yates, once thought to be by Stuart but now unattributed, is owned by the National Gallery of Art, Washington, D.C.; see Miles 1995, pp. 367–68.

29

30. WILLIAM BAYARD

1793−94
Oil on canvas, 36 x 28 in. (91.4 x 71.1 cm)
Princeton University Art Museum, Princeton,
New Jersey; Gift of Viscountess Eccles (2004-37)

Fig. 71. *Elizabeth Cornell Bayard*, 1793−94. Oil on canvas, 36 x 28 in. (91.4 x 71 cm). Private collection

1. On Bayard, see *DAB*, vol. 1, pt. 2, pp. 72−73; Mrs. Anson Phelps Atterbury, *The Bayard Family: An Address Read Before the New York Branch of the Order of Colonial Lords of Manors in America, April, 1927* (Baltimore, 1928). Bayard's papers are held in the Bayard, Campbell, Pearsall Papers, Manuscripts and Archives Division, New York Public Library, Astor, Lenox and Tilden Foundations.
2. When Bayard's cousin James McEvers later joined the business, the name was changed to Bayard, LeRoy, and McEvers.
3. *DAB*, vol. 1, pt. 2, p. 73.
4. P.M., "Obituary: William Bayard," *Evening Post*, September 19, 1826. See also the obituary in the *Commercial Advertiser*, September 19, 1826.
5. The portrait of William Bayard is not listed in Mason 1879; it is listed in Park 1926, pp. 142−43, no. 69. The portrait of Elizabeth Bayard is listed in Fielding 1929, p. 133.

The principal member of what would become New York's premier mercantile operation was thirty-five years old when he sat for Stuart. William Bayard (1759−1826), whose father of the same name was also a merchant, descended from an old New Jersey family with British roots and extensive landholdings in North America.[1] In 1783 he married Elizabeth (see fig. 71), one of the five beautiful Cornell sisters who came with their mother to New York from New Bern, North Carolina, in 1781, shortly after the death of their father, Samuel. Elizabeth's sister Hannah married Bayard's friend Herman LeRoy, and together the Bayards and the LeRoys converted family relations into business opportunities with the establishment of Bayard and LeRoy, New York's leading commercial house for more than forty years; in the 1820s they would secure the loans required to develop the Erie Canal.[2] Beginning in December 1786, the firm explored all the opportunities in the postrevolutionary era. They traded principally with England, the Caribbean, and South America in every lucrative commodity from medicines to silk, liquor to spices, and hardware to real estate. In 1789 they spent over $500,000 in depreciated southern state securities and subsequently doubled their money when the federal government bought out the state deficits. The Panic of 1792 hurt Bayard, but he was among the first to recover with his unique blend of financial savvy and personal relations. One of his biographers called it the "Bayard magnetism," a special blend of charm and intelligence: "He had a reputation for mildness of temper and charm of manner in addition to the unusual business acumen which made him one of the wealthiest men in the country."[3] And later, at his death, even after years of privateering, speculation, and deal making, Bayard was eulogized as "a model of mercantile integrity and correctness."[4] A member of the close-knit family network of Bayards, Pearsalls, and Kembles, he was also related by marriage to the Livingstons (see cat. 31), Van Cortlandts, and Stuyvesants of New York. He was brother-in-law to Matthew Clarkson (see fig. 60), who married a third Cornell sister, and cousin to John Jay (see cat. 32).

Bayard's was the sort of portrait Stuart painted easily, a softly modeled and highly decorative image with an inspired palette of pastel hues.[5] Stuart experimented with the composition as he worked, making changes in the lower quadrant that remain engagingly visible. The inkwell is painted twice. The papers and Bayard's hands changed during the process, and a quill is but an outline of an intention. Most revelatory of all is the bottom edge and right side of the picture, where the skirt of Bayard's wool coat is folded as if bunched against the back of a chair—but there is no chair. While these elements define the painting as unresolved, Stuart's virtuosic finish of the figure of Bayard seems to require nothing else.

Bayard's portrait bears comparison with Stuart's second portrait of Gabriel Manigault, the Charlestonian who, insisting on a plain, dark coat in his portrait got a dismal result and then allowed the painter to have his way, which meant a fancy waistcoat in an inspired composition (fig. 62). Stuart captured Bayard's magnetic personality with color and design while maintaining his serious character with a dignified composition: the working merchant dressed in an ensemble fit for a dandy. The warm rose of the background curtain and table cover sets off Bayard's apple green coat and complements his pale pink gold-spotted waistcoat. To counter any charge of pridefulness in clothing, he has left his sleeve button undone, a mark of Bayard's carelessness and hence humanity.

CRB

30

31. ROBERT R. LIVINGSTON

1793–94
Oil on canvas, 36 ³/₈ x 28 ³/₈ in. (92.4 x 72.1 cm)
Clermont State Historic Site, Germantown, New
York; New York State Office of Parks, Recreation
and Historic Preservation (CL.1974.56.a.b)

Fig. 72. *Mrs. Robert R. Livingston*, 1793–94.
Oil on canvas, 36 x 28 in. (91.4 x 71.1 cm).
Private collection (photo: Museum of the City
of New York)

Robert R. Livingston (1746–1813) and his six siblings had probably the wealthiest parents in New York State: Robert R. Livingston—lawyer, Supreme Court judge, and prosperous landholder—and Margaret Beekman, heiress of the fortune accumulated by her parents, Colonel Henry and Janet Beekman of Rhinebeck, New York.[1] His own fortunes rose still further after his marriage in 1770 to Mary Stevens, daughter of John Stevens of New Jersey, and when his father and his father-in-law both died in 1775, vast tracts of tenanted land, most of it in the Hudson River Valley and the Catskills, became his. By that time he had begun practicing law with his cousin John Jay (see cat. 32), with whom he had graduated from Kings College (now Columbia University) in 1765. He left private law practice as he assumed a succession of government appointments: recorder of the City of New York, member of the Provincial Congress from Dutchess County, leader of the New York delegation to the Second Continental Congress, and Chancellor of the State of New York, a position he held from 1777 to 1813.

Livingston held prominent position after prominent position with scant advancement; he suffered the humiliation of being by turns esteemed and then overlooked. He sat on the committee to draft the Declaration of Independence, but there is no evidence that he ever worked on the document. He wrote part of the constitution for New York State, a text largely attributed to Jay. In 1781, Congress elected Livingston Secretary of Foreign Affairs but then sent Jay to London to negotiate the treaty. Livingston all but breached his longtime friendship with Jay by lambasting the treaty in the *New York Argus* under the pseudonym Cato and resigned as Secretary of Foreign Affairs; Jay succeeded him in 1783. On April 3, 1789, Chancellor Livingston administered the oath of office to George Washington as first president and proclaimed in his booming voice "Long Live George Washington, President of the United States" but was not offered a position in the federal government; the post he coveted, that of chief justice, went to Jay. Washington attempted to assuage Livingston with an offer to send him abroad as Minister to France, but Livingston turned it down recognizing it as an effort to move him farther away from the center of power. In 1798, he accepted the nomination to oppose Jay in the race for governor of New York and lost resoundingly. In 1801, he took from President Jefferson the office that he had refused from Washington, and as Minister to France he was involved in negotiating the Louisiana Purchase, although the ultimate achievement in that agreement was James Madison's.

A key diplomat and a republican aristocrat, Livingston epitomized the era's ruthlessly elitist grandee who worked for the government on his own terms, even as he tended to his tenants and his true interests: agricultural experimentation, Merino sheep breeding, and steam navigation. Wrote one biographer: "Livingston embodied the contradictions of the new nation. Neither a feudal baron exploiting his domains and tenants, nor a fully modern capitalist, he was something in between: an entrepreneurial agrarian protector who improved, rather than enlarged, his landholdings, who merchandized his products, and who seriously pursued and financed scientific and technological innovation."[2] The Chancellor, as he was known to family and friends to distinguish him from all of the other Roberts and Livingstons in the "complex cousinage" of great New York clans, cherished his service for the state, and it was in that role that he sat for Stuart.

In a highly traditional three-quarter-turn-at-desk pose, Livingston sits in an upholstered mahogany armchair, the very image of an aristocratic gentleman of the old school

1. *ANB*, vol. 13, pp. 774–76; George Dangerfield,
   Chancellor Robert R. Livingston of New York,
   1746–1813 (New York: Harcourt, Brace, 1960).
2. *ANB*, vol. 13, p. 776.

31

3. On the Livingston portraits, see Mason 1879, p. 216; Park 1926, pp. 481–84, nos. 495–99. In addition to cat. 34, the portraits of Robert R. Livingston are in the New-York Historical Society, the Museum of the City of New York, and the U.S. Department of State. In addition to fig. 72, portraits of Margaret Beekman Livingston are in the New-York Historical Society; the New York State Office of Parks, Recreation, and Historic Preservation; and the Senate House State Historic Site, Kingston, N.Y. See also Ruth Piwonka, *A Portrait of Livingston Manor, 1686–1850* (Germantown, N.Y.: Friends of Clermont, 1986), pp. 57, 167, for an extensive listing of these works and copies after Stuart.

4. Undated letter from Margaret Beekman Livingston to Catharine Livingston Garrettson, Livingston Papers, New-York Historical Society.

with black coat, white shirt, no adornments, and powdered hair pulled back with a black ribbon. An imposingly large man with a florid complexion, he got from Stuart the sort of factual image that would have bolstered his ego. Stuart accurately showed Livingston with one blue and one hazel eye, just as he captured the verity of the work at hand. Livingston holds a document marked "Council of Revision" and rests his fist atop another, the "Constitution of S.N.Y.," showing that he was at work to amend the document that Jay, and not he, had pushed through the state congress. Such a detailed passage would have required complicity between Livingston and Stuart, who although indebted to Jay, might have hoped to engage Livingston's influence as well in his bid to obtain a sitting with President Washington. By 1794, Jay was closer in position to the president, but Livingston wielded significant influence as Washington continued to offer him diplomatic positions. Stuart's work for the Livingstons was also prestigious and lucrative in its own right: he painted several versions of the Chancellor's portrait, along with four of his mother (see fig. 72).[3] The work furthered his reputation in New York and may have attracted clients. Mrs. Livingston wrote to her daughter about the "many gentlemen [who] have been to see the old face and while I was sitting sent up their names and wished to be permitted to come in . . . everybody says so striking a likeness."[4]

CRB

32. JOHN JAY

1794
Oil on canvas, 51½ x 40⅛ in. (130.8 x 101.9 cm)
National Gallery of Art, Washington, D.C.; Lent by Peter A. Jay

1. Pickering 1817 (October 29).
2. The robes were identified by Professor Richard B. Morris; information communicated by Ene Sirvet of the Papers of John Jay, Columbia University, New York, letter to Ellen Miles, March 6, 1974.
3. On the portrait, see Mason 1879, pp. 205–7; Park 1926, p. 436, no. 437; John Jay Ide, *The Portraits of John Jay (1745–1829), First Chief Justice of the United States* (New York: New-York Historical Society, 1938), p. 26, no. 7.
4. This letter, quoted in Mason 1879, p. 206, and Whitley 1932, p. 92, is one of two about Stuart's portraits of Jay that have not been located by the editors of the Papers of John Jay; see their Web site, http://www.columbia.edu/cu/lweb/eresources/archives/jay/, no. 6558. In the George Champlin Mason Papers (Rhode Island Historical Society, Providence) is a letter from Jay's descendant John Jay, August 23, 1878 (transcribed by Laura Mills), in which the text is also quoted; he had "chanced upon two letters of Mrs. Jay."
5. John Jay Papers, Rare Book and Manuscript Library, Columbia University, no. 6560.
6. Ibid., no. 6561.
7. Ibid., no. 6564.
8. Quoted in Mason 1879, p. 206, and Whitley 1932, p. 92, this letter, like the earlier letter, has not been

John Jay (1745–1829) was one of the few people Stuart knew in New York when he arrived from Dublin in the spring of 1793. Stuart later told Henry Pickering that "He [Stuart] was an entire stranger at New York. He knew however one person—& that one was Mr. Jay! He repaired as soon as he could to the mansion of that gentleman, but was chagrined not to find him at home. They afterwards met however, & Mr. Jay remained his firm friend. Mr. S. [Stuart] had seen Mr. Jay in London, & had painted his portrait—& what is more remarkable, had prognosticated his future greatness."[1]

Stuart's extraordinary gift of characterization through physiognomic accuracy combined with creative choice of pose is well represented here. In this dramatic image, Jay, lawyer, statesman, and author of the Federalist Papers with Alexander Hamilton and James Madison, is seated, looking off to our right. His left hand rests on a book, and his right hand is in his lap. As first chief justice of the United States, appointed by President Washington in 1789, Jay wore an academic robe from Harvard College, which gave him an honorary doctor of laws degree in 1790.[2] His stern, chiseled face, with its sharply defined chin and receding hairline, contrasts dramatically with the swirl of the red and black robes. The bright red of the robe brings Jay's rosy cheeks and pale forehead to life, while his graying hair contrasts with the strong black of the gown. The pale rose-colored curtain and a column behind Jay are muted echoes of these colors.

Stuart began the portrait sometime before May 12, 1794, when Jay left for London to negotiate with England a treaty known subsequently as the Jay Treaty.[3] This negotiation addressed issues of defense and trade that were left unresolved by the Treaty of Paris in 1783 at the end of the American Revolution, for which Jay had also served as a commissioner. Sarah Livingston Jay's letters to her husband show that Stuart had not finished the portrait before Jay's departure. Remaining in New York, she wrote Jay in London on August 2, 1794, "Would you believe that Stuart has not yet sent me your picture? I call

Fig. 73. Gilbert Stuart and John Trumbull, *John Jay*, 1784/1818. Oil on canvas, 50½ x 40 in. (128.3 x 101.6 cm). National Portrait Gallery, Smithsonian Institution, Washington, D.C. (NPG.74.46)

Fig. 74. *John Jay*, 1784–94. Oil on canvas, 50½ x 41½ in. (128.3 x 105.4 cm). Diplomatic Reception Rooms, U.S. Department of State, Washington, D.C. (72.47)

located by the editors of the Jay Papers, Columbia University. It is not listed on the Web site.

9. Jay Papers, no. 13075.

10. Mason 1879, p. 206, and Whitley 1932, p. 92.

11. Peter A. Jay, letter to John Jay, July 8, 1808, Jay Papers, no. 6131. Evans (1999, p. 147 n. 12) discusses this portrait as an example of Stuart's occasional carelessness in painting drapery.

12. Jay left England on January 22, 1784, writing to Stuart from Paris about the portraits and frames on February 22; the letter is in the Joseph Downs Collection of Manuscripts and Printed Ephemera, Winterthur Library, Winterthur, Del., and was

upon him often. I have not hesitated telling him that it is in his power to contribute infinitely to my gratification, by indulging me with your portrait; he has at length resumed the pencil and your nephew [probably Peter Jay Munro] has been sitting with your robe for him; it is now nearly done, and is your very self. It is an *inimitable picture*, and I am all impatience to have it to myself. He begged me to remind you of the promise you made him the day he breakfasted with you. There is an excellent engraver in New-York, and Stuart has been solicited to permit him to copy that portrait of yours by a very respectable number of citizens, for which reason he has asked and obtained my consent."[4] She mentioned the picture again at the end of her letter of September 27, "Have you set yet for yr. picture—Stewart has not yet gratified me by sending the one he has taken of you."[5] On October 11 she also mentioned portraits, referring to their son Peter Augustus Jay, who was with his father in London, "Have you yet sat for your picture? You & Peter are silent about it, but I hope you do not repent your promise. Stewart still keeps your portrait."[6] And on November 12, "I have not been able yet to get yr. picture from Stewart—have you sat for a Miniature—Would it not be worth while for Peter likewise to sit."[7] Finally, on November 15 she reported, "Just as I had laid aside my pen to take tea, Mr. Stuart arrived with your picture. He insisted on my promising it should be destroyed when he presented me with a better one, which he said he certainly would, if you would be so obliging as to have a mask made for him."[8] By December 5 she had hung the portrait in the dining room. "Your picture as I mentioned formerly I've recd. it hangs in the dining-room where the little prints used to hang, & you cannot imagine how much I am gratified by having it."[9] When Mrs. Jay wrote to Jay in London on November 15, 1794, she added news about Stuart: "In ten days hence he is to go to Philadelphia, to take a likeness of the President."[10] Jay had provided Stuart with a letter of introduction to George Washington, which enabled the relatively unknown artist to paint his first portrait of the president (see "The Portraits of George Washington"). Jay's name appears on Stuart's 1795 list of people wishing a portrait of Washington.

It is possible that Stuart did not complete the robes in the portrait. This could explain the rapidly painted, awkward areas of the robe along Jay's left shoulder and arm. In 1808, Peter Jay described the painting to his father as unfinished: "I have put up your portrait by Stuart which you were so kind as to give me. It is an excellent likeness but the unfinished state of the Drapery makes it look ill, & I wish to have that part compleated by some other painter. For that purpose I will be obliged to you, if you will be so good, as to bring with you when you next come to Rye, your Chief Justice's Robes."[11] If this is so, it was not the first time that Stuart left portraits of Jay unfinished. Ten years earlier, after Jay negotiated the Treaty of Paris, he was in London for several months and commissioned two portraits of himself from Stuart. One was intended as a gift for William Bingham (see cat. 53), Jay's host. Stuart left the portraits unfinished, pawning them when he went to Dublin three years later.[12] John Trumbull retrieved the portraits, probably when he accompanied Jay to London as his secretary in 1794. He completed both portraits, according to Unitarian minister Horace Holley, who saw one of the portraits at Trumbull's house in New York in 1818: "The John Jay, which Mr. Trumbull has, is the painting of himself and of Mr. Stewart. Mr. Trumbull bought it for ten guineas of a broker in London, who had it in pledge among many others. Mr. Stewart painted the head, and Mr. Trumbull the rest. It is nearly the whole length, a sitting figure. The face was painted in 1784. Mr. Jay had paid Mr. Stewart for two half lengths, but neither was finished till Mr. Trumbull found them at a broker's & gave twenty guineas for the two. Mr. Jay has the other one himself."[13] The portrait that Trumbull kept for himself depicts

32

Fig. 75. Cornelius Tiebout after Gilbert Stuart and John Trumbull, *John Jay*, 1795. Engraving, 12⅜ x 8¾ in (31.3 x 22.2 cm). National Portrait Gallery, Smithsonian Institution, Washington, D.C. (78.238)

Jay in a brown coat and a white waistcoat (fig. 73). Engraved by Asher B. Durand as by Stuart and Trumbull, it has always been recognized as the work of both painters.[14] The second portrait that Stuart began in 1784 also shows Jay seated (fig. 74), but he wears a black silk suit, and the arms are positioned differently. Horace Holley offers the only evidence that Trumbull had a role in completing the painting, which otherwise has always been attributed to Stuart.[15] The portrait was engraved in London by Cornelius Tiebout, an American artist studying with English engraver James Heath. The head-and-shoulders print (fig. 75), published in London on April 1, 1795, credits the portrait to "Gabriel Stuart," just as Heath would credit the full-length Lansdowne portrait of Washington a few years later (see cat. 45).

Jay probably brought this earlier portrait with him from London when he returned to New York in May 1795. Whether it was finished is unclear. That fall, when miniaturist Walter Robertson asked for a sitting for a portrait, Jay, recently elected governor of New York, wrote that he had two portraits of himself by Stuart which Robertson could copy, describing one as unfinished.[16] Robertson pursued the idea of a sitting, writing on April 15, 1796, that "he is very desirous of having his portrait for the purpose of being engraved as a companion to two prints of the President and Col. Hamilton. Mr. Robertson has already sketched the Governors features from an unfinished portrait of Mr. Stewart's, and now takes the liberty of requesting to know at what time his Excellency could make it convenient to honor him with a sitting."[17] His plan to make an engraving was not realized. In 1798, Tiebout, now returned to New York, made a similar request, distinguishing between the earlier portrait, which he had engraved in London, and the later portrait. Jay wrote his son Peter Augustus from Albany to arrange for Tiebout to borrow the portrait.[18] Again, the project did not result in an engraving.

Jay's final experience with Stuart was equally beset with problems. In 1801 the New York Common Council asked Jay to sit for his portrait. Although Stuart agreed to do the portrait, he delayed coming to New York, and Jay was requested to sit instead for John Vanderlyn.[19] A month later, Peter Augustus Jay wrote his father that Vanderlyn "is said to be one of the best portrait painters in the world—far superior to Stuart."[20] Ultimately, the full-length portrait was painted in 1805 by John Trumbull.[21] Jay's problematic dealings with Stuart over his portraits is ironic given his critical role in providing the artist with an introduction to Washington. Perhaps the only portrait of Washington by Stuart that he owned was "a Portrait of the late President engraved from a painting of Stewart," which was shipped to New York merchant William Constable in July 1797 with the portraits of Washington that Constable had commissioned (see cat. 47).[22] Jay thanked John Vaughan, who had shipped the portraits, writing that he was "much obliged by this Mark of your Brothers attention, as well by as your Care respecting it."[23] Jay's nephew Peter Jay Munro, who sat for the robes in this portrait, later acquired Stuart's full-length of Washington known as the Munro-Lenox portrait (cat. 49).

EGM

published in Richard B. Morris, ed., *John Jay, the Winning of the Peace: Unpublished Papers, 1780–1784* (New York: Harper and Row, 1980), pp. 696–97.

13. Horace Holley, visit of February 11, 1818, "A Journey from Boston in Massachusetts to Lexington in Kentucky, commenced February 3rd 1818 by Horace Holley," p. 50, Horace Holley Papers, William L. Clements Library, University of Michigan, Ann Arbor.

14. On this portrait, see Mason 1879, pp. 205–7; Park 1926, pp. 434–35, no. 436; Ide, *Portraits of John Jay,* p. 18, no. 3; Evans 1999, pp. 53, 139 n. 23. Some sources indicate that Jay's son Peter Augustus Jay sat for the figure so that Trumbull could complete this portrait.

15. Mason 1879, pp. 205–7; Park 1926, p. 437, no. 438; Ide, *Portraits of John Jay,* p. 12, no. 2; Clement E. Conger et al., *Treasures of State: Fine and Decorative Arts in the Diplomatic Reception Rooms of the U.S. Department of State* (New York: Harry N. Abrams, 1991), pp. 392–93. Park, who wrote that the portrait was "received by the family from Stuart on 5 December, 1794," was unaware of Holley's manuscript. Park also lists two replicas of this portrait, p. 438, nos. 439 (now owned by the Brook Club, New York) and 440 (John Jay Homestead State Historic Site, Katonah, N.Y.).

16. Jay, letter to Robertson, November 30, 1795, Jay Papers, no. 8952.

17. Jay Papers, no. 7076.

18. John Jay, letter to Peter Augustus Jay, April 16, 1798, Jay Papers, no. 7347.

19. John B. Coles, letter to John Jay, February 6, 1802, Jay Papers, no. 13018.

20. Peter Augustus Jay, letter to John Jay, March 8, 1802, Jay Papers, no. 6101.

21. Irma B. Jaffe, *John Trumbull, Patriot-Artist of the American Revolution* (Boston: New York Graphic Society, 1975), pp. 169–76.

22. Jay, letter to John Vaughan, July 31, 1797, Jay Papers website, no. 8169; also John Vaughan Papers, B/V 462, American Philosophical Society, Philadelphia. Constable had written Vaughan on July 25, 1797, on receiving the portraits, "The Pictures are safely landed & the Box for Govr. Jay sent him," "William & James Constable Account Book: 1797–1799" (labeled and inventoried as an account book, this is actually a letterbook), Constable-Pierrepont Family Papers, vol. 32, p. 244. Manuscripts and Archives Division, New York Public Library, Astor, Lenox and Tilden Foundations. A handwritten, annotated copy of Constable's letter is in the "Pierrepont Family, Papers relating to Gilbert Stuart's 'Portrait of George Washington,'" Brooklyn Museum Library Collection, New York.

23. Jay Papers, no. 8169.

33. MATILDA STOUGHTON DE JAUDENES Y NEBOT

1794
Oil on canvas, 50 5/8 x 39 1/2 in. (128.6 x 100.3 cm)
The Metropolitan Museum of Art, New York;
Rogers Fund, 1907 (07.76)

34. JOSEF DE JAUDENES Y NEBOT

1794
Oil on canvas, 50 5/8 x 39 1/2 in. (128.9 x 101.00 cm)
The Metropolitan Museum of Art, New York;
Rogers Fund, 1907 (07.75)

34

1. Albert Ten Eyck Gardner, "Fragment of a Lost Monument," *The Metropolitan Museum of Art Bulletin*, n.s. 6 (March 1948), p. 190.

2. On Jaudenes, see Enrique Fernández y Fernández, "Spain's Contribution to the Independence of the United States," *Review Interamericana* 10 (fall 1980), pp. 1–24; Enrique Fernández y Fernández, "Esboza biográfico de un ministro ilustrado, Diego de Gardoqui y Arriquibar (1735–1798)," *Hispania: Revista Española de Historia* 49 (May–August 1989), pp. 713–30.

During the early years of the American republic, aspiring diplomats hoped their involvement in its affairs would see their fortunes rise with those of the new nation. Josef de Jaudenes y Nebot was a minor Spanish official who intended to inflate his meager governmental commission into much more. Scholars have described him as a "dandy and spendthrift," a "swarthy Spanish provocateur," "arrogant," "slippery," "shifty," and even "cruel."[1] He married a girl who could advance his career, and he recognized the potential benefit of sitting for the nation's preeminent painter, an artist who could amplify his stature through visual clues and might get him closer to the president.

Born March 25, 1764, in Valencia, Josef was the son of Antonio de Jaudenes y Amat and Emilia Nebot.[2] He was dispatched to New York in May 1785 along with José Ignacio de Viar as assistant to the first Spanish minister plenipotentiary, Don Diego de

3. The paintings are not listed in Mason 1879; see Park 1926, pp. 432–34, nos. 434, 435.

4. So rare is this phenomenon in Stuart's oeuvre that in 1907, after the paintings were acquired by the Metropolitan Museum, they were deemed copies after lost Stuart originals; see John Caldwell and Oswaldo Rodriguez Roque, *American Paintings in The Metropolitan Museum of Art*, vol. 1, *A Catalogue of Works by Artists Born by 1815* (New York: Metropolitan Museum of Art, 1994), p. 169; Kenyon Cox, "Two Portraits by Stuart," *Bulletin of The Metropolitan Museum of Art* 11 (April 1907), pp. 64–69.

5. Washington, Providence 1967, p. 71.

6. Stuart's "list of gentlemen who are to have copies of the Portrait of the President of the United States," April 20, 1795; see "The Portraits of George Washington" below.

Gardoqui y Arriquibar. When Gardoqui returned to Spain in October 1790, Jaudenes and Viar became joint chargés d'affairs ad interim, and they moved to Philadelphia. Secretary of State Thomas Jefferson presented Jaudenes to President Washington in July 1791. Jaudenes conferred on matters pertaining to the territory of Spanish Louisiana, navigation on the Mississippi River, and trade rights, but continuing disagreements, with no compromise in sight, caused negotiations to be transferred to Madrid in 1795. Jaudenes, however, stayed in the United States with his American wife and with his sights set on becoming a permanent Spanish envoy to this country. He had wooed the daughter of the Spanish consul in Boston, John "Don Juan" Stoughton, and his wife, Esther Fletcher, a courtship that got him closer to the commanding figure in Spanish-American relations at the time. Jaudenes married sixteen-year-old Matilda Stoughton (1778–after 1822) in New York, her hometown, in the spring of 1794, and while there arranged with Stuart to have the union proclaimed in a pair of portraits.

Stuart took yet another opportunity in New York to display his talents, this time in response to a patron who required the trappings of ceremony and wealth.[3] Beneath the ostentatious gloss of these pictures, they are strikingly formulaic compositions, replete with proper iconography—his masculine ones, some papers, a walking stick, a sword; her feminine ones, an ivory fan, some little books, a portrait miniature. Both pictures find countless matches in the more rococo examples in Sir Joshua Reynolds's oeuvre. With quickly filled-in backgrounds, these compositions were not a challenge for Stuart's talents, and on this rare occasion he made the clothing and jewelry carry the character of his sitters.[4] The faces are vapid, and the context is literal rather than inspired, leaving the viewer to take inventory of the myriad effects Stuart could achieve with his brush. With a degree of technical resourcefulness and skill unknown in America, Stuart painted elaborate portraits for elaborate sitters, executing the costumes swiftly and likely without the sitters after having painted their heads in just the right complementary positions.

Jaudenes's dark blue velvet coat over scarlet waistcoat and breeches are resplendent with silver embroidery and buttons, an outfit that stood out in the United States as aristocratic and extraordinary. Hers has the same effect, an ensemble that is a billowing confection of silks, diamonds, and seed pearls, and her coronet-shaped headdress a none too subtle manifestation of her changed life. Her costume is not Spanish, but rather English embellished for sumptuous distinction. Such difference or otherness in dress was probably what the patrons had ordered from Stuart because it was how they dressed. At a party hosted by Mrs. John Jay, Margaret Manigault (see fig. 63) noticed that "Mr. and Mrs. Jaudenes were there, as fine as little dolls." And a year later, in Philadelphia, a guest at a dinner given by President Washington remarked that Mrs. Jaudenes was "brilliant with diamonds."[5]

Señora de Jaudenes's characterization in her portrait is difficult to assess because, with her elaborate coiffure, snowflake *piochas* (hairpins), and inordinately complicated gown, she is like a doll, dressed up and lovely to see. If she seems constrained and ill at ease in her costume, that has only added to the idea that her husband was wicked and conniving. By keeping up appearances and showing off his pretty young wife, Jaudenes kept up with his scheme, and from Stuart, who knew how pendant portraits worked, he purchased the means to display Matilda as his accoutrement, yet another adornment that could advance his career. When Stuart took orders for his portraits of Washington, Jaudenes placed his name second on the subscription list with a request for five pictures, no doubt planning to send them to political allies in Spain.[6] He also commissioned a full-length portrait of the president by Josef Perovani (fig. 106) and purchased for the

7. Gardner, "Fragment of a Lost Monument," p. 190.

8. The inscriptions on his portrait are, at upper right, the Jaudenes arms and *Don Josef de Jaudenes y Nebot / Comisario Ordenador de los / Reales Exercitos y Ministro Em / biado de su Magestad Catholi / ca Cerca de los Estados Unidos / de America. / Nació en la ciudad de Valen / cia Reyno de España el 25 de / Marzo de 1764*; at lower right, *G. Stuart, R.A., New York, Sept. 8, 1794.* The inscriptions on her portrait are, at upper left, the Stoughton arms and *Doña Matilde Stoughton / de Jaudenes. Esposa. / de Don Josef de Jaudenes. / y Nebot Comisario Ordena– / dor de Los Reales Exercitos / de Su Magestad Catholica / y su Ministro Embiado cerca / de los Estados Unidos de / America. / Nacio en la Ciudad de / Nueva-York en los Estados / Unidos el 11 Enero de / 1778*; at lower left, *G. Stuart, R.A., New York, Sept. 8, / 1794.*

large sum of $2,000 a lifesize marble bust of Washington from the Italian sculptor Giuseppe Cerrachi (The Metropolitan Museum of Art) as a gift for his Spanish mentor Manuel Godoy.[7] However, his political ambitions were crushed when, without his advance knowledge, Don Carlos María Martínez de Yrujo (see cat. 66) was appointed envoy extraordinaire and minister plenipotentiary. Jaudenes resigned his commission on April 25, 1796, and sailed for Spain, with his Stuart portraits, on July 24, 1796. He returned to his family's ancestral estate, a vineyard near Palma, Majorca. Jaudenes served as quartermaster for the Royal Armies and was created a knight of the order of Charles III on July 14, 1803.

Just how much stock Jaudenes put in his Stuart portraits can be gauged by the fact that they were further adorned with family crests and the false signature of the artist with R.A., for Royal Academician, inscriptions that tally the international score: the marriage of a Spanish man and an American woman, painted by an artist who had been accepted into the British system.[8]

CRB

Stuart in Philadelphia (1794–1803)

1. Edgar P. Richardson, "The Athens of America, 1800–1825," in Russell F. Weigley, ed., *Philadelphia: A 300-Year History* (New York: W. W. Norton and Co., 1982), p. 218. For Philadelphia in the years of Stuart's residence, see ibid., pp. 208–57; Richard G. Miller, "The Federal City, 1783–1800," in *Philadelphia*, pp. 155–207. On the decorative arts in Philadelphia at this time, see Beatrice B. Garvan, *Federal Philadelphia: The Athens of the Western World*, exh. cat. (Philadelphia: Philadelphia Museum of Art, 1987). Also useful is Robert J. Gough, "The Philadelphia Economic Elite at the End of the Eighteenth Century," in Catherine E. Hutchins, ed., *Shaping a National Culture: The Philadelphia Experience, 1750–1800* (Winterthur, Del.: Henry Francis du Pont Winterthur Museum, 1994), pp. 15–43.

2. Margaret L. Brown, "Mr. and Mrs. William Bingham of Philadelphia: Rulers of the Republican Court," *Pennsylvania Magazine of History and Biography* 61 (1937), p. 307, quoting Henry Wansey, *An Excursion to the United States of North America in the Summer of 1794*, 2nd ed. (Salisbury, Eng., 1798), p. 57.

Detail of cat. 37, *George Washington* (the Gibbs-Channing-Avery portrait)

Philadelphia in 1800 was the largest city in the United States, with a population of almost sixty-eight thousand.[1] English textile merchant Henry Wansey in 1794 compared it with other American and British cities: "Boston is the Bristol, New York the Liverpool, and Philadelphia the London of America."[2] This city of merchants was designed by its founder William Penn on a grid plan that ran from the Delaware River westward to the Schuylkill River. The central city in Stuart's day was on the Delaware River, where interstate and international shipping brought newcomers and goods from Europe and Asia. Philadelphia was the state capital from 1776 to 1799 and served as the meeting place of the Constitutional Convention of 1787 that established the structure of the new American federal government. More important for Stuart's career, Philadelphia served as the temporary capital of the United States from 1790 to 1800, before the federal government moved to the new city of Washington, on the Potomac River. Because of its importance as a trading center and its federal status, Philadelphia saw visitors as diverse as French planters from Santo Domingo and French nobility, including the duc d'Orléans, later King Louis-Philippe of France, fleeing the French Revolution and its aftermath; members of the state government and the federal Congress; European businessmen and investors; and representatives of foreign governments, including those representing Native Americans. The home of the Bank of North America, whose founders and officers included the wealthy city merchants Robert Morris, Thomas Fitzsimmons, Thomas Willing, and William Bingham (see cat. 53), the city was also the site of the new federal Bank of the United States, established in 1791. Not surprisingly, one major activity of these and other merchants was speculation in land and establishment of new cities and towns in Pennsylvania, as well as in New York, Maine, the District of Columbia, and Georgia.

Stuart went to Philadelphia in late November 1794 expressly to paint George Washington's portrait. To his uncle Philadelphia merchant Joseph Anthony (see fig. 76), whose business contacts included William Bingham, John Vaughan (see fig. 80), and Thomas Willing, all of whom had a role in Stuart's career, Stuart explained, "I should have been with you before this time had not a smart attack of the fever and Ague prevented me. Fortunately for me I feel so well recover'd as to [be] able to promise myself that pleasure while the weather is fine, perhaps in less than three weeks. The object of my journey is only to secure a picture of the President, & finish yours. My other engagements are such as totally precludes the Possibility of my encouraging the most Distant Idea that any other application

Fig. 76. *Joseph Anthony*, 1794. Oil on canvas, 36 x 28 in. (91.5 x 71 cm). National Gallery of Art, Washington, D.C.; Andrew W. Mellon Collection (1942.8.11)

3. Stuart, letter to Joseph Anthony, November 2, 1794 (original unlocated), photostat, Massachusetts Historical Society, Boston. The letter is quoted, with some changes in spelling and capitalization, in Whitley 1932, p. 93; Mount 1964, p. 183. The bank books of Joseph Anthony and Son for 1793–99 are in the Meredith Family Papers, Ms. 1509, Historical Society of Pennsylvania, Philadelphia.

4. Dunlap 1834, vol. I, p. 196.

5. Wolcott reported this to Connecticut poet John Trumbull; see draft of a letter from Wolcott to Trumbull, May 17, 1800, Papers of Oliver Wolcott Jr., vol. II, no. 48, Connecticut Historical Society, Hartford (quoted in cat. 49 below).

6. Eisen 1932, p. 7, places Stuart first at Fourth and Market Streets, and then at Tenth and Chestnut. Neither is confirmed by contemporary city directories. The second, probably an error for Fifth and Chestnut, is from Robert Gosman, "Biographical Sketch of John Vanderlyn, Artist" (manuscript, 1848–49), transcribed in Louise Hunt Averill, "John Vanderlyn, American Painter (1775–1852)" (Ph.D. diss., Yale University, 1949), pp. 292–338. On Vanderlyn's presence at Stuart's studio at that time, see cat. 35.

7. Charles Francis Jenkins, *Washington in Germantown* (Philadelphia: William J. Campbell, 1905), pp. 297–312, discusses Stuart in Germantown and illustrates the house and studio, which had been rebuilt as a one-story building after a fire and was torn down five years before he wrote.

8. Thomas Boylston Adams, letter to Abigail Adams, May 31, 1801, Adams Papers, Massachusetts Historical Society, quoted in Oliver 1967, p. 133. Adams had gone to Stuart's

can have any effect at present."[3] Sometime in 1795, Stuart painted his first portrait of Washington, known today as the Vaughan portrait type (see cat. 35). Its success and the commission of two additional, new portraits of Washington (cats. 39, 45) by Martha Washington and William Bingham brought high visibility and prominence to Stuart. Many of his other sitters in Philadelphia had close connections with the president and his wife, including Martha Washington's granddaughter Elizabeth Parke Custis Law (cat. 50) and Sarah Morton (cat. 60). Sitters also included national figures like John Adams and his wife, Abigail Adams (cats. 59, 58), in the city because of the federal government; international visitors like the vicomte de Noailles (cat. 54) and Samuel Gatliff (cat. 56), drawn by political or economic opportunities; and local citizenry like Quaker merchant Edward Penington and his wife (cats. 62, 63), his niece Ann (cat. 64), and the members of the Willing family, including Mary Clymer (cat. 52) and her sister the illustrious Anne Bingham (cat. 51). Some of them also bought a portrait of Washington. William Dunlap's comment about Stuart's work is very appropriate for the Philadelphia years: "He left us the features of those who have achieved immortality for themselves, and made known others who would but for his art have slept in their merited obscurity."[4]

With the exception of the lifesize full-length portraits of George Washington (see cats. 45–47), Stuart's portraits in Philadelphia most often were painted on canvas measuring about 30 by 25 inches, a standard English canvas size known in the eighteenth century as a "three-quarter length." Stuart used this size, his smallest, to show figures to the waist, with one or two hands visible, often occupied in some activity such as writing or holding a book. In Philadelphia he rarely made use of the 36-by-28-inch kit-cat canvas (one example is his portrait of his uncle Joseph Anthony) or the 50-by-40-inch half-length format, both of which he had used very effectively for portraits painted in Britain and New York. This suggests that he was making smaller paintings in order to complete more commissions, in addition to trying to fill the demand for replicas of his portraits of Washington. Despite the smaller format, however, his characterizations continued to be inventive and individualistic, and he seems to have succeeded in representing the individual personalities of those who sat for him. Also in Philadelphia, Stuart began to use wood panels instead of canvas, probably beginning in 1800 with his portrait of Horace Binney (fig. 77). He told Oliver Wolcott Jr. that wood panels were particularly valuable in warmer climates for portraits that would hang in public places.[5]

Stuart seems to have established his first Philadelphia home and studio in a house owned by William Moore Smith, a lawyer and the son of Dr. William Smith (see cat. 61), on the southeast corner of Fifth and Chestnut Streets, a half-block from the State House (now Independence Hall). George Washington had at least one sitting for the so-called Lansdowne portrait (see cat. 45) at this house, on April 12, 1796. When writing to confirm the appointment, in a note addressed to "Mr. Stuart, Chesnut Street," Washington described the residence as "your own house."[6] Stuart's family had joined him by this time; his wife's description of Washington as he arrived for a sitting was later recorded by their daughter Jane (see cat. 45). In the summer of 1796 Stuart moved his home and studio to

Fig. 77. *Horace Binney*, 1800. Oil on wood, 29 x 23¾ in. (73.5 x 60.5 cm). National Gallery of Art, Washington, D.C.; Gift of Horace Binney (1944.3.1)

Germantown house to rescue Abigail Adams's portrait from a sheriff's sale of Stuart's property (see cats. 58, 59).

9. Robert Gilmor Jr., *Memorandums Made in a Tour to the Eastern States in the Year 1797* (Boston: Trustees of the Boston Public Library, 1892), p. 6.

10. Dunlap 1834, vol. 1, p. 206.

11. William R. Smith, letter to John A. McAllister, Mineral Point, [Pa.?], November 24, 1858, McAllister Manuscripts, Library Company of Philadelphia. Mount (1964, p. 219), says that Stuart and his family stayed at Smith's during the yellow fever epidemic in the late summer of 1797.

12. Stuart, letter addressed "Dear Sir," February 16, 1801, Gratz Collection, Historical Society of Pennsylvania. The letter, concerning payment for the portrait of George Washington commissioned by the State of Connecticut, is quoted in Morgan and Fielding 1931, pp. 268–69. The recipient has been identified in the past as Jonathan Trumbull, a member of the committee that commissioned the portrait. However, because the rest of the correspondence was with Oliver Wolcott Jr., another member of the committee, this letter was also undoubtedly written to Wolcott. See Ellen G. Miles, "'Memorials of great & good men who were my friends': Portraits in the Life of Oliver Wolcott, Jr.," *Proceedings of the American Antiquarian Society* 107, pt. 1 (1998), esp. pp. 118–22.

13. About the farm, see Evans 1999, p. 89.

14. Sally McKean Yrujo, letter to "Mr. Stewart," December 4, 1801, Society Collection, Historical Society of Pennsylvania. The identity of the writer and the subject of the letter identify the recipient as Gilbert Stuart.

15. James Robinson, *The Philadelphia Directory, City and County Register, for 1802* (Philadelphia, 1801), p. 232.

Germantown, north of Philadelphia, to escape the large number of visitors who came to see his work.[7] There he leased a house with a stable, whose second floor became his studio or "painting room," as described by Thomas Boylston Adams in 1801.[8] George and Martha Washington visited Stuart there in January 1797, at the end of the president's second term of office, at which time he reportedly gave the artist permission to keep their unfinished portraits (see cats. 38, 39) in order to make replicas. Another visitor, in July 1797, was Robert Gilmor Jr. of Baltimore, who called on Stuart in Germantown to see the version of the Lansdowne portrait painted for William Bingham (see cat. 46). "Stewart . . . received us in the most welcome manner, offered us refreshments and conducting us to his painting room which he had fitted up in his stable."[9] And it was from the window of this second-floor studio that Stuart threatened to throw artist William Winstanley when he came with his proposal that Stuart give "the last touch" to the copies of the Lansdowne that Winstanley had painted (see cat. 47).

Another reason for moving to Germantown was the danger of contracting yellow fever in the city in the late summer and fall. The first epidemic in Philadelphia had occurred in August 1793. In early September 1797, because of the danger of illness in the city, members of the Willing family joined their in-law William Bingham at his country house, Lansdown, where they were painted by Stuart (see cats. 51, 52). In 1798, engraver David Edwin and miniaturist Benjamin Trott were Stuart's neighbors "near the Falls of the Schuylkill" during that summer's epidemic.[10] This suggests that Stuart's association with Dr. William Smith had begun by this time, for when Stuart was painting the portrait of Smith, in 1801 or 1802, he "resided in Dr Smith's old mansion on the Hill opposite the Falls," near the Schuylkill River, according to Smith's grandson.[11] It was after seeing Stuart at Smith's home in the summer of 1802 that Dr. Benjamin Rush proposed that Stuart paint "a gallery of portraits of sick people labouring under such diseases as shew themselves in the features, and countenance" as an aide in the study of medicine (see cat. 61). In the meantime, Stuart had begun making payments on a farm in Pottsgrove, Pennsylvania, stocking it with Durham cows. He referred in February 1801 to this "small farm for my family," for which payment was due on March first.[12] He lost the whole investment of $3,442 when the seller died and there was no written evidence that Stuart had made payments.[13] By late 1801, Stuart again had a studio in Philadelphia. Sally McKean Yrujo addressed him as "Mr. Stewart. Front Street" on December 4, 1801, when she asked to postpone a sitting.[14] He is listed as "Charles G. Stewart, portrait painter" at 392 North Front Street in a city directory for 1802, which was published in 1801.[15]

Numerous other artists flocked to Philadelphia in the 1790s, no doubt because of its mercantile and political importance. The organizational skills of Charles Willson Peale, the most talented of them, brought the first permanent museum into being and also the first artists' society. Peale's museum featured natural science, art, and history displays, including his important gallery of portraits "of celebrated Personages." Artists in the city in the 1790s included Americans John Trumbull, returning from Europe with new plans for his history paintings, as well as Edward Savage and Benjamin Trott. European artists included Giuseppe Ceracchi, Adolph Ulrich Wertmüller, John James Barralet, David Edwin,

16. On artists in Philadelphia in this decade, see especially *Philadelphia: Three Centuries of American Art*, exh. cat. (Philadelphia: Philadelphia Museum of Art, 1976), pp. 149–91.

17. On the Columbianum, see Lillian B. Miller, ed., *The Selected Papers of Charles Willson Peale and His Family* (New Haven: Yale University Press, 1983–), vol. 2, pp. 101–13.

18. Walter Robertson, as chairman of the Columbianum, letter to Benjamin Rush, February 4, 1795, Benjamin Rush Papers, Historical Society of Pennsylvania, Philadelphia, courtesy of Brandon Fortune.

19. Stuart's letter, unlocated today, is quoted in Mason 1879, p. 28.

20. "Minutes of the Proceedings of the President & Directors of the Pennsylvania Academy of the Fine Arts," meetings of October 8, 1807, and March 15, 1812, pp. 15, 44, Archives of the Pennsylvania Academy of the Fine Arts, Philadelphia; microfilm, Archives of American Art, Smithsonian Institution, Washington, D.C.

21. The complex world of interlocking businesses in London in the 1780s is described in Marcia Pointon, *Hanging the Head: Portraiture and Social Formation in Eighteenth-Century England* (New Haven: Yale University Press, 1993), pp. 36–52.

22. On this court case, see Evans 1999, pp. 86, 148–49 n. 20.

23. Eliza Cope Harrison, ed., *Philadelphia Merchant: The Diary of Thomas P. Cope, 1800–1851* (South Bend, Ind.: Gateway Editions, 1978), p. 124, entry dated June 10, 1802.

James Sharples, C. B. J. Févret de Saint-Mémin, and Walter Robertson, with whom Stuart had traveled from Dublin. Many came to the United States with an interest in republican government, an admiration for George Washington, and, of course, a hope for important commissions.[16] In January 1795, a group of these artists, including Peale, Robertson, landscapist William Birch, and architect Samuel Blodget Jr. (who later assisted Stuart in the design of the backgrounds of his Lansdowne portrait of Washington and his portrait of William Smith) founded the short-lived Association of Artists in America. The group planned to establish a school of the arts, which they called the Columbianum, or American Academy of the Fine Arts.[17] Appointments to its faculty included Dr. Benjamin Rush as Professor of the Theory and Practice of Pictorial Physiognomy.[18] However, their ranks split over the issue of governance, with Peale's group favoring a democratic model, and a second group, described as "eight foreigners" in the account in the *Aurora* (February 26, 1795), envisioning a hierarchical model like the royal academies of Europe. After the split, the group that was led by Peale held an exhibition of their work in May at the State House. Stuart was elected a member of the academy shortly before this exhibition, writing the members in thanks on May 9, "It is particularly flattering to me to be thought worthy of choice in any society among my countrymen, but more especially when that society is formed of artists."[19] Although the Columbianum failed, the idea led to the establishment of the Pennsylvania Academy of the Fine Arts in 1805. Stuart became an honorary member in 1807, and in 1812 he was elected a Pennsylvania Academician along with other notable artists, including Charles Willson Peale, Thomas Sully, Benjamin West, and Washington Allston.[20]

Despite this activity, the city could not offer Stuart a setting like the one he had known in London, with its public exhibitions, framers, engravers, printsellers, and avid patrons of the arts.[21] And federal America was not always sympathetic to Stuart's assumptions about the artist and his status in society. For example, he struggled to protect his copyright of the Washington portraits, arguing first with William Bingham about James Heath's engraving of the Lansdowne portrait, and then with John E. Sword, whose Cantonese copies of the Athenaeum portrait, made as reverse paintings on glass and sold in the city, led to a lawsuit and a court victory for Stuart in 1802.[22] Descriptions of Stuart emphasize his artistic gifts, his storytelling, and his unreliability. For instance, merchant Thomas Pym Cope described Stuart in June 1802: "His countenance bespeaks a nervous, versatile mind. Like many other men of preeminent genius, he is his worst foe. His passions are impetuous, nor does he appear very regardful to control them. His conversation was lively, vehement & free."[23] By this time, Stuart was considering a move to the new federal capital, Washington, D.C. After an exploratory visit in August 1802, he transferred his portrait-painting business there in December 1803.

EGM

The Portraits of George Washington

Stuart returned to America in March 1793 with the intention of painting a portrait of George Washington.[1] After spending a year and a half in New York, he went to Philadelphia in November 1794, taking a letter of introduction to the president from John Jay (see cat. 32).[2] On November 15, Jay's wife wrote to him that "in ten days hence [Stuart] is to go to Philadelphia, to take a likeness of the President."[3] According to William Dunlap, "Soon after his arrival in Philadelphia, Mr. Stuart called on the president, and left Mr. Jay's letter and his own card. Some short time after, . . . he found a note from Mr. Dandridge, the private secretary, inviting him to pass that evening with the president. He went accordingly."[4]

On April 20, 1795, Stuart compiled a list of the names of thirty-two men who had commissioned a total of thirty-nine portraits of President Washington. The presence of English and New York patrons, including the Marquis of Lansdowne, Viscount Cremorne, Benjamin West, John Jay, and Aaron Burr, suggests that Stuart already had some commissions for portraits of Washington before he went to Philadelphia to arrange sittings with the president. The names with some payments are noted on "A list of gentlemen who are to have copies of the Portrait of the President of the United States":[5]

J. Wharton, Esq.	1	Mr. Crammond	2
Don Jos. DeJaudennes	5	Mr. T. Barrow, N.Y.	1
Marquis of Lansdowne	1	John Craig, Esq. 100	1
Lord Viscount Cremorne	1	John Stoughton, Esq.	1
B. West, Esq., P.R.A.	1	Kearney Wharton	1
Mess. Pollock, N.Y. 100	2	Casaubon, Esq. 153 M.I.	1
I. Vaughan, Esq. 200	2	Meredith, Esq.	1
Col. Burr, N.Y. 100	1	Blodget, Esq.	1
——Mead, Esq.	1	I. Swan, Esq	1
Greenleaf, Esq. 100	1	Smith, Esq., S.C.	1
Wm. Hamilton, Esq.	1	Crammond, Esq.	1
Mr. Chief Justice Jay	1	Doctor Stevens	1
Col. Read	1	Scott, Esq., Lancaster	1
Mr. Holmes, 100	1	Grant, Esq. Susqueha'a	1
Mr. Fitzsimons, 100	1	Will'm Ludwell Lee	
Mr. Necklin	1	Greenspring, Va.	1
Gen. Lee	1		

Stuart's portraits of Washington were a success from the start. He painted three distinct portraits from life, the so-called Vaughan (waist-length, right side of face; see cat. 35), Athenaeum (left side of face; cat. 39), and Lansdowne (full-length, left side of face; cat. 45) portraits,[6] and made numerous replicas of them (see cats. 36, 37, 40–44, 46, 47). During his entire career, Stuart painted at least one hundred versions of the different compositions, most of them based on the unfinished Athenaeum portrait. With these portraits, as with those of less famous sitters, he employed his expert method of capturing individual likeness, which was based on a talent for bringing out each sitter's personality through conversation and on his close observation of the face. And he infused each portrait with his belief in theories of physiognomy and his study of anatomy.

1. Dorinda Evans (1999, pp. 60–73) includes a very thorough accounting of Stuart's portraits of Washington. The most complete cataloguing of the individual portraits can be found in Park 1926, pp. 845–94, nos. 1–111 (based closely on Fielding 1923); Morgan and Fielding 1931, pp. 211–361, nos. 1–106; Eisen 1932, list not numbered but very inclusive. Morgan and Fielding list an additional sixty-nine portraits by Washington attributed to Stuart and forty-nine copies by known artists. Critical early writings about Stuart's portraits of Washington are Dunlap 1834, vol. 1, pp. 197–206; J. Stuart 1876. Adam Greenhalgh's documentation of Stuart's portraits of Washington has been very helpful in this research.

2. Dunlap 1834, vol. 1, p. 196; J. Stuart 1876, p. 369. The letter has never been located or published.

3. Sarah Livingston Jay, letter to John Jay in London, November 15, 1794, quoted in Mason 1879, p. 206; Whitley 1932, p. 92; Mount 1964, p. 184. These authors did not identify their source, the letter is unlocated, and it is not reproduced on the Web site of the John Jay Papers, Rare Book and Manuscript Library, Columbia University, New York, http://www.columbia.edu/cu/lweb/eresources/archives/jay.

4. Dunlap 1834, vol. 1, p. 197, recording information "from the artist to whom Stuart related the circumstance"; J. Stuart 1876, p. 369.

5. J. Stuart 1876, p. 373, and published frequently in sources about Stuart and his portraits of Washington.

6. Mason (1879, pp. 89–90) and Elizabeth Bryant Johnston (*Original Portraits of Washington including Statues, Monuments, and Medals* [Boston: James R. Osgood and Co., 1882], pp. 80, 83, 84) appear to be the first writers to refer to all three life portraits by the terms "Vaughan," "Athenaeum," and "Lansdowne," although earlier writers, including Henry T. Tuckerman (*The Character and Portraits of Washington* [New York: G. P. Putnam, 1859], pp. 53–58), had referred to the Athenaeum and the Lansdowne life portraits by the names of the owners.

Fig. 78. *George Washington*, 1795. Oil on canvas, 29¼ x 24 in. (74.3 x 60.9 cm). The Frick Collection, New York

7. *The Frick Collection: An Illustrated Catalogue*, vol. 1, *Paintings* (New York: Frick Collection, 1968), pp. 3–4.

8. Mount 1964, p. 188; Eisen 1932, p. 8; Mason 1879, p. 26, respectively.

9. The letter, owned by the Earl of Rosebery, is on long-term loan to the National Portrait Gallery, Washington, D.C.; see note 19 below.

Stuart's first life portrait of Washington, representing him turned to the viewer's right, no longer survives; it may have resembled most closely the early replica in the Frick Collection (fig. 78).[7] The version that was identified from the 1850s until recently as the life portrait, known as the Vaughan portrait after its first owner (see cat. 35), has given this name to its replicas. Because few copies or engravings were made of this composition, it is less familiar than the other portraits. Modern writers suggest three sites for the sittings, but there is no evidence supporting any particular one: Washington's own house, the State House (now known as Independence Hall), and the house of William Moore Smith, where the only documented sitting for the Lansdowne portrait took place the following year, on April 12, 1796.[8] The date of a sitting for the first portrait is equally uncertain. A note added by Stuart to a letter of April 11, 1796, to him from George Washington to arrange for sittings for the Lansdowne portrait says that the first portrait was painted "in ye winter season."[9] Jane Stuart, the artist's daughter, who was born in 1812 and was thus was not an eyewitness, wrote that it was painted "toward the spring of 1795."[10] Washington was in Philadelphia during that winter and early spring.[11] In this scenario, the list of commissions would postdate the sittings.

Rembrandt Peale gave a different date for the sittings for the first portrait and a different narrative, however, changing some details as he repeated it over a twenty-five-year period. He summed up his memory of events in his 1850s lecture "Portraits of Washington." Describing his own sittings with Washington "in the Autumn of 1795," Peale said, "[Washington] could not sit the next day—Mrs. Washington informing me that he was engaged to sit to Mr. Stuart, an Artist from Dublin, who had just come from New York for the purpose."[12] This version appears to agree with a story published by William Dunlap in 1834, although Dunlap indicated that Stuart had already had a sitting.[13] The sittings for the Peales probably took place after Washington's return on October 20, 1795, from Mount Vernon, where he had gone on September 8. He remained in Philadelphia through the winter and spring, until June 13, 1796.[14] Rembrandt Peale and his brother Raphaelle left for Charleston, South Carolina, in November, and there on December 3, they advertised an exhibition of portraits that included "a Portrait of the President of the United States painted the first of last month being the last which has been taken from that distinguished Patriot."[15] Stuart's first portrait of Washington is very similar to the ones painted by Rembrandt Peale and his father, Charles Willson Peale, at these sittings.[16] They show Washington with a long, oval face, the same oval face seen in portraits painted a year earlier, in the fall of 1794, by Swedish painter Adolph Ulrich Wertmüller (Philadelphia Museum of Art) and Irish miniaturist Walter Robertson (versions at Tudor Place Foundation, Washington, D.C., and at Mount Vernon).

When Stuart painted Washington in 1795, the president was sixty-three years old and in the middle of his second term of office. Stuart subscribed to prevailing theories about physiognomy, which held that a study of the outward body could reveal a person's inner qualities, or character, and in the portrait, he sought to depict Washington so that his character would be successfully conveyed to viewers. Dunlap wrote of Stuart's difficulties in representing Washington's mind, or, we might say, personality:

Stuart has said that he found more difficulty attending the attempt to express the character of Washington on his canvas than in any of his efforts before or since. It is known that by his colloquial powers, he could draw out the minds of his sitters upon that surface he was tasked to represent; and such was always his aim. But Washington's mind was busied within. During the sitting for the first mentioned portrait [Vaughan], Stuart could not find a subject, although he tried many, that could elicit the expression he knew must accord with such features and such a man. He was more fortunate in the second attempt, and probably not only had more self-possession, but had inspired his sitter with more confidence in him, and a greater disposition to familiar conversation.[17]

Stuart made between twelve and sixteen replicas of this first image[18] and abandoned it after he received commissions to paint new portraits of Washington (cats. 39 [Athenaeum portrait], 45 [Lansdowne portrait]). The fate of the original is indicated in the note Stuart added to his letter of April 11, 1796, from Washington, when he sent it to Samuel Williams, an American merchant in London, then the owner of the Lansdowne portrait. Stuart dictated the note to Williams's brother: "In looking over my papers to find one that had the Signature of Geo. Washington, I found this asking me when he should sit for his portrait, which is now owned by Samuel Williams of London, I have thought it proper it should be his especially as he owns the only original painting I ever made of

10. J. Stuart 1876, p. 369.

11. On October 28, 1794, he returned to Philadelphia from the military expedition to western Pennsylvania organized to quell the Whiskey Rebellion and stayed until he went to Mount Vernon on April 14, 1795. He returned again on May 2 and remained until July 15, when he again went home to Virginia, traveling back on August 11. See James Thomas Flexner, *George Washington: Anguish and Farewell (1793–1799)* (Boston: Little, Brown and Co., 1972), pp. 183, 208, 216, 221.

12. "Rembrandt Peale's Lecture on Washington and His Portraits," Eisen 1932, pp. 308–9; the full lecture is transcribed on pp. 297–323, from a copy made in 1865 by Harriet Cany Peale, the artist's wife, from Peale's manuscript of 1858. Peale gave the same information in a letter to Charles Edwards Lester, March 16, 1846, Charles Henry Hart Autograph Collection, Archives of American Art, Smithsonian Institution, Washington, D.C.

13. Dunlap 1834, vol. 1, p. 206.

14. Donald Jackson and Dorothy Twohig, eds., *The Diaries of George Washington* (Charlottesville: University Press of Virginia, 1976–79), vol. 6, pp. 208–27.

15. Lillian B. Miller, ed., *The Selected Papers of Charles Willson Peale and His Family* (New Haven: Yale University Press, 1983–), vol. 2, p. 132.

16. See Lillian B. Miller, *In Pursuit of Fame: Rembrandt Peale, 1778–1860*, exh. cat. (Washington, D.C.: National Portrait Gallery, Smithsonian Institution, in association with the University of Washington Press, Seattle, 1992), pp. 32–33.

17. Dunlap 1834, vol. 1, p. 197–98.

18. Fielding 1923, pp. 113–28, lists fourteen examples; Park 1926, pp. 845–53, lists Fielding's fourteen as nos. 1–14, and adds two; Morgan and Fielding 1931, pp. 250–59, list the same sixteen as Park; Eisen 1932, pp. 39–48, also lists those sixteen. I have not closely examined all of them. At least twelve of these are sound attributions. Two Vaughan portraits not mentioned in these sources are a portrait at the Homeland Foundation, Amenia, N.Y., and a portrait in a New York private collection, which was on loan to the National Portrait Gallery, Washington, in 1977–85, when it was in the collection of J. William Middendorf.

19. George Washington, letter to Gilbert Stuart, "Monday Evening 11th Apl 1796," collection of the Earl of Rosebery; the letter is on long-term loan to the National Portrait Gallery, Washington. It was first published in 1833 in the *New York Post*, according to [Henry T. Tuckerman], "Original Portraits of Washington," *Putnam's Monthly Magazine of American Literature, Science and Art* 6 (October 1855), p. 346. It is reproduced in Eisen 1932, p. 59, pl. 5; Morgan and Fielding 1931, pp. 358–59; *George Washington* 2002, p. 45.

20. Evans (1999, p. 141 n. 4) points out that later that year, Stuart told Henry Pickering (1817 [October 29]) the same information.

21. Dunlap 1834, vol. 1, p. 197.

22. J. Stuart 1876, p. 369.

Washington except one I own myself [the Athenaeum portrait]. I painted a third but rubbed it out. I now present this to his Brother Timo. Williams, for sd. Samuel. Boston 9th Day March 1823. G. Stuart." Timothy Williams added, "N.B. Mr. Stuart painted in ye winter season, his first portrait of Washington, but destroyed it. The next portrait was ye one now owned by S. Williams; the third Mr. S. now has—two only remain as above stated."[19] The statement that there were only two surviving life portraits of Washington had already appeared in an article titled "Stuart's Picture of Washington," in the *Boston Intelligencer, and Morning and Evening Advertiser* on August 2, 1817.[20] According to Dunlap, writing about the first portrait, "Not satisfied with the expression, [Stuart] destroyed it, and the president consented to sit again."[21] And Jane Stuart later wrote that Stuart's "admiration and respect were so great, that he could not feel at ease in his presence, and he ultimately erased this picture."[22]

EGM

35. George Washington (The Vaughan Portrait)

1795

Oil on canvas, 28³/₄ x 23³/₄ in. (73 x 60.5 cm)
National Gallery of Art, Washington, D.C.;
Andrew W. Mellon Collection (1942.8.27)

1. Annotation to a letter to Stuart from George Washington, April 11, 1796, concerning a sitting for the Lansdowne portrait, dictated by Stuart in 1823 before he sent the letter to the then owner of that painting. The letter is in the collection of the Earl of Rosebery, on long-term loan to the National Portrait Gallery, Washington.

2. Morgan and Fielding 1931, p. 229; summary of their identification of the painting as the life portrait, pp. 229–35; catalogued as their "Vaughan Type" no. 1, p. 250; documentary evidence for the identification, pp. 347–52. In their opinion, while that evidence is inconclusive, no other version is a better candidate for the life portrait. On the present portrait, see also Fielding 1923, p. 114, no. 1; Park 1926, p. 845, no. 1; Eisen 1932, p. 39; Mount 1964, pp. 186–95; Miles 1995, pp. 201–6; Evans 1999, pp. 60–61, 63. All sources except Miles 1995 identify this portrait as the life portrait.

3. Rembrandt Peale, letter to Charles Edwards Lester, March 16, 1846, Charles Henry Hart Autograph Collection, Archives of American Art, Smithsonian Institution, Washington, D.C. He repeated this in his lecture "Washington and His Portraits," reprinted in Eisen 1932, p. 311.

4. The copy (New York Public Library) is inscribed *R. Peale from Stuart's first Portrait.* Peale wrote Harrison on February 16, 1859 (archives of the National Gallery of Art, Washington), that the

Scholars have struggled over the issue of the life version and replicas of Stuart's first portrait of President George Washington, the so-called Vaughan type looking to the right, particularly because Stuart himself in 1823 described the Lansdowne portrait (cat. 45) as "the only original painting I ever made of Washington except one I own myself [the Athenaeum portrait, cat. 39]. I painted a third but rubbed it out."[1] In the 1850s, the present painting at the National Gallery of Art, a replica of Stuart's first portrait, was identified as the life portrait. According to John Hill Morgan and Mantle Fielding, "the claim rests largely on letters and statements of the artist, Rembrandt Peale."[2] Peale had said that Stuart made only five copies of this first portrait before selling the original to English landscape painter William Winstanley, "who took it to England."[3] After Philadelphia collector Joseph Harrison purchased the portrait and brought it back from England, Peale borrowed it to make a copy for his lectures on portraits of Washington.[4] Although Winstanley did own a version of the Vaughan portrait and made copies of it,[5] we now know that the Vaughan portrait at the National Gallery is a replica, acquired by its first owner from Stuart in 1795.

The painting, by its provenance, is identifiable with one of the two commissioned by Philadelphia merchant John Vaughan, who is on Stuart's 1795 "list of gentlemen who are to have copies of the Portrait of the President of the United States" as "I. Vaughan, Esq. 200 2," indicating that he paid $200 for two copies. About this time, Stuart also painted a portrait of Vaughan (fig. 80). Vaughan sent the portrait of Washington to his father, Samuel Vaughan, a merchant in London. Engraved in 1796 (fig. 81), it was included in volume 3 of the translation from the French of Johann Caspar Lavater's Essays on Physiognomy, Designed to Promote the Knowledge and the Love of Mankind, published in London in 1798.[6] The essays present Lavater's theories about the analysis of a person's character and personality from study of the shape of the face and its individual features. The engraving of Stuart's Washington is inscribed "Engraved by T. Holloway

Fig. 79. Robert Field after Gilbert Stuart, *George Washington*, ca. 1800. Watercolor on ivory, 3⅛ x 2⁷⁄₁₆ in. (7.9 x 6.2 cm). The Metropolitan Museum of Art, New York; Bequest of Charles Allen Munn, 1924 (24.109.90)

portrait was the "first Original portrait painted by Stuart in September 1795, at the same time that Washington sat to me," and suggested that after taking it to England, Winstanley "doubtless sold it to Wm. Vaughan, from whose Nephew you bought it." See Miles 1995, p. 202.

5. Winstanley took Stuart's painting to Washington, D.C., according to Anna Maria Thornton; "Diary of Mrs. William Thornton, 1800–1863," *Records of the Columbia Historical Society* (Washington) 10 (1907), p. 163 (July 5, 1800). A watercolor-on-ivory miniature copy of Winstanley's Stuart by Robert Field (fig. 79) shows that it was indeed a version of the Vaughan type; on Field's copies, see Harry Piers, *Robert Field: Portrait Painter in Oils, Miniature and Water-Colours and Engraver* (New York: Frederic Fairchild Sherman, 1927), pp. 157–66. According to Mrs. Thornton ("Diary of Mrs. William Thornton," pp. 214, 217–18), on November 24 the miniaturist borrowed "of Mr Winstanley Genl Washington's picture by Stewart to copy in Miniature." Martha Washington gave this miniature to Tobias Lear, Washington's private secretary, according to its former owner Charles A. Munn (1908, p. 60, facing illus.). Winstanley's example of Stuart's Vaughan is not located, and while several Vaughan-style portraits of Washington have been attributed to Winstanley, none is firmly documented.

6. Wick 1982, pp. 58–59.

7. Johann Caspar Lavater, *Essays on Physiognomy, Designed to Promote the Knowledge and the Love of Mankind*, translated from the French edition of the German original by Henry Hunter (London: Printed for John Murray, Henry Hunter, and Thomas Holloway, 1789–98), vol. 3, pp. 435–36.

from a Picture painted by Mr. Stuart in 1795 in the possession of Samuel Vaughan Esqr. Published as the act directs by T. Holloway and the other Proprietors Novr. 2, 1796."

In the French edition, Lavater discussed two engravings of portraits of Washington after paintings by Charles Willson Peale and on them based his analysis of Washington's physiognomy. They are also included in the English edition. Lavater mentioned his "distrust in the resemblance of engraved portraits; and I believe I have likewise said, that I consider the images of illustrious men, in general, nearly as so many caricatures. I do not know the person meant to be represented in this Print, but he has performed great atchievements, atchievements which excite astonishment . . . is it possible to withhold the character of greatness from the man who impresses this character on his actions? . . . [W]ould not the Physiognomist be eager to know the features of him, whom Providence selected as the instrument of effecting a revolution so memorable?" Lavater, although he knew Washington only by his reputation, concluded his analysis of the portraits, "Every thing in this face announces the good man, a man upright, of simple manners, sincere, firm, reflecting and generous."[7] While these words are a reading of Peale's images, not of Stuart's, in the English edition Stuart's portrait would have been seen in this context.[8]

Stuart most likely intended this portrait of Washington to be engraved for this English edition of Lavater's *Essays*. The subscribers to this translation included several people closely associated with Stuart:[9] John Vaughan, Benjamin West (see cat. 12), Dr. William Cruikshank, James Heath (see fig. 35), John Hall (see cat. 11), William Sharp, John Boydell (see "The Boydell Pictures" and cats. 10–14), Luke White of Dublin, whose portrait Stuart painted while there (fig. 47), as well as Henry Fuseli, who wrote the preface to the English edition of the first volume and coordinated the engravings for the publication.[10] Dorinda Evans has pointed out that Stuart's interest in physiognomy is indicated by "the language that he used in discussing Washington's appearance," which is "decidedly Lavateresque."[11] For example, Isaac Weld Jr., an Englishman traveling in America and Canada in 1795–97, recorded:

Mr. Stewart, the eminent portrait painter, told me, that there are features in his [Washington's] face totally different from what he ever observed in that of any other human being; the sockets of the eyes, for instance, are larger than what he ever met with before, and the upper part of the nose broader. All his features, he observed, were indicative of the strongest and most ungovernable passions, and had he been born in the forests, it was his opinion that he would have been the fiercest man amongst the savage tribes. In this Mr. Stewart has given a proof of his great discernment and intimate knowledge of the human countenance; for although General Washington has been extolled for his great moderation and calmness, during the very trying situations in which he has so often been placed, yet those who have been acquainted with him the longest and most intimately, say, that he is by nature a man of a fierce and irritable disposition, but that, like Socrates, his judgment and great self-command have always made him appear a man of a different cast in the eyes of the world.[12]

If Stuart intended the Vaughan portrait for the Lavater publication, this would explain the special care he used in painting the face, while treating the shirt ruffle with less attention than in his other replicas of the portrait. Washington's face in this example has a masklike treatment and is painted with a considerable amount of white pigment that is visible particularly in the X-ray (fig. 82). Details are carefully added on the surface with thin, dark lines below the mouth and around the eyes. The red tones of the back-

35

Fig. 80. *John Vaughan*, ca. 1795. Oil on canvas, 30⅛ x 25¼ in. (76.5 x 64.1 cm). The Bayou Bend Collection of the Museum of Fine Arts, Houston (B.61.55)

Fig. 81. Thomas Holloway after Gilbert Stuart, *George Washington*, 1796. Engraving, 9 x 7¾ in. (23 x 19.7 cm). National Portrait Gallery, Smithsonian Institution, Washington, D.C. (NPG.79.139)

Fig. 82. X-ray of cat 35

8. Egon Verheyen and Dorinda Evans assumed that the comparison included the engraving of Stuart's portrait, but if the text is a translation from the French edition, as stated in the publication, this would not be possible; see Verheyen 1989, pp. 134–36; Evans 1999, p. 66.

9. Lavater, *Essays on Physiognomy*, vol. 1, "List of Subscribers." The list includes "Mr. Charles Stuart" and "Mr. Charles Stuart, Bank." Might the first be Gilbert Stuart?

10. According to the entry on Thomas Holloway (1748–1827) in *DNB*, vol. 9, p. 1074, the edition of Lavater was "illustrated with about eight hundred plates executed by Holloway himself, Bartolozzi, Blake, and other good engravers, under the direction of Henry Fuseli, R.A."

11. Evans (1999, p. 67) discusses Stuart as priding himself "on his own ability as a physiognomist."

12. Isaac Weld Jr., *Travels through the States of North America, and the Provinces of Upper and Lower Canada during the Years 1795, 1796, and 1797* (London: Printed for John Stockdale, 1807), vol. 1, pp. 105–6; partially quoted in Evans 1999, p. 67.

13. Evans 1999, p. 140 n. 3.

14. "Technical notes" for the entry on this portrait in Miles 1995, p. 201.

15. J. Stuart 1876, p. 370.

16. Evans 1999, pp. 140–41 n. 3.

17. Anne L. Poulet, *Jean-Antoine Houdon: Sculptor of the Enlightenment*, exh. cat. (Washington, D.C.: National Gallery of Art in association with the University of Chicago Press, 2003), p. 267; see the entry on the marble-bust version of Washington's portrait (Los Angeles County Museum of Art), pp. 263–68.

ground were added up to the edge of the lighter color of the hair and do not extend underneath the hair. Evans saw the "rather erratic aureole around the head," visible in the X-ray, as evidence that this painting is the life portrait. The aureole "could well be a thin smear of residue from a rubbing out, which in parts was probably total."[13] However, National Gallery of Art conservator Ann Hoenigswald interpreted this roughened area as a possible result of changes in the red background.[14] The painting might have been reworked to conform for physiognomic reasons to the only portrait of Washington that Stuart admired more than his own, that done in 1785 by French sculptor Jean-Antoine Houdon: "Houdon's bust came first, and my head of him [i.e., the Athenaeum portrait] next. When I painted him, he had just had a set of false teeth inserted, which accounts for the constrained expression so noticeable about the mouth and lower part of the face. Houdon's bust does not suffer from this defect. I wanted him as he looked at that time [1785]."[15] In Evans's interpretation of changes from initial to final brushwork, as documented by the X-ray, she noticed that there are alterations of "the far eye, the upper lip, the shading under the chin, and the placement of the highlight on the tip of the nose. Perhaps the most telling revision concerns the philtral ridges of Washington's upper lip. These ridges, defining the indentation of the lip, are quite distinctive in that they are remarkably widely spaced. They appear in Houdon's life mask (Pierpont Morgan Library, New York), done from a mold of Washington's face, and in the x-radiograph but not in the final Vaughan portrait."[16]

Houdon made his life mask of Washington at Mount Vernon, then returned to France to work on the full-length lifesize marble statue commissioned by the State of Virginia, which was installed in 1796 in the rotunda of the Virginia State Capitol, where it can be seen today. Before he left, he made a low-fired clay bust for George Washington, which is at Mount Vernon (fig. 83), and a plaster cast for Benjamin Franklin (unlocated).[17] Years later, in Boston, Stuart made a pencil drawing of the profile of Houdon's portrait of Washington, one of the few of Stuart's drawings to survive

Fig. 84. Gilbert Stuart, *Sketch of George Washington from Houdon's Bust*, 1820–28. Graphite pencil on paper, 3¾ x 3 in. (9.5 x 7.6 cm). Museum of Fine Arts, Boston; Gift in memory of Charlotte Hervoches du Quilliou (28.362)

Fig. 83. Jean-Antoine Houdon, *George Washington*, 1785. Terracotta, H. 22 in. (55.9 cm). Mount Vernon Ladies' Association

18. The drawing, according to its inscription, was made in the presence of George Brimmer and given in 1836 to Horatio Greenough. The outline is indented, suggesting that it was made with a mechanical device, perhaps a drawing instrument such as a pantograph or physiognotrace.

19. Verheyen (1989, pp. 127–39) compared Stuart's achievement with Rembrandt Peale's, especially regarding Peale's "Porthole" portrait (1824–25; U.S. Capitol, Washington, D.C.).

(fig. 84).[18] His interest in the Houdon portrait as an accurate representation of Washington is not surprising. To a physiognomist, a life mask is the most truthful form of portrait because it is cast directly from the person and is not subject to artistic interpretation. It seems possible that Stuart adjusted his own portrait of Washington based on observations of Houdon's portrait not only to capture an accurate likeness for his own purposes but also to create a reliable image for the interpretive context of publication in Lavater's volume.[19]

EGM

36. GEORGE WASHINGTON

1795
Oil on canvas, 29⅛ x 24⅛ in. (74 x 61.3 cm)
Private collection

1. Gustavus A. Eisen, "Stuart's Three Washingtons," *International Studio* 76 (February 1923), p. 390. For the portrait, see Charles I. Landis, "Some Oldtime Lancaster Portraits of Washington," *Papers Read before the Lancaster County Historical Society* 21, no. 2 (1917), pp. 29–34; Charles A. Munn, *Three Types of Washington Portraits: John Trumbull, Charles Wilson Peale, Gilbert Stuart* (New York: Privately printed, 1908), pp. 54–58 (Munn had recently acquired the portrait); Charles Henry Hart, "Tracing the Pedigrees of Stuart's Washingtons." *New York Sun,* January 21, 1917, sec. 5, p. 4; Fielding 1923, p. 117, no. 4, illus. facing p. 20; Park 1926, pp. 847–48, no. 4; Morgan and Fielding 1931, p. 252, no. 4, illus. facing p. 254; Eisen 1932, p. 47. The portrait was exhibited at the M. H. de Young Memorial Museum, San Francisco, in 1935; see *Exhibition of American Painting*, exh. cat. (San Francisco, 1935), no. 38; and by M. Knoedler and Co., New York, in 1936: see *Masterpieces of American Historical Portraiture*, exh. cat. (New York, 1936), p. 11, no. 1.

2. These portraits are discussed in Park 1926, pp. 847–53, nos. 3, 5–9, 11, 15, and 16; Morgan and Fielding 1931, pp. 250–59, with the same catalogue numbers. Eisen (1932, pp. 39–48) provides some additional documentation. The painting at the Homeland Foundation and the one in a private New York collection are not listed in these sources. Park no. 10 (Mead Art Museum, Amherst College, Amherst, Mass.) may be a later copy of no. 11 (University of Virginia). In addition, for the portrait at Winterthur (Park no. 3), see Edgar P. Richardson, *American Paintings and Related Pictures in the Henry Francis du Pont Winterthur Museum* (Charlottesville: University Press of Virginia, 1986), pp. 92–94, illus. Harvard's portrait (Park no. 6) is published in *Philadelphia: Three Centuries of American Art*, exh. cat. (Philadelphia: Philadelphia Museum of Art, 1976), pp. 170–71, no. 140, illus. The Coleman portrait (Park no. 9; private collection) is reproduced in Barbara J. Mitnick and William S. Ayres, *George Washington: American Symbol*, exh. cat. (New York: Hudson Hills Press in association with the Museums at Stony Brook and the Museum of Our National Heritage, 1999), p. 12, pl. 4.

3. Park 1926, p. 851, no. 12; Morgan and Fielding 1931, p. 256, no. 12.

4. The provenance of the portrait is discussed in Landis, "Some Oldtime Lancaster Portraits of Washington," pp. 29–34. The portrait was purchased after Scott's death by Edward Brien of Lancaster (d. 1816) and is listed in the inventory of

Among the replicas that Stuart painted of the Vaughan portrait of George Washington, this very fine example was described by Gustavus Eisen as "painted with a perfect technic and great simplicity."[1] The coloring of this portrait, depicting the president in a black suit with black buttons against a red background, is characteristic of all but two of the Vaughan replicas (see cat. 37). The replicas include the two additional examples in this exhibition (cats. 35, 37), as well as the William Bingham portrait at the Henry Francis du Pont Winterthur Museum (fig. 85); the Camperdown portrait in the Frick Collection, New York (fig. 78); the Fisher family portrait at Harvard University (fig. 86); the General Henry Lee portrait at Colonial Williamsburg, Virginia; the Vaughan-Sinclair portrait at the National Gallery of Art (fig. 87); the Coleman family portrait in a private collection (fig. 88); the Tucker-Rives portrait at the University of Virginia, Charlottesville (fig. 89); the Phillips-Brixey portrait at the Metropolitan Museum (fig. 90); the John Jacob Astor painting at the Indiana University Library, Bloomington; a painting with a Boston provenance now owned by the Homeland Foundation, Amenia, New York (fig. 93); and another in a New York private collection.[2] One unlocated example was painted for General John Eager Howard.[3]

The first owner of the present portrait was Alexander Scott (d. 1810) of Lancaster, Pennsylvania, a member of the Pennsylvania legislature in 1797–1800.[4] His name appears on Stuart's 1795 "list of gentlemen who are to have copies of the Portrait of the President of the United States" (see "The Portraits of George Washington") as "Scott, Esq., Lancaster." Scott is one of only three people on the list of thirty-two men commissioning thirty-nine paintings whose purchase can be connected with an identified portrait of the Vaughan type. The others are John Vaughan (see cat. 35) and General Henry Lee (for the painting at Colonial Williamsburg).[5]

The known portraits of the Vaughan type were undoubtedly painted within a relatively short period of time in 1795. One cataloguer of Stuart's portraits of Washington attempted to group the paintings into subtypes on the assumption that such close study might indicate where each version fits in relationship to the others in the sequence of the copies.[6] However, this charting assumed that the portrait painted for John Vaughan was the life portrait, which is now questioned (see cat. 35). Also, it now seems likely that Stuart painted more than one replica at a time. There are subtle variations among examples that initially seem identical. The differences are probably due to Stuart's own creative impulse to give variety to the images, and also perhaps to the work of an assistant in some areas.

In a close study of their compositional details, seven of the versions, including this portrait, have characteristics which suggest that they can be grouped together as the earlier paintings of the series. Excluding the portrait for which the series is named (cat. 35), this group includes this privately owned example, the Vaughan-Sinclair (National Gallery), the Phillips-Brixey (Metropolitan Museum), and the paintings owned by the Frick Collection and Harvard University. The portraits at Colonial Williamsburg and Winterthur are close to these in appearance. Ignoring the color differences in the Frick painting (see cat. 37), these paintings have notable compositional similarities, including a long, thin, somewhat angular face and elaborate folds in the shirt ruffle. The Frick and Harvard pictures have a distinct background with a curtain and a pink and blue sky. The painting at Winterthur also has a curtain and some sky, while the Vaughan-Sinclair has

Fig. 85. *George Washington*, 1795. Oil on canvas, 28¾ x 23½ in. (73 x 59.7 cm). Henry Francis du Pont Winterthur Museum, Winterthur, Del. (59.0857)

Fig. 86. *George Washington*, 1795. Oil on canvas, 29 x 24 in. (73.7 x 61 cm). Harvard University Portrait Collection, Cambridge, Mass.; Gift of Sidney F. Tyler to the University (H631)

Fig. 87. *George Washington* (the Vaughan-Sinclair portrait), 1795. Oil on canvas, 29⅛ x 24⅛ in. (73.8 x 61.1 cm). National Gallery of Art, Washington, D.C.; Andrew W. Mellon Collection (1940.1.6)

Fig. 88. *George Washington*, 1795. Oil on canvas, 29 x 24 in. (73.7 x 61 cm). Private collection

Fig. 89. *George Washington*, 1795. Oil on canvas, 30 x 25 in. (76.2 x 63.5 cm). University of Virginia, Charlottesville

Fig. 90. *George Washington* (the Phillips-Brixey portrait), 1795. Oil on canvas, 29 x 23¾ in. (73.7 x 60.3 cm). The Metropolitan Museum of Art, New York; Bequest of Richard De Wolfe Brixey, 1943 (43.86.1)

his estate. Brien's granddaughter Anna Rogers Reilly sold the portrait to Charles Allen Munn in 1907. Hart ("Tracing the Pedigrees of Two of Stuart's Washingtons") discussed the confusion of this provenance with that of a portrait of Washington acquired by Alexander Smith Cochran.

5. Park 1926, p. 849, no. 7. Park identified his no. 13, pp. 851–52, as having belonged to William Ludwell Lee, also on the list. I have not traced that portrait.

6. Eisen (1932, pp. 22–37) discussed the Vaughan types in detail and included drawings of the varieties of shirt ruffles and queue ribbons.

hints of a curtain but no sky. In other details, such as the pattern of the hair curls and the size and shape of the queue ribbons, these pictures differ slightly. In some the hair curls are soft, while in others their ends are described by oval shapes. Most of the queue ribbons are narrow. Also, in comparison to others, the coat of the Phillips-Brixey version is very flat.

A second, smaller group includes the example at the University of Virginia, the Coleman portrait (in a private collection), and the painting at the University of Indiana. These share a flat red background with no curtain, shirt ruffles that are simpler than the previous group, and a wide queue ribbon. Given their similarity in details to the first group, it can be suggested that they closely follow the first examples in date of execution. A third group, consisting of the Gibbs-Channing-Avery picture (cat. 37), the

36

painting owned by the Homeland Foundation, and a painting in a private collection in New York, has distinctly different characteristics. Details such as the serrated hair ribbon, the execution of the heavily painted curls in the powdered hair, and the paintings' provenances suggest that while they may have been begun in Philadelphia before Stuart abandoned this type of portrait of Washington, they were completed later in Boston.

EGM

37. GEORGE WASHINGTON (THE GIBBS-CHANNING-AVERY PORTRAIT)

Begun 1795, completion date unknown
Oil on canvas, 30¼ x 25¼ in. (76.8 x 64.1 cm)
The Metropolitan Museum of Art, New York;
Rogers Fund, 1907 (07.160)

1. See Fielding 1913, p. 115, no. 2; Park 1926, pp. 845–46, no. 2; Morgan and Fielding 1931, pp. 236, 251 no. 2, 352–53; Eisen 1932, p. 44; Samuel P. Avery, *Some Account of the "Gibbs-Channing" Portrait of George Washington, Painted by Gilbert Stuart* (New York: Privately printed, 1900); John Caldwell and Oswaldo Rodriguez Roque, *American Paintings in The Metropolitan Museum of Art*, vol. 1, *A Catalogue of Works by Artists Born by 1815* (New York: Metropolitan Museum of Art, 1994), pp. 175–77.
2. See Miles 1999, pp. 38–39, on these changes.
3. On this portrait, see Park 1926, p. 848, no. 5; Morgan and Fielding 1931, p. 253, no. 5; *The Frick Collection: An Illustrated Catalogue*, vol. 1, *Paintings* (New York: Frick Collection, 1968), pp. 3–4.
4. Gustavus A. Eisen, "Stuart's Three Washingtons," *International Studio* 76 (February 1923), pp. 388–89.
5. A version in a private collection appears to be a very early copy of the painting now in the Frick Collection. It was catalogued in Morgan and Fielding 1931, p. 314, no. VII, as attributed to Stuart, with the notation that neither author had seen the painting.
6. William Sullivan, *Familiar Letters on Public Characters, and Public Events, from the Peace of 1783, to the Peace of 1815*, 2nd ed. (Boston: Russell, Odiorne, and Metcalf, 1834), pp. 75, 76.
7. Washington's list of clothing, dated May 6, 1797, is published in John C. Fitzpatrick, ed., *The Writings of George Washington from the Original Manuscript Sources 1745–1799* (1931–44; reprint, Westport, Conn.: Greenwood Press, 1970), vol. 35, p. 442 n., from a photocopy at the Library of Congress of a memorandum compiled by Washington; the original is unlocated.

Among the replicas of the Vaughan portrait, this example, known by the names of its successive owners, may contain evidence of the appearance of the life portrait, which Stuart "rubbed out."[1] Washington is seated in front of a green curtain instead of the red curtain of the other Vaughan replicas. Further, though he is now seen in a black coat, a close examination of the painting by Dorothy Mahon in the Paintings Conservation Department of the Metropolitan Museum confirms the presence of a reddish brown underlayer beneath the black coat, which suggests that Washington was initially depicted wearing a chestnut brown coat that was perhaps not fully realized before it was painted over with black. In addition, an X-ray (fig. 92) reveals the use of white paint to depict the yellow metal buttons that Stuart overpainted in black.[2] In these details—the brown coat and the yellow buttons—this portrait is similar to Stuart's portrait of Washington in the Frick Collection, New York, which was acquired by Henry Clay Frick in 1918 from the estate of Adam Philip Haldane Duncan, third Earl of Camperdown (figs. 78, 92).[3] It has been suggested that the portrait at the Frick was given by Samuel Vaughan to Admiral Adam Duncan (1731–1804), created Viscount Duncan of Camperdown in 1797 after his victory at the Battle of Camperdown.[4] A comparison of the two paintings in the Metropolitan Museum's conservation laboratory on July 28, 2003, showed that the Frick painting is better conceived and painted, very fresh in its execution, with more effort in the highlighting on the coat, the shading around the arm, and the touches around the eyes. In it Washington's head is tilted slightly to the right as compared to other Vaughan-type images. Although details such as the outline of the shirt ruffle are identical in the Frick and the Metropolitan Museum paintings, the shading and highlighting are more carefully executed in the Frick version, while apparently painted more quickly in the Metropolitan version.[5]

How do we explain the different coloring of these two versions and the change of coat color in the Metropolitan version? A change in the color of the coat from black to brown does not make chronological sense since the overwhelming majority of the portraits of Washington by Stuart show him in his black velvet suit. But a change from brown to black suggests that the Metropolitan and the Frick paintings are the early versions and reflect the appearance of the "rubbed out" life portrait (see cat. 35). Possibly the change from a brown coat to the black velvet suit that Washington wore on public occasions was an iconographic decision: brown may have been the color of the coat Washington was actually wearing when he sat for the life portrait. A contemporary observer wrote of Washington's appearance at his formal Tuesday receptions: "On entering [the visitor] saw the tall manly figure of Washington clad in black velvet; his hair in

37

Fig. 91. X-ray of cat. 37

Fig. 92. X-ray of fig. 78

Fig. 93. *George Washington*, ca. 1795. Oil on canvas, 29¼ x 24 in. (74.3 x 61 cm). Homeland Foundation, Incorporated, Amenia, N.Y.

8. Information from Carol Borchert Cadou, Curator, George Washington's Mount Vernon, e-mail message to the author, September 22, 2003.

9. Miles 1999, pp. 26–28, illus.

10. Quoted in Avery, *Some Account of the "Gibbs-Channing" Portrait*, p. 5.

11. Charles Henry Hart, "Stuart's Lansdowne portrait of Washington," *Harper's New Monthly Magazine* 93 (August 1896), 1896, p. 378.

12. The portrait at the Homeland Foundation, not listed by sources for Stuart's portraits of Washington, including Park 1926, Morgan and Fielding 1931, and Eisen 1932, has a Boston rather than a Philadelphia provenance; its earliest owner was a man named John Joy. Its last private owner was Chauncey D. Stillman, who created the Homeland Foundation in 1938 and bequeathed it in 1989 to the foundation.

full dress, powdered and gathered behind in a large silk bag; yellow gloves on his hands; holding a cocked hat with a cockade in it, and the edges adorned with a black feather about an inch deep. He wore knee and shoe buckles; and a long sword, with a finely wrought and polished steel hilt, which appeared at the left hip; the coat worn over the sword, so that the hilt, and the part below the folds of the coat behind, were in view. The scabbard was white polished leather." By contrast, "when Mrs. Washington received visiters, [Washington] did not consider *himself* as visited. He was then as a private gentleman, dressed usually in some colored coat and waistcoat, (the only one recollected was brown, with bright buttons,) and black, on his lower limbs. He had then neither hat nor sword."[6] A list that Washington compiled in 1797 of his own clothing included "1 Full Suit . . . dark brown; 1 Ditto . . . lighter [brown]."[7] A brown suit that belonged to Washington still survives at Mount Vernon.[8] After painting the life portrait and one replica, perhaps Stuart left a second replica (the Gibbs-Channing-Avery version) unfinished and painted the rest of the replicas showing Washington in the black coat that was his public dress as president. Of the portraits made of Washington during his presidency, only one other, by Scottish artist Archibald Robertson, painted in 1791–92 (Colonial Williamsburg), shows him in a coat other than black. Robertson's miniature depicts Washington wearing a plum-colored coat.[9]

Such a change in the color of the coat supports the tradition in the Gibbs family that their portrait remained for some time in Stuart's studio and was retouched by the artist before the family acquired it. Dr. William F. Channing, who sold the portrait to Samuel P. Avery in 1889, wrote that the portrait was "sold by Stuart, at an early date, to his warm personal friend, Colonel George Gibbs (died 1833) of New York, with the statement that it was on the easel while Washington was sitting, and worked upon from life."[10] Charles Henry Hart wrote in 1896 that Stuart "retained the Gibbs picture by him for several years, and is said to have disposed of it to Colonel Gibbs as his best work, and only out of personal friendship."[11] Since the Gibbs family had close connections to Stuart from their origins in Newport, the idea that Gibbs acquired the portrait at a date later than 1795 is plausible. At that point, Stuart would have completed it to conform to other presidential images of Washington. Another indication of a slightly later completion date is the sawtooth queue ribbon, which is not typical of the Vaughan portraits and appears first on the earlier examples of the Athenaeum portrait such as the one owned by the Huntington Gallery (cat. 40), and on the Constable-Hamilton half-length (cat. 48), both painted in 1797. A later origin might also be true of the version of the Vaughan portrait owned by the Homeland Foundation, Amenia, New York (fig. 93), which has a Boston provenance and which, despite its traditional coloring with a red curtain, appears most similar to the Gibbs version, suggesting that Stuart may have kept the Gibbs portrait long enough to have made a replica later in Boston.[12]

EGM

38. MARTHA WASHINGTON (THE ATHENAEUM PORTRAIT)

1796
Oil on canvas, 48 x 37 in. (121.9 x 94 cm)
Jointly owned by the National Portrait Gallery,
Smithsonian Institution, Washington, D.C.
(NPG.80.116); and the Museum of Fine Arts,
Boston (1980.2), William Francis Warden Fund,
John H. and Ernestine A. Payne Fund,
Commonwealth Cultural Preservation Trust

39. GEORGE WASHINGTON (THE ATHENAEUM PORTRAIT)

1796
Oil on canvas, 48 x 37 in. (121.9 x 94 cm)
Jointly owned by the National Portrait Gallery,
Smithsonian Institution, Washington, D.C.
(NPG.80.115); and the Museum of Fine Arts,
Boston (1980.1), William Francis Warden Fund,
John H. and Ernestine A. Payne Fund,
Commonwealth Cultural Preservation Trust

1. The Athenaeum portrait of Washington and the replicas are catalogued in Fielding 1923, pp. 152–245, nos. 33–124 (ninety-two examples, including the life portrait); Park 1926, pp. 862–94, nos. 31–111 (eighty-one examples, including the life portrait); Morgan and Fielding 1931, pp. 223–24, 240–49, 273–311 nos. 34–106 (seventy-three examples, including the life portrait). Morgan and Fielding (1931, pp. 324–38) also list additional examples, which they chose not to "make an attribution except as indicated" (p. 312). Eisen's study of the portraits and the replicas and copies is found in Eisen 1932, pp. 135–92. The Athenaeum portraits are discussed in Evans 1999, pp. 63–67. The Athenaeum portrait of Martha Washington is catalogued in Park 1926, pp. 788–89, no. 882.

2. Rembrandt Peale, letter to Charles Edwards Lester, March 16, 1846, Charles Henry Hart Autograph Collection, Archives of American Art, Smithsonian Institution, Washington, D.C.

3. Rembrandt Peale, letter to unidentified "Dear Sir," May 7, no year indicated, Robert C. Graham Collection of Artists Letters, Archives of American Art.

4. "Rembrandt Peale's Lecture on Washington and His Portraits," Eisen 1932, p. 311.

5. William T. Oedel, "John Vanderlyn: French Neoclassicism and the Search for an American Style" (Ph.D. diss., University of Delaware, 1981), pp. 31–41. Bill Oedel also kindly gave me copies of a recent draft of his book-length study of Vanderlyn, which is in preparation. Vanderlyn's copy of Stuart's portrait of Benson is at The Metropolitan Museum of Art; his copy of Burr's

Stuart never completed this pair of portraits of George and Martha Washington, commissioned by Mrs. Washington for Mount Vernon. They remained in his possession and were acquired by the Boston Athenaeum after his death in 1828. They are now known as the Athenaeum portraits.[1] It is likely that Stuart began at least the portrait of President Washington before April 12, 1796, the only documented sitting for the Lansdowne portrait (cat. 45), which it closely resembles in the face. Rembrandt Peale recalled in 1846 that the Athenaeum was "painted I believe in March 1796" before the full-length Lansdowne.[2] He repeated this in detail: "The whole length for Landsdowne was not his <u>Second</u>—that in the Atheneum is the 2^d begun for Mrs. Washington—The 3^d being copied from his 2^d with <u>one</u> sitting in the Summer of 96—from the life—Thus making it, in some degree his 3^d Portrait."[3] He later added details to this record in his lecture on portraits of Washington: "Soon after my return to Philadelphia, in the Spring of 1796, Mr. Stuart exhibited his Portrait of Washington. It was of the Head-size, 25 by 30 inches, with a Crimson Curtain Background—advantageously displayed in a Room of the City Hall—and was much visited, as it well deserved to be, being a beautiful work of Art, tho' not to me a satisfactory likeness. . . . It is here necessary to state that this was not the Portrait Mr. Stuart began in the Autumn of 1795."[4]

An early copy of the Athenaeum portrait attributed to the young American artist John Vanderlyn (Senate House, Kingston, N.Y.) supports this timing. Vanderlyn worked briefly for Stuart in New York in 1794 and made copies of his portraits of Egbert Benson and Aaron Burr (fig. 61). In 1795 Burr paid Vanderlyn's expenses to live with Stuart in Philadelphia and work as Stuart's studio assistant. Vanderlyn moved to Philadelphia about mid-July 1795 and remained with Stuart until the late spring of 1796. He learned painting techniques from Stuart by observing his work, preparing canvases, and blocking out, or "dead coloring," the basic arrangements of shapes, especially, apparently, for the replicas of Stuart's portraits of Washington.[5] On April 20, 1796, Vanderlyn wrote Peter Van Gaasbeek in Kingston, "I have not made any copy of the President for myself yet, but will ask [Stuart's] consent which if he does not object to, will paint it before I come home (that is) within a fortnights time. Mr. S. has 100 Dolls. for a Portrait of the president which is his price for painting a likeness here now."[6]

However, Washington's grandson George Washington Parke Custis and Stuart's daughter Jane wrote that the original Athenaeum portraits were painted after the original Lansdowne. Custis wrote in 1852, "After the sittings for the picture [for] the Marquis

38

39

Detail of cat. 38

Detail of cat. 39

portrait, at the Princeton University Art Museum, Princeton, N.J., is listed in Park 1926, pp. 190–91, no. 129, as a replica by Stuart.

6. John Vanderlyn Papers, Senate House State Historic Site, Kingston, N.Y. (microfilm, Archives of American Art), quoted in Oedel, "John Vanderlyn," p. 39.

7. George Washington Parke Custis, letter to George W. Childs, July 1, 1852, reprinted in the *New York Daily Tribune*, August 10, 1852, quoted in Mabel Munson Swan, *The Athenaeum Gallery, 1827–1873: The Boston Athenaeum as an Early Patron of Art* (Boston: Boston Athenaeum, 1940), pp. 82–83.

8. J. Stuart 1876, p. 370.

9. Mount (1964, pp. 200–201) proposed that the 50-by-40-inch Athenaeum portrait of Washington was initially commissioned by Bingham. However, this theory does not explain the existence of the pendant portrait of Martha Washington, which Mount (p. 202) described simply thus: "its purpose is obscure."

of Lansdowne, the chief declared that he would sit no more for any one. Mrs. Washington, desirous of having an original by Stuart, to place among the family pictures at Mount Vernon, entreated the chief to sit once more for her, Stuart being desirous of painting another original with a view to some improvements. The bargain was concluded; Stuart was to make certain copies, and then the last original was to have been handed over to Mrs. Washington."[7] And Jane Stuart wrote in 1876, "After this picture was completed for Lord Lansdowne, Washington gave a commission to paint the portraits of himself and Mrs. Washington. As my father was, at this time, inundated with visitors, he found it impossible to attend to his profession, and moved from Chestnut street, Philadelphia, to a country home in Germantown, where he transformed a barn into a painting-room. Here Washington sat for the portrait now at the Athenaeum, Boston."[8]

Washington is posed to face to the viewer's left, while Martha faces slightly to the viewer's right, so that when the compositions were finished, the two figures would turn toward each other. The sizes of the canvases, which are close to the standard 50-by-40-inch "half-length" canvases, and the positions of the head, slightly off-center, suggest that Stuart may originally have conceived the images as seated portraits.[9] If so, perhaps this portrait would have resembled the portrait that William Constable commissioned for Alexander Hamilton (cat. 48) or Stuart's later portraits of Thomas Jefferson and James Madison (cats. 76, 77). Stuart discussed the concept of balancing the compositions of portraits of a married couple with Henry Pickering in 1817, when painting a portrait of Pickering's mother. According to Pickering, Stuart "placed a chair for my Mother on his left hand. I thought, said I, you would have placed my Mother on the other side, as you usually do, & expressed a wish that he would. He wished to know my reason. I told him I had a portrait of my Father, painted by Mr. Waldo of New York, & that he had been taken in the position he was about to place my Mother. It is usual said I, for husband & wife to treat one another with civility in the presence of others, & they ought to be taken looking at each other."[10] For Washington's portrait, he also lightly sketched the white of the President's shirt and the black of his coat and queue ribbon. He depicted both sitters against an aureole of dark paint that enabled him to select colors for the face that would give a successful illusion of volume, a practice visible in unfinished eighteenth-century English portraits. In Washington's portrait, the warm tones of the sitter's face contrast with his white powdered hair and his blue eyes. Stuart applied the subtly varied skin tones in separate, unblended touches of the brush that enliven the surface. This technique is visible even in the shaded areas under the chin, where Stuart alternated darker and lighter flesh tones to indicate shadow and reflected light. With Martha Washington's portrait, he completed the face but only lightly sketched in her white cap.

There are several stories about the sittings. Mrs. Basil Hall, who visited Stuart in Boston in 1827, recorded one of Stuart's reminiscences:

In [Stuart's] painting-room there is an original painting he did of Washington, merely a head, the figure and drapery left unfinished. He amused us exceedingly by the account he gave us of the embarrassment at first as to how he was to get on with it, he found it such hard work to make General Washington speak on light subjects; however he resolved to try at all hazards to make him laugh, and accordingly told him the old Joe Miller story of King James II's journey to gain popularity, in the course of which he arrived somewhere that the Mayor of the place was Baker and no speechmaker and had to be prompted, so that when his friend jogged his elbow and said, "Hold up your head and look like a man," the blundering Mayor repeated the admonition to the King. This stupid story had the desired effect, "and from that time," said Mr. Stuart, "I had him on a pivot and could manage him nicely."[11]

According to Custis, "the President was awakened when the painter began to talk about horses,"[12] a favorite subject of the president, who was a very fine horseman. Jane Stuart repeated this reminiscence.[13] Samuel Lorenzo Knapp also wrote of Stuart's difficulties in painting Washington:

In the chair for the painter, Washington was apt to fall into a train of thought, and become abstracted from the things around him, and of course most of the likenesses of him, show more of gravity of muscle, than of the divinity of intelligence. When he sat to Stuart, as the latter has often stated, an apathy seemed to seize him, and a vacuity spread over his countenance most appalling to the painter. The best portrait painter of the age, was now to take the likeness of the greatest man of all ages; and the artists and the patriots of all countries were interested in it. To have failed in getting a good likeness would have been death to the artist's fame, and a perpetual source of mortification to the people of the country. Stuart was, like Washington, not easily overcome; he made several fruitless attempts to awaken the heroick spirit in him, by talking of battles, but in vain; he next tried to warm up the patriot and sage, by turning the conversation to the republican ages of antiquity; this was equally unsuccessful. At length the painter struck on the master key, and opened a way to his mind which he has so happily transferred to the canvass with the features of his face. In the whole of this picture, in every limb, as well as feature, the martial air of the warrior chief, is admirably mingled with the dignity and majesty of the statesman and sage.[14]

10. Pickering 1817 (October 29).
11. Whitley 1932, pp. 208–9, quoting Margaret Hall Hunter and Una Pope-Hennessy, eds., *The Aristocratic Journey; being the outspoken letters of Mrs. Basil Hall written during a fourteen months' sojourn in America, 1827–1828* (New York: G. P. Putnam's Sons, 1931).
12. According to Whitley 1932, p. 99.
13. J. Stuart 1876, p. 370.
14. Samuel Lorenzo Knapp, *American Cultural History, 1607–1829: A Facsimile Reproduction of Lectures on American Literature, 1829*, introduction and index by Richard Beale Davis and Ben Harris McClary (Gainesville, Fla.: Scholars' Facsimiles and Reprints, 1961), p. 194. There are a number of errors, such as the idea that the portrait was painted in Washington, D.C. It is also unclear whether Knapp is thinking of the Lansdowne or the Athenaeum portrait.

Stuart's ability to read character in his sitter's physiognomy enabled him, he believed, to detect that Washington had a fierce temper. Stuart, according to his daughter, remarked one day to General Henry Lee that Washington "had a tremendous temper, but held it under wonderful control. General Lee breakfasted with the President and Mrs. Washington a few days afterward. 'I saw your portrait the other day—a capital likeness,' said the General, 'but Stuart says you have a tremendous temper.' 'Upon my word,' said Mrs. Washington, coloring, 'Mr. Stuart takes a great deal upon himself, to make such a remark.' 'But stay, my dear lady,' said General Lee, 'he added, that the President had it under wonderful control.' With something like a smile, General Washington remarked, 'He is right.'"[15]

Stuart believed that he had succeeded in representing Washington more successfully in this second portrait than he had in the first, the original of the Vaughan portrait. He admitted having some difficulty with Washington's jaw, however. The square shape of Washington's jaw and the bulge around the mouth differ noticeably from Washington's oval face as seen in portraits by other artists. The distortion resulted from a new set of false teeth made by James Gardette, a Philadelphia dentist, about the time Stuart painted this portrait. Jane Stuart later reported that, of other artists' portraits of Washington, her father admired most that made by French sculptor Jean-Antoine Houdon, done earlier in Washington's life: "When I painted [Washington], he had just had a set of false teeth inserted, which accounts for the constrained expression so noticeable about the mouth and lower part of the face. Houdon's bust does not suffer from this defect. I wanted him as he looked at that time."[16] Rembrandt Peale, in a letter to Isaac J. Greenwood, grandson of John Greenwood, the dentist who had made a set of teeth for Washington in 1790, wrote that "Washington sat to me in the Autumn of 1795—and at the same time sat to Stuart, having then in his mouth the Teeth made by your Grandfather in 1790. Not satisfied with this Portrait, Stuart painted another Portrait in the spring of 1796, when the General had in his mouth an Ivory Sett made by James Gardette, which caused his mouth to be changed."[17] Washington's difficulty with the teeth made by Gardette is confirmed by his letter to John Greenwood on January 20, 1797. Writing about a set of teeth that he had returned to Greenwood to be repaired, he asked that they be sent back "as soon as possible for although I now make use of another sett, they are both uneasy in the mouth and bulge my lips out in such a manner as to make them appear considerably swelled. . . . [N]othing must be done to them which will, in the *least* degree force the lips out than more than *now* do, as it does this too much already; but if both upper and lower teeth were to incline inwards more, it would shew the shape of the mouth better, and not be the worse in any other respect."[18]

The only reference to Stuart found in Washington's writings, in addition to the letter he wrote to Stuart about sitting for the Lansdowne portrait in April 1796,[19] is an annotation in his diary for January 7, 1797, that he "Road to German Town with Mrs. Washington to see Mr. Stuarts paintings."[20] Stuart asked Washington's permission to keep the unfinished portrait in order to fulfill the commissions he received for replicas, which would provide a steady income. According to John Neagle, "Mrs. Washington called often to see the general's portrait, and was desirous to possess the painting. One day she called with her husband, and begged to know when she might have it. The general himself never pressed it, but on this occasion, as he and his lady were about to retire, he returned to Mr. Stuart and said he saw plainly of what advantage the picture was to the painter, (who had been constantly employed in copying it, and Stuart had said he could not work so well from another;) he therefore begged the artist to retain the paint-

15. J. Stuart 1876, p. 371.
16. Ibid., p. 370. Jane Stuart was referring to the time Houdon made his portrait, which was 1785.
17. Rembrandt Peale, letter to Isaac J. Greenwood, March 27, 1859, in Greenwood, "Remarks on the Portraiture of Washington," *Magazine of American History* 2, no. 1 (January 1878), p. 37.
18. John C. Fitzpatrick, ed., *The Writings of George Washington from the Original Manuscript Sources, 1745–1799* (1931–44; reprint, Greenwood Press, Westport, Conn., 1970), vol. 35, pp. 370–71.
19. George Washington, letter to Gilbert Stuart, April 11, 1796, collection of the Earl of Rosebery, on long-term loan to the National Portrait Gallery, Washington.
20. Donald Jackson and Dorothy Twohig, eds., *The Diaries of George Washington* (Charlottesville: University Press of Virginia, 1976–79), vol. 6, p. 229.

21. John Neagle, quoted in Dunlap 1834, vol. 1, p. 198.

22. J. Stuart 1876, p. 370.

23. Morgan and Fielding (1931, pp. 282–83, no. 49) list a portrait of Washington that they described as painted for Martha Washington and inherited by Washington's nephew George Steptoe Washington. When they wrote, the work was owned by Wharton Sinkler of Philadelphia; it now belongs to the Philadelphia Museum of Art. The idea that it belonged to Martha Washington has been discredited by researchers at Mount Vernon.

24. C. M. Harris, ed., *Papers of William Thornton* (Charlottesville: University Press of Virginia, 1995–), vol. 1, pp. 529–30. Thornton is referring to a Stuart portrait of Washington that Winstanley had purchased (unlocated); Winstanley believed it was the original of the Vaughan portraits.

25. This letter, in a private collection, is described in a memorandum on file at Mount Vernon; see ibid., p. 531 n.

26. On painted copies, see Morgan and Fielding 1931, pp. 339–46; Eisen 1932, pp. 193–97. For engravings, see Wick, 1982; William S. Baker, *The Engraved Portraits of Washington* (Philadelphia: Lindsay and Baker, 1880); Charles Henry Hart, *Catalogue of the Engraved Portraits of Washington* (New York: Grolier Club, 1904).

27. John Neal, "Randolph, a Novel" (1823), in *Observations on American Art: Selections from the Writings of John Neal (1793–1876)*, ed. Harold Edward Dickson (State College: Pennsylvania State College, 1943), p. 2.

ing at his pleasure." [21] And Jane Stuart: "When General and Mrs. Washington took their last sittings my father told Washington it would be of great importance to him to retain the originals, to which Washington replied: 'Certainly, Mr. Stuart, if they are of any consequence to you; I shall be perfectly satisfied with copies from your hand, as it will be impossible for me to sit again at present.'" [22] However, Stuart never delivered the originals, or any copies, to the family. Jane Stuart recalled that copies were made for Mount Vernon but she did not know where they were by the time she wrote her articles about her father in 1876. [23] After Washington's death, his friend William Thornton complained, in a letter of January 6, 1800, to the English artist William Winstanley:

I have never seen Mr. Stewart's paintings of the late illustrious Washington, and shall with peculiar pleasure view the painting with which you mean to honor our new city. I am sorry to be obliged to observe that the late General and his lady thought themselves extremely ill used by Mr. Stewart, who promised repeatedly *the original painting to them,* and always spoke of it as appertaining to them, *but never sent it, though frequently solicited. He also took Mrs. Washington's portrait but keeps it unfinished. The original of the General I think ought to be Mrs. Washington's—and I think Mr. Stewart has not acted honorably in disposing of it. I admire his genius and abilities but his inattention to the General's family certainly was ungrateful after the General sat so repeatedly to serve Mr. Stewart—and to have possessed the original picture would have been to Mrs. Washington one of the highest gratifications, now it would be a signal consolation. Make me a promise you will not take the original out of this country. You know that the Marquis of Lansdowne has a full-length by Stewart, therefore another original is of less consequence there than here. Promise my good friend to deposit that original here, if it be the original of originals, for Stewart you know has sold many originals. We will compensate you in one way or another. I pray you also use all your influence with Stewart to induce him to fulfil his promise to Mrs. W. It will do him great credit yet, and as I know he must have good qualities with such great genius call these good (but latent) qualities forth.* [24]

Tobias Lear, Washington's private secretary, wrote to Stuart on March 10, 1800, on behalf of Martha Washington to plead that the portrait of her husband be sent to her, offering to pay the usual price. [25] Instead, the portraits remained with Stuart. Although he never made replicas of the portrait of Mrs. Washington, his portrait of the first president became the best-known image of him in the nineteenth century through Stuart's own replicas, as well as those painted, engraved, and lithographed by other artists. [26] As writer and critic John Neal wrote in 1823, "Stuart says, and there is no fact more certain, that he [Washington] was a man of terrible passions; the sockets of his eyes; the breadth of his nose and nostrils; the deep broad expression of strength and solemnity upon his forehead, were all a proof of this. So, Stuart painted him; and, though a better likeness of him were shown to us, we should reject it; for, the only idea that we now have of George Washington, is associated with Stuart's Washington." [27]

EGM

40. GEORGE WASHINGTON

1797
Oil on canvas, 28¹/₂ x 23⁵/₈ in. (72.4 x 60 cm)
The Huntington Library, Art Collections, and
Botanical Gardens, San Marino, California; Gift
of Mrs. Alexander Baring (39.1)

Stuart made approximately seventy-five head-and-shoulders replicas of the Athenaeum portrait (cat. 39) over the course of his long career. They all depict Washington in a black velvet suit and a white shirt with a ruffle of lace or linen. Of the five included in this exhibition, this is the earliest (see cats. 41–44). While some writers about these portraits, notably John Hill Morgan and Mantle Fielding in 1931 and Gustavus Eisen in 1932, have tried to group these replicas into types, their exercise is futile except for the most general observations. As part of their groupings, Morgan and Fielding focused on the shapes of the faces without discussing the rest of the compositional details, while Eisen tried to describe all variations, including the twists and turns of the shirt ruffle and the shapes of the queue ribbons. Morgan and Fielding ultimately noted that

[t]he various canvases of the Athenaeum Type, which compose the largest class of Stuart's Washington portraits, cannot be said to be replicas of the Athenaeum Head for not one is a replica in the strict meaning of the word. "Replica" is defined as "A work of art made in exact likeness of another and by the artist himself." All portraits showing the left side of the face, eyes front, have heretofore been called "replicas" of the Athenaeum Head, which they certainly are not. It would seem as if Stuart, who, during the period of 1795–7, was in Philadelphia and, no doubt, seeing Washington constantly, was creating in these variations more or less original compositions, representing a somewhat different conception of Washington's face. In no other way can their variety be satisfactorily explained.[1]

Of more importance for studies of Stuart's work than the charting of the varieties of Athenaeum portraits is the striking fact that in many cases, if not in most, the original owners of the portraits were people who had other connections to Stuart. They sat to the artist for their own portraits, or they commissioned portraits of family members, or they were allied with Stuart's patrons through business or politics. The purchaser of this portrait is a good example. Charles Baring (1774–1865) of Courtland, Devon (England), was a nephew of Francis Baring, a founder of the London banking firm of John and Francis Baring and Company.[2] Although Charles was in Philadelphia in the 1790s, his life is not as well documented as that of his illustrious cousin Alexander Baring, later first Baron Ashburton, who at this time was serving as his father's agent in America in the firm's purchase of lands in Maine from William Bingham (see cat. 53) in 1796. Another cousin, Alexander Baring's brother Henry Baring, was also in the United States in the 1790s.[3] Of the three, only Charles Baring settled there permanently.

His acquisition of the portrait is described by his son Alexander Baring: "In 1797 my Father, Charles Baring, was in Philadelphia. . . . Gilbert Stuart . . . expressed the wish to paint my Father's portrait. However, my Father persuaded him to paint, instead, a portrait of General Washington. . . . The portrait in my possession, painted for my father, is one of the first replicas of the 'Athanaeum Portrait' of George Washington."[4] The portrait remained in his family until it was donated to the Huntington. Because of the longevity of both Charles Baring, who married his second wife in 1847, and his son Alexander Baring (1848–1932), the donor of the portrait to the Huntington in 1939, Louise T. Baring, Alexander Baring's widow, was only its third owner.[5]

The image of Washington is similar in details of the composition to others painted during Stuart's Philadelphia years, including the figure in the larger portrait known as the Constable-Hamilton portrait (cat. 48), which was completed by the summer of 1797.

1. Morgan and Fielding 1931, p. 240.
2. Charles Baring's father was Charles Baring (1742–1829), younger brother of Sir Francis Baring (1740–1810) and partner with his older brother John (1730–1816) in the Exeter branch of the firm, John and Charles Baring and Company. On the Barings, see Ralph W. Hidy, *The House of Baring in American Trade and Finance* (Cambridge, Mass.: Harvard University Press, 1949), pp. 10, 44, 487 n. 25; *Burke's Genealogical and Heraldic History of the Landed Gentry*, 18th ed. (London: Burke's Peerage, 1965–72), vol. 3, p. 387. Philip Ziegler, *The Sixth Great Power: Barings, 1762–1929* (London: Collins, 1988), pp. 15–19, 22–24, 366 appendix I, fig. 1 (family tree).
3. Hidy, *House of Baring*, pp. 43–45. In 1803 Henry Baring became a partner in the House of Baring.
4. Alexander Baring, *My Recollections, 1848–1931* (Santa Barbara, Calif.: Schauer Printing Studio, 1933), pp. 192–93.
5. Baring and his first wife, Susan Hayward, widow of South Carolinian John Hayward, were married in November 1797; he married his second wife, Constance Dent, daughter of John Herbert Dent of the United States Navy, in 1847. They lived in Flat Rock, N.C.
6. The example of the Historical Society of Pennsylvania, formerly owned by British consul Gilbert Robertson, is listed in Park 1926, p. 866, no. 36; Morgan and Fielding 1931, pp. 275–76, no. 36. The Historical Society's pictures have recently been transferred to the Atwater Kent Museum of Philadelphia.

40

7. Park 1926, pp. 864–65, no. 35; Morgan and Fielding 1931, pp. 274–75, no. 35. The portrait was ordered from Stuart, December 27, 1799, and delivered in 1803. According to the 1803 report of the committee appointed to acquire the portrait, which included Benjamin Latrobe, it was painted "about 6 years ago."

8. Park 1926, p. 885, no. 84; Morgan and Fielding 1931, p. 302, no. 86.

Similar head-and-shoulders examples are owned by the Historical Society of Pennsylvania (fig. 94),[6] the American Philosophical Society (fig. 95),[7] and the United States Capitol (fig. 96), a painting that formerly belonged to Edward Penington (see cat. 63).[8] Morgan and Fielding described this group: "In all canvases of this type, the face is rounder, the nose longer and more aquiline and the expression different from the Athenaeum head. All are carefully and thoroughly painted and done probably about 1798. The majority show the saw-toothed queue ribbon, dark eyes and lace jabot. All

Fig. 94. *George Washington,* 1796–1803. Oil on canvas, 29 x 24 in. (73.7 x 61 cm). Historical Society of Pennsylvania Collection, Atwater Kent Museum of Philadelphia

Fig. 95. *George Washington,* 1797–1803. Oil on canvas, 29¼ x 24¼ in. (74.3 x 61.5 cm). American Philosophical Society, Philadelphia (58.P.25)

Fig. 96. *George Washington* (the Edward Penington portrait), 1796–1803. Oil on canvas, 28¾ x 23⅝ in. (73 x 60 cm). U.S. Senate Collection, United States Capitol, Washington, D.C.; Purchased by the Joint Committee on the Library, 1886 (31.00004)

which have been traced so far to purchasers in this period (1796–1798) or to original Pennsylvania owners (who might have made their purchases during Stuart's residence in Philadelphia and Germantown), and all of the left side of the face found in England are of this [t]ype. . . ."[9] Like these portraits, the painting owned by the Huntington has a face that seems more rectangular than the original Athenaeum, as well as a slightly turned-down mouth, a long torso that reflects the possibility that it was copied from a portrait showing more of Washington's figure, a large, lace shirt ruffle, and a queue ribbon with a sawtooth outline. In this painting the overall technique demonstrates careful drawing with the brush; in this it is very similar to the Constable-Hamilton portrait (cat. 48). The loose treatment of the hair, with gray wisps painted over the area of ground that is left unpainted, and the very flat and sketchy quality of the coat indicate that it is a replica.

9. Morgan and Fielding 1931, p. 242.

The handling of the translucent lace of the shirt ruffle, in its striking inventiveness, is very characteristic of Stuart's brilliant technique. The lace is painted to indicate that it falls over the lapels of Washington's black coat. A close look reveals that Stuart only painted the dark color of the coat up to the outer edges of the lacy area. After painting the white lace in the space reserved for it, Stuart added dabs of gray-black paint within the lace pattern to suggest the presence of the dark coat behind it. Finally, he added small dots of white along the curved edges of the lace as they overlap the black coat. While it is clear that the artist had already worked out the general placement of the colors, here and in other early examples the variety and freshness of the brushwork are particularly noticeable. The large swirls of the lace shirt ruffle are frequently repeated with variations and short cuts in other pictures made in Philadelphia, including the example in the U.S. Capitol that formerly belonged to Edward Penington and the example at the National Gallery of Art (fig. 98) that formerly belonged to William MacDonald of Baltimore, which in other respects have more in common with the example at the Sterling and Francine Clark Art Institute (cat. 41).

EGM

41. GEORGE WASHINGTON

1796–1803
Oil on canvas, 28⅞ x 24 in. (73.5 x 61.1 cm)
Sterling and Francine Clark Art Institute,
Williamstown, Massachusetts (1955.16)

1. The portrait was catalogued in Margaret C. Conrads, *American Paintings and Sculpture at the Sterling and Francine Clark Art Institute* (New York: Hudson Hills Press, 1990), pp. 195–96. It is not included in Park 1926 but is listed in Fielding 1923, p. 203, no. 82, as owned by Robert S. Clark in Paris, and with the same owner in Morgan and Fielding 1931, p. 326, no. XXXII, in a list of attributed portraits that the authors had not seen. It is also listed in Eisen 1932, p. 185. It was included in the exhibition "America: The New World in 19th Century Painting," Österreichische Galerie Belvedere, Vienna, March 17–June 20, 1999, and briefly discussed in Marc Simpson, "'A Big Anglo-Saxon Total': American and British Painting, 1670–1890," in *America: The New World in 19th Century Painting*, exh. cat., ed. Stephan Koja (Munich, London, New York: Prestel, 1999), pp. 61 fig. 6, 214. I thank Adam Greenhalgh for his assistance with this portrait.
2. The report is by Michael Heslip, Williamstown Regional Art Conservation Laboratory, July 25, 1987.
3. Park 1926, p. 889, no. 96; Morgan and Fielding 1931, p. 308, no. 100.

This replica of Washington's portrait, like that at the Huntington (cat. 40), was painted in Philadelphia, as indicated by its provenance,[1] but it is most likely a slightly later example. Differences in details include a less intricate shirt ruffle and less sense of the body as a solid form. The areas painted with white, including the face, the stock, the lace, and the hair are depicted in a thick impasto, with a special effort in details of the face. According to a recent conservation report, the "flesh tones of the face cover the under design of transparent brown drawing."[2] The brown drawing was probably part of Stuart's copying process, although thin brown lines can sometimes be seen on the surface of the paintings as final touches. Portraits similar to this one include the example in the William A. Clark Collection at the Corcoran Gallery of Art (fig. 97),[3] the portrait at the United States Capitol formerly owned by Colonel John Chesnut of South Carolina, who sat for Stuart in Philadelphia,[4] and the example at the National Gallery of Art (fig. 98) that was once owned by William MacDonald of Baltimore.[5] The intense blue eyes of this version recall George Washington Parke Custis's remark that Stuart painted Washington's eyes a deep blue, adding, "In a hundred years they will have faded to the right color."[6]

The first owner of the present painting was Thomas Lloyd Moore (d. 1819) of Philadelphia, who served in several Pennsylvania regiments during the Revolutionary War, reaching the rank of major, and in the United States Infantry as a lieutenant colonel in 1799–1800. George Washington, who dined at Moore's house in 1787, referred to him in 1783 as among "the best Officers who were in the Army."[7] As is true of other portraits of Washington by Stuart, this one was owned by a member of a family, social, business circle that included patrons of the artist. Moore's daughter Eliza married Richard Willing, son of Thomas Willing, who was painted by Stuart about 1795 (private collection).[8] Stuart also painted portraits of Thomas Willing's five daughters (see cats. 51, 52). When Moore's grandson Thomas Moore Willing offered the portrait for sale in

4. Park 1926, p. 885, no. 83; Morgan and Fielding 1931, p. 302, no. 85.

5. Park 1926, p. 881, no. 73; Morgan and Fielding 1931, pp. 295–96, no. 73; Miles 1995, pp. 235–37.

6. Quoted in Tuckerman 1870, p. 54; also quoted in Evans 1999, p. 143 n. 16.

7. Francis B. Heitman, *Historical Register of Officers of the Continental Army during the War of the Revolution, April, 1771, to December, 1783* (rev. ed., 1914; addenda by Robert H. Kelby; reprint, Baltimore: Genealogical Publishing Co., 1973), p. 400; Donald Jackson and Dorothy Twohig, eds., *The Diaries of George Washington* (Charlottesville: University Press of Virginia, 1976–79), vol. 5, pp. 169, 240; Conrads, *American Paintings and Sculpture at the Clark Art Institute*, p. 196.

8. Park 1926, pp. 825–26, no. 926.

9. Thomas Moore Willing, letter to Lewis Rogers, his agent in New York, October 19, 1845; a photocopy of the letter is in the curatorial file for this painting, Clark Art Institute.

10. George Heard Hamilton, Director, Clark Art Institute, letter to Lord Monk-Bretton, February 3, 1970, curatorial files, Clark Art Institute. Margaret Conrads (*American Paintings and Sculpture at the Clark Art Institute*, p. 196) provides details of this provenance: R. L. Paterson, 1845; Charles Paterson, by descent; Mrs. Elizabeth S. Clark, ca. 1905; Stephen C. Clark, 1909; Robert Sterling Clark, by 1911.

11. The signature was compared with examples on letters in the Cadwalader Family Papers, Ms. 1454, Historical Society of Pennsylvania, Philadelphia. For example, a similar signature can be seen on the letter Willing wrote to George Cadwalader, June 15, 1844, George Cadwalader Correspondence.

12. The research by George Heard Hamilton, former director of the Clark, is discussed in Conrads, *American Paintings and Sculpture at the Clark Art Institute*, pp. 195–96. The provenance of the portrait is given in a letter to Hamilton from Lord Monk-Bretton, February 11, 1970, curatorial files, Clark Art Institute. The portrait is listed in Fielding 1923, p. 180, no. 59; Park 1926, p. 876, no. 60; Morgan and Fielding 1931, pp. 287–88, no. 59.

13. Lord Monk-Bretton, letter to Hamilton, February 11, 1970, curatorial files, Clark Art Institute.

Fig. 97. *George Washington*, 1796–1803. Oil on canvas, 29⅞ x 24½ in. (75.9 x 62.2 cm). The Corcoran Gallery of Art, Washington, D.C.; William A. Clark Collection (26.172)

Fig. 98. *George Washington*, 1796–1803. Oil on canvas, 29 x 24¼ in. (73.6 x 61.4 cm). National Gallery of Art, Washington, D.C.; Gift of Jean McGinley Draper (1954.9.2)

1845, he described it as "The picture of Washington which . . . was painted for my grandfather Col: Moore by Stewart & Washington gave it one sitting at Stewart's request because my grandfather stood for the legs when Stewart painted one of his full length pictures of Washington. I believe it was that one ordered by Mr. Bingham & which I think is in the possession of the Marquis of Lansdowne. Most of the pictures of Washington are copies by Stewart of his first picture, and this picture has the additional merit of having recd one sitting from Washington himself. This Mrs. Moore frequently told me & boasted much of its excellence."[9] Willing's claim that Moore stood for Stuart for the pose of Washington in the Lansdowne portrait is not reflected in discussions of that portrait in the literature (see cat. 45), and the claim of this replica to life sittings is spurious.

The portrait's early provenance seems to be accurate. Willing's letter was provided to the purchaser of the portrait in December 1845, R. L. Paterson, whose niece Theresa Le Roy Paterson later provided copies of this and other relevant letters to Stephen C. Clark after it was acquired by his mother, Mrs. Alfred Corning Clark. Stephen Clark's brother Robert Sterling Clark was the owner by 1911.[10] A misreading of the signature on the letter as "W. Willing" led to attempts to identify the seller as William Willing. Moore did not have a grandson named William Willing, however, and the signature is definitely that of Thomas Moore Willing, who signed his letters "T. M. Willing."[11] Adding to doubts that the seller was Thomas Moore Willing was the discovery that a similar provenance had been provided for a portrait of Washington sold by Thomas Moore Willing in 1841 to Joshua Bates of Boston, a business associate of Baring Brothers who immigrated to the United States. The second Baron Monk-Bretton purchased the portrait in 1912 from Bates's grandson Victor Van De Weyer, who was Monk-Bretton's wife's uncle.[12] Its most recent owner of record is John Charles Dodson, third Baron Monk-Bretton, of Sussex, England.[13] It has not been possible to determine whether both portraits were owned by Thomas Lloyd Moore.   EGM

41

ca. 1803

Oil on canvas, 29¼ x 24 in. (74.3 x 61 cm)

The Corcoran Gallery of Art, Washington, D.C.;

Bequest of Mrs. Benjamin Ogle Tayloe (02.3)

1. Mason 1879, p. 107. J. Stuart (1876, p. 373) wrote that it was painted for Tayloe.

2. Elizabeth Bryant Johnston, *Original Portraits of Washington, including Statues, Monuments, and Medals* (Boston: James R. Osgood, 1882), p. 101.

3. On this portrait, see [Henry T. Tuckerman], "Original Portraits of Washington," *Putnam's Monthly Magazine* 6 (1855), p. 345; Tuckerman 1870, p. 116; Fielding 1923, p. 167, no. 46; Park 1926, p. 871, no. 47; Morgan and Fielding 1931, pp. 280–81, no. 46; Eisen 1932, pp. 174–77; *A Catalogue of the Collection of American Paintings in the Corcoran Gallery of Art* (Washington, D.C.: Corcoran Gallery of Art, 1966–73), vol. 1, p. 28. Adam Greenhalgh was very helpful in cataloguing this portrait of Washington.

4. Park 1926, pp. 739–41, nos. 822, 823.

5. Park 1926, p. 886, no. 85; Morgan and Fielding 1931, pp. 302–3, no. 87.

6. Eisen 1932, p. 180.

7. Park 1926, p. 880, no. 70; Morgan and Fielding 1931, p. 294, no. 70.

8. Park 1926, p. 882, no. 74; William Kloss and Doreen Bolger, *Art in the White House: A Nation's Pride* (Washington, D.C.: White House Historical Association in cooperation with the National Geographic Society, 1992), p. 349.

9. Park 1926, p. 870, no. 46; Morgan and Fielding 1931, p. 280, no. 45; John Caldwell and Oswaldo Rodriguez Roque, *American Paintings in The*

According to George Mason, his early biographer, Stuart took this portrait with him to Washington, D.C., when he moved there from Philadelphia in 1803.[1] Elizabeth Bryant Johnston added in 1882 that he took it "as an example of his skill, when he came to paint Jefferson and his cabinet."[2] The portrait was purchased by John Tayloe of Mount Airy, Richmond County, Virginia, owner of the Octagon House in Washington, D.C., designed by Stuart's friend William Thornton.[3] Stuart painted portraits of Tayloe and his wife, Ann Ogle Tayloe (private collection), in 1804.[4]

This example of the Athenaeum replicas appears to have been painted with less effort than his earlier ones in the exhibition (cats. 40, 41). Its more abbreviated shirt ruffle is linen rather than lace, thus requiring less elaborate brushwork, and the coat is very flat. As in earlier examples, the areas of white—the powdered hair and the shirt ruffle—are painted in reserved spaces and the surrounding dark colors are painted up to the contours. After painting the jagged areas of shadow in the shirt ruffle with gray, Stuart added slight touches of white highlights to its edges. As before, he used fine touches of red-brown pigment to give detail to the eyes.

The painting is similar to a group of portraits owned by patrons in Philadelphia, Baltimore, and Washington. The portraits with a Philadelphia provenance include examples at the Pennsylvania Academy of the Fine Arts, bequest of Paul Beck, warden of the port of Philadelphia;[5] the Everson Museum of Art, Syracuse, New York (fig. 99), owned first by John Richards, agent for Baring Brothers in America;[6] and the National Portrait Gallery, London (fig. 100), owned by Charles Cotesworth Pinckney, minister to France from 1796 to 1798.[7] Also in the group is the portrait owned by Robert Barry of Baltimore, now with the White House Historical Association (fig. 101),[8] and the Carroll-Havemeyer portrait (The Metropolitan Museum of Art), which first belonged to Daniel Carroll of Duddington Manor, Washington, D.C.[9] Although all of the early owners of these portraits could have acquired them in Philadelphia, Barry and Carroll could also have acquired theirs from Stuart in Washington. While this suggests that

Fig. 99. *George Washington*, ca. 1803. Oil on canvas, 28¾ x 24 in. (73 x 61 cm). Everson Museum of Art, Syracuse, N.Y. (P.C.76.35)

Fig. 100. *George Washington*, ca. 1803. Oil on canvas, 28¾ x 23¾ in. (73 x 60.3 cm). National Portrait Gallery, London (NPG 2041)

Fig. 101. *George Washington*, ca. 1803. Oil on canvas, 30 x 25 in. (76.2 x 63.5 cm). White House Historical Association (White House Collection), Washington, D.C.; Gift of Mr. and Mrs. Charles Payson in memory of Pvt. Daniel Carroll Payson (949.3496.1)

42

Metropolitan Museum of Art, vol. 1, *A Catalogue of Works by Artists Born by 1815* (New York: Metropolitan Museum of Art, 1994), pp. 186–88.
10. Morgan and Fielding 1931, p. 246.

some were painted in Washington, there is no evidence for this. According to John Hill Morgan and Mantle Fielding, "All canvases which can be traced to a possible purchaser during Stuart's residence in Washington (1803–1805) are of this type. The face . . . shows clearly the development from the Atheneaum Head into the Boston canvases."[10]

EGM

43. George Washington

ca. 1820
Oil on wood panel, 26¼ x 21 in. (66.7 x 53.3 cm)
Museum of Art, Rhode Island School of Design,
Providence; Public Subscription Fund (22.220)

1. Mason 1879, p. 221; Fielding 1923, p. 160, no. 39;
   Park 1926, p. 868, no. 40; Morgan and Fielding
   1931, p. 278, no. 40; Eisen 1932, p. 171.
2. Morgan and Fielding 1931, p. 246.
3. Park 1926, pp. 871–72, no. 49; Morgan and
   Fielding 1931, pp. 281–82, no. 48.
4. Park 1926, p. 874, no. 55; Morgan and Fielding 1931,
   p. 285, no. 54.
5. Park 1926, p. 869, no. 42; Morgan and Fielding
   1931, p. 278, no. 41, illus.
6. *DAB*, vol. 6, pp. 370–71.
7. See Park 1926, pp. 506–7, nos. 526, 527 (Anna
   Powell Mason), and pp. 671–72, nos. 741, 742
   (Miriam Clark Mason, Mrs. David Sears).
8. See Park 1926, pp. 512–13, nos. 532, 533.
9. Mason 1879, p. 221.

This replica of Stuart's Athenaeum portrait is one of a distinct group of copies of the Athenaeum portrait whose provenances indicate that they were painted after Stuart's move to Boston in 1805.[1] The faces, which are round in comparison to earlier replicas, are painted in a softer manner. The clothing includes the usual black coat, a very quickly painted, abbreviated lace shirt ruffle, and a small queue ribbon rather than a large bow. According to John Hill Morgan and Mantle Fielding, "All of the canvases, except No. 28 [*Washington at Dorchester Heights*, fig. 159], at present known to have been painted after 1805, are of this type."[2] The group includes examples at the Huntington (fig. 102), painted in 1819 for Isaac McKim of Boston;[3] at the National Gallery of Art, Washington, in the Gibbs-Coolidge series (fig. 103);[4] and at Kykuit (fig. 104), purchased from Stuart in about 1820 by Dr. George C. Shattuck of Boston.[5] Like the portrait here, some of them are on wood panel of the smaller size characteristic of Stuart's later work in Boston. This suggests a date for this portrait that is later than Park's estimate of about 1805.

The first owner of this portrait was Jonathan Mason (1756–1831), who served as United States Senator from Massachusetts from November 1800, after the resignation of Senator Benjamin Goodhue, to March 1803.[6] Stuart painted portraits of Mason's daughters Anna Powell Mason (fig. 136) and Miriam Clark Mason in Washington in 1804–5.[7] He may also have painted Mason and his wife, Susannah Powell Mason (fig. 137), at this time.[8] Senator Mason then persuaded Stuart to move to Boston.[9] He no doubt told Stuart that he would find sitters eager to be painted by him. In Boston Stuart later painted portraits of Mason's third daughter, Susan Powell Mason Warren (unlocated), and her husband, Dr. John Collins Warren (cat. 83).

EGM

Fig. 102. *George Washington*, 1819. Oil on canvas, 27 x 22 in. (68.6 x 55.9 cm). Huntington Library, Art Collections, and Botanical Gardens, San Marino, Calif. (19.11)

Fig. 103. *George Washington*, ca. 1821. Oil on wood, 26⅜ x 21⅝ in. (67 x 55 cm). National Gallery of Art, Washington, D.C.; Gift of Thomas Jefferson Coolidge IV in memory of his great-grandfather Thomas Jefferson Coolidge, his grandfather Thomas Jefferson Coolidge II, and his father, Thomas Jefferson Coolidge III (1979.5.1)

Fig. 104. *George Washington*, ca. 1820. Oil on canvas, 30¼ x 25¼ in. (76.8 x 64.1 cm). National Trust for Historic Preservation, Kykuit, Pocantico Hills, N.Y.

43

44. GEORGE WASHINGTON

1825
Oil on canvas, 30 x 25 in. (76.2 x 63.5 cm)
The Walters Art Museum, Baltimore (37.151)

1. A photograph of this receipt (unlocated) is reproduced in Edward S. King, "Stuart's Last Portrait of Washington: Its History and Technique," *Journal of the Walters Gallery* 9 (1946), p. 85; this article presents a full discussion of the painting, including X-radiography, pp. 80–96. The portrait is also listed in catalogues of the Walters Art Gallery collection, including, most recently, Edward S. King and Marvin C. Ross, *Catalogue of the American Works of Art* (Baltimore: Trustees of the Walters Art Gallery, 1956), pp. 10–11, no. 34; as well as in Mason 1879, p. 107; Elizabeth Bryant Johnston, *Original Portraits of Washington, including Statues, Monuments, and Medals* (Boston: James R. Osgood and Co., 1882), p. 102; Samuel P. Avery, *Some Account of the "Gibbs-Channing" Portrait of George Washington, Painted by Gilbert Stuart* (New York: Privately printed, 1900), pp. 16–17. As King noted ("Stuart's Last Portrait of Washington"), the portrait was identified as two different paintings by cataloguers of Stuart's work: in Fielding 1923, as no. 61, p. 182, and as no. 76, p. 197; in Park 1926, as no. 62, p. 877, and no. 76, p. 882; in Morgan and Fielding 1931, as no. 61, p. 289, and as no. 76, p. 297; in Eisen 1932, pp. 184 and 187, all of this suggesting that Gilmor owned two portraits of Washington by Stuart. King cleared up the confusion in correspondence with Morgan in 1941 (copies in the curatorial files, Walters Art Museum).
2. Stuart's receipt and the letter from Truman were acquired by Madeleine Vinton Dahlgren when she purchased the portrait in 1872. In 1885 she sent them to Samuel P. Avery, agent for the next owner of the portrait, William T. Walters; see King, "Stuart's Last Portrait of Washington," pp. 84, 95–96 nn. 11, 14.
3. Lance Lee Humphries, "Robert Gilmor, Jr. (1774–1848): Baltimore Collector and American Art Patron" (Ph.D. diss., University of Virginia, 1998), vol. 2, p. 36, quoting Robert Gilmor's catalogue of his collection, begun in 1823.
4. Johnston, *Original Portraits of Washington*, p. 102; Avery, *Some Account of the "Gibbs-Channing" Portrait*, p. 17. King ("Stuart's Last Portrait of Washington," p. 84) wrote that he did not find the document, assuming it was a letter from Stuart himself to Gilmor.
5. Dunlap 1834, vol. 1, pp. 198–99.

Stuart painted his last replica of the Athenaeum portrait for Baltimore art collector Robert Gilmor Jr. (1774–1848). Stuart's receipt for payment for this portrait reads, "Received 12 Aug 1825 of Rob Gilmor, Esq., per R Truman, one hundred & fifty Dollars for a portrait of General Washington. $150—G Stuart."[1] Gilmor received a letter dated August 18, 1825, from Robert Truman about the shipping of the portrait: "I received in [due] course your esteemed favour of 30 June & I have the pleasure to say that the Portrait is finished: enclosed is the receipt for its cost. I have been with Daggett & he will have the case ready & attend to its shipping by the Helen Hallett, which will leave this [place] on Saturday. I leave Town for Lebanon this day or would have had the Mate's Receipt & I could not have it shipped previously, as Mr. Stuart did not think it sufficiently dry. As to price he has but one, for I mentioned to him that it was not so much an object with you, as the goodness of the copy, & he [replied], I will do all I can for Mr. Gilmor, but I have but one price: you will, I think, be pleased."[2] The painting is listed in Gilmor's catalogue of his collection as by "Gabriel Stewart," with the name "Gilbert" added above; he noted that it was "Painted for me by Stewart."[3] Elizabeth Johnston in 1882 and Samuel P. Avery in 1900 wrote that the painting was accompanied by a letter from Stuart. Avery, however, also wrote that Gilmor had Stuart's receipt "and some lines saying that, painting it for such a distinguished amateur, he had taken especial pains with it, and hoped Mr. Gilmor would be pleased."[4] This seems to be a description of Truman's letter.

The portrait is very loosely painted and, as Stuart's last replica of the Athenaeum portrait, has been the subject of some discussion. According to John Neagle, "Mr. Stuart told me one day when we were before this original portrait, that he never could make a copy of it to satisfy himself, and that at last, having made so many, he worked mechanically and with little interest. The last one I believe ever made by him, was for Mr. Robert Gilmor, of Baltimore. I asked him if he ever intended to finish the coat and back-ground of the original picture? To this he replied, 'No: and as this is the only legacy I can leave to my family, I will let it remain untouched.'"[5] Recently, Dorinda Evans suggested that it is possible that most of the portrait was made by an assistant, "given the demand and the tediousness of copying." To Evans,

his last known copy of the Athenaeum head . . . has a strange overall softness, almost a smudged effect in form and color, that makes it unconvincing as by him; his hand is possibly in evidence only in some minor touches, as in the incongruously prominent penciling around the tip of the nose and around the eyes. That Stuart should retouch an assistant's copy to make it his own, as appears to be the case here, is, in fact, consistent with his training in London and under West. The man who ordered the portrait, Robert Gilmor, a wealthy merchant and art patron in Baltimore, offered to pay more for a better-than-usual copy but Stuart replied that there was only once price, meaning he would not increase his participation.[6]

However, while the technique of the face is very soft, the representation of the lace shirt ruffle is consistent with the other renditions of the Athenaeum portrait that Stuart painted in his later years (see cat. 43). Stuart had good reason to make a special effort for Gilmor, whose personal connection with the artist began almost thirty years earlier, when Gilmor as a young man visited Stuart's Germantown studio on July 27, 1797. There

44

6. Evans 1999, p. 84. She added (p. 148 n. 16) that this copy "arouses suspicion also because Jane Stuart was working closely with her father at the time, and he spoke of her as the best copyist of his work."

7. Robert Gilmor Jr., *Memorandums Made in a Tour to the Eastern States in the Year 1797* (Boston: Trustees of the Boston Public Library, 1892), p. 6.

8. Robert C. Alberts, *The Golden Voyage: The Life and Times of William Bingham, 1752–1804* (Boston: Houghton Mifflin Co., 1969), pp. 114–15, 138, 224–26, 415.

he saw the second version of the Lansdowne portrait, which was painted for William Bingham, and heard Stuart's plans to make replicas of the portrait (see cat. 46). In addition to his comments about the Lansdowne portrait, Gilmor wrote, "There were a number of other portraits unfinished of distinguished characters, which were very excellent. As a portrait painter Stewart is not excelled I believe by any man living. He has the appearance of a man who is attached to drinking, as his face is bloated & red. He possesses a good deal of humour & related several very interesting anecdotes respecting the Historical painter Trumbul and the Player Kemble. On leaving him he desired we

9. On these portraits, see Park 1926, pp. 351–53, nos. 332, 334. On the portrait of Robert Gilmor Sr., see Humphries, "Robert Gilmor, Jr.," vol. 2, pp. 34–35; Sona K. Johnston, *American Paintings, 1750–1900, from the Collection of the Baltimore Museum of Art* (Baltimore: Baltimore Museum of Art, 1983), pp. 146–47. On the portrait of Gilmor Jr., see *American Paintings in the Museum of Fine Arts, Boston* (Boston: Museum of Fine Arts, 1969), vol. 1, pp. 260–61, no. 950.

would on our return pay him another visit and view the progress he was making in his copies, for which purpose he had retired from the busy interruptions he was liable to in Philad[a] to the calm and pleasant retreat of Germantown."[7] Gilmor's entrée to Stuart's studio, paved by the vicomte de Noailles (see cat. 54), undoubtedly came about because of his father's business partnership with William Bingham (see cat. 53), Stuart's most important patron in Philadelphia.[8] Although Gilmor Jr. was never painted by Stuart, the artist portrayed his father, Robert Gilmor Sr. (1803; Baltimore Museum of Art), and his nephew Robert Gilmor III (Museum of Fine Arts, Boston). The youngest Gilmor was painted when he was a student at Harvard College (class of 1828), about the time Stuart completed this last portrait of Washington for his uncle.[9]

EGM

45. George Washington (The Lansdowne Portrait)

1796

Oil on canvas, 97 1/2 x 62 1/2 in. (247.7 x 158.8 cm)
National Portrait Gallery, Smithsonian Institution, Washington, D.C.; acquired as a gift to the nation through the generosity of the Donald W. Reynolds Foundation (NPG.2001.13)

Painted for William Petty, first Marquis of Lansdowne (1737–1805), in 1796 as the gift of wealthy Philadelphia merchant William Bingham and his wife, Anne Willing Bingham (see cats. 53, 51), this portrait, known as the Lansdowne portrait, is Stuart's grandest American accomplishment.[1] It was quickly recognized as the best pictorial summation of Washington's public role as first president of the United States. Its immediate success led to commissions for replicas (see cats. 46, 47) and unauthorized painted and engraved copies. As with Stuart's other life portraits of Washington, conclusions about its early history are made difficult by the lack of documentation and by discrepancies in the existing documentation. It is unclear, for example, whether the initial commission came from the Marquis of Lansdowne, whose name appears on Stuart's 1795 list of those wishing portraits of Washington (see "The Portraits of George Washington") or from Bingham. According to Jane Stuart, the commission for the painting was from Lord Lansdowne, after Stuart had painted his first portrait of Washington, known as the Vaughan portrait (see cat. 35): "Lord Lansdowne gave him a commission to paint for him a whole-length of Washington to take to England. Mr. Bingham, a resident of Philadelphia, called upon Stuart, and was very solicitous of having the honor of presenting the picture to his Lordship. Stuart, knowing the extreme fastidiousness of the English nobility, declined; but Mr. Bingham persuaded him that it would be considered a compliment, and then hurried him so to complete it, that Stuart was made seriously ill by the effort."[2] William Dunlap, quoting artist John Neagle, who knew Stuart, recorded the same information.[3] However, when Stuart drafted a letter to the Marquis of Lansdowne in 1800 about the engraving of the portrait, he wrote, "It was, therefore, with peculiar pleasure, that I found myself invited by Mr. Bingham to take the portrait of President Washington, to be presented to your Lordship."[4] A third suggestion is that of Jonathan Mason Jr., the son of one of Stuart's significant Boston patrons, who stated that Stuart "came to America at the suggestion of the house of Barings, Alexander (Lord Ashburton) and brother to paint the father of his country for their father-in-law Mr. Bingham of Philadelphia."[5] Another key figure in this transatlantic exchange was

1. On the Lansdowne portrait, see Dunlap 1834, vol. 1, pp. 198–206; Mason 1879, pp. 87–105; Elizabeth Bryant Johnston, *Original Portraits of Washington, including Statues, Monuments, and Medals* (Boston: James R. Osgood and Co., 1882), pp. 80–90; Charles Henry Hart, "Stuart's Lansdowne Portrait of Washington," *Harper's New Monthly Magazine* 93 (August 1896), pp. 378–86; Fielding 1923, pp. 89–98, 133, no. 17; Park 1926, pp. 854–55, no. 19; Morgan and Fielding 1931, pp. 223, 238, 261 no. 19, 356–59; Eisen 1932, pp. 69–73, 93–106; Mount 1964, pp. 198–216; Evans 1999, pp. 63, 67–69, and extensive notes, pp. 141–44; *George Washington* 2002. Writers up to and including Mount (1964) described the painting at the Pennsylvania Academy of the Fine Arts (cat. 46) as the original, although Morgan and Fielding (1931, pp. 356–59) also offered strong evidence in favor of the portrait painted for Lansdowne as the original. For a detailed provenance of the Lansdowne portrait, see Margaret C. S. Christman, "The Story of the Lansdowne Washington," in *George Washington* 2002, pp. 42–75.
2. J. Stuart 1876, p. 369.
3. Dunlap 1834, vol. 1, p. 203.

4. The unlocated draft of the letter, which was never sent, is quoted in Mason 1879, pp. 95.

5. Jonathan Mason Jr., "From the Recollections of an Octogenarian," Joseph Downs Collection of Manuscripts and Printed Ephemera, Winterthur Library, Winterthur Del.

6. "The whole length for Lansdowne was not his <u>Second</u>—that in the Atheneum is the 2^d begun for Mrs. Washington—The 3^d being copied from his 2^d with <u>one</u> sitting in the Summer of 96—from the life—Thus making it, in some degree his 3^d portrait. The Whole length, of course, was <u>first Original</u> Picture, as engraved"; Rembrandt Peale, letter to an unidentified "Dear Sir," May 7, no year given, Robert C. Graham Collection of Artists Letters, Archives of American Art, Smithsonian Institution, Washington, D.C.

7. The letter, owned by the Earl of Rosebery, is on long-term loan to the National Portrait Gallery, Washington, D.C.; see Christman, in *George Washington* 2002, p. 44, illus. p. 45. Mount (1964, pp. 200–201) suggested that this sitting was for the Athenaeum portrait, which he believed was the initial commission by Bingham. He also wrote (p. 204) that the full-length portrait was painted at Stuart's Germantown studio. However, it is more likely that Stuart moved to Germantown to paint the replicas; see Robert Gilmor Jr., *Memorandums Made in a Tour to the Eastern States in the Year 1797* (Boston: Trustees of the Boston Public Library, 1892), p. 6.

8. George Washington Parke Custis, letter to Thomas Carberry, April 7, 1839, in "Original Documents," *Magazine of American History* 13 (January–June 1885), p. 583.

9. George Washington Parke Custis, *Recollections and Private Memoirs of Washington*, with a memoir of the author by his daughter and illustrative and explanatory notes by Benson J. Lossing (New York: Derby and Jackson, 1860), p. 521 n.

10. William R. Smith, letter to John A. McAllister, November 24, 1858, McAllister Manuscripts, Library Company of Philadelphia.

11. Mason 1879, p. 92.

12. Ibid., citing Mrs. William Bingham Clymer.

13. Ibid. According to Mount 1964, p. 206, the cast was made with the help of Charles Willson Peale; he cited Charles Coleman Sellers, *Charles Willson Peale*, vol. 2, *Later Life (1790–1827)* (Philadelphia: American Philosophical Society, 1947), p. 94. Editors of the Peale Family Papers at the National Portrait Gallery have not found the source of Sellers's information.

the charming, socially perceptive Anne Willing Bingham. She was able to persuade George Washington to sit for the portrait at a time when he had grown impatient with artists and their requests for sittings. Her fondness for Lord Lansdowne and her gratefulness for his social courtesies when she and her husband were in London during the years 1783–86 are referred to in his letters to Lansdowne, and she was the person Lansdowne thanked on receiving the portrait.

When and how many times Washington posed for the portrait is not recorded. The usual practice for artists in England was at least three sittings, perhaps lasting about two hours each. The sitter's time was usually limited to posing for the face and perhaps the hands. Rembrandt Peale remembered that Stuart, had only one sitting for the Lansdowne portrait.[6] A letter from Washington to Stuart, written on April 11, 1796, documents the sitting: "Sir, I am under promise to Mrs. Bingham, to set for you tomorrow at nine oclock, and wishing to know if it be convenient to you that I should do so, and whether it shall be at your own house, (as she talked of the State House) I send this note to you, to ask information. I am Sir Your Obedient Servt, G. Washington."[7] The sitting took place at the house at the southeast corner of Fifth and Chestnut Streets, in Philadelphia, owned by W. Moore Smith.

Following English practice, Stuart did not expect Washington to pose for the figure. Instead there were stand-ins, which may explain why Washington's grandson George Washington Parke Custis later commented, "The Head of Stuart is incomparably the best likeness of the Chief in his latter days, but in the person, that great Master of Portrait Painting failed entirely. . . . Stuart has given a plumpness, or fleshiness. . . . Washington was never fleshy, as witness his weight." Custis wrote that Washington estimated his own weight at about 210–220 pounds and said that his height was about six feet and that he was "of extraordinary breadth of frame, and a matchless combination of bone and muscle."[8] The shape of his body in the Lansdowne portrait is broader than this description suggests. Contemporaries recorded the names of three men who might have posed for Stuart. One of these, according to historian Benson J. Lossing, was "a small man named Smith, with whom Stuart boarded in Philadelphia."[9] This would have been William Moore Smith, whose son wrote John A. McAllister in 1858, "I am glad that Rembrandt Peale recollects the fact of Gilbert Stuart having a painting room in my fathers house—the circumstance of my Father <u>standing</u> for the full length figure, I conceive to be highly probable, as he was not only <u>in the house</u>, when, at least <u>one</u> of the pictures of Washington was painted, but W. Moore Smith was certainly a more graceful man in his proportions, and carriage, than Michael Keppele."[10] However, McAllister wrote George Champlin Mason, Stuart's biographer, in the 1870s, that a man named "Alderman Keppele stood for the figure. I had this from his daughter."[11] A third story related that the vicomte de Noailles was the model for the figure (see cat. 54).[12] Stuart may also have used casts to complete some aspects of the painting. Custis said that "the hands were painted from a wax cast of Stuart's own hand, which was much smaller than Washington's."[13]

The formal oratorical pose and the scale of the portrait, as well as the use of objects to represent thematic material, are hallmarks of the tradition of European portrait painting. Stuart was experienced at painting full-length portraits, having created several during his years in England and Ireland, and he was familiar, although perhaps not completely comfortable, with their challenges. This portrait is a striking departure from the image of Washington in earlier full-length portraits painted during the American Revolution by Charles Willson Peale and later by John Trumbull, who depicted

Washington in uniform, as commander in chief of the Continental army. Stuart's portrait instead points to Washington's civilian leadership. Except for the direction of his gaze, his face is reproduced from the Athenaeum portrait, carrying with it the physiognomic meanings of that portrait as seen by Stuart and his contemporaries (see cat. 38).

The clothing Washington wears points to his civilian role as president. He is dressed in a black velvet suit, the type of suit that he wore on public occasions. Choice of dress was one of the many protocol decisions made by the first president. Precedents included Thomas McKean of Pennsylvania, who, as president of Congress, had worn a "rich black velvet suit, a sword at his side," for the arrival of the French army in Philadelphia in 1781.[14] Jane Stuart recalled, "I have heard my mother say that the first time she saw [Washington], he entered the hall door, as she passed from the entry to the parlor, and that she thought him the most superb-looking person she had ever seen. He was then dressed in black velvet, with white lace ruffles, etc., exactly as Stuart's picture represented him."[15] For informal public occasions, Washington wore coats that were of other colors than black, such as brown (see cat. 37). The lace ruffles on the shirt at the neck and wrists were separate pieces of fabric attached to the shirt. According to Jane Stuart, Mrs. Washington had given the artist "a piece of lace, such as the General wore, to paint from."[16] Also in the Lansdowne portrait, Washington rests his left hand on the hilt of a sword. Its handle is wrapped in gold ribbon and has a gold tassel; its scabbard has a red ribbon attached with a metal buckle.[17] Although the sword was probably of military origin, Washington used it at this time for ceremonial purposes. Jane Stuart recalled that the vicomte de Noailles gave Stuart a "superb silver-mounted rapier" so that he could include it in the painting.[18]

Other pictorial elements carry additional meaning about the man and the time in which the painting was made. The neoclassical decorative elements of the furniture, which did not exist, are derived from the Great Seal of the United States, authorized by Congress in 1782 and still in use today. The oval medallion on the back of the armchair is draped with laurel, a symbol of victory, and its shield is like the one borne by the eagle on the Great Seal, a blue horizontal field with thirteen stars above thirteen alternating red and white vertical stripes. William Barton, one of the designers of the seal, described the shield in 1782 as representing the thirteen original states, individually and as a confederation. Two eagles at the top of the table leg are in upright positions, each holding a bundle of arrows—a symbol of war—in one claw like the eagle on the seal, but neither holds the olive branch, symbol of peace, in the other claw. Under the table are large books titled *General Orders*, *American Revolution*, and *Constitution & Laws of the United States*. These refer to past events: Washington's roles as commander of the American colonial army and as president of the Constitutional Convention of 1787 during the debates over the structure of the new government. The books on the table are titled *Federalist* and *Journal of Congress*. The Federalist Papers, written in 1787–88 by John Jay, James Madison, and Alexander Hamilton and published anonymously, discussed details of the new American Constitution, while the Journals of Congress recount the everyday actions and votes of Congress beginning in 1789. Also on the table are two blank papers and a silver inkwell with a quill pen. The inkwell, in the shape of an ark resting on figures of recumbent dogs, is engraved with the Washington family coat of arms. On the table as well is Washington's black hat with a black cockade. The color of a cockade could be a political symbol, as used, for example, by supporters of John Adams who marched in Philadelphia in 1798 with Federalist black cockades in their hats.[19] It is not documented, however, that Washington's black cockade was a political symbol.

14. Robert C. Alberts, *The Golden Voyage: The Life and Times of William Bingham, 1752–1804* (Boston: Houghton Mifflin Co., 1969), p. 109.

15. J. Stuart 1876, p. 372.

16. Ibid.

17. A sword very much like this one is at Mount Vernon.

18. Jane Stuart, quoted in Mason 1879, p. 92.

19. Alberts, *Golden Voyage*, p. 336.

20. As Dorinda Evans (1999, p. 67) points out, "Except for its specific associations, the work is consistent with a tradition of portraiture for aristocrats and royalty."

21. Park 1926, p. 50, citing Charles Henry Hart; Evans 1999, p. 67.

22. William R. Smith, letter to John A. McAllister, November 24, 1858, McAllister Manuscripts, Library Company of Philadelphia.

23. Mason 1879, pp. 99–100. This suggests that Stuart had not finished the original Lansdowne when Constable and McCormick saw it in the fall of 1796, unless perhaps McCormick had visited Stuart earlier in the year.

24. *The Time Piece*, February 7, 1798, quoted in Whitley 1932, p. 108; Morgan and Fielding 1931, p. 360.

25. William Bingham, Account Book, Bingham, W., Manuscripts, Lilly Library, Indiana University, Bloomington. The page is undated but appears from the other entries, which refer to portraits of the Bingham family, and from the accounts on adjacent pages, to be from 1797; see fig. 108.

26. William Bingham, letter to Rufus King, November 29, 1796, in Charles R. King, ed., *The Life and Correspondence of Rufus King* (New York: G. P. Putnam's Sons, 1896), vol. 2, p. 112. The original letter is in "American Political Letters, 1796–1799," Rufus King Papers, vol. 41, New-York Historical Society, according to Evans 1999, p. 143 n. 17.

27. Lord Lansdowne, letter to Anne Willing Bingham (the recipient's name and the date of the letter are not on the document), Bingham, W., Manuscripts, Lilly Library.

28. *Oracle and Public Advertiser* (London), May 15, 1797, quoted in Whitley 1932, pp. 99–100.

29. See *DNB*, vol. 15, pp. 1005–13.

30. Frederick S. Allis Jr., ed., *William Bingham's Maine Lands, 1790–1820* (Boston: Colonial Society of Massachusetts, 1954), vol. 1, p. 79; Alberts, *Golden Voyage*, pp. 114–15.

31. Alberts, *Golden Voyage*, pp. 124–25.

32. Ibid., pp. 125–26; Margaret L. Brown, "William Bingham, Eighteenth Century Magnate," *Pennsylvania Magazine of History and Biography* 61 (1937), p. 289.

33. For Vaughan's comment that he had introduced the Binghams to Lord Lansdowne, see Vaughan's notation on a letter he received from Lord Lansdowne, ca. 1791, Benjamin Vaughan Papers, American Philosophical Society, Philadelphia. For Vaughan's role in Paris, see Craig C. Murray, *Benjamin Vaughan (1751–1835): The Life of an American Intellectual* (Ph.D. diss., Columbia University, 1972; New York: Arno Press, 1982), pp. 73–179.

34. *DNB*, vol. 1, pp. 1195–96; Philip Ziegler, *The Sixth Great Power: Barings, 1762–1929* (London: Collins, 1988), pp. 28–42.

35. Ralph W. Hidy, *The House of Baring in American Trade and Finance: English Merchant Bankers at Work, 1763–1861* (Cambridge, Mass.: Harvard University Press, 1949), pp. 14, 22.

The setting, a portico-like space with a wall, columns, a curtain, and an open sky behind the figure is one found often in the European tradition of state portraits. The foreground, an ambiguous space that is furnished and carpeted, repeats compositions used for portraits of monarchs, bishops, admirals, and other public figures.[20] Charles Henry Hart suggested that the source for the setting was Pierre-Imbert Drevet's engraving of a portrait of Bishop Jacques-Bénigne Bossuet (fig. 105) painted by Hyacinthe Rigaud; Dorinda Evans agreed.[21] To compose these areas of the painting, Stuart had the assistance of architect Samuel Blodget Jr., son-in-law of William Smith (see cat. 61). Smith's grandson William R. Smith wrote in 1858, "I wish to call Mr [Rembrandt] Peales attention to the <u>adjuncts</u> to the <u>full length portrait</u> of Washington—I believe that the Books Papers, Drapery, Table, Chair &c in this Picture . . . were designed and sketched by Samuel Blodget of Philad^a, who was a Son-in-law of Dr Smith."[22] For the carpet, Stuart copied a rug that he purchased, according to Daniel McCormick, who accompanied his friend William Constable to Philadelphia to see Stuart at work on Constable's version of the Lansdowne full-length (see cat. 47).[23] Even the stormy sky and the rainbow in the background are symbolic. A newspaper advertisement for the 1798 exhibition in New York of the version of the full-length portrait of Washington owned by Gardiner Baker (fig. 110) described the president as "surrounded with allegorical emblems of his public life in the service of his country, which are highly illustrative of the great and tremendous storms which have frequently prevailed. These storms have abated and the appearance of the rainbow is introduced in the background as a sign."[24]

William Bingham paid Stuart $1,000 for the portrait.[25] The finished, framed painting was shipped to England in November 1796.[26] Lansdowne's praise for it on arrival was effusive. He wrote to Mrs. Bingham: "A very fine portrait of the greatest man living in a magnificent frame found its way into my hall, with no one thing left for me to do regarding it, except to thank the amiable donor of it. It is universally approv'd and admir'd, and I see with satisfaction, that there is no one who does not turn away from every thing else, to pay their homage to General Washington. Among many circumstances which contribute to enhance the value of it, I shall always consider the quarter from whence it comes as most flattering, & I look forward with the greatest pleasure to the time of shewing you and Mr. Bingham where I have plac'd it."[27] An article in the London *Oracle and Public Advertiser* on May 15, 1797, was very enthusiastic:

GENERAL WASHINGTON

The portrait presented by the President to the Marquis of Lansdowne is one of the finest pictures we have seen since the death of Reynolds. Stuart painted it, who, if he had done nothing more, established a first-rate fame by his picture of Kemble.

To many a description of the person of General Washington will be new: the picture enables us from its fidelity to describe it very correctly. The figure is above the middle height, well proportioned, and exceedingly graceful. The countenance is mild and yet forcible. The eye, of a light grey, is rendered marking by a brow to which physiognomy attaches the sign of power. The forehead is ample, the nose aquiline, the mouth regular and persuasive. The face is distinguishable for muscle rather than flesh, and this may be said of the whole person. The dress he wears is plain black velvet; he has his sword on, upon the hilt of which one hand rests while the other is extended, as the figure is standing and addressing the Hall of Assembly. The point of time is that when he recommended

Fig. 105. Pierre-Imbert Drevet after Hyacinthe Rigaud, *Bishop Jacques-Bénigne Bossuet*, 1723. Mezzotint, 19½ x 13½ in. (49.5 x 34.3 cm). British Museum, London

36. Hidy, *House of Baring*, p. 18. On Francis Baring, see Ziegler, *Sixth Great Power*, pp. 15–77; Hidy, *House of Baring*, pp. 12–23. Details of his career in Parliament, in seats under Lansdowne's control, are discussed in R. G. Thorne, *The House of Commons 1790–1820* (London: Secker and Warburg for the History of Parliament Trust, 1986), vol. 3, pp. 140–41.

37. David Mannings and Martin Postle, *Sir Joshua Reynolds: A Complete Catalogue of His Paintings* (New Haven: Yale University Press, 2000), vol. 1, pp. 173–74, no. 543. The posthumous portrait of Dunning is based on an earlier portrait by Reynolds; see ibid., p. 173, no. 540, unlocated.

38. Jay had returned to Paris when he wrote Stuart on February 22, 1784, about the portraits and frames; his letter, in the Joseph Downs Collection of Manuscripts and Printed Ephemera, Winterthur Library, is published in Richard B. Morris, ed., *John Jay, the Winning of the Peace: Unpublished Papers, 1780–1784* (New York: Harper and Row, 1980), pp. 696–97.

39. French economist André Morellet described Lansdowne's portrait as unfinished in his letter to Lansdowne dated December 24, 1784, in Jeffrey Merrick and Dorothy Medlin, eds., *André Morellet (1727–1819) in the Republic of Letters and the French Revolution* (New York: P. Lang, 1995), p. 549, no. 252; Whitley (1932, pp. 59–60) quotes the London *World* for April 18, 1787. The portrait is unlocated. The first version of Barré's portrait is owned by the Brooklyn Museum; a second version is at the National Portrait Gallery, London. I thank Teresa Carbone for sharing the draft of her catalogue entry on the painting for *American*

inviolable union between America and Great Britain. The background is made up of a state chair, columns of the hall, and some clouds. . . .

The liberality of his Lordship [the Marquis of Lansdowne] has consigned it to the graver, but we cannot resist the pleasure of describing the effect which the picture produced upon us. It is at his Lordship's house in Berkeley Square.[28]

The commission of the painting celebrated the political and social alliance of a small group of American and British statesmen and investors whose lives had been intertwined since 1783, when William Bingham was introduced to William Petty, the second Earl of Shelburne, who would be created first Marquis of Lansdowne in December 1784, taking the title from his lands near Bath that included Lansdowne Hill.[29] Bingham, in London during 1783–86, was intent on making private commercial arrangements.[30] He also hoped for a treaty between America and England that would permit open trade.[31] His views agreed with those of Lansdowne, who was in favor of liberalizing Britain's trade policies with the United States.[32] Lansdowne, as Lord Shelburne, had completed his short term of office as prime minister in February 1783, having engineered the preliminary peace treaty with America. The man who introduced them was London merchant Benjamin Vaughan, a Unitarian with radical political views, who became Prime Minister Lord Shelburne's personal representative to the American treaty commissioners in Paris in the summer of 1782.[33] Shelburne's political circle also included member of Parliament and political activist Isaac Barré and Francis Baring, founder and partner in the London merchant banking firm of John and Francis Baring and Company and a director of the East India Company.[34] Barré and Shelburne had been political allies since 1761; Barré, like Shelburne, opposed the taxation of the American colonies. Baring, who had business connections with the Philadelphia firm of Thomas Willing and Robert Morris before the American Revolution, became private adviser to Shelburne in matters of trade in 1782;[35] they agreed on a policy of "the freest possible trade with the United States and for American shipping."[36] Baring celebrated their political alliance in 1787 by commissioning Sir Joshua Reynolds's triple portrait of Lansdowne and Barré with Baring's brother-in-law John Dunning, first Baron Ashburton (private collection).[37] These men were well known to the American commissioners, including John Jay, who negotiated the Treaty of Paris during 1782–83, which formally ended the American Revolution.

John Jay was apparently the first of this group to have his portrait painted by Stuart. He sat during the winter of 1783–84, and before returning to Paris, he commissioned Stuart to paint a replica as a gift for Bingham (Stuart left these portraits unfinished; see cat. 32).[38] By December 1784 Stuart had begun a portrait of Lansdowne, finished by 1787, and in 1785 he painted Barré (fig. 17).[39] He also began a group portrait of the Bingham family sometime during their stay in London (see cat. 53). And about 1787 Stuart painted Landowne's eldest son, John Henry Petty, Earl Wycombe (private collection), member of the House of Commons for Chipping Wycombe from 1786 to 1802, who became the second Marquis of Lansdowne at his father's death in 1805.[40] Earl Wycombe went to America in the fall of 1791 to investigate his father's claim to land invested in by his great-grandfather political economist Sir William Petty.[41] He took a letter from his father, dated July 4, 1791, to George Washington, whom he met in Georgetown on October 17. Shortly afterward, Washington wrote Lansdowne that he had received the letter, "presented to me by Lord Wycombe . . . so worthy and intelligent a young nobleman." He continued, "This Country has a grateful recollection of the Agency your Lordship had in settling the dispute between Great Britain and it; and fixing the

Fig. 106. Josef Perovani, *George Washington*, 1796. Oil on canvas, 86⅝ x 57⅛ in. (220 x 145 cm). Museo de la Real Academia de Bellas Artes de San Fernando, Madrid (693)

Paintings in the Brooklyn Museum: Artists Born by 1876 (forthcoming, 2005).

40. For the second marquis, see Thorne, *House of Commons 1790–1820*, vol. 4, pp. 788–89. The portrait was formerly in the collection of Major James Hanbury and was sold at Christie's, London, June 20, 1947, lot 90.

41. For Wycombe's visit to the United States, see his letters to his father, Papers of William Petty, second Earl of Shelburne, later Marquis of Lansdowne (1737–1805), British Library, London, formerly in the collection of the Earl of Shelburne, Bowood, Wiltshire, microfilm no. 42 (box 141), fols. 1–46, William L. Clements Library, University of Michigan, Ann Arbor. His letter of November 8, 1791, comments on the claim to lands acquired by their ancestor Sir William Petty. I particularly thank Arlene Shy of the Clements Library for her assistance with research on the Marquis of Lansdowne, his son Earl Wycombe, and Sir Francis Baring. She is preparing a biography of Lansdowne.

42. Wycombe, letter to Lansdowne, Hampton, Va., October 28, 1791, Papers of William Petty, second Earl of Shelburne, Bowood, microfilm no. 42 (box 141), Clements Library; George Washington, letter to Lansdowne, November 7, 1791, Papers of William Petty, second Earl of Shelburne, Bowood, microfilm no. 24 (box 73), fols. 82–83, Clements Library.

boundary between them. It is to be wished that the same liberal policy was pursued, and every germe of discontent removed that they might be reciprocally beneficial to each other; their Laws, Language and Customs being much assimilated."[42]

After Bingham and his wife and daughters returned to Philadelphia in 1786, he remained in contact with Lansdowne, Baring, and Vaughan. His letters discussed political and economic issues and their mutual admiration of Washington and reiterated their interest in American independence and open trade. During 1793–96 Bingham was involved in two interrelated commercial enterprises: acquisition and sale of extensive acreage in Maine, and passage of a new treaty with England that would allow greater transatlantic trade. The commission for Stuart's full-length portrait of Washington came about in this context. Negotiations for a long-hoped-for new treaty with Britain began in 1794. Known today after its negotiator, John Jay, the treaty addressed issues left unresolved by the Treaty of Paris, including trade in the West Indies and the British occupation of military posts along the northwest borders of the United States.[43] Jay went to London in June 1794 and submitted a treaty draft to British Prime Minister Lord Grenville on September 30; it was signed on November 19. When the treaty was sent back to the United States for ratification by the Senate, Bingham, elected to the Senate in February 1795, rallied the support of American merchants. On December 8, 1795, after Congress reconvened in the new Congress Hall next to the State House, Washington supported the treaty in his annual address. Success of the treaty, which went into effect on February 29, 1796, was critical to Bingham's negotiation to sell to European investors some of the extensive lands in Maine he purchased in 1793 in partnership with General Henry Knox.[44] Hoping to interest Sir Francis Baring in this investment, he had sent William Jackson, a former army officer who had served recently as a private secretary to George Washington, to England as his representative in the negotiations in 1793.[45] The negotiations were slowed by the uncertainties in international trade and finance caused by events of the French Revolution, and Jackson, after two years in Europe, returned to the United States without a completed sale. In the late fall of 1795, Baring sent his son Alexander Baring (1774–1848), a brilliant young banker who was later created Baron Ashburton, to investigate the Maine lands proposal.[46] Baring arrived in Boston on November 29 and was in Philadelphia by mid-January; on February 15, 1796, the final agreement was spelled out. Bingham would sell part of the lands in Maine to Baring, with Baring providing a loan until the contract was finalized.[47]

Because the commission of the full-length of Washington occurred in the midst of the debates on both sides of the Atlantic about the Jay Treaty and the sale of land in Maine, it is likely that Washington's pose alludes to his address to Congress on December 8, 1795, his annual message, which included references to the Jay Treaty and other treaties.[48] The paper, pen, and inkwell suggest the signing of a document, perhaps the Jay Treaty. According to the 1798 advertisement for the exhibition of Gardiner Baker's version, the painting showed "A full-length of General Washington (large as life) represented in the position of addressing Congress the last time, before his retirement from public life."[49] In the past, writers assumed that this referred to Washington's farewell address to Congress at the end of his presidency, which in fact was published and not delivered by him in person. However, the portrait's oratorical pose was described specifically in the London *Oracle and Public Advertiser* on May 15, 1797, as a reference to Washington's support of the Jay Treaty: "The figure is standing and addressing the Hall of Assembly. The point of time is that when he recommended inviolable union between America and Great Britain."[50]

43. On the Jay Treaty, see Samuel Flagg Bemis, *Jay's Treaty: A Study in Commerce and Diplomacy* (New York: Macmillan Co., 1923); Jerald A. Combs, *The Jay Treaty: Political Battleground of the Founding Fathers* (Berkeley: University of California Press, 1978); Richard B. Morris and Jeffrey B. Morris, eds., *Encyclopedia of American History*, 7th ed. (New York: Harper Collins, 1996), pp. 143–44. The text of the treaty is in Bemis, *Jay's Treaty*, pp. 321–45.

44. Allis, *William Bingham's Maine Lands*, vol. 1, pp. 288–376; Alberts, *Golden Voyage*, pp. 228–36; Hidy, *House of Baring*, pp. 28–29.

45. On Jackson, see *ANB*, vol. 11, pp. 778–79. Jackson married Anne Bingham's sister Elizabeth Willing in 1795 after returning from England.

46. Ziegler, *Sixth Great Power*, p. 31. On Alexander Baring, see ibid., pp. 44–125; Thorne, *House of Commons 1790–1820*, vol. 3, pp. 138–40; *DNB*, vol. 1, pp. 1110–11. He married the Binghams' daughter Ann Louisa in 1798, and his brother Henry married Maria Bingham in 1802; see Alberts, *Golden Voyage*, pp. 346, 419. For a succinct summary of his role in the purchase of the Maine lands, see Hidy, *House of Baring*, pp. 28–29.

47. On the purchase, see Alberts, *Golden Voyage*, pp. 268–84; for the agreement dated February 15, 1796, see Baring's letter to Bingham, February 15, 1796, in Allis, *William Bingham's Maine Lands*, vol. 1, pp. 672–74.

48. In her recent interpretation, Dorinda Evans (1999, p. 67) described the theme of the painting as a timeless one of "benevolent governance," appropriate as a portrait painted for Lansdowne, who was not only a central figure in the negotiations of the Treaty of Paris and the Jay Treaty but also a "political philosopher."

49. *The Time Piece*, February 7, 1798, quoted in Whitley 1932, pp. 107–8; Morgan and Fielding 1931, p. 360.

50. *Oracle and Public Advertiser* (London), May 15, 1797, quoted in Whitley 1932, p. 100.

51. Von Erffa and Staley 1986, pp. 218–19, no. 105, illus. p. 50.

52. Trumbull, letter to Jay, December 10, 1794, John Jay Papers, Rare Book and Manuscript Library, Columbia University, New York, no. 7201; quoted from the Papers of John Jay Web site, http://www.columbia.edu/cu/lweb/eresources/archives/jay.

53. Isadora Rose-de Viejo, *The Portrait of George Washington by Josef Perovani*, Obras del museo de la Real Academia de San Fernando, 1 (Madrid: Ediciones El Viso, 1998).

54. *Life and Correspondence of Rufus King*, vol. 2, p. 199, from the Rufus King Papers, vol. 41, "American Political Letters, 1796–1799," New-York Historical Society.

55. *Commercial Advertiser* (New York), June 27, 1800, quoting "The Monthly Magazine for March"; Rita Susswein Gottesman, *The Arts and Crafts in New York, 1800–1804* (New York: New-York Historical Society, 1965), pp. 50–51. Whitley (1932, p. 103) quotes David Kennedy's advertisements for the sale of the engraving in Philadelphia newspapers in the summer of 1800.

Thus, if the portrait refers to the Jay Treaty and this powerful alliance of British and American politicians and merchant bankers, it can be seen as an example of the use of portraits to celebrate political alliances, especially at times of international treaties. Contemporary portraits that were intended to commemorate treaties include Benjamin West's group portrait *Signing of the Preliminary Treaty of Peace in 1782*, begun in 1783–84 but never completed. The painting (Henry Francis du Pont Winterthur Museum) includes the portraits of the American delegation.[51] In 1794, at the time of the signing of the Jay Treaty, the question of portraits came up again. John Trumbull, who served as Jay's secretary in London during the negotiations, commented on the English practice of giving portraits at such occasions in his letter of December 10, 1794, to Jay:

Mr. Burges informed me that it was the established Custom here to present to the Foreign Minister who concluded a Treaty the Portrait of the King, elegantly set; "and on this Occasion," added he, "I have by Lord Grenville's direction already given Orders to the King's Jeweller to have the Picture, and Box which is to enclose it, finished immediately. It is also customary to make a proportional present to the Secretary of such Minister; and these are given on the Exchange of the Ratifications." I answer'd that I believed it to be otherwise with us; and that the Officers of the United States were even prohibited to receive Presents of any kind, from any foreign Prince or State. I submit to your Judgement how far my Answer was right; and how far it was intended by the Constitution to prohibit the Ministers of the United States receiving Presents of this Nature.[52]

Another important treaty, the Treaty of San Lorenzo between the United States and Spain, signed in 1795, was celebrated in a manner similar to the commission for the Lansdowne portrait. In 1796, Josef de Jaudenes y Nebot (see cat. 34), Spanish representative to the United States, commissioned a full-length portrait of George Washington as a gift to the Spanish secretary of state, Manuel Godoy (fig. 106). Painted in Philadelphia by Italian-born artist Josef Perovani, the portrait shows the influence of the Lansdowne portrait in Washington's frontal standing pose and in his black velvet suit and his sword, although his face appears closer to portraits by Charles Willson Peale.[53]

The final chapter in the highly charged commission of the Lansdowne portrait of Washington occurred when it was engraved by English printmaker James Heath, leading to the alienation of the artist from William Bingham, his wealthy patron. Bingham wrote Rufus King on July 10, 1797, about plans for an engraving: "I received your Letter of April 26th, with several inclosures from the Marquis of Lansdown, who, I am pleased to find, is much gratified with the Portrait of the President. Stewart has been much disappointed in his Hopes relative to Profits, which he expected to derive from this Picture. He had wrote to his friend West, requesting him to engage an able artist to execute an Engraving therefrom, which, from the general admiration the picture attracted, might have been disposed of to great advantage in this Country. He has not heard from Mr. West, & he is fearful that Lord Landown's obliging character may induce him to permit some other artist to take off the Impression."[54] The print, published on January 1, 1800, shortly after Washington's death, was praised in American newspaper notices (fig. 107). "The leading Portrait is one copied from Stuart by Heath, and which in point of resemblance is said by those who have seen the General, to be uncommonly faithful. Indeed Stuart's fidelity to his original is so great, that we scarcely ever see a Portrait from his Pencil, that could not be immediately identified."[55] According to the inscription on the print, the work was "Painted by Gabriel Stuart 1797," an error that was supremely

Fig. 107. James Heath after Gilbert Stuart, *George Washington*, 1800. Engraving, 19⅞ x 13⅛ in. (50.6 x 33.3 cm). National Portrait Gallery, Smithsonian Institution, Washington, D.C. (NPG.81.55)

frustrating to Stuart because he had not given permission for Heath to make the engraving.[56] Further, it disrupted his plans to have an engraving made by William Sharp, probably arranged through Benjamin West. Stuart later showed George Washington Parke Custis the copperplate by Sharp.[57]

The story of Heath's engraving was recounted by Dunlap as told to him by Neagle: "Mr. Bingham had not made it a condition with the marquis that a copy-right should be secured for the benefit of the painter; indeed he never mentioned Mr. Stuart's wish, intending by the next vessel, to beg this provision for the painter's benefit, as an after thought, which would not appear to lessen the value of the present. But this proved too late for poor Stuart. When the next vessel arrived, Heath had made his copy under the sanction of the owner, and his design was already on the copper. The matter, however, was never broached to Stuart, and he told me that the first he knew of it was in Mr. Dobson's book-store, in Second-street, Philadelphia." When Mr. Dobson opened a box of the engravings, sent to him to sell on commission, Stuart was startled to see the unauthorized reproduction of his own painting.[58] Stuart then visited Bingham; artist James Barton Longacre later recorded Stuart's comments: "on asking Mr. Bingham how he proposed to compensate him for the injury he had sustained by the publication of the print, Mr. Bingham replied, 'Have you anything to show for it?' which ended their inter-course, Stuart leaving him abruptly and indignantly without further remark."[59] And Jane Stuart wrote, "The engraving was exceedingly bad, and, as some one has said, a libel both upon Stuart and Washington. This was a severe mortification to the artist, in many ways, he being annoyed at having so imperfect a representation of his art circulated among his old friends and admirers in England. He requested Mr. Bingham to secure a copyright, which he agreed to do. But he did not attend to the business, and now began all Stuart's trouble with regard to copyright, spurious pictures, etc."[60]

Stuart drafted a letter to Lord Lansdowne, which he apparently never sent; the draft was among his papers after his death:

The liberality with which you have uniformly patronized the Arts, and a grateful recol-lection of my personal obligation for your approbation and countenance, have inspired a hope that your Lordship will receive with indulgence the representation of an injury, to which I have recently been exposed under the apparent sanction of your name. As a resource to rescue myself from pecuniary embarrassment, and to provide for a numerous family at the close of an anxious life, I had counted upon the emoluments that might arise from a portrait of George Washington, engraved by an artist of talent. It was, therefore, with peculiar pleasure, that I found myself invited by Mr. Bingham to take the portrait of President Washington, to be presented to your Lordship; as I knew of no one in whose hands it could be placed with more propriety and advantage, nor one on whom I could more confidently rely to secure the rights and promote the interest of the artist.

I . . . expressly stipulated with [Mr. Bingham's] agent in the transaction, that no copy should be taken of the picture, nor should any engraving be allowed but with my consent, and for my benefit. Scarcely, however, had the picture been received by your Lordship, when I had the mortification to find an engraving promised to the public; and soon afterward, at a moment when the sensibility of Europe, as well as of America, was keen-ly excited by the death of General Washington, the print was published in England and in the United States; executed by Mr. Heath, for the emolument of himself and Mr. Barry, of New-York; and stated to be taken "from the original picture, by Gilbert Stuart, in the collection of the Marquis of Lansdowne." Thus, without my privilege and partici-

56. On the engraving, see Wick 1982, pp. 59–61, fig. 40.
57. Evans 1999, p. 144 n. 20, citing Park 1926, pp. 50–51 n.; Custis, *Recollections and Private Memoirs of Washington*, p. 522; J. Stuart 1876, p. 370.
58. Neagle, quoted in Dunlap 1834, vol. 1, pp. 204–5; and in Mason 1879, pp. 93–94. On Neagle's visit to Stuart in Boston, see Robert W. Torchia, *John Neagle: Philadelphia Portrait Painter*, exh. cat. (Philadelphia: Historical Society of Pennsylvania, 1989), pp. 30–32. In addition to Dunlap, Torchia cites a diary fragment for October 18, 1824–March 12, 1831, Historical Society of Pennsylvania.
59. "Extracts of the Diary of James B. Longacre," *Pennsylvania Magazine of History and Biography* 29, no. 2 (1905), p. 140. Longacre visited Stuart in Boston in 1825 with John Neagle.
60. J. Stuart 1876, 369–70.

61. The unlocated draft of the letter is quoted in Mason 1879, pp. 95–96; with this draft was found one for a letter to "Mr. Barry," whom Stuart believed was involved in making the engraving, pp. 96–97.
62. J. Stuart 1876, p. 369.

pation, despoiled of the fair fruits of an important work, and defeated in the great object of my professional pursuit, your Lordship will readily allow me the privilege to complain. There is something due to my feelings as a man, and to my character as an artist; and to repel, as far as it is practicable, the wrong that has been committed, I have issued proposals for a superior engraving, from a portrait intended to be fixed at Mount Vernon, and I address myself respectfully to your Lordship, to inquire into the source of my misfortune.[61]

The engraving was a sore subject for Stuart for the rest of his life. Jane Stuart noted, in relation to Stuart's feelings about the Heath engraving and his control of his habit of swearing, "all that I can remember, is that when the engraving was alluded to, he would walk up and down the room, taking tremendous pinches of snuff."[62]

EGM

46. George Washington

1796–97
Oil on canvas, 96 x 60 in. (243.8 x 152.4 cm)
Signed lower left on the edge of the book under the table: G Stuart 1796
Pennsylvania Academy of the Fine Arts, Philadelphia; Bequest of William Bingham (1811.2)

Stuart painted this replica of the Lansdowne full-length for William Bingham, who commissioned the original (see cat. 45).[1] Evidence that the painting is a replica and not the original can be found in Robert Gilmor Jr.'s description of the portrait when he saw it in Stuart's studio in the summer of 1797, as well as in the entry for the payment for the portrait in William Bingham's account book. In late July 1797, Gilmor, the son of Bingham's business partner Robert Gilmor of Baltimore, was visiting Philadelphia.

In the morning of the 27th we rode out to breakfast at Mr. Nichlin's and from thence went to Germantown to see Stewart's painting of the late [i.e., former] President. We should have disappointed in this had not I taken care to get a letter of introduction to him from General de Noailles who was intimate with him & for whom Stewart entertained a great respect. His wife met us at the door and said Mr S. was out:—I requested she would send the note I had to him wherever he was; I told her I should stay but a few days in Philad[a] & should be very much disappointed if I could not see Mr. Stewart's performance. She at length invited us into the parlour and left the room; in a few minutes Stewart came in, received us in the most welcome manner, offered us refreshments and conducting us to his painting room which he had fitted up in his stable. The Picture he had there of the President was the first copy he had made of the celebrated full length which he had painted for Mrs. Bingham intended as a present to the Marquis of Lansdown. It was supposed one of the finest portraits that ever was painted. This copy was for Mr Binghams own use and from which Stewart told us he had engaged to finish copies to amount of 70 or 80,000 Drs at the rate of 600 Drs a copy.[2]

Bingham, in his personal account book, recorded payments to Stuart totaling $2,200 for "family Pictures & a Copy of Genl Washington" (fig. 108; see also cats. 51–53).[3] While the year is not written on this page in Bingham's account book and only some of the payments have specific dates, the payments appear to have been made toward the end of 1796 and in 1797.[4]

1. Dunlap 1834, vol. 1, pp. 203–5; Mason 1879, p. 100; Elizabeth Bryant Johnston, *Original Portraits of Washington, including Statues, Monuments, and Medals* (Boston: James R. Osgood and Co., 1882), p. 87; Charles Henry Hart, "Stuart's Lansdowne Portrait of Washington," *Harper's New Monthly Magazine* 93 (August 1896), pp. 378–86; Fielding 1923, p. 132, no. 16; Park 1926, p. 854, no. 18; Morgan and Fielding 1931, pp. 238, 260, 355–61; Eisen 1932, pp. 109–10; Washington and Providence 1967, p. 77, no. 28; *In this Academy: The Pennsylvania Academy of the Fine Arts, 1805–1976, a Special Bicentennial Exhibition* (Philadelphia: Pennsylvania Academy of the Fine Arts, 1976), p. 293, no. 152.
2. Robert Gilmor Jr., *Memorandums Made in a Tour to the Eastern States in the Year 1797* (Boston: Trustees of the Boston Public Library, 1892), p. 6.

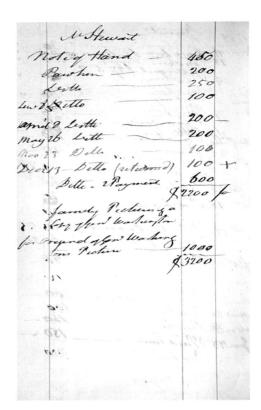

Fig. 108. Page in William Bingham's Account Book listing payments to Stuart. Bingham, W., Manuscripts, Lilly Library, Indiana University, Bloomington

A theory that the Pennsylvania Academy's version of the Lansdowne portrait was the original received its greatest promotion from Charles Henry Hart, who published this opinion in 1896 after examining the painting and after corresponding with Sir George Scharf, director of the National Portrait Gallery, London, about the version painted for Lord Lansdowne, which was then owned by Archibald Philip Primrose, the fifth Earl of Rosebery.[5] Hart's opinion was based on "the intrinsic evidence of the picture's originality, its freedom and animation, and upon the important fact that it is signed and dated."[6] Until recently most authors agreed.[7] Scharf examined the Lansdowne version twice for Hart, in 1892 and 1893, when it was in the London home of Lord Rosebery. Scharf wrote to Hart that "The only test applicable to the two pictures of Washington you now refer to would be to see whether either of them contains a <u>pentimento</u>, that is when the artist had made an alteration and painted something quite different over it, traces of the former design are generally perceptible on looking sideways in a particular light."[8]

These changes are among the hallmarks of the Lansdowne original (cat. 45). By contrast, in the Pennsylvania Academy portrait, the areas that are beautifully painted, characteristic of Stuart's best work, are the face, hands, hair, shirt ruffle, and lace at the sleeves. However, some differences in the technique can be seen in the gray outlining on Washington's left thigh and in the slight lack of detail in the face, especially around the jaw and chin. The furniture and drapery have the appearance of being copied: the perspective is sometimes incorrect and, for example, the position of the front left leg of the chair and details of the drapery on the table are imprecise. The heavy orange-red impasto used to highlight details of the gilded eagles and table leg does not seem characteristic of Stuart's work. The carpet is very loosely and imprecisely painted and appears less intense in color than in the original. These differences may indicate the hand of an assistant, but the painting was done too late for this assistant to have been John Vanderlyn, who worked in Stuart's studio from the summer of 1795 to the late spring of 1796.[9] The "late 18th century gold leaf portrait frame" with "a triple reeded top molding with cross straps occurring at 12 inch intervals, a plain deep cove, a bead and flat liner," probably went with painting directly from Bingham to the Pennsylvania Academy.[10] The painting, listed in the inventory of Bingham's estate that was filed by his executors in 1807, "was removed to the Bank of the United States for safe-keeping." At the request of the Pennsylvania Academy to his executors, the painting was transferred there in 1811, the bequest of William Bingham.[11]

EGM

3. William Bingham, Account Book, Bingham, W., Manuscripts, Lilly Library, Indiana University, Bloomington.

4. Lilly Library Curator of Manuscripts Saundra Taylor wrote about the dating that "Bingham seems to have jumped around the pages, entering things of an earlier date between pages of a later year's account. . . . I would say you have a choice of 1797, 1798, or 1799, but I would probably go with the 1797"; e-mail message to Ellen Miles, April 11, 2003.

5. Hart, "Stuart's Lansdowne Portrait," pp. 378–86.

6. Ibid., p. 380.

7. In "The White House Full Length *Portrait of George Washington* by Gilbert Stuart: Conservation Treatment Report and Commentary," Washington Conservation Studio, Kensington, Md., October 1978, Marion F. Mecklenburg and Justine S. Wimsatt carefully examined the Pennsylvania Academy's painting in relation to the versions at the White House and the Brooklyn Museum, as well as the Lansdowne portrait itself, then on loan to and now owned by the National Portrait Gallery, Washington, D.C. They concluded that the version at the National Portrait Gallery was the original. They believed, however, that the Pennsylvania Academy portrait was perhaps less developed than the Brooklyn Museum one, and

therefore it could be the third, not the second, in the sequence. Evans (1999, p. 141 n. 5) concurs.

8. Sir George Scharf, letter to Charles Henry Hart, December 16, 1893; copy, "Icon Notes—George Washington," Heinz Archive, National Portrait Gallery, London (text © National Portrait Gallery).

9. William T. Oedel, "John Vanderlyn: French Neoclassicism and the Search for an American Art" (Ph.D. diss., University of Delaware, 1981), pp. 31–41.

10. The file on the painting at the Pennsylvania

Academy of the Fine Arts includes a report on the frame by R. Wayne Reynolds, November 1985.

11. Mason 1879, p. 100. See also "Minutes of the Proceedings of the President & Directors of the Pennsylvania Academy of the Fine Arts," p. 34, December 24, 1810, Archives of the Pennsylvania Academy of the Fine Arts, microfilm, Archives of American Art, Smithsonian Institution, Washington, D.C.; and "Report of Comm on obtaining Stuart's Washington from Bingham Estate," March 14, 1811, Archives of the Pennsylvania Academy of the Fine Arts.

1796–97

Oil on canvas, 96⅛ x 60¼ inches (244 x 153 cm)

Brooklyn Museum, New York; Dick S. Ramsay Fund and Museum Purchase Funds (45.179)

1. J. Stuart 1876, p. 373; Mason 1879, pp. 97–100, 105; Elizabeth Bryant Johnston, *Original Portraits of Washington, including Statues, Monuments, and Medals* (Boston: James R. Osgood and Co., 1882), pp. 85–87; Fielding 1923, p. 134, no. 18; Park 1926, pp. 855–56, no. 20; Morgan and Fielding 1931, pp. 261–62, no. 20; Eisen 1932, pp. 93–97, 111; Evans 1999, p. 83. Teresa Carbone kindly shared her catalogue entry for this portrait, drafted for *American Paintings in the Brooklyn Museum: Artists Born by 1876* (forthcoming, 2005).

2. On Constable, see William A. Davis, "William Constable: New York Merchant and Land Speculator, 1772–1803" (Ph.D. diss., Harvard University, 1955); and on his portrait by Stuart, see John Caldwell and Oswaldo Rodriguez Roque, *American Paintings in The Metropolitan Museum of Art*, vol. 1, *A Catalogue of Works by Artists Born by 1815* (New York: Metropolitan Museum of Art, 1994), pp. 178–79.

3. Davis, "Constable," pp. 229–30.

4. "Mrs. H. B. Pierrepont's original Memorandum of the History of the Stuart full length & half length Washington," 1849, George Washington Portrait Collection, Manuscripts and Archives Division, New York Public Library, Astor, Lenox and Tilden Foundations. A typed copy dated 1878 is in the "Pierrepont Family, Papers Relating to Gilbert Stuart's 'Portrait of George Washington,'" Brooklyn Museum Library. Her narrative is summarized in Mason 1879, pp. 97–98.

5. "Mrs. H. B. Pierrepont's original Memorandum," [pp. 2–3].

6. A photocopy of this receipt, now unlocated, is in the George Washington Portrait Collection, New York Public Library; a copy is in the "Pierrepont Family, Papers," Brooklyn Museum Library. The receipt reads:

    Wm. Constable Esqr To G Stuart Dr
    1796
    Nov   To one portrait of said WC Dr. 100–
    1797
    July 4   " one do [ditto] of the late President of the
    *   United States at full length   500*
    *   " one do half length   250*
    *   Dr. 850 Dollars*

    Philadelphia 13 July 1797 Received of Richd Soderstrom Esqr through the hands of John Vaughan Esqr the above Sum in full of all demands against them and the abovementioned Wm. Constable Esqr.
    *   G Stuart*
    Dimensions given by Mr Stuart
    5 feet x 8 feet
    3.4 – 4.3

Stuart painted this replica of the Lansdowne portrait of Washington for William Kerin Constable (1752–1803), a New York merchant and landowner.[1] Born in Dublin, Ireland, and raised in the colony of New York, Constable settled in Philadelphia after the American Revolution, marrying Ann White in 1782. In 1784 he moved to New York City, where he built a thriving business in partnership with John Rucker and later with James Constable, his brother. Their company "became the greatest merchant house in New York" in the 1790s.[2] After he spent the years 1792–95 in Europe, where he sold large blocks of New York State land that he and other investors had purchased, he returned to New York on the same ship with John Jay, arriving in early June 1795.[3]

Constable's daughter Anna Maria Pierrepont later recorded the story of the commission of this painting.[4] She wrote that on a trip to Philadelphia, Constable arranged to have Stuart "take his likeness for his family" (fig. 109).

Gilbert Stuart was at the time of my Fathers visit, painting a full length portrait of Washington for Mr Bingham (who presented it to the Marquis of Lansdown). My Father was so much pleased with it, that he engaged Stuart to paint one for him at the same time, as the Genl was giving him sittings, Stuart who was well acquainted with my Father, promised both pictures should be worked upon alternately, so that both should be originals. Mr. Trott the artist who painted a minature of my Father (which I have) told me that Stuart had only sketched the hand of the General & that he held his own hand for him to paint from. Daniel McCormick who died in NYK 1834 aged 94, was a friend of Stuarts and being under many obligations to my Father used his influence to induce Stuart to bestow very particular care & attention upon the picture which was considered more highly finished in its details than was usual for Stuart. My Father went twice [added in pencil: from New York] to Philadelphia in his chariot & four, taking Mr. McC with him, to watch the progress of the painting; and to encourage the procrastinating artist, they had him invited to many dinner parties among friends, & by great perseverance obtained their wishes & before the picture was sent to NYK Stuart painted a half length from it, which my Father presented to his friend General Hamilton. A large party of friends assembled at our house in Broad Way (which then stood where the Astor now stands) our neighbours being, Colonel Burr, Walter Rutherford Grand Father to Mrs. Peter A Jay, and Richard Harrison the emminent Lawyer to look at "the Picture"— "Gentlemen said my Father there is the man" and they responded, "The man himself". Daniel McCormick said he had seen Stuart purchase the Turkey carpet on which the Genl stood and it was a fac simile.[5]

A receipt signed by Stuart records the prices for this painting, Constable's own portrait, and a second portrait of Washington, which Constable gave to Alexander Hamilton (cat. 48).[6]

The sequence of this replica in relationship to Bingham's replica is unclear. The invoice suggests that Constable's own portrait was finished by November 1796. Although Constable's sittings are not themselves documented, he did make a trip to Philadelphia in October 1796.[7] An additional story told about Daniel McCormick, a New York

7. In a letter of December 19, 1796, to Joseph Anthony and Son, Constable noted, "when I was at Phila last Octo^r," "William Constable: Letter-book for 1794–1797," Constable-Pierrepont Family Papers, vol. 4, p. 332, Manuscripts and Archives Division, New York Public Library, Astor, Lenox and Tilden Foundations (hereafter Constable Papers). All of the Constable account books cited below are in this collection. In "William & James Constable Account Book: Accounts Current, 1791–1799," Constable Papers, vol. 34, p. 141, Constable recorded on October 6, 1796, an expense for "Medicines for the horses going to Phila 15s."

8. Mason 1879, pp. 99–100.

9. Marion F. Mecklenburg and Justine S. Wimsatt, "The White House Full Length *Portrait of George Washington* by Gilbert Stuart: Conservation Treatment Report and Commentary," Washington Conservation Studio, Kensington, Md., October 1978, p. 15. They proposed that the Brooklyn painting was the second in the sequence.

10. "Mrs. H. B. Pierrepont's original Memorandum," [p. 3].

11. "William & James Constable Account Book: 1797–1799" (a letterbook, not an account book), Constable Papers, vol. 32, p. 244. A handwritten, annotated copy of this letter is in the "Pierrepont Family, Papers," Brooklyn Museum Library.

12. "William & James Constable Account Book: Accounts Current, 1791–1799," Constable Papers, vol. 34, p. 168. The same payments are recorded on a loose sheet from an account book for 1797; see folder marked "Accounts 1797," in "William and James Constable Accounts, 1792–1803," Constable Papers, box 6. The payment for shipping the pictures is also in "William and James Constable, Petty Cash Book, 1793–July 1797, Constable Papers, vol. 37 (unpaginated), for July 25, as $4.25. The payment of $900 to Richard Soderstrom is also recorded in "William and James Constable Cash Book, 1791–1797," Constable Papers, vol. 36, p. 131, in two payments of $400 and $500, and in "William and James Constable Journal, 1791–1799," Constable Papers, vol. 40, p. 583.

13. "William & James Constable Account Book: Accounts Current, 1791–1799," Constable Papers, vol. 34, p. 144; "William and James Constable Cash Book, 1791–1797 (August)," Constable Papers, vol. 36, p. 111.

14. The best source on Baker remains Robert M. McClung and Gale S. McClung, "Tammany's Remarkable Gardiner Baker," *New-York Historical Society Quarterly* 42 (April 1958), pp. 142–69.

15. "William & James Constable Account Book: 1797–1799," Constable Papers, vol. 32, p. 307. See also "William and James Constable Cash Book, Sept. 1797–June 1801," Constable Papers, vol. 38, p. 13.

16. "William & James Constable Account Book: 1797–1799," Constable Papers, vol. 32, p. 320.

17. "William and James Constable Cash Book, Sept. 1797–June 1801," Constable Papers, vol. 38, p. 13. This consists of a double entry; on the left side under the category "Cash" is the entry "Dec. 1797:

merchant, supports the suggestion that Constable made two additional trips with him to see the progress of the Lansdowne paintings: "One day he met Mr. Stuart carrying a Turkey rug, and asked him what he was going to do with it. Stuart replied that it was for his studio. 'You extravagant dog,' said McCormick, 'why did you not buy a Kidderminster for your studio? It would have answered as well.' 'Some day, McCormick, you will say that I have done right.' When the picture, in which the rug is skillfully introduced, was finished, and while Mr. McCormick was looking at it, Stuart nudged him with his elbow and said, 'Well, McCormick, what do you say to my rug?' 'You have done right,' was the reply."[8] If this story is true, the visits must have taken place before the original was completed and shipped to London, which occurred by the end of November 1796 (see cat. 45). It also indicates that the painting for Constable was begun in the fall of 1796.

Because the Lansdowne painting (cat. 45) and the Bingham (cat. 46) and Constable replicas have not been seen together since they were painted, comparisons are based on photographs. In photographs, the Bingham version and the Constable version are much the same. Treatment of furniture details, the patterns and abbreviations in the folds of the red drapes, and the colors and patterns of the rug are very similar. When Marion F. Mecklenburg and Justine S. Wimsatt carefully examined these three Lansdowne paintings and the one at the White House (fig. 110) in 1978, they concluded that there were slight compositional changes in the tabletop and in Washington's legs in the Constable painting, suggesting that the artist was still working out details of the composition. They noted that the Constable painting was "more developed than the Bingham and White House versions in terms of density and brilliance of color. The first indications of the artist relying on a less developed style for the drapery, cloth, and rug are presented. Some passages are altered in much the same way as those in the Lansdowne but to a lesser degree—compositional development is still in progress."[9] This would support Mrs. Pierrepont's memory that Daniel McCormick "used his influence to induce Stuart to bestow very particular care & attention upon the picture which was considered more highly finished in its details than was usual for Stuart."[10]

After Stuart was paid, the three pictures for Constable were shipped to New York. They arrived by July 25, 1797, when Constable wrote to John Vaughan about the payment: "We understand from Mr. Soderstrom that after passing the Drafts on us for paying Mr. Stewart the latter returned $150 which Mr. Soderstrom informs us is in your Hands & we have therefore taken the Liberty of drawing upon you for that Amount at 3d/s to order of Charles Wilkes Esqre which you will please honour. The Pictures are safely landed & the Box for Govr. Jay sent him."[11] Constable's account books record that on July 25, 1797, he paid for "Freight & Cartage of Pictures from Philadelphia 4.50," and on July 28 he paid "R. Soderstram's drafts for Pictures of the President 900} Deduct, returned 150} 750."[12] The previous December 13, he had paid "To R. Soderstrom's Draft for a Picture &c £52," an amount which is recorded in a separate cashbook as $130.[13] This may explain why the sum of $150 was returned.

Constable's account books also document his role in the commission of the version of the Lansdowne portrait painted for Gardiner Baker, manager of the Tammany Society's museum in New York (fig. 110).[14] On December 9, 1797, four months after paying for his own portraits, Constable wrote to John Vaughan in Philadelphia, "We received yours of 1st Inst. & the Picture has been safely received. Mr. Baker complains of a Breach of Contract on the Part of Mr. Stewart & begs some accomodation as to

21 To J. Vaughan recd. Of G. Baker 200," and on the right side, under the category "Contra" is the entry "Dec. 1797: 23 By J Vaughan remitted to him 200."

18. "William & James Constable Account Book: 1797–1799," Constable Papers, vol. 32, p. 336.

19. Mount (1964, p. 216), quotes the letter from Timothy Pickering to Pinckney, dated July 22, 1797, recording that he paid for the portrait that morning (Massachusetts Historical Society). Mount (1964, p. 263), said that Pinckney's picture was later resold by Stuart to Baker, as does William Kloss and Doreen Bolger, *Art in the White House: A Nation's Pride* (Washington, D.C.: White House Historical Association in cooperation with the National Geographic Society, 1992), pp. 68–69, but this cannot be confirmed. The price is repeated in Pickering's letter to McHenry, December 13, 1804, McHenry Papers, William L. Clements Library, University of Michigan, Ann Arbor. This letter is quoted in Park 1926, p. 880, with the recipient unidentified; Whitley 1932, pp. 114–15, with the recipient correctly identified; Mount 1964, p. 263, with the recipient incorrectly identified as William Loughton Smith.

20. Baker's advertisement for the exhibition in *The Time Piece*, February 7, 1798, is quoted in Morgan and Fielding 1931, p. 360; Whitley 1932, pp. 107–8.

21. Kloss and Bolger, (*Art in the White House*, pp. 66–69) give this history for the portrait. It is discussed in Whitley 1932, pp. 108–9; Morgan and Fielding 1931, pp. 318–20, as no. XV, attributed to Stuart. In addition, Morgan and Fielding's note VI, pp. 359–61, gives details of its early exhibition history in New York and Boston.

22. Anna Maria Thornton, letter to Dolley Madison, August 24, 1802, in David B. Mattern and Holly C. Shulman, eds., *The Selected Letters of Dolley Payne Madison* (Charlottesville: University of Virginia Press, 2003), pp. 50–51.

23. Dunlap 1834, vol. 1, pp. 201–2. Evans (1999, pp. 85–86, 148 nn. 18, 19) gives the history of William Winstanley's relationship with Stuart. Her position is that the White House portrait is not by Stuart and that the painting that belonged to Baker is unlocated. She points out that the phrase "but he had bargained for it" suggests that Stuart somehow made it possible for Winstanley to make the copy. On Winstanley, see Dunlap 1834, vol. 1, pp. 394–95; J. Hall Pleasants, *Four Late Eighteenth Century Anglo-American Landscape Painters* (1942; reprint, Worcester, Mass.: American Antiquarian Society, 1943), pp. 117–40; Edward J. Nygren, *Views and Visions: American Landscape before 1830*, exh. cat. (Washington, D.C.: Corcoran Gallery of Art, 1986), pp. 28, 30–31, 304. The comment does suggest that Stuart did not paint the entire portrait. However, Baker acquired the painting in 1797, probably earlier than Winstanley's contact with Stuart.

24. Dunlap 1834, vol. 1, p. 200.

25. The portrait at Catholic University of America, Washington, D.C., which formerly belonged to the Catholic Club of New York, is listed as by Stuart in

Fig. 109. *William Kerin Constable*, 1796. Oil on canvas, 28 5/8 x 23 1/2 in. (72.7 x 59.7 cm). The Metropolitan Museum of Art, New York; Bequest of Richard De Wolfe Brixey, 1943 (43.86.2)

the Time of Payment, upon which Subject he addresses you at this time & we wait your Directions how to act."[15] In his next letter, written on December 23, Constable wrote Vaughan, "In consequence of yours of 18th We sent the Inclosure to Baker, who we have settled with & inclose you a Bank Note for $200 & his own at 60 d/s endorsed by John Bailey for $300 which We have no doubt will be paid when due. The charge of Freight &c He also paid."[16] The bank note for $200 had been paid to Constable by Baker two days earlier, indicating that Baker paid Vaughan, through Constable, a total of $500.[17] The last letter to Vaughan on the subject that is recorded in the letterbook is dated January 11, 1798, "We wrote you 23 Ult. inclosing Bank Notes for 200 Dlrs. & G. Baker's for $300 to which we have as yet no reply & request to know if that Letter reached you safely."[18] The $500 price is less than the cost of the earlier replica for Bingham, although it is the same price as Constable's full-length of Washington. This was also the price paid for a replica commissioned by Charles Cotesworth Pinckney, which was paid for on July 22, 1797.[19]

Baker placed this portrait of Washington on exhibition in February 1798.[20] Baker died in September 1798, and his painting was purchased two years later, in July 1800, for the White House, for $800.[21] Stuart subsequently disavowed it on several occasions, the first in 1802, when he visited Washington, D.C. Anna Maria Thornton wrote Dolley Madison in 1802, "We have been gratified by seeing the celebrated Stewart, he came down with Mr Thornton and was here every day while he staid. . . . He denies most pointedly having painted the picture in the President's house, and says he told Genl: Lee that he did not paint it—but he had bargained for it."[22] William Dunlap wrote that William Winstanley, a British landscape painter working in New York and Philadelphia, substituted his own copy of the portrait when hired to pack Baker's canvas for shipment to Washington.[23] According to Dunlap, Stuart and Winstanley met for the first time when Winstanley went to Stuart's Germantown studio with a business proposition:

"I have been copying your full-length of Washington; I have made a number of copies; I have now six that I have brought on to Philadelphia; I have got a room in the state-house, and I have put them up; but before I show them to the public, and offer them for sale, I have a proposal to make to you. . . . It would enhance their value, you know, if I could say that you had given them the last touch. Now, sir, all you have to do is to ride to town, and give each of them a tap, you know, with your riding-switch—just thus, you know. . . . And we will share the amount of the sale." [Stuart replied,] "Did you ever hear that I was a swindler?" . . . The painter rose to his full height. "You will please to walk down stairs, sir, very quickly, or I shall throw you out at the window."[24]

Fig. 110. Attributed to Gilbert Stuart, *George Washington*, 1797. Oil on canvas 95 x 59¾ in. (241.3 x 151.9 cm). White House Historical Association (White House Collection), Washington, D.C. (800.1290.1)

Park 1926, pp. 857–58, no. 23; Morgan and Fielding 1931, p. 320, no. XVI (Morgan did not accept the attribution); Eisen 1932, pp. 114–15. The portrait at Washington and Lee University, Lexington, Va., known as the Ramdoolal Dey portrait for its first owner, a merchant in India, is listed in Eisen 1932, pp. 110–11; and the portrait in a private collection, formerly owned by the Art Institute of Chicago, is listed as by Stuart in Morgan and Fielding 1931, pp. 262–63; Eisen 1932, pp. 114–15. Park (1926, pp. 856–57, no. 21) erroneously conflated the Chicago portrait with the one owned by Baker. A fourth copy, in the U.S. Capitol, appears to be the work of a different painter, judging from technique and from details of the composition. It may be a later copy, dating from about 1818, the year it was given by Richard Meade to the U.S. Embassy in Madrid. On this painting, see Morgan and

Because of this anecdote and the story of the painting at the White House, Winstanley is at times mentioned informally as the artist likely to have painted three early full-size copies of the Lansdowne portrait, which are now owned by Catholic University, Washington and Lee University, and a private collector.[25] If Dunlap's anecdote is correct in its details and Winstanley did indeed make the copies before coming to Philadelphia, the source of his copies was probably Baker's version of the Lansdowne. Winstanley in 1798 had some connection with Baker's museum. According to Charles Willson Peale, who visited the museum in June 1798, Baker had "purchased a whole length of General Washington in a Very superb Frame which he exhibits with an Elegant Musickcal Clock & a large Crusifix and several Landscapes lent him by Mr. Winstanley, and sundry small whole lengths of distinguished characters in the french Revolution, Prints &c in a Room lent him in the Tontine City Tavern."[26] Winstanley could have made his copies at this time, before taking them to Stuart in Philadelphia. Such timing would agree with his purchase of

Fielding 1931, pp. 264–65, no. 23; Eisen 1932, p. 115.

26. Charles Willson Peale, diary excerpt, June 1798, New York, in Lillian B. Miller, ed., *The Selected Papers of Charles Willson Peale and His Family* (New Haven: Yale University Press, 1983–), vol. 2, pp. 221–23; quotation is on p. 222.

27. "Second Exhibition of the American Academy of the Fine Arts (continued)," *American Monthly Magazine and Critical Review* 1 (July 1817), p. 200. On this exhibition, see Carrie Rebora Barratt, "The American Academy of the Fine Arts, New York, 1802–1842" (Ph.D. diss., City University of New York, 1990), vol. 1, p. 348.

28. "Stuart's Picture of Washington," *Boston Intelligencer, and Morning and Evening Advertiser,* August 2, 1817, p. 2.

29. *New-York Evening Post,* August 16, 1817, p. 2, in response to the reprinting of the Boston article in the *New-York Evening Post,* August 7, 1817.

a copy of the Vaughan portrait from Stuart, which he took to Washington, D.C., in 1800 (see cat. 35).

In 1817 Constable's portrait was exhibited at the second exhibition of the American Academy of the Fine Arts in New York. A reviewer in the *American Monthly Magazine and Critical Review* compared it to the portrait owned by Peter Jay Munro (see cat. 49).[27] This review was reprinted in the *Boston Intelligencer, and Morning and Evening Advertiser,* and the writer of the accompanying commentary believed that the portrait in the exhibition must have been "a spurious copy, by another hand" and that only six full-lengths of Washington had been painted by Stuart: one for Lord Lansdowne, one owned by Peter Jay Munro, one owned by the town of Boston, and the others for "individual states."[28] The author of the original review responded in a letter published in the *New-York Evening Post* commenting that the picture in question was the one "painted for Mr. Constable by Mr. Stewart, and still belongs to the family of the original proprietor" and noting that another full-length had been painted by Stuart for Gardiner Baker.[29]

EGM

48. GEORGE WASHINGTON (THE CONSTABLE-HAMILTON PORTRAIT)

1797
Oil on canvas, 50 x 40 in. (127 x 101.6 cm)
The New York Public Library, Astor, Lenox and Tilden Foundations

1. On this portrait, see Mason 1879, p. 98; Elizabeth Bryant Johnston, *Original Portraits of Washington, including Statues, Monuments, and Medals* (Boston: James R. Osgood and Co., 1882), pp. 86–87; Fielding 1923, p. 147, no. 29; Park 1926, pp. 855, 861–62, no. 30; Morgan and Fielding 1931, pp. 242–43, 270–71, no. 30; Eisen 1932, pp. 125–26; Evans 1999, p. 83.

2. "Mrs. H. B. Pierrepont's original Memorandum of the History of the Stuart full length & half length Washington," 1849, George Washington Portrait Collection, Manuscripts and Archives Division, New York Public Library, Astor, Lenox and Tilden Foundations.

New York City merchant William Kerin Constable commissioned this portrait as a gift for Alexander Hamilton, Secretary of the Treasury during George Washington's first term as president. Stuart had recently painted a portrait of Constable himself (fig. 109) and was completing for Constable a replica of the Lansdowne portrait (cat. 47), from which this work is also derived.[1] Constable's daughter Anna Maria, wife of Hezekiah Beers Pierrepont, mentioned this commission in her memorandum about the full-length.[2] While Alexander Hamilton's descendants believed that the portrait was given by Washington to Hamilton, the invoice in Constable's papers and the recollections of Constable's daughter confirmed that Constable did indeed commission the portrait.[3] Stuart received payment for the three paintings, including the portrait of Constable, on July 13, 1797,[4] and the paintings were shipped to New York, arriving on July 25, when Constable wrote to John Vaughan, in Philadelphia.[5] The details of Constable's payments are recorded in his account books. On July 25, 1797, he paid for "Freight & Cartage of Pictures from Philadelphia 4.50," and on July 28 he paid "R. Soderstram's drafts for Pictures of the President 900} Deduct, returned 150} 750."[6] The dimensions of the canvas are those of a traditional half-length portrait in the eighteenth-century English practice of portrait painting. Canvases were prepared to this size by retailers of artists' materials. Normally, as in the present work, a half-length showed the figure to about the knees. Also typical is the pricing: half the price of a full-length. Stuart's price for a replica of the Lansdowne full-length was $500, and the price for this painting was $250.

This portrait is derived from the Lansdowne (cat. 45), with significant changes to the pose and background that give it additional significance. As in the Lansdowne

3. Neal Richmond, "A Provenance Controversy: Did Washington Present a Stuart Portrait to Alexander Hamilton?" *New York Public Library Bulletin* 61 (1957), pp. 63–72. The portrait was bequeathed by his grandson Alexander Hamilton to the Astor Library.

4. Stuart's signed receipt is now unlocated. A copy is in the George Washington Portrait Collection, New York Public Library (see cat. 47, note 6).

5. Constable, letter to John Vaughan, July 25, 1797, "William & James Constable Account Book: 1797–1799" (a letterbook, not an account book), Constable-Pierrepont Family Papers, vol. 32, p. 244, Manuscripts and Archives Division, New York Public Library, Astor, Lenox and Tilden Foundations (hereafter Constable Papers). A handwritten, annotated transcript of this letter, referring correctly to the source as a letterbook, is in the "Pierrepont Family, Papers," Brooklyn Museum Library.

6. "William & James Constable Account Book: Accounts Current, 1791–1799," Constable Papers, vol. 34, p. 168. The same payments are recorded on a loose sheet from an account book for 1797; see folder marked "Accounts 1797," in "William and James Constable Accounts, 1792–1803," Constable Papers, box 6. The payment for shipping the pictures is also in "William and James Constable, Petty Cash Book, 1793–July 1797," Constable Papers, vol. 37 (unpaginated), for July 25, as $4.25. The payment of $900 to Richard Soderstrom is also recorded in "William and James Constable Cash Book, 1791–1797," Constable Papers, vol. 36, p. 131, in two payments of $400 and $500, and in "William and James Constable Journal, 1791–1799," Constable Papers, vol. 40, p. 583.

7. Roger B. Stein, *Seascape and the American Imagination*, exh. cat. (New York: Clarkson N. Potter in association with the Whitney Museum of American Art, 1975), pp. 27, 133 n. 31.

8. Mary-Jo Kline, ed., *Alexander Hamilton: A Biography in His Own Words* (New York: Newsweek, 1973), p. 335.

9. Hamilton, letter to Washington, July 9–11, 1795, quoted in ibid., pp. 335–36. For the full text of Hamilton's "Remarks on the Treaty of Amity, Commerce and Navigation lately made between the United States and Great Britain," see Harold C. Syrett, ed., *The Papers of Alexander Hamilton* (New York: Columbia University Press, 1961–87), vol. 18, pp. 404–54.

10. For a discussion of the articles and their authorship (ten additional essays were written by Rufus King), see the introductory note to the first article, in the *Papers of Alexander Hamilton*, vol. 18, pp. 475–79.

Fig. 111. Pierre-Imbert Drevet after Hyacinthe Rigaud, *Samuel Bernard*, 1729. Mezzotint, 24 x 16½ in. (60.8 x 42 cm). The New York Public Library, Astor, Lenox and Tilden Foundations; Miriam and Ira D. Wallach Division of Art, Prints, and Photographs, Print Collection

portrait, the president is dressed in a black velvet suit, with a white shirt and white lace shirt ruffles. His powdered hair is tied in a queue with a saw-toothed black ribbon. He is seated in a chair similar to the one behind him in the Lansdowne portrait, and across his lap rests a similar sword with a gold ribbon. And in the near background are a masonry wall with a column and a swirling drape with two tassels. In other respects the image is unlike the Lansdowne: Washington is seated, and he holds a document, illegible except for his signature, *G. Washington*. The background seascape is unprecedented in Stuart's portraits of Washington. While the intermediary curtain and column and the background scene appear to be based on Pierre-Imbert Drevet's engraving of Hyacinthe Rigaud's portrait of Samuel Bernard (fig. 111), closer examination suggests that the seascape may portray a specific event. The large ship bears a red and white striped flag at the stern. The ship's position in relation to the other ships and the red and black smoke nearby indicate a naval battle, as yet unidentified.

Roger Stein has commented, "That this rare seascape *Washington* came into the possession of Alexander Hamilton is suggestive, considering Hamilton's interest in the sea and American commercial policy."[7] More specifically it may be that if the purpose of the Lansdowne portrait commission was to thank Lord Lansdowne for his support of the American cause during the revolution as well as the signing of the Jay Treaty, this gift from Constable, a New York merchant-trader, to Hamilton, a leading New York Federalist, recognizes Hamilton's support of the treaty. In the summer of 1795, after the U.S. Senate ratified all but the twelfth article of the treaty, "new British captures of American ships made Washington reluctant to sign the agreement, and he sought Hamilton's opinion."[8] Hamilton advised Washington privately that the treaty would preserve peace. "With peace, the force of circumstances will enable us to make our way sufficiently fast in Trade. War at this time would give a serious wound to our growth and prosperity."[9] Hamilton also supported the treaty publicly in a series of twenty-eight articles published in New York newspapers from July 22, 1795 through January 9, 1796, which he signed with the pseudonym Camillus.[10] Washington signed the treaty on August 14, 1795.

EGM

48

49. George Washington (The Munro-Lenox Portrait)

ca. 1800

Oil on canvas, 95 x 64 in. (241.3 x 162.6 cm)
Signed on the table brace, to the right of the table
leg, as if the rest of the name were covered by the
drape: G. St
The New York Public Library, Astor, Lenox and
Tilden Foundations

Fig. 112. *George Washington*, 1800–1801. Oil on canvas, 96 x 60 in. (243.8 x 152.4 cm). State of Rhode Island and Providence Plantations

This portrait is the first of four identical full-length paintings for which Stuart revised the Lansdowne composition.[1] The setting, including the chair and draped table, the books, the inkwell, hat, and document on the table, and the columns and drapery with a distant clearing sky and rainbow all repeat the Lansdowne composition, and Washington is depicted in the same black suit. However, Stuart turned Washington's body toward his right and repositioned his feet. Washington's right hand rests on the document on the table next to him, rather than being held out in an oratorical gesture. In addition, the positions of the sword and his left hand were altered. These changes make a more dramatic and elegant image, and the thinner, more elongated figure may be truer to Washington's physique. Other changes include a cooler hue for the background drapery and substitution of a floor of brown, yellow, and green tiles, which, as Dorinda Evans noted, imitates the floor in the engraving of Hyacinthe Rigaud's portrait of Bishop Bossuet (fig. 105).[2]

The New York Public Library portrait is considered the original of these four works. It was painted completely by Stuart, who told Henry Pickering in 1817 that "he had made one copy of [the Lansdowne portrait], & that that is in the possession of Peter Jay Munroe Esq."[3] The portrait has been known since at least the 1930s as the Munro-Lenox portrait for its two nineteenth-century owners, Peter Jay Munro and James Lenox. Munro (1767–1833), nephew of John Jay, met Stuart in New York in 1794 when he posed for Stuart in John Jay's robes to enable Stuart to finish the portrait (see cat. 32).[4] The New York Public Library portrait was described in the *Boston Intelligencer* for August 2, 1817, as "The copy done for an individual gentleman, . . . the one now in possession of Peter Jay Munroe, Esq. who we understand purchased it in England. It was painted for a London banker by order of the British Consel General. The banker wished only a *half length*; but by mistake it was made a *full length*."[5] James Lenox acquired the portrait in 1845 from Munro's descendants. The portrait became part of the Lenox Library, which he established in 1870. After his death, the Lenox Library merged with the Astor Library and the Tilden Trust to become the New York Public Library.

While the details of the early history of this painting are not known, the story of the three replicas, made for the states of Rhode Island and Connecticut, is well documented. The first description of the portrait is found in Stuart's advertisement for the engraving in the *Aurora*, a Philadelphia newspaper, on June 12, 1800:

Gilbert Stuart, having been appointed by the Legislatures of Massachusetts and Rhode Island to prepare full length Portraits of the late General Washington, takes this mode to apprise the citizens of the United States of his intention to Publish Engravings of General Washington, from the Mount Vernon Portrait, executed, upon a large scale, by an eminent Artist. This advertisement (which has been suspended from motives of delicacy towards the afflicted family of Mount Vernon,) is deemed to be peculiarly necessary, as Mr. Stuart has the mortification to observe, that without any regard to his property, or feelings, as an Artist, an engraving has been recently published in England; and is now offered for sale in America, copied from one of his Portraits of General Washington. Though Mr. Stuart cannot but complain of this invasion of his Copy-right (a right always held sacred to the Artist, and expressly reserved on this occasion, as a provision for a numerous family), he derives some consolation from remarking, that the manner of

Fig. 113. *George Washington*, 1800–1801. Oil on canvas, 96 x 60 in. (243.8 x 152.4 cm). Connecticut State Library / State Archives, Hartford (PG 500)

executing Mr. Heath's engraving, cannot satisfy or supercede the public claim, for a correct representation of the American Patriot. . . . a full length engraving of General Washington, shall be delivered to each subscriber at the price of Twenty Dollars. . . . [E]ngravings from his Portraits of the President [John Adams] and Vice President [Thomas Jefferson] are likewise preparing . . . and will be published in the course of a few weeks.[6]

Recent publications have identified the "Mount Vernon Portrait" as the Munro-Lenox portrait. Evans wrote that this appellation may have come about because Stuart was "seeming to update the likeness with reference to the location of Washington's retirement. It is also possible that he intended initially to give the picture to the Washington family at Mount Vernon, perhaps to release himself from his obligation—which had become particularly pressing with Washington's death—to deliver the Athenaeum portrait."[7] However, the wording of the advertisement, "from the Mount Vernon Portrait," could refer to the facial image itself rather than the full composition, indicating that Stuart thought of the Munro-Lenox painting as based on the unfinished life portrait (the Athenaeum portrait; cat. 38), commissioned by Martha Washington for Mount Vernon. In that portrait Washington looks directly at the viewer, whereas in the Lansdowne portrait, Washington looks into the distance over the viewer's left shoulder. Even though Washington's face is longer here than in the Athenaeum and Lansdowne portraits, this distinction offers insight into the way Stuart thought about portraits: the face is the portrait; the rest is additional imagery. Evans also proposed that Stuart hoped that an engraving of this portrait would compete with Heath's engraving of the Lansdowne portrait (see cat. 45).[8]

The two replicas for Rhode Island were voted for by the state's General Assembly on March 1, 1800: "The citizens of this State . . . Do Resolve, That two portraits of [General George Washington] drawn at full length by some eminent artist, with suitable frames, be procured at the expence of the State, and that one of them be placed in the Senate chamber in each of the State Houses of Newport and Providence."[9] In May 1801, the General Assembly authorized payment of $1,200 for the two portraits.[10] According to Mantle Fielding, "When the portraits were finished they were framed and placed in the care of Joseph Anthony & Co. of Philadelphia, by whom they were shipped to Rhode Island on board Gibbs and Channing's sloop 'Eagle.' The pictures were received in Newport in October, 1801. They met with an enthusiastic reception and for weeks their exhibition drew crowds of admirers from all portions of the state."[11] The original frames, which are still on the portraits, were made in Philadelphia by Martin Jugiez, who charged $30 for "making 2 large frames for the Portrait of Genl Washington

1. The Munro-Lenox portrait and its three replicas are discussed in Fielding 1923, pp. 138–42, nos. 22–25; Park 1926, pp. 858–60, nos. 24–27; Morgan and Fielding 1931, pp. 265–69, nos. 24–27; Eisen 1932, pp. 83–85; Mount 1964, pp. 225–30, 235; Evans 1999, pp. 69–71.
2. Evans 1999, p. 69.
3. Pickering 1817 (November 10), quoted in ibid.
4. Morgan and Fielding (1931, p. 265) gave the name "Munro-Lenox" to this painting to distinguish it from versions of the Lansdowne portrait. They explained (p. 266 n.) that this type had been wrongly called "The Teapot Type," an error made by writers about engravings of Washington's portraits. On Munro, see *Appleton's Cyclopaedia of American Biography*, rev. ed., ed. James Grant Wilson and John Fiske (New York: D. Appleton and Co., 1898), vol. 4, p. 461.
5. "Stuart's Picture of Washington," *Boston Intelligencer and Morning and Evening Advertiser*, August 2, 1817, p. 2. The most famous banker associated with Stuart was Sir Francis Baring, but there is no documentation to connect him with this commission.
6. Alfred Coxe Prime, comp., *The Arts and Crafts in Philadelphia, Maryland, and South Carolina: Gleanings from Newspapers*, pt. 2, *1786–1800* (1929–32; reprint, New York: Da Capo Press, 1969), pp. 34–35.
7. Evans 1999, pp. 69, 71. Mount (1964, p. 228) first proposed the identification of the Munro-Lenox portrait as the Mount Vernon portrait referred to in the advertisement.

@ 15 Drs ea," $120 for "Carving 2 trophies of War, @ 60 Dolls ea," and $210 for "Gilding the frames & trophies @ 105 ea." [12] The elaborate carvings (see fig. 112) include the state shield with the word HOPE and an anchor at the center, with an eagle above, and flags, swords, cannon, cannon balls, and oak branches to each side.

The portrait for the State of Connecticut (fig. 113) was voted by that state's General Assembly in May 1800.[13] It was completed by February 16, 1801, when Stuart wrote to Oliver Wolcott Jr., representative of the committee designated by the assembly to commission the portrait.[14] Wolcott's correspondence with and on behalf of the committee reveals something of Stuart's reputation and practice. When the committee asked Wolcott to determine Stuart's price for a full-length, Wolcott responded, "I have understood that Mr. Stewart has usually demanded One Thousand Dollars, for full length Portraits of Genl. Washington." He added a caveat: "Mr. Stewart is under many engagements and has sometimes failed in punctuality. The demand for his Portraits is increasing & he may possibly expect somewhat more than the sum I have mentioned."[15] After an interview with the artist, he reported, "The price of One Thousand Dollars for Portraits, mentioned in my letter of yesterday, was I find his demand for <u>originals</u>—he will if desired engage to furnish two well finished <u>duplicates</u> of an excellent original Portrait for Twelve hundred Dollars, exclusive of frames, the expense of which is estimated at Two hundred Dollars more." He added, "Mr. Stewart observes, that the heat of our Climate will destroy Canvas, exposed in a public building, in about Twenty years & he recommends Mahogany Pannells, in lieu of Canvass. He says that the Pannells can be so constructed as not to warp or crack. I should suppose his judgement founded on experience ought to be relied upon." Wolcott said that "the proposed Portraits will be five feet wide & eight feet long, surrounded by a plain gilded frame of nine Inches in Width. If a Contract is soon formed, the work will be ready for delivery at the end of the present year."[16] Contracts were drawn up and sent to Stuart, delivered to him by William Bingham. Stuart "evaded signing them [and] . . . returned them without his Signature observing that he had come to a resolution to have inserted in every contract for any of his paintings, that he reserved to himself the entire and exclusive privilege of copyright & publishing prints of them."[17] Although Wolcott apparently did amend the contracts, ultimately only one portrait was painted. The receipt for payment, signed by Stuart, dated April 4, 1801, is for $600.[18]

When the replica of the Lansdowne portrait painted for William Constable (cat. 47) was exhibited at the American Academy of the Fine Arts in New York in 1817, Munro's full-length, not in the exhibition, was compared favorably with it in a review in the *American Monthly Magazine and Critical Review*: "We have seen a full length portrait of Washington, by Stewart, giving another view of the face, and another attitude, beyond all comparison preferable to this. It is in the possession of Peter Jay Munroe, Esq. We lament that the engraving had not been made from Mr. Munroe's, rather than Lord Lansdown's picture. It is not only a better picture, but it is much more like the person and face of Washington. In No. 52 [the painting on exhibition], a disagreeable protuberance of the under lip may be observed, and a deficiency of chin very unfavourable to the physiognomy."[19] In a reprint of the review in the *Boston Intelligencer*, the accompanying commentary questioned whether the exhibited painting was in fact by Stuart and launched a discussion about how many full-lengths Stuart had painted of Washington and whether they were all alike. The writer described the Lansdowne portrait as one of only two "*original* heads of Washington" by Stuart and went on to say, "About five *full length* copies only by Stuart's own hand have been given to the world. Most of these

8. Evans 1999, p. 144 n. 19.

9. Rhode Island General Assembly, February Session, 1800, Rhode Island Colony Records, vol. 15, pp. 640–41, Rhode Island State Archives, Providence. The documentation for these portraits is quoted in James L. Yarnall, "The Full-Length Portrait of George Washington by Gilbert Stuart in the Newport Colony House," *Newport History: Journal of the Newport Historical Society* 72–73 (fall 2003–spring 2004), pp. 150–59. For the portrait in Providence, see also *Most Admirable: The Rhode Island State House* (Providence: Rhode Island State House Restoration Society, 2002), p. 60. I thank Kevin A. Carvalho, Department of Administration, State of Rhode Island, for providing photocopies of this documentation and for arranging for the authors to see the paintings in Providence and Newport. John A. Woods of South Windsor, Conn., was very helpful with this research, as was Kenneth Carlson, Reference Archivist, Rhode Island State Archives.

10. Authorization of payment of $1,200 is found in the Journal of the Rhode Island Senate, May 1801, Rhode Island Colony Records, vol. 16, p. 32, Rhode Island State Archives.

11. Fielding 1923, pp. 139–40.

12. Jugiez is listed as a carver and gilder at 25 Walnut Street, Philadelphia, in *The New Trade Directory for Philadelphia, Anno 1800* (Philadelphia, 1799), p. 43. The second name on the invoice is difficult to read, but appears to be "Owants." No identification could be made for this person.

The framers in Philadelphia also provided the "Packing Cases & packing," "Porterage," and "Bills lading" for "a total of $389.55. In addition the committee members were reimbursed for the costs of shipping one portrait and frame to the Providence State House on the ship "Rising States" for $10, and trucking the crates from the ship to "a store near the Court House," fifty cents. Their bill, dated Philadelphia, November 23, 1801, was submitted to the committee that commissioned the portrait, which paid them and was reimbursed; see "John Maybins bill for Washingtons Portraits, 1801," "Accounts Allowed," February 1802, Rhode Island State Archives. Approval to pay these expenses was voted by the Assembly in February 1802; see February Session, 1802, at Providence, Rhode Island Colony Records, vol. 16, p. 133, Rhode Island State Archives.

The expenses of putting up the portraits in the state houses in Newport and Providence were paid for in June 1802. For approval to reimburse these expenses, voted by the Assembly in June, see Rhode Island Colony Records, vol. 16, p. 187, Rhode Island State Archives; for the bills, see "Accounts Allowed," June 1802, Rhode Island State Archives.

13. On this portrait, in addition to the references in note 1 above, see Wilson H. Faude, "Old State House, Hartford, Connecticut," *Antiques* 117 (March 1980), pp. 626–33, illus. p. 631; and Ellen G. Miles, "'Memorials of great & good men who were my friends': Portraits in the Life of Oliver Wolcott, Jr.," *Proceedings of the American Antiquarian Society* 107, pt. 1 (1998), pp. 118–21. Connecticut initially also voted to commission a second portrait for the state house in New Haven, but only one portrait was painted.

14. The letter is in the Gratz Collection, Historical Society of Pennsylvania, Philadelphia; it is quoted in Morgan and Fielding 1931, pp. 268–69 (described as unlocated). The addressee was simply "Dear Sir," who has been identified as John Trumbull, a member of the committee. However, the rest of the correspondence was with Wolcott, suggesting that this too was written to Wolcott.

15. Draft of a letter from Wolcott to Trumbull, May 16, 1800, Papers of Oliver Wolcott Jr., vol. 11, no. 47, Connecticut Historical Society, Hartford; quoted in Miles, "Memorials of great & good men who were my friends," p. 120.

16. Draft of a letter from Wolcott to Trumbull, May 17, 1800, Wolcott Papers, vol. 11, no. 48,

Connecticut Historical Society; quoted in Miles, "Memorials of great & good men who were my friends," pp. 120–21.

17. Israel Whelen, Wolcott's agent in the transaction with Stuart, letter to Wolcott, August 6, 1800, Wolcott Papers, vol. 15, no. 108, Connecticut Historical Society. Bingham and Wolcott also exchanged letters at this time, when Bingham was at Lansdown, his country estate; see Wolcott Papers, vol. 15, no. 106. Whelen's letter about the revised drafts of the contracts is dated August 13, 1800, Wolcott Papers, vol. 15, no. 111.

18. The signed receipt is in the Connecticut State Archives, Hartford, no. 920/St91w; a copy was provided by John A. Woods and Kevin Carvahlo.

19. "Second Exhibition of the American Academy of the Fine Arts (continued)," *American Monthly*

have been done for individual states, (none however for the state of New-York) one for an individual gentleman, and one for the town of Boston."[20] The writer also stated that Munro's portrait was "an exact copy" of the Lansdowne and "does *not* give 'another view of the face' nor represent Washington 'in another attitude.'" This information, of course, is not correct. The five full-length copies that the Boston writer referred to were Munro's portrait, the three replicas of it, and a completely different full-length, painted for the city of Boston in 1806. That portrait, *Washington at Dorchester Heights* (fig. 159), is the only lifesize full-length portrait that Stuart painted of Washington in his general's uniform.[21] In response to this *Boston Intelligencer* commentary, the *American Monthly Magazine* reviewer published a letter listing two additional full-lengths, the one on exhibition painted for William Constable (cat. 47) and the one painted for Gardiner Baker.[22] No doubt because of the interest created by this exchange, Munro's full-length of Washington was exhibited at the American Academy that fall after Stuart was elected an honorary member.[23]

EGM

Magazine and Critical Review 1 (July 1817), p. 200.

20. "Stuart's Picture of Washington," *Boston Intelligencer and Morning and Evening Advertiser*, August 2, 1817, p. 2.

21. On this portrait, see Fielding 1923, p. 45, no. 27; Park 1926, p. 860, no. 28; Morgan and Fielding 1931, p. 269, no. 28; *American Paintings in the Museum of Fine Arts, Boston* (Boston: Museum of Fine Arts, 1969), vol. 1, pp. 247–48, no. 915; Evans 1999, pp. 86–87.

22. *New-York Evening Post*, August 16, 1817, p. 2, in response to the reprinting of the Boston article in the *New-York Evening Post*, August 7, 1817.

23. Carrie Rebora, "The American Academy of the Fine Arts, New York, 1802–1842" (Ph.D. diss., City University of New York, 1990), vol. 2, pp. 350, 509.

50. ELIZABETH PARKE CUSTIS LAW

1796
Oil on canvas, 28¼ x 23½ in. (71.8 x 59.7 cm)
Collection of Katherine S. Merle-Smith

Research for and drafts of this entry were done by
Christopher H. Jones.
1. Mary V. Thompson, draft entry on Elizabeth
   Parke Custis Law for the *Dictionary of Virginia
   Biography*, ed. John T. Kneebone et al. (Richmond:
   Library of Virginia, 1998–), vol. 3, forthcoming
   2005. She has determined that Eliza died on
   December 31, 1831; her death previously has been
   given as 1832. On Washington's stepchildren, see
   also *Burke's Presidential Families of the United States
   of America*, 2nd ed. (London: Burke's Peerage,
   1981), pp. 16–17.
2. Elizabeth Parke Custis, letter to Washington,
   September 7, 1794, in Edmund Law Rogers,
   "Some New Washington Relics: II. From the
   Collection of Edmund Law Rogers, Esq." *Century
   Illustrated Monthly Magazine* 40 (May 1890), p. 23.
3. George Washington, letter to Elizabeth Parke
   Custis, September 14, 1794, in John C. Fitzpatrick,
   ed., *The Writings of George Washington from the
   Original Manuscript Sources, 1745–1799* (1931–44;
   reprint, Westport, Conn.: Greenwood Press, 1970),
   vol. 33, pp. 500–501.
4. Martha Washington, letter to Fanny Bassett
   Washington, April 6, 1795, in Joseph E. Fields,
   comp., *"Worthy Partner": The Papers of Martha
   Washington* (Westport, Conn.: Greenwood Press,
   1994), p. 284.

Fig. 114. Walter Robertson, *George Washington*,
1794. Watercolor on ivory, 3 x 2⅜ in. (7.6 x 6 cm).
Courtesy of Stewart P., Cameron B., and Brian
H. McCaw

Elizabeth Parke Custis (1776–1831), known to her family as Eliza or Betsy, was the oldest
surviving child of Martha Washington's son John Parke Custis and his wife, Eleanor
Calvert.[1] After her father died during the American Revolution, she and her sister
Martha lived with their mother and stepfather, Dr. David Stuart. Custis's two younger
children, Eleanor and George Washington Parke Custis, were adopted by their grandparents, Martha and George Washington, and lived at Mount Vernon, where Elizabeth
was a frequent visitor. She expressed her closeness to her grandparents when she wrote
Washington on September 7, 1794, to ask for his portrait, saying she "had *no other wish*
nearer my *heart* than that of possessing your likeness. . . . It is my first wish to have it in
my power to contemplate, at all times, the features of one, who, I so highly respect as
the Father of his Country and look up to with grateful affection as a parent to myself
and family."[2] He gave her a miniature of himself by Irish artist Walter Robertson (fig. 114)
and questioned her in a teasing tone whether "the contemplation of an inanimate thing,
whatever might be the reflections arising from the possession of it, can be the *only* wish
of your heart." His grandfatherly letter, about "emotions of a softer kind, to wch. the
heart of a girl turned of eighteen, is susceptible," comments on romantic love and its
place in marriage in relation to other "necessary ingredients," including the future husband's "good sense, good dispositions, and the means of supporting you in the way you
have been brought up."[3] In 1795 Eliza asked if she could join her grandparents in
Philadelphia. Her grandmother agreed, but worried about her health: "Betsy Custis told
me, she wished to stay with me, and I wrote to her mother for her permission which she
redily gave—She seemed to be very grave I was in hope that being in the gay world
would have a good effect on her, but she seems to wish to be at home—and very much
by herself—she takes no delight to goe out to visit—she would not go with Nelly and
myself to the assembly last week she dont like to go to church every sunday thinks it too
fatiguing—to be always to be indisposed she often complains of not being well—she
took ill when she first came here—but is much better and looks better tho she does not
like to be told so—the girls have lived so long in solatude that they do not know how to
get the better of it—Betsy seems so reconciled to be alone."[4]

Within a year after moving to Philadelphia, however, Eliza announced her plans to
marry Thomas Law (1756–1834), an Englishman twice her age who had recently arrived
in America.[5] The son of Edmund Law, bishop of Carlisle, Law lived in India from 1773
to 1791, serving in administrative positions with the East India Company and accumu-
lating a sizable fortune. Drawn to America in part because of George Washington's
fame, he went in 1794 to New York, where he met real estate promoter James Greenleaf.
Almost immediately Law purchased 2,400,000 square feet of property in the District of
Columbia at a price that yielded a large profit for Greenleaf and his partners, Robert
Morris and John Nicholson. This prompted President Washington, who had yet to meet
Law, to ask: "Lately, a Gentleman from England, has paid, or is to pay £50,000 for 500
Lots.—Will it not be asked, why are speculators to pocket so much money? Are not the
Commissioners as competent to make bargains?"[6] Law and Eliza presumably were
introduced when he went to Philadelphia in 1795, after this purchase, to meet the president.[7] When she informed Washington of her engagement to Thomas Law, he responded, "I therefore proceed to assure you—if Mr. Law is the man of your choice . . . that
you find, after a careful examination of your heart, you cannot be happy without him—

50

5. On Law, see *DNB*, vol. 11, pp. 676–77, which has some errors; and Allen C. Clark, *Greenleaf and Law in the Federal City* (Washington, D.C.: Press of W. F. Roberts, 1901). On his English family, see Peter Townend, ed., *Burke's Genealogical and Heraldic History of the Peerage, Baronetage, and Knightage*, 104th ed. (London: Burke's Peerage, 1967), pp. 872–74, "Baron Ellenborough"; Law's older brother Edward became first Baron Ellenborough in 1802, the year he became chief justice.

6. George Washington, letter to Daniel Carroll,

that your alliance with him meets my approbation . . . accompanied with my fervent wishes that you may be as happy in this important event as your most sanguine imagination has ever presented to your view."[8] To Law, he was more direct: "No intimation of this event, from any quarter, having been communicated to us before, it may well be supposed that it was a matter of Surprize. This being premised, I have only to add . . . my approbation, in which Mrs. Washington unites."[9] Washington was sufficiently concerned about Law's motives and prospects that he wrote to David Stuart suggesting that, as her stepfather, he require Law to "make a settlement upon her previous to marriage; of her own fortune if no more," allowing her to keep control of her own inheritance.[10]

Fig. 115. *Thomas Law*, ca. 1796. Oil on canvas, 29 x 24 in. (73.7 x 61 cm). Private collection

The couple was married in March 1796 at her mother's home in Virginia, in what her sister Nelly described as "quite a private wedding, & we have had no dancing or parties of any kind."[11]

Family tradition says that Stuart painted Eliza's portrait in Philadelphia in February 1796, shortly before her marriage, at the time Stuart was painting the portrait of George Washington known today as the Athenaeum portrait (cat. 38). He may also have painted his portrait of Law at this time (fig. 115).[12] According to Jane Stuart, whenever Eliza Custis "could find an opportunity, [she] would accompany [Washington] to my father's painting-room. She has said to me, with great satisfaction: 'I was present during many of the sittings, and have seen the likeness of the dear General grow under your father's pencil.'"[13] According to descendants, "While Stuart was painting the portrait of Washington she entered the room, coming from a walk, and stood with arms folded regarding the artist at work," the pose that Stuart represented in the painting.[14] Her brown dress, worn with an open-weave white fichu or scarf, her slightly untidy hair, and her bare arms crossed in front, with her left hand holding a straw hat with a red ribbon, all suggest casual, spontaneous motion, as does her figure, turned to the side, set in an open landscape. Even Stuart's brushwork—the fichu painted with lines that he may have completed with the butt end of the brush, the dark shadow of the scarf knot added as the last step—suggests quick completion. The crossed-arm pose is rare in his work and usually was reserved for his portraits of men. Examples include those of John Philip Kemble (National Portrait Gallery, London), Luke White (fig. 47), Colonel John Chesnut (Denver Art Museum), and Sir Robert Liston (National Gallery of Art, Washington), as well as its unusual variation in *The Skater* (cat. 6). Her expression seems to fit what her father described as her "Proud spirit."[15] Others, too, throughout her life, saw her as strong-willed with unpredictable emotions and behavior. Her aunt Rosalie Stier Calvert, in a retrospective look back on this time of her life, recalled, "Since childhood, Mrs. L demonstrated a violent and romantic disposition. Her father recognized that her singular personality would bring her unhappiness and he tried to correct it, but he died while she was still very young. . . .When Mrs. L entered society, she was very pretty, rich, and quite intelligent. Her relatives and connections were the most respectable. Consequently, she was greatly admired and flattered. She never cared about the compliments she was given on her beauty, but she was always very vain about her mind and knowledge."[16]

The Laws took up residence in the new federal city where Law built several houses for investment.[17] Their only child, Eliza, was born in 1797. In 1803 Law went to England to raise money for a canal project; soon after his return, the couple separated; they were divorced in 1811 and Law was granted custody of their daughter.[18] Eliza's aunt Rosalie Calvert wrote to her own mother in Belgium with the news: "Mrs. Law and her husband separated amicably. I believe this is the most peculiar affair of this sort that has ever taken place. . . . You know he has always been a little crazy, and I think she is too."[19] Rosalie, who soon lost patience with Eliza, described her marriage to Mr. Law as "against the wishes of all her relatives. Never were two people less suited to live together, but during the life of her grandmother Mrs. Washington, to whom she was most attached, they restrained themselves in order to spare her pain. . . . Mrs. L's biggest fault

January 7, 1795; in Clark, *Greenleaf and Law*, p. 92. On Law's purchase, see also Bob Arnebeck, *Through a Fiery Trial: Building Washington, 1790–1800* (Lanham, Md.: Madison Books, 1991), pp. 250–53.

7. On Eliza Custis and Thomas Law, see Charles Moore, *The Family Life of George Washington* (Boston: Houghton Mifflin Co., 1926), pp. 104–15.

8. Washington, letter to "Betsey" Custis, February 10, 1796, Pierpont Morgan Library, New York, on the Web site of the George Washington Papers, http://gwpapers.virginia.edu; in *Writings of George Washington*, vol. 34, pp. 457–58. Her letter to Washington is unlocated.

9. Washington, letter to Thomas Law, February 10, 1796, Pierpont Morgan Library, http://gwpapers .virginia.edu; *Writings of George Washington*, vol. 34, pp. 458–59.

10. Washington, letter to David Stuart, February 7, 1796, in *Writings of George Washington*, vol. 34, p. 454.

11. Eleanor Parke Custis, letter to Elizabeth Bordley, May 13, 1796, in Patricia Brady, ed., *George Washington's Beautiful Nelly: The Letters of Eleanor Parke Custis Lewis to Elizabeth Bordley Gibson, 1794–1851* (Columbia: University of South Carolina Press, 1991), p. 28.

12. On Law's portrait, see Park 1926, p. 463, no. 473; Park dates it to ca. 1800. However, an earlier date

at the time of their marriage has been suggested; see *The Mount Vernon Ladies Association of the Union, Annual Report 1983* (Mount Vernon, Va., 1983), pp. 16, 35.

13. J. Stuart 1876, p. 372.

14. On the family tradition about the portrait, see Charles Henry Hart, *Historical Descriptive and Critical Catalogue of the Works of American Artists in Collection of Herbert L. Pratt, Glen Cove, L.I.* (New York, 1917), pp. 37–38, no. 10. The portrait is catalogued in Mason 1879, p. 212; Park 1926, pp. 464–65, no. 474. It is included in Washington, Providence 1967, p. 78, no. 29.

15. Eliza Custis, letter to David Baillie Warden, the American consul in Paris, April 20, 1808, Warden Papers, Maryland Historical Society, Baltimore, in William D. Hoyt Jr., "Self-Portrait: Eliza Custis, 1808," *Virginia Magazine of History and Biography* 53, no. 2 (1945), p. 95. We appreciate the assistance of Mount Vernon Librarian Barbara McMillan, who directed us to a wealth of material on Eliza Custis, and of the library's Research Specialist, Mary V. Thompson, who shared her as yet unpublished entry on Elizabeth Parke Custis Law for the *Dictionary of Virginia Biography*.

16. Rosalie Stier Calvert, letter to Isabelle van Havre, February 18, 1805, in Margaret Law Callcott, ed. and trans., *Mistress of Riversdale: The Plantation Letters of Rosalie Stier Calvert, 1795–1821* (Baltimore: Johns Hopkins University Press, 1991), p. 111.

17. According to Thomas Froncek, ed., *The City of Washington: An Illustrated History by the Junior League of Washington* (New York: Alfred A. Knopf, 1977), pp. 71–72, they rented a house at Sixth and

is that she has such a high opinion of herself that she is contemptuous of everyone else. Of all her relatives only my husband has her trust and the power to tell her the truth about herself . . . In her tastes and pastimes she is more man than woman and regrets that she can't wear pants."[20] When conveying the news of her separation to her friend Anna Cutts (see cat. 71), Sally McKean Yrujo (see cat. 65) bluntly described Eliza as Law's "Amazonian wife."[21] Eliza styled herself "Mrs. Custis" and began a life in which she described herself as "the most lonely and desolate of mortals," living at times in Washington, Philadelphia, and Alexandria, Virginia.[22] Shortly after learning of her death in Richmond, Virginia, in 1831, Thomas Law maintained that "she always Loved me—after our separation when I was sick, she burst into my room & insisted upon nursing [me]—how painful to think with a deranged mind she could not command her temper or conduct."[23] Stuart's portrait successfully captures her youthful energy and beauty while suggesting the complex elements of her personality that would influence her life's course.

EGM

N Streets SW, which was built in 1796. It is now part of the residential complex called Tiber Island.

18. Moore, *Family Life of Washington*, p. 107.

19. Rosalie Stier Calvert, letter to Mme H. J. Stier, July 30, 1804, in *Mistress of Riversdale*, pp. 92, 93 n. 4.

20. Rosalie Stier Calvert, letter to Isabelle van Havre, February 18, 1805, in *Mistress of Riversdale*, p. 111.

21. Sally McKean Yrujo, letter to Anna Cutts, June 28, 1804, transcription of lost original, Cutts Family Collection of Papers of James and Dolley Madison, microfilm 14326, Manuscript Division, Library of Congress, Washington, D.C.

22. Elizabeth Custis, letter to David Baillie Warden, quoted in Elswyth Thane, *Mount Vernon Family* (New York: Crowell-Collier Press, 1968), p. 58.

23. Thomas Law, letter to his nephew Charles Rumbold, January 10, 1832, Thomas Law Papers (#2801), Tracy W. McGregor Library, Special Collections, University of Virginia Library, Charlottesville.

51. ANNE WILLING BINGHAM

1797
Oil on canvas, 30 x 25 in. (76.2 x 63.5 cm)
Signed and dated lower left: G. Stuart 1797
Private collection

Research for and drafts of this entry were done by Christopher H. Jones.

1. Abigail Adams, letter to her sister Mary Smith Cranch, September 30, 1785, American Antiquarian Society, Worcester, Mass., quoted in Robert C. Alberts, *The Golden Voyage: The Life and Times of William Bingham, 1752–1804* (Boston: Houghton Mifflin Co., 1969), p. 151. On Anne Bingham, see especially Margaret L. Brown, "Mr. and Mrs. William Bingham of Philadelphia: Rulers of the Republican Court," *Pennsylvania Magazine of History and Biography* 61 (July 1937), pp. 286–324; Alberts, *Golden Voyage.*

2. The portrait of Anne Bingham was acquired in 1963 from M. Knoedler and Co. and Julius Weitzner, who purchased it from a London dealer. It is not listed in Mason 1879 or in Park 1926, who catalogued a second version, with slight differences, that was owned in 1879 by T. F. Bayard and in 1926 by Mrs. J. Gardner Bradley; see Mason 1879, p. 139; Park 1926, pp. 155–56, no. 85. The portrait was exhibited in 1989 at the National Portrait Gallery, Washington; see Margaret C. S. Christman, *The First Federal Congress, 1789–1791,* exh. cat. (Washington, D.C.: Smithsonian Institution Press, 1989), p. 201.

3. The children of Thomas and Anne McCall Willing are listed in Thomas Willing Balch, *Willing Letters and Papers* (Philadelphia: Allen, Lane and Scott, 1922), pp. lix–lx; Alexander Du Bin, ed., *Willing Family and Collateral Lines of Carroll-Chew-Dundas-Gyles-Jackson-McCall-Moore-Parsons-Shippen* (Philadelphia: Historical Publication Society, 1941), pp. 10–12. Of thirteen children, ten survived to adulthood.

4. The Binghams' years in Europe are described in detail in Alberts, *Golden Voyage,* pp. 121–56.

5. Susan Branson discusses Anne Bingham's salons in *These Fiery Frenchified Dames: Women and Political Culture in Early National Philadelphia* (Philadelphia: University of Pennsylvania Press, 2001), pp. 133–40.

6. On the house, see Alberts, *Golden Voyage,* pp. 157–64; Wendy A. Nicholson, "Making the Private Public: Anne Willing Bingham's Role as a Leader of Philadelphia's Social Elite in the Late Eighteenth Century" (master's thesis, University of Delaware, 1988).

7. Joshua Francis Fisher, quoted in Alberts, *Golden Voyage,* pp. 213–14.

Anne Willing Bingham, described by Abigail Adams as "taken altogether . . . the finest woman I ever saw," was among the most widely admired American women of her era.[1] Her portrait and the pendant portrait of William Bingham (fig. 116) were painted in the summer of 1797 at Lansdown, the Binghams' country house near Philadelphia, with other family portraits (see cat. 52).[2] Over the course of that year Bingham paid Stuart $1,600 for "family pictures," as recorded in his personal account book (see cat. 53 and fig. 108). Stuart's portrait captures Anne's self-assurance and sensuality. Her posture, her elaborate hairstyle, and the rich black velvet of her dress, with its revealing neckline, convey a subtle imperiousness, while her direct gaze conveys her self-confidence. The red upholstery of the chair and the red cover on the table contrast effectively with her black dress. The large gold pendant that she wears on a gold chain, the jeweled pin that gathers the sleeve of her dress, and her gold earring add to the richness of the image.

Anne Bingham (1764–1801), called Nancy, was the eldest daughter of Philadelphia merchant Thomas Willing and his wife, Anne McCall. She grew up with her four sisters and five brothers in a large extended Philadelphia family that included relatives in the McCall, Shippen, Powel, and Francis families, many of them living nearby.[3] In 1780 she married William Bingham, who had already begun to amass one of the greatest fortunes of the day. With the marriage he gained access to the Willing family's considerable political, social, and economic influence. In 1783 Anne and William Bingham went to Europe, where for three years they lived in London and Paris, and traveled to The Hague, Bath, Switzerland, and Italy.[4] Mrs. Bingham's charms opened many doors as did their wealth, and contemporaries commented on her beauty and preference for French fashions. In London, shortly before returning to America in 1786, Anne was presented at court on the celebration of Queen Charlotte's birthday.

The Binghams returned to Philadelphia with the intention of continuing their cosmopolitan European lifestyle. When the city became the temporary capital of the federal government in 1790, Anne combined her wealth and personal connections to successfully transplant to America the salon society she had experienced in Paris.[5] The Binghams' grand Philadelphia residence, Mansion House, was furnished to facilitate social events of a style and scale new to Philadelphia.[6] The events attracted "all that was distinguished and accomplished in the country," observed her cousin Joshua Francis Fisher, who added that "certainly there never was in our country a series of such distinguished *réunions.* Brilliant balls, sumptuous dinners and constant receptions."[7] The receptions at the Mansion House became political salons of a type unprecedented in the new republic. Guests included political leaders from the state and federal government, including George Washington, who was a frequent guest. After a visit on May 21, 1787, he noted in his diary, "Dined, and drank Tea at Mr. Binghams in great Splendor."[8] Their contemporaries most admired Anne Bingham's ability to charm and welcome her guests. Samuel Breck noted that "Mrs. Bingham's conversational cleverness in French and English, graceful manners, and polite tact in doing the honors of her splendid establishment, rendered it exceedingly attractive."[9] For entertaining, William Bingham purchased specialty foods, wine, and china from France. At the same time, for his wife, he purchased face cream, powder, artificial flowers, feathers and other hair ornaments, and gloves.[10] Her taste was praised by some, questioned by others. Julian Niemcewicz, a Polish statesman who was in America in 1797–99, wrote about his visit to the Binghams, "One mounts a staircase of white native marble. One enters an immense room with a

Fig. 116. *William Bingham*, 1797. Oil on canvas, 30 x 25 in. (76.2 x 63.5 cm). Private collection

sculptured fireplace, painted ceiling, magnificent rug, curtains, armchairs, sofas in Gobelins of France. The dinner is brought on by a French cook; the servants are in livery, the food served in silver dishes, the dessert on Sevres porcelain. The mistress of the house is tall, beautiful, perfectly dressed and has copied, one could not want for better, the tone and carriage of a European lady. . . . In a word, I thought myself in Europe."[11] Another visitor, John Marshall, later chief justice of the United States, wrote his wife in July 1797, after attending a dinner at the Binghams' country seat. Following his description of the service, he commented on Anne Bingham's gown, which is very similar in its sleeve detail to the one she wears in Stuart's portrait. "Mrs. Bingham is a very elegant woman who dresses at the height of fashion. I do not however like that fashion. The sleeve [does] not reach the elbow or the glove come quite to it. There is a vacancy of three or four inches & just [above] the naked elbow is a gold clasp."[12]

Anne Bingham belonged to a generation of women who questioned the roles that society and custom had accorded them. Her father's family included strong-willed women, like her aunt Elizabeth Willing Powel, who was known to "eagerly and passionately" argue politics with Washington.[13] In 1799 Mrs. Powel paid bookseller Thomas Dobson "one Dollar and a half in full for Wollstonecrafts Letters."[14] This was probably a copy of *Letters Written during a Short Residence in Sweden, Norway, and Denmark* (London, 1796), by noted English feminist Mary Wollstonecraft. Anne Bingham was a patron of Susanna Rowson, an English actress in America who wrote about women's lives and dedicated her first novel written in America, *The Trials of the Human Heart* to "Mrs. Bingham."[15] Mrs. Bingham expressed her strongly held ideas about the roles women could play in the new political world in a letter to Thomas Jefferson, who had become a friend of the Binghams in Paris, where he was American minister. He wrote on February 7, 1787, to ask if she does not "find the tranquil pleasures of America preferable to the empty bustle of Paris," and went on to describe the frivolous concerns of the daily life of a woman in French society. She wrote in answer:

I agree with you that many of the fashionable pursuits of the Parisian Ladies are rather frivolous, and become uninteresting to a reflective Mind; but the Picture you have exhibited, is rather overcharged. . . . The state of Society in different Countries requires corresponding Manners and Qualifications. . . . In what other Country can be found a Marquise de Coigny, who, young and handsome, takes a lead in all the fashionable Dissipation of Life, and at more serious moments collects at her House an assembly of the Literati, whom she charms with her Knowledge and her bel Esprit. The Women of France interfere in the politics of the Country, and often give a decided Turn to the Fate of Empires. Either by the gentle Arts of persuasion, or by the commanding force of superior Attractions and Address, they have obtained that Rank and Consideration in society, which the Sex are intitled to, and which they in vain contend for in other Countries. We are therefore bound in Gratitude to admire and revere them, for asserting our Privileges, as much as the Friends of the Liberties of Mankind reverence the successfull Struggles of the American Patriots.[16]

8. Donald Jackson and Dorothy Twohig, eds., *The Diaries of George Washington* (Charlottesville: University Press of Virginia, 1976–79), vol. 5, p. 159.

9. Samuel Breck, "Recollections of the Members of the American Philosophical Society," American Philosophical Society, quoted in Alberts, *Golden Voyage*, p. 213.

10. Alberts, *Golden Voyage*, p. 215.

11. Julian Ursyn Niemcewicz, *Under Their Vine and Fig Tree: Travels through America in 1797–1799, 1805*, trans. and ed. Metchie J. E. Budka, Collections of the New Jersey Historical Society at Newark, vol. 14 (Elizabeth, N.J.: Grassman Publishing Co., 1965), p. 37.

12. John Marshall, letter to Mary Marshall, July 14, 1797, William C. Stinchcombe and Charles T. Cullen, eds., *The Papers of John Marshall*, vol. 3 (Chapel Hill: University of North Carolina Press, 1979), p. 102.

13. James Thomas Flexner, *George Washington and the New Nation, 1783–1793* (Boston: Little, Brown and Co., 1970), p. 321, quoted in Branson, *These Fiery Frenchified Dames*, p. 135.

14. Papers of Elizabeth Willing Powel, box 5, folder 13, receipts, 1799, Powel Family Papers, Ms. 1582, Historical Society of Pennsylvania, Philadelphia.

15. Patricia L. Parker, *Susanna Rowson* (Boston: Twayne Publishers, 1986), pp. 87–88. Susanna

51

Fig. 117. *Constantin-François Chasseboeuf, Comte de Volney*, 1797. Oil on canvas, 29 x 23⅛ in. (73.8 x 58.6 cm). Pennsylvania Academy of the Fine Arts, Philadelphia; Gift of Mrs. Thomas Bayard (1922.8)

Anne and William Bingham met Stuart in London in 1784 or 1785, when they commissioned a family portrait; the picture was left unfinished, some say, because she and the artist disagreed about the composition. In 1796 she was the catalyst for Stuart's critical access to George Washington that resulted in the first sitting for the Lansdowne portrait (see cat. 45). The Marquis of Lansdowne, whom she had charmed when in London, thanked her for the portrait the following spring. Her portrait and those of her husband and sisters were painted in 1797. The series of portraits of the five Willing sisters especially reveals Stuart's exceptional talents for physiognomic likeness and characterization (see also cat. 52).

In her portrait Stuart shows Mrs. Bingham marking her place in a book called *VOYAGE EN SYRIE* with the index finger of her left hand; other volumes rest on the table nearby. The book she holds is no doubt a copy of *Voyage en Syrie et en Égypt, pendant les années 1783, 1784, et 1785*, by French geographer Constantin-François Chasseboeuf, comte de Volney, which was first published in 1787 in Paris, with a London edition the same year and a New York edition in 1798.[17] The comte de Volney came to America in 1795 for three years, after his imprisonment during the Reign of Terror. While in Philadelphia, he was a frequent guest of the Binghams, where the English merchant Thomas Twining, great-grandson of the founders of Twinings tea company, met "the celebrated Monsr. Volney" in April 1796.[18] According to Anne Bingham's niece Mary Clymer, Stuart painted his portrait of Volney (fig. 117) at Lansdown when he was painting members of the Willing family in the summer of 1797. "He wished to be taken with open throat, as Voltaire is represented, but from some cause the artist did not gratify him. . . . Volney was in German town & used to walk over daily to Landsdown where he taught Mr Bingham's daughters French so that the Artist was familiar with his appearance & character."[19]

The portrait captures Anne in her early thirties, only a few years before her untimely death. She became seriously ill after the birth of their only son, William, in December 1800. Her doctors diagnosed her condition as consumption and ordered a sea voyage in hopes that a warmer climate would be beneficial. Her father noted on April 14, 1801, "My daughter Bingham left . . . for Lisbon . . . accompanied by Mr. Bingham, her daughter Maria, & her Sisr Abigail reduced by a defluction on her breast to the lowest State of debility, My Daughter is induced to try this Voyage as the last hope for relief. May God grant success to the attempt & restore to health & to her family, this Amiable, deserving & beloved Woman, justly esteemed an Ornament to Society & an honor to her Sex." On May 26 he sadly noted, "This day Mr. Bingham return'd from Bermuda where my dear daughter died on the 11th of May 1801."[20] William Bingham left Philadelphia for England in August with his two daughters and Ann Louisa Bingham's husband, Alexander Baring; William Bingham, his son, remained in Philadelphia with relatives, too young to travel. The contents of the Mansion House were sold at auction in 1805 in Philadelphia, after Bingham's death in England the previous year.[21]

EGM

Rowson, who wrote plays, novels, and tracts with strong feminist sentiments, opened Boston's first academy for young women that featured a rigorous curriculum including geography, history, navigation, and music; see *ANB*, vol. 19, pp. 12–13.

16. Thomas Jefferson, letter to Anne Willing Bingham, February 7, 1787, and Mrs. Bingham, letter to Jefferson, June 1, 1787, in Julian P. Boyd, ed., *The Papers of Thomas Jefferson*, vol. 11 (Princeton, N.J.: Princeton University Press, 1955), pp. 122, 392–93. This is one of the few letters of hers that survives (Massachusetts Historical Society).

17. Charles Coulston Gillespie, ed., *Dictionary of Scientific Biography* (New York: Charles Scribner's Sons, 1970–80), vol. 14, pp. 68–69.

18. Alberts, *Golden Voyage*, pp. 306–7, 314–15, 338; Thomas Twining, *Travels in India a Hundred Years Ago, with a Visit to the United States*, ed. William H. G. Twining (London: James R. Osgood, McIlvaine and Co., 1893), p. 369, quoted in Alberts, *Golden Voyage*, p. 314. Twining later discussed his travels in India with Volney when they were both in Baltimore; see Twining, *Travels*, pp. 414–16.

19. Miss Mary Willing Clymer, daughter of Mrs. Mary Willing Clymer, Trenton, N.J., letter to George Champlin Mason, ca. 1878, George Champlin Mason Papers, Rhode Island Historical Society, Providence, transcription by Laura Mills. The portrait is listed in Mason 1879, p. 274; Park 1926, p. 779, no. 870. Mount (1964, p. 223) suggested that the portrait was commissioned by William Bingham.

20. Notations by Thomas Willing, John William Wallace Papers, PHi 686, vol. 4, p. 153, Historical Society of Pennsylvania. On her death, see also Alberts, *Golden Voyage*, pp. 411–13.

21. The advertisement for the auction, published in the *United States Gazette*, November 16, 1805, contained the only inventory of the furnishings of Mansion House; see Alberts, *Golden Voyage*, appendix 4, pp. 467–73.

52. MARY WILLING CLYMER

1797
Oil on canvas, 29 x 23 in. (73.7 x 58.4 cm)
Signed and dated lower left, above the book:
G Stuart 1797
The Barker Welfare Foundation, Chicago

Research in secondary sources and early drafts for
this entry were done by Christopher H. Jones.

1. The portraits of Dorothy, Elizabeth, and Abigail
   are listed in Park 1926, p. 331, no. 306 (Dorothy
   Willing Francis), p. 430, no. 432 (Elizabeth Willing
   Jackson), pp. 593–93, no. 633 (Abigail Willing
   Peters). For Dorothy's portrait, see also *The John
   Brown House Loan Exhibition of Rhode Island
   Furniture,* exh. cat. (Providence: Rhode Island
   Historical Society, 1965), pp. 158–59, no. 104. For
   the portraits of Elizabeth and Abigail, see also
   Nancy Fresella-Lee, comp., Jacolyn A. Mott, ed.,
   *The American Paintings in the Pennsylvania
   Academy of the Fine Arts* (Philadelphia:
   Pennsylvania Academy of the Fine Arts in associ-
   ation with the University of Washington Press,
   Seattle, 1989), pp. 141 no. 1293, 142 no. 1308.
2. Charles Francis Adams, ed., *Letters of Mrs. Adams,
   the Wife of John Adams,* 4th ed. (Boston: Wilkins,
   Carter, and Co., 1848), p. 351, quoted in Robert C.
   Alberts, *The Golden Voyage: The Life and Times of
   William Bingham, 1752–1804* (Boston: Houghton
   Mifflin Co., 1969), p. 212.
3. There are two versions of this portrait. This version is catalogued in Park 1926, p. 221, no. 165.
   Mason (1879, p. 160) referred to it as an unlocated
   version for which Mary Clymer "gave the artist
   three sittings." The second version was catalogued
   in Mason 1879, pp. 159–60; Park 1926, p. 222, no. 166.
   It was owned by the sitter's daughter Mary
   Willing Clymer, of Trenton, N.J., in 1879 and is
   now in a private collection, on loan recently to
   Independence National Historical Park,
   Philadelphia. It is not signed.
4. James R. MacFarlane, *George Clymer, His Family
   and Descendants* (Sewickley, Pa.: Privately printed,
   1927), p. 15. Her next child, Anne Willing, was
   born in December 1797. Of eight children, six survived to adulthood.
5. Mason 1879, p. 160; he described the fabric as an
   "East India plaid cotton handkerchief." Park (1926,
   p. 221) repeated the story, saying that her sisters
   tied the turban on her head "in order to give her
   portrait more color."
6. The invoices are in the John William Wallace
   Papers, PHi 686, vol. 4, pp. 172, 174, Historical
   Society of Pennsylvania, Philadelphia, a collection
   that includes documents of the Willing family.
   According to the *Oxford English Dictionary,* 2nd

Stuart's portrait of Mary Willing Clymer (1770–1852) is one of five that he painted of the daughters of Thomas and Anne McCall Willing of Philadelphia. The other four represent Anne Willing Bingham (cat. 51); Elizabeth Willing, who married William Jackson in 1795; Dorothy Willing, who married her cousin Thomas Willing Francis in 1794; and Abigail Willing, who married Richard Peters in 1804.[1] Abigail Adams charac- terized them in 1790 as these "beautiful sisters," part of a "constellation of beauties" that dazzled Philadelphia.[2] The five portraits, a stunning series, point up two of Stuart's main talents as a portrait painter: close observation of facial features; and individual characterizations through compositional choices. The portraits are most successful when Stuart responded favorably to the sitters, as apparently was the case in this instance.

By the time Stuart painted Anne Bingham and Mary Clymer in 1797, he was well known to the Willing and Bingham families. He had painted the Binghams in London (see cat. 53) and was commissioned by William Bingham in 1796 to paint the full-length portrait of George Washington known as the Lansdowne portrait (cat. 45). Of the two sisters' portraits, that of Anne Willing Bingham, the eldest sister, is the more direct, as apparently fit her personality. Stuart's characterization of Mary suggests a more reticent sitter.[3] Her features are similar to Anne's: an oval face, large eyes under slightly arcing eyebrows, a long thin nose, broad mouth, and a slightly pointed chin. However, her pose and dress are less assertive and more modest. Mary is turned slightly to the left, seated in a large armchair upholstered in crimson velvet and damask. She wears a long-sleeved white muslin dress with ruffles that are held closed at the neck with a wide green ribbon. Earrings are her only jewelry. Her curly hair is powdered, accentuating her pale complexion. Her somber expression may be a sign of her mourning for the death of her second child, three-month-old Louise Ann, in January 1797, the year the portrait was painted.[4] The colorful addition of the red, green, and white plaid East India cotton scarf, worn as a turban, was said later to have been the suggestion of Stuart and Anne Bingham, "as she was a pale brunette."[5] It is an appropriate addition for a portrait of a daughter of Thomas Willing, whose successful mercantile activities at this time included trade with India. His papers from 1797 include invoices from Calcutta merchants that document the firm's purchase of "calliacat" handkerchiefs as well as shirts, pantaloons, jackets, buttons, and tape.[6]

The characterizations of the other three Willing sisters repeat elements of these two portraits, with variations. All are depicted seated, their hands in their laps, against plain backgrounds that set off the busy details of their clothes and hair. Elizabeth Jackson and Abigail Peters (figs. 118, 119) wear white dresses similar to Mary's and look directly at the viewer, while Dorothy Francis (private collection), in a black dress like Anne's, looks pensively off to the side. Their powdered hair is arranged in elaborate curls, and Elizabeth wears a white lace turban. Bright accents appear in the portraits of Abigail and Dorothy, who are seated in gilt armchairs upholstered in red. There are books or writing materials on nearby tables, and Dorothy holds a fluffy lapdog. Although only the portraits of Mary and Anne are signed and dated, it is evident that the five sisters were painted about the same time. In early September 1797 Stuart was painting portraits at the Binghams' country estate near Philadelphia, described by visitor Robert Gilmor Jr., who stayed with them for about a week. "Company were continually visiting Lansdowne, & added to its own made a most sociable society. During the day I either

Fig. 118. *Elizabeth Willing Jackson*, 1797. Oil on canvas, 29⅜ x 24¼ in. (74.5 x 61.6 cm). Pennsylvania Academy of the Fine Arts, Philadelphia; Bequest of Ann Willing Jackson (1876.2.1)

Fig. 119. *Abigail Willing Peters*, 1797. Oil on canvas, 28½ x 24½ in. (72.4 x 62.2 cm). Pennsylvania Academy of the Fine Arts, Philadelphia; Gift of Mr. and Mrs. John White Field (1887.1.8)

ed., the term "calico," which was often corrupted, refers to all kinds of cotton cloth imported from the East, principally India, and often included fabrics dyed with bright, gay colors.

7. Robert Gilmor Jr., *Memorandums Made in a Tour to the Eastern States in the Year 1797* (Boston: Trustees of the Boston Public Library, 1892), p. 22.

8. Miss Mary Willing Clymer, daughter of Mrs. Mary Willing Clymer, Trenton, N.J., to George Champlin Mason, ca. 1878, George Champlin Mason Papers, Rhode Island Historical Society, Providence, transcription by Laura Mills.

9. Thomas Willing's portrait, dated ca. 1795, is listed in Park 1926, pp. 825–26, no. 926.

10. Thomas Willing Francis's portrait, dated ca. 1800, is listed in Park 1926, p. 330, no. 305.

11. According to Miss Mary Willing Clymer, her daughter, letter to George Champlin Mason, ca. 1878, Mason Papers, Rhode Island Historical Society, transcription by Laura Mills; published in Mason 1879, p. 160.

12. On Dr. Gregory, see *DNB*, vol. 8, p. 545.

13. Mary Sumner Benson, *Women in Eighteenth Century America: A Study of Opinion and Social Usage* (New York: Columbia University Press, 1935), p. 60. Cynthia A. Kierner describes Gregory's treatise as the most influential of its kind in late-eighteenth-century America; see Kierner, "Hospitality, Sociability, and Gender in the Southern Colonies," *Journal of Southern History* 62 (1996), p. 472.

14. Jay Fliegelman, *Prodigals and Pilgrims: The American Revolution against Patriarchal Authority, 1750–1800* (Cambridge: Cambridge University Press, 1982), p. 39. For a discussion of Gregory, see pp. 44–51.

amused myself with hunting or retired to the Library where Stuart the painter was engaged in painting the whole family."[7] Mary Clymer's daughter recorded about 1878 that "Mr. Stuart had the best opportunity of taking these pictures [of her mother and the comte de Volney; see cat. 51] & many others of the Willing family, as he was at the time living in Germantown from whence he could walk over to Landsdown Mr Bingham's country place where the Willing family sought refuge in consequence of the prevalence of yellow fever in Phil[adelphia]."[8] Perhaps the sisters' portraits were also among the "family Pictures" paid for by Bingham that year (see cat. 53). They apparently were not part of a series of members of the large Willing family, for although Stuart did paint Thomas Willing, none of his five sons was painted.[9] (Their mother, Anne McCall Willing, had died in 1781.) In addition, there are pendant portraits of only two of the sisters' husbands, William Bingham himself (fig. 116) and Thomas Willing Francis (private collection), whose portrait is less elaborate and could have been painted later.[10] Neither William Jackson nor Henry Clymer was painted by Stuart, and Abigail was not married when the portraits were painted.

The book that Mary holds was later identified by her as "Gregory's letters of advice to young ladies."[11] This is undoubtedly *A Father's Legacy to His Daughters*, by John Gregory, a Scottish physician whose letters were first published posthumously in Edinburgh in 1774.[12] Reprinted in America beginning in 1775, Gregory's volume went through fifteen editions over the next twenty-one years, and excerpts were included frequently in periodicals.[13] The book, one of the most popular in America during and after the revolution, "set forth the ideal education of a daughter."[14] Its chapters include discussions of religion, behavior, amusements, friendship, love, and marriage. The book conveyed the views of writers of the Scottish Enlightenment, "defining rights in terms of duties."[15] The inclusion of the book seems appropriate for a portrait of Mary Willing Clymer, whose relationship to her father, as seen through surviving family papers, indicates his generosity and, at the same time, her dependence on his wealth and social position. In July 1792 he gave her a cash gift of 1,000 pounds, as well as bank stock and

52

property in and around Philadelphia valued at 6,000 pounds, recorded in the "List of Property given to Mary Willing by her Father Thos. Willing as a mark of his affection."[16] Three and a half years later, on January 6, 1796, following her marriage to Henry Clymer and the birth of her eldest child, Eliza, her father wrote, "My very dear Molly, I congratulate you on the coming in of a new year; & most sincerely do I wish you, and yr. little family, much good health, and the most perfect happiness thro' the Course of this, & many succeeding One's—You are favour'd in the possession of a fine healthy & lovely babe—She is a pleasing addition to the Number of my descendants, & most heartily welcome to my family Circle. I hope she may ever deserve your attachment and tender affections, as well as you have done mine." He also sent a gift of $160 for "Pin & Pocket Money—It is a tribute of affection, from a heart devoted to your comfort & happiness."[17]

Mary's husband, Henry Clymer, was the son of George Clymer, a successful Philadelphia merchant and banker and signer of the Declaration of Independence, who, like Thomas Willing, provided generously for his children.[18] Although Henry Clymer, a graduate of Princeton College, studied law and was a member of the Philadelphia bar, management of family properties became the focus of his career. These responsibilities required that he and Mary leave behind the familiar social networks of Philadelphia and move with their children to a succession of homes in Bucks County, Morrisville, Northumberland, and Wilkes-Barre, Pennsylvania, as well as in Trenton, New Jersey.[19] Whether as a result of mismanagement or misfortune, Mary and Henry seem to have found their resources inadequate to meet their needs. About 1819 she wrote her father a somewhat strained letter from Trenton, which she annotated as "in answer to one in which my Father tells me it is no longer convenient to him to give me $300 a year which sum he had before allowed me": "The distance at which we have so long been separated is very far from having lessened my respect & affection for you & it has always been to me a matter of regret that I have been precluded from that personal intercourse with you that all your other children have had the happiness to enjoy. It has always been my wish to possess your approbation & affection. . . . I am very far from intending to trespass on you but when it is found convenient to resume the payment of the sum heretofore allowed me I shall be thankful to you for it. I was happy to hear from Nancy that you continue so well & beg you to accept my dear sir the best wishes of your affectionate Daughter."[20] Thomas Willing's response to his daughter's request is unknown. However, at his death in 1821 the majority of his substantial estate was divided among his eight surviving children, presumably relieving Mary of her lingering financial concerns.[21]

EGM

15. Rosemarie Zagarri, "The Rights of Man and Woman in Post Revolutionary America," *William and Mary Quarterly*, ser. 3, 55 (1998), p. 213.

16. Hare-Willing Family Papers, American Philosophical Society, Philadelphia.

17. The letter is quoted in Thomas Willing Balch, *Willing Letters and Papers* (Philadelphia: Allen, Lane and Scott, 1922), pp. 219–20.

18. *ANB*, vol. 5, pp. 90–92.

19. MacFarlane, *George Clymer*, p. 15.

20. Mary Willing Clymer, letter to Thomas Willing, January 12, no year, Society Collection, Historical Society of Pennsylvania. The letter can be dated to 1819–21 since the Clymers moved to Trenton in 1819 and Thomas Willing died in 1821.

21. Burton Alva Konkle, *Thomas Willing and the First American Financial System* (Philadelphia: University of Pennsylvania Press; London: Humphrey Milford, Oxford University Press, 1937), p. 215.

53. WILLIAM BINGHAM

1797
Oil on canvas, 44⅞ x 34⅝ in. (114 x 88 cm)
ING Bank NV, London Branch (PT011)

1. The biography on William Bingham by Robert C. Alberts, *The Golden Voyage: The Life and Times of William Bingham, 1752–1804* (Boston: Houghton Mifflin Co., 1969), remains the most complete study of this important American. Very short summations of his life and importance can be found in *DAB*, vol. 1, pp. 278–79; *ANB*, vol. 2, pp. 797–98.

2. Thomas Twining, *Travels in India a Hundred Years Ago, with a Visit to the United States*, ed. William H. G. Twining (London: James R. Osgood, McIlvaine and Co., 1893), p. 363.

3. Alexander Baring, letter to Hope and Co., Amsterdam bankers, February 26, 1796, copy to Sir Francis Baring, Baring Archive, ING Bank NV, London Branch, DEP 3.1, no. 24. This quote appears in Alberts, *Golden Voyage*, p. 283, with other comments by Baring about Bingham; it is also quoted in Frederick S. Allis Jr., ed., *William Bingham's Maine Lands, 1790–1820* (Boston: Colonial Society of Massachusetts, 1954), vol. 1, pp. 644–45, n. 9.

4. Abigail Adams, letter to her daughter Abigail Adams Smith, April 11, 1798, quoted in Margaret L. Brown, "Mr. and Mrs. William Bingham of Philadelphia: Rulers of the Republican Court," *Pennsylvania Magazine of History and Biography* 61 (July 1937), p. 316, who cites *Journal and Correspondence of Miss Adams, Daughter of John Adams, Second President of the United States*, edited by her daughter (New York, London: Wiley and Putnam, 1841–42), vol. 2, pp. 153–54.

5. The Binghams took the unfinished painting with them when they returned. Anne Bingham later gave it to her brother-in-law Henry Clymer who, with the advice of Thomas Sully, arranged to have it cut into three sections. See Mason 1879, pp. 137–39; Park 1926, pp. 151–52, 154–55, nos. 80, 81, 84; Alberts, *Golden Voyage*, pp. 149–50. Park dated the painting to 1784, probably because of the apparent age of the younger child, who had been born in London the previous year.

William Bingham (1752–1804), arguably Stuart's most important patron in Philadelphia, was highly successful as a merchant and investor, and in Federalist politics.[1] He made a considerable fortune during the American Revolution while serving as representative of the new American government in the West Indies. In 1780 he married Anne Willing (see cat. 51), daughter of his business partner Thomas Willing. Involved in almost everything of financial interest in Pennsylvania, Bingham became a very successful merchant in the international trade, a stockholder in the Bank of North America, and an investor in land in New York State and Maine. Elected as a senator from Pennsylvania in 1795, he was described by the young English merchant Thomas Twining in April 1796 as "the principal person in Philadelphia, and the wealthiest, probably, in the Union."[2] Bingham was a controversial figure. Alexander Baring, later first Baron Ashburton, became acquainted with Bingham in 1796 on a visit to America to advise his father and other investors about the purchase of land in Maine that Bingham owned. He wrote in a report that Bingham was "not generally liked, being rather too high & proud for this country, where but very little will do. . . . He is undoubtedly the richest man in this country & his affairs are not embarrassed or likely to become so by further speculations. He is a timid & cautious man. His property cannot be short of £4 or 500/m sterl[g], his expenses annually about £5,000 sterl[g]. The house he lives in with ground round it is estimated worth near £50/m sterl[g]."[3] In 1798 Abigail Adams, who first met the Binghams in Europe in the 1780s, described him with an even more critical eye: "Money, Money is his sole object, and he feels the weight of it; he is not without some talents, but they are all turned to gain; for that he would make sacrifices, which a man who considers the honour and independence of his country at stake, would sooner sacrifice his life than submit to. I am warranted in saying this from his public conduct. Yet in company he is a social pleasant man, and always seemed good humored."[4]

Bingham and Stuart met in London in 1783 or 1784, when Bingham was in England at the end of the revolution to set up arrangements for trade with the British. In London in 1784 or 1785 Stuart began a group portrait of Bingham and his wife, Anne, with their daughters Ann Louisa and Maria Matilda, leaving it unfinished, possibly because of a disagreement with Mrs. Bingham about the composition.[5] After Bingham returned to Philadelphia in 1786, he maintained an interest in the work of Stuart and other American artists abroad, as his letter of November 12, 1792, to Italian sculptor Giuseppe Ceracchi indicates. Ceracchi, who went to Philadelphia in 1791 hoping to win the commission from the U.S. Congress for an equestrian monument of George Washington, had returned to Rome. Bingham wrote:

I think you did this Country great Injustice when you attempted to draw a Comparison between it & Europe, relative to the Cultivation of the Arts & Elegance. Our Fortunes are So inferior to those of the Europeans, that however Strongly our Taste & Inclination may prompt us to Support & encourage them, yet the Means of doing it effectually, are wanting. Even those American artists, whom Nature has endowed with more than a common Portion of her Gifts, (such as West, Copley, Trumbull, Stewart etc) are compelled to seek the Recompense of their Superior Talents in foreign Countries, where the Power of rewarding them exists with the Inclination. However, from the rapid rise of this Country, & its increasing resources, I have little doubt of a considerable Change speedily taking place relative to the Encouragement of Works of Genius & Taste.[6]

Bingham's interest in the arts was decidedly international. In 1792 he commissioned from Francesco Lazzarini a full-length statue of Benjamin Franklin, which was carved in Carrara, Italy, and installed in the facade of the Library Company, Philadelphia.[7] He also was an early patron of English miniaturist William Russell Birch, who went to Philadelphia in 1794 with a letter of introduction from Benjamin West.[8] Stuart and Bingham met again after Stuart arrived in Philadelphia in 1794 to paint George Washington's portrait. Bingham acquired a replica of his first life portrait of the president (fig. 85). In the spring of 1796 he commissioned Stuart's lifesize full-length Washington known as the Lansdowne portrait (cat. 45), as well as a replica for himself (cat. 46). In 1797 Stuart painted this full-length of Bingham as well as a pair of portraits of William (fig. 116) and Anne (cat. 51).[9] He was at work on portraits of family members at Lansdown, the Binghams' country estate, in early September 1797, according to a young visitor, Robert Gilmor Jr., son of Bingham's Baltimore business partner Robert Gilmor. Gilmor, who had visited the Binghams earlier in the summer, described the house: "It is a most superb place, and supposed to be the best country house in America. It commands a noble view of the Schuylkill & the seats in the neighbourhood, & at a distance the steeples of some of the churches in Philad[a]."[10]

In Stuart's small full-length, a type rare in the artist's work (see cat. 54), Bingham is seen standing in the entrance hall of a large building that is assumed to be his Philadelphia mansion.[11] Located at the northwest corner of Third and Spruce Streets, the large residence, which no longer exists, was designed in imitation of the London house of George Montagu, the fourth Duke of Manchester, in Manchester Square, now the home of the Wallace Collection.[12] Bingham sent a plan for the house to his father-in-law Thomas Willing from London, and construction was probably almost completed when the Binghams returned in 1786. English merchant Thomas Twining described the exterior of the house in April 1796: "His house stood alone, and occupied, with the gardens attached to it, a spacious piece of ground. It was by far the handsomest residence in the city."[13] While its exterior is known from William Birch's engraving *View on Third Street from Spruce Street, Philadelphia*, there are no images of the interiors to compare with the background of the portrait. Any evidence about the first-floor hall comes from descriptions by visitors, who reported that the floor was of marble in a mosaic pattern. Bingham, in the only full-length that Stuart completed of him, stands at the entrance. He is dressed in a black suit with a long coat, and his powdered hair is tied in a black queue ribbon. His cheeks have a rosy tinge. A table covered with a red drape, with books, papers, and an inkwell, and several chairs appear next to him in the foreground. Holding a rolled document, he gestures with his right hand beyond paired columns and a green drape to the hall itself, whose walls have decorative relief sculptures set between pilasters. The sculpture nearest Bingham, beyond the columns, is a relief of a classical draped figure of a woman. The ceiling is a barrel vault with coffers and arched clerestory windows through which can be seen a hint of blue sky. The inventory made when the house's contents were sold in 1805 after Bingham's death lists, in the hall, pedestals with busts of Voltaire and Rousseau, four bronze figures with no identifications, "1 Female figure composition stone," as well as "2 Marble medallions in gilt frames" and "3 busts of Franklin," in addition to a large lamp and twelve Windsor chairs.[14]

In his personal account book, Bingham recorded payments to Stuart totaling $2,200 for "family Pictures & a Copy of Genl Washington" (see fig. 108). This sum did not

6. William Bingham Letterbook 1791–1793, pp. 370–72, William Bingham Papers, PHi AM 0244, Historical Society of Pennsylvania, Philadelphia, partially quoted in Alberts, *Golden Voyage*, p. 290. For the most recent study of Ceracchi's work, see *Giuseppe Ceracchi: Scultore Giacobino, 1751–1801*, exh. cat., Palazzo dei Conservatori, Rome (Rome: Artemide Edizioni, 1989).

7. Alberts, *Golden Voyage*, pp. 208–9; Charles Coleman Sellers, *Benjamin Franklin in Portraiture* (New Haven: Yale University Press, 1962), pp. 203–5.

8. Alberts, *Golden Voyage*, pp. 308–9.

9. The bust-length portrait of Bingham is described in Mason 1879, p. 139; Park 1926, pp. 152–53, no. 82; it is illustrated in Alberts, *Golden Voyage*, as the frontispiece (detail) and facing p. 174.

10. Robert Gilmor Jr., *Memorandums Made in a Tour to the Eastern States in the Year 1797* (Boston: Trustees of the Boston Public Library, 1892), p. 5. On the house, see Alberts, *Golden Voyage*, pp. 222, 282, 309–11, 320, 440–41. There are no drawings of the interior of the house, which was damaged by fire in 1854 and later destroyed. Two sketches of the exterior survive—by Robert Gilmor Jr. and by William Russell Birch.

11. On the portrait, see Margaret L. Brown, "William Bingham, Eighteenth Century Magnate," *Pennsylvania Magazine of History and Biography* 61 (October 1937), illus. facing p. 394, dated ca. 1797; Alberts, *Golden Voyage*, illus. facing p. 367, dated 1797; John Orbell and Jane Waller, comps., *The Art of ING Barings* (London: Baring Brothers, 2000), pp. 82–83. The portrait is not listed in Mason 1879, Park 1926, or Mount 1964.

12. On the Mansion House, see Alberts, *Golden Voyage*, pp. 157–64, 440; a fire damaged the building in 1847 when it was used as a hotel, and it was torn down.

13. Twining, *Travels in India*, p. 363.

14. The inventory, which appeared in the advertisement of the sale in the *United States Gazette*, November 16, 1805, is published in Alberts, *Golden Voyage*, appendix 4, pp. 466–73.

53

15. William Bingham, Account Book, Bingham, W., Manuscripts, Lilly Library, Indiana University, Bloomington.
16. While the account book page that lists payments to Stuart is not dated, Lilly Library Curator of Manuscripts Saundra Taylor suggested 1797 (see cat. 46, note 4); e-mail message to Ellen Miles, April 11, 2003.
17. "Extracts of the Diary of James B. Longacre," *Pennsylvania Magazine of History and Biography* 29, no. 2 (1905), p. 140.
18. John Neagle, quoted in Dunlap 1834, vol. 1, p. 205. This was probably a study for the London family group, published in Alberts, *Golden Voyage*, facing p. 366.

include the additional $1,000 that he paid "for original of Genl Washingtons Picture," listed separately.[15] The payments appear to have been made toward the end of 1796 and in 1797.[16] Bingham paid $600 as the price of his copy of the full-length of Washington (cat. 46), leaving a balance of $1,600, a very large sum for the three known portraits of Bingham and his wife. The two smaller images of the Binghams would have cost $100 each, Stuart's price at the time for portraits measuring 30 by 25 inches. This full-length portrait on a canvas measuring 50 by 40 inches might have cost $250, the price William Constable paid in 1797 for the portrait of Washington on a canvas that size (cat. 48). Thus Bingham must have paid for the other known family portraits of Mrs. Bingham's four younger sisters, Elizabeth Willing Jackson, Mary Willing Clymer, Dorothy Willing Francis, and Abigail Willing Peters (see cat. 52 and figs. 118, 119).

Stuart's relationship with Bingham ended abruptly in 1800 over the question of permission given to James Heath to engrave the Lansdowne portrait of Washington (see fig. 107). American engraver James Barton Longacre later recorded the encounter, writing that Stuart "called on Mr. Bingham and reminded him of the stipulation under which he had parted with the portrait, the fact of which was not denied. But on asking Mr. Bingham how he proposed to compensate him for the injury he had sustained by the publication of the print, Mr. Bingham replied—'Have you anything to show for it?'—which ended their intercourse, Stuart leaving him abruptly and indignantly without further remark."[17] John Neagle told William Dunlap that after Stuart and Bingham quarreled, "the painter left unfinished [the] painting that he had commenced for the Bingham family. I saw one beautifully painted head of Mrs. Bingham, on a *kit cat* lead coloured canvass with nothing but the head finished. The rest was untouched."[18] After Anne Bingham's death in 1801, Bingham moved to London with his daughters, Ann Louisa who had married Alexander Baring in 1798, and Maria who would marry Alexander's brother Henry Baring in 1802. Bingham died in Bath, England, on February 6, 1804.

EGM

54. LOUIS-MARIE, VICOMTE DE NOAILLES

1798

Oil on canvas, 50 x 40 inches (127 x 101.6 cm)
Signed and dated lower left: G. Stuart 1798
The Metropolitan Museum of Art, New York;
Purchase, Henry R. Luce Gift, Elihu Root Jr.
Bequest, Rogers Fund, Maria DeWitt Jesup Fund,
Morris K. Jesup Fund and Charles and Anita Blatt
Gift, 1970 (1970.262)

1. On this portrait, see especially John K. Howat, "'A Young Man Impatient to Distinguish Himself': The Vicomte de Noailles as Portrayed by Gilbert Stuart," *The Metropolitan Museum of Art Bulletin*, n.s. 29 (March 1971), pp. 327–40; John Caldwell and Oswaldo Rodriguez Roque, *American Paintings in The Metropolitan Museum of Art*, vol. 1, *A Catalogue of Works by Artists Born by 1815* (New York: Metropolitan Museum of Art, 1994), pp. 183–85. Additional biographical information is from *ANB*, vol. 16, pp. 467–68.

2. Howat, "A Young Man," p. 338.

3. Caldwell and Rodriguez Roque, *American Paintings*, p. 184.

4. Letters to John Howat in 1971, curatorial files, Department of American Paintings and Sculpture, The Metropolitan Museum of Art, indicate disagreement among military historians about whether Noailles is represented as a colonel or as a *maréchal de camp*. American historians Frederick P. Todd and Col. John R. Elting identified the uniform as that of a colonel of the regiment of the Chasseurs d'Alsace. Elting added that as a general officer Noailles's uniform would have been a long blue coat with red cuffs and collar, and white breeches. Col. M. McCarthy of the Musée de l'Armée, Paris, instead stated that the uniform was that of the new regiment, the Chasseurs à cheval des Alpes, and that a general officer was permitted to wear his regimental uniform, with the gold embroidery of a general officer and a red vest, as seen here.

5. On Noailles and the Binghams, see Robert C. Alberts, *The Golden Voyage: The Life and Times of William Bingham, 1752–1804* (Boston: Houghton Mifflin Co., 1969), esp. pp. 285–86.

Stuart painted this dashing portrait of French army officer Louis-Marie, vicomte de Noailles (1756–1804) in Philadelphia, where Noailles lived from 1793 to 1802.[1] The small full-length portrait, very rare in Stuart's work, is painted on a canvas the size that Stuart usually used for a large figure represented in three-quarters view. Stuart skillfully rendered the details of Noailles's face and figure, as well as the figure of the attendant, the two horses, and the background view. Noailles's uniform, that of a French cavalry regiment (Chasseurs à cheval), is depicted in such detail that one suspects Stuart was copying the actual uniform, taken by Noailles to Philadelphia. He carries a nonregulation Polish karabela saber. His attendant, unidentified but carefully characterized, awaits the colonel's next command. At their feet is a scene of thistles, a snake, and the skull of a horse, reminders of battlefields and mortality.[2] It has been suggested that Noailles appears again in the background scene, as commander riding at the head of the regiment, as fires destroy a hilltop fortress in the distance.[3] The careful treatment of all aspects of the portrait recalls the historical paintings of Benjamin West, Stuart's teacher in London, as well as John Trumbull's recent studies for his history paintings of the American Revolution and his small full-length portraits of George Washington.

The portrait celebrates Noailles's military leadership during the early years of the French Revolution, before his self-imposed exile from France in 1792. Noailles is probably represented as colonel of the Chasseurs à cheval d'Alsace, the cavalry regiment that he commanded from March 1788. While the background scene has not been firmly identified, it may represent the defeat by his regiment of an insurrection at Colmar in May 1791. It has been suggested that he may instead be depicted as *maréchal de camp*, the general army rank to which he was promoted when the regiment was redesignated the first Chasseurs à cheval des Alpes in 1791. However, during his subsequent military service in 1792, after the French Assembly had declared war against Austria, Noailles saw French army troops mutiny near Lille on April 29 and subsequently experienced military defeat, events that are not likely to be memorialized in a portrait. A third possibility is that he is depicted as *maréchal de camp*, with the background scene of the victory at Colmar that explains his promotion.[4]

Brother-in-law of the marquis de Lafayette, Noailles as a young officer was eager to join in the fight against the British in North America and served in a French siege at Grenada in 1779, for which he was awarded the Cross of Saint-Louis. He came to North America with General Rochambeau's army in 1780, during the American Revolution; he was later introduced to George Washington and represented the French army in drawing up the terms of the surrender of General Lord Cornwallis in 1781 at Yorktown. Returning to France, he served in the National Assembly in 1789, where, as a political liberal, he proposed the restructuring of taxes and the suppression of the privileges and titles of the French nobility, and served as president of the assembly in 1791. As the French Revolution intensified, he served with the army again before fleeing to England as the political structure of France crumbled. His wife was later guillotined.

Noailles went to Philadelphia in 1793. He became a close associate of William and Anne Bingham, whom he had met in Paris ten years earlier, and lived at the Binghams' Philadelphia mansion.[5] He formed a partnership with another French émigré to purchase land on the Susquehanna River in northeastern Pennsylvania from Bingham's partner Robert Morris for a French émigré community called Azilum or Azylum. The

6. Thomas Twining, *Travels in India a Hundred Years Ago, with a Visit to the United States*, ed. William H. G. Twining (London: James R. Osgood, McIlvaine and Co., 1893), pp. 363–64.

7. Alexander Baring, letter to Sir Francis Baring, dated "Novr 1796," Baring Archive, ING Bank NV, London Branch, DEP 3.1, no. 37, London, in Twining, *Travels in India*, p. 363.

8. Mason 1879, p. 92, citing Jane Stuart.

9. Breck is quoted in Howat, "A Young Man," p. 337; Alberts, *Golden Voyage*, p. 286. Mason (1879, p. 92) cited Mrs. William Bingham Clymer as the source for Noailles standing in for Washington. Eisen (1932, pp. 70–73) suggested that he posed for the Munro-Lenox portrait of Washington (cat. 49), in which the president's figure is turned to one side.

10. Robert Gilmor Jr., *Memorandums Made in a Tour to the Eastern States in the Year 1797* (Boston: Trustees of the Boston Public Library, 1892), p. 6.

11. Gilmor, *Memorandums*, pp. 21–23. Gilmor's visits are discussed in Alberts, *Golden Voyage*, pp. 309–11.

young English tea merchant Thomas Twining, visiting Philadelphia on his return home from India, noted that when he went to the Binghams' on April 7, 1796, he found "a large party. Besides Mr. and Mrs. Bingham and their two daughters, were Count de Noailles, Count Tilley, Mr. Alexander Baring, and others."[6] Baring, who had recently arranged the purchase by the Baring Brothers firm in London of land that Bingham owned in Maine, described Noailles to his father, Sir Francis Baring, in November 1796 as "perfectly a man of honor, & a bon compagnon but no merchant & has no idea of business beyond what you would suppose a metamorphosis from a French Viscount who has passed all his time in the army would produce. . . . He is a man I found it desirable to conciliate, exclusive of his disposition & manners being an inducement, from his very great influence in the Bingham family from certain female reasons you will easily understand, & he was of service to me in my negotiations."[7]

Noailles's association with Bingham brought him in contact with Stuart. In 1796 Noailles gave the artist a "superb silver-mounted rapier" for inclusion in the Lansdowne portrait of George Washington, commissioned that year by Bingham (cat. 45).[8] Noailles, described by Philadelphian Samuel Breck as a man of perfect form, "tall, graceful, the first amateur dancer of the age," may also have served Stuart as a stand-in for the figure of the president.[9] In July 1797 he provided young Robert Gilmor Jr. of Baltimore, son of Bingham's partner Robert Gilmor, with a letter of introduction to Stuart, enabling the young man to visit the artist's studio in Germantown on July 27 "to see Stewart's painting of the late President."[10] On Gilmor's return in September from his tour of New England, he was greeted by Noailles, who took him to Lansdown, the Binghams' country house, carefully avoiding Philadelphia itself because of a yellow fever outbreak. At Lansdown Gilmor discovered that Stuart was occupied in painting portraits of members of the Bingham family.[11] Noailles's portrait, painted the following year, is very similar to Stuart's small full-length of Bingham (cat. 53) in scale and in carefully handled brushwork. Noailles, who never returned to France, may have had the portrait painted for his children. After his legal status as a French citizen was restored in 1800, Noailles went to the island of Saint Dominique (Santo Domingo), where he received a commission as brigadier general. He died the following year of wounds received in a naval battle with the English. Bingham visited Noailles's family in France in 1802 after he moved to England following Anne Bingham's death.

EGM

54

55. JOHN BILL RICKETTS

ca. 1795–99

Oil on canvas, 29³/₈ x 24¹/₄ in. (74.6 x 61.5 cm)

National Gallery of Art, Washington, D.C.; Gift of Mrs. Robert B. Noyes in memory of Elisha Riggs (1942.14.1)

The research for and early drafts of this entry were done by Christopher H. Jones.

1. Pickering 1817 (October 29).

2. Ricketts's advertisement is quoted in James S. Moy, *John B. Ricketts' Circus, 1793–1800* (Ph.D. diss., University of Illinois at Urbana-Champaign, 1977; Ann Arbor: UMI Microfilm, 1977), p. 8. Information on Ricketts's circus is drawn principally from Moy's dissertation, and from the entry on the portrait in Miles 1995, pp. 208–11.

3. Quoted in Robert C. Smith, "A Portuguese Naturalist in Philadelphia, 1799," *Pennsylvania Magazine of History and Biography* 78 (January 1954), p. 94.

4. Quoted in Miles 1995, p. 210, from Isaac John Greenwood, *The Circus, Its Origin and Growth prior to 1835, with a Sketch of Negro Minstrelsy*, 2nd ed. (New York: W. Abbatt, 1909), p. 79.

5. Washington mentioned the first visit in his letter to Mr. and Mrs. Samuel Powel, April 24, 1793; see Joseph E. Fields, comp., *"Worthy Partner": The Papers of Martha Washington* (Westport, Conn.: Greenwood Press, 1994), p. 248. Moy, "Ricketts' Circus," p. 64, records a newspaper account of Ricketts's toast to Washington when the president visited the circus on July 13, 1793. His attendance on both dates was noted by Jacob Hiltzheimer in his diary, quoted in William S. Baker, "Washington after the Revolution, 1784–1799," *Pennsylvania Magazine of History and Biography* 20, no. 3 (1896), pp. 356, 360.

6. George Washington Parke Custis, *Recollections and Private Memoirs of Washington* (Philadelphia: J. W. Bradley, 1861), p. 486.

7. *Gazette of the United States*, January 23, 1797, quoted in Donald Jackson and Dorothy Twohig, eds., *The Diaries of George Washington* (Charlottesville: University Press of Virginia, 1976–79), vol. 6, p. 232; "Washington's Household Account Book, 1793–1797," *Pennsylvania Magazine of History and Biography* 31 (1907), p. 337.

8. William S. Baker, "Washington after the Revolution, 1784–1799," *Pennsylvania Magazine of History and Biography* 21, no. 2 (1897), p. 188.

9. *Diaries of George Washington*, vol. 6, p. 235, entry dated February 22, 1797.

10. Baker, "Washington after the Revolution," (1897), pp. 192–93, quoting *Claypoole's American Daily Advertiser*.

11. Washington's Account Book, Ledger C, entry dated January 26, 1797, Morristown National

Like many of Stuart's Philadelphia sitters, circus owner and performer John Bill Ricketts was an admirer of George Washington. He was the proprietor and star attraction of America's first circus, which he established shortly after his arrival in Philadelphia in October 1792. Stuart apparently knew Ricketts before the performer arrived in America, telling Henry Pickering in 1817 that when he came back to America from Dublin, "he meant to have sailed for Philadelphia, but hearing that Ricketts, the equestrian, had determined to embark in the same vessel, with all his horses, & dancing devils, & little devils, (company which neither he nor his family had been accustomed to associate with) he immediately renounced the project. He then took passage in a vessel bound to New York."[1] In Philadelphia, Ricketts advertised that he "respectfully acquaints the public, that he has erected at considerable expense a circus, situated at the corner of Market and Twelfth Streets where he proposes instructing Ladies and Gentlemen, in the elegant accomplishments of riding."[2] On April 3, 1793, he offered his first equestrian performance, and in May he introduced tightrope dancer "Seignior Spinacuta" and a clown. Closing the season there in July, he moved to New York for the summer; in December he moved the company to Charleston, South Carolina. The circus returned to Philadelphia in 1794 and again in 1795, when he built Ricketts's New Amphitheatre, a large round wood building at the corner of Sixth and Chestnut Streets. The building was almost one hundred feet in diameter and could accommodate six or seven hundred spectators. It had a conical roof and was illuminated for evening events by a chandelier. Hipólito José da Costa, a Portuguese naturalist who visited Philadelphia in 1798–99, described the building as "a kind of theater called the circus, which is a circular building with boxes all around it. It is here that they have exhibitions of acrobatics and performing horses, etc."[3] Equestrian performers now included Ricketts's brother Francis Ricketts as well as Matthew Sully, an English actor working in America, and his son, Matthew Jr., who joined Ricketts's performers in 1795. Matthew Sully Sr. was the father of American artist Thomas Sully.

Ricketts, described in 1794 as "perhaps the most graceful, neat, and expert public performer on horseback, that ever appeared in any part of the world,"[4] was a favorite performer of George Washington. The president first visited the circus only a few weeks after its opening in April 1793 and again in July.[5] Ricketts admired Washington's horsemanship and said of him, according to Washington's grandson George Washington Parke Custis, "I delight to see the general ride, and make it a point to fall in with him when I hear that he is abroad on horseback—his seat is so firm, his management so easy and graceful, that I, who am a professor of horsemanship, would go to him and *learn to ride*."[6] On January 24, 1797, only a short time before Washington's retirement to Mount Vernon, he attended Ricketts's presentation of "a variety of performances, at the Pantheon BY DESIRE OF THE PRESIDENT OF THE UNITED STATES"; as recorded in his accounts, he "pd for 8 tickets of admission to Rickett's Circus . . . 8.00."[7] The amphitheater was the scene of the celebration of Washington's birthday on February 22, 1797, which was described in *Claypoole's American Daily Advertiser* as "a Ball on the occasion at Rickett's Amphitheatre, which for Splendor, Taste and Elegance, was, perhaps, never excelled by any similar Entertainment in the United States."[8] Washington described the event as "an elegant entertainmt. given on my birth night."[9] Washington was again at Ricketts's amphitheater on March 4, five days before his departure for Mount Vernon,

55

Historic Park, Morristown, N.J.; copy provided by the editors of the Papers of George Washington, University of Virginia, Charlottesville.

12. Smith, "Portuguese Naturalist in Philadelphia," pp. 97–98.

13. This portrait is listed in Mason 1879, p. 151, as "Breschard, the Circus-Rider"; Park 1926, pp. 634–35, no. 691, as "Mr. Rechart (or Rickart)." Park's identification was based on two inscriptions on

for a farewell dinner hosted by the "Merchants of Philadelphia."[10] In January 1797, Washington had sold his "white horse Jack" to Ricketts for $150.[11] Two years later, Hipólito José da Costa observed on a visit to the circus that "one of the horses which I saw best was a white one, which is said to have been President Washington's campaign horse in the late war. He was sold to these comedians for them to do their tricks with."[12]

Stuart's sense of humor is on display in the portrait, left unfinished because of the artist's impatience with the sitter.[13] When painting Ricketts, Stuart sketched in the head the painting, which were added later. They also identify the sitter as a friend of the artist; see Miles 1995, pp. 208–11.

14. Handbill for August 4, 1797, Harvard Theatre Collection. Cornplanter was named after the renowned Seneca leader. The horse in the portrait is identified as Cornplanter in Washington, Providence 1967, p. 65, no. 20.

15. J. Thomas Scharf and Thompson Westcott, *History of Philadelphia, 1609–1884* (Philadelphia: L. H. Everts and Co., 1884), vol. 2, p. 1044.

16. Moy, "Ricketts' Circus," p. 23; Miles 1995, p. 210.

17. Edward Biddle and Mantle Fielding, *The Life and Works of Thomas Sully* (1921; reprint, New York: Da Capo Press, 1970), p. 259, nos. 1471, 1472; the first was painted in May, and the second in November.

18. Tuckerman 1870, p. 110.

Fig. 120. Ricketts's playbill for an Albany, N.Y., performance on August 4, 1797. Harvard Theatre Collection, Cambridge, Mass.

of a horse, with Ricketts's hand around its muzzle. This horse could be Cornplanter, described in Ricketts's playbill for an Albany, New York, performance on August 4, 1797 (fig. 120): "Mr. Ricketts will exhibit a GRAND PERFORMANCE with the Broad Sword . . . upon the Celebrated Horse, Cornplanter, who is thoroughly trained for the purpose," and "ride with Master Hutchins on his shoulders, in the attitude of A FLYING MERCURY."[14] Stuart completed only Ricketts's head, set against a small area of darker background color to permit the modeling of highlights and shadows of the face as the work progressed. Stuart at some point playfully added the details of a second horse's head on this aureole, touches that would have been covered when the painting was completed. However, Stuart did not complete the painting. "Ricketts, the circus-rider, sat to him, and the artist becoming angry at the equestrian, who gave him a good deal of trouble by his want of promptitude and the delays which occurred, is said to have dashed his paintbrush into the face of the portrait, declaring that he would have nothing more to do with him."[15]

After Ricketts's circus building was destroyed in a spectacular fire on the night of December 17, 1799, which possibly was caused by a lighted candle in a storage area, Ricketts found rebuilding difficult. He went with his company to the West Indies after a last American performance on April 24, 1800. He decided to return to England about 1803, and his ship was lost at sea.[16] The unfinished portrait was owned after his death by his brother Francis and probably was copied by Thomas Sully, whose register lists two portraits of "Mr. Ricketts" painted in 1807 (now unlocated). One was a small portrait 12 by 10 inches, "copied from a painting," and the other was a bust-length portrait, which measured 24 by 20 inches.[17] Stuart's portrait was later admired by artists. According to Henry Tuckerman, it became one of the "unfinished heads much prized by art-students as indicative of his method of painting."[18]

EGM

56. SAMUEL GATLIFF

ca. 1798
Oil on canvas, 29¹/₈ x 24¹/₈ in. (74.1 x 61.3 cm)
Pennsylvania Academy of the Fine Arts,
Philadelphia; Bequest of Dr. Ferdinand Campbell
Stewart (1899.9.1)

57. ELIZABETH CORBIN GRIFFIN GATLIFF AND HER DAUGHTER ELIZABETH

ca. 1798
Oil on canvas, 29¹/₄ x 24 in. (74.3 x 61 cm)
Pennsylvania Academy of the Fine Arts,
Philadelphia; Bequest of Dr. Ferdinand Campbell
Stewart (1899.9.2)

Initial research on the Gatliffs was done by Margaret Christman; the first draft was written by Christopher H. Jones.

1. On the portraits, see Mason 1879, pp. 183, 192; Charles Henry Hart, "Gilbert Stuart's Portraits of Women: Mrs. Samuel Gatliff (Elizabeth Corbin Griffin)," *Century Illustrated Monthly Magazine* 57 (March 1899), pp. 696–97; Park 1926, pp. 342–43, nos. 318, 319.

2. Sarah Wentworth Apthorp Morton, "To Mr. Stuart, on His Portrait of Mrs. M.," *The Port Folio* 3 (June 18, 1803), p. 1.

3. Cornelius William Stafford, *The Philadelphia Directory for 1798* (Philadelphia, 1798), p. 60; Cornelius William Stafford, *The Philadelphia Directory for 1799* (Philadelphia, 1799), p. 58; *The New Trade Directory for Philadelphia, Anno 1800* (Philadelphia, 1799), p. 106; Cornelius William Stafford, *The Philadelphia Directory for 1801* (Philadelphia, 1801), p. 99; James Robinson, *The Philadelphia Directory, City and County Register, for 1802* (Philadelphia, 1802), p. 97; James Robinson, *The Philadelphia Directory, City and County Register, for 1803* (Philadelphia, 1803), p. 97. The advertisement appeared in the *Gazette of the United States* (Philadelphia), on January 3, 7, and 10, 1803, p. 2. The *Oxford English Dictionary* identifies the fabrics as woven wools used to make clothing and curtains.

4. The notice of their wedding appeared in *Claypoole's Daily Advertiser* (Philadelphia), November 25, 1796; see "Historical and Genealogical Notes: Griffin-Campbell," *William and Mary Quarterly* 7, no. 1 (July 1898), p. 60.

5. "Historical and Genealogical Notes: Griffin-Campbell," pp. 60-61. On this portrait, see Mason 1879, p. 192; Park, pp. 342–43, no. 319.

6. Park 1926, pp. 373-74, no. 362.

7. Eleanor Parke Custis Lewis, letter to Elizabeth Bordley Gibson, August 3, 1826, in Patricia Brady,

These portraits of English merchant Samuel Gatliff and his wife, Elizabeth, with their daughter Elizabeth, are heartwarming images from Gatliff's otherwise troubled life in America.[1] Gatliff appears frail and thin. His slight smile, arched eyebrows, and blue-gray eyes directed at the viewer give him a look of naïveté and uncertainty. He is seated at a table covered with a red cloth and holds papers in his right hand, a pose reminiscent of poet Sarah Morton's descriptions of Stuart's portraits of merchants: "patient plodding, and with wealth content, / The man of commerce counts his cent per cent."[2] He is fashionably dressed in a double-breasted blue jacket with a darker collar and brass buttons. The fabric of his double-breasted white waistcoat has a decorative diagonal weave, and one collar of the waistcoat falls open on top of the blue coat. His hair is powdered gray and tied with a small queue ribbon. In contrast to this cool, elegant portrait, the double image of Elizabeth Gatliff and their daughter Elizabeth is one of warmth and affection. The little girl is seated on her mother's lap. Their tender gestures and Mrs. Gatliff's contented expression convey their close relationship. Mother and daughter look alike, with large brown eyes, brown hair, and rosy complexions. Mrs. Gatliff's loosely fitted white gown contrasts with a pale yellow drape over her left arm. Her chestnut hair falls around her face in a very informal style. She is seated in a chair upholstered in red, in front of a red curtain; a blue sky with pink and white clouds is visible in the left distance. Her arms encircle her young daughter, also dressed in white, and the child rests her pudgy right hand on her mother's arm. Small wisps of babyish brown hair peek out from the white bonnet that envelops her chubby face, and the pearls of her necklace reflect the pale pink of her skin.

Samuel Gatliff (1773/74–1806) was a partner in an English woolen manufacturing firm at Larchfield Mill, near Huddersfield, Yorkshire, in the English Midlands. He is listed as a merchant at 124 Spruce Street in Philadelphia city directories for 1798–1803, advertising "thirty bales of stuffs" for sale in 1803 in the *Gazette of the United States*, including "Bombazettes, Moreens, Durants, Callimancoes, [and] Several bales superfine dark blue broad cloths."[3] The earliest record of his life in America is his marriage to Elizabeth Corbin Griffin in Williamsburg, Virginia, in November 1796, when he was described as "of Philadelphia."[4] Elizabeth Griffin (1779–1853) was the only daughter of Elizabeth Braxton Griffin and Samuel Griffin of Williamsburg, and granddaughter of Carter Braxton, a prominent Virginia planter, politician, and signer of the Declaration of Independence.[5] Her father, a lawyer who represented Virginia in Congress from 1789 to 1795, was also painted by Stuart in Philadelphia (fig. 121).[6] Elizabeth's circle of friends included George Washington's granddaughter Eleanor Parke Custis (Lewis), who mentioned her years later as among "my dear & good friends."[7]

Gatliff, while perhaps a successful merchant, overextended his personal credit. His English business partner Pim Nevins went to Philadelphia in 1802 to rescue the firm

56

ed., *George Washington's Beautiful Nelly: The Letters of Eleanor Parke Custis Lewis to Elizabeth Bordley Gibson, 1794–1851* (Columbia: University of South Carolina Press, 1991), p. 182.

8. Eliza Cope Harrison, ed., *Philadelphia Merchant: The Diary of Thomas P. Cope, 1800–1851* (South Bend, Ind.: Gateway Editions, 1978), p. 136, entry dated December 31, 1802.

9. Pim Nevins, "Journal, 1802–1803," American

from financial distress. Philadelphia merchant Thomas Pym Cope described Nevins's visit as necessitated "by the misconduct of his resident partner here, L. Gatliff, who, it seems, has in his private speculations absorbed so much of the funds of the House as to have compelled his partner to stop the manufactury at home & discharge several hundred workmen who were dependent on them for bread."[8] Nevins recorded Gatliff's life in America in great detail in a journal of his trip, providing the only glimpse we have of this man and, occasionally, his family. A week after Nevins arrived with his son in New

57

Philosophical Society, Philadelphia, entry dated
June 11, 1802. The cataloguing abstract at
http://www.amphilsoc.org/library/mole/n/
nevins.htm gives the location of the mill in
England.

10. Nevins, "Journal," pp. 19–20, entry dated June 13,
1802.

11. Ibid., p. 95, entry dated November 6, 1802.

12. Ibid., p. 151, entry dated December 18, 1802.

York on June 3, 1802, he was in Frankford, Pennsylvania, near Philadelphia, and dined
with the Gatliffs, who lived "in a rural Spot situated on the side of a hill near the banks
of that beautiful romantic River the Schuilkil." [9] Nevins was impressed by the "quantity
of land belonging to each Estate" and the fact that "the proprietors who many of them
having Houses in the City, have also Country Houses situated in considerable Tracts of
Land wch does not yet have a price proportionate to its real value, for at this unfortunate juncture, the Estates of many Merchts here, who twelve months ago lived in

Fig. 121. *Samuel Griffin*, ca. 1800. Oil on canvas, 29 x 24 in. (73.7 x 61 cm). Pennsylvania Academy of the Fine Arts, Philadelphia; Bequest of Dr. Ferdinand Campbell Stewart (1899.9.3)

13. Ibid., pp. 173–74, entry dated January 23, 1803.

14. Ibid., p. 29, entry dated June 19, 1802.

15. Ibid., p. 93, entry dated November 2, 1802. Park 1926, p. 342, indicates that they had four daughters.

16. Nevins, "Journal," pp. 186, 188, entries dated February 9 and 10, 1803.

17. Ibid., p. 190, entry dated February 15, 1803.

18. Gatliff was buried at Saint Peter's Church, Philadelphia, on October 14, 1806; see "Internments Reported to the Board of Health, 1806," *Pennsylvania Vital Records: From the Pennsylvania Genealogical Magazine and the Pennsylvania Magazine of History and Biography* (Baltimore: Genealogical Publishing Co., 1983), vol. 3, p. 15.

19. "William Byrd III House Historical Report," 1990, Research Report Series, Colonial Williamsburg Foundation, Williamsburg, Va., p. 5. Griffin had purchased the house from the widow of William Byrd III in 1778.

20. Susan Bowdoin, letter to Robert Wash, March 8, 1811, John D. Rockefeller Jr. Library, Colonial Williamsburg Foundation.

21. St. George Tucker, letter to Robert Wash, October 2, 1812, Tucker-Coleman Papers, box 32, Manuscripts and Rare Books Department, Earl Gregg Swem Library, College of William and Mary, Williamsburg, Va.

22. *George Washington's Beautiful Nelly*, p. 182.

23. Elizabeth (Gatliff) Campbell, letter to Mrs. Robert Hare, October 27, 1824, Hare Papers, American Philosophical Society. Susan, their fourth daughter, died in 1822; *Enquirer* (Richmond), October 22, 1822, information courtesy of George H. Yetter, Associate Curator, Architectural Drawings and Research Collections, Colonial Williamsburg Foundation.

Splendor & considered themselves qualified so to do, are & will be to be sold, to satisfy in part the claims of angry creditors whose sufferings will be felt severely not only here but in Great Britain." [10]

During his almost yearlong visit, Nevins recorded the details of Gatliff's life as a merchant, and his own efforts to extract the partnership from its financial difficulties. Because of yellow fever, he was unable to go into the city of Philadelphia until November 6. [11] A Quaker, he also visited Friends' meetings in the area. On December 18, he noted, "The friends of this City are hospitable & kind to us, yet time begins to hang very heavy, having little to do, yet no prospect of getting liberated soon, for the more I view my affairs the more discouraging my prospect appears of getting them settled so as to get home to my family & business." [12] On January 23, 1803, he recorded the "uncommonly high" state of his spirits, "notwithstanding the embarrass'd state of my affairs, wch sometimes leads my mind into the wilderness, sometimes I hope to be reestablished in business at Leeds & at other times it appears if my lot was to be cast in this country. I never look for being settled down with my Children in Larchfield again." [13] Nevins saw Gatliff often, and though he dined frequently with the Gatliffs, he rarely commented about Elizabeth Gatliff. He wrote soon after his arrival, "Tea at Sam W. Fisher's on our way to S. Gatliffs where we spent the eveng pleasantly. I have often heard his wife highly spoken of but not more so than she seems to merit." [14] He commented on the birth of one of the Gatliffs' four daughters that November, "After dinner got to Saml Gatliff's, where we found . . . a little female Stranger added to S.G's family just two weeks ago." [15]

By February 1803 Nevins's relationship with Gatliff had deteriorated. Following "a very unpleasant interview with a person [Gatliff] with whom I have had close & large connection in business, as well as near friendship," Nevins concluded on February 9 that his partner's conduct was driven by "a heart designing to do me injury." The next day he recorded, "I told him I could look in his face & once thot it was the face of an honest Man but now look at the face of a Rogue. I ask'd him for my property in his hands wch he told me he would not give me." [16] The acrimony between the men led Nevins, who felt himself "duped, insulted & deceived," to seek the assistance of British Consul General, Phineas Bond, in negotiating the dissolution of their partnership. [17] After the dissolution of the partnership on March 23, Nevins returned to England. Gatliff died three years later at the age of thirty-two. [18]

After Gatliff's death, Elizabeth returned to Williamsburg with their daughters to live in her father's house. [19] After her father's death, she took in boarders, including her future husband, Ferdinand Stuart Campbell, who taught mathematics at the College of William and Mary. Contemporaries give us a more personal view of her than Pim Nevins did. Robert Wash learned from Susan Bowdoin that "Mr. Campbell boards at Mrs. Gatliffs; he is a charming young Man in all eyes. . . . Mrs. Gs elegant conversation will no doubt sooth his woes!" [20] St. George Tucker gave Wash the news of their marriage: "Mr Campbell (Brother of Frederic Campbell whom you knew) a very respectable young Gentleman . . . not long after married the beautiful Mrs. Gatliff, a <u>Widow</u>, <u>nine years older</u> than himself. Mark that, and tremble for yourself! . . . The grammar school has been discontinued and Mr Campbell is now professor of Mathematics." [21] Nelly Custis also referred to the difference in their ages: "*I cannot avoid envying Betsy Campbell, altho' not for her juvenile Spouse,* believe me." [22] After the marquis de Lafayette visited Williamsburg in 1824, Mrs. Campbell wrote her Philadelphia friend Mrs. Hare about her daughter Elizabeth: "Our Town was in a bustle at the arrival of Lafayette. My Elisa:th was called upon to arrange his rooms, and the Dining room in the Raleigh

24. Letters in the Campbell Family Papers, 1802–1879, Virginia Historical Society, Richmond, further document the family. We thank Frances S. Pollard, Director of Library Services, for her timely assistance with this collection.

25. Park 1926, p. 342; "Archaeological Report, William Byrd III House," p. 5; Hart, "Stuart's Portraits of Women: Mrs. Gatliff," p. 696.

Tavern. I am told she did it with very great taste. The General embraced my three girls, & kissed them (an honor on them alone). Why, I know not, unless he was told they were Col. Griffin's Grand-daughters."[23] Campbell taught mathematics at William and Mary until 1833.[24] He assumed the last name Campbell Stewart when he became heir to the estates of the Stewarts of Ascog House, Scotland. By 1839 they had moved to Philadelphia, where Elizabeth Campbell Stewart died in 1853.[25]

EGM

58. ABIGAIL SMITH ADAMS

ca. 1800–1815
Oil on canvas, 28⅞ x 23½ in. (73.4 x 59.7 cm)
National Gallery of Art, Washington, D.C.; Gift of
Mrs. Robert Homans (1954.7.2)

59. JOHN ADAMS

ca. 1800–1815
Oil on canvas, 29 x 24 in. (73.7 x 61 cm)
National Gallery of Art, Washington, D.C.; Gift of
Mrs. Robert Homans (1954.7.1)

1. Receipt for payment by Abigail Adams, signed by Gilbert Stuart and dated May 20, 1800, Adams Papers, microfilm no. 397, Massachusetts Historical Society, Boston, quoted in Oliver 1967, p. 132. Quotations from the Adams Papers are from the microfilm edition, by permission of the Massachusetts Historical Society. Oliver published the documentation on these portraits that is found in the Adams Papers. He discussed Stuart's paintings and all known replicas and copies, including engravings and lithographs, pp. 132–78, and also listed them in a separate catalogue, pp. 251–58. The portraits are also discussed in Miles 1995, pp. 211–16, which gives provenance, exhibitions, and earlier catalogue entries in Mason 1879 and Park 1926. Laura Mills has provided transcriptions from the Adams Papers and other archival sources.

2. *Journal of the House* 18 (May 1797–March 1798), p. 130, entry dated June 20, 1797, Massachusetts State Library, Boston, transcribed by Laura Mills, who noted that the *Journal of the Senate* recorded the same order on June 23, 1797, p. 102.

3. Evans 1999, p. 101, describes this portrait as "a belatedly finished version of a one-sitting sketch."

Stuart's portraits of John Adams (1735–1826) and Abigail Smith Adams (1744–1818) are the most memorable pendant portraits of these forceful personalities. Stuart began the paintings in Philadelphia sometime before May 20, 1800, when he was paid $100 for Mrs. Adams's portrait, but he did not finish them until 1815, in Boston. Only the persistence of their son John Quincy Adams led to their completion.[1] In 1800 Adams was in his last year as president of the United States. His portrait, family members later said, was commissioned by the Massachusetts Legislature for the new Massachusetts State House. While no documentation has been found to support the specific request of the state legislature for Adams's portrait, the Massachusetts House had voted on June 20, 1797, "an order directing the agents for building the New State House to procure suitable portraits of the late Governor [John] Hancock, [James] Bowdoin and [Samuel] Adams to be preserved in some proper place in said building."[2] However, the Adamses' portraits, when completed in 1815, instead became the property of their son John Quincy Adams. Letters documenting the attempts by family members to persuade Stuart to finish the paintings indicate that they thought highly of the portraits but, at the same time, were critical of Stuart as an individual and as a businessman.

The portrait of John Adams is essentially a depiction of him in 1815, not in 1800.[3] When Stuart stopped working on the portraits, Adams's portrait was barely begun. He described it in March 1804 to his Dutch friend Francis Adrian Van der Kemp: "I satt to him, at the request of our Massachusetts Legislature. But have never seen any Thing of the Picture but the first Sketch."[4] However, the characterization was apparently already in place. Horace Binney, a Philadelphia lawyer whose portrait Stuart painted in 1800 (fig. 77), reported, "'Stuart thought highly of his portrait of John Adams.' Showing it one day to [me], 'Look at him,' said [Stuart]. 'It is very like him, is it not? Do you know what he is going to do? He is just going to sneeze.'"[5] Mrs. Adams's image, the stern face of a woman in her mid-fifties, was more complete. Its appearance when still unfinished is recorded in a copy painted by an unidentified artist sometime between 1800 and 1815 (fig. 122).[6] William Smith Shaw, the son of her sister Elizabeth Smith Shaw, wrote to

58

She sums up the history of the portrait, p. 153 n. 15.

4. John Adams, letter to Francis Adrian Van der Kemp, March 3, 1804, Francis Adrian Van der Kemp Collection, Historical Society of Pennsylvania, Philadelphia; letterbook copy, Adams Papers, quoted in Oliver 1967, p. 134. Adams had told Van der Kemp about the portrait in a letter dated December 14, 1802, Van der Kemp

Mrs. Adams on May 25, 1800: "Your likness has attracted much company to Stewarts and has as many admirers as spectators. Stewart says, he wishes to god, he could have taken Mrs. Adams when she was young, he believes he should have a perfect Venus."[7] In May 1801, after the Adamses had settled in Quincy, Massachusetts, in retirement, their son Thomas Boylston Adams, in Philadelphia, rescued the paintings from possible sale by the sheriff, with other possessions of the artist, for repayment of a debt.

59

Collection, Historical Society of Pennsylvania;
letterbook copy, Adams Papers, quoted in Oliver
1967, pp. 133–34.

5. Mason 1879, p. 142, quoting Binney's nephew
Horace Binney Wallace. For Binney's portrait, see
Miles 1995, pp. 219–21.

6. Oliver 1967, pp. 137–38, 140, and fig. 65, believed
that the uncompleted portrait was the life study.

I felt alarmed for the safety of your portrait & my father's. . . . I found however, upon my arrival, that my father's picture had not been seized or levied upon, but that your's had, and upon my assurance, that the picture was already paid for, the Sheriff consented to withdraw your representative, from the fangs of the law. I left the portrait in Stuart's hands, but I have no idea it will ever be finished. . . . There is no appearance of any thing more having been done towards finishing the painting, than when I saw it a twelvemonth,

Fig. 122. Unidentified artist after Gilbert Stuart, *Abigail Adams*, 1800–1815. Oil on canvas, 22 x 18 in. (55.9 x 45.7 cm). Massachusetts Historical Society, Boston

However, it appears instead to be a copy, by an unknown artist, presumably made when it was still in Stuart's studio; see Miles 1995, p. 214.

7. William Smith Shaw, letter to Abigail Adams, May 25, 1800, Adams Papers, microfilm no. 397, quoted in Oliver 1967, p. 137.

8. Thomas Boylston Adams, letter to Abigail Adams, May 31, 1801, Adams Papers, microfilm no. 400, partially quoted in Oliver 1967, p. 133.

9. Abigail Adams, letter to Thomas Boylston Adams, June 12, 1801, Adams Papers, microfilm no. 401, quoted in Oliver 1967, p. 133.

10. John Quincy Adams, letter to Abigail Adams, December 19, 1804, Adams Papers, microfilm no. 403, quoted in Oliver 1967, p. 134.

11. Abigail Adams, letter to John Quincy Adams, December 30, 1804, Adams Papers, microfilm no. 403, quoted in Oliver 1967, p. 134.

12. The first of several entries that Rev. Stephen Peabody made in his diary about these portrait commissions is dated September 1, 1809; entries from the diary, owned by the American Antiquarian Society, Worcester, Mass., were transcribed by Laura Mills.

13. Rev. Peabody, diary, entry dated October 13, 1809, American Antiquarian Society.

14. Ibid., entry dated October 18, 1809.

15. Ibid., entry dated October 19, 1809.

16. In ibid., entries for August 29, August 30, September 3, and September 4, 1811, Rev. Peabody discussed his attempts to obtain a finished portrait of his wife by Stuart.

17. John Quincy Adams, letter to John Singleton Copley, April 29, 1811, letterbook copy, Adams Papers, microfilm no. 135, quoted in Oliver 1967, p. 135. On this portrait, see ibid., pp. 23–38; Jules

or more, ago. . . . Moreover I know he is an oddity & I never could deal with such character, for if men will take offence, when you exact from them, only justice & fidelity, I never could discover wherein they differ from knaves. . . . It so happened, that your picture was the only one seized, as it was in his house & not in his <u>Stable</u>, which he occupies as his painting room.[8]

Mrs. Adams answered, "I know not what to do with that strange man Stewart. The likeness is said to be so good, both of your Father and of me, that I shall regret very much if he cannot be prevaild upon to finish them as our Children may like to look upon our Likeness when the originals are no more seen."[9]

The family's second failed attempt to obtain the portraits took place late in 1804. Asking his mother for the receipt for payment of the portrait, John Quincy Adams wrote from Washington, D.C., on December 19, "Stuart is now here, and perhaps if I had the right to call on him for the picture he might be induced to finish it, under the apprehension, that it would be liable to injure his reputation by its being exhibited in the owner's possession, in its unfinished state. At any rate, it is so excellent a likeness, that being the only one extant of you, I am very anxious to have it in our own power; by whomsoever of us it may rightfully belong."[10] Mrs. Adams forwarded the receipt on December 30, 1804, and commented, "I have thoughts of writing him a few lines when you call upon him for the portrait. I wish he could be prevaild upon to execute the one of your Father, which was designed for the State House in Boston. Genius is always eccentrick, I think. Superiour talents give no security for propriety of conduct; there is no knowing how to take hold of this Man, nor by what means to prevail upon him to fulfill his engagements."[11]

In 1809, after Stuart had moved to Boston, there was a third attempt to convince him to complete at least the portrait of Mrs. Adams. Her brother-in-law the Reverend Stephen Peabody, second husband of her sister Elizabeth Smith Shaw, visited Stuart with the idea of having his and his wife's portraits painted.[12] While he decided to commission his own portrait from Boston artist John Johnston, who charged $30, rather than Stuart, who charged $100, he noted on October 13: "By the solicitations of Wm Shaw and her friends she has concluded to have her portrait taken by Stewart, on their paying ye extra expence."[13] His diary entries indicate that Mrs. Adams was sitting again at this time. Peabody noted on October 18, "Called at Stewart's & found Mam and Mrs. Adams had been there on Monday & he had gotten their portraits under way. I saw them both and believe will be good."[14] On the 19th he "walked up to Stewart's where I met with Mam & Sister Adams. Their likenesses begin to look well."[15] Even after these sittings, however, the portraits remained unfinished. In 1811 the Reverend Peabody tried again, unsuccessfully, to convince Stuart to finish the portrait of his wife. On September 3 he noted, "I went to Stewart's he is a whistling fellow, and I shall not be able to get Mam's portrait at this time."[16]

Also in 1811 John Quincy Adams sought to finally obtain the full-length portrait of his father painted in London by John Singleton Copley in 1783 (Fogg Art Museum, Cambridge, Mass.). He told Copley that "Mr. Stewart was engaged by the Legislature of Massachusetts to paint one to be placed in the Hall of the House of Representatives, and . . . actually took a likeness of the face. But Mr. Stewart thinks it the prerogative of genius to disdain the performance of his engagements, and he did disdain the performance of that."[17] At the same time he wrote his brother Thomas Boylston Adams, "This reminds me of the two portraits, of my father and mother, which that, I know not what

Fig. 123. *Elizabeth Smith Shaw Peabody*, 1809/15. Oil on wood, 26¾ x 21¼ in. (67.9 x 54 cm). Arizona State University Art Museum, Tempe; Gift of Oliver B. James

David Prown, *John Singleton Copley*, vol. 2, *In England 1774–1815* (Cambridge, Mass.: Harvard University Press, 1966), p. 300.

18. John Quincy Adams, letter to Thomas Boylston Adams, March 29, 1811, Adams Papers, microfilm no. 411, quoted in Oliver 1967, p. 134.

19. John Quincy Adams, letter to Thomas Boylston Adams, May 13, 1811, Adams Papers, microfilm no. 411, quoted in Oliver 1967, p. 135.

20. Park 1926, pp. 578–79, no. 618, quotes the receipt for $120.

21. Abigail Adams, letter to Abigail Adams Shaw, June 6, 1815, Kaller's American Gallery, New York, transcription by Seth Kaller.

22. Abigail Adams, letter to John Quincy Adams, June 8, 1815, Adams Papers, microfilm no. 424, partially quoted in Oliver 1967, p. 137. She continued, "Two years since, he took your Aunt Peabody, at her sons request, since her death he has finished it, and an admirable likeness it is."

23. Nathalie Rothstein, curator emerita, Textile Furnishings and Dress, Victoria and Albert Museum, London, "What Silk Shall I Wear? Fashion and Choice in Some 18th and Early 19th Century Paintings in the National Gallery of Art," lecture, National Gallery of Art, Washington, D.C., September 16, 1990, described Mrs. Adams's cap and embroidered net shawl as fashionable in 1815.

24. Photocopy of unlocated original receipt for $100, dated June 14, 1815, Artists' Letters, Joseph Downs Collection of Manuscripts and Printed Ephemera, Winterthur Library, Winterthur, Del.

25. Stuart's bill, dated December 9, 1815, Adams Papers, microfilm no. 428, in Oliver 1967, p. 135.

26. See Miles 1995, p. 214, for a discussion of the canvases.

27. Oliver believed that the earlier portrait of Adams was the painting then owned by John F. Seymour,

to call him, Stuart has so shamefully kept, and which I wish you could get once more out of his hands, as you once rescued them from the Sheriff at Philadelphia."[18] On May 13, he wrote Thomas again: "I never think of this subject without feeling against Stuart an indignation, which I wish I could change into contempt. If there was another portrait painter in America, I could forgive him. I beg of you to try to get the portrait he has of my mother, and to buy of him that of my father for me. If he will finish it, I will gladly give him his full price for pictures of that sort for it."[19]

Finally John Quincy Adams's insistence that his father sit to Stuart for his portrait and the death of Mrs. Peabody on April 9, 1815, compelled Stuart to complete the three paintings. Mrs. Peabody's son William Smith Shaw paid Stuart on May 26, 1815, for her portrait (fig. 123).[20] John Adams was persuaded by Shaw to sit again. Mrs. Adams wrote to her niece Abigail Adams Shaw about all three portraits:

I have had a melancholy, and yet delightful pleasure, in viewing at Stuarts the admirable likeness of your beloved Mother, and my dear Sister. He has finished it, and it is so like to her very character, that, you will contemplate it, with reverence, respect and veneration, indeed with all those tender emotions, which so correct, a view of her features must inspire. I was tempted to apply to Stuart the lines addressed to the memory of the Great painter Sir Godfrey Kneller. "Stuart by Heaven, and not a master taught whose Art was nature, and whose pictures thought." I rejoice that she was prevailed upon to sit for her portrait, it will be more precious to her Friends who survive her, than if it had been taken in the prime and vigor of youth. That which was twenty years past, taken for me, serves only to remind me of the ravages of time and the decays of Nature, the Image of time past, my grandchildren will never know it, nor the present generation. Mr. JQA has several times written to request his Father to Sit to Stuart for his likeness. by the persuasion of your Brother, who is getting a copy of one formerly taken by him he has consented, and I have accompanied him three days for the purpose. I think Stuart will be happy in his likeness, although nine years older than I am, he retains his countance much better than I do.[21]

She also wrote her son John Quincy Adams, "Your father is gone, to comply with a request made by you through your Brother, to sit to Stuart for his portrait—if he gets a good likeness, as I think it promises, you will value it more than if it had been taken, in youth or Middle Age. He has promised to finish that which twenty years ago he took for me, but now, no more like me than that of any other person. I am sure my Grand Children will never know it and therefore I cared not whether he ever finishd it. It has however a strong resemblance of you."[22]

Adams's finished portrait shows him as he looked in 1815, at the age of eighty. Although Mrs. Adams's was completed with a cap and shawl of the style of that period, her face is no doubt the one painted in 1800.[23] Shaw paid Stuart for two paintings of Adams. Stuart signed a receipt for $100 from Shaw on June 14, 1815, for "a portrait of the Hon. John Adams."[24] A second invoice to William Smith Shaw for $100 "for Mr. Adams portrait" is dated December 9, 1815, and was paid on January 31, 1816, to Stuart's friend Isaac P. Davis.[25] One payment is for the portrait now paired with that of Mrs. Adams, painted on exactly the same size and type of canvas as hers.[26] The original "sketch," the "one formerly taken by him" as Mrs. Adams described it to her niece Abigail, would now lie under the finished portrait.[27] The other payment was for the copy that Shaw owned. This could be the painting acquired after his death by the

Fig. 124. Attributed to Gilbert Stuart Newton, *John Adams*, ca. 1815. Oil on wood, 26 x 20¾ in. (66.2 x 52.8 cm). Boston Athenaeum

Fig. 125. Attributed to Nicholas-Eustache Maurin after Gilbert Stuart, *John Adams*, 1828. Lithograph, 16 x 12 in. (40.6 x 30.5 cm). National Portrait Gallery, Smithsonian Institution, Washington, D.C. (NPG.87.58.2)

Fig. 126. *John Adams*, ca. 1821. Oil on wood, 26 x 21½ in. (66 x 54.5 cm). National Gallery of Art, Washington, D.C.; Ailsa Mellon Bruce Fund (1979.4.1)

and now owned by the National Portrait Gallery, Washington; see Oliver 1967, pp. 141–44 and fig. 67. Instead, it is an early copy; see Miles 1995, p. 214. Evans (1999, p. 153 n. 15) agreed, writing that Oliver's "candidate for the earlier portrait is not persuasive."

28. On that portrait, see Oliver 1967, pp. 151, 152, and fig. 69.

29. That Newton copied Stuart's portrait is documented by a statement in John Stevens Cogdell's diary, vol. 3, entry for September 15, 1816, Downs Collection, Winterthur Library, transcribed by Laura Mills: "I went this morng with Mr Coolidge to Mr Newtons Room in Boston—his copy of John Adams from a head of Gilbert Stewart was the only good thing in the room it was a rough exhibition of that style which has bewildered all artists & been the wonder of all who have been fortunate enough to see any paintings of this great master." For a copy by Newton, see Oliver 1967, pp. 176–77 and fig. 89.

30. Adams, letter to Joseph Delaplaine, March 5, 1816, letterbook copy, Adams Papers, microfilm no. 122, partially quoted in Oliver 1967, p. 150. On Delaplaine's project, see Gordon Marshall, "The Golden Age of Illustrated Biographies: Three Case Studies," in Wendy Wick Reaves, ed., *American Portrait Prints: Proceedings of the Tenth Annual American Print Conference* (Charlottesville: University Press of Virginia for the National Portrait Gallery, Smithsonian Institution, 1984), pp. 28–45, 72.

31. See Delaplaine, letter to William Smith Shaw, August 21, 1817, and John Quincy Adams, letter to Delaplaine, December 15, 1817, letterbook copy, Adams Papers, both quoted in Oliver 1967, p. 150.

32. John Quincy Adams, diary, entry dated September 27, 1821, Adams Papers, microfilm no. 35, quoted in Oliver 1967, p. 161.

Boston Athenaeum (fig. 124), where he had served as librarian.[28] Attributed to Stuart when it was copied by Bass Otis in 1817 for an engraving by James Barton Longacre, it has been attributed to Gilbert Stuart Newton, Stuart's nephew, since at least 1834.[29] It was apparently the version that John Adams thought Stuart possessed when he referred to it in 1816, when Philadelphia publisher Joseph Delaplaine asked to borrow Stuart's portrait of Adams to engrave for his publishing project, *Repository of the Lives and Portraits of Distinguished Americans* (1816–18). Adams replied on March 5, "The portrait taken by Mr Stewart is the property of John Quincy Adams, my Son, taken by his order, often repeated, for six years, from St. Petersburg & paid for by his property. I have no right in it, or power over it. Most certainly it will never go from under my roof, with my consent, untill it is delivered into his hand. But if the picture <u>was</u> my property, I should feel a delicacy for the painter. It would be painful for me to engrave it without his consent. Mr. Stewart possesses another portrait as like it as any two objects in nature or Art are alike."[30] Although Shaw corresponded with Delaplaine about that second painting, it was never engraved for Delaplaine's project.[31] Stuart himself, however, copied it in 1821 for a new commission from Boston framer and printseller John Doggett for a series of portraits of the first five American presidents. On September 27, John Quincy Adams recorded that Shaw "came out with Stewart the painter, who brought with him the copy he had made of Shaw's portrait of my father, and to whom my father gave a sitting of two or three hours. They returned this afternoon to Boston. Stewart paints this picture for a Mr. Doggett, as one of the five Presidents of the United States. He is to paint them all for him."[32]

Unfortunately, Doggett's version of Adams's portrait was one of the three of the series of presidential portraits that was destroyed by fire at the Library of Congress in 1851 (see cat. 87), and its appearance is known today only from the lithograph (fig. 125). Stuart painted another version of the portrait about this time for George Gibbs Jr. for a similar series of presidential portraits known today as the Gibbs-Coolidge series (fig. 126). Two years later, at John Quincy Adams's request, Adams sat again for Stuart, for his last portrait by the artist (cat. 90).

EGM

60. SARAH WENTWORTH APTHORP MORTON

ca. 1800–1802
Oil on canvas, 29⅛ x 24⅛ in. (74 x 61.3 cm)
Worcester Art Museum, Worcester, Massachusetts;
Gift of the Grandchildren of Joseph Tuckerman
(1899.2)

This unfinished portrait of American poet Sarah Morton (1759–1846) is one of Stuart's most sensual, expressive images.[1] Its creation is a part of a complex tale of the close friendship of Stuart with two sitters, Mrs. Morton and John Dunn, a lawyer from Killaly, Ireland, who came to America in 1797–1802 to study Native North American languages.[2] Stuart painted three portraits of each sitter, keeping this swiftly repainted, unfinished portrait of Mrs. Morton and an unfinished painting of Dunn. His fondness for Mrs. Morton and his extraordinary talent for capturing gesture and personality are in evidence in this portrait, as Stuart recorded Mrs. Morton in a spontaneous gesture. The sketchy quality of the painting conveys the illusion of motion rarely conveyed in portraits of this period. Whichever the original gesture—putting on, or taking off, the transparent white veil—the impression to the modern viewer is one of revealing the face of the exquisitely beautiful Mrs. Morton.

The painting was developed in two distinct stages. Stuart began as he would with any composition, lightly describing her face, her dark curls, and her jewelry—a necklace and an earring—without fully resolving the details. He also painted her arms, which cross in front of her body at the lower edge of the painting, clearly visible in the infrared reflectogram (fig. 127). A dark area above her left arm, perhaps the beginning of a black dress, now covered with white, also belongs to the first stage. In the second stage, Stuart changed the planned composition to record her spontaneous gesture, which undoubtedly caught Stuart's eye the same way that Eliza Law's entrance in the artist's studio is reflected in her portrait (cat. 50). Stuart repositioned Mrs. Morton's arms, raised to hold the transparent veil, outlining them with a cool umber pigment on top of the unfinished background. He filled in some of the white area of the veil and painted out her left arm with white as he gave shape to her white dress. The background is completed as a blue sky with clouds and perhaps some suggestion of landscape to the left.

1. On this portrait, of which Mason (1879) was unaware, see Park 1926, p. 534–36, no. 561; Evans 1999, p. 110; and Laura Mills's fine essay on the painting, with documentation and conservation notes, in "Early American Paintings in the Worcester Art Museum," the museum's online catalogue, found at www.worcesterart.org/Collection/Early American.

2. The full story of the commissions is described in Harris 1964. On Dunn, who served as member of the Irish Parliament from 1790 to 1797, see Harris 1964, pp. 215–18; Miles 1995, pp. 216–19; Mills, "Early American Paintings in the Worcester Art Museum," pp. 6–7. On Sarah Morton, see Emily Pendleton and Milton Ellis, *Philenia: The Life and Works of Sarah Wentworth Morton, 1759–1846* (Orono, Maine: University Press, 1931), as well as the shorter entries in Edward T. James, ed., *Notable American Women, 1607–1950: A Biographical Dictionary* (Cambridge, Mass.: Belknap Press of Harvard University Press, 1971), vol. 2, pp. 586–87; *ANB*, vol. 15, pp. 961–63. Her collection of poetry, *My Mind and Its Thoughts, in Sketches, Fragments, and Essays* (Boston: Wells and Lilly, 1823), was reprinted in a facsimile edition (Delmar, N.Y.: Scholars' Facsimiles and Reprints, 1975), with an introduction by William K. Bottorff.

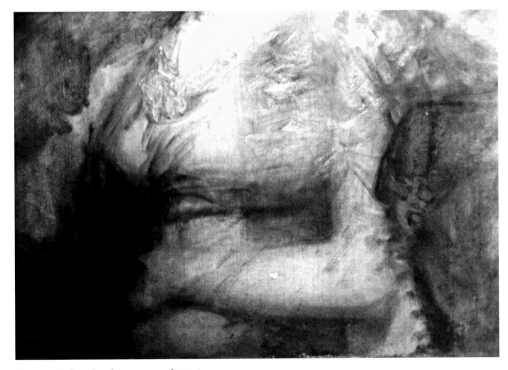

Fig. 127. Infrared reflectogram of cat. 60

Fig. 128. *Sarah Wentworth Apthorp Morton*, ca. 1800–1802. Oil on canvas, 29¼ x 24 in. (74.3 x 61 cm). Museum of Fine Arts, Boston; Juliana Cheney Edwards Collection (39.681)

Fig. 129. *Sarah Wentworth Apthorp Morton*, ca. 1800–1802. Oil on wood, 29½ x 24 in. (74.9 x 61 cm). Henry Francis du Pont Winterthur Museum, Winterthur, Del. (63.77)

3. On this portrait, oil on canvas, 29¼ by 24 in., see Mason 1879, pp. 225–26; Park 1926, pp. 536–37, no. 562; *American Paintings in the Museum of Fine Arts, Boston* (Boston: Museum of Fine Arts, 1969), vol. 1, pp. 245–46, no. 910.

4. On this portrait, see Mason 1879, pp. 225–27; Park pp. 537–38, no. 563; Edgar P. Richardson, *American Paintings and Related Pictures in the Henry Francis du Pont Winterthur Museum* (Charlottesville: University Press of Virginia, 1986), pp. 94–95; Harris 1964. After Dunn's death, his family sent this portrait to Mrs. Morton. She sold the portrait of Dunn to George W. Brimmer on August 12, 1828, for $150. The receipt (Sarah Wentworth

The portrait is closely related to Stuart's two completed portraits of Mrs. Morton and is very likely to be the original life portrait. While the others are finished images that depict Mrs. Morton seated, wearing a black dress, the representation of her face is the same in all three paintings. The more demure of the two, painted for her or her family (fig. 128), shows her in the black dress with a brown and green shawl, her hair arranged at the back of her head. Her simple jewelry includes her wedding ring and a red clasp on the sleeve of her black dress.[3] The second (fig. 129), which was painted for Dunn, has a more complex, and more personal imagery.[4] Here Mrs. Morton's long, dark curls fall loosely around her face. Her jewelry includes three strands of pearls and a bracelet on her left wrist that she touches with her right hand. On the table are the tools of a writer: an inkwell, some papers, and a book. Behind the table is a sculpture of George Washington, derived from Jean-Antoine Houdon's portrait bust.

Stuart probably painted the three portraits of Mrs. Morton sometime between 1800 and 1802, during one of the visits that Mrs. Morton and her husband, Perez Morton, made to Philadelphia from Massachusetts. At the time Perez Morton, a lawyer, was representing the Boston proprietors of Yazoo River land in Georgia. His visits to the national capital, first to Philadelphia in 1800 and then to Washington, resulted in a formal petition to Congress in 1804.[5] The Mortons' presence in Philadelphia in April 1800 is referred to in a letter to Abigail Adams's nephew William Smith Shaw from Arthur M. Walter in Boston, dated April 24: "Mr & Mrs Morton are with you. Are you sufficiently acquainted with them to send me any thing on their return?"[6] Shaw's report to Walter on May 10, that "Congress intends adjourning on Monday[.] Many of the gentlemen have already left the City & many go to morrow," indicates that Morton was in Philadelphia during sessions of Congress that year.[7] The suggestion that Mrs. Morton sit for Stuart could have been made by Dunn, whose portrait Stuart painted about 1798. He arrived in Boston sometime in 1797, before his election as a corresponding member of the Massachusetts Historical Society on December 1, 1797.[8] He may have sought out Mrs. Morton because of her published poem, "Ouâbi; or, The Virtues of Nature: An Indian Tale in Four Cantos" (1790). He was in Philadelphia by January 9, 1798, when he sent George Washington a copy of Mrs. Morton's recently published *Beacon Hill. A Local Poem, Historic and Descriptive* (Boston Athenaeum). It was a gift from the author, who had expressed her admiration of the president in the poem. Dunn apologized for the tardy delivery because of "Delays on the Road." On the flyleaf he inscribed his own poem, paying tribute to Mrs. Morton and Washington, the combined theme of the version of Mrs. Morton's portrait that Dunn owned.[9] Dunn, described by Jane Stuart many years later as one of the people who frequented the studio when Stuart was painting Washington,[10] gave one version of his own portrait to Mrs. Morton (Museum of Fine Arts, Boston), returning to Ireland by mid-March 1802 with the other (National Gallery of Art, Washington).[11]

Mrs. Morton praised Stuart's portraits of her in her forty-four line poem "To Mr. Stuart, on his portrait of Mrs. M." published in *The Port Folio* on June 18, 1803.

Stuart, the portraits speak, with skill divine; / Round the bright Graces flows the waving line. / Expression in its finest utterance lives, / And a new language to creation gives. / Each varying trait the gifted artist shews, / Wisdom majestic in his bending brows; / The warrior's open front, his eye of fire, / Or when the charms of bashful youth retire; / Or patient plodding, and with wealth content, / The man of commerce counts his cent per cent. / 'Tis character *that breathes, 'tis* soul *that twines / Round the rich*

60

Morton Document, #8048, Clifton Waller Barrett Library, Special Collections, University of Virginia Library, Charlottesville) says it was painted "about 1798."

5. His appointment as representative of the Boston proprietors is described in Harris 1964, p. 213.

6. Arthur M. Walter, Boston, to William Smith Shaw, [Philadelphia], April 24, 1800, William Smith Shaw Papers, box 4, Boston Athenaeum, B.A.2a; the Shaw papers were researched and transcribed by Laura Mills.

7. William Smith Shaw, Philadelphia, to Arthur M. Walter, Boston, May 10, 1800, William Smith Shaw Papers, box 4.

8. *Proceedings of the Massachusetts Historical Society* 1 (1791–1835), p. 109, where he is described as "John Dunn, LL.D., of Killaly, Ireland." He was nominated at the October 31 meeting; see ibid., p. 108.

9. The inscriptions are quoted by Appleton P. C. Griffin, comp., *A Catalogue of the Washington Collection in the Boston Athenaeum* ([Cambridge: University Press]; Boston Athenaeum, 1897), p. 147. Dunn's letter is dated Philadelphia, January 9, 1798. A copy of this poem that is transcribed with a manuscript collection, "Poems by Sarah Morton" (Huntington Library, San Marino, Calif., HM6272) is titled "To Mrs. M." from "John Dunn of Dublin, M.P."

10. J. Stuart 1876, p. 371.

11. Dunn was elected to the Royal Irish Academy on March 16, 1802. On his portraits, see *American Paintings in the Museum of Fine Arts, Boston*, vol. 1, pp. 245–46, no. 909; Miles 1995, pp. 216–19. Stuart kept the unfinished portrait of Dunn; see Park 1926, pp. 294–95, no. 256; Miles 1995, pp. 216–19.

12. Sarah Wentworth Apthorp Morton, "To Mr. Stuart, on his portrait of Mrs. M.," *The Port Folio* 3 (June 18, 1803), p. 1. The poem is published in full, with Stuart's response, in Mason 1879, pp. 226–27. She included the poem in her collection, *My Mind and Its Thoughts*, pp. 74–76, with a new title, "To Mr. Stuart, upon seeing those portraits which were painted by him at Philadelphia in the beginning of the present century," with some changes of words and phrases in the poem.

13. Stuart, "To Mrs. M—," *The Port Folio* 3 (June 18, 1803), p. 1.

14. *The Port Folio* 3 (June 18, 1803), p. 1.

canvas, trac'd in living lines, / Speaks in the face, or in the form display'd, / Warms in the tint, and mellows in the shade. / Those touching graces, and that front sublime, / Thy hand shall rescue from the spoil of Time. / Thence the fair victim scorns the threatening rage, / And stealing steps of slow, advancing Age; / Still on her cheek the rose of beauty blows, / Her lip's full tint its breathing crimson shows. / Like the Magician's wand, thy pencil gives / Its potent charm, and every feature lives; / Quick as the powerful eye's transcendant ray / Steals the soft glance, and bids the heart obey, / Thy fine perceptions flow, by heaven design'd, / To reach the thought, and pierce the unfolded mind; / Through its swift course the rapid feeling trace, / And stamp the sovereign Passion on the face. / E'en me, by thy enlivening grace array'd, / Me, born to linger in Affliction's shade, / Hast thou, kind artist, with attraction drest, / With all that Nature in my soul express'd. // Go on—and may Reward thy cares attend, / The friend of Genius must remain thy friend; / Though sordid minds with impious touch presume / To blend thy laurels with the Cypress gloom, / With tears of grief its shining leaves to fade, / Its fair hope withering in the cheerless shade, / The well earn'd meed with sparing hand deny, / And on thy talents gaze with dubious eye. / Genius is Sorrow's child, to Want allied, / Consol'd by Glory, and sustain'd by Pride; / Unknown—unfelt—unshelter'd—uncaress'd— / In walks of life, where worldly passions rest.[12]

Stuart's response of thirty-four lines, "To Mrs. M—," was published with her verses.

Who would not glory in the wreath of praise, / Which M——n offers in her polish'd lays? / I feel their cheering influence at my heart, / And more complacent I review my art; / Yet, ah, with Poesy, that gift divine, / Compar'd, how poor, how impotent is mine! / What though my pencil trace the hero's form, / Trace the soft female cheek, with beauty warm; / No farther goes my power; 'tis thine to spread / Glory's proud ensign o'er the hero's head; / 'Tis thine to give the chief a deathless name, / And tell to ages, yet unborn, his fame— / 'Tis thine to future periods to convey / Beauty enshrin'd in some immortal lay. / No faithful portrait now Achilles shows, / With Helen's matchless charms no canvas glows; / But still in Homer's mighty verse pourtray'd, / Ne'er can her beauty, or his glory fade. / Nor wonder, if, in tracing charms, like thine, / Thought and expression blend a rich design; / 'Twas heaven itself that blended in thy face, / The lines of Reason, with the lines of Grace; / 'Twas heaven that bade the swift idea rise, / Paint thy soft cheek, and sparkle in thine eyes: / Invention, there could, justly, claim no part, / I only boast the copyist's humbler art. / Mid varied scenes of life, howe'er deprest, / This blest reflection still shall soothe my breast; / M——n commends—and this alike outweighs / The vulgar's censure, or the vulgar's praise. / With such distinction, wrapt in proud content, / No more my adverse fortune I lament; / Enough for me, that she extends her meed, / Whose approbation is applause, indeed.[13]

In his accompanying commentary, *Port Folio* editor Joseph Dennie praised Stuart and described Mrs. Morton's portrait as "one of his [Stuart's] most beautiful, captivating, and highly finished performances . . . his spirited portrait of the impassioned and ingenuous features of a Lady, whose rank is high in the Monarchy of Letters, and whose conversation powers, and attractive graces, are the delight of that society, whom she gladdens by her presence."[14]

In their poetry, Stuart and Mrs. Morton both refer to personal anguish. Mrs. Morton described herself as "born to linger in Affliction's shade," while Stuart described

15. Morton, *My Mind and Its Thoughts*, pp. 76, 213–14. On Stuart's portraits of Fisher Ames and Isaac Hull, see Park 1926, pp. 99–100 no. 14, 418–19 no. 419. A copy of Hull's portrait by an unidentified artist is at The Metropolitan Museum of Art; see John Caldwell and Oswaldo Rodriguez Roque, *American Paintings in The Metropolitan Museum of Art*, vol. 1, *A Catalogue of Works by Artists Born by 1815* (New York: Metropolitan Museum of Art, 1994), pp. 196–97. The story of the portrait of Mrs. Hull is recounted in Jonathan Mason Jr., "Recollections of a Septuagenarian," vol. 2, pp. 21–24, Joseph Downs Collection of Manuscripts and Printed Ephemera, Winterthur Library, Winterthur, Del.

16. "Poems by Sarah Morton," Huntington Library, HM 6272, pp. 213–14.

17. *The Port Folio*, n.s. 4 (November 21, 1807), p. 335.

18. Swan 1938, pp. 308–9, identified the year of the single sheet of entries, which had been published in Mason 1879, p. 46, without that information.

19. On Charlotte Morton Dexter's portrait, finished by an unidentified artist, see Miles 1995, pp. 279–81.

her "wreath of praise" as encouragement. Mrs. Morton's sorrows arose in part from her husband's affair with her sister, which led to a public scandal in 1788. Already a poet by that time, she published her first verses, "Invocation to Hope," in 1789. Using the pseudonyms "Constantia" and "Philenia," she continued to write and publish poetry to at least 1823, becoming known as "the American Sappho," after the Greek poetess. She celebrated Stuart's work in verse at least three more times. Her "Inscription, for the portrait of Fisher Ames, painted con amore by Stuart" (ca. 1807; National Portrait Gallery) includes a reference to Ames's famed 1796 speech in defense of the Jay Treaty. In her poem titled "To Gilbert Stuart, on his intended portrait of Mrs. H, the beautiful wife of one of the Naval Heroes of the U.S.," she wrote about a portrait of the wife of Commodore Isaac Hull, which Stuart left unfinished.[15] Her verse "To Mr. Stuart solicited by his Friend to give his own Portrait" is undated and apparently remained unpublished.[16] Unsigned verses published in the *Port Folio* on November 21, 1807, "Lines, On Seeing the portrait of a lady, recently taken by Mr. Stuart" may also be hers.[17] Her visit to Stuart's studio on April 27, 1808, is recorded on a page of the artist's appointment book that survived at least until the late 1870s.[18] Her daughter Charlotte and Andrew Dexter were sitting for their portraits that week, before their marriage in June 1808. Mrs. Morton's last recorded visit to Stuart's studio was in 1825, when she saw the unfinished portrait of Charlotte, who had died in 1819.[19]

EGM

61. WILLIAM SMITH

ca. 1801–2

Oil on canvas, 37 x 60 in. (94 x 152.4 cm)
On loan to the University of Pennsylvania Art Collection, Philadelphia, courtesy of A. J. Brinton (1950.0001-L)

The first drafts of this entry were written by Christopher H. Jones.

1. On the portrait, see Mason 1879, pp. 257–58; Park 1926, pp. 701–3, no. 778; Michael Quick, no. 23, in Quick, Marvin Sadik, and William H. Gerdts, *American Portraiture in the Grand Manner: 1720–1920*, exh. cat. (Los Angeles: Los Angeles County Museum of Art, 1981), p. 116; Evans 1999, pp. 83, 147 n. 13.

2. William R. Smith, letter to John A. McAllister, November 24, 1858, McAllister Manuscripts, Library Company of Philadelphia. Mount (1964, p. 219) says that Stuart and his family stayed at Smith's during the yellow fever epidemic in the late summer of 1797.

3. The engraving appears as the frontispiece of volume 1 of *The Works of William Smith, D.D., Late Provost of the College and Academy of Philadelphia*, 2 vols. (Philadelphia: Hugh Maxwell and William Fry, 1803), published shortly after Smith's death.

Stuart's portrait represents the much admired and eccentric Dr. William Smith (1727–1803), provost of the College of Philadelphia, in retirement at the end of his long life as an educator and clergyman.[1] Seated at a desk with books, papers, and an inkwell, he holds a quill pen, poised in the act of writing. He wears the black academic robe and crimson hood that denote his doctor of divinity degree. Stuart carefully depicted Smith's face, with its soft, ruddy skin, and his gray hair with black curls in the shadows. His right hand, holding the pen, is also closely observed, with highlights on the fingertips, and the lower contours of the fingers outlined with red-brown, on top of local color, as a shading technique. To the left is a large brass theodolite, a surveying instrument with a telescope to measure horizontal and vertical angles, and a compass lies partly hidden under the papers; these reflect Smith's lifelong interest in science. The painting's unusual horizontal format allows space for the expansive desk, the theodolite, and the landscape background.

Stuart and Smith knew each other well. Stuart lived in the house owned by Smith's son William Moore Smith in Philadelphia, where at least one sitting with George Washington took place for the full-length Lansdowne portrait (see cat. 45). After Stuart moved to Germantown, he and his family lived for a time in one of the houses on Smith's property, according to Smith's grandson.[2] The dates of the sittings for Smith's portrait are not known. David Edwin engraved the likeness for the posthumous publication of Smith's sermons in 1803 (fig. 130).[3] The inscription on the engraving, *William Smith D.D. Æt: 75*, suggests that the portrait was made during the year leading up to Smith's seventy-fifth birthday on September 7, 1802.[4] Edwin vividly described meeting Smith when the engraving was commissioned:

I thank James Green of the Library Company for checking their copy of this publication for the engraving and its inscription, and for his assistance in dating the portrait. For a discussion of Smith's plans to publish his own writings, see Albert Frank Gegenheimer, *William Smith: Educator and Churchman, 1727–1803* (Philadelphia: University of Pennsylvania Press, 1943), pp. 219–20.

4. On the portrait and engraving, see Horace Wemyss Smith, *Life and Correspondence of the Rev. William Smith, D.D.* (1879–80; reprint, New York: Arno Press, 1972), vol. 2, pp. 413–14, 449. Edwin was paid $45 for the engraving by Smith's executors. The engraving is catalogued in Mantle Fielding, *Catalogue of the Engraved Work of David Edwin* (Philadelphia: Privately printed, 1905), p. 38, no. 183; David McNeely Stauffer, *American Engravers upon Copper and Steel* (1907; reprint, New York: Burt Franklin, 1964), vol. 2, p. 146, no. 877.

5. This reminiscence is quoted in Dunlap 1834, vol. 2, p. 69.

6. This biography is based on the entries in *DAB*, vol. 9, pp. 353–57; *ANB*, vol. 20, pp. 305–6.

7. Martin P. Snyder, *City of Independence: Views of Philadelphia before 1800* (New York: Praeger Publishers, 1975), pp. 222–24. Snyder reproduces a

About the year 1801 I had the happiness of forming an acquaintance with Mr. Gilbert Stuart. It took place on my undertaking to engrave a portrait of Dr. Smith, (of the Pennsylvania University) from Mr. Stuart's painting. The first meeting I had with the Doctor on the subject of the plate that was to be engraved, I shall not readily forget. The Doctor had been a school-master; and although ignorant of the art of engraving, undertook to examine me on my capabilities. He was old, hasty, and very irritable. He began in a broad Scotch dialect, by asking me if I could draw. But when we came to the price of the plate, I thought the poor Doctor would have gone distracted. He ran out and in the room, throwing at me angry and reproachful glances; and ended with the determination of paying me only half of my demand, which I accepted, considering the connection I should form with Mr. Stuart, by undertaking the work, of more value to me than any sum the doctor could pay me for the plate.[5]

Born in Aberdeen, Scotland, William Smith attended the University of Aberdeen and went to New York in 1751 as a tutor.[6] In 1753 he published an essay on education called *A General Idea of the College of Mirania*, which led to his appointment to the faculty of the Academy of Philadelphia. After the academy was reorganized as the College of Philadelphia, he was appointed its provost and taught mathematics and natural sciences. A member of the intellectual and political leadership of Philadelphia, he was an early patron of the American artist Benjamin West. Smith was also an ordained minister in the Church of England and in 1759 received doctor of divinity degrees from Oxford University and the University of Aberdeen. When the Pennsylvania General Assembly revoked the college's charter during the American Revolution because of the Tory views of its leadership, Smith became rector of Chester Parish, Chestertown, Maryland. There he established Kent School, chartered in 1782 as Washington College. Efforts to restore the charter of the College of Philadelphia succeeded in 1789, and Smith resumed his position as provost for two years, until the college became part of the reorganized University of Pennsylvania.

The landscape in the background of the portrait represents the panoramic view from Smith's home on a hillside overlooking the Schuylkill River, with whitewater highlights

Fig. 130. David Edwin after Gilbert Stuart, *William Smith*, 1801–2. Engraving. The Library Company of Philadelphia

Fig. 131. Infrared reflectogram of cat. 61

61

view from the western shore by George Isham Parkyns, which shows the falls but not Smith's home. Snyder (ibid., p. 221) wrote that Parkyns "seated himself by the corner of an old mill on the west side," perhaps the long building on the riverbank in the background of Smith's portrait.

8. On Smith's land on the Schuylkill River, see Edwin Iwanicki, "The Village of Falls of Schuylkill," *Pennsylvania Magazine of History and Biography* 91 (July 1967), pp. 331–33. The property was on the hill above what is now the intersection of Ridge Avenue and Indian Queen Lane in the Germantown section of Philadelphia, according to Karie Diethorn, Chief Curator, Independence National Historic Park, e-mail message to Christopher H. Jones, October 6, 2003.

9. Smith described his home in a "TO BE LETT For the *Summer Season*, or for one year," advertisement appearing in the *Pennsylvania Gazette*, April 28, 1784. A similar ad, for the summer or "a short Term of Years," had been placed in the *Gazette* on March 16, 1774.

10. Park 1926, p. 158, no. 88, dating her portrait ca. 1798.

11. William R. Smith, letter to John A. McAllister, November 24, 1858, McAllister Manuscripts, Library Company of Philadelphia.

on the falls in the foreground and hills on the far side.[7] Smith retired to this property on the eastern bank of the Schuylkill River, north of Philadelphia, which he had purchased over a period of time beginning in 1757.[8] In 1784 he advertised for lease his "large and commodious mansion house . . . situate at the Falls of Schuylkill, and commanding a grand and extensive prospect of the river and many adjacent country seats."[9] The landscape view in the portrait was designed by Samuel Blodget Jr., an architect and the husband of Smith's daughter Rebecca Smith, whose portrait was also painted by Stuart (Pennsylvania Academy of the Fine Arts, Philadelphia).[10] According to Smith's grandson William R. Smith,

It is well known that Stuart paid little regard to the <u>adjuncts</u> of a picture, Books, Dress, Instruments, Curtains or Drapery and back ground landscape. In his picture of my Grandfather Dr. Wm. Smith . . . there are philosophical instruments, a globe &c and a view of the Falls of Schylkill—the picture was painted at that place, as Stuart then resided in Dr. Smith's old mansion on the Hill opposite the Falls. In this connection I wish to call Mr Peales attention to the <u>adjuncts</u> to the <u>full length portrait</u> of Washington— I believe that the Books Papers, Drapery, Table, Chair &c in this Picture, as well as the various ornamental portions of the above portrait of Dr. Smith, were designed and sketched by Samuel Blodget of Philada, who was a Son-in-law of Dr Smith. By the way, Dr. Smith's picture is very singular in shape, for in order to admit of the <u>ornaments</u> &c it is about 3 1/2 feet high, and near 6 feet in width.[11]

The landscape is thinly painted with a wash. Faint, very precise lines are visible through the oil paint, outlining the hills and riverbank and detailing the leafy boughs of trees,

Fig. 132. Jesse Ramsden, "plain" theodolite, illustrated in George Adams, *Geometrical and Graphical Essays* (London, 1791), pl. 16. Special Collections, Smithsonian Institution Libraries, Washington, D.C.

the furrows in a distant field, and the rocks in the river, as if the image was transferred from a drawing. It is not known whether Blodget or Stuart drew the outlines, which also describe the two buildings on the far shore, including the windows of the larger building. These contour lines are especially visible when the painting is examined with an infrared camera (fig. 131), which also reveals a small building hidden in the trees on this side of the river, above the inkwell and Smith's right hand.

The theodolite, too, appears to have been drawn before it was painted. Lines seem to outline the legs of the instrument and the two telescopes, although here the paint is applied more thickly, with highlights and shadow, making the drawing more difficult to detect. When examined with infrared reflectography, the books also appear to have been outlined. The theodolite has sometimes been interpreted as a reference to one of Smith's most notable scientific accomplishments, the observation with David Rittenhouse of the transit of Venus on June 3, 1769.[12] However, Smith did not own a theodolite, and while it would be possible to use one in astronomical observations, the theodolite depicted here dates from later than 1769. Recently Brandon Fortune and Deborah Warner have successfully argued that the image was taken from an engraved illustration published in George Adams's catalogue *Geometrical and Graphical Essays* (London, 1791) of a theodolite made by London instrument maker Jesse Ramsden (fig. 132).[13] The position of the instrument in the painting exactly duplicates the engraving, and the few visible traced lines support the idea that the image comes from a two-dimensional source rather than from an actual instrument. Also, the theodolite as depicted is larger than its true size. The authors interpret the inclusion of the theodolite as an assertion of Smith's "scientific and mathematical skill" in a disagreement with engineer and architect Benjamin Latrobe over the design of a system that would supply Philadelphia's water, part of Smith's postretirement interest in establishing a reliable canal system in Pennsylvania.

Smith figured in two subsequent proposals for portraits by Stuart that were never realized. Dr. Benjamin Rush's commission was the more ambitious. He presented this idea to Smith on August 10, 1802, in answer to a letter in which Smith referred to their recent meeting, "when I had the Pleasure of a short Visit from You, at my House in the Country, as my <u>Friend</u> and <u>Physician</u> (the celebrated Artist, <u>Gilbert Stuart Esq</u>, being present with us, and the conversation turning upon old times . . .)."[14] Rush wrote Smith,

Your villa will hereafter have an additional hold upon my memory, by being the place where I first met a man whose talents for conversation have commanded nearly as much admiration as his pencil, I mean the celebrated Mr. Stewart. Thirty years ago I communicated to Mr Peale a wish to see a gallery of portraits of sick people labouring under such diseases as shew themselves in the features, and countenance. These are chiefly madness—melancholy—fatuity—consumption—Dropsey—Jaundice, Leprosy—Gutta Rosea—Stone—Cancer—Colic, Dysentary, small pox—measles,—Scarlet fever, and plagues of all kinds. . . . By means of a gallery of portraits such as I have hinted at, the Study of medicine might be much aided, and benevolent Sympathies be excited in persons, who from education, Situation, or too much Sensibility, are precluded from seeing the originals in sick rooms or hospitals.

Suppose you suggest the idea of such an Undertaking to Mr. Stewart. If in revolving it in his mind, he should feel any fear of being infected with the last named disease [yellow fever], you may assure him from much higher Authority than mine, that the yellow fever is <u>not</u> contagious, and spreads only through the medium of an Atmosphere rendered

12. Washington, Providence 1967, p. 84.
13. Brandon Brame Fortune, with Deborah J. Warner, *Franklin and His Friends: Portraying the Man of Science in Eighteenth-Century America*, exh. cat. (Washington, D.C.: Smithsonian National Portrait Gallery in association with the University of Pennsylvania Press, Philadelphia, 1999), pp. 93–97.
14. William Smith, letter to Benjamin Rush, August 5, 1802, Miscellaneous Letters, Benjamin Rush Papers, 22 Rush Ms. 49, Historical Society of Pennsylvania, Philadelphia.

15. Rush, letter to Smith, August 10, 1802, William Smith Papers, UPT 50 S664, box 3, FF10, University of Pennsylvania Archives, Philadelphia. Brandon Fortune called my attention to these letters after finding a letterpress copy of Rush's letter to Smith in Rush's papers at the Historical Society of Pennsylvania.

16. The letter is quoted in Mason 1879, p. 258, as among Stuart's papers; H. W. Smith, *Life and Correspondence of the Rev. William Smith, D.D.,* vol. 2, p. 447.

impure by putrid exhalations. A patient in the Country therefore, who had carried the disease from our city, might be approached, viewed, and painted with as much Safety as a person in the Gout, or tooth ach[e].[15]

These paintings were never painted. Nor was the one that Smith commissioned in February 1803, when he wrote Stuart about a portrait of his son William Moore Smith: "By Dr. Rush's order I am now wholly confined to my bed-chamber. . . . I beg the pleasure and comfort of a short visit from you in a day or two. My son, in two or three weeks, will embark for England. I shall never see him again, as I believe. He has consented to sit to you for his picture before he goes. I shall pay you cash down, as we may agree. An answer *per* bearer is requested by Your affectionate Wm. Smith."[16] Smith died three months later.

EGM

62. HELENA LAWRENCE HOLMES PENINGTON

1803
Oil on wood, 29 x 23¾ in. (73.7 x 60.3 cm)
Collection of Judith and Steaven K. Jones

63. EDWARD PENINGTON

1802
Oil on wood, 29 x 23¾ in. (73.7 x 60.3 cm)
Historical Society of Pennsylvania Collection, Atwater Kent Museum of Philadelphia; Bequest of Edward Carey Gardiner (HSP.1954.1)

Christopher H. Jones contributed to the research and writing of this entry.

1. The portraits, catalogued in Mason 1879, p. 237; Park 1926, p. 582, nos. 621, 622, have been separated since at least 1879. Penington's portrait is also catalogued in Nicholas B. Wainwright, comp., *Paintings and Miniatures at the Historical Society of Pennsylvania* (Philadelphia: Historical Society of Pennsylvania, 1974), p. 202. The reverse of the frame is inscribed *Edward Penington aetat 36 Stewart pinx. 1802 (cost $100).* For the portrait of Mrs. Penington, see Ilene Susan Fort with Trudi Abram, *American Paintings in Southern California Collections: From Gilbert Stuart to Georgia O'Keeffe,* exh. cat. (Los Angeles: Los Angeles County Museum of Art, 1996), p. 33.

2. "Edward Penington's Day Book, 1799–1806," unpaginated, Edward Carey Gardiner Collection, Ms. 227A, Historical Society of Pennsylvania, Philadelphia.

Toward the end of his decade in Philadelphia, Stuart painted these sympathetic portraits of the sugar merchant and arts patron Edward Penington (1766–1834) and his wife, Helena Holmes Penington (1769–1852).[1] Penington noted the payments in pounds in his daybook. On January 8, 1803, he "pd Gilbert Stuart for my Portrait 37.10," and on March 26, 1803, he "pd Mr Stuart yesterday for Mrs P portrait 37.10."[2] On February 24, he "pd Charles Vivant for 2 frames for Portraits 10/10/0," probably the frames that are still on the portraits.[3] Stuart also painted Penington's niece Ann Penington in 1805 (cat. 64) and was commissioned to copy a portrait of Penington's mother from a drawing by English artist James Sharples, who worked in Philadelphia in the 1790s. On September 13, 1803, Penington "pd G Stuart for Portrait of my mother which he is to copy from one of Sharples's"; the price was 37/10/0. A pencil note adds, "portrait never painted & money never ret[urned]?" A purchase not recorded in the daybook is the replica of Stuart's Athenaeum portrait of George Washington that he also owned (fig. 96).[4]

The portraits complement each other in color and pose. Helena Penington's portrait shows her seated in an armchair upholstered in red and turned toward her husband. She wears a low-cut white dress with a ruffled bodice and a black shawl with lace trim. She has chestnut brown hair and brown eyes, and her only visible jewelry is a gold earring, which Stuart highlighted. The portrait of Edward Penington is a study in gray and black, with touches of red. Penington wears a black coat, and his dark hair is pulled back in a queue. The powder gives his hair a gray appearance. Seated in a chair with red upholstery, Penington holds a letter addressed to him. Its red wax seal, the red of the

62

3. "Edward Penington's Day Book, 1799–1806." When paying for his portrait on January 8, Penington noted, "pd Mr Devant for Frame to do [ditto]," but crossed this out later with the annotation "See Feby 24." Vivant is listed as a gilder at 19 North Sixth Street, Philadelphia, in James Robinson, *The Philadelphia Directory, City and County Register, for 1802* (Philadelphia: William W. Woodward, 1802), p. 249.

4. Park 1926, p. 885, no. 84; Morgan and Fielding 1931, p. 302, no. 86.

5. "Edward Penington's Day Book, 1799–1806."

chair, and pink touches on his cheeks and hands are the few carefully orchestrated points of bright color in the portrait. His white cravat with its crisp folds and gray shadows is plain, probably muslin, similar to the "6 muslin Cravats" he bought for £2 5s. on April 15, 1800. He wears a pair of silver-rimmed spectacles, perhaps the ones for which he paid "18/9" on November 27, 1801, or the "pair Silver mounted Spectacles with green Glasses added" that he purchased for £3 7s 6d on June 21, 1802, from Philadelphia merchant John McAllister.[5] In 1802 McAllister and his partner advertised that they had "considerably enlarged their assortment of Spectacles in gold, silver, steel, tortoise shell, &c. Besides the common convex glasses, they have them with green glasses for weak eyes, likewise with concave glasses for those that are near-sighted."[6]

63

6. *Pennsylvania Gazette and Daily Register*, advertisement, courtesy Deborah Jean Warner, Smithsonian National Museum of American History, Washington, D.C. Scottish woodworker John McAllister established a cane shop in Philadelphia in 1781, and by 1800 he had added a whip manufactory to his enterprise and was importing and marketing spectacles. His shop made frames for Thomas Jefferson, Charles Willson Peale, and Rubens Peale, among others; see Charles Willson Peale, letter to Thomas Jefferson, March 12, 1807, in Lillian B. Miller, ed., *The Selected Papers of Charles Willson Peale and His Family* (New Haven: Yale

Edward Penington and Helena Holmes, the daughter of James Holmes of New York, were married in 1798 at Mulberry Hill, Monmouth County, New Jersey. Her family history is not well documented. Penington was a Quaker whose London ancestor Edward Penington (1667–1701) came to Philadelphia in 1698 as surveyor-general of Pennsylvania.[7] With land grants from William Penn, the Penington family became major property owners in Bucks County, Pennsylvania, and nearby New Jersey. Edward was the seventh child of Edward Penington (1726–1796) and Sarah Shoemaker.[8] His father moved the family to Philadelphia, where he invested in property and owned a sugar refinery. During the revolution the elder Edward Penington opposed war and armed resistance and, with other wealthy Quaker merchants, was exiled in 1777 to

Fig. 133. Samuel Lewis, *A Deception*, ca. 1805–9. Ink and graphite on paper, 16 x 10¾ in. (40.6 x 27.3 cm). Private collection

Winchester, Virginia as a suspected loyalist. In 1781, after his return, he was among several who refused on religious grounds to illuminate their homes as part of Philadelphia's celebration of Cornwallis's defeat at Yorktown.

His son Edward's interests were in the arts, rather than politics. While continuing the family's sugar refining business with his brother Isaac, Penington recorded in the entries of his daybook every personal expense, including visits to the theater, purchases of paintings, drawings, prints, and books, as well as clothing and other items such as quarterly payments to a barber and powder for his hair.[9] He attended plays frequently during the theater season. He listed the names of the plays and his companions, including his wife and his niece Ann, in his daybook. Sometimes he added comments on the plays, noting for example on November 27, 1801, "Jealous Wife (good) + Maid of the Oaks (Poor)." Among the paintings and prints he purchased were "Portrait of a Man Clean[in]g Fish" by "Brekelenkamp," a "fruit piece" by Van Pool, William Birch's series of "20 Prints coloured of views in Philad=," an engraving of Washington, a "Picture of Penn's Treaty," and a portrait of Jefferson, the last two probably also prints. On June 19, 1800, he "pd Mr. Birch for painting my family [coat of] arms," and on October 16 he paid Henry Reynolds for "framing a Coat of Arms." On July 3, 1800, he recorded a payment of 7/6 for "Seeing Museum &c" and visited a wax works on February 20, 1801. Of singular interest is his payment on July 27, 1805, to "Samuel Lewis for a print [crossed out] representation of different objects with the Pen." Lewis was a Philadelphia writing instructor and cartographer. A known example of his work in trompe l'oeil, or "deception," as it was then termed, is an ink-and-graphite drawing of a board on which envelopes, letters, and other papers are held in place by two colored ribbons.[10] Among the papers depicted in this work is a printed paper wrapper from Penington's sugar refinery (fig. 133), a possible allusion to Penington's patronage.

Penington's purchase of Lewis's work coincided with his early support of the Pennsylvania Academy of the Fine Arts, founded in 1805. He noted in his daybook on July 23, 1805, "paid Dr. Glentworth for my Subscription to the Academy of Fine Arts 11/5." He served on the academy's board of directors beginning in 1807 and was engaged in 1810 in attempts to foster the cooperation of the academy with the short-lived Society of Artists of the United States.[11] Philadelphia artist Charles Robert Leslie cited Penington as one of the patrons of his early work at this time, enabling him to go to England in 1811 to study painting.[12] He was also a member of the American Philosophical Society, as was his father, his brother Dr. John Penington, and his brother-in-law Dr. Benjamin Smith Barton. He was a subscriber to the Library Company and belonged to a musical group called the Harmonic Society.[13] While serving on the managing board of the Pennsylvania Hospital, he assisted in the functions of the hospital library and in the restoration of the pedestal of a statue of William Penn.[14] He also assembled a personal library of "some 6000 Volumes in the Different Departments of Literature and Sciences."[15] Edward and Helena Penington had six sons, two of whom, John and Henry Penington, continued his literary interests, John as an author and book dealer, and Henry, a lawyer, as editor of a law dictionary.[16]

EGM

University Press, 1983–), vol. 2, pp. 1006–8; Robert Wilson Torchia with Deborah Chotner and Ellen G. Miles, *American Paintings of the Nineteenth Century*, pt. 2 (Washington, D.C.: National Gallery of Art, 1998), pp. 52–54, Rembrandt Peale, *Rubens Peale with a Geranium*, 1801.

7. For a history of the Penington family, see John W. Jordan, ed., *Colonial Families of Philadelphia* (New York: Lewis Publishing Co., 1911), vol. 2, pp. 579.

8. On Edward Penington (1726–1796), see Jordan, *Colonial Families*, vol. 2, pp. 577–79; *ANB*, vol. 17, pp. 288–89.

9. "Edward Penington's Day Book, 1799–1806."

10. See William H. Gerdts, "A Deception Unmasked: An Artist Uncovered," *American Art Journal* 18, no. 2 (1986), pp. 4–23; this example of Lewis's work was owned by members of the Peale family.

11. "Minutes of the Proceedings of the President & Directors of the Pennsylvania Academy of the Fine Arts," p. 30, August 20, 1810, Archives, Pennsylvania Academy of the Fine Arts, Philadelphia; microfilm, Archives of American Art, Smithsonian Institution, Washington, D.C. For the founding of the artists' society, see "Minutes of the Board of Fellows of the Society of Artists of the United States Established at Philadelphia. 1810," Archives of the Pennsylvania Academy of the Fine Arts; microfilm, Archives of American Art.

12. Dunlap 1834, vol. 1, pp. 241–42.

13. "Penington's Day Book"; he paid "15." (pounds, presumably) annual dues to the Library Company on May 5, 1800, and joined the Harmonic Society on January 25, 1803.

14. Thomas G. Morton, *The History of the Pennsylvania Hospital, 1751–1895* (1895; reprint, New York: Arno Press, 1973), pp. 334, 353, 405–7.

15. S. Austin Allibone, *A Critical Dictionary of English Literature and British and American Authors* (Phila-

delphia: J. B. Lippincott Co., 1888), vol. 2, p. 1549.

16. Jordan, *Colonial Families*, vol. 2, p. 579; *Appleton's Cyclopaedia of American Biography*, ed. James Grant Wilson and John Fiske, rev. ed. (New York: D. Appleton and Co., 1898–1900), vol. 4, pp. 710–11.

64. ANN PENINGTON

1805

Oil on canvas, 29 x 23¹/₂ inches (73.7 x 59.7 cm)
Signed and dated lower left: G. Stuart
Bordentown 1805
*Philadelphia Society for the Preservation of
Landmarks, The Powel House; Bequest of Miss
Frances Wister*

Christopher H. Jones contributed to the research
and writing of this entry.
1. On the portrait, see Mason 1879, p. 237; Charles
   Henry Hart, "Gilbert Stuart's Portraits of Women:
   Nancy Penington," *Century Illustrated Monthly
   Magazine* 56 (August 1898), pp. 544–45; Park, 1926,
   p. 581, no. 620; Washington, Providence 1967, p. 88,
   no. 38.
2. Hart, "Stuart's Portraits of Women: Nancy
   Penington," p. 544.
3. Anne Verplanck, Curator of Prints and Paintings,
   Henry Francis du Pont Winterthur Museum,
   Winterthur, Del., has indicated that this silhou-
   ette is very similar to those made at Peale's muse-
   um. On the museum silhouettes, see especially
   Lillian B. Miller, ed., *The Selected Papers of Charles
   Willson Peale and His Family* (New Haven: Yale
   University Press, 1983–), vol. 2, pp. 475–85.
4. Anne Verplanck discusses the Quaker preference
   for silhouettes in *Facing Philadelphia: the Social
   Function of Silhouettes, Miniatures, and
   Daguerreotypes, 1760–1860* (Ph.D. diss., College of
   William and Mary, 1996; Ann Arbor: UMI
   Microform, 1997), chap. 2, pp. 66–117.
5. Washington, Providence 1967, p. 88.
6. "Edward Penington's Day Book, 1799–1806,"
   unpaginated, Edward Carey Gardiner Collection,
   Ms. 227A, Historical Society of Pennsylvania,
   Philadelphia. Theater visits in 1803 are noted in
   the entries dated February 17, March 10, and
   March 21; and on March 26, 1803, he noted a
   theater visit when he included "2 nieces" among
   his companions.
7. Hart ("Stuart's Portraits of Women: Nancy
   Penington," p. 544) described her grave marker in
   Bordentown: "In memory of Ann Penington,
   daughter of Isaac and Sarah Penington, who
   departed this life October 28th 1806, in the 22nd
   year of her age."

Stuart painted this portrait of twenty-year-old Quaker Ann Penington (1784/85–1806) in New Jersey, adding one of his rare inscriptions in the lower left of the canvas.[1] Stuart painted the portrait while visiting his wife and children, who lived in Bordentown, New Jersey, during the years 1803–5, when he worked in Washington, D.C. He was probably on his way to Boston at this time. The portrait is one of his most striking images of a beautiful young woman, made the more evocative by the fact that she died the following year of consumption. Ann, wearing a black velvet dress with a low bodice, is seated in a gilded armchair with red upholstery. Her auburn hair is arranged in ringlets at the back of her head. She looks directly at the viewer. In the background, seen through the window on the left, is a river with cliffs and trees, and a blue sky with pink and gray clouds. Art historian Charles Henry Hart, the source of much of the information about this painting, described Stuart's landscape background as a view of the banks of the Delaware River.[2]

Ann holds a silhouette framed in a gold case, which she wears around her neck on a long gold chain. The silhouette has stylistic features characteristic of those made with the physiognotrace in Charles Willson Peale's Philadelphia museum, including the depiction of the wisps of hair and the shape of the silhouette's lower edge, which often is a formal signature of the cutter.[3] Stuart painted at least three other portraits of women wearing small portraits as jewelry. Matilda de Jaudenes wears a miniature in her portrait (cat. 33). Sally McKean Yrujo wears a painted miniature, probably of her father, on a chain similar to Ann Penington's (cat. 65). And Sarah Shippen Lea wears a miniature of her son Robert, pinned over her heart and also attached to a chain (fig. 134); that miniature is a reduced image of a portrait by Adolph Ulrich Wertmüller. Ann Penington's miniature differs in the choice of a silhouette, often preferred by Quakers.[4] Recently it has been suggested that the framed silhouette could represent Ann's half sister, Elizabeth Harvey, her mother Sarah Penington's daughter from her earlier marriage to Thomas Harvey; Elizabeth married John Wister in 1798.[5] However, the profile itself appears to be that of an older woman with a double chin, and possibly wearing a cap, and is more likely to be an image of Ann's mother.

Ann, or Nancy, as she was known, was the daughter of Sarah and Isaac Penington, who lived in the township of Chesterfield, Burlington County, New Jersey. Her father and his brother Edward Penington (see cat. 63) were partners in a sugar refinery in Philadelphia that was founded by her grandfather Edward, a prominent Quaker merchant. Glimpses of her life are found in her uncle Edward Penington's record of theater visits in Philadelphia. "Nancy P" went to the theater with her uncle Edward at least once in 1801 and in 1802, and in 1803 she joined her uncle's theater parties several times. On February 16 she attended the theater with her uncle, "Aunt Sally," and "S. P. Nesbit" (Sarah Penington Nesbit, her cousin), when they saw "Dramatist & Children in Wood." She went again on March 9 with her uncle and cousin Sarah, to see "Busy Body & Bernards Benefit." On March 19 with "S.P.N." and a "Miss Watmough," they saw "School for Scandal & Blue Beard."[6] The idea that Stuart would paint her portrait could have arisen on these visits with Edward Penington, for he had recently paid for his own portrait by Stuart and would soon pay for his wife's. However, Ann's father, Isaac Penington, died on April 28, which could have led to a postponement.

Ann's illness would have increased the urgency. She died of consumption (pulmonary tuberculosis) on October 28, 1806, "in the 22nd year of her age."[7] In her will

8. Ann Penington's will, originally filed in the Surrogate's Office, Burlington County, N.J., is now at the New Jersey State Archives, Trenton; it is available on microfilm at the Historical Society of Pennsylvania. Her will is helpful in identifying family members and relatives.

9. The family's sad history is found in the inscriptions transcribed from the gravestones in the "Hopkinson Burying-ground," Bordentown, N.J.; a son, William Penington, died in 1797. See Charles Henry Hart, "Notes and Queries: Penington," *Pennsylvania Magazine of History and Biography* 21 (January 1898), pp. 504–5.

10. Sarah Penington's will, originally filed in the Surrogate's Office, Burlington County, N.J., is now at the New Jersey State Archives, Trenton; it is available on microfilm at the Historical Society of Pennsylvania. Saint-Mémin's portrait, dated 1802, is listed in Ellen G. Miles, *Saint-Mémin and the Neoclassical Profile Portrait in America* (Washington, D.C.: National Portrait Gallery, Smithsonian Institution Press, 1994), p. 369, no. 647.

11. William Rotch Wister, letter to George Champlin Mason, July 9, 1878, George Champlin Mason Papers, Rhode Island Historical Society, Providence; transcribed by Laura Mills.

Fig. 134. *Sarah Shippen Lea*, ca. 1798. Oil on canvas, 29⅛ x 24 in. (74 x 60.9 cm). The Corcoran Gallery of Art, Washington, D.C.; Anonymous gift (1979.77)

dated October 24, 1806, Ann designated her mother as the principal beneficiary of her estate, after certain specific cash bequests were paid. She also specified that on her mother's death, "the whole of the residue of my estate real and personal" would go to "my Sister Elizabeth Wister, my Uncle Edward Pennington and my Aunt Mary Barton," and their heirs.[8] Ann's mother died the following January (1807), leaving no descendants.[9] She also left her estate to Elizabeth Wister, after making specific bequests, including, to Edward Penington, a portrait of her husband, Isaac, which was probably the drawing made by Charles Balthazar Julien Févret de Saint-Mémin.[10] Neither will mentions Stuart's portrait. The idea that it was painted for Elizabeth Wister seems to have developed among her descendants, to personalize the bequest. Elizabeth Wister's grandson stated in 1878 that "the picture was no doubt painted for Miss P. for the purpose of presentation to my Gdmother [grandmother]," and that it was said in the family to have been "an excellent likeness."[11] However, without documentation for the sittings or record of payment for the portrait, its early history remains unknown, except for the inscription, *G. Stuart Bordentown 1805.*

EGM

64

Stuart in Washington (1803–5)

1. Anna Maria Thornton, letter to Dolley Madison, August 24, 1802, in David B. Mattern and Holly C. Shulman, eds., *The Selected Letters of Dolley Payne Madison* (Charlottesville: University of Virginia Press, 2003), pp. 50–51.

2. On Stuart in Washington, see Mount 1971–72, and a brief overview in Evans 1999, pp. 90–91, 150 nn. 1, 2.

3. The studio is described in John C. Van Horne and Lee W. Formwalt, eds., *The Correspondence and Miscellaneous Papers of Benjamin Henry Latrobe* (New Haven: Yale University Press for the Maryland Historical Society, 1984–88), vol. 1, p. 327 n. 4, as on lot 15, which faced C street, in the middle of the block, according to the diagram in *Maps of the District of Columbia and City of Washington, and Plats of the Squares and Lots of the City of Washington* (Washington, D.C.: A. Boyd Hamilton, 1852), p. 75. Kyra Swanson researched Latrobe's relationship with Stuart, especially the studio he built for the artist; Sarah Efird Stephens searched for a map that would locate the studio. There are no known images of the studio.

4. Latrobe, letter to John Lenthall, September 26, 1803, in *Correspondence and Miscellaneous Papers of Latrobe*, vol. 1, p. 326. The text may have read "frames"; the document as reproduced in the fiche edition appears to have a loss in the paper; see *The Papers of Benjamin Henry Latrobe*, microtext ed. (Clifton, N.J.: James T. White and Co. for the Maryland Historical Society, 1976), fiche 170/G1.

5. Latrobe, letter to John Lenthall, December 13, 1803, in *Papers of Latrobe*, fiche 170/G1.

6. Anna Maria Thornton, diary, entry for December 7, 1803, Papers of Anna Maria Brodeau Thornton, Manuscript Division, Library of Congress, Washington, D.C.; for some of her notations, especially about her portrait and that of William Thornton by Stuart, painted in 1804, see Miles 1995, pp. 240–46.

7. For the portrait of John Randolph, see Miles 1995, pp. 249–53. On the portrait of Fenwick, see *Selections from the Collection of the Carolina Art Association* (Charleston, S.C.: Carolina Art Association, 1977), p. 84.

Detail of cat. 68, *Elizabeth Patterson Bonaparte*

Stuart first considered moving to Washington in 1802, as Anna Maria Thornton, wife of William Thornton, mentioned in a letter to Dolley Madison that August: "We have been gratified by seeing the celebrated Stewart, he came down with Mr Thornton and was here every day while he staid, he was in search of a house and talks of coming this winter with his family—I hope he may, I shall then hope to get some good pictures to copy after."[1] When he made the move in December of the following year, he went without his family, who instead settled on a farm in Bordentown, New Jersey.[2] Before his arrival, his friend Benjamin Latrobe, surveyor of public buildings in Washington, designed a one-story structure for Stuart that consisted of two rooms, one for exhibiting portraits and one for painting. The studio was a block north of Pennsylvania Avenue on C Street NW, between Four and a Half and Sixth Streets, on square 491.[3] Latrobe's letter of September 26, 1803, to John Lenthall, clerk of the works at the Capitol, who was constructing the studio, provides the only description of the rooms: "There should be a simple washboard in both Mr. Stuart's rooms. You may look into your tool Chest for the design. It is I think necessary, to keep the Picture frame from hurting the Wall. As to the battening I think both the Shew room and painting room will want it on the North, and East sides: For we all know how injurious damp is to pictures. On the North no battening would be wanted below the Shed roof were it not for the projection of plaistering which it will occasion."[4] On December 13, Latrobe alerted Lenthall that Stuart "has departed for Washington. . . . [Y]ou will see one of the greatest, if not the most pleasing, originals in the United States."[5] Mrs. Thornton had already recorded his arrival on December 7 and would record his visits with the Thorntons and their visits to his studio while he was in Washington.[6]

Stuart's portrait practice in Washington was an extension of his experience in Philadelphia. His sitters were similar. Some people were involved with the federal government or were in the city because it was the capital, including President Thomas Jefferson (cats. 77–79), Secretary of State James Madison, Dolley Madison, her sister and brother-in-law Anna Payne Cutts and Richard Cutts (cats. 69–71, fig. 146), Congressman John Randolph of Roanoke, Virginia (National Gallery of Art, Washington), and Lieutenant John Roger Fenwick of the United States Marines (fig. 141).[7] Europeans included diplomats Edward Thornton and the Yrujos (cats. 65, 66), Irish merchant James Barry and his family (figs. 147, 149, 150), and Jerome Bonaparte (cat. 67), while local residents included the Van Nesses (cats. 74, 75), the Tayloes, and members of the Custis and

8. Anna Maria Thornton noted in her diary on March 5, 1804, "I went from Stewart's room with Mrs. Morton & Miss Spear to the [House of] Representatives." On March 6, she went to the Senate with Mrs. Morton.

9. Anna Maria Thornton, diary, entry for June 14, 1804; see Miles 1995, p. 241.

10. Rosalie Stier Calvert, letter to her mother, Mme Henri Joseph Stier, March 1804, in Margaret Law Callcott, ed., *Mistress of Riversdale: The Plantation Letters of Rosalie Stier Calvert* (Baltimore, London: Johns Hopkins University Press, 1991), p. 80.

11. Rosalie Stier Calvert, letter to her mother, May 12, 1804, in *Mistress of Riversdale*, p. 83.

12. Transcription of an unlocated original letter to Anna Payne Cutts, May 7, 1804, Cutts Family Collection of Papers of James and Dolley Madison, microfilm 14326, Manuscript Division, Library of Congress. The transcriber attributed the letter to "a friend of Mrs Cutts," who may in fact have been Dolley Madison herself.

13. The quotation comes from Stuart's legal petition in 1802 to the United States Circuit Court for the District of Eastern Pennsylvania regarding copies made in China of his Athenaeum portrait of George Washington, in which he explained that copies were a source of income for himself and his family; see Richardson 1970. Evans (1999, p. 90) points out that this new plan of Stuart's was "an extension of his experience with the Athenaeum likeness."

14. Lillian B. Miller, ed., *The Selected Papers of Charles Willson Peale and His Family* (New Haven: Yale University Press, 1983–), vol. 2, p. 693.

15. Diary entry, undated, *Selected Papers of Charles Willson Peale and His Family*, vol. 2, p. 698. On the portrait of Priestley, see Park 1926, p. 612, no. 680, as painted in England; and *Correspondence and*

Washington families, including Eleanor Parke Custis Lewis and her half-sister Ann Calvert Robinson, as well as Maryland residents Elizabeth Patterson Bonaparte, Elizabeth Beltzhoover Mason, and John Carroll, Bishop of Baltimore (cats. 68, 72, 73). Also in Washington were several sitters from Philadelphia, including Eleanor Lewis's sister Elizabeth Law (cat. 50), her husband, Thomas Law (fig. 115), and Stuart's admirer Sarah Morton (cat. 60), who visited his studio on March 5, 1804, when she came to the city with her husband, Perez Morton.[8]

In Washington, Stuart painted about forty portraits in eighteen months, mainly of the 30-by-25-inch, waist-length size. The portraits show quick completion, with less elaborate brushwork than the Philadelphia pictures, no doubt because Stuart had little assistance, if any, and prepared his own materials, including "grinding colors," as Mrs. Thornton noted in her diary.[9] At the same time, Stuart maintained his ability to capture likeness and personality, varying these small portraits considerably. Stuart seems to have been busiest in the first six months of 1804. Rosalie Stier Calvert (fig. 135), the Belgian wife of landowner and state legislator George Calvert of Riversdale, Maryland, described him in March: "The painter Stuart—whose paintings Charles [her brother Charles Jean Stier] admired so much—is in Washington, and I think he has improved. That is to say, he has changed his manner, which was very rude, and has settled down somewhat. He finishes [his paintings] quickly and has a lot of work."[10] She visited his studio in May with her daughter Caroline and reported that he "has a fine collection of portraits."[11] A contemporary described him at this time as "all the rage, he is almost worked to death, and everybody afraid that they will be the last to be finished."[12]

Stuart was apparently planning to exhibit "portraits of great and eminent personages" in his studio and sell copies.[13] He took at least one replica of the Athenaeum portrait of George Washington with him (see cat. 42); he may have taken the original Athenaeum portrait as well. About two weeks after his arrival, he accepted half payment for a portrait of Thomas Jefferson, probably a replica (see cat. 77). When he painted a new portrait of Jefferson more than a year later, Stuart kept it with the intention of making an engraving. He also planned to engrave the portraits of Bishop John Carroll (cat. 73) and the English scientist and political theorist Joseph Priestley, a commission for the American Philosophical Society that he had begun in Philadelphia. After Charles Willson Peale visited Stuart in his studio in early June 1804, he noted in his diary that Priestley's portrait was "very like though quite an unfinished picture, and it is very doubtful when it will be compleated as Mr. Steuart is seldom in a hurry to finish his pictures."[14] Peale, Thornton, and Latrobe all tried to persuade Stuart to finish the portrait and have it engraved. When Peale visited Stuart's studio again a few days later, he noted that Stuart wished to "have a Print made by [David] Edwin from it & had stipulated to give the Society their choise of purchasing a print for each resident member and such a number as they might want to present to the societies in Europe with whom our Society hold Correspondence & that after this the plate to be the property of Edwin & himself to make what profit they would with the sale to Strangers."[15] However, once finished, the portrait was not delivered to the society and instead became the property of T. B. Barclay of Liverpool, a relative of Priestley.

Papers of Latrobe, vol. 2, p. 27 n. 3 It is illustrated in Mount 1971–72, p. 103.

16. On the portrait, described as "painted by Stuart this past summer," see Rosalie Stier Calvert's letter to her father, H. J. Stier, May 19, 1805, in *Mistress of Riversdale*, p. 119; George Calvert later reported that Stuart had spent two weeks at Riversdale when painting their portraits. As an uncle of Martha Washington's Custis grandchildren, Calvert often entertained members of the late president's family.

17. For Stier's list of his paintings, see *Mistress of Riversdale*, appendix, pp. 395–97.

18. Charles Willson Peale, letter to Angelica Peale, August 2, 1807, in *Selected Papers of Charles Willson Peale and His Family*, vol. 2, p. 1025.

19. See *Correspondence and Miscellaneous Papers of Latrobe*, vol. 2 (1805–10), p. 26; and Latrobe's letters to John P. Van Ness and William Duncanson, September 13, 1804, reproduced from Latrobe's letterbooks in *Papers of Latrobe*, fiche 35/C3, 35/C4.

20. The portraits are listed in Park 1926, pp. 506–7, no. 526 (dated to Washington, 1804), and p. 671, no. 741 ("Mrs. David Sears," dated to Boston, 1806).

21. For these portraits, see Park 1926, pp. 512–13, nos. 532, 533, where they are dated "Washington, 1805."

22. *Selected Papers of Charles Willson Peale and His Family*, vol. 2, p. 785.

23. On the portrait, see ibid., pp. 785–86, 795, 797. Peale began the portrait on January 30 and finished it a few days later.

24. Rembrandt Peale, letter to Stuart, March 24, 1806, ibid., pp. 949.

25. Latrobe, letter to John Vaughan, March 12, 1805, in *Correspondence and Miscellaneous Papers of Latrobe*, vol. 2, pp. 24–25.

That summer Stuart painted George Calvert and a double portrait of his wife, Rosalie, and their daughter Caroline (fig. 135) at their home, Riversdale.[16] Probably this was the occasion when Stuart saw some of the European paintings owned by Mrs. Calvert's father, Henri Joseph Stier, who had brought his collection of Flemish, Dutch, and Italian pictures to America when he fled the French invasion of Belgium in 1794. The collection of sixty-three paintings included works by Anthony van Dyck and Peter Paul Rubens.[17] According to Charles Willson Peale, "one Box only was allowed to be opened, to see the state of them & repacked by Mr. Stewart."[18] By September 1804, Stuart was delinquent in the rent he owed Latrobe, who in turn owed the money to John Peter Van Ness (see cat. 75), owner of the property.[19] He presumably continued to paint, although no portraits are firmly documented to the fall of 1804. At Christmastime he painted portraits of Anna Powell Mason (fig. 136) and Miriam Clark Mason, daughters of Massachusetts Senator Jonathan Mason, who paid Stuart $200 for the portraits, which he described in his diary as "perfect likenesses."[20] He probably also painted Senator Mason and his wife, Susannah Powell Mason (fig. 137), at this time.[21] On January 11, 1805, Charles Willson Peale visited Stuart again, with his son Rembrandt Peale, and they "were amused with him & his painting all the morning."[22] Peale painted a portrait of Stuart at this time (fig. 1).[23] Rembrandt Peale later wrote to Stuart in Boston, thanking him for conversations in which Stuart had "freely explained to me some of the principles of the Art, which have assisted me much."[24]

Stuart's lessened productivity was apparently a result of illness. He had suffered from malaria the previous summer, and the return of the illness in the early spring of 1805 was a great concern to Latrobe, who wrote John Vaughan (see fig. 80) on March 12:

Stuart however is in a deplorable condition. All last Summer he had a violent Ague and fever. This now returned upon him, and he cannot paint at present. I fear indeed that he will lay his bones at Washington, and it seems of the highest importance that some of his family should attend him. He is miserably off, though his life and his residence are of his own choice. He has one Man Servant, who does exactly as he pleases, and is seldom with him. He has shut himself up in a little building never intended for an habitation but only for a painting room; where he boards himself, after a fashion, with the assistance of his Manservant, when he can get him to the place, and where he sleeps. The house is remarkably comfortable and warm, but in the present state of the drainage of the city the situation must be unhealthy in warm weather. I could do nothing with him not even get him to paint my own portrait, which, if he ever paints it, will cost me 1.000 Dollars, and more. He had resolved when I last saw him to finish the pictures he had on hand, which he thought he could do in six weeks, begin no new ones, and move off to the Northward. But should he continue sick there will be an end of all his exertions, and I think he runs a great risk of dying for want of good nursing where he is. I shall write to him, but he is a Man that answers no letters. Thank heaven, at least my family ought to thank heaven, that I have no Genius, if this is the orbit in which Genius must move. And indeed it generally is so.[25]

Latrobe wrote Stuart the next day about plans to make a new engraving of a portrait of George Washington. He joked about Heath's engraving of the Lansdowne, referring to the misattribution on the engraving to "Gabriel" Stuart

Fig. 135. *Rosalie Stier Calvert and Her Daughter*, 1804. Oil on canvas, 29 x 23½ in. (73.7 x 59.7 cm). The Maryland Historical Society, Baltimore (1991.58.2)

Fig. 136. *Anna Powell Mason*, 1804. Oil on canvas, 32⅝ x 26¾ in. (82.9 x 67.9 cm). Private collection

Fig. 137. *Susannah Powell Mason*, 1805. Oil on wood, 28¾ x 23½ in. (73 x 59.7 cm). Collection of Erving and Joyce Wolf

26. Latrobe, letter to Stuart, March 13, 1805, ibid., pp. 26–27.

27. Merry's note, with payment for $200, which probably also included payment for his portrait, is recorded in Park 1926, p. 523, no. 548; Merry's portrait is listed in Park 1926, p. 522, no. 547.

28. Latrobe, letter to Charles Willson Peale, July 17, 1808, in *Correspondence and Miscellaneous Papers of Latrobe*, vol. 2, pp. 105. Latrobe complained to John Randolph, letter of April 13, 1808, that Stuart, "the greatest painter we have seen, was a profligate spendrift"; ibid., p. 592

29. Latrobe, letter to Jefferson, May 19, 1811, in *Correspondence and Miscellaneous Papers of Latrobe*, vol. 3, p. 92; for the context and Latrobe's address to the society, see pp. 65–91.

30. *Correspondence and Miscellaneous Papers of Latrobe*, vol. 3, p. 93 n. 10; see also *The Annual Exhibition Record of the Pennsylvania Academy of the Fine Arts, 1807–1870* (Madison, Conn.: Sound View Press, 1988), p. 217.

(see cat. 45) and advised, "Let me . . . intreat you to leave that sink of your health, your Genius, and your interests, Washington. I often am angry with you for having staid so long. Get into the packet at Georgetown if you cannot bear a carriage, get any where, but get away. . . . God bless You and give you resolution to start off to a climate more healthy and less tainted with fraud, speculation, marsh miasmata, and the insolence of clerkships."[26]

Stuart left Washington in July 1805, after he was paid for his portrait of Elizabeth Merry (Museo Lázaro Galdiano, Madrid), wife of the British envoy Anthony Merry, on July 3. Merry complimented the artist for exerting "his known talents with so much success."[27] Stuart stopped in New Jersey to see his family and to paint Ann Penington's portrait (cat. 64), then went to Boston. Latrobe was bitter that Stuart left without paying the rent due on the studio. When he wrote Charles Willson Peale on July 17 about the new Pennsylvania Academy of the Fine Arts, he added, "That greatest of our Artists, and most unprincipled of our Citizens (by the bye he is no American citizen) Stuart, is not I suppose of your number, and his absence is no loss, I believe."[28] In May 1811, on the occasion of the First Annual Exhibition of the Society of Artists in Philadelphia, Latrobe wrote Thomas Jefferson, "Stuart has sent nothing. This admirable painter and worthless man is, I am told, at last making money at Boston. There are some of his old pictures in the exhibition."[29] One of these was a portrait of "Washington, whole length (1796)," no doubt the version of the Lansdowne Washington that had recently been transferred to the Pennsylvania Academy of the Fine Arts from William Bingham's estate (see cat. 46).[30]

EGM

65. SARAH McKEAN, MARQUESA DE CASA YRUJO

1804
Oil on canvas, 29½ x 24½ in. (74.9 x 62.2 cm)
Collection of Mr. and Mrs. Thomas R. McKean

66. DON CARLOS MARÍA MARTÍNEZ DE YRUJO Y TACÓN, MARQUÉS DE CASA YRUJO

1804
Oil on canvas, 29½ x 24½ in. (74.9 x 62.2 cm)
Collection of Mr. and Mrs. Thomas R. McKean

The research and first drafts for this entry are by Christopher H. Jones.

1. Anna Maria Brodeau Thornton, diary, January 30, 1804, Anna Maria Brodeau Thornton Papers, Manuscript Division, Library of Congress, Washington, D.C. Edward Thornton was the British chargé d'affairs at this time; see David B. Mattern and Holly C. Shulman, eds., *The Selected Letters of Dolley Payne Madison* (Charlottesville: University of Virginia Press, 2003), p. 43.

2. Lillian B. Miller, ed., *The Selected Papers of Charles Willson Peale and His Family* (New Haven, London: Yale University Press, 1983–), vol. 2, p. 693.

3. Robert Werlich, *Orders and Decorations of All Nations: Ancient and Modern, Civil and Military*, 2nd ed. (Washington, D.C.: Quaker Press, 1974), pp. 392–93; Roberdeau Buchanan, *Genealogy of the McKean Family of Pennsylvania* (Lancaster, Pa.: Inquirer Printing Co., 1890), p. 137. It has not been possible to determine when he was awarded the knighthood. He was referred to as "Chevalier" and signed letters with this title as early as 1797.

4. Mason 1879, pp. 177–78; Park 1926, pp. 300–302, nos. 264, 267; Mount 1971–72, pp. 94, 96, 125. The portraits are listed in the inventory of the estate of Sarah McKean, 1820, Thomas McKean Papers, Ms. 405, Historical Society of Pennsylvania, Philadelphia, as "2 Paintings of the Marquis & Marchio⁵ de Yrujo" valued at $20. Stuart also painted Thomas McKean; see Park 1926, p. 516, no. 538.

5. On this pair of portraits, see Park 1926, pp. 301 no. 265, 303 no. 268; Charles Henry Hart, "A Spanish Opponent of the Louisiana Purchase: Chevalier d'Yrujo," *Century Magazine* 64 (1902)," p. 109; William C. Bendig, "Spain's Unknown Stuarts," *Art Gallery* 19 (June–July 1976), pp. 80, 101. A third pair of paintings is in the collection the Duke of Sotomayor's uncle, the marqués de la Romana, Madrid; see Park 1926, pp. 301 no. 266, 303 no. 269; Bendig, "Spain's Unknown Stuarts," p. 101. Hart ("Spanish Opponent of the Louisiana Purchase," p. 109) wrote that "each is a different and original portrait."

6. J. Thomas Scharf and Thompson Westcott, *History of Philadelphia, 1609–1884* (Philadelphia:

The portrait of Don Carlos Martínez de Yrujo y Tacón (1763–1824) was one of the first that Stuart painted in Washington. On January 30, 1804, Anna Maria Thornton, wife of architect William Thornton, noted in her diary: "Mr. Stuart came in the Carriage with Dr. T. brought his pictures of Mr Eᴰ Thornton & the Marquis Yrujo."[1] The pendant portrait of Sarah McKean, marquesa de Casa Yrujo (1777–1841), called Sally, was finished by June 1804, when Charles Willson Peale saw the paintings at Stuart's studio: "This morning in Viewing Mr. Gabrial Stewerts Paintings, amongst them was a very excellant portrait of the Marquis Casa de Eyrugo (minister of Spain) and his Lady, the latter was a very handsome picture but not so strikingly like as that of the Marquis."[2] In his portrait, Yrujo, a Knight Grand Cross of the Order of Charles III, wears the badge of the order, an "eight-pointed gold-rimmed blue and white enamelled cross . . . suspended from a gold laurel wreath," on a blue-and-white striped ribbon.[3] He was created marqués de Casa Yrujo in 1803, the year before the portrait was painted. Sally Yrujo is depicted in a white dress with bodice and sleeves trimmed with pearls, and she wears a necklace of two strands of pearls. Seated in an armchair, she holds a fan.

This pair of portraits, showing Sally Yrujo on the left and her husband on the right, remained with her parents and their descendants in the United States.[4] Another pair of portraits, distinctly different and with the figures reversed, was taken to Spain, probably in 1808, when the sitters left the United States (figs. 138, 139).[5] That the present pair (cats. 65, 66) was painted in Washington can be suggested by the style of Yrujo's coat, which is slightly later than the style of the coat in the other portrait, and by the close similarity of the portrait of Sally Yrujo to other portraits of women that Stuart painted in Washington. It has the same compositional simplicity as his portraits of Dolley Madison (cat. 70) and Mrs. Thornton (fig. 145), painted in Washington in the spring of 1804, and is virtually identical to that of Elizabeth Mason (cat. 72), also painted about this time.

By contrast, the earlier portraits of the Yrujos, in their more elaborate depiction of clothing and background, are consistent with Stuart's work in Philadelphia. In that pair, Sally Yrujo wears a similar white dress with a more elaborate ruffle, and her hair, which is more intricately fashioned, is decorated with a red rose, perhaps in a Spanish fashion. She wears a miniature, probably of her father, on a gold chain, an adornment seen also in Stuart's portraits of Mrs. Thomas Lea (fig. 134) and Ann Penington (cat. 64). Yrujo, seated and turning his head to the side, with his left elbow resting on the curved arm of the chair, resembles the description of his appearance at John Adams's inauguration in 1797: "of middle size, of round person, florid complexion, and hair powdered like a snow-ball."[6] Evidence of the possible date of the earlier paintings' execution is a letter from Sally Yrujo to Stuart, December 4, 1801, in Philadelphia: "Madame d'Yrujo presents her respects to Mr. Stewart & informs him, she is very sorry it will not be in her

65

66

Fig. 138. *Don Carlos María Martínez de Yrujo y Tacón, Marqués de Casa Yrujo*, ca. 1801. Oil on canvas, 30¾ x 31⅞ in. (78.1 x 81 cm). Collection of the Duke of Sotomayor, Spain

Fig. 139. *Sarah McKean, Marquesa de Casa Yrujo*, ca. 1801. Oil on wood, 30¾ x 31⅞ in. (78.1 x 81 cm). Collection of the Duke of Sotomayor, Spain

L. H. Everts and Co. 1884), vol. 2, p. 913, quoting William McKoy, who is not further identified; this is also quoted in Hart, "Spanish Opponent of the Louisiana Purchase," p. 109.

7. Sally McKean Yrujo, letter to "Mr. Stewart, Front Street," December 4, 1801, Society Collection, Historical Society of Pennsylvania.

8. Hart, "Spanish Opponent of the Louisiana Purchase," p. 109; Buchanan, *Genealogy of the McKean Family*, pp. 133–39; *Enciclopedia universal ilustrada europeo-americana* (Madrid: Espasa-Calpe, 1931), vol. 12, p. 13; Victor Herrero Mediavilla, ed., *Archivo biográfico de España, Portugal e Ibero-américa, 1960–1995* (Munich: K. G. Saur, 1998), microform, frame 238.

9. G. S. Rowe, *Thomas McKean: The Shaping of an American Republicanism* (Boulder: Colorado Associated University Press, 1978), pp. 295–300; Buchanan, *Genealogy of the McKean Family*, pp. 133–39. In a letter dated August 3, 1797, to Dolley Madison, Sally McKean refers to Yrujo as "our amiable friend the Chevalier"; David B. Mattern et al., eds., *The Papers of James Madison*, vol. 17 (Charlottesville: University Press of Virginia, 1991), pp. 37–38.

10. Anne Hollingsworth Wharton, *Salons Colonial and Republican* (Philadelphia: J. B. Lippincott, 1900), p. 154, quoting an unidentified witness; this story is also quoted by Buchanan (*Genealogy of the McKean Family*, p. 134), who suggests that the dinner was given by George Washington and who cites a letter from George Champlin Mason in the *New York Evening Post*, March 24, 1879, for identification of the guests.

11. Harrison Gray Otis, letter to his wife, Sally Foster Otis, April 10, 1798, Harrison Gray Otis Papers, 1691–1870, Massachusetts Historical Society, Boston (reference and photocopy courtesy of Laura Mills).

12. For letters discussing the presumed end of his appointment and its continuation by Jefferson, see

power to wait on Mr. Stewart to day, as she is sick with a head ache, will be glad to know at what hour it will be convenient for her to wait on him to morrow."[7]

Yrujo arrived in Philadelphia in 1796 as envoy of the king of Spain, Charles IV. He succeeded Josef de Jaudenes y Nebot (see cat. 34), who had represented Spain's interests since 1791.[8] Jaudenes introduced him to Thomas McKean, Pennsylvania's chief justice and later its governor. Two years later, Yrujo married McKean's daughter Sarah.[9] The couple first met at a dinner party in June 1796, at which the guests are said to have included Stuart as well as a number of his future sitters, among them Anne Bingham (cat. 51), her sister Mary Clymer (cat. 52), the comte de Volney (fig. 117), and British ambassador Robert Liston and his wife (both, National Gallery of Art, Washington): "Among the first to arrive was Chief Justice McKean, accompanied by his lovely daughter, Miss Sally McKean. Miss McKean had many admirers, but her heart was still her own. . . . The next to arrive was Señor Don Carlos Martinez de Yrujo, a stranger to almost all the guests. He spoke with ease, but with a foreign accent, and was soon lost in amazement at the grace and beauty of Miss McKean."[10] Their marriage in 1798 was described by Harrison Gray Otis to his wife: "Yesterday morning at eight o'clock the Spanish Envoy Mr. Yrujo finished & executed his treaty with Miss McKean in the Romish Chapel—The ceremony was performed with due Castilian and diplomatic Gravity, after which the parties went into the country where it is probable, they threw off their Robes of Office, & cemented the new alliance."[11]

Yrujo assumed a high public profile as a combative advocate for Spain's interests and diplomatic prerogatives, using the partisan press and anonymously published pamphlets to advance his positions. His activities, including bitter, personal attacks on his opponents that resulted in a series of libel suits, brought him into conflict with President Adams, who sought his recall.[12] Yrujo lobbied the incoming administration of Thomas Jefferson to support his reappointment and complained to Jefferson's secretary of state, James Madison, regarding his plight, describing his circumstances as moving "like a Gipsie family from place to place" because of the uncertainty of his tenure as minister.[13] His diplomatic mission was extended by Jefferson, who may have been swayed by a letter from Thomas McKean requesting that Yrujo be retained: "I love him as a child

Yrujo, letters to James Madison, March 20 and May 18, 1801, in Robert J. Brugger et al., eds., *The Papers of James Madison: Secretary of State Series*, vol. 1 (Charlottesville: University Press of Virginia, 1986), pp. 31–32, 194–95.

13. Yrujo, letter to James Madison, September 4, 1801, in Mary A. Hackett et al., eds., *The Papers of James Madison: Secretary of State Series*, vol. 2 (Charlottesville: University Press of Virginia, 1993), pp. 84–85.

14. McKean, letter to Thomas Jefferson, March 21, 1801, in Rowe, *Thomas McKean*, p. 321.

15. On this subject, see Yrujo, letters to James Madison, September 4 and 27, and October 12, 1803, in David B. Mattern et al., eds., *The Papers of James Madison: Secretary of State Series*, vol. 5 (Charlottesville: University Press of Virginia, 2000), pp. 378, 464, 513–15.

16. Yrujo, letter to Thomas McKean, November 20, 1803, Thomas McKean Papers, Ms. 405, Historical Society of Pennsylvania.

17. Examples of printed invitations with this title are in the Thomas McKean Papers, Ms. 405, Historical Society of Pennsylvania.

18. Merrill D. Peterson, *Thomas Jefferson and the New Nation* (New York: Oxford University Press, 1970), pp. 730–34.

19. Jefferson, letter to William Short, January 23, 1804, in "Documents: Jefferson to William Short on Mr. and Mrs. Merry, 1804," *American Historical Review* 33 (July 1928), pp. 832.

20. Buchanan, *Genealogy of the McKean Family*, p. 137.

21. Latrobe, letter to Lewis DeMun, August 21, 1808, in John C. Van Horne et al., eds., *The Correspondence and Miscellaneous Papers of Benjamin Henry Latrobe* (New Haven: Yale University Press for the Maryland Historical Society, 1986), p. 649.

22. Henry Adams, *History of the United States during the First Administration of Thomas Jefferson* (1889; reprint, New York: Charles Scribner's Sons, 1931), vol. 1, p. 426.

and never expect to see my daughter again after their departure for Europe."[14] In Washington Yrujo found himself quickly at odds with the new administration over the acquisition of Louisiana and Florida. He was vehemently opposed to the Louisiana Purchase, maintaining that Spain retained rights in the territory and that France could not sell land it did not own.[15] He confided to his father-in-law on November 20, 1803, "I wish Luisiana was at the bottom of the Sea for the good of Spain, of the United States, & of myself," and commenting about the new capital city, "We are all very well altho not reconcil'd yet to the inconveniences of Washington."[16]

In Washington Sally Yrujo counted among her friends Betsy Bonaparte, Dolley Madison, and Mrs. Madison's sister Anna Payne Cutts, all three of whom sat for Stuart (cats. 68, 70, 71). Her marriage, like that of Mrs. Bonaparte's, was one that joined an American woman and a member of European nobility. After her husband was ennobled, she used the title "Marchioness de Casa Yrujo."[17] In addition to their differences over Louisiana, Yrujo feuded with Jefferson, who was determined to dispense with European formality, over the protocol of the entry and the seating of diplomats and their wives at dinners with government officials. Both Yrujo and the British minister Anthony Merry found Jefferson's attitudes and actions insulting.[18] According to Jefferson, the Merrys and the Yrujos "claim at private dinners (for of public dinners we have none) to be first conducted to dinner and placed at the head of the table above all other persons citizens or foreigners, in or out of office. we say to them, no; The principle of society with us, as well as of our political constitution, is the equal rights of all . . . nobody shall be above you, nor you above anybody, pele-mele is our law."[19] By 1805 the accumulated acrimony led Secretary of State Madison to request of Spain's foreign ministry that Yrujo be recalled, which the marqués resisted: "I intend remaining in the city, four miles square, in which the Government resides, as long as it may suit the interests of the King my master, or my own personal convenience."[20] The defiant diplomat returned to Philadelphia, where he stubbornly remained, occasionally attacking Madison in the press, until his departure with his family for Spain in 1808. That voyage entailed some difficulties, which architect Benjamin Latrobe noted in a letter: "Mr. Burr is in England, and so is the Marquis D'Yrujo, he having been captured on his passage to France and carried in. This is, I think, a most fortunate misfortune for the little Marquis, to whom I wish every possible good, as a little cunning accomplished generous intriguer, an employment for which his natural disposition however is somewhat too honest."[21] Historian Henry Adams concluded eight decades later that Yrujo had "needed only the contrast of characters such as those of Pickering or Madison to make him the most entertaining figure in Washington politics."[22]

EGM

67. JEROME BONAPARTE

1804
Oil on canvas, 28¼ x 23½ in. (71.8 x 59.7 cm).
Private collection

Research for and early drafts of this entry are by
Themis Chryssostomides.

1. The portrait is discussed in Mason 1879, p. 146;
   Park 1926, pp. 159–60, no. 90; and John B. Boles,
   ed., *Maryland Heritage: Five Baltimore Institutions
   Celebrate the American Bicentennial* (Baltimore:
   Maryland Historical Society, 1976), p. 93, no. 65.
2. For a brief biographical entry on Jerome
   Bonaparte, see Magnus Magnusson, ed.,
   Cambridge Biographical Dictionary (Cambridge:
   Cambridge University Press, 1990), p. 175.
   Biographical information on this period of Jerome
   Bonaparte's life is detailed in Sidney Mitchell, *A
   Family Lawsuit: The Story of Elisabeth Patterson
   and Jérôme Bonaparte* (New York: Farrar, Straus
   and Cudahy, 1958), pp. 21–68. A short discussion
   of Jerome's marriage is also found in Alan Schom,
   Napoleon Bonaparte (New York: Harper Collins,
   1997; Harper Perennial ed., 1998), pp. 384–88.
3. Quoted in Mitchell, *A Family Lawsuit*, p. 28.
4. This miniature, which belonged to Betsy
   Patterson, is part of a collection of miniatures
   donated to the Maryland Historical Society in

This unfinished portrait of Jerome Bonaparte (1784–1860), the youngest brother of
Napoleon Bonaparte, first consul of France, was painted in Washington in 1804, shortly
after his marriage to Elizabeth Patterson of Baltimore (see cat. 68).[1] A lieutenant in the
French navy on duty in Martinique, Jerome Bonaparte was sent for his own safety to
Norfolk, Virginia, in mid-July 1803, during the Napoleonic Wars, when his commanding officers feared he could be captured at sea by the British.[2] The British admiralty had
circulated a description of Bonaparte, who was traveling under the alias "M. Albert": "20
to 23 years old, slim figure, dark complexion, height 5 feet 6 inches, black hair short and
stiff. He sometimes wears a wig and powder."[3] A miniature painted about this time,
possibly in the Caribbean before he arrived in the United States, shows him in his
French navy uniform (fig. 140).[4]

Bonaparte arrived in Georgetown, District of Columbia, on July 22. He planned to
ask the American government to provide passage to Spain, but by the end of August he
was in Baltimore as a guest of Captain Joshua Barney, a naval hero of the American
Revolution who had served more recently in the French Navy. There, that autumn, he
fell in love with Elizabeth Patterson, known as Betsy. The engagement, according to
Rosalie Stier Calvert (see fig. 135), was opposed by her parents: "Jerome, the great man's
brother, has been here for some time and commands no respect. People insult him at
every opportunity. He was courting Miss Patterson of Baltimore, but her parents refused
to consent to the marriage. The young lady threatened to run away with him, [so] they
gave in. . . . She is a most extraordinary girl, given to reading Godwin on the rights of
women, etc., in short, a modern *philosophe*."[5] The marqués de Yrujo (see cat. 66) served
as Bonaparte's representative in the negotiations with the Pattersons.

French chargé d'affaires Louis-André Pichon opposed the marriage, writing her parents that according to French law Bonaparte needed the consent of his mother, his only

Fig. 140. Unidentified artist,
Jerome Bonaparte, ca. 1800.
Watercolor on ivory, 2⅝ x 1⅞ in.
(6.67 x 4.76 cm). The Maryland
Historical Society, Baltimore;
Gift of Mrs. Charles Joseph
Bonaparte (xx-5-58)

Fig. 141. *John Fenwick*, ca. 1804. Oil on canvas, 29 x 24⅜
in. (73.8 x 61.8 cm). Gibbes Museum of Art/Carolina
Art Association, Charleston (68.27)

67

1922 by the widow of her grandson Charles Joseph Bonaparte; see Elle Shushan, "Amours en miniatures," *Connaissance des Arts*, no. 534 (December 1996), pp. 106–11.

5. Rosalie Stier Calvert, letter to her mother, Mme H. J. Stier, November 1803, in Margaret Law Callcott, ed. and trans., *Mistress of Riversdale: The Plantation Letters of Rosalie Stier Calvert, 1795–1821* (Baltimore: Johns Hopkins University Press, 1991), p. 62.

6. For the legal documents concerning this marriage and subsequent divorce, see especially Mitchell, *A Family Lawsuit*.

living parent, because he was under twenty-five. Despite this, they were married on December 24, 1803, in Baltimore, by Bishop John Carroll (see cat. 73).[6] Early in 1804 the couple visited Washington, D.C., attending private parties at which the marriage and Mme Bonaparte's French fashions caused a stir. John Quincy Adams, who saw them at Pichon's on the evening of January 7, 1804, recorded in his diary: "Pichon is profoundly mortified at the marriage of Jerome. He says it is impossible the First Consul should put up with it—'tis a marriage against many laws, many usages, many opinions, and many prejudices, personal, official, and national, of the First Consul. Jerome is not of age; he is an officer; he is the First Consul's brother. The marriage will undoubtedly be broken."

7. Allan Nevins, ed., *The Diary of John Quincy Adams, 1794–1845: American Political, Social, and Intellectual Life from Washington to Polk* (New York: Charles Scribner's Sons, 1951), p. 22, entry dated January 7, 1804; this passage is quoted in Mitchell, *A Family Lawsuit*, p. 44.

8. Park 1926, p. 160, recorded the inscription.

9. Quoted in Mason 1879, p. 144.

10. On their Atlantic voyage, see Dorothy M. Quynn and Frank F. White Jr., "Jerome and Betsy Cross the Atlantic," *Maryland Historical Magazine* 48 (September 1953), pp. 204–14, which publishes the log of the voyage kept by the ship's captain.

11. Whitley 1932, p. 125.

12. Elizabeth Patterson Bonaparte, letter to Robert Gilmor Jr., September 30, 1807, private collection, courtesy of Lance Humphries. Previous authors assumed that she was trying to obtain her own portrait; see Eugene L. Didier, *The Life and Letters of Madame Bonaparte* (New York: Charles Scribner's Sons, 1879), pp. 39–40; Whitley 1932, p. 124; Mount 1964, p. 282.

But Pichon hopes it will not affect the national honor. He has given express warnings of all these facts to the lady's parents. But they have such an *inconceivable infatuation . . .* that make it they must; and it was really the young man who was seduced."[7]

Stuart probably began his portrait of Bonaparte in February 1804, when he began Mme Bonaparte's. They may have been introduced to Stuart by the marqués de Yrujo, or by Mme Bonaparte's friend Robert Gilmor Jr. An inscription on the back of the canvas reads, *JEROME NAPOLEON Frère du grand NAPOLEON: L'An 1804 G. Stuart. Pinxt.*[8] The painting offers a rare opportunity to observe Stuart's methods, since the portrait, like that of John Bill Ricketts (cat. 55), is in its early stages. Bonaparte's face is more finished than other areas of the portrait but lacks Stuart's final highlighting touches. Stuart laid in Bonaparte's powdered hair with dark color, then painted over it with broad gray and white brushstrokes; he broadly painted the shirt collar as well. This allowed him to choose contrasting tones for the face. The rest of the portrait is only blocked in. While the dark shape of the coat is in place, the gold epaulette is indicated with only a first layer of color. The white area and the dark patch on the right are a continuation of the clothing. Bonaparte's uniform would probably have been the same or similar to the one he is wearing in the contemporary miniature by an unidentified artist. The finished portrait of Bonaparte might have resembled, in reverse, Stuart's portrait of Lieutenant John Fenwick of the United States Marines, painted in Washington at this time (fig. 141).

Stuart left both the Bonapartes' portraits unfinished and refused to deliver them. Jane Stuart later recalled, "Jerome Bonaparte, the husband of Madame Bonaparte, was anxious to have her portrait completed, it having been in an unfinished state for some time; but as sitters were crowding in upon my father, this request could not be immediately complied with. Bonaparte deemed it an insult to be so neglected, and when the two came together—Bonaparte and Stuart—the painter thought that the remarks addressed to him were impertinent; the result was Bonaparte could not get possession of his own or his wife's portrait on any terms. He sent his friends to offer any price, but these offers made no impression on Stuart."[9]

Napoleon, who proclaimed himself emperor of France in May 1804, did not recognize Jerome Bonaparte's marriage. He ordered Pichon not to advance funds to Jerome and demanded that he return to France without Miss Patterson. Determined to reconcile his situation, Jerome made several attempts to leave American ports, which failed because of the likelihood of capture by the British at sea. At last he sailed for France with Betsy—who was pregnant—in March 1805 in a brig that her father purchased for the purpose.[10] When they arrived in Lisbon in April, Bonaparte went ashore to travel to Milan to see Napoleon. Mme Bonaparte intended to land in France or Holland but was denied permission. She was forced to go to England, where their son, Jerome Napoleon Bonaparte, was born on July 7, 1805.

Prohibited from visiting France, she returned home that fall. By the time she arrived in Baltimore, Stuart had moved to Boston, taking with him the couple's two unfinished portraits. In August 1807, the young American painter Thomas Sully, who was studying with Stuart, accidentally stepped on the painting of Bonaparte. He recalled that Stuart remarked, "You needn't mind. It's only a —— French barber."[11] About this time, Mme Bonaparte enlisted Robert Gilmor Jr. to persuade Stuart to give up her husband's unfinished portrait; she did not, apparently, ask for her own portrait as well. After Gilmor retrieved the painting, Mme Bonaparte wrote to thank him: "I entreat you to accept my acknowledgments for your successful application to Stuard for the portrait. An act as flattering to me, as it is pleasing & which augments if possible, the sentiments of regard, by which I have ever been actuated towards you. Steward has hitherto remained inexorable to all our solicitations; & his prompt acquiescence in your demand affords a proof of the estimation, in which you are held, by this distinguished artist. You will, I flatter myself, have the goodness to retain the picture in your possession, until my arrival in Town: where I shall have the honor of personally offering you my thanks."[12] She signed the letter "Eliza Bonaparte" and continued to use this name even after the marriage was annulled in a French ecclesiastical court in 1806. In 1807 Bonaparte, already proclaimed a French prince, was crowned king of Westphalia and married Princess Catherine of Württemberg. He served as a French army commander during Napoleon's invasion of Russia (1812) and at Waterloo (1815). After Napoleon's defeat, Bonaparte lived in exile, returning to France in 1847.

EGM

68. ELIZABETH PATTERSON BONAPARTE

1804
Oil on canvas, 28 x 24 in. (71.1 x 61 cm)
Private collection

Early drafts of this entry are by Themis Chryssostomides.
1. Sidney Mitchell, *A Family Lawsuit: The Story of Elisabeth Patterson and Jérôme Bonaparte* (New York: Farrar, Straus and Cudahy, 1958), provides a modern, well-documented biography of Elizabeth Patterson Bonaparte. Biographical essays are included in Edward T. James, ed., *Notable American Women, 1607–1950: A Biographical Dictionary* (Cambridge, Mass.: Belknap Press of Harvard University Press, 1971), vol. 1, pp. 192–94; *ANB*, vol. 3, pp. 157–58. William Patterson is listed in the *DAB*, vol. 7, pp. 309–10. Many letters and other documents are in the extensive collection of Elizabeth Patterson Bonaparte Papers, 1802–79, Ms. 142, H. Furlong Baldwin Library, Maryland Historical Society, Baltimore. Others, now unlocated, were published in Eugene L. Didier, *The Life and Letters of Madame Bonaparte* (New York: Charles Scribner's Sons, 1879). Our thanks for her assistance with this research go to Helen Jean Burn of Baltimore, who shared her extensive knowledge of the Bonaparte Papers with us.
2. Pichon, letter to Charles-Maurice de Tallyrand-Périgord in Paris, February 20, 1804, in *Pièces a Consulter pour S.A.I. le Prince Napoléon contre Mme. Elisabeth Paterson M. Jerôme Bonaparte (Paterson)*

This triple portrait, unique in Stuart's work, depicts Elizabeth Patterson Bonaparte (1785–1879), known as Betsy, the daughter of Baltimore shipping merchant William Patterson and his wife, Dorcas Spear.[1] The portrait was painted soon after her marriage on December 24, 1803, to Jerome Bonaparte (see cat. 67), youngest brother of Napoleon Bonaparte, at the time the first consul of France, in a ceremony performed by Bishop John Carroll of Baltimore (see cat. 73). The date of the sitting is well documented. The French chargé d'affaires, Louis-André Pichon, wrote from Washington on February 20, 1804, "M. Jérôme Bonaparte est revenu ici depuis huit jours. L'objet de son voyage est de faire peindre son épouse par Stewart" (Jerome Bonaparte has been here eight days. The object of his trip is to have his wife's portrait painted by Stewart).[2] Stuart's unfinished study shows Mme Bonaparte in three poses on a canvas of the size that he usually used for portraits of a single figure shown at waist length.[3] In the central image, probably Stuart's initial design, Mme Bonaparte looks directly at the viewer, her Cupid's-bow mouth in a slight smile, rouge on her cheeks, her brown hair in ringlets covering her forehead and eyebrows. On the left, he added a playful image of his subject peeking out from behind the first portrait and, to the right, a more formal neoclassical profile. These images all convey Stuart's fascination with this beautiful, captivating young woman.

Stuart was not alone in his admiration. Indeed, the Bonapartes had become the talk of the capital city, not only because of their controversial marriage but especially because Mme Bonaparte dressed in the latest and most risqué French fashions, which her husband imported for her from Paris. A sheer French evening dress that she owned, once believed to be her wedding dress (fig. 142), is a good indication of the new styles that she wore.[4] Margaret Bayard Smith, wife of Samuel Harrison Smith, editor of the *National Intelligencer*, described Mme Bonaparte's scandalous appearance at a party that her aunt Margaret Smith Smith, wife of Secretary of the Navy Robert Smith, gave for her:

But of Mad'm—I think it no harm to speak the truth. She has made a great noise here, and mobs of boys have crowded round her splendid equipage to see what I hope will not often be seen in this country, an almost naked woman. An elegant and select party was given to her by Mrs. Robt. Smith; her appearance was such that it threw all the company into confusion, and no one dar'd to look at her but by stealth; the window shutters being left open, a crowd assem-

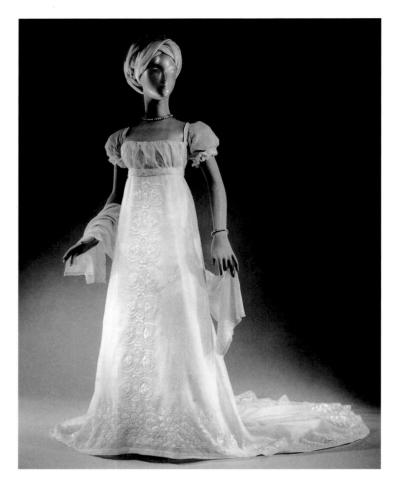

Fig. 143. Attributed to Thomas Sully, *Elizabeth Patterson Bonaparte*, ca. 1805–10. Watercolor on ivory, 3¹³⁄₁₆ x 3½ in. (9.7 x 8.9 cm). The Metropolitan Museum of Art, New York; Purchase, Dodge Fund and funds from various donors, 2000 (2000.359)

Fig. 142. Evening dress owned by Elizabeth Patterson Bonaparte, ca. 1804–5. White mull. The Metropolitan Museum of Art, New York; Purchase, Gifts in memory of Elizabeth N. Lawrence, 1983 (1983.6.1)

(Paris: Renou et Maulde, 1861), p. 15, no. 10. This publication recounts Jerome Bonaparte's side at the time of the lawsuit by Betsy Patterson Bonaparte to obtain part of Bonaparte's estate for their son. It includes transcriptions of letters written by Pichon to the French government and others at the time of the marriage. A copy is in the Elizabeth Patterson Bonaparte Papers, Ms. 142, Maryland Historical Society.

3. The portrait is described in Mason 1879, pp. 144–45; Park 1926, pp. 160–62; Whitley 1932, pp. 122–25.

4. Jean L. Druesedow, *In Style: Celebrating Fifty Years of the Costume Institute*, exh. cat. (New York: Metropolitan Museum of Art, 1987), p. 26.

5. Margaret Bayard Smith, letter to Jane Bayard Kirkpatrick, January 23, 1804, in Gaillard Hunt, ed., *The First Forty Years of Washington Society* (New York: Charles Scribner's Sons, 1906), pp. 46–47.

6. Rosalie Stier Calvert, letter to her mother, Mme H. J. Stier, March 2, 1804, in Margaret Law Callcott, ed. and trans., *Mistress of Riversdale: The Plantation Letters of Rosalie Stier Calvert, 1795–1821* (Baltimore: Johns Hopkins University Press, 1991), p. 78. She described her own portrait in a letter to her father in May 1805; see ibid., p. 119 and frontispiece.

7. Law's verses are quoted, with a set of more polite verses, in *Mistress of Riversdale*, pp. 78–79.

bled round the windows to get a look at this beautiful little creature, for every one allows she is extremely beautiful. Her dress was the thinnest sarcenet and white crepe without the least stiffening in it, made without a single plait in the skirt, the width at the bottom being made of gores; there was scarcely any waist to it and no sleeves; her back, her bosom, part of her waist and her arms were uncover'd and the rest of her form visible. She was engaged the next evening at Madm P's, Mrs. R. Smith and several other ladies sent her word, if she wished to meet them there, she must promise to have more clothes on.[5]

Rosalie Stiers Calvert, painted by Stuart with her daughter Caroline in the summer of 1804 (fig. 135), also attended the party and described Mme Bonaparte as "wearing a dress so transparent that you could see the color and shape of her thighs, and even more!"[6] She sent her mother some rather nasty verses by Thomas Law, another guest at this party, who was married to Eliza Custis Law (see cat. 50), niece of Mrs. Calvert's husband, George. Law's verses, about Mme Bonaparte's appearance that night, begin: "I was at Mrs. Smith's last night / And highly gratified my self / Well! What of Madame Bonaparte / Why she's a little whore at heart."[7] Law sent a more admiring poem about Stuart's portrait to Mme Bonaparte on February 14. Sally McKean, marquesa de Yrujo, also painted by Stuart at this time (cat. 65), forwarded Law's poem with his note. Law's note and poem indicate that Stuart originally planned a full-length work:

*Mde. Bonaparte having come to the city, that Mr. Stewart might paint her full length, it was observed that upon the portrait's arrival at Paris, the Venus de Medicis would be thrown into the Seine for its superiority. But instead of a full length it was afterwards determined that Mr. Stewart should draw three heads of Mde. Bonaparte in one picture, viz a full face, two thirds of the face & a profile. From this circumstance arose the follow*ᵍ *lines by Mr. Law.*

68

8. Thomas Law, note and verses to Betsy Patterson Bonaparte, forwarded by Sally McKean Yrujo with a letter to Mme Bonaparte, February 14, 1804, Elizabeth Patterson Bonaparte Papers, Ms. 142, Maryland Historical Society.

9. Josephine Seaton, *William Winston Seaton of the National Intelligencer* (1871; reprint, [New York]: Arno, 1970), p. 90, quoted in Mason 1879, p. 144.

10. Anna Maria Brodeau Thornton, diary, entry dated February 14, 1804, Papers of Anna Maria Brodeau Thornton, Manuscript Division, Library of Congress, Washington, D.C.

11. Baron de Maupertuis, letter to Elizabeth Patterson Bonaparte, 1804, Elizabeth Patterson Bonaparte Papers, Ms. 142, Maryland Historical Society. Maupertuis is described in a letter from Pichon to the "Ministre des relations extérieures," January 4, 1804, as a relative of Jerome Bonaparte's mother whom Bonaparte had encountered in New York and taken with him to Baltimore; see *Pièces a Consulter pour S.A.I. le Prince Napoléon*, pp. 12–13, no. 8.

12. Baron de Maupertuis to Elizabeth Patterson Bonaparte, "Vers adressés à Madame Bonaparte En lui envoyant les letters à Émilie," Baltimore, 1804; Elizabeth Patterson Papers, Ms. 142, Maryland Historical Society. Mme Bonaparte also saved his love poem titled "Le Curedent—à Madame Bonaparte." I am grateful to Patricia Svoboda of the National Portrait Gallery and her collaborators Cheryl Tennille, Nicole Becker, and Susan Cohen for their transcriptions and translations of these documents. I also thank Philip Conisbee, Senior Curator of European Paintings, National Gallery of Art, for his helpful comments on the translation.

13. Samuel Lorenzo Knapp, *American Cultural History, 1607–1829: A Facsimile Reproduction of Lectures on American Literature, 1829*, introduction and index by Richard Beale Davis and Ben Harris McClary (Gainesville, Fla.: Scholars' Facsimiles and Reprints, 1961), p. 198.

14. Mason 1879, p. 144.

The painter won't oerwhelm the sculptor's art / For Venus' Statue we no longer fear, / The matchless form of Mde. Bonaparte / Will not by Stewart at full length appear. // But ah! the picture with three heads in one / With so much fervor idolized will be / I tremble, lest our faith should be undone / By this new captivating Trinity. [8]

That Stuart at first considered a different composition was also suggested some years later by Sarah Gales Seaton, wife of William Seaton, associate editor of the *National Intelligencer*: "To [her] mental gifts was added a beauty of a Greek yet glowing type, which not even the pencil of Stuart adequately portrayed in the exquisite portrait that he wished might be buried with him; nor yet on his other canvas, which, with its dainty head in triple pose of loveliness, still smiles in unfading witchery." [9]

On February 14, 1804, William and Anna Maria Thornton, good friends of Stuart, "went to Mr. Stewart's painting room to see Mde Bonaparte's picture." [10] Also in February, Baron de Maupertuis, an acquaintance of Jerome Bonaparte's from the West Indies and a guest of the Bonapartes in Baltimore, wrote Mme Bonaparte about having her portrait painted: "Mr votre peintre atil deja commencé son bel ouvrage, je trouve qu'il entreprend une forte besogne; quand on n'a qu'un portrait ordinaire a faire, en le flattant un peu presque toujour on reussit a plaire au modele, mais avec vous, cest la nature dans toute la verité qu'il faut rendre, et les meilleurs pinceaux sont presque toujour faibles en pareil cas" (Has your painter already started his beautiful work? I find that he undertakes a difficult job. When one has only to do an ordinary portrait, by flattering a little one almost always succeeds in pleasing the model. But with you, it is Nature in all truth that he must render, and the best brushes are almost always deficient in such a situation). [11] The infatuated Maupertuis also sent her a copy of "les lettres à Émilie" (probably the popular *Lettres à Émilie, sur la Mythologie*, by Charles-Albert Demoustier), along with a verse about her having her portrait painted:

Si jamais vous avez l'aimable fantaisie / de voir sous le pinceau s'animer vos attraits / pour peintre addressez vous à l'auteur d'émilie, / il pétrit la nature en fesant ses portraits. / que ne puis je suivant ses traces / peindre ainsi l'amour et les grâces? / gardez vous cependant de trop cher lui payer / pour un original une simple copie! / Car peut-être il pourrait pour ne pas se tromper / Vous calquer sans façon sur la belle Émilie. (If ever you fancy to see your charms / come alive under a brush, / choose the author of Émilie as a painter, / he molds nature while making his portraits. / I wish I could, as he does, / depict love and the Graces? / Be careful however not to pay him too dearly / the price of an original for a mere copy! / For he might, in order not to err, / Offhandedly turn you into a copy of the beautiful Émilie.) [12]

Stuart left the much-admired portrait unfinished, apparently because he became annoyed with Jerome Bonaparte's interference. The writer Samuel Knapp later recounted that "He would not bear any flippant connoisseur about him. Numerous instances have been related, and many of them believed, of his having resented a hasty word from men of the first standing in society, by refusing to finish a picture, and nothing would ever induce him to touch it again. One of these pictures, on which a dandy criticism produced a quarrel, and which is unfinished still, is one of exquisite beauty; it is three views of the beautiful face of a celebrated dame, who was then just married to a foreign magnate. It is but justice, however, to say, that it was not the lady who made the offensive remarks, but her dapper husband, who found fault with the drapery. 'That you can buy,' said the indignant artist, 'at any milliner's shop in the city.'" [13] Jane Stuart related that Bonaparte was impatient with Stuart's delays in finishing the portrait. [14]

15. Sarah Morton, letter with poem enclosed to Elizabeth Patterson Bonaparte, Dorchester, August 12, 1804, addressed "Madame Bonaparte / Care of the French Commissary of Commercial relations, New-York," Elizabeth Patterson Bonaparte Papers, Ms. 142, Maryland Historical Society:

As round the pure unruffled Stream,
*   Which loves the shining Vale to lave,*
More bright the bordering Florets seem,
*   Reflected by the lucid Wave.*

So in the Charms which deck thy Form,
*   The Graces of thy Soul we find,*
That Blush, from Nature's Pencil warm,
*   Is but the Bounty of thy Mind.*

That Voice, which like the vernal Breeze,
*   With balmy Health, & Fragrance fraught,*
Each animated Sense to please,
*   Was from thy heavenly Temper caught.*

And though thy Bosom's downy Throne
*   The Whiteness of the Dove impart,*
E'en that, the Critick's Eye will own,
*   Is not more spotless than thine Heart.*

The finish'd Form, the speaking Eyes,
*   To <u>Sense</u> & <u>Diffidence</u> are due,*
While <u>that</u> their brilliant Glance supplies,
*   From <u>this</u> the modest Graces grew.*

Thence <u>he</u>, whom Queens were proud to claim.
*   Proud his imperial Hopes to share,*
Gives to thy Love his glorious Name,
*   And finds his happiest Empire there.*

No longer then the adoring Train
*   Shall boast that blooming Charms alone,*
Can with despotic Empire reign,
*   And make the subject Heart their own.*

But gazing on thy perfect Face,
*   To all thy beauteous Self resign'd,*
Will, in that polish'd Mirror, trace
*   Each faultless Feature of thy Mind.*

16. The list is on a loose sheet of paper in an account book with expenses from a trip to England in 1815, Elizabeth Patterson Bonaparte Papers, Maryland Historical Society, Ms. 142.

17. See Dorothy M. Quynn and Frank F. White Jr., "Jerome and Betsy Cross the Atlantic," *Maryland Historical Magazine* 48 (September 1953), pp. 204–14.

18. This story is told in Whitley 1932, p. 125. This probably occurred on Sully's three-week visit to Stuart in August 1807, which is described in detail in Morgan 1939, p. 36.

Later in 1804, the Bonapartes toured Boston, New York, and Philadelphia. In Boston they visited Stuart's friend Sarah Morton (see cat. 60), who wrote Mme Bonaparte, "I parted from you, my amiable Friend, with even more Regret than I had anticipated," and enclosed an eight-stanza poem in praise of her beauty as the outward expression of "Each faultless Feature of thy Mind."[15] Bonaparte purchased jewelry for his wife, which she later inventoried as "1804. Bought at Boston 1 pair Diamond Earrings 1,000 by my husband for me," and "1804 at Phila 1 ring 120 by same J. Bonaparte."[16] In March 1805, the Bonapartes sailed for France, hoping to persuade Napoleon to accept their marriage, which he had opposed. When their ship reached Lisbon, Bonaparte went ashore to travel to Milan, where he could confront Napoleon. Mme Bonaparte, who was six months pregnant, sailed to England, where their son, Jerome Napoleon Bonaparte, was born on July 7, 1805.[17] Despite efforts of her family and his friends, the couple remained apart, and Mme Bonaparte and her son returned to Baltimore that September. The Bonapartes' marriage was annulled in a French ecclesiastical court in 1806, and Mme Bonaparte was awarded a yearly pension of $12,000. She was granted a divorce by Maryland statute in 1813. She returned to Europe after Napoleon's overthrow, seeking for her son both legitimacy and a good marriage.

By the time of her return to Baltimore in 1805, Stuart had moved to Boston, taking with him her unfinished portrait and that of Bonaparte, also unfinished. In 1807, with the help of her friend Robert Gilmor Jr., she was able to reclaim Jerome's portrait but hers remained in the studio. Continued requests for her portrait led Stuart to threaten, as reported by Thomas Sully, that "if he were bothered any more about it he would put rings through the nose, and send it to any tavern-keeper who would hang it up. He would have done it too for he was not a man to flinch from anything of that kind."[18] Samuel Colleton Graves saw her portrait in Boston in 1808 and sent Mme Bonaparte a poem.[19] A miniature copy of the portrait, possibly painted by Sully in Stuart's studio, is owned by the Metropolitan Museum (fig. 143).[20]

Stuart's young daughter Jane also saw and admired it: "The garret where these discarded pictures were heaped was my playroom when a child, and this beautiful sketch of Madame Bonaparte was the idol that I worshiped. The stretcher had been taken from it, and the canvas, unrolled, was lying on the floor." At the age of thirteen, as she later remembered, she tried to copy the portrait. A fire in the kitchen chimney brought her father to the attic. He was astonished at her attempt and then advised, "You must not mix your colors with turpentine; you must have some oil."[21]

William Patterson retrieved his daughter's unfinished portrait when he visited Stuart's Boston studio about 1820 to have his own portrait painted.[22] Jane Stuart recalled that "In the course of the conversation with Stuart, this picture was mentioned, when the painter had it brought down from the garret. Mr. Patterson was delighted with it, and my father presented it to him, which he could ill afford to do, to convince the world that he did not value his work as much as he did his position as an artist."[23] Mme Bonaparte thanked her father in a letter dated January 8, 1822: "I am very glad Stuart has given up the picture, and obliged to you for your taking the trouble of getting it from him. It is the only likeness that has ever been made of me. My other pictures are quite as like any one else as me."[24]

Stuart seems also to have begun a portrait of her son, Jerome, when he was a student at Harvard College. The young man, nicknamed "Bo," wrote to his grandfather William Patterson from Rotterdam on June 16, 1826, about his attempts to persuade Stuart to finish it: "I called upon him frequently for six months before I left Boston, to hurry him,

19. Samuel Colleton Graves, poem to Elizabeth Patterson Bonaparte, June 21, 1808, Elizabeth Patterson Bonaparte Papers, Ms. 142, Maryland Historical Society:

To Madame Bonaparte; Lines written after having seen her portrait—
Blessing the hand whose various hue Could imitate the form—Moore

By Stuart's skill, I fondly trace
The beauties of Eliza's face,
Though she alas is far remov'd,
By art *her image here's renew'd.*
Here I can view, the silky hair
Which floats upon her forhead fair,
And here behold her piercing eyes,
Where sparkling animation lies,
Here, on her cheeks, the roses blow
Well blended with the lily's snow,
The lips are of a vermil hue,
And each beauteous feature's true;
Yet, is the painter's best design
Not equal to her form divine;
For though the bosom brightly swell,
Can love within that bosom dwell?
Although the lips are vermil bright,
By utt'rance they cannot delight,
And though the cheeks like hers, are fair,
They want her smile to dimple there.
Yet when the likeness was display'd,
Oh! How I bless'd the Grecian maid
Who in an age quite unrefin'd,
By love instructed, taught mankind
To trace by such an easy mode,
And bring to memory's abode,
The strict resemblance of a form,
Which wants but life alone to warm:
But more I bless'd that sacred thrill,
Which could the precious thought instill
And only wish'd, the tender flame
From whence the happy impulse came,
Had added licence, to impart
A spark of feeling to the heart,
And given power, to improve
That spark of feeling into love.

20. A copy in pastel by Georges d'Almaine, 1856, is owned by the Maryland Historical Society.
21. The story is recounted in Mason 1879, p. 145.
22. On his portrait, see Park 1926, pp. 577–78, no. 617.
23. Mason 1879, pp. 144–45.
24. Elizabeth Patterson Bonaparte, letter to William Patterson, Rome, January 8, 1822, quoted in Didier, *Life and Letters of Madame Bonaparte*, p. 88. Mount (1964, pp. 313–14) says, without indicating a source, that the damages the portrait suffered

but without success. Perhaps now that I am away he may be prevailed upon to finish it at once. When I left Boston, I was on excellent terms with Stuart; but he is so capricious that he may possibly be offended at my having left the country without having given him any notice of it."[25] He wrote from Rome in 1827 advising that if Stuart were not well enough to finish the portrait, his grandfather should take it in its present condition, since the head was finished; another artist could complete the rest.[26]

Patterson kept the portrait until his death in 1835. He complained about his daughter's behavior in his will: "The Conduct of my daughter Betsy has through life been so disobedient, that in no instance has she ever consulted my opinion or feelings, indeed she has caused me more anxiety & trouble than all my other children put together & her folly & misconduct has occasioned me a train of Expence that first & last has cost me much money, under such circumstances it would not be reasonable, just or proper, that she should at my death inherit and participate in an equal proportion with my other Children in an equal division of my Estate. Considering however the weakness of human nature & that she is still my Daughter it is my Will & pleasure to provide for her." He bequeathed to her the house in which she was born, a house by the Market Street Bridge, three brick houses on Market Street, and her portrait: "that of my daughter Betsy in a groope of three faces painted by Stewart."[27] The unequal distribution of Patterson's estate caused a rift between Mme Bonaparte and her brothers. After her father's death she lived in Baltimore in a boardinghouse and invested in Baltimore real estate with considerable success. After Jerome Bonaparte's death in 1860, Mme Bonaparte sued unsuccessfully to claim part of his estate for their son.[28] The portraits were separated in the late nineteenth century.

EGM

when the portrait was in Stuart's studio were repaired by Thomas Sully.

25. Jerome Napoleon Bonaparte, letter to William Patterson, June 16, 1826, quoted in Didier, *Life and Letters of Madame Bonaparte*, p. 183. The portrait is mentioned in Mason 1879, p. 146; Mason was unable to locate it.

26. Jerome Napoleon Bonaparte, letter to William Patterson, February 12, 1827, paraphrased in Didier, *Life and Letters of Madame Bonaparte*, pp. 204.

27. "Last Will and Testament of William Patterson," August 20, 1827, p. 10, clause 9, manuscript copy, March 16, 1835, William Patterson Papers, 1798–1835, Ms. 145, H. Furlong Baldwin Library, Maryland Historical Society.

28. Her narrative in defense of this claim is presented in the publication by the Cour Impériale de Paris, Première Chambre, *Appel du jugement de la première Chambre du Tribunal de première instance de la Seine, du 15 février 1861: M. Jérome-Napoleon Bonaparte et Mme Élisabeth Patterson contre S.A.I. le Prince Napoléon* (Paris: Pillet fils ainé, 1861); her late husband's case is presented in *Pièces a Consulter pour S.A.I. le Prince Napoléon.* Copies of both are found in the Elizabeth Patterson Bonaparte Papers, Ms. 142, Maryland Historical Society.

69. James Madison

1804
Oil on canvas, 29½ x 24⅝ in. (74.9 x 62.4 cm)
The Colonial Williamsburg Foundation,
Williamsburg, Virginia; Gift of Mrs. George S.
Robbins (1945-23, A&B)

70. Dolley Payne Todd Madison

1804
Oil on canvas, 29⅛ x 24⅛ in. (74.1 x 61.3 cm)
The White House, Washington, D.C.

Research for this catalogue entry was begun by
Edurne Poggi-Aranda and completed by Emily
Burns, who wrote the first draft.

1. For a brief biography of James Madison, see *ANB*,
   vol. 14, pp. 306–12.

2. For brief biographies of Dolley Madison, see
   Edward T. James, ed., *Notable American Women,
   1607–1950: A Biographical Dictionary* (Cambridge,
   Mass.: Belknap Press of Harvard University Press,
   1971), vol. 2, pp. 483–85; *ANB*, vol. 14, pp. 302–4.
   Also very useful is Conover Hunt-Jones, *Dolley
   and the "great little Madison"* (Washington, D.C.:
   American Institute of Architects Foundation,
   1977), as is the most recent publication on Dolley
   Madison, David B. Mattern and Holly C.
   Shulman, eds., *The Selected Letters of Dolley Payne
   Madison* (Charlottesville, London: University of
   Virginia Press, 2003).

3. Dolley Madison, letter to Elizabeth Collins Lee,
   1794, quoted in Allen C. Clark, *Life and Letters of
   Dolley Madison* (Washington, D.C.: Press of W. F.
   Roberts Co., 1914), p. 19; Hunt-Jones, *Dolley and
   the "great little Madison,"* p. 1.

4. For a description of Dolley Madison's role in
   Washington at the time of Stuart's visit, see
   David B. Mattern and Holly C. Shulman, "A
   Washington Education, 1801–1809," in *Selected
   Letters of Dolley Payne Madison*, pp. 38–48; Hunt-
   Jones, *Dolley and the "great little Madison,"* pp. 21–
   27. Political and social life in Washington at the
   time is also described in Catherine Allgor, *Parlor
   Politics* (Charlottesville: University Press of
   Virginia, 2000), chap. 1, pp. 4–47.

This exhibition offers the rare opportunity to temporarily reunite Stuart's portraits of James and Dolley Madison, which have been in separate collections since 1849. James Madison (1751–1836), elected fourth president of the United States in 1808, was secretary of state in Thomas Jefferson's administration when Stuart painted the portraits.[1] A Virginian, Madison was a delegate to the Constitutional Convention in 1787. He played a critical role in the formation of the Constitution of the United States and was co-author of the Federalist Papers with Alexander Hamilton and John Jay. Elected to the first federal congress in 1788, he served four terms. He met his now legendary spouse, Dolley Payne Todd (1768–1849), in 1794 in Philadelphia, where she had moved from Virginia with her family, who were Quakers.[2] Her first husband, John Todd Jr., and their younger son, William Temple Todd, had died of yellow fever the previous year. Before her introduction to Madison, she wrote her friend Elizabeth Collins Lee, "Thou must come to me, Aaron Burr says that the great little Madison has asked to be brought to see me this evening."[3] They were married on September 15, 1794. After Madison's congressional term ended in 1797, they lived at Madison's Virginia home, Montpelier. When he became Jefferson's secretary of state in 1801, they moved to Washington, the new capital city. There Mrs. Madison became a key member of the political and social circle that included members of Jefferson's government, the diplomatic corps, investors and real estate developers, and members of prominent local families. Her elegance, warmth, and openness engaged all who met her, and she occasionally served as hostess at events held by President Jefferson, a widower.[4]

Stuart painted the portraits of the Madisons in the spring of 1804.[5] He was then in great demand, as a contemporary explained: "Stuart is all the rage, he is almost worked to death, and everybody [is] afraid that they will be the last to be finished. He says 'the ladies come and say "Dear Mr. Stuart, I am afraid you will be very much tired, you really must rest when my picture is done."' Mrs. Robert Smith [wife of the secretary of the navy] is sitting now, so is Mr. Madison."[6] Mrs. Madison wrote to her sister Anna Payne Cutts on May 20, "Steward has taken an admirable picture of Mr. Madison—his & mine are finished—Mrs R Smiths is nearly done but she does not like it tho tis verry like her."[7]

Stuart painted the Madisons turned slightly toward each other, each sitter looking directly at the viewer. The paintings mirror each other also in choice of color, with emphasis on red, black, and gold. The Madisons are seated, their hands in their laps, in identical gilded chairs upholstered in red velvet. Mrs. Madison wears a high-waisted white dress with a low-cut bodice, a French style then in fashion; the dress is trimmed with gold ribbon, and she wears a three-strand gold necklace. Her hair is arranged in

69

5. James Madison's portrait is discussed in Mason 1879, pp. 218–19; Park 1926, p. 496, no. 515; Theodore Bolton, "The Life Portraits of James Madison," *William and Mary Quarterly*, ser. 3, 8 (January 1951), pp. 41–42. On Mrs. Madison's portrait, see Mason 1879, pp. 218–19; Park 1926, pp. 499–500, no. 519; Evans 1999, pp. 75, 76, 79, 90; William Kloss, *Art in the White House: A Nation's Pride*, suppl., *Acquisitions 1992–2002* (Washington, D.C.: White House Historical Association, 2002), pp. 6–7.

the popular neoclassical style, pulled back in a chignon with loose ringlets framing the face.[8] In the background are a red curtain and a column, with a cloudy blue sky beyond. In his portrait, Madison wears a black suit with a white shirt and cravat. The red curtain and shelves of books in the background add brightness to the painting.

These portraits are similar to the other pairs of portraits of married couples that Stuart undertook on arrival in Washington, which include those of the marqués de Yrujo and his American wife, Sally McKean Yrujo (cats. 65, 66), who was Mrs. Madison's close friend from Philadelphia; Anna Payne Cutts (cat. 71) and her husband, Richard (fig. 146); the Madisons' friends William and Anna Maria Thornton (figs. 144, 145); and John and

70

6. Transcription of an unlocated original letter to
Anna Payne Cutts, May 7, 1804, Cutts Family
Collection of Papers of James and Dolley
Madison, microfilm 14326, Manuscript Division,
Library of Congress, Washington, D.C. The tran-
scriber attributed the letter to "a friend of Mrs
Cutts," who may have been Dolley Madison her-
self.
7. Dolley Madison, letter to Anna Payne Cutts,
May 20, 1804, in *Selected Letters of Dolley Payne
Madison*, p. 56, from the Mary Estelle Elizabeth
Cutts Papers, Schlesinger Library, Radcliffe

Ann Ogle Tayloe (both, private collection), for whom Thornton designed the residence
now known as Octagon House. In each pair, Stuart posed husband and wife to face
toward each other. (For Henry Pickering's conversation with Stuart in 1817 about this
traditional way of depicting husband and wife, see cats. 38, 39.) The poses of the
Madisons are especially similar to those of the Thorntons, although the color schemes
and backgrounds differ. Stuart began Thornton's portrait in March and his wife's in
May; he finished them in June.[9] Two days after her last sitting on June 24, Mrs.
Thornton visited Stuart's studio with "Mr. & Mrs. M," as she often referred to the
Madisons. In late July, Mrs. Thornton, who in 1802 had hoped that Stuart would

Fig. 144. *William Thornton*, 1804. Oil on canvas, 28 ⅞ x 24 ⅜ in. (73.2 x 61.9 cm). National Gallery of Art, Washington, D.C.; Andrew W. Mellon Collection (1942.8.25)

Fig. 145. *Anna Maria Thornton*, 1804. Oil on canvas, 28 ⅞ x 24 ⅛ in. (73.2 x 61.3 cm). National Gallery of Art, Washington, D.C.; Andrew W. Mellon Collection (1942.8.26)

College (earlier sources incorrectly dated this letter to June 3, 1804). In an earlier letter, ca. May 8,
to her sister in the same collection, she also seems
to refer to the portraits, but the text is unclear
because the top third of the page is torn. The transcription in *Selected Letters of Dolley Payne
Madison*, p. 54, reads, "finished—& hers . . . nearly
done—quite pritty he has made us." A portrait of
Margaret Smith (Mrs. Robert) Smith that is
attributed to John Wesley Jarvis (private collection) appears from photographs to be by Stuart.

8. Michele Majer, "American Women and French
Fashion," in Katell le Bourhis, ed., *The Age of
Napoleon: Costume from Revolution to Empire, 1789–
1815*, exh. cat. (New York: Metropolitan Museum
of Art, 1989), p. 235.

9. Miles 1995, pp. 240–46.

10. Anna Maria Brodeau Thornton, diary, July 26,
1804, Papers of Anna Maria Brodeau Thornton,
Manuscript Division, Library of Congress. For
details of the visits and sittings recorded in Mrs.
Thornton's diary, see Miles 1995, pp. 240–46.

11. Evans 1999, p. 90.

12. For illustrations of these portraits, see Hunt-Jones,
Dolley and the "great little Madison," pp. 12 fig. 17, 33
fig. 36, 56 fig. 48.

13. Dolley Madison, letter to Margaret Bayard Smith,
January 17, 1835, in *Selected Letters of Dolley Payne
Madison*, p. 308.

14. [Dolley Madison], letter to Anna Payne Cutts,
May 1804; transcription of unlocated original,
Cutts Family Collection of Papers of James and
Dolley Madison, microfilm 14326, Manuscript
Division, Library of Congress, quoted partially in
Evans 1999, p. 90. A version with a few differences
in spelling and word choice is quoted in Clark,
Life and Letters of Dolley Madison, pp. 73–74, dated
about June 5. While identification of the letter's
author is considered uncertain, it seems to be pro-
vided in the letter itself with the question recorded

provide her with "good pictures to copy after," noted that she "began yesterday to try to copy Mr. & Mrs. M's pictures by Stuart."[10]

Dorinda Evans attributes the formulaic quality of the portraits from Stuart's stay in Washington to the artist's "strained finances."[11] The similarity among portraits is most pronounced in those of women; his compositions in the portraits of Mrs. Madison, the marquesa de Yrujo, and Elizabeth Mason (cat. 72) are almost identical. Also, these women wear nearly identical white, high-waisted dresses, and their hairstyles are the same. However, in his portraits painted in Washington, as in the rest of Stuart's work, the interpretations of personality are almost always present, if very subtle. Thus Madison's portrait quite success-fully reflects his introspective, serious nature, while Mrs. Madison's clearly expresses her outgoing personality. Stuart's representation of her, with a direct gaze and a slight smile, is very like that of her by three other artists: James Peale, in an unlocated miniature that was painted in 1794; Bass Otis in 1816 (New-York Historical Society); and Joseph Wood in 1817 (Virginia Historical Society, Richmond).[12] This suggests that these artists all conveyed her personality successfully. Mrs. Madison's only known comment about Stuart's portrait came years later, in 1835. She sent Margaret Bayard Smith "an Engraving from Stuarts Portrait which tho' indifferently executed, is a better likeness than Mr Wood's."[13]

At the time Stuart painted the Madisons' portraits, Mrs. Madison hoped that Stuart would remain in Washington. She wrote her sister Anna Payne Cutts, "Dr. & Mrs. Thornton sat yesterday to Stuart for the last time. He has now nearly finished all & says he means to go immediately to Boston, but he has been going these two years—He is a man of genius, and therefore does everything differently from other people—He travels to the Southward on his way Northward. I hope he will be here next winter as he has bought a square to build a Temple on."[14] Years later, in 1812, she commented on the lack of a good portrait painter in the city to her friend Ruth Barlow in Paris: "I wish I could gratify you my dear friend, with the Portraits you mention, but I see little prospect of doing so. Steward is far from us & we have no Painter of skill in this quarter."[15] Thomas Jefferson would also sound this theme to Stuart in 1814 (see cat. 78).

During the War of 1812, Mrs. Madison played a critical role in the rescue of the ver-sion of Stuart's Lansdowne portrait of George Washington that hung in the White

in Clark's version, "Where will you celebrate the Fourth of July my dear sister?"

15. Dolley Madison, letter to Ruth Barlow, ca. April 19, 1812, in *Selected Letters of Dolley Payne Madison*, p. 164.

16. See cat. 47 for Stuart's denial of authorship of the painting.

17. Dolley Madison, letter to Lucy Payne Washington Todd, August 23, 1814, in *Selected Letters of Dolly Payne Madison*, pp. 193–94. Later (February 11, 1848), Mrs. Madison wrote to Robert G. L. De Peyster, one of the men to whom she had given the portrait, about the incident; see ibid., p. 387.

18. Dolley Madison, letter to Christopher Hughes, March 20, 1828, ibid., p. 273.

19. On provenance, see note 5 above. Madison's portrait was acquired by Colonial Williamsburg in 1945. Mrs. Madison's portrait was owned by the Pennsylvania Academy of the Fine Arts, Philadelphia, from 1899 to 1994, when it was acquired for the White House.

House (fig. 110).[16] In August 1814, as the British army advanced on Washington, Mrs. Madison remained in the President's House (as the White House was then called) with Colonel Charles Carroll of Bellevue and "his hundred men, who were stationed as a guard in the enclosure." On August 23, when she could hear cannon nearby during the battle at Bladensburg, she wrote her sister, "Our kind friend, Mr. Carroll, has come to hasten my departure, and is in a very bad humor with me because I insist on waiting until the large picture of Gen. Washington is secured, and it requires to be unscrewed from the wall. This process was found too tedious for these perilous moments; I have ordered the frame to be broken, and the canvass taken out it is done, and the precious portrait placed in the hands of two gentlemen of New York, for safe keeping. And now, dear sister, I must leave this house, or the retreating army will make me a prisoner in it, by filling up the road I am directed to take."[17]

Stuart's portraits of the Madisons were also rescued from the British advance. Mrs. Madison wrote in 1828, "There ware upon the Walls two or three Engravings, by Edwin of Mr Madison and myself, with large Portraits of both, by Stewart—the latter, were removed before the British entered, and the former, we understood, were taken by the destroyers of the building."[18] The portraits were hung at Montpelier after Madison's presidency ended in 1817 and remained there until after his death, when Dolley Madison moved back to Washington, D.C. At her death in 1849, Madison's portrait became the property of Judge Edward Coles, his former private secretary, and Mrs. Madison's became the property of her niece Anna Payne Causten.[19] The full-length portrait of Washington was returned to the White House.

EGM

71. ANNA PAYNE CUTTS

1804

Oil on canvas, 29 x 24 1/8 in. (73.8 x 61.3 cm)

The White House, Washington, D.C.

Research for this catalogue entry was begun by Edurne Poggi-Aranda and completed by Emily Burns, who wrote the early drafts.

1. Anna Payne's life is closely intertwined with that of her famous sister Dolley Payne Madison; their letters and details of their lives are well documented in Ethel Stephens Arnett, *Mrs. James Madison: The Incomparable Dolley* (Greensboro, N.C.: Piedmont Press, 1972); David B. Mattern and Holly C. Shulman, eds., *The Selected Letters of Dolley Payne Madison* (Charlottesville: University of Virginia Press, 2003).

Anna Payne (1779–1832), the youngest sister of Dolley Payne Madison, was born in Virginia and moved with her parents and siblings to Philadelphia in 1783.[1] Eleven years younger than Dolley, Anna lived with her older sister until she married Congressman Richard Cutts (1771–1845) of Massachusetts in Washington, D.C., on March 31, 1804.[2] Stuart probably painted Anna Cutts and her husband (fig. 146) about the time of their marriage, which took place a few days after the end of the first session of the Eighth Congress. They left for Boston in April. The next opportunity to sit for Stuart would have been during the second session of Congress, which met from November 5, 1804, to March 3, 1805.

In her portrait, Mrs. Cutts sits with her hands in her lap and looks at the viewer with a slight smile on her lips. Her hair is arranged in a style popular at this time, described recently as "long and bunched in ringlets on the crown, in the style of ancient Greece."[3] She wears a white dress with a low-cut bodice. A rose-colored shawl with gold fringe falls off her shoulders, filling the foreground. The style of her dress reflects the popularity of French fashions in Washington. Dolley Madison noted the influence of Alexandrine-Émilie Brongniart, wife of the French chargé d'affaires Louis-André Pichon, on her own choice of styles.[4] Mrs. Madison wrote her sister in 1805 that

2. On Cutts, see *Biographical Directory of the American Congress, 1774–1971* (Washington, D.C.: Government Printing Office, 1971), pp. 818–19. The Massachusetts district that Cutts represented is in present-day Maine.

3. Vanda Foster, *A Visual History of Costume: The Nineteenth Century* (London: B. T. Batsford, 1984), p. 12.

4. On the taste for French fashions at this time, see Michele Majer, "American Women and French Fashion," in Katell le Bourhis, ed., *The Age of Napoleon: Costume from Revolution to Empire, 1789–1815*, exh. cat. (New York: Metropolitan Museum of Art, 1989), esp. pp. 217–23.

5. Dolley Madison, letter to Anna Cutts, May 22, 1805, in *Selected Letters of Dolley Payne Madison*, p. 60; on their friendship, see ibid., p. 46.

6. Sally McKean, marquesa de Yrujo, letter to Anna Cutts, Philadelphia, June 28, 1804, transcription, Cutts Family Collection of Papers of James and Dolley Madison, microfilm 14326, Manuscript Division, Library of Congress, Washington, D.C. Dolley Madison, in her letter to Anna Cutts, May 20, 1804, mentions the marquesa's friendship; see *Selected Letters of Dolley Payne Madison*, pp. 58–59.

7. Richard D. Cutts, letter to George Champlin Mason, August 9, 1878, George Champlin Mason Papers, Manuscripts Division, Rhode Island Historical Society, Providence, with thanks to Rick Stattler, Manuscripts Curator and Library Director. This information was repeated in Mason 1879, p. 166; Park 1926, p. 249–50.

8. Harriet Taylor Upton, *Our Early Presidents, Their Wives and Children* (Boston: D. Lothrop Co., 1890), p. 202.

9. Anne Hollingsworth Wharton, *Social Life in the Early Republic* (1902; reprint, New York: Benjamin Blom, 1969), pp. 143–44.

10. This story is quoted in Mason 1879, p. 141, from a manuscript written by Binney's nephew Horace Binney Wallace, of Binney's recollections of his sittings with Stuart. The original manuscript has not been located. The term pencil refers to Stuart's paintbrush. On this portrait, see Miles 1995, pp. 219–21.

11. Pickering 1817 (November 10).

12. Dolley Madison, letter to Richard D. Cutts and James Madison Cutts, April 5, 1845, private collection, 1966; transcript, Office of the Curator, White House, Washington, D.C.

Madame Pichon "shews me everything she has, & would fain give me of *every thing*—she decorates herself according to the french Ideas & wishes me do so two."[5] Mrs. Madison sat for Stuart in a similar dress and wrote to her sister about Stuart's portraits of herself and her husband (cats. 69, 70). Sally McKean, marquesa de Yrujo (see cat. 65), also mentioned Stuart in one of her letters to Anna: "I cannot quit [writing about] the beloved place until I tell you that Stuart is still buisy, and has been bored to death by the quizzical Dr:—— to make haste and finish his picture before the weather became hotter and he became sunburnt: is that not a good one!"[6]

Fig. 146. *Richard Cutts*, 1804–5. Oil on canvas, 29 x 24¼ in. (73.7 x 61.6 cm). Virginia Historical Society, Richmond

Behind Mrs. Cutts is a billowing green curtain that forms exaggerated eyes, nose, and mouth, while the base of a column forms the chin. It is said to represent Stuart in profile. Comments about the profile date from about seventy-five years after the portrait was painted. In 1878 Richard D. Cutts, one of Anna's sons, wrote George Champlin Mason, Stuart's biographer: "The portrait of my Mother, painted by Stuart, was considered by him as one of his best efforts; so much so that in the drapery, he drew his own profile, but so gently blended that not one in three would notice it, unless their attention was specially drawn thereto. Before leaving Wash[n], he addressed a note to my Mother, thanking her for some service that she had been to him, & alluding to his opinion of the portrait & to his profile."[7] Stuart added to the portrait when Mrs. Cutts said to him "during a sitting, that it was a thousand pities there should be no portrait of himself made for his friends, [and] he replied that he would paint himself in upon the canvas of her portrait."[8] They debated about the most expressive feature of the face: "Mr. Stuart gave his verdict in favor of the nose, while Miss Payne contended for the superior claims of the eyes and mouth. Stuart, who greatly relished a joke, even at his own expense, presented to his sitter the next morning a canvas upon which *his own* profile, the long nose somewhat exaggerated, occupied the place of the usual drapery in the background, inquiring, with a triumphant smile, whether he had not proved that the nose was the most expressive feature of the face."[9] Stuart's letter to Mrs. Cutts is not located today.

Other visitors to Stuart's studio recorded the artist's belief that the nose was the telling feature of a face, among them the young Philadelphia lawyer Horace Binney, who sat for his portrait in 1800 (fig. 77): "'On the day when I was sitting to him the second time,' said Mr. Binney, 'I said to Stuart, "What do you consider the most characteristic feature of the face? You have already shown me that the eyes are not; and we know from sculpture, in which the eyes are wanting, the same thing."' Stuart just pressed the end of his pencil against the tip of his nose, distorting it oddly. 'Ah, I see, I see,' cried Mr. Binney."[10] Stuart also commented on noses to Henry Pickering in 1817: "In speaking of the features of the face, Mr. S. said he considered the nose the most important; the eyes confer character—the mouth imparts expression."[11] Stuart's self-portrait in silhouette, if deliberate, may also have been an allusion to the popularity at the time of profile

71

13. For King's copies, see Virginius Cornick Hall Jr., *Portraits in the Collection of the Virginia Historical Society: A Catalogue* (Charlottesville: University Press of Virginia, 1981), p. 65; Andrew J. Cosentino, *The Paintings of Charles Bird King (1785–1862)* (Washington, D.C.: Smithsonian Institution Press, 1977), p. 131, nos. 59, 60; Conover Hunt-Jones, *Dolley and the "great little Madison"* (Washington, D.C.: American Institute of Architects Foundation, 1977), p. 21.

portraiture, especially those by Charles Balthazar Julien Févret de Saint-Mémin, who was at work in Washington in 1804.

Richard Cutts served in Congress from 1801 to 1813 and was second comptroller of the Treasury Department, from 1817 to 1829. After his death, Dolley Madison resolved a family dispute over which of her sister's two sons would inherit Stuart's portraits of their parents, deciding that each would retain one original and one copy, which would be painted by Charles Bird King.[12] King's copy of Mrs. Cutts's portrait is owned by the Virginia Historical Society, Richmond, and his copy of the portrait of Cutts is privately owned.[13]

EGM

72. ELIZABETH BELTZHOOVER MASON

1804
Oil on canvas, 29 x 24 in. (73.8 x 61 cm)
The Cleveland Museum of Art, Cleveland, Ohio;
Gift from J. H. Wade (1921.428)

Stuart's portrait of Elizabeth Beltzhoover Mason exemplifies why he was so much in demand in Washington for his portraits of women. She appears very sensual, quite voluptuous, and the portrait's rich colors are wonderfully orchestrated.[1] Mrs. Mason wears a white Empire dress trimmed with pearls on the bodice and sleeves, and a pearl necklace. The brown of her eyes and her chestnut hair, which is decorated with pearls, is complemented by the rich wine red of the upholstery on the chair, and the pale rose curtain brings out the pink of her lips and cheeks. Her arms, crossed, rest in her lap, her wedding ring clearly visible.

While the commission is not documented, the portrait can probably be dated to the spring of 1804 by its similarity to others that Stuart painted at that time. The portrait closely resembles Stuart's portraits of Sally McKean, marquesa de Yrujo (cat. 65), Dolley Madison (cat. 70), and Anna Maria Thornton (fig. 145), all painted in Washington in the first half of 1804. Mrs. Mason's dress and hairstyle, with its chignon and ringlets, closely resemble those worn by the marquesa de Yrujo. The sitter's pose is a subtle variation on those in the portraits of Dolley Madison and Sally McKean Yrujo. Mrs. Mason is seated, turned to the right, in an upholstered armchair, in front of a curtain and a distant landscape, much as the marquesa de Yrujo is depicted; in this portrait, the artist has added a column has behind the figure, giving an additional sense of volume. Similar chairs appear in the portraits of Mrs. Thornton, her husband, William Thornton (fig. 144), Mrs. Madison, and the marquesa de Yrujo. And in its use of the background curtain as well as a landscape, the portrait resembles that of Ann Barry (fig. 147), also painted in Washington.[2] However, there are differences. Stuart has conveyed a more sensuous impression of soft flesh in her portrait than in the others through details such as the tight bodice of her dress and the highlights and shadows of the fingers of her left hand as they rest on her right arm. The upward tilt of Mrs. Mason's head and her slightly downward glance at the viewer seem also to be part of this characterization, not a formula.

1. Mason 1879, p. 221; L[awrence] P[ark], "Portrait of Mrs. John Thomson Mason by Gilbert Stuart," *Bulletin of the Cleveland Museum of Art* 8 (December 1921), pp. 154–55; Park 1926, pp. 510–11, no. 531; Mount 1971–72, p. 96; Evans 1999, p. 76. Park (1926, p. 510) suggested that the portrait was painted because Mrs. Mason's father was a "Hollander who settled in this country and became intimate with Stuart," but no documentation has been found for this. The Brooklyn Museum owns an oval copy of the portrait by an unidentified artist (33.250).
2. On the portraits of the Thorntons, Ann Barry, and her sister Mary Barry, also painted in Washington, see Miles 1995, pp. 230–35, 240–46.
3. Her birth date, February 23, 1781, and death date, June 30, 1836, were provided by John Kilbourne of the Maryland Historical Society, Baltimore, in 1963, to Mrs. Lammot DuPont Copeland for Gunston Hall, where she was a regent and curator of records. Her family's involvement with the Evangelical Lutheran Congregation is recorded in the Norris Harris Church Register file, Maryland Historical Society, based on original records retained by the church in Hagerstown.
4. On Mason, see *Appleton's Cyclopaedia of American Biography*, ed. James Grant Wilson and John Fiske (New York: D. Appleton and Co., 1900), vol. 4, p. 242, which gives his birth date as 1764. His correct date of birth, March 15, 1765, and the date of his death, December 10, 1824, which are used in later sources, were provided by John Kilbourne of the Maryland Historical Society, as detailed in note 3. On the Mason family, see Pamela C. Copeland and Richard K. MacMaster, *The Five George Masons: Patriots and Planters of Virginia and Maryland* (Charlottesville: University Press of Virginia, 1975), including table 1, a family tree, between pp. 268 and 269; Mason Family Genealogy on the Gunston Hall Plantation Web site (www.gunstonhall.org/masonweb). For the date of their marriage, see Mrs. Copeland's letter of June 8, 1976, to the Cleveland Museum of Art, which gives a descendant as the source.
5. See entries on Stevens Thomson Mason and Thomson Mason in *DAB*, vol. 6, pp. 374–77.

Fig. 147. *Ann Barry*, 1804–5. Oil on canvas, 29¼ x 24 in. (74.3 x 61 cm). National Gallery of Art, Washington, D.C.; Gift of Jean McGinley Draper (1954.9.3)

72

6. Thomas J. C. Williams, *A History of Washington County, Maryland, from Its Earliest Settlements to the Present Time, including a History of Hagerstown* (1906; reprint, Baltimore: Regional Publishing Co., 1968), vol. 1, pp. 131–32; vol. 2, p. 908. The property, left to him or his brother Abraham Barnes Thomson Mason, was the source of later discord. Family documents are among the papers of his son in the John Thomson Mason Jr. Collection, 1774–1882, Ms. 2224, H. Furlong Baldwin Library, Maryland Historical Society. A letter from John T. Mason, to Mann Page Jr., August 11, 1787, in the John D. Rockefeller Jr.

Elizabeth Beltzhoover (1781–1836) was the daughter of Melchior and Elisabeth Beltzhoover of Hagerstown, Maryland. Her father had settled there by 1770, when he helped to found the Evangelical Lutheran Church.[3] In 1797 she married John Thomson Mason (1765–1824), a nephew of Revolutionary War era statesman George Mason IV of Gunston Hall.[4] His father, Thomson Mason, had served in the colonial Virginia Assembly, and his brother Stevens Thomson Mason was a United States senator from Virginia in 1795–1803.[5] John Thomson Mason studied law at William and Mary College and settled in Hagerstown.[6]

Although the couple made their home at Montpelier, their estate in Hagerstown, Mason's law practice required considerable travel and led him to establish an office in

Library, Colonial Williamsburg Foundation, Williamsburg, Va., indicates that he was studying law at William and Mary. His law career is referred to in the entry on his nephew John Thomson Mason (son of his brother Stevens Thomson Mason), in Hugh Blair Grigsby, *The History of the Virginia Federal Convention of 1788*, ed. R. A. Brock (Richmond: Virginia Historical Society, 1891), vol. 2, pp. 268–69.

7. Mason in Leonard Town, letter to his wife, May 20, 1810, and Mrs. Mason, letter to Mason in Annapolis, December 7, 1813, John Thomson Mason Jr. Papers, Ms. 2224, Maryland Historical Society.

8. John Thomson Mason Jr. Papers, Ms. 2224, box 1, Maryland Historical Society.

9. Elizabeth Mason, letter to her daughter Mary Barnes Mason "at Mr. Bronaughs George Town," March 3, 1811, Mason Family Manuscripts Collection, Gunston Hall Plantation, Mason Neck, Va.

10. Dumas Malone, *Jefferson the President: Second Term, 1805–1809* (Boston: Little, Brown and Co., 1974), pp. 35, 37.

11. Elizabeth Armistead Thomson Mason Wharton, "Memorandum," undated, Mason Family Manuscripts Collection, Gunston Hall Plantation.

Georgetown, District of Columbia.[7] His presence in Georgetown and his political connections in the administrations of Thomas Jefferson and James Madison no doubt provided the opportunity for his wife to sit for Stuart. A possible reference to the painting in family manuscripts is in "An Invoice of things to be sent to George Town," dated 1808, which lists enough furnishings for a small house or series of rooms. On the list, which includes furniture, dishes, "Mrs. Mason's Looking Glass," carpeting, and saddles, are "the pictures of Col. J. Barnes & Mrs. Mason," presumably the portrait of Elizabeth Mason and one of her husband's uncle John Barnes.[8] It appears, however, that his wife and their seven children lived primarily at Montpelier. In 1811, Mrs. Mason wrote from Montpelier to their eldest daughter, Mary Barnes Mason, who was at school in Georgetown, "I have given up the thoughts of visiting you this spring, but have not given up the pleasure of seeing you. You are to come home at Easter."[9] Although at times Mason was offered political appointments in the district or federal government, he either refused them or held them for only a short time. In about 1805 Mason turned down Jefferson's request that he serve as the United States attorney general.[10] In 1816 he ran for the Senate as the Democratic-Republican candidate against Robert Goodloe Harper but lost by one vote. Other than Stuart's portrait and the rare letter to or from Mrs. Mason, there is little personal documentation of her life. The only description of her is brief, found in a document written after her death by her daughter Elizabeth, who notes that she was "honoured, beloved, and lamented by all who knew her."[11]

EGM

73. BISHOP JOHN CARROLL

1804–5
Oil on canvas, 29 x 24 in. (73.7 x 61 cm)
Georgetown University Library, Washington, D.C.; Special Collections Division, Gift of Judge Pacificus Ord, 1895

This entry was researched and drafted by Sarah Efird Stephens.

1. On Carroll, see Annabelle M. Melville, *John Carroll of Baltimore: Founder of the American Catholic Hierarchy* (New York: Charles Scribner's Sons, 1955); Thomas O'Brien Hanley, S.J., ed., *The John Carroll Papers*, 3 vols. (Notre Dame, Ind.: University of Notre Dame Press, 1976); *ANB*, vol. 4, pp. 461–63; Thomas W. Spalding, *John*

John Carroll (1736–1815), the son of Maryland colonial merchant Daniel Carroll and his wife, Eleanor Darnall, studied abroad at the Jesuit College of Saint Omer in Flanders, entered the novitiate of the Society of Jesus in 1753, and was ordained in 1761.[1] After teaching and traveling in Europe, he returned to Maryland in 1774. His second cousin Charles Carroll of Carrollton, Maryland, was the only Roman Catholic signer of the Declaration of Independence. John Carroll played a major role in the establishment of the Roman Catholic Church in America, petitioning the pope in 1788 to create a bishopric, to be elected by the American clergy. In 1790 he was named the first Catholic bishop in the United States for the new diocese of Baltimore. Instrumental in the founding and growth of several Catholic educational institutions, including Georgetown College (now Georgetown University) in the District of Columbia, and Saint Mary's Seminary in Baltimore, he was named the country's first archbishop by Pope Pius VII in 1808, when Baltimore was made a Roman Catholic archdiocese.

Stuart painted Carroll when he was bishop of Baltimore.[2] Almost seventy years old, Carroll wears a dove gray robe and a large gold cross. The soft flesh of his face, with its rosy red cheeks and wispy gray shadows, is deftly described. His forehead has strong highlighting, his gray eyes are directed at the viewer, and his lips appear pursed, as if he is about to speak. The grays of his hair and robe are set against the warm tones of the

73

Carroll Recovered: Abstracts of Letters and Other Documents Not Found in the John Carroll Papers (Baltimore: Cathedral Foundation Press, 2000). On the Carroll family and Catholicism in America, see Joseph T. Durkin, S.J., and Annabelle M. Melville, "Catholicism and the Carrolls in Early Maryland," in Ann C. Van Devanter, *"Anywhere So Long As There Be Freedom": Charles Carroll of Carrollton, His Family and His Maryland*, exh. cat. (Baltimore: Baltimore Museum of Art, 1975), pp. 83–99.

2. The portrait is listed in Mason 1879, pp. 156–57; Park 1926, pp. 203–4, no. 143; Erik Larsen, *Catalogue of the Art Collection, Georgetown University* (Washington, D.C.: Georgetown University, 1963), pp. 85–86; Van Devanter, *"Anywhere So Long As There Be Freedom,"* pp. 200–201, 316.

3. Park 1926, p. 204. John Davis (2001, p. 314 n. 3) contrasts the portrait with the more active image of Bishop Cheverus (cat. 89).

4. Mason (1879, p. 156) was the first to write that the portrait was painted at Robert Barry's request.

5. Biographical information on Robert Barry is recorded in the file on this portrait in the J. Hall Pleasants Studies, no. 3461, Maryland Historical Society, Baltimore.

6. On James Barry, see Allen C. Clark, "Captain James Barry," *Records of the Columbia Historical Society of Washington, D.C.* 42–43 (1942), pp. 1–16; and correspondence between Barry and John Carroll, in *John Carroll Papers.*

7. Allen C. Clark, *Greenleaf and Law in the Federal City* (Washington, D.C.: W. F. Roberts, 1901), p. 237.

8. Anna Watkins, "James Barry and His Chapel," *Catholic Historical Society of Washington Newsletter*, January–March 1998, pp. 8–15.

9. Spalding, *John Carroll Recovered*, p. 236.

10. The portraits of Barry and his daughters are catalogued in Park 1926, pp. 133–35, nos. 57, 58, 60; the portrait of Joanna Gould Barry is not recorded in Park. For a more extensive study of the portraits of Mary and Ann Barry, see Miles 1995, pp. 230–35.

11. John C. Van Horne and Lee W. Formwalt, eds., *The Correspondence and Miscellaneous Papers of Benjamin Henry Latrobe* (New Haven: Yale University Press for the Maryland Historical Society, 1984–88), vol. 1, pp. 476–77.

12. *John Carroll Papers*, vol. 2, p. 520.

13. Van Devanter, *"Anywhere So Long As There be Freedom,"* pp. 204–5. A painting of Carroll, once attributed to Jeremiah Paul (owned by the Archdiocese of Baltimore; ibid., pp. 202–3, illus.), is now attributed to Joshua Johnson; see Carolyn J. Weekley and Stiles Tuttle Colwill with Leroy Graham and Mary Ellen Hayward, *Joshua Johnson: Freeman and Early American Portrait Painter*, exh. cat. (Williamsburg, Va.: Abby Aldrich Rockefeller Folk Art Center; Baltimore: Maryland Historical Society, 1987), p. 148, no. 60, illus.

14. Barry's will, filed in New York City, December 6, 1809, described him as "of the City of New York";

red curtain, which is tied with a gold cord ending in tassels. The books behind Carroll allude to his interest in education, and his index finger marks a page in the book that Lawrence Park called a breviary.[3] Stuart's portrait of the elderly bishop conveys an image of quiet dignity.

The commission of the portrait has been ascribed to Baltimore merchant Robert Barry (1775–1838) because the portrait was in his estate.[4] Barry emigrated from Ireland to New York, then moved to Baltimore, where from 1805 to 1821 he was a trustee of Baltimore Cathedral.[5] It is more likely, however, that his uncle James Barry (1755?–1808) commissioned the portrait. James Barry was born in Ireland and worked in India, where he met Englishman Thomas Law.[6] After arriving in New York

Fig. 148. William S. Leney and Benjamin Tanner after J. Paul, *The Most Reverend John Carroll, D.D., First Archbishop of Baltimore*, 1812. Engraving, 19½ x 15¾ in. (49.5 x 40 cm). National Portrait Gallery, Smithsonian Institution, Washington, D.C. (NPG. 74.58)

sometime in the early 1790s, Barry and Law became partners in real estate investments in Washington. In 1796 Barry was a trustee of the prenuptial financial arrangement between Law and Eliza Parke Custis (see cat. 50).[7] He lived in Baltimore until 1800 and served as local consul for Spain and Portugal. He then moved to the new capital, where he built a wharf and store on the Anacostia River, called the Eastern Branch of the Potomac, with a house nearby. He also had a country house at Poplar Point, across the Anacostia River. In 1806 he helped found Saint Mary's Chapel, one of the first Roman Catholic churches in Washington.[8] Barry, his wife, Joanna Gould Barry, and their daughters Ann (d. 1808) and Mary (d. 1805) became close friends of Bishop Carroll in Baltimore. Barry was a member of the first board of trustees of the Baltimore Cathedral congregation, which elected Carroll president at its first meeting on December 29, 1795.[9] Carroll oversaw the education of Mary Barry in Baltimore after the family moved to Washington.

In Washington, Stuart painted the portraits of Barry (fig. 149), his wife, Joanna (unlocated), and their two daughters (figs. 147, 150).[10] Barry may have known of Stuart's arrival in the city from Law, whose portrait Stuart had painted (fig. 115), or from the marqués de Yrujo, one of the artist's first clients in the city (see cat. 66). Yrujo had served as representative for Jerome Bonaparte in the negotiations for his marriage to Betsy Patterson in Baltimore on Christmas Eve, 1803, at which Carroll officiated (see cats. 67, 68). And soon Carroll met architect Benjamin Latrobe, who had designed and built a "painting room" for Stuart in Washington. Latrobe wrote to Carroll on April 10, 1804, with a discussion of flaws in the existing architectural plans for a new Roman Catholic cathedral in Baltimore and an offer to prepare his own plan.[11] Latrobe soon became the principal architect for the project.

Carroll sat for Stuart in Washington; his involvement with Georgetown College and other church administrative matters took him frequently to the city. In addition, his brother Daniel Carroll had been one of the city's first commissioners and a distant relative, Daniel Carroll of Duddington, was a landowner. Carroll's only reference to his portrait is in his letter of July 9, 1806, to James Barry: "Mr. [Jeremiah] Paul is a painter of eminence, who has recommended himself very much by his performance here. He was

Fig. 149. *James Barry*, 1804–5. Oil on canvas, 28¾ x 24 in. (73 x 61 cm). Princeton University Art Museum, Princeton, N.J.; Bequest of Aileen Osborn Webb (Mrs. Vanderbilt Webb)

Fig. 150. *Mary Barry*, 1804–5. Oil on canvas, 29¼ x 24¼ in. (74.3 x 61.6 cm). National Gallery of Art, Washington, D.C.; Gift of Jean McGinley Draper (1954.9.4)

a copy of the will was filed on July 17, 1811, with the Register of Wills, District of Columbia. Joanna Barry's will, filed October 22, 1811, is also with the Register of Wills, District of Columbia.

15. On Hurley, see *John Carroll Papers*, vol. 2, p. 482 n. 1.

16. The sale of the portrait is recorded in "Robert Barry's Account of Sales," Account of Sales, D.M.P. book 21, 1838, fol. 69, Register of Wills, Baltimore City (courtesy of Lance Humphries), as "[Painting of] Archbishop Carroll" to L. Rogers for $205.

17. News of the acquisition was announced in the *Georgetown College Journal* 23 (July 1895), p. 109.

18. Will of Joanna Barry, 1811, office of the Register of Wills, District of Columbia; Clark, "Captain James Barry," p. 13. The sale of the portrait is recorded in "Robert Barry's Account of Sales," Account of Sales, D.M.P. book 21, 1838, fol. 69; Register of Wills, Baltimore City (courtesy of Lance Humphries), as "Painting of Washington," sold to L. Rogers for $120. On the portrait, see also Park 1926, p. 882, no. 74; William Kloss and Doreen Bolger, *Art in the White House: A Nation's Pride* (Washington, D.C.: White House Historical Association in cooperation with the National Geographic Society, 1992), p. 349.

anxious to take my portrait, with a view of engraving it, to which I would not consent, out of delicacy for Stuart. But as he will never probably execute his *professed* intention, & Mr. Paul, a good judge, will employ an artist of great merit for the engraving, I have referred him to you for permission."[12] An engraving by William S. Leney and Benjamin Tanner published in Baltimore in 1812 (fig. 148) is inscribed *Painted by J. Paul*. The similarity of the image to Stuart's, with a change in the vestments that probably reflects Carroll's new status as archbishop, suggests that Paul's role was primarily that of copyist.[13]

While Stuart's painting of Carroll is not mentioned in James Barry's will, the portrait and six others by Stuart are specifically listed in the will of his widow, who died in 1811.[14] She bequeathed to the "Reverend Mr. Michael Hurly the Portrait of the Reverend Bishop Carroll done by Steward"; Hurley was an influential Roman Catholic priest in Philadelphia.[15] To her husband's nephew James David Barry she bequeathed "his Uncles, my Own, and my two dear Children's likenesses done by Steward," and to Eliza Law, daughter of Thomas Law, she left "her father's likeness done by Steward." She willed "the portrait done by Steward of General Washington" to her brother Garrett Gould. She also bequeathed $500 to Bishop Carroll, who was an executor of her will. While no record has been found concerning transfer of ownership of the portrait of Carroll from Reverend Hurley to James Barry's nephew Robert Barry, the portrait was included in the sale of Robert Barry's estate in 1838, at which it was purchased by Lloyd Nicholas Rogers of Druid Hill, Baltimore.[16] Judge Pacificus Ord of Washington, D.C., purchased the painting in 1895 from Rogers's daughter Eleanor Rogers Goldsborough for Georgetown University.[17] At the sale of Robert Barry's estate, Rogers also purchased the portrait of George Washington; it is the painting now at the White House (fig. 101).[18]

EGM

74. MARCIA BURNES VAN NESS

1805
Oil on canvas, 29¼ x 27⅞ in. (74.3 x 70.8 cm)
Collection of Richard Hampton Jenrette (589)

75. JOHN PETER VAN NESS

1805
Oil on canvas, 29⅛ x 24½ in. (74 x 62.2 cm)
Collection of Richard Hampton Jenrette (486)

John Peter Van Ness (1770–1846) was born near Kinderhook in Columbia County, New York. He attended Columbia College in New York City and read law. A protégé of Aaron Burr (see fig. 61), he went to Washington in 1801 after his election to the House of Representatives as a Democratic-Republican.[1] There he married Marcia Burnes (1782–1832), daughter of David Burnes, who owned a large portion of the land that is now the downtown area of Washington.[2] At her father's death in 1799, she inherited most of his estate.[3]

75

Edurne Poggi-Aranda did much of the initial
research on these portraits; early drafts of the entry
are by Emily Burns.

1. *Biographical Directory of the American Congress,
   1774–1971* (Washington, D.C.: U.S. Government
   Printing Office, 1971), p. 1852; Susan L. Klaus,
   "'Some of the Smartest Folks Here': The Van
   Nesses and Community Building in Early
   Washington," *Washington History* 3 (fall–
   winter 1991–92), pp. 23–45, 92–94; Frances
   Carpenter Huntington, "The Heiress of
   Washington City: Marcia Burnes Van Ness, 1782–
   1832," *Records of the Columbia Historical Society of
   Washington, D.C.*, 1969–70, pp. 80–101; Allen C.
   Clark, "General John Peter Van Ness, a Mayor of
   the City of Washington, His Wife, Marcia,
   and Her Father, David Burnes," *Records of the
   Columbia Historical Society, Washington, D.C.* 22
   (1919), pp. 125–205.
2. On Burnes, see Richard Hampton Jenrette,
   Adventures with Old Houses (Charleston, S.C.:

John Peter Van Ness wrote to his brother William Peter Van Ness on March 7, 1802, shortly before the wedding, "I wrote you a few days since that there was a prospect of my getting married before I returned home from this place. The prospect is still the same. And if my own feelings & sentiments and those of the Lady whom I have in view continue as they now are this event will [crossed out: probably] take place. The Lady's reputation, merit & prospects are all unimpeachable. She has a well improved mind & possesses personal accomplishments. I trust I shall do nothing that will dissatisfy my friends. I have consulted my own heart, and exercised all the prudence I am master of. . . . She is certainly a Girl of good sense, and personal accomplishments."[4] Aaron Burr wrote William Peter Van Ness the same day, "John (your brother meaning) is in a good Way. He has laid Siege to a charming Girl with an immense fortune and . . . will bear her off from forty rivals. He has really managed with wonderful address. It is probable that they will marry about the 6 or 8th apr [?]. But I strongly recommend to you to say not one Word on the subject, even to your father till you hear further from me. The Rivals would raise hell to defeat him if they suspected his good fortune."[5] Van Ness's friends in Washington included Dolley Madison and her sister Anna Payne Cutts, also

Wyrick and Co., 2000), p. 102; Klaus, "Some of the Smartest Folks Here," p. 24. Burnes's property, which he inherited from his father and grandfather, extended from H Street NW to Constitution Avenue, and from Third Street NW to Eighteenth Street NW.

3. Allen C. Clark, *Life and Letters of Dolley Madison* (Washington, D.C.: Press of W. F. Roberts Co., 1914), p. 251. The inheritance was worth about $1.5 million at the time, $14 million in 1991; see Klaus, "Some of the Smartest Folks Here," p. 26.

4. John Peter Van Ness, letter to William Peter Van Ness, March 7, 1802, William Peter Van Ness Papers, Ms. 74-569, Manuscripts and Archives Division, New York Public Library, Astor, Lenox and Tilden Foundations.

5. Aaron Burr, letter to William Peter Van Ness, March 7, 1802, Misc. Mss. Burr, Aaron, New-York Historical Society.

6. John Peter Van Ness, letter to William Peter Van Ness, March 5, 1802, William Peter Van Ness Papers, New-York Historical Society.

7. John Peter Van Ness, letter to William Peter Van Ness, May 12, 1802, William Peter Van Ness Papers, Ms. 74-569, New York Public Library.

8. For their address, see Klaus, "Some of the Smartest Folks Here," p. 27.

9. Now reunited, the portraits were separated for at least seventy years; see Jenrette, *Adventures with Old Houses*, p. 102. On Van Ness's portrait, see Mason 1879, p. 273; Park 1926, pp. 774–75, no. 864; "Museums and Collections: The Corcoran Gallery of Art, Washington, D.C.," *American Art Review* 2, no. 11 (1881), p. 211; Dinitia Smith, "An Estate Lives On, Thanks to Apples," *New York Times*, November 1, 2001, p. F9; Jenrette, *Adventures with Old Houses*, pp. 102–3. On Mrs. Van Ness's portrait, which was unknown to Mason and Park, see Jenrette, *Adventures with Old Houses*, pp. 102–3; Junior League of Washington, Thomas Froneck, ed., *The City of Washington: An Illustrated History* (New York: Alfred A. Knopf, 1977), p. 58.

10. For this portrait, see Park 1926, p. 523, no. 548, illus. On chemisettes, see Vanda Foster, *A Visual History of Costume: The Nineteenth Century* (London: B. T. Batsford; New York: Drama Book Publishers, 1984), pp. 31, 142.

11. The invoice is in the John Peter Van Ness Papers, box 2, folder 2, New-York Historical Society. The papers are part of the Van Ness–Philip Papers.

12. Cynthia D. Earman, "A Census of Early Boardinghouses," *Washington History* 12 (spring–summer 2000), pp. 118–21. In 1804–5, Stelle ran a hotel at A and First Streets NE. Between 1805 and 1809, he operated a hotel in Carroll's Row, at A and East Capitol Streets SE.

13. Klaus, "Some of the Smartest Folks Here," p. 30. John Peter Van Ness's papers at the New-York Historical Society include a number of pleas from merchants and tradesmen.

14. Klaus, "Some of the Smartest Folks Here," pp. 28–29; Huntington, "The Heiress of Washington City," p. 88.

painted by Stuart (cats. 70, 71); in his letter of March 5, 1802, to his brother regarding the upcoming event, he wrote, "I wish you would arrange your business so that either yourself & Mrs. Van Ness or yourself alone could pay this place a visit by about the first of April. Mrs. Madison and Miss Paine are frequently enquiring about you both and would be very happy to see you, as well as your other friends here."[6] Marcia Burnes and John Peter Van Ness were married in May 1802, as John Peter Van Ness reported to his brother: "I can now inform you that on the 9th Inst. I was married to Miss Marcia Burnes of this place. . . . She is a Lady who unites in herself all those personal & mental charms & qualifications which are eminently calculated to secure all that happiness which connexions of this kind are intended to produce."[7]

When Stuart painted the Van Nesses, they lived at Twelfth and D Streets NW, within walking distance of Stuart's studio.[8] In his portrait, John Peter Van Ness, in a black coat with a white shirt and shirt ruffle, is seated in an armchair upholstered in red.[9] He appears a more forceful personality than his wife, who faces him, seated in an identical chair with darker upholstery. She wears a black dress with a sheer white chemisette inside the low-cut bodice. Stuart depicted the chemisette asymmetrically as a frame for her heart-shaped face and graceful neck. Elizabeth Merry, wife of British envoy Anthony Merry, wears an identical white chemisette tucked into the bodice of her black dress in Stuart's portrait of her (Museo Lázaro Galdiano, Madrid), the last he painted in Washington.[10] The portraits of both Van Nesses appear quickly painted and have plain backgrounds without landscape or curtain details. This and the July date on an invoice from Stuart to John Peter Van Ness suggest that the portraits may have been among the last ones Stuart painted before leaving the city. The amount on the invoice, $100, could represent either payment for one of the Van Ness portraits or the second installment for the two portraits.[11] The invoice, signed by Stuart, reads:

> *Washington City July 12th 1805*
> *Mr. John P. Vanness*
> *Sir*
> *Please to pay to Mr. Pontius D. Stelle or order one hundred Dollars on Sight*
> *and you will much oblige*
> > *Yr. Hum. Servt.*
> > *Gilbert Stuart*
> *$100*

Stelle, who ran a hotel on Capitol Hill, was paid almost a year later; the endorsement on the reverse reads, "Recd the within May 26 1806 of J. P. Van Ness.—Pontius D. Stelle." A possible explanation for Stuart's specifying payment to Stelle is that he may have boarded at Stelle's hotel and owed him for lodging or meals.[12] A complicating aspect of Van Ness's debt may have been the fact that he was, in effect, Stuart's landlord, since he owned the property on which Benjamin Latrobe had built Stuart's studio (see "Stuart in Washington"). Actively involved in managing his wife's real estate, Van Ness was often late in paying his bills, and while "considered a wealthy man . . . he was often cash poor."[13]

Van Ness gave up his congressional seat in 1803. His appointment in the District of Columbia militia became a political issue because it was a federal position and holding two federal posts was not permitted by the Constitution.[14] He became a central figure in the growth and social life of the capital city, and he would serve as mayor from 1830 to 1834. He and others, including Henry Dearborn (see cat. 84), organized the first theater

15. John Peter Van Ness, letter to David Parish, April 25, 1815, Misc. Mss. Van Ness, Peter, New-York Historical Society. Parish had recommended architect Joseph Jacques Ramée for the position.
16. Clark, "General John Peter Van Ness," p. 157.
17. Clark, *Life and Letters of Dolley Madison*, p. 256. According to Clark, the *Daily National Intelligencer* for September 10, 1832, called Mrs. Van Ness "the guardian of the Orphan and the benefactress of the Poor." On her death and public funeral, see Klaus, "Some of the Smartest Folks Here," p. 42.

in Washington in 1803, and, again with Dearborn as well as Thomas Law (see fig. 115) and James Madison (see cat. 69), he was a subscriber to the city's dancing assembly in 1805. Serving as a major general in the militia during the War of 1812, Van Ness was involved in the reconstruction of Washington's public buildings that were burned by the British in 1814. In 1815 he hired Latrobe as architect for the rebuilding of the Capitol, explaining, "we considered that as Mr. Latrobe, whose professional talents are acknowledgedly great, had, from his former agency in the erection and completion of the Capitol, necessarily a knowledge of circumstances details and facts connected with the Building which must be useful to whoever undertakes the rebuilding of it, & which can not be known to others, that therefore it would be most adviseable to re-employ him."[15] The Van Nesses also hired Latrobe to design a new house for them on a large plot of land at the corner of Seventeenth and C Streets NW, which was begun in 1815. In 1821 their only child, Ann, married Arthur Middleton of Charleston, South Carolina.[16] Ann and her infant daughter died in 1823 following childbirth. Marcia Van Ness became increasingly involved in local charities, especially as director of the Washington Female Orphan Asylum, of which she was a founder after the War of 1812, and she died in 1832 while nursing cholera victims.[17]   EGM

76. JAMES MADISON

1805–7
Oil on canvas, 48½ x 39¾ in. (123.29 x 101 cm)
Bowdoin College Museum of Art, Brunswick, Maine; Bequest of the Honorable James Bowdoin III (BCMA 1813.054)

1. On the portrait of Madison for Bowdoin, see Mason 1879, p. 219; Park 1926, p. 497, no. 516; Theodore Bolton, "The Life Portraits of James Madison," *William and Mary Quarterly*, ser. 3, 8 (1951), pp. 30–31, 42; Marvin S. Sadik, *Colonial and Federal Portraits at Bowdoin College* (Brunswick, Maine: Bowdoin College Museum of Art, 1966), pp. 164–66; Richard H. Saunders III, "James Bowdoin III (1752–1811)," in Kenneth E. Carpenter et al., eds., *The Legacy of James Bowdoin III* (Brunswick, Maine: Bowdoin College Museum of Art, 1994), p. 22; Linda J. Docherty, "Preserving Our Ancestors: The Bowdoin Portrait Collection," in *Legacy of James Bowdoin III*, p. 68; Susan E. Wegner, "Copies and Education: James Bowdoin's Painting Collection in the Life of the College," in *Legacy of James Bowdoin III*, pp. 143, 148, 156; Evans 1999, p. 150 n. 4.

In 1805 Stuart received a commission from James Bowdoin III for a pair of portraits of Thomas Jefferson and James Madison, his secretary of state.[1] An admirer and political supporter of Thomas Jefferson, Bowdoin had written to Jefferson soon after his inauguration as president in 1801, expressing interest in a political appointment. He reiterated this interest to Henry Dearborn, a fellow landowner in Maine and Jefferson's secretary of war, who informed him in November 1804 that he had been appointed minister to the court of Spain.[2] Preparing for his departure, Bowdoin wrote Dearborn on March 25, 1805: "I shall be much obliged to you to procure me the portraits of Mr. Jefferson and Mr. Madison if a good painter can be found at Washington, and they should be willing to take the trouble of sitting therefor. I should be glad to have them sent to one of the Atlantic ports of Spain subject to my order. Mr. Winthrop will pay your draft on presentment for the amount of ye Painter's bill. I should like to have them done by Stuart, could he be induced to execute them, as well he is able. They need not be framed, as I can procure more fashionable and better frames in Europe. Please to let ye pictures be half length and of a size to match each other."[3]

Stuart posed the seated figures so that, when the portraits are displayed together, the two men turn toward each other, with Jefferson's head slightly higher than Madison's, as Madison was shorter. Madison's position on the left was dictated by his pose in the life portrait that Stuart painted for the Madisons the previous year. His body is in a more frontal pose than in the earlier portrait, and his glance is to the viewer's right, in the direction of Jefferson. The positioning of Madison's head is essentially the same, as seen in the shape of his powdered hair and coat collar.[4] He rests his arm on a table covered with a red drape. On the table are a few books, and behind Madison are a column and a red curtain in front of a

Fig. 151. *James Bowdoin*, ca. 1805. Oil on canvas, 29⅞ x 24¾ in. (75.9 x 62.9 cm). Bowdoin College Museum of Art, Brunswick, Maine; Bequest of Mrs. Sarah Bowdoin Dearborn (1870.006)

Fig. 152. *Sarah Bowdoin*, ca. 1805. Oil on canvas, 30⅛ x 25⅛ in. (76.5 x 63.8 cm). Bowdoin College Museum of Art, Brunswick, Maine; Bequest of Mrs. Sarah Bowdoin Dearborn (1870.007)

plain wall. Jefferson, who was painted to be positioned on the right, is also seated at a table draped with red, his hand on a paper next to some books; he looks directly at the viewer (cat. 77). The background of his portrait includes a curtain, a column, and sky with clouds.

Bowdoin did not spell out his reasons for commissioning these portraits in his letter. A recent assessment observes that the portraits were "originally intended to hang in the official residence in Madrid. For [Bowdoin], the appointment as Jefferson's minister to Spain marked the high point of his public career. Although his diplomatic mission proved unsuccessful, the Stuart commission provides ample evidence that he understood and respected the power of portraiture in the public sphere."[5] Precedents in Stuart's work for such diplomatic use of portraits can be seen in the portraits of George Washington, notably the one sent to the Marquis of Lansdowne in London in 1796 after the signing of the Jay Treaty (cat. 45). Charles Cotesworth Pinckney commissioned a version of that portrait to be sent to France when he went there as minister from the United States (see cat. 47). Bowdoin, moreover, knew firsthand the value of original works of art. He had inherited from his father, James Bowdoin II, the governor of Massachusetts from 1785 to 1787, a small collection that included mythological paintings, as well as prints and family portraits.[6] The Bowdoins had also commissioned portraits of themselves since about 1725, including works by John Smibert, Robert Feke, Joseph Blackburn, and John Singleton Copley, to which would soon be added portraits by Stuart, John Trumbull, and Edward Greene Malbone. Bowdoin also collected portraits of "worthies," as paintings of poets, philosophers, and statesmen had been known since the Renaissance; he had ten mezzotints of sculptures of ancient worthies, including Homer.[7]

Bowdoin's interest in collecting continued with his appointment abroad. Before leaving for Spain, he wrote Jefferson to offer his services as agent in acquiring paintings and sculpture in Europe. (He also offered the president a marble sculpture then believed to be of Cleopatra but now known as *Ariadne*, which Jefferson accepted.)[8] Later, in France, Bowdoin bought for himself a portrait of the comte de Mirabeau, the French statesman, and he tried to acquire some marble busts from Italy.[9]

Bowdoin arrived in Spain in poor health and soon left for London, where he learned that he should go to Paris to fulfill his primary mission, negotiating the American purchase of West Florida. By this time Stuart had begun the portraits of Jefferson and

2. On Bowdoin, see Sadik, *Colonial and Federal Portraits at Bowdoin College*, pp. 135–42; Saunders, "James Bowdoin III," pp. 1–31; *ANB*, vol. 3, pp. 274–75.

3. Bowdoin, letter to Dearborn, March 25, 1805, quoted in Sadik, *Colonial and Federal Portraits at Bowdoin College*, pp. 155–56. The paintings are of dimensions that eighteenth-century artists called "half length" because the canvas size was half of a full-length, lifesize canvas.

4. Sadik briefly discusses the positioning of the figures in *Colonial and Federal Portraits at Bowdoin College*, p. 166.

5. Docherty, "Preserving Our Ancestors," p. 68.

6. On Bowdoin's collection, see Wegner, "Copies and Education," pp. 141–85.

7. Ibid., pp. 148–49.

8. His letter, dated March 22, 1805, is quoted by Saunders and Wegner, who also discuss the sculpture; see Saunders, "James Bowdoin III," pp. 16–18, illus.; Wegner, "Copies and Education," pp. 143–44, illus. The sculpture is at Monticello.

9. See Saunders, "James Bowdoin III," pp. 21–22; Wegner, "Copies and Education," pp. 148–49, 174, no. 37.

Fig. 153. *James Madison*, 1821. Oil on canvas, 40 x 32 in. (101.6 x 81.3 cm). Mead Art Museum, Amherst College, Amherst, Mass.; Bequest of Herbert L. Pratt (1945.82)

Fig. 154. *James Madison*, ca. 1821. Oil on wood, 25 ¾ x 21 ⅜ in. (65.3 x 54.3 cm). National Gallery of Art, Washington, D.C.; Ailsa Mellon Bruce Fund (1979.4.2)

10. Dearborn, letter to Winthrop, June 27, 1805, quoted in Sadik, *Colonial and Federal Portraits at Bowdoin College*, p. 156.

11. Winthrop, letter to Bowdoin, August 14, 1807, quoted ibid., p. 161.

12. Bowdoin, letter to Winthrop, July 21, 1807, quoted ibid., p. 146.

13. Bowdoin, letter to Winthrop, October 13, 1807, quoted ibid., p. 161.

14. Saunders, "James Bowdoin III," p. 22.

15. The portrait of James Bowdoin III is believed to be a copy of the miniature (Bowdoin College Museum of Art) painted by Edward Malbone before Bowdoin left for Europe, while that of Sarah Bowdoin was painted from life but its date is uncertain; see Sadik, *Colonial and Federal Portraits at Bowdoin College*, pp. 144–55; Saunders, "James Bowdoin III," p. 17; Docherty, "Preserving Our Ancestors," pp. 59, 69.

16. On this portrait, see Mason 1879, p. 219; Park 1926, pp. 497–98, no. 517; Bolton, "Life Portraits of James Madison," p. 43; Lewis A. Shepard and David Paley, *A Summary Catalogue of the Collection at the Mead Art Gallery* (Middletown, Conn.: Distributed by Wesleyan University Press, 1978), pp. 196–97.

17. Stuart's remark was recorded by Alpheus Spring Packard (a member of the Bowdoin faculty); see Sadik, *Colonial and Federal Portraits at Bowdoin College*, p. 159, citing "Catalogue of Paintings in the Picture Gallery at Bowdoin College," ca. 1855, Bowdoin College Museum of Art. See also "Gilbert Stuart's Lost 'Catalogue' of the Paintings of James Bowdoin III," in *Legacy of James Bowdoin III*, p. 177.

18. On the Gibbs version, see Miles 1995, pp. 275–77.

Madison that Bowdoin had commissioned. On June 27, Dearborn, in Washington, wrote to Thomas L. Winthrop, husband of Bowdoin's niece Elizabeth Temple Winthrop, "By Mr. Bowdoins request I engaged Mr. Stuart to take a half length portrait of the President of the U.S. and one of Mr. Madison. Mr. Stuart has nearly completed them and will take them with his other effects to Boston and when completed will deliver them to you, to be forwarded to Mr. Bowdoin, and as Mr. Bowdoin requested me to draw upon you for the expence of the two portraits, I take the liberty of requesting you to pay Mr. Stuart the amount of his bills when presented."[10] Stuart completed the portraits after moving to Boston that summer. On August 14, 1807, Winthrop wrote to Bowdoin, "The Pictures of Mr. Jefferson & Mr. Madison remain with Mr. Stewart; you have omitted to give any directions respecting them."[11] However, Bowdoin had resigned from his appointment in May, after negotiations in Paris were unfruitful, and he returned home the following April without ever serving as minister in Spain. While in Paris, he filled a request from Stuart, which he sent to the artist through Thomas Winthrop: "a number of pencils [brushes] agreably to Mr. Stewart's request . . . [and] an assortment of impalpable colours, wch I understand are equally good & much more economical than colours ground in oil: in this case Mr. Stewart will put ye oil to ye colours as he wants them."[12] He notified Winthrop on October 13, 1807, that "With respect to Mr. Jefferson's and Mr. Madison's pictures, I wish them to be retained to be put up in my house."[13] The portraits were hung in Bowdoin's Boston home on his return.[14] Bowdoin bequeathed them to the college, named in honor of his father, that he endowed in Brunswick, Maine. The college also owns Stuart's portraits of Bowdoin and his wife, Sarah (figs. 151, 152).[15]

Stuart saw the portraits of Madison and Jefferson again in 1821. After receiving a commission from Boston framer and gilder John Doggett to paint a series of portraits of the first five presidents of the United States, Stuart went to Bowdoin College to copy the portrait of Madison.[16] (Of Doggett's series, only the portraits of Madison [fig. 153] and Monroe [cat. 87] survive.) Upon seeing his portraits of Madison and Jefferson at Bowdoin College, he declared "that he regarded them as good as originals."[17] While making the copy for Doggett, he also painted a smaller version for George Gibbs Jr. for a similar series of portraits of the first five presidents (fig. 154).[18]

EGM

77. THOMAS JEFFERSON

1805–7

Oil on canvas, 48 ½ x 39 ⅞ in. (123.2 x 101.3 cm)
Bowdoin College Museum of Art, Brunswick,
Maine; Bequest of the Honorable James
Bowdoin III (BCMA 1813.055)

This portrait of Thomas Jefferson (1743–1826), third president of the United States, was painted for James Bowdoin III at the beginning of Jefferson's second term.[1] The highly political commission, with the pendant portrait of James Madison, Jefferson's secretary of state, was intended for a diplomatic setting (see cat. 76). As Bowdoin requested, the paintings are "half length and of a size to match each other."[2] They were composed to be seen with Jefferson on the right, a position dictated by Madison's in the life portrait Stuart had already painted (cat. 69), which he copied for this commission. Jefferson is seated in a red-upholstered Directoire chair next to a red-draped table with papers and books. His body is turned to our left, and he looks directly at the viewer. In the background are a red drape, a column, and some sky with clouds. This is the largest of Stuart's portraits of Jefferson.

Jefferson had commissioned a portrait from Stuart in 1800, but it may never have been completed and does not survive.[3] Stuart may have hoped to finish it when he went to Washington, D.C., in December 1803; shortly after his arrival, he accepted partial payment from "S. Smith," probably Maryland Senator Samuel Smith, for a different portrait of Jefferson, which he apparently never painted.[4] Years later, Jefferson wrote, "With respect to mr Stuart, it was in May 1800, I got him to draw my picture, and immediately after the last sitting I paid him his price, he was yet to put the last hand to it, so it was left with him. when he came to Washington in 1805. he told me he was not satisfied with it, and therefore begged me to sit again, and he drew another which he was to deliver me instead of the first, but begged permission to keep it until he could get an engraving from it. I soon after got him to sketch me in the Medallion form, which he did on paper with Crayons. altho a slight thing I gave him another 100. D. [dollars] probably the treble of what he would have asked. this I have; it is a very fine thing altho' very perishable."[5] On June 18, 1805, after the medallion portrait (cat. 79) was completed, Jefferson wrote Stuart about the paintings: "Th: Jefferson pre[sents his compliments to Mr. Stewart,] and begs leave to send [him the inclosed for the trouble he gave him] in taking the head á [la antique. Mr. Stewart seemed to contemplate] having an engraving m[ade either from that or the first portrait;] he is free to use the on[e or the other at his choice; the one not pro]posed to be used Th: J. [will be glad to receive at Mr. Stewart's con]venience; the other wh[en he shall be done with it]."[6] Stuart kept the large portrait of Jefferson, although he did deliver the medallion portrait. And, as with the paintings of George Washington (cat. 39) and John Adams (cat. 59), the subsequent history of the portrait of Jefferson resulted in a frustrated client.

Bowdoin's painting is one of five versions that resulted from Jefferson's sittings for Stuart in 1805. Four survive, and the fifth was destroyed by fire in 1851. There is considerable uncertainty over which is the life portrait. The five works are: 1) this portrait, painted for James Bowdoin, finished in 1807;[7] 2) a bust-length painting on canvas measuring 30 by 25 inches, owned by James Madison (fig. 155), completed most likely before Stuart left Washington in 1805 and certainly delivered by 1806;[8] 3) the head-and-shoulders painting known as the Edgehill portrait, sent to Jefferson in 1821 (cat. 78); 4) a similar painting in the series of presidential portraits painted for George Gibbs Jr. (fig. 156);[9] 5) the version that was part of the series commissioned by Boston framer and gilder John Doggett; destroyed by fire at the Library of Congress in 1851, it is known today only from the lithograph attributed to Nicholas-Eustache Maurin (fig. 157).[10] While

1. Stuart's portraits of Jefferson have been documented by a number of authors, beginning in 1898 with Charles Henry Hart, "The Life Portraits of Thomas Jefferson," *McClure's Magazine* 11 (May 1898), pp. 47–55; followed by Park 1926, pp. 439–42, nos. 441–46 (no. 447, p. 443, is now identified as a copy by Matthew Harris Jouett). The subsequent writers have been Fiske Kimball, "The Life Portraits of Jefferson and Their Replicas," *Proceedings of the American Philosophical Society* 88, no. 6 (1944), pp. 497–534 (the section on Stuart's portraits, pp. 512–23, reproduces Kimball, "The Stuart Portraits of Jefferson," *Gazette des Beaux-Arts*, ser. 6, 23 [January–June 1943], pp. 329–44); Marvin S. Sadik, *Colonial and Federal Portraits at Bowdoin College* (Brunswick, Me.: Bowdoin College Museum of Art, 1966), pp. 155–64; Meschutt 1981; Alfred L. Bush, *The Life Portraits of Thomas Jefferson* (Charlottesville, Va.: Thomas Jefferson Memorial Foundation, 1987). The last is the most recent edition of a study first published in 1962 with the same title; the material was also published as "The Life Portraits of Thomas Jefferson," in William Howard Adams, ed., *Jefferson and the Arts: An Extended View* (Washington, D.C.: National Gallery of Art, 1976), pp. 9–100. Evans's (1999) discussion of Jefferson's portraits is found on pp. 91–92, 104–5, 150–51 n. 4, 153–54 n. 18.

For documents in the Thomas Jefferson Papers, Library of Congress, I have quoted from Series I: General Correspondence, 1651–1827, using the images of the letters on the American Memory Web site at the Library of Congress: http://memory.loc.gov. I thank T. Jefferson Looney, Editor, and Lisa Francavilla, Editorial Assistant, Papers of Thomas Jefferson: Retirement Series, Thomas Jefferson Memorial Foundation, Charlottesville; Susan R. Stein, Curator, Monticello; and Martha J. King, Associate Editor, Papers of Thomas Jefferson, Princeton University, for help with Jefferson's correspondence about these portraits.

2. Bowdoin, letter to Henry Dearborn, March 25, 1805, quoted in Sadik, *Colonial and Federal Portraits at Bowdoin College*, pp. 155–56.

3. For the 1800 portrait, see Kimball, "Life Portraits of Jefferson and Their Replicas," p. 512; Bush, *Life Portraits of Thomas Jefferson*, pp. 45–47, no. 14, illustrating an engraving published in London by Vernor and Hood. Meschutt (1981, p. 3) and Evans (1999, p. 150 n. 4) do not accept the engraving as

after Stuart's 1800 portrait of Jefferson. Meschutt agrees with Noble Cunningham's conclusion that the English engraving is in fact a reverse of Rembrandt Peale's first portrait of Jefferson; see Noble E. Cunningham Jr., *The Image of Thomas Jefferson in the Public Eye: Portraits for the People, 1800–1809* (Charlottesville: University Press of Virginia, 1981), pp. 41–43.

4. The receipt for $50, dated December 22, 1803, Harrison Gray Otis Papers Papers, 1691–1870, Massachusetts Historical Society, Boston, is quoted in Mount 1964, p. 263. Sadik (*Colonial and Federal Portraits at Bowdoin College*, p. 162 n. 4), Meschutt (1981, p. 3 n. 3), and Evans (1999, p. 150 n. 4) all suggest that Smith's version was never painted, while Mount (1964) believed that it was the original of the 1800 portrait and that Stuart fraudulently sold it to Smith, who was the brother of Robert Smith, Jefferson's secretary of the navy.

5. Jefferson, letter to Henry Dearborn, July 5, 1819, polygraph copy, Thomas Jefferson Papers, Library of Congress.

6. Jefferson, letter to Stuart, June 18, 1805, quoted in Kimball, "Life Portraits of Jefferson and Their Replicas," p. 512, from Hart, "Life Portraits of Thomas Jefferson," p. 48; partially quoted in Bush, *Life Portraits of Thomas Jefferson*, p. 61. The surviving left-hand section of the letter (outside the square brackets) is in the Manuscript and Ephemera Collection, Museum of the City of New York, gift of Mrs. J. Percy Sabin (37.300.10).

7. Park 1926, p. 439, no. 441; Sadik, *Colonial and Federal Portraits at Bowdoin College*, pp. 155–64; see also Kimball, "Life Portraits of Jefferson and Their Replicas"; Bush, *Life Portraits of Thomas Jefferson*; Meschutt 1981.

8. Park 1926, p. 441, no. 444; see also Kimball, "Life Portraits of Jefferson and Their Replicas"; Bush, *Life Portraits of Thomas Jefferson*; Meschutt 1981.

9. Park 1926, p. 442, no. 445; as well as Kimball, "Life Portraits of Jefferson and Their Replicas"; Bush, *Life Portraits of Thomas Jefferson*; Meschutt 1981. In Miles 1995, p. 266, I proposed that the Gibbs series was painted about 1821. Evans (1999, p. 153 n. 18) does not agree with this dating, proposing 1815–17.

10. Park 1926, p. 442, no. 446; see also Kimball, "Life Portraits of Jefferson and Their Replicas"; Bush, *Life Portraits of Thomas Jefferson*; Meschutt 1981.

11. Kimball, "Life Portraits of Jefferson and Their Replicas," p. 516. Sadik (*Colonial and Federal Portraits at Bowdoin College*, p. 163 n. 12) and Meschutt (1981) both recount the history of this debate. A different painting was proposed as the life portrait by its owner, Orland Campbell, but this theory has not been accepted by others; see *The Lost Portraits of Thomas Jefferson Painted by Gilbert Stuart Recovered and Studied by Orland and Courtney Campbell*, exh. cat., Mead Art Building, Amherst, Mass. (Mass.?: Amherst College?, 1959).

12. See Sadik, *Colonial and Federal Portraits at Bowdoin College*, pp. 159, 163 n. 12; Bush, *Life Portraits of Thomas Jefferson*, pp. 57–59.

13. See Mount 1964, p. 290; Meschutt 1981, p. 13.

Fig. 155. *Thomas Jefferson*, 1805. Oil on canvas, 30 x 25 in. (76.2 x 63.5 cm). Colonial Williamsburg Foundation

Fig. 156. *Thomas Jefferson*, ca. 1821. Oil on wood, 26 x 21½ in. (66 x 54.5 cm). National Gallery of Art, Washington, D.C.; Gift of Thomas Jefferson Coolidge IV in memory of his great-grandfather Thomas Jefferson Coolidge, his grandfather Thomas Jefferson Coolidge II, and his father, Thomas Jefferson Coolidge III (1986.71.1)

Lawrence Park in 1926 thought that the Bowdoin painting was the life portrait, the Edgehill was described as the life portrait in 1944 by Fiske Kimball, director of the Philadelphia Museum of Art.[11] Alfred Bush, who first wrote about the life portraits of Jefferson in 1962, and Marvin Sadik, former director of the National Portrait Gallery, writing in 1966, agreed with Kimball.[12] Charles Merrill Mount in 1964 and David Meschutt in 1981 suggested instead that the portrait in Madison's collection is the life portrait.[13] Dorinda Evans proposed in 1999 that the life portrait was the painting on a canvas measuring about 50 by 40 inches that Henry Pickering saw in Stuart's Boston studio in 1817: "I saw a head of Mr. Jeffersons at Mr. Stuart's today for the first time. Mr. S. told me it was executed at one sitting. It appears to be a fine likeness. It is intended to be a *three-quarters*. For this size his price is $300. I observed to Mr. S. that I should not know precisely what size a picture would be, from the terms used by painters. He immediately took a piece of chalk & described the different sizes as follows—the smallest compartment being first delineated, & the other lines added. The smallest compartments are *Heads*— Both together form a *Kitcat*—Two Kitkats make a *Three-Quarters*—& two Three Quarters constitute a whole length Portrait. Thus—" (fig. 158).[14] Evans proposed that

Fig. 157. Attributed to Nicholas-Eustache Maurin after Gilbert Stuart, *Thomas Jefferson*, 1828. Lithograph, 11½ x 9⅝ in. (29.2 x 24.5 cm). National Portrait Gallery, Smithsonian Institution, Washington, D.C. (NPG.87.58.3)

77

14. Pickering 1817 (November 4). This comment about Jefferson's portrait is cited and partially quoted in Evans 1999, p. 151 n. 4. Pickering's terms are not correct. He confused the kit-cat format with the three-quarter size (30 x 25 in.). In fact, two "heads" were cut from a "three-quarters" canvas, and two "three-quarters" canvases were cut from a "half-length" (50 x 40 in.).

15. Evans 1999, pp. 104, 150–51 n. 4.

16. Meschutt 1981, p. 13, citing William Dunlap's diary entry for February 15, 1806; Dunlap borrowed the painting to copy it.

17. Jefferson, letter to Joseph Delaplaine, May 20, 1816, polygraph copy, Thomas Jefferson Papers, Library of Congress.

18. Kimball ("Life Portraits of Jefferson and Their Replicas," p. 518) cites eight examples that he found illustrated in Park 1926; Sadik, *Colonial and Federal Portraits at Bowdoin College*, p. 161.

19. Cunningham, *Image of Thomas Jefferson in the Public Eye*, pp. 87–92, engraving illus. p. 89.

20. Pickering 1817 (November 4).

21. Jefferson, letter to Henry Dearborn, March 26, 1820; Jefferson, letter to Joseph Delaplaine, May 3, 1814; polygraph copies, Thomas Jefferson Papers, Library of Congress.

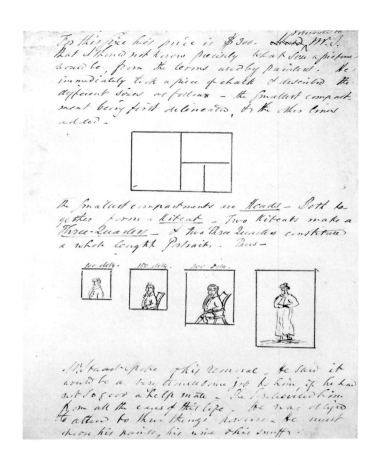

Fig. 158. Henry Pickering, diagrams of painting sizes and prices, 1817. Ink on paper. The Pickering Foundation, Salem, Mass. (photo: Peabody Essex Museum, Salem)

this was the portrait Stuart sold to John Doggett in 1821. She noted that Doggett and artist Washington Allston considered the pictures of Adams and Jefferson that Stuart painted for Doggett to be among Stuart's best perhaps because both were painted from life sittings.[15]

This theory is very plausible, given Pickering's description of the painting. Stuart would have derived the other versions from this original. The version owned by James Madison was completed and delivered before Stuart left Washington; it was in Madison's possession by early 1806.[16] Jefferson wrote of it in 1816, "I have no doubt that the copy of my portrait at the President's residence in Orange (3. miles off the stage road) is as good as the original in the possession of Stewart."[17] Stuart finished the portrait for James Bowdoin in Boston in 1807, according to correspondence between Bowdoin and Thomas Winthrop (see cat. 76). Moreover, Stuart used this type of chair only in portraits that he painted soon after his arrival there.[18] In March 1807 Robert Field published a bust-length engraving of the portrait, with a column in the background, which was advertised for sale in the Boston *Independent Chronicle*.[19] The final two versions were painted years later for Jefferson (cat. 78) and for George Gibbs Jr.

Stuart spoke of Jefferson's charm to Henry Pickering in 1817: "Mr. S. mentioned Mr. Jefferson's companionable talents. They had long been friends, tho' they differed in politicks. Mr. J. knew very well how to please his guests—he presided with grace & ease & dignity at his own table. Mr. S. said slily that Mr. Jefferson took very good care not to make a too great display of his learning."[20] Jefferson preferred the portrait that Stuart had begun in 1800 to the one painted in 1805; "there was something pleasanter in the aspect of that portrait & which I liked better than the second drawn at Washington." Jefferson knew, however, that Stuart considered the later one "the best of the two."[21]

EGM

78. THOMAS JEFFERSON (THE EDGEHILL PORTRAIT)

1805/21

Oil on wood, 26 ⅛ x 21 in. (66.4 x 53.3 cm)
Jointly owned by Monticello, the Thomas Jefferson
Foundation, Incorporated, Charlottesville, Virginia
(1982-53), and the National Portrait Gallery,
Smithsonian Institution, Washington, D.C.
(NPG.82.97); purchase funds provided by the
Regents of the Smithsonian Institution, the Trustees
of the Thomas Jefferson Foundation, Incorporated,
and the Enid and Crosby Kemper Foundation

1. On this portrait, see Park 1926, pp. 440–41, no. 443; Fiske Kimball, "The Life Portraits of Jefferson and Their Replicas," *Proceedings of the American Philosophical Society* 88, no. 6 (1944), pp. 516–20; Marvin S. Sadik, *Colonial and Federal Portraits at Bowdoin College* (Brunswick, Maine: Bowdoin College Museum of Art, 1966), pp. 159–61, 163 n. 12; Meschutt 1981, pp. 8–9; Alfred L. Bush, *The Life Portraits of Thomas Jefferson* (Charlottesville, Va.: Thomas Jefferson Memorial Foundation, 1987), pp. 57–59; Susan R. Stein, *The Worlds of Thomas Jefferson at Monticello* (New York: Harry N. Abrams in association with the Thomas Jefferson Memorial Foundation, 1993), pp. 113, 138–39; Evans 1999, pp. 92, 151 n. 4. Also see cat. 77, note 1, for a discussion of the manuscript sources.

2. On Delaplaine, see Gordon M. Marshall, "The Golden Age of Illustrated Biographies: Three Case Studies," in Wendy Wick Reaves, ed., *American Portrait Prints: Proceedings of the Tenth Annual American Print Conference* (Charlottesville: University Press of Virginia, 1984), pp. 29–45, 72.

3. Jefferson, letter to Joseph Delaplaine, May 30, 1813, polygraph copy, Thomas Jefferson Papers, Library of Congress, Washington, D.C.

4. Jefferson, letter to Delaplaine, May 3, 1814, polygraph copy, Thomas Jefferson Papers, Library of Congress.

5. Jefferson, letter to Stuart, August 9, 1814, Rosenbach Museum and Library, Philadelphia; the first half of the letter is quoted in Kimball, "Life Portraits of Jefferson and Their Replicas," p. 512; Meschutt 1981, p. 6.

This portrait is known today as the Edgehill portrait from its ownership by Jefferson's descendants, the Randolphs, at Edgehill, Albemarle County, Virginia. It was described as Stuart's life portrait by Fiske Kimball in 1944, a conclusion with which Alfred Bush and Marvin Sadik agreed.[1] While Jefferson believed that he received the life portrait from his sittings for Stuart in 1805, Stuart instead apparently belatedly fulfilled the commission with a copy.

Jefferson's attempts to obtain the painting from Stuart began in earnest in 1813, because of a request from Philadelphia publisher Joseph Delaplaine for a portrait that could be engraved for his proposed publication *Repository of the Lives and Portraits of Distinguished American Characters.*[2] Jefferson's letters document his respect for Stuart's talent and his patience with the artist, although he was relieved when he finally obtained the painting. Thinking that Stuart had two life portraits, one from sittings in 1800 and one from sittings in 1805 (see cat. 77), Jefferson wrote Delaplaine in May 1813, "mr Stuart has drawn two portraits of me, at different sittings, of which he prefers the last. both are in his possession. he also drew a third in water colours, a profile in the medallion stile [cat. 79], which is in my possession. mr Rembrandt Peale also drew a portrait in oil colours on canvas while I lived in Washington. of the merit of these I am not a judge, there being nothing to which a man is so incompetent as to judge of his own likeness. he can see himself only by reflection, and that of necessity full-faced or nearly so."[3] He wrote Delaplaine again in 1814: "The two original portraits of myself taken by mr Stewart, after which you enquire, are both in his possession at Boston. One of them only is my property. the President [Madison] has a copy from that which Stewart considered as the best of the two; but I believe it is at his seat in this state."[4] Jefferson then wrote Stuart, reiterating what he understood was their agreement, that Stuart would keep the painting until a print could be made, which Jefferson thought had been done, having seen a print of it. He went on to say that Delaplaine was asking permission to engrave it, and, in order to obtain the painting finally for himself, he proposed, "I have therefore authorised him to ask for the portrait in your possession, to copy his print from it, & return it to me." Jefferson continued:

With a high veneration for your talents, & sincere good wishes that they might have abundant employment for the establishment of your own happiness and fame, I learned with pleasure the extensive work in which you were engaged in Boston. yet nature having spread with pretty equal hand her gifts of worth and wisdom over the different parts of the Union, it would have been more consonant with her plan, & our wishes, that your talents should have been applied to their commemoration with the same equal hand. your former central position was more favorable to this, and certainly you could never there have been without more than you could do. I do not think, with some, that man is so far the property of society as that it may command the use of his faculties without regard to his own will or happiness: but it is at least to be wished that the inclination should generally be coupled with the power of aiding the reasonable objects of those with whom we live; and I am not without a hope that you will resume the function of leaving to the world your own excellent originals rather than copies from inferior hands of characters of local value only. pardon these observations. they flow not merely from considerations of public concern, but equally from great personal regard, and the desire that the employment of your talents should be worthy of their dignity. I add with great sincerity assurances of my high respect and consideration.[5]

78

6. Bush, *Life Portraits of Thomas Jefferson*, pp. 64–67, no. 20.

7. Jefferson, letter to Henry Dearborn in Boston, October 27, 1818, polygraph copy, Thomas Jefferson Papers, Library of Congress.

8. Dearborn, letter to Jefferson, November 6, 1818, Thomas Jefferson Papers, Library of Congress, incorrectly cited in Kimball, "Life Portraits of Jefferson and Their Replicas," p. 514, and some later authors as written on November 16 rather than on November 6.

9. Dearborn, letter to Jefferson, June 24, 1819, and Jefferson, letter to Dearborn, July 5, 1819 (polygraph copy), Thomas Jefferson Papers, Library of Congress.

Apparently nothing came of Jefferson's request, for Delaplaine instead commissioned Philadelphia artist Bass Otis in 1816 to paint Jefferson's portrait for him to engrave.[6]

Four years later Jefferson renewed his effort to obtain the portrait from Stuart. He wrote to Henry Dearborn (see cat. 84), who had arranged the sittings in 1805, asking if he could, "without involving yourself in offence with Stewart, obtain thro' any channel, a frank and explicit declaration on what ground he detains my portrait? for what term? and whether there is to be an end of it? I think he has now had it 10. or 12. years. I wrote to him once respecting it, but he never noticed my letter."[7] Stuart's answer, conveyed to Dearborn by Dearborn's son Henry A. S. Dearborn, was that "he could not finish it in cold weather, but would certainly complete it in the Spring."[8] After Dearborn wrote to Jefferson in June 1819 that "I suspect that you have paid him in part, or in full, in advance," Jefferson replied with a history of his portraits (see cat. 77).[9] The discussion continued for another year and offers insight into Stuart's attitude toward the life portrait,

10. Dearborn, letter to Jefferson, January 20, 1820, Thomas Jefferson Papers, Library of Congress.

11. Jefferson, letter to Dearborn, February 5, 1820, polygraph copy, Thomas Jefferson Papers, Library of Congress.

12. Dearborn, letter to Jefferson, March 3, 1820, Thomas Jefferson Papers, Library of Congress.

13. Jefferson, letter to Dearborn, March 26, 1820, polygraph copy, Thomas Jefferson Papers, Library of Congress.

14. Evans 1999, p. 151 n. 4; Henry A. S. Dearborn's letter about shipment of the portrait, dated May 21, 1821, is quoted in Kimball, "Life Portraits of Jefferson and Their Replicas," p. 516.

15. Jefferson, letter to Henry Dearborn, August 17, 1821, polygraph copy, Thomas Jefferson Papers, Library of Congress.

16. On Jouett's copies, see William Barrow Floyd, *Matthew Harris Jouett: Portraitist of the Ante-Bellum South*, exh. cat. (Lexington, Ky.: Transylvania University, 1980), pp. 14, 69.

17. See Evans 1999, p. 151 n. 4, for her discussion of the Edgehill portrait as a late replica.

18. Kimball, "Life Portraits of Jefferson and Their Replicas," p. 516, quoting Mrs. Randolph's granddaughter Mrs. William B. Harrison, who said that Stuart assured her grandmother it was the original.

19. For three of these, see Robert G. Stewart, *A Nineteenth-Century Gallery of Distinguished Americans*, exh. cat. (Washington, D.C.: Smithsonian Institution Press for the National Portrait Gallery, 1969), p. 45; Virginius Cornick Hall Jr., comp., *Portraits in the Collection of the Virginia Historical Society: A Catalogue* (Charlottesville: University Press of Virginia, 1981), p. 127; Clarence Winthrop Bowen, ed., *The History of the Centennial Celebration of the Inauguration of George Washington as First President of the United States* (New York: D. Appleton and Co., 1892), p. 484, illus. facing p. 21. A painted copy by Asher B. Durand (ca. 1835; New-York Historical Society) also shows a dark background, but the Edgehill version may not be the source; see *Catalogue of Portraits in the New-York Historical Society* (New Haven: Yale University Press, 1974), vol. 1, pp. 399–400.

20. Bush, *Life Portraits of Thomas Jefferson*, p. 59, noting that the dark background can be seen in reproductions made when it was owned by Burton Harrison, 1902–27.

which he apparently had always thought of as painted for himself, as the first stage to completing the Bowdoin commission. Dearborn wrote Jefferson, "feeling a little out of patience, I observed to him that I would inform you that you must never expect to have it. I then indicated his having received pay for it, he said that you paid him one hundred dollars for one that you now have in your home, and that he received one hundred dollars for a Medallion, but had received nothing for the one he now has, that he painted this for himself, that he had no commission from any one to paint it, I was too much out of temper to say any thing more to him and retired."[10] And Jefferson replied, "he must have spoken without reflexion when he supposed it in my possession and hanging in my hall. the peculiarities of his temper and ideas render him a difficult subject to handle. in the inclosed letter I have endeavored to bring his recollection to rights as softly as I can. with respect to the 1st canvas portrait I thought it a good one, and should have been contented with it, had he not himself been dissatisfied with it; and still if he chuses to deliver that instead of the 2d if he will finish and deliver it I shall be satisfied."[11] Dearborn responded that Stuart "now ownes that he had been mistaken, & that he has received one hundred dollars for the portrait, which you have not received, and only wants to know whether you would prefer a common portrait or one of half the length of the Body, the former at $100, the latter $300."[12] Jefferson advised Dearborn, "I shall be perfectly content to recieve the original he drew in Philadelphia in 1805 [Jefferson presumably meant 1800], which was of the common size (what the painters call, I believe, a bust) it will suit me better than a half length, as it will range better in the line of my other portraits, not one of which is half length. I have no doubt that mr Stuart's justice will think me entitled to the original, & not merely a copy. there was something pleasanter in the aspect of that portrait & which I liked better than the second drawn at Washington."[13]

As Dorinda Evans suggests, Jefferson's preference for the smaller size, to agree with the other portraits of himself that he owned, probably led Stuart to paint the Edgehill portrait, an entirely new bust-size replica, which he sent to Jefferson the following year.[14] Jefferson thanked Dearborn on August 17, 1821.[15]

The close similarity of the details in this version to the one painted for George Gibbs Jr. (fig. 156) makes a persuasive case that both date from this late period. In particular, the two paintings show Jefferson without his hair tied in the queue ribbon that is a feature of the Bowdoin and Madison versions (cat. 77, fig. 155); the queue ribbon also appears in the portrait that Kentucky artist Matthew Harris Jouett copied in Stuart's Boston studio in 1816.[16] In addition the Edgehill and Gibbs portraits are both painted on wood panels of the dimensions that Stuart used in Boston but not in Washington, and, as Evans pointed out, the head in the Edgehill painting is "outlined in the manner Stuart used for replicas."[17] While Jefferson was satisfied to end the long, drawn-out business deal, his daughter Martha Jefferson Randolph remembered later that when the portrait arrived, the paint on the coat was still fresh and she wondered if it was a replica.[18] The portrait also had a dark background, as seen in nineteenth-century copies, including an engraving by J. B. Forrest published in 1835, a painting by Louis Mathieu Didier Guillaume of about 1858 (Virginia Historical Society, Richmond), a book reproduction of 1892, and a painted copy by Edward Caledon Bruce (1896; private collection).[19] Alfred Bush commented that "subsequently this dark ground and a considerable amount of repainting has been removed to reveal the delicate, transparently painted surface of the original."[20] The result is a very fresh image of the third president.

EGM

79. Thomas Jefferson (The Medallion Portrait)

1805

Grisaille of aqueous medium on blue laid paper on canvas, 18 x 18-3/8 in. (46 x 46.7 cm)

Fogg Art Museum, Harvard University Art Museums, Cambridge, Massachusetts; Gift of Mrs. T. Jefferson Newbold and family, in memory of Thomas Jefferson Newbold, Class of 1910 (1960.156)

The best life portrait of Jefferson that Stuart painted may be this unique profile, quickly done on paper with a water-based paint.[1] The medallion portrait is a tribute to Jefferson's patience with Stuart and his admiration for the artist's talents. After sitting for Stuart for the portrait commissioned by James Bowdoin (cat. 77), the president sat for this portrait, known as the medallion portrait, painted at his request.[2] Writing to Philadelphia publisher Joseph Delaplaine in 1813 about the portraits Stuart had made of him, Jefferson described this work as "in water colours a profile in the medallion stile, which is in my possession."[3] Jefferson's admiration for Stuart's talents is clear in their exchanges at the time the portrait was painted. At his visit to Stuart's studio on June 7, 1805, when a sitting for this or the earlier large portrait may have taken place, the two discussed colors for the floor of the entrance hall at Monticello. The next day Jefferson sent James Dinsmore, a joiner at Monticello, a paint sample given him by Stuart: "After writing to you yesterday, I was at the painting room of mr Stewart (the celebrated portrait painter) who had first suggested to me the painting a floor green, which he had himself tried with fine effect. he observed that care should be taken to hit the true *grass-green*, & as he had his pallet & colours in his hand, I asked him to give me a specimen of the colour, which he instantly mixed up to his mind, and I spread it with a knife on

1. The portrait is catalogued in Park 1926, p. 440, no. 442; and is discussed also in Fiske Kimball, "The Life Portraits of Jefferson and Their Replicas," *Proceedings of the American Philosophical Society* 88, no. 6 (1944), pp. 512, 521; David Meschutt, "Gilbert Stuart's Portraits of Thomas Jefferson," *American Art Journal* 13 (winter 1981), pp. 15–16; Alfred L. Bush, *The Life Portraits of Thomas Jefferson* (Charlottesville, Va.: Thomas Jefferson Memorial Foundation, 1987), pp. 60–63; Noble E. Cunningham Jr., *The Image of Thomas Jefferson in the Public Eye: Portraits for the People, 1800–1809* (Charlottesville: University Press of Virginia, 1981), pp. 92–95, Susan R. Stein, *The Worlds of Thomas Jefferson at Monticello* (New York: Harry N. Abrams in association with the Thomas Jefferson Memorial Foundation, 1993), p. 141; Evans 1999, pp. 91–92. Bush (*Life Portraits of Thomas Jefferson*, p. 61) explained that the drawing is "executed in gouache—opaque watercolor—over a lightly indicated crayon drawing on hand-made laid paper . . . mounted on thin linen, which in turn is mounted on modern artist's canvas and varnished."

2. Jefferson, letter to Henry Dearborn, July 5, 1819, polygraph copy, Thomas Jefferson Papers, Library of Congress, Washington, D.C.

3. Jefferson, letter to Delaplaine, May 30, 1813, polygraph copy, Thomas Jefferson Papers, Library of Congress. On Delaplaine, see Gordon M. Marshall, "The Golden Age of Illustrated Biographies: Three Case Studies," in Wendy Wick Reaves, ed., *American Portrait Prints: Proceedings of the Tenth Annual American Print Conference* (Charlottesville: University Press of Virginia, 1984), pp. 29–45, 72.

4. Jefferson, letter to James Dinsmore, June 8, 1805, in Charles T. Cullen and Martha T. Briggs, *Th. Jefferson, a Life with Letters: An Exhibition Honoring the 250th Anniversary of the Birth of the Sage of Monticello* (Chicago: Newberry Library, 1993), p. 4. I thank Susan Stein, Curator, Monticello, and Martha J. King, Associate Editor, Papers of Thomas Jefferson, Princeton University, for assistance in locating and transcribing this letter.

5. "A Varnish for mahogany furniture from Gilbert Stuart," n.d., Thomas Jefferson Papers, Library of Congress.

6. James A. Bear Jr. and Lucia C. Stanton, eds., *Jefferson's Memorandum Books: Accounts, with Legal Records and Miscellany, 1767–1826,* Papers of Thomas Jefferson, second series (Princeton, N.J.: Princeton University Press, 1997), vol. 2, p. 1156. Kimball ("Life Portraits of Jefferson and Their

the inclosed paper."[4] This may also have been when Stuart gave Jefferson a recipe for varnish for mahogany furniture, which survives in Jefferson's handwriting.[5]

Jefferson paid for the portrait on June 18, noting in his memorandum book: "Pd. Gilbert Stewart for drawing my portrait 100. D."[6] Painted only a year after the profile portrait by Charles Balthazar Julien Févret de Saint-Mémin (1804; Worcester Art Museum), the portrait shows Jefferson with a short haircut of the type then fashionable in France. While the older fashion, in which a man's hair was pulled back and tied in a queue, had political associations with the Federalists, the short haircut became a political gesture that was distinctly pro-Jefferson, a neoclassical style with antecedents found on Roman coins and in Roman sculpture.[7] The medallion portrait was delivered to Jefferson sometime before Stuart left Washington in the summer of 1805. William Birch saw it at the President's House (now the White House) about October 1805 and borrowed it to make a drawing, which was engraved by David Edwin in 1809.[8]

The profile was considered by family and friends one of the best likenesses of Jefferson. To Horatio G. Spafford, Jefferson wrote that it was "deemed the best which has been taken of me."[9] William Dunlap asked permission to copy it, as did William Thornton and Charles Bird King (National Portrait Gallery, Washington).[10] Thornton wrote that the portrait was "one of the finest [he] ever saw."[11] Jefferson's daughter Martha Jefferson Randolph is said to have commented that the profile "best gives the shape of his magnificent head and its peculiar pose."[12] After Jefferson's death in 1826, his collection was sent to Boston, where it was exhibited at the Athenaeum and sold. However, the medallion portrait was reserved from the sale and became the property of Jefferson's descendants in the Coolidge family.[13] Either this or the Edgehill portrait (cat. 78) was included in the exhibition of Stuart's work in 1828 at the Athenaeum, listed as "THOMAS JEFFERSON. The original head, painted for Mr. JEFFERSON."[14]

EGM

Replicas," p. 512) dated this payment to June 7, 1805, a date that has been repeated by subsequent authors on this portrait.

7. On the profile of Jefferson, see Ellen G. Miles, *Saint-Mémin and the Neoclassical Profile Portrait in America* (Washington D.C.: National Portrait Gallery, Smithsonian Institution Press), pp. 130–31 illus., 326–27. In 1801 American commanding general James Wilkinson ordered the army to cut their queues; see ibid., pp. 186–87.

8. Cunningham, *Image of Thomas Jefferson in the Public Eye*, pp. 93–95.

9. Jefferson, letter to Horatio Gates Spafford, February 21, 1815, Coolidge Collection of Thomas Jefferson Manuscripts, 1705–1826, Massachusetts

Historical Society, Boston, quoted in Bush, *Life Portraits of Thomas Jefferson*, p. 62; Cunningham, *Image of Thomas Jefferson in the Public Eye*, p. 95.

10. On the copies, see Bush, *Life Portraits of Thomas Jefferson*, pp. 62–63.

11. Quoted in Bush, *Life Portraits of Thomas Jefferson*, p. 62.

12. Quoted ibid.

13. Robert F. Perkins Jr. and William J. Gavin III, comps. and eds., *The Boston Athenaeum Art Exhibition Index, 1827–1874* (Boston: Boston Athenaeum, 1980), p. 135, no. 314; and Bush, *Life Portraits of Thomas Jefferson*, p. 62.

14. Boston 1828, p. 7 no. 137.

Stuart in Boston (1805–28)

Stuart moved to Boston in July 1805 at the invitation of United States Senator Jonathan Mason of Massachusetts, who, along with his wife, Susannah Powell (fig. 137), and daughters Anna (fig. 136) and Miriam, sat for Stuart in Washington, D.C. Eager to bring such a remarkable and famous painter to his constituency, Mason promised Stuart commissions from his family and friends in Boston, a relatively small city in which nearly all members of elite society were connected to the senator in some way. More than this, Mason reportedly pledged to use "his influence with his connexions and the public at large as sitters," effectively offering Stuart an introduction to the entire town.[1] Stuart also had his own group of family members and acquaintants. Sarah Apthorp Morton (see cat. 60) was in Boston, with her circle of potential clients. Isaac P. Davis, a wealthy manufacturer of cables and cordage for constructing rope walks who cultivated friendships with many artists, became devoted to Stuart and his work.[2] Former president John Adams and his wife, Abigail, now lived in nearby Quincy; Stuart still had not delivered their portraits, which he had begun in Philadelphia five years earlier (cats. 58, 59). Stuart's mother lived in Boston with his sister, Anne Stuart Newton, who was raising a large family and running a boarding school for girls. Stuart's oldest friend, Benjamin Waterhouse, was now a distinguished surgeon in Cambridge. It could be said that Stuart was coming home.

After having followed the national government from place to place—from New York to Philadelphia to Washington—Stuart might have looked forward to Boston as a respite from the political arena. Dolley Madison remarked to her sister Anna Payne Cutts (see cats. 70, 71), "[Stuart] is a man of genius, and therefore does every thing differently from other people—He travels to the Southward on his way Northward," implying that Boston was always his ultimate destination.[3] Stuart would live in Boston for twenty-three years, until his death in 1828, although the announcement of his arrival in Boston's *Columbian Centinel* for July 31, 1805, presented him as a visitor: "Mr. Stuart, the celebrated painter, who has immortalized his fame by his masterly portrait of our deceased Washington, is now on a visit to this town from Philadelphia."[4] In 1808, he told Waterhouse that he would leave Boston soon for it was "too cold a climate for his constitution."[5] Not being the sort who made decisions based on the weather, Stuart never left because there was every reason to stay.

He did, however, move around quite a bit. Upon arrival he boarded at Chapotin's Hotel on Broad Street. When his wife and five children joined him in 1806, he moved to a home on Washington Street, which suited until about 1808 or

1. Jonathan Mason Jr., "Recollections of an Octogenarian," Joseph Downs Collection of Manuscripts and Printed Ephemera, Winterthur Library, Winterthur, Del. See Theodore Sizer, ed., *The Autobiography of Colonel John Trumbull, Patriot-Artist, 1756–1843* (New Haven: Yale University Press, 1953), p. 239; Whitley 1932, p. 126.
2. "Isaac P. Davis," *Memorial Biographies of the New England Historic Genealogical Society* 2 (1881), pp. 327–34.
3. [Dolley Madison], letter to Anna Payne Cutts, May 1804; transcription of unlocated original, Cutts Family Collection of the Papers of James and Dolley Madison, microfilm 14326, Manuscript Division, Library of Congress, Washington, D.C.
4. Quoted in Whitley 1932, p. 126.
5. Waterhouse quoted by Charles Willson Peale, letter to Rembrandt Peale, September 11, 1808, Peale Family Papers, Letterbook 9, American Philosophical Society, Philadelphia.

Detail of cat. 91, *Josiah Quincy*

6. For the addresses, see Dunlap 1834, vol. 1, p. 208; Park 1926, p. 195; Whitley 1932, pp. 150, 157; Eliza Susan Quincy, letter to George Champlin Mason, September 21, 1878, George Champlin Mason Papers, file of Eliza Quincy's letters, Manuscripts Division, Rhode Island Historical Society, Providence.

7. John Quincy Adams, letter to Thomas Boylston Adams, May 13, 1811, quoted in Oliver 1967, p. 135.

8. Quoted in S. G. W. Benjamin, *Art in America: A Critical and Historical Sketch* (New York: Harper and Brothers, 1880), p. 20. See also Pickering 1810, 1817 (October 4).

1809, when Sarah Morton's friend Hepzibah Clarke Swan (see cat. 81) offered a better house with a large L-shaped studio on Devonshire Street in Roxbury, just on the Boston Neck. About 1817 Stuart moved to Washington Place on Fort Hill in Medford, and by late 1824 he was living in Essex Street in Boston.[6] Sitters seem to have made their way to him, wherever he was; he never traveled, except to Brunswick, Maine, in 1821, and possibly once to Newport to see his hometown.

By the turn of the century, Stuart was the finest artist in America. As John Quincy Adams put it to his brother Thomas Boylston Adams, both of whom were annoyed with Stuart for failing to finish their portraits of their parents, John and Abigail, "If there was another portrait painter in America, I could forgive him."[7] Stuart might have painted in any city he pleased; the sitters would have come to him. Boston had a strong tradition of commissioned private portraits, and Stuart had little competition. He was the first fine painter in town since the departure of John Singleton Copley (see cat. 13) in 1775.

In some respects, Stuart took up where Copley had left off, fulfilling a desire not only for portraits but also for help in deciding how clients should look in their pictures. Much had changed in Boston since before the Revolutionary War, but the social aspects of portrait painting—group visits to the studio and commissions between friends—and the awareness of the value of a portrait in a home were virtually the same. Stuart looked anew at Copley's work and understood how it had captivated Bostonians. On seeing his portrait of the Gloucester merchant Epes Sargent (National Gallery of Art, Washington), Stuart marveled: "Prick that hand and blood will spurt out!"[8] They were poles apart in temperament and personality,

Fig. 159. *Washington at Dorchester Heights*, 1806. Oil on panel, 107 ½ x 71 ¼ in. (273.4 x 181 cm). Museum of Fine Arts, Boston; Deposited by the City of Boston (30.76a)

Fig. 160. *Paul Revere*, 1813. Oil on panel, 28¼ x 22½ in. (71.8 x 57.2 cm). Museum of Fine Arts, Boston; Gift of Joseph W. Revere, William B. Revere, and Edward H. R. Revere (30.782)

Fig. 161. *Rachel Walker Revere*, 1813. Oil on panel, 28¼ x 22⅜ in. (71.8 x 56.8 cm). Museum of Fine Arts, Boston; Gift of Joseph W. Revere, William B. Revere, and Edward H. R. Revere (30.783)

but Stuart assumed Copley's role, taking commissions from some of his former sitters, including Paul Revere and his wife (figs. 160, 161). The thorny Mrs. Basil Hall visited Stuart with her entourage in October 1827, afterward reporting that he "amused us exceedingly" with accounts of George Washington, David Hume, and Voltaire.[9] Stuart took in work for repair and the presence in his studio of works assigned to Dürer, Canaletto, and Poussin, along with his ever ready commentary, attracted still more visitors.[10] His extraordinary powers of conversation made him a fixture on the social circuit; many of his clients invited him to dinners and parties, extending their relationships with the artist beyond the professional environment.[11] But, of course, those who owned a Stuart portrait truly had cachet.

Stuart revitalized the social practice of portrait exchange with its mutual commissions and gift giving. Hepzibah Swan, whose husband, James, sat for Stuart in Philadelphia a decade before, was among the first on the painter's doorstep, with orders for portraits of herself, her friends Generals Henry Knox (cat. 80) and Henry Jackson, her children, their spouses, and some in-laws. Mrs. Morton brought in her soon-to-be-married daughter and her neighbors John and Mary Babcock Gore, who ordered portraits for their home of Bishop Cheverus (cat. 89) and the Reverend John Sylvester Gardiner. The merchant Samuel Parkman commissioned a monumental image of George Washington at Dorchester Heights (fig. 159) and ordered portraits of himself and his wife and daughter. And so it went, a stream of kith and kin. The only extant page of Stuart's appointment book records that during the week of April 25, 1808, he saw ten or more people each day, including sitters, escorts, companions, and visitors—in addition to the occasional tradesman or service person, such as Mr. Shaw who came to tune the artist's harpsichord on April 27.[12] The South Carolina connoisseur John Cogdell visited Stuart in 1825, having heard that everyone called to see him, and was enthralled by his unfinished works: "I am more enraptured with his work than I ever was before."[13]

9. See Margaret Hall Hunter and Una Pope-Hennessy, eds., *The Artistocratic Journey; being the outspoken letters of Mrs. Basil Hall written during a fourteen months' sojourn in America, 1827–1828* (New York: G. P. Putnam's Sons, 1931), October 14, 1827, pp. 93–94.

10. Pickering 1817 (August 19).

11. See, for example, Whitley 1932, p. 190, for a description of a dinner on October 1, 1825, at the home of Josiah Quincy, which President-elect John Quincy Adams, Isaac P. Davis, Stuart, and others attended.

12. Swan 1938.

13. John S. Cogdell, diaries and letterbooks, 1808–1841, September 22, 1825, Joseph Downs Collection of Manuscripts and Printed Ephemera, Winterthur Library, Winterthur, Del.

Fig. 162. *Elizabeth Tuckerman Salisbury*, ca. 1810. Oil on wood, 32½ x 26¼ in. (82.6 x 66.7 cm). Worcester Art Museum, Worcester, Mass.; Gift of Stephen Salisbury III (1901.29)

For the pleasure of a portrait, Stuart's clients were undeterred by high prices (he charged between $120 and $150 for a bust-length image), delays, and delinquency.[14] He was also irregular in his studio practice. Eliza Susan Quincy accompanied a friend to her appointment at Stuart's on March 13, 1816, only to find that Stuart had taken another sitter.[15] Stuart also abandoned commissions, as John Quincy Adams gossiped to Copley (both artists had received commissions for a full-length portrait of his father, John Adams). Copley finished his, but Stuart did not: "Mr. Stuart thinks it the prerogative of genius to disdain the performance of his engagements, and he did disdain the performance of that."[16] An unidentified visitor to Stuart's studio in 1807 commented, "I was impressed too with the wayward capriciousness of genius which would frequently design without deigning to finish, and leave the most interesting sketch of the 'human countenance divine,' just beginning like a rosebud to unfold its perfections on the canvas, to be penciled out at pleasure by the imagination of the disappointed beholder."[17]

Yet Stuart had the capacity to amaze visitors, and the finished works were almost uniformly brilliant. As he grew older, Stuart adopted a shorthand version of the painterly methods of his best English portraits: fluid, swift strokes in thin glazes that captured a reality deeper than mere likeness. He worked quickly, finishing, for example, the lifesize portrait of Washington at Dorchester Heights in nine days and his colleague John Trumbull's portrait in less than three weeks (cat. 85). His brush glided over the surface of his favorite prepared panels, which were North Carolina yellow pine or West Indian mahogany texturized by dragging a toothed plane-iron diagonally over the wood. The texture was similar to that of a twill-weave canvas, and it has been suggested that Stuart used these panels because canvas may have been expensive or scarce due to various congressional nonimportation acts alternately enforced and repealed from 1807 and throughout the War of 1812.[18] In fact, he used panels even when canvas was available and the war was over. Many of his finest Boston works, such as *Elizabeth Tuckerman Salisbury* (fig. 162), were executed on scored wood.

Numerous artists visited Stuart in Boston, some staying to learn what they could. Thomas Sully, who would soon corner the portraiture market in Philadelphia, visited Stuart in 1807 to "gather some instruction from his practice."[19] According to Sully, "He was kind and communicative, and I derived much information from him." Jacob Eichholtz, also from Philadelphia, came the same year to show Stuart his portrait of the banker Nicholas Biddle (private collection): "I had a fiery trial to undergo. My picture was placed alongside the best of his hand, and that lesson I consider the best I ever received; the comparison was, I thought, enough, and if I had vanity before I went, it 'all left me' before my return."[20] Henry Sargent took frequent walks with Stuart on the Boston Common and learned by listening: "I never argued with him for as he was a vain proud man and withal quick tempered I chose rather to preserve his friendship as an artist."[21] Others less deferential also came to call. John Wesley Jarvis, New York's leading portraitist, who received the plum commission to paint six large portraits of the heroes of the War of 1812, paid a visit in 1814, perhaps to assess his competition. A flamboyant type known for his fur coats and huge hounds that carried his packages, Jarvis went to Stuart's lavishly dressed: "He had buff gloves—buff jacket—

14. Mrs. Peabody, who sat for Stuart in 1810, mentioned the price of $120 to her son, William Shaw, quoted in Whitley 1932, p. 144. On the the price of $150, charged to John Trumbull, see cat. 85.

15. Eliza Susan Quincy, journal, September 16, 1814–September 30, 1821, entry for March 13, 1816, Eliza Susan Quincy Papers, Rhode Island Historical Society.

16. John Quincy Adams, letter to Copley, April 29, 1811, quoted in Martha Babcock Amory, *The Domestic and Artistic Life of John Singleton Copley, R.A.* (Boston: Houghton, Mifflin and Co., 1882), p. 90.

17. Letter from an unidentified writer, published in *The Emerald*, 1807, quoted in Whitley 1932, p. 138.

18. Marcia Goldberg, "Textured Panels in American 19th Century Painting," *Journal of the American Institute for Conservation* 32 (1993), pp. 33–42.

19. Thomas Sully, "Memoirs of the Professional Life of Thomas Sully Dedicated to His Brother Artists Philadelphia November 1851," Historical Society of Pennsylvania, Philadelphia.

20. Quoted in Whitley 1932, pp. 141–42.

21. Quoted in Swan 1938, p. 309.

22. Dunlap 1834, vol. 1, pp. 211–12.

23. Mary Tyler Peabody Mann, letter to Miss Rawlins Pickman, January 27, 1825, Horace Mann Papers, microfilm reel 37, Massachusetts Historical Society, Boston. On Jane Stuart, see Mary E. Powel, "Miss Jane Stuart, 1812–1888," *Bulletin of the Newport Historical Society*, no. 31 (January 1920), pp. 1–16; and the results of a survey of her oeuvre conducted in 2002, curatorial files, Department of American Paintings and Sculpture, The Metropolitan Museum of Art.

24. Jouett 1816.

25. Allston, quoted by John Neal from the *Monthly Magazine*, 1826, in Whitley 1932, p. 205.

26. In addition to fig. 4, Neagle's portraits of Stuart are in the Historical Society of Pennsylvania Collection, Atwater Kent Museum of Philadelphia; and the Museum of Art, Rhode Island School of Design, Providence.

27. In addition to fig. 5, Goodridge's portraits of Stuart are in the National Portrait Gallery, Washington, D.C., and the Museum of Fine Arts, Boston.

28. *Columbian Centinel*, December 3, 1825, quoted in Whitley 1932, p. 191. See also David Meschutt, *A Bold Experiment: John Henri Isaac Browere's Life Masks of Prominent Americans* (Cooperstown, N.Y.: New York State Historical Association, 1988), pp. 23–24.

29. The request to Stuart for "Portraits of distinguished Patriots" is recorded in a document written by James Savage, April 25, 1825, with a postscript recording a unanimous vote, April 29, 1825, signed by Josiah Quincy, Mayor, Boston City Archives and inscribed by him on the verso. Stuart died before he began the project.

Mayor Quincy also commissioned a posthumous portrait of his father. In his will, Quincy said the portrait of his father was painted about 1826; will of Josiah Quincy, proved August 29, 1864, Massachusetts State Archives, no. 45572; Mason 1879, pp. 244–46. The portrait is on loan to the Museum of Fine Arts, Boston, from a descendant.

buff waistcoat and trowsers—and buff shoes," said Stuart to a mutual friend, the engraver David Edwin.[22] Edwin told Jarvis that Stuart had remarked on his clothing, and on his next visit, Jarvis wore all black. Stuart said, "So! I caused him to put his buff in mourning." John Vanderlyn, the rising star on the New York portrait scene, who had begun his career copying Stuart's portrait of Aaron Burr (fig. 61) some twenty years earlier, spent only a day in 1817.

Stuart never claimed any artist as his student, although nearly every American artist of the next generation credited him or his works in the development of their own. Stuart's daughter Jane could perhaps be regarded as a legitimate student because of her constant proximity to him. Yet little is known of her actual training, she was only sixteen when he died, and he disclaimed any report of instruction.[23] His nephew Gilbert Stuart Newton certainly studied with him before going to London. James Hubbard, the silhouettist, learned to paint in Stuart's studio. The portraitist and decorative painter John Penniman ground colors for Stuart and copied his Athenaeum portrait of Washington (cat. 39). Matthew Harris Jouett came from Lexington, Kentucky, to spend the summer of 1816 with Stuart. He sketched and painted in the studio and conducted a series of interviews; his notes provide the best information about Stuart's technique, art-historical knowledge, and approach to his work.[24] The artist Washington Allston, who sat for Stuart about 1820 (cat. 88), valued his opinions greatly. Allston said, "Stuart's word in the art is law and from his decision there is no appeal."[25] Chester Harding, James Frothingham, and Francis Alexander spent time with Stuart during the mid-1820s, becoming such skilled imitators of his style that they picked up his clientele after his death.

A few artists asked to take Stuart's portrait, not only to preserve his craggy countenance but also to spend some time with him and to compare their efforts with his. John Neagle's sitting with Stuart (see fig. 4) was profitable, and he returned to Philadelphia a much improved painter for the effort.[26] The miniaturist Sarah Goodridge, who painted him three times (see fig. 5), adapted his oil-painting techniques to watercolor, the result of which was a range of stunningly saturated and controlled works.[27] The sculptor John H. I. Browere took a cast of Stuart's face (fig. 3), as he had done for other distinguished public figures including Adams and Jefferson. The *Columbian Centinel* assured its readers that "nothing of a painful or unpleasant nature was experienced by Mr. Stuart on the occasion."[28]

Stuart's fame was enhanced by his connection to the first five presidents of the United States, all of whom sat for him. In 1821 the Boston gilder and framer John Doggett proposed that Stuart paint for him a series of presidential portraits, which would be engraved for sale (on the series, see cat. 87). In April 1825, Mayor Josiah Quincy, also a Stuart sitter (cat. 91), and his Board of Aldermen wanted a series of portraits of "distinguished patriots" for display at the newly renovated Fanueil Hall. Their mandate "to employ the best artist" in America was bureaucratic code for asking Stuart to paint the pictures.[29] They ordered from him images of Samuel Adams, Benjamin Franklin, John Hancock, Joseph Warren, and several others. It was the largest commission Stuart had received since 1785, when John Boydell had asked him for fifteen portraits of artists (see cats. 10–14). The thirty-year-old artist who completed the work for Boydell was now nearly seventy,

30. See Boston 1828. See also Mabel Munson Swan, *The Athenaeum Gallery, 1827–1873: The Boston Athenaeum as an Early Patron of Art* (Boston: Boston Athenaeum, 1940), p. 64.
31. Quoted in Whitley 1932, pp. 214–15.
32. "Gilbert Stuart," *Boston Daily Advertiser*, July 22, 1828.

and although he accepted Quincy's commission, he never began it; after three years waiting in vain, Quincy recorded, "death put an end to all hopes from him."

After the artist's death, Quincy and twenty-two other Bostonians raised money to purchase Stuart's unfinished portraits of George and Martha Washington (cats. 38, 39) for the Boston Athenaeum. The sale helped Stuart's family, left destitute at his demise. Isaac Davis proposed a benefit memorial exhibition at the Athenaeum and, with the help of Washington Allston and others, organized the loan of more than two hundred works from various owners for what was the first retrospective display of Stuart's work.[30] The artists of Philadelphia, led by Sully, wore mourning arm bands for a month and offered a testimonial: "His object was to counterfeit the soul—to throw the intelligence of expression in to the face of his picture, to catch the thoughts and 'living manners as they rise'— to draw to a focus and to embody the history of the disposition, and with such eloquent touches that a glance at his copy was sufficient to afford an understanding of the mind of the original."[31] In his obituary of Stuart for the *Boston Daily Advertiser*, Allston eloquently captured his mentor: "On almost every subject, more especially on such as were connected with his art, his conversation was marked by wisdom and knowledge; while the uncommon precision and eloquence of his language seemed even to receive an additional grace from his manner, which was that of a well-bred gentleman. . . . He never suffered the manliness of his nature to darken with the least shadow of jealousy, but where praise was due, he gave it freely, and gave too with a grace which showed that, loving excellence for its own sake, he had a pleasure in praising. To the younger artists he was uniformly kind and indulgent, and most liberal of his advice, which no one ever properly asked but he received, and in a manner no less courteous than impressive."[32]

CRB

80. HENRY KNOX

1806

Oil on wood, 47⅞ x 38⅝ in. (121.6 x 98.11 cm)
Museum of Fine Arts, Boston; Deposited by the
City of Boston (L-R 30.76b)

1. Eleanor P. DeLorme, "Attribution and Laboratory Analysis in Portraiture, the Master and the Student," *American Art Review* 3, no. 2 (1976), p. 123; DeLorme 1979b, pp. 382–89.

2. See Henry Jackson, Boston, to Henry Knox, May 16, 1790, Henry Knox Papers, P17, microfilm reel 26, Massachusetts Historical Society, Boston.

3. William Eustis, Boston, letter to David Cobb, November 16, 1794, David Cobb Papers, microfilm reel 1, Massachusetts Historical Society.

4. *ANB*, vol. 17, pp. 833–43; North Callahan, "Henry Knox: American Artillerist," in George Athan Billias, ed., *George Washington's Generals and Opponents: Their Exploits and Leadership* (New York: Da Capo Press, 1994), pp. 239–59; Michael Darryl Carter, "Nationbuilding and the Military: The Life and Career of Secretary of War Henry Knox, 1750–1806" (Ph.D diss., West Virginia University, 1997); Alan Taylor, "From Fathers to Friends of the People: Political Personas in the Early Republic," *Journal of the Early Republic* 11, no. 4 (1991), pp. 465–91; Miriam Lochman, "Henry Knox: A Man in the Shadows of History," *Daughters of the American Revolution Magazine* 123, no. 7 (1989), pp. 612–15, 646–48; George Washington Nordham, "The Friendship of George Washington and Henry Knox," *Daughters of the American Revolution Magazine* 119, no. 2 (1985), pp. 100–103; Doris Ricker Marston, "A Noble Train of Artillery," *New England Galaxy* 11, no. 3 (1970), pp. 20–27.

5. *ANB*, vol. 17, p. 833.

6. E. B. Winthrop, letter to Sarah Bowdoin, July 4, 1806, Winthrop Papers, microfilm reel 21, Massachusetts Historical Society.

7. The painting is listed in Mason 1879, p. 211; Park 1926, pp. 459–60, no. 468.

8. "Poems by Sarah Morton," HM6272, Huntington Library, San Marino, Calif.

9. Sarah Morton, Dorchester, to "Mr. General Knox," Montpelier, August 15, 1806, Gilder-Lehrman Collection, New-York Historical Society.

10. Advertisement, *Monthly Anthology and Boston Review* 4 (February 1807), p. 111.

11. Peale painted several versions of his portrait of Knox, including a miniature now at The Metropolitan Museum of Art.

12. "The Stuart Gallery," *Evening Gazette*, August 2, 1828, p. 2; *Catalogue of the Second Exhibition of Paintings in the Athenaeum Gallery* (Boston: Boston Athenaeum, 1828), no. 125, "General Knox [lent by] Mad. Swan"; Boston 1828, no. 70, "Gen. Knox."

Among the first of Stuart's Boston patrons, Hepzibah Clarke Swan (see cat. 81) commissioned a series of eight portraits of family and friends that would complement the portrait the artist had executed of her husband, James, in Philadelphia a decade before. She arranged appointments for Henry Knox (1750–1806) and Henry Jackson (1747–1809), the distinguished generals who stayed with the Swans during the Siege of Boston, defending their property.[1] After the revolution, the two friends continued to watch over her, especially when her husband's real estate speculations took him to Europe for extended periods and eventually landed him in prison in Paris. In 1790, Jackson sent Knox, then secretary of war, the itinerary of Mrs. Swan's trip from Boston to Paris, with a proposed strategy meant to safeguard her against any eventuality, especially if something happened to her husband and she was left alone in Europe.[2] Jackson—*le général* to Mrs. Swan—lived in the Swans' Dorchester house but kept up appearances by renting rooms at a Boston boarding house. One friend wrote to another about the liaison between Jackson and Mrs. Swan, "This the world would call scandal, but to you I know it to be sweet incense."[3]

Knox acted as escort while Jackson watched over the house and children during her absence. The two generals were at the core of her lively ménage for nearly thirty years, and Stuart's portraits recorded something of the nature of their friendship. The bust-length portrait of Jackson (private collection) is relatively modest, conceived without reference to the sitter's profession—no uniform, accoutrements, or narrative allusions. Jackson's head radiates the affability and care the man brought to the Swan household. A smaller and more intimate portrait than any of the ones painted of the Swan family, it is in fact a devotional image. Mrs. Swan's true monument to Jackson came after his death: he was interred in her garden in a tomb—where she later joined him—surmounted by a grand obelisk. Knox's likeness, on the other hand, is as large as its subject and rich with iconographic references to his achievements. Jackson's portrait is private, Knox's public; the former took care of her at home, while the other looked out for her in the larger world.

Knox's biographers describe him as hefty and jovial, the sort of man who filled a room. Knox's girth was matched by his strength, which was put to use early in the Revolutionary War loading heavy artillery for transport.[4] Knox had taken an interest in armaments as a boy, when to support his widowed mother, he opened the London Book-Store in Boston, which catered to a clientele of British officers by keeping a stock of volumes on military history and tactics. He read in his inventory, became an expert in engineering and weapons, and joined the local artillery company in 1768. The loss of two fingers on his left hand in a hunting accident in the summer of 1773 made him self-conscious—he concealed his hand in his pocket or in a handkerchief—but did not affect his career, for George Washington commissioned him as a colonel in the new American army in 1775 and made him head of artillery for twelve companies. The twenty-five-year-old Knox oversaw the transport of cart cannons, shot, howitzers, and muskets three hundred miles across the frigid Berkshire Mountains from the captured arsenal at Fort Ticonderoga to Washington's camp at Cambridge. This firepower enabled Washington to drive the British out of Boston—the very episode recorded in Stuart's grand portrait of Washington at Dorchester Heights (fig. 159), which Stuart would have been working on for Fanueil Hall when Knox sat for him.[5] Knox's combination of brains and brawn led to

Fig. 163. Charles Willson Peale, *Henry Knox*, 1783. Oil on canvas, 24 x 20 in. (61 x 50.8 cm). Independence National Historical Park, Philadelphia

Fig. 164. Attributed to Gilbert Stuart, *Henry Knox*, ca. 1820. Watercolor on ivory, 3⅜ x 2¾ in. (8.6 x 7 cm). Worcester Art Museum, Worcester, Mass.; Eliza S. Paine Fund (1988.170)

13. Minutes of the Mayor and Board of Aldermen, May 2, 1831, vol. 9, p. 91; and draft of the letter from the Board of Aldermen to William Sullivan, May 10, 1831, Boston City Archives, Dorchester, Mass. The city placed the Faneuil Hall portraits on permanent loan to the Museum of Fine Arts, Boston, in 1876; "Faneuil Hall Paintings," May 22, 1876, Board of Aldermen, docket documents, Boston City Archives.

14. The Jane Stuart copy is unlocated. Other copies are by James Harvey Young, U.S. Department of the Army, Washington, D.C.; Albert Gallatin Hoyt, Bowdoin College Museum of Art, Brunswick, Me.; Elkanah Tisdale, miniature, Museum of Fine Arts, Boston; Charles Henry Granger, State House, Augusta, Maine.; Margaret

his swift promotion to brigadier general in 1776 and major general in 1782 (among the youngest in the Continental Army), and in December 1783 Washington named him interim commander-in-chief for a period of six months. Knox became secretary of war in 1785 by congressional appointment and kept that post in the new government in 1789. Knox's pet project was the establishment of a national militia, which never came to fruition, and he spent much of his energy overseeing Native American affairs. Implicated in the disastrous Indian Wars in the Northwest Territory and a participant in the disappointing Indian negotiations of 1792–94, Knox was no longer regarded as an always successful diplomat, and he seems to have strained his professional relationship with Washington by his continued absence from the capital. He resigned his cabinet post at the end of December 1794 but remained in Philadelphia.

Knox kept a townhouse in Boston and, for his retirement, built Montpelier, a mansion on the Saint George River in Thomaston, Maine, where his wife, Lucy Flucker, had inherited a vast tract of land. Lucy Knox's flamboyance matched her size—she was almost as large as her husband—and she gave lavish parties and loved fine clothing. The Knoxes traveled to Boston often, and their visits were noted in the press. In March 1806, Knox was in Boston for the thirtieth anniversary of Evacuation Day (the holiday commemorating the British decamping from Boston in March 1776), and he returned for July 4 festivities, as reported by E. B. Winthrop to Sarah Bowdoin in Paris: "Mr. and Mrs. Knox are in Town . . . & are as fat & Jolly as when you saw them."[6] It would have been on these trips that General Knox sat for Stuart.[7] In August 1806 Knox's friend Sarah Wentworth Apthorp Morton (see cat. 60) wrote an ode entitled "For the Portrait of General Knox Exhibited at Mr. Stuart's painting room," urging the general to spend more time in Boston.[8] Unpersuaded, Knox was back home by August 15, 1806, when Mrs. Morton wrote to him "the loss of your society is much felt and regretted in Boston."[9] It was his last trip to the city; Knox died on October 25 at Montpelier. Stuart seems to have finished the picture in early October 1806. The engraver and miniature painter Robert Field proposed a print after "a very excellent likeness by Stuart, taken but a few weeks before [Knox's] decease."[10]

As he had done in his picture of Horatio Gates (cat. 26), Stuart portrayed Knox in the current issue of a blue-and-buff general's single-breasted uniform, rather than in the earlier version he had worn at the height of his career. He places his left hand on a cannon, noting his prowess and hiding his missing fingers. His right arm is akimbo, fist to hip, drawing back his coat front to reveal the paunch that was evident throughout his career. For Mrs. Swan's parlor, Stuart created an image as imposing as it is genial, overtly masculine while abidingly sensitive.

Knox had previously been painted by Edward Savage (Philipse Manor Hall, Yonkers, N.Y.) and by Charles Willson Peale (fig. 163), a portrait copied by Peale's nephew Charles Peale Polk (National Portrait Gallery, Washington), but Stuart's commanding image had the advantage of being the last portrait of the general.[11] Mrs. Swan's family lent the portrait to the Boston Athenaeum exhibition honoring Stuart's death in 1828.[12] In 1831 the family gave the portrait to the city of Boston; the Board of Aldermen hung it in Fanueil Hall "where it may remain by the side of Washington of whom Knox was the personal friend, and companion in glory."[13] This public display allowed the picture to be copied by many artists, among them Jane Stuart, the artist's daughter.[14]

Perhaps the most compelling version of the portrait is the watercolor-on-ivory miniature attributed to Stuart (fig. 164). The Bostonian Edward Appleton, whose family once owned the piece, told the historian Charles Henry Hart that his aunt the miniatur-

80

Bushine Preble, Patton Museum, Armor Branch Museum, Fort Knox, Ky.; Kenneth Frazier, West Point Museum, U.S. Military Academy, West Point, N.Y.; Robert S. Chase, after 1930, for display at the Knox house, Montpelier, Thomaston, Me.; unidentified artists, Faneuil Hall, Boston, and Detroit Institute of Arts. On the last, see Dorinda Evans, in Nancy Rivard Shaw et al., *American Paintings in the Detroit Institute of Arts* (New York: Hudson Hills Press, 1991), p. 291.

15. See Susan E. Strickler, *American Portrait Miniatures: The Worcester Art Museum Collection* (Worcester, Mass.: Worcester Art Museum, 1989), p. 108.

16. Goodridge also painted a miniature of Knox (Bowdoin College Museum of Art).

ist Sarah Goodridge attempted to make a tiny copy of the portrait of Knox about 1820 when she was studying with Stuart.[15] It was said that Stuart, growing impatient with the young artist, took a piece of ivory and set an example for her. The inscription on the back would seem to confirm the tale: *General Henry Knox / Painted by Gilbert / Stuart for Miss / Sarah Goodridge / the miniature painter to show / her how to do it.* Set against this are the questions of why Knox's portrait was back in Stuart's studio in 1820 and how Stuart could paint miniatures when he had never done so before. The broad hatch-work technique and the aspect of the head, high and off center on the ivory, however, have been cited as proof that the work is indeed by Stuart.[16]   CRB

81. HEPZIBAH CLARKE SWAN

ca. 1806
Oil on wood, 32⅝ x 26½ in. (82.9 x 67.3 cm)
Museum of Fine Arts, Boston; Bequest of Miss
Elizabeth Howard Bartol (27.539)

1. Martha Babcock Amory, *The Domestic and Artistic Life of John Singleton Copley, R.A.* (Boston, New York: Houghton, Mifflin and Co., 1882), pp. 103–4.
2. On Hepzibah and James Swan, see DeLorme 1979b; Howard C. Rice, "James Swan: Agent of the French Republic, 1794–1796," *New England Quarterly* 10 (September 1937), pp. 464–86; James Kirker, "Bullfinch's Houses for Mrs. Swan," *Antiques* 86 (October 1964), p. 68; Eleanor P. DeLorme, "James Swan's French Furniture," *Antiques* 107 (March 1975), p. 452.

Hebzibah Clarke Swan (1757–1825) turned heads, it seems, at home in Boston and abroad. She was noticed on the streets of London in the 1790s, "arrayed in all the elegance of the French capital, and attracting every eye by her grace and fancied resemblance to the ill-fated Marie Antoinette, . . . daintily attired, with a self-possession and assurance which her companions vainly endeavored to acquire, as they were forced with some diffidence, to attend so conspicuous a dame."[1] Mrs. Swan was indeed conspicuous: in society, in politics, and in the lives of a number of men, including Gilbert Stuart, who had her to thank for plum commissions, countless connections, and even a place to live. Before the age of twenty, she had inherited vast fortunes from her father, the merchant Barnabas Clarke, and from a close family friend William Dennie, giving her the wherewithal to live in the manner to which she was not merely accustomed but, some would say, destined.[2] Cosmopolitan and intelligent, a devoted friend and watchful parent, Madame Swan—as she was known—was charismatic, not least because of her money but in good measure because of her charm. A neighbor to Jonathan Mason, the man most responsible for bringing Stuart to Boston, Mrs. Swan sought out Stuart on his arrival in 1805 to commission images of her friends Generals Henry Knox (cat. 80) and Henry Jackson, pictures that, in a curious ménage à trois, joined the one he had painted of her husband, James Swan (fig. 165), about 1795 in Philadelphia. In her home, each portrait was a surrogate for the man himself: her imposing protector Knox, her thoughtful companion Jackson, and her distant, estranged husband.

James Swan (1754–1831) was a member of the Sons of Liberty who fought in the Battle of Bunker Hill, served in the artillery with Knox, and later rose to the rank of colonel. Aided by his wife's fortune, he became perhaps the most successful and notorious player in international commerce during the postwar era. The Swans shared a

Fig. 165. *James Swan*, ca. 1795. Oil on canvas, 29 x 24 in. (73.6 x 61 cm). Museum of Fine Arts, Boston; Bequest of Miss Elizabeth Howard Bartol (27.538)

81

3. DeLorme 1979b, p. 368.

4. The painting is listed in Mason 1879, p. 263; Park 1926, pp. 731–32, no. 814.

5. Swan 1938, p. 308.

6. *Mrs. John Clarke Howard (Hepzibah Clarke Swan)*, Museum of Fine Arts, Boston; *Dr. John C. Howard*, Boston Medical Library; *James Keadie Swan*, Montpelier Memorial, Thomaston, Maine; *Mrs. William Sullivan (Sarah Webb Swan)*, Yale University Art Gallery, New Haven; *James Sullivan*, Museum of Fine Arts, Boston.

7. Eleanor P. DeLorme, "Attribution and Laboratory Analysis in Portraiture, the Master and the Student," *American Art Review* 3, no. 2 (1976), pp. 122–32, compares and discusses the portrait by Kitty Swan in relation to the original by Stuart. See also Robert Taylor, "Discovering a 'Mrs. Jack'—long before her time," *Boston Sunday Globe*, November 9, 1975. Park (1926, p. 505) illustrates Kitty's portrait of Mrs. Swan, but his description matches the Stuart portrait.

passion for frivolous and slightly scandalous entertainments, and with their friends the Perez Mortons (see cat. 60), the Harrison Gray Otises, the Isaac Winslows, and others, they founded Sans Souci, a private social club for card playing and dancing; the club was satirized in Mercy Otis Warren's *Sans Souci, alias Free and Easy; or An Evening's Peep into a Polite Circle*, a play that opened in Boston in January 1785 (Mrs. Swan was portrayed as Mrs. Brilliant). In general, the Swans' deepest passion was for things French, which they parlayed into not only a lavish way of life, but also a business. Swan became a broker of French luxury goods on the American market, making and losing fortunes as the financial tide flowed and ebbed and finally in July 1808 landing in a French prison for twenty-two years. Swan's fate was not entirely grim: at the prison of Sainte-Pélagie he kept a wine cellar, luxuriated in a bathtub filled with strawberries, and entertained friends and mistresses but not his wife.[3] Mrs. Swan had gone abroad with him several times in the 1780s and 1790s but never saw him again after his final return to France in 1798.

Hepzibah Swan may have commissioned Stuart's portrait of her husband in 1795, when he was just back from seven years abroad. Or Swan contacted the artist himself, recognizing that as the painter closest to Washington and his circle, Stuart was auspiciously placed. Swan added his name to Stuart's "list of gentlemen who are to have copies of the Portrait of the President of the United States" (see "The Portraits of George Washington"). Stuart's Boston portrait of Hepzibah Swan is not conceived as a pendant to that of her husband: they both face the same way, the size and scale differ, and the painting styles are dissimilar. The portrait of James, so fluid and lightly handled, appears almost unfinished when compared to the impeccably controlled, porcelain-finished portrait of Hepzibah. Stuart meticulously picked out the detail in the lace of Mrs. Swan's gown and mantilla and the wood grain on her bergère.[4] This high-maintenance doyenne of Boston society was herself pendant to no one man, and yet her portrait does find a companion in that of Jackson, the man most often associated with Mrs. Swan while her husband was otherwise engaged.

Stuart probably painted Mrs. Swan's portrait in 1806, about the same time as those of Jackson and Knox. She visited him again two years later with her daughter, as recorded on the single extant page of Stuart's sitting book. On April 24, 1808, Stuart wrote, "Rubbed in Mrs. Howard's . . . background" and for April 29 "Mrs. Swan and Mrs. Howard . . . Mrs. and Miss Knox."[5] These entries refer to portrait sittings for Hepzibah Swan Howard, who was accompanied to Stuart's by her mother, and for Miss Caroline Knox, who came with her mother, Mrs. Henry Knox, the general's widow. Caroline Knox soon married Mrs. Swan's son, James Keadie Swan, who also sat for Stuart that year. In addition, Mrs. Swan arranged for her middle daughter, Sarah Swan Sullivan, to sit for Stuart, and Sarah's father-in-law, the governor of Massachusetts, James Sullivan, also came for his portrait.[6] All told, Mrs. Swan was responsible for bringing at least nine commissions to Stuart.

Mrs. Swan's eldest daughter, Christiana (Kitty) Keadie Swan (1777/78–1867), painted a portrait of her mother after Stuart's image that was mistakenly attributed to Stuart until the late 1970s.[7]

CRB

82. Lydia Smith

ca. 1808–10
Oil on wood, 32⅛ x 28¾ in. (81.5 x 73 cm)
Private collection

Among the eight portraits that Stuart painted for Barney Smith's family, the one of Lydia (1786–1859), so full of charm and narrative detail, stands out.[1] While those of Lydia's parents, brother, sister, and others are strong characterizations with the requisite flourish, Lydia's picture apparently warranted special effort, whether by her father's request or of Stuart's own volition. Lydia wears a simple white gown, a severe style in Boston. On a young lady who had been abroad, however, especially one known for her daring taste in clothing, its high fashion—empire waist, scooped décolletage, and cinched-up sleeves—would have been striking. Her mother wrote, "Now as to fashions you know she is a fickle creature. . . . Lydia has invented something very pretty for herself which are in the Grecian style and when she wears them the fashion is admired."[2] The artist's conception recalls his double portrait of Anna Dorothea Foster and her cousin (cat. 21), in which, as here, the signal element is the direct and comely gaze of an attractive young woman displaying her accomplishments. Lydia Smith has been drawing with a porte-crayon on a large sheet of paper that rests on her portfolio, thick with other sketches ready to slip out but for the ribbon closures at top and side. She pauses and turns her lovely heart-shaped face toward her admirer. Lydia has propped the portfolio against a pianoforte. This layering of her artistic and musical talents, and contained in the limited space of the composition, offers a sense of her all in one glance.

It was contemporary practice for young women to engage in genteel pastimes to attract a suitor and to attest to a family's prosperity, and Lydia's portrayed skills were real attainments, acquired at considerable expense in Saint-Germain-en-Laye, France.[3] There she studied under the renowned Madame Campan, a clever teacher who knew well that a young woman's studies strengthened her ability to run a home. Madame Campan once extolled the accomplishments of one of her students: "a girl . . . who expresses herself . . . in English and German as in her own language; who is acquainted with all that composes an extensive and solid education; has the greatest execution on the piano-forte . . . and who paints heads and landscapes in oil, so well as to find it a useful resource against great reverses of fortune. To these arts she unites the greatest skill in all the works of her sex, from the simple seam to the art of making artificial flowers; and yet this union of different talents so little destroys her taste for the modest occupations of the household."[4]

Stuart's portrait of Lydia has traditionally been dated to about 1805, which would make it among the first pictures he painted upon arriving in Boston. Yet Stuart arrived in late July of that year and Lydia left for her studies at the end of September, leaving little time for the portrait. Moreover, Stuart would have had to anticipate Lydia's future talents, for lessons in drawing and piano were part of the reason she went abroad.[5] She and her mother stopped first in London, where she was delighted to have a piano in her room but humbled by her feeble ability to play it: "I have been attempting to renew the little knowledge that I possess—the new sounds reviv'd a thousand remembrances dear to me the first chords I struck thril'd in my very soul but it was a long time before I could proceed with my song." Within about a year, Lydia was enrolled at Madame Campan's, where she gained facility not only on the keyboard but also on the harp. She studied speech, learned French, and proved herself quite talented in drawing. At her school's annual exhibition in 1807, she received a gold medal from Napoleon for the best work after the antique.[6] Lydia returned home to Boston in the spring of 1808 and left again about two years later. This is most likely the period during which she sat for the portrait that catalogues her newly acquired skills. Lydia would have been about twenty-two at the time—older than she appears in Stuart's picture. Yet the blush of youth depicted would have recommended her for marriage, and the occasion for the portrait may indeed have been her father's desire to record his daughter's qualifications.

A date for the portrait of about 1808 to 1810 also accords with the image in Lydia's drawing: it is a woman with a plumed headdress, similar to those worn by her mother and aunt when they sat for Stuart about 1809. It may be that Lydia drew while her relatives sat; this sort of studio activity was quite popular. Stuart did not finish Lydia's mother's portrait until 1818, when she wrote to her daughter, "Mr. Stuart has finished my portrait and I think he has done ample justice to it. He says you ought to thank him for not finishing it before you went away for you would have ruined it by carrying it so far."[7]

1. The portrait is listed in Mason 1879, p. 251 (Mrs. John Russell); Park 1926, pp. 697–97, no. 774. The other family portraits are of Barney Smith and his wife, Ann Otis Smith (both with R. H. Love Galleries, Chicago, in 1981); their son, Henry Barney Smith (private collection); their daughter Lucinda Smith Otis (unlocated) and her husband, George Alexander Otis (Glen Burnie Museum, Winchester, Va.); Barney's brother, Abiel Smith, and his wife, Lydia Otis Smith (both with Jan Herda in 1999).
2. Ann Smith, London, letter to Lucinda Otis, Boston, June 13, 1811, copy in the bound volume of Ann Smith copies of letters, 1805–12, Jonathan Russell Papers, box 3, Massachusetts Historical Society, Boston.
3. See Davida Tenenbaum Deutsch, "The Polite Lady: Portraits of American Schoolgirls and Their Accomplishments," *Antiques* 135 (March 1989), p. 243; Ann Bermingham, "Elegant Females and Gentlemen Connoisseurs: The Commerce in Culture and Self-Image in Eighteenth-Century England," in Bermingham and John Brewer, eds., *The Consumption of Culture 1600–1800: Image, Object, Text* (London: Routledge, 1995), pp. 489–513.
4. M. Maigne, ed., *The Private Journal of Madame Campan* (Philadelphia: A. Small, 1825), pp. 217–18.
5. Lydia Smith's diary, September 26–27, 1805, written in the form of a letter to her friend Anna Lothrop, Jonathan Russell Papers, box 4, Massachusetts Historical Society. All further quotations from Lydia Smith are from this source.
6. See Amelia E. Russell, "Recollections of Europe in 1817," Jonathan Russell Papers, box 5, Massachusetts Historical Society.

7. Ann Smith, letter to Lydia Smith, Stockholm, March 24, 1818, Vose Galleries, Boston, file on Stuart.

8. "Wedding of Lydia and Jonathan Russell," *Columbian Centinel*, April 5, 1817.

9. Eliza Susan Quincy's diary, July 21, 1819, Quincy Family Papers, Massachusetts Historical Society.

10. Lydia Smith's diary, undated (ca. December 1805), Massachusetts Historical Society.

11. Jonathan Russell, Ghent, letter to Amelia Russell, Philadelphia, December 24, 1814, Jonathan Russell Papers, box 1, Massachusetts Historical Society.

The distance Lydia would have carried her mother's portrait was from Boston to Stockholm. She moved there with her husband, Jonathan Russell (1771–1832), United States minister to Sweden, in August 1817, several months after their wedding.[8] They had met in London in 1811. The recently widowed Russell, with four children, had become chargé d'affaires at the American embassy, and Lydia was enjoying her second sojourn abroad, this time with artistic guidance from Stuart's friends Washington Allston and Charles Bird King, and his teacher Benjamin West, who gave her his palette as a token of his esteem and directed her to copy portraits by Sir Joshua Reynolds and landscapes by Claude Lorrain.[9] By the time she married Russell, Lydia was thirty-one, a veritable old maid. Perhaps the very abilities that should have recommended her to men made her remote. Her accomplishments may have been an end in themselves rather than a conduit to efficient housekeeping. Her proficiency in fine art, especially, veered toward a professional vocation. She was demanding of herself, once writing about her music studies that "if I cannot attain at least superiority I had rather remain in ignorance entirely" and describing the "mortification of an unavailing attempt" to paint a perfect picture.[10] Russell may have been attracted to Lydia's determination. In 1814, before they married, he sent his daughter Amelia to her for instruction in various arts, counseling Amelia, "You know, however, that a little learning is a dangerous thing & if you taste you must drink deep."[11]

Lydia Smith made a copy of her portrait by Stuart, which is still held in her family.

CRB

83. JOHN COLLINS WARREN

1812
Oil on wood, 32½ x 26 in. (82.6 x 66 cm)
Collection of the Warren Family

Laura Mills did extensive archival research for this entry, and Christopher H. Jones located the publication in which the drawing of the heart appeared and wrote early drafts of the entry.

1. On John Warren, see *ANB*, vol. 22, pp. 723–24; on the Warren family, see Rhoda Truax, *The Doctors Warren of Boston: First Family of Surgery* (Boston: Houghton Mifflin Co., 1968).

2. *ANB*, vol. 22, pp. 726–27.

3. On Park Row, see Harold Kirker, *The Architecture of Charles Bulfinch* (Cambridge, Mass.: Harvard University Press, 1969), pp. 180–85.

4. The portrait is catalogued in Mason 1879, p. 275; Park 1926, pp. 786–87, no. 880. Mount (1964, pp. 282–83) applied to this portrait a story about Stuart's reaction to an unidentified sitter's elaborate clothing; however, Mount did not give a source for the story, saying only that he thought the sitter was Dr. Warren after seeing a photograph of his portrait.

By the time Stuart painted this portrait, Boston physician John Collins Warren (1778–1856) was fully engaged in a medical career that would establish him as one of America's preeminent surgeons. He was born into a family of medical professionals. His father, John Warren, was a founder of Harvard Medical School in 1782 and its first professor of anatomy and surgery.[1] His uncle Joseph Warren, also a physician, was an important political figure in the early protests against British rule and died in 1775 at the battle of Bunker Hill.[2] John Collins Warren graduated from Harvard College in 1797, and after an apprenticeship with his father, he studied medicine and surgery in London, Edinburgh, and Paris for three years. He received a medical degree from the University of St. Andrews, Scotland. In 1802 he returned to Boston, where he joined his father's practice. He also performed surgeries in an office in his home at 2 Park Street, Boston, one of several houses called Park Row, designed by Charles Bulfinch.[3] He was appointed adjunct professor of anatomy and surgery at Harvard Medical School in 1809 and was instrumental in the school's reorganization when it moved from Cambridge to Boston in 1810.

Stuart's portrait shows Warren stylishly dressed in a black coat with a white shirt, shirt ruffle, and cravat.[4] His direct gaze, arched eyebrows, and upswept reddish brown hair give an air of alertness and self-assurance. He is seated in a chair upholstered in red, at a table draped in red, in front of columns, a red curtain, and a shelf with books. His

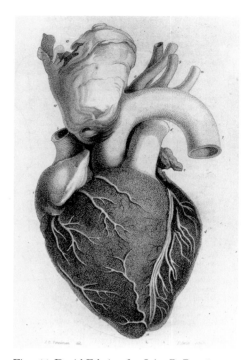

Fig. 166. David Edwin after John R. Penniman, *Diseased Heart.* Engraving, published in the *New England Journal of Medicine and Surgery, and the Collateral Branches of Science* 1 (April 1812), between pp. 120, 121 (photo: National Library of Medicine, Bethesda, Md.)

folded arms rest on several pieces of paper on the table, and in his left hand he holds a drawing of a human heart. This unusual image helps to date the portrait to 1812, when the drawing was published as an engraved illustration (fig. 166) for an article by Warren in the new periodical *New England Journal of Medicine and Surgery, and the Collateral Branches of Science*, of which Warren was cofounder.[5] Warren described this illustration of a diseased heart that he examined in a postmortem of a patient who died in August 1811: "The plate, which accompanies this case, represents about half the extent of the largest aneurismal tumour. Such a view as would have exhibited the tumour more completely, must have concealed its connection with the aorta."[6] Warren's grandson, also named John Collins Warren, wrote in 1881, "The idea of the heart was suggested to the artist by seeing an engraving of that organ lying upon my grandfathers table at the time of their first interview—said engraving being prepared for an article on the heart of which he was the author—It was strongly objected by his mother but subsequently allowed to remain."[7]

The published engraving is inscribed *J. R. Penniman del. Edwin sculp.* The artist, John R. Penniman (1783–1830/34), a Boston portrait and ornamental painter, was an assistant in Stuart's studio, where he ground colors and made at least one copy of the Athenaeum portrait of George Washington.[8] The engraver, David Edwin, an Englishman whose entire career took place in Philadelphia, had met Stuart in 1801 when he engraved Stuart's portrait of Dr. William Smith (see cat. 61). Thomas Foster of Philadelphia made the arrangements for Edwin to engrave Penniman's drawing of the diseased heart, writing Warren on March 2, 1812, "I recd your letter of the 29th ult., with the drawing accompanying it yesterday (Sunday), & have this morning called on several engravers. . . . I could not find one (except Edwin) who could begin the plate before next month. . . . Under these circumstances I concluded that it was best to engage Edwin to make the plate—As there is a great possibility that it will be finished soon enough to appear in the next number of the journal. . . . I trust you will approve of the decision. . . . He has the reputation of a man of punctuality."[9] Edwin had previously engraved two anatomical illustrations of human hearts by Penniman for Warren's book *Cases of Organic Diseases of the Heart*, pub-

5. John Collins Warren, "Cases of Organic Diseases of the Heart and Lungs," *New England Journal of Medicine and Surgery, and the Collateral Branches of Science* 1, no. 2 (April 1812), pp. 120–30. We thank Stephen J. Greenberg, History of Medicine Division, National Library of Medicine, Bethesda, Md., and Peter Rawson, Francis A. Countway Library of Medicine, Harvard Medical School, Boston, for assistance in locating the article and other publications by Warren. Park (1926, p. 787) gave the date of the portrait as 1807 based on the engraving of the portrait by S. A. Schoff in Edward Warren, *The Life of John Collins Warren, M.D., Compiled Chiefly from His Autobiography and Journals* (Boston: Ticknor and Fields, 1860), vol. 1, frontispiece. Schoff inscribed the engraving *G. Stuart Pinxt. 1807 S.A.Schoff Sc.*
6. Warren, "Cases of Organic Diseases," p. 123.
7. John Collins Warren, letter to Dr. Edwin Howard Brigham, November 18, 1881, B MS c 5.3, Boston Medical Library in the Francis A. Countway Library of Medicine.
8. On Penniman, see George C. Groce and David H. Wallace, *The New-York Historical Society's Dictionary of Artists in America, 1564–1860* (New Haven: Yale University Press, 1957), p. 498; Morgan 1939, pp. 33–35.

Drs Stewart Gilbert Contra. Crs
Amt. in June, Augt. & Sept. 1815 $15.00 1817 Nov.
Drs Skinner William S. Contra. Crs
Amt. fr. Oct. 1814 to Oct. 1816 $27.50 $27 50 $27 50
Dr. Stuart Mrs. G.
1828 Aug 2 V S $3.— $3

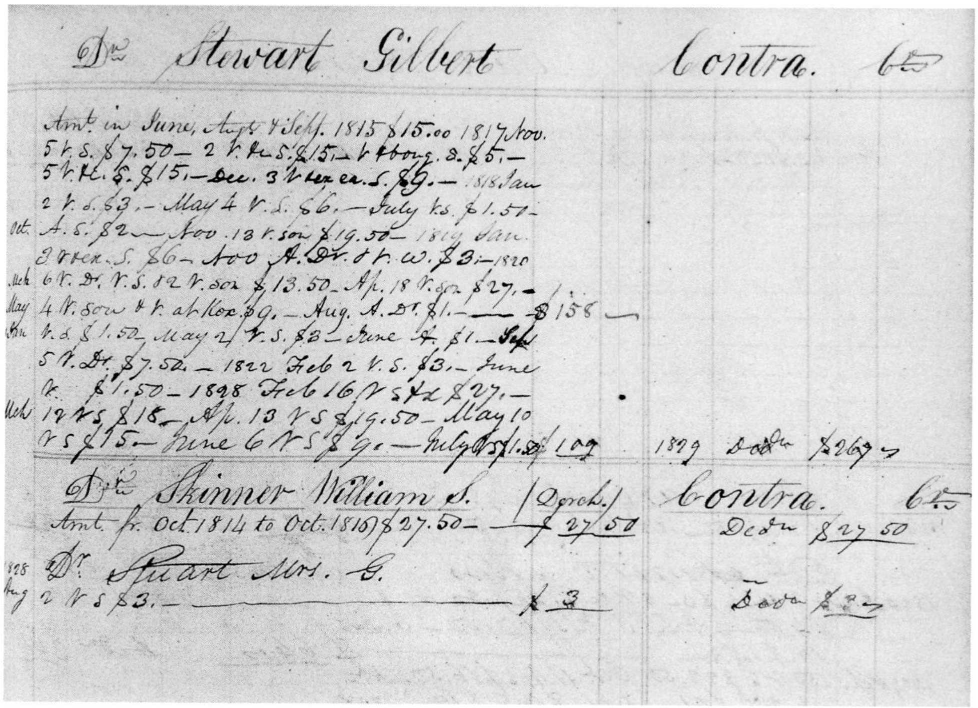

Fig. 167. Entry in John Collins Warren's medical account book that records his account with Gilbert Stuart. John Collins Warren Papers, vol. 54, Massachusetts Historical Society, Boston

83

9. Thomas Foster, letter to John C. Warren, M.D.,
March 2, 1812, John Collins Warren Papers, vol. 8,
Massachusetts Historical Society, Boston.

10. These engravings are listed in David McNeely
Stauffer, *American Engravers upon Copper and
Steel*, pt. 2, *Check-list of the Works of the Earlier
Engravers* (1907; reprint, New York: Burt Franklin,
1964), p. 158, no. 941. A brief biography of Edwin
is in ibid., pt. 1, *Biographical Sketches*, pp. 76–77.
Penniman and Edwin also cooperated in produc-
ing a certificate for the Massachusetts Medical
Society; see Mantle Fielding, *American Engravers*

lished in Boston in 1809 by Thomas B. Wait and Company, which also details evidence of
heart disease after postmortem examinations of patients.[10]

Stuart's introduction to Warren was probably through Warren's father-in-law,
Jonathan Mason, whose daughter Susan Powell Mason married Warren in 1803.[11] Stuart
painted portraits of Mason (unlocated) and his wife, Susannah Powell Mason (fig. 137),
and of Mason's daughters Anna Powell Mason (fig. 136) and Miriam Clark Mason
(unlocated) in Washington in the winter of 1804–5, and Mason encouraged the artist to
move to Boston. Warren could also have learned of Stuart through the artist's Newport
friend Colonel George Gibbs (see cat. 37), who returned from Europe in 1802 on the

upon Copper and Steel, suppl./pt. 3, Biographical Sketches and Check Lists of Engravings (1917; reprint, New York: Burt Franklin, 1961), p. 104, no. 424.

11. Mount (1964, p. 377) listed a portrait of Mrs. Warren, on a wood panel cut down to 18 by 14¾ inches, Museum of Fine Arts, Springfield, Mass. However, the museum has no record of this portrait, which is otherwise unpublished. The Warrens had seven children, including a son John who became mentally unstable and was disavowed by his father; see Truax, The Doctors Warren, pp. 133–35.

12. John Collins Warren, Medical Account Book, ca. 1817–40, John Collins Warren Papers, 1783–1923, vol. 54, Massachusetts Historical Society.

13. Morgan 1934, p. 92.

14. On the hospital building, see Kirker, Architecture of Charles Bulfinch, pp. 311–17.

15. See Anthony A. Walsh, "Phrenology and the Boston Medical Community in the 1830s," Bulletin of the History of Medicine 50 (1976), pp. 261–73.

16. For the first daguerreotype, see the on-line catalogue of the exhibition "A Family Practice: The Warrens of Harvard Medical School," Countway Library of Medicine (http://www.countway.med.harvard.edu/rarebooks/warrens/index.html), where it is credited to Harvard Medical Library. The second is illustrated in Sotheby's, New York, sale cat., April 18, 1996, lot 13.

same ship as Warren. Another mutual friend was Sarah Morton (see cat. 60), whose poetic tribute to Warren was published in 1823 in My Mind and Its Thoughts, in Sketches, Fragments, and Essays. Warren served as Stuart's family physician: his medical account book records the amounts he charged the artist for almost every year from 1815 through 1822, and in 1828 for each month from February through July; Stuart died on July 9, 1828.[12] The entries give specific dates, amounts, and coded identifications, for example in 1817, "Nov. 5, V. S. $7.50," and in 1818, "Nov. 13 V. son $19.50" (fig. 167). The probate account for Stuart's estate detailed a debt of $132 for "Dr. Warren's bill for the last sickness of deceased."[13]

In 1815, after his father's death, Warren became Hersey Professor of Anatomy and Surgery at Harvard Medical School. He was a founder of Massachusetts General Hospital and served as its chief surgeon after it opened in 1821.[14] A pioneer in surgical techniques, Warren advocated the use of ether anesthesia, operating successfully with it in 1846. He was also interested in paleontology; he assembled a mastodon skeleton, about which he published The Mastodon Giganteus of North America in 1852–55. Another interest was the study of the shape and structure of the skull and brain, termed craniognomy by Franz Joseph Gall, to whose work he was introduced as a student in Paris in 1801.[15] Warren published his own research on comparative anatomy in 1822 and was instrumental in arranging for the visit of Gall's pupil phrenologist Johann Christoph Spurzheim to Boston in 1832. After Spurzheim died suddenly, Warren performed a public autopsy at the Massachusetts Medical College, as Harvard Medical School was known. He later acquired Spurzheim's collection of skulls and casts from the Boston Phrenological Society. Many of these materials are now part of the Warren Anatomical Museum (Francis A. Countway Library of Medicine, Boston), formed with Warren's bequest of his collection of anatomical specimens and medical equipment. Two daguerreotypes of Warren show him with anatomical materials. These photographs are in the tradition of Stuart's depiction, one with his hand on a skull, the other with two anatomical specimens from his collection—a wax model of a human heart and the skeleton of a human fetus.[16]

EGM

84. HENRY DEARBORN

1812–13

Oil on wood, 28⅛ x 22¾ in. (71.5 x 57.8 cm)

The Art Institute of Chicago; Friends of American Art Collection (1913.793)

1. The painting is listed in Mason 1879, pp. 170–71; Park 1926, pp. 268–69, no. 224. See also Judith A. Barter et al., American Arts at the Art Institute of Chicago: From Colonial Times to World War I (Chicago: Art Institute of Chicago, 1998), p. 139.

2. ANB, vol. 6, p. 301. For Dearborn's biography, see also Richard A. Erney, The Public Life of Henry Dearborn (New York: Arno Press, 1979); "The Life and Services of Henry Dearborn," The New World 7 (July 8, 15, 29; August 5, 19, 1843), pp. 11, 35–37, 105–7, 132–34, 197–200.

The splendid aspect of Stuart's portrait of Henry Dearborn (1751–1829), with sculptural face and richly wrought uniform, reveals nothing of Dearborn's trials and tribulations, and perhaps that is the way it was meant to be.[1] In print, he is remembered as inadequately prepared for the responsibility he was given, with no experience in tactical planning, no strong leadership capabilities, and a near inability to conceive a strategy. For example, it was said that he excelled as "a loyal and discriminating follower rather than as an effective and courageous leader."[2]

The son of a New Hampshire farmer, Dearborn became a doctor and small-town politician before embarking on a military career. At the outbreak of the Revolutionary War, he became a captain in his state's first regiment, fought at Bunker Hill, and subsequently took part in nearly every major campaign of the war. He rose to the rank of lieutenant colonel and was well liked among the troops. In 1787 Dearborn was appointed major general of the Massachusetts militia. Five years later, he was elected to the United States

84

3. Francis S. Drake, *The Town of Roxbury: Its Memorable Persons and Places, Its History and Antiquities* (Roxbury, Mass., 1878), p. 337.

4. Sarah M. Dearborn, letter to [W. Raymond Lee], December 27, 1878, George Champlin Mason Papers, file D, Manuscripts Division, Rhode Island Historical Society, Providence. This letter was enclosed with Lee's of January 2, 1879, to Mason. The portraits of Henry Alexander Scammell Dearborn and Hannah Swett Lee Dearborn are in the Bowdoin College Museum of Art, Brunswick, Me. Stuart also painted Dearborn's daughter, Julia, and her husband,

Congress and aligned himself with Thomas Jefferson, who in 1801 appointed him secretary of war, a post Dearborn retained during Jefferson's two terms as president. Dearborn carried out the Military Peace Establishment Act of 1802, essentially a Republican retrenchment policy that called for a reorganization of military staff in order to break the Federalist hold on the army. He reduced hierarchical structure, set up new recruiting methods, revamped the training program, and helped establish an officer-training school at West Point. At the end of Jefferson's administration, Dearborn requested and received appointment as collector of customs at the Port of Boston, a lucrative and fairly undemanding position.

Three years later, in January 1812, he accepted President James Madison's appointment as senior major general of the United States Army, which put him in charge of the

Fig. 168. J. B. Binon, *Henry Dearborn*, 1818. Marble, 23 x 22½ x 11¼ in. (58.4 x 57.2 x 28.6 cm). Chicago Historical Society (1896.8.a-b)

Joshua Wingate. See Park 1926, p. 383, nos. 930, 931.

5. Stuart painted two replicas of the Dearborn portrait (Portland Museum of Art, Portland, Me., and Henry Ford Museum, Dearborn, Mich.). Several artists copied the Stuart portrait, including John Neagle (Pennsylvania Academy of the Fine Arts, Philadelphia), Walter M. Brackett (U.S. Department of the Army, Washington, D.C.), and Ulysses Dow Tenney (State House, Concord, N.H.).

6. Barter et al., *American Arts at the Art Institute of Chicago*, p. 139.

7. Pierre Berton, letter to Milo Naeve, March 2, 1982, files of the Department of American Arts, Art Institute of Chicago.

major theater of the War of 1812: the northeastern sector between the Niagara River and the New England coast. Dearborn was way out of his depth and saw heavy casualties and little military gain. Not all the failures were his fault, but they occurred on his watch. In April 1813, illness compelled him to pass his command to another, but he was nonetheless incensed when in July Madison relieved him of duty.

According to Francis S. Drake, the nineteenth-century town historian for Roxbury, Massachusetts, where Dearborn and Stuart both lived in the 1810s, the general sat for his portrait "in three sittings of an hour each," then was "hastily summoned to the chief command on the northern frontier."[3] Dearborn left home in early February 1812 for strategy sessions in Washington, and did not return to the Boston area until after his discharge in July 1813. His granddaughter-in-law, Sarah Dearborn, recalled that Stuart painted the general along with his son Henry A. S. Dearborn and his son's wife, Hannah Swett Lee Dearborn, in 1812.[4] All three portraits are the same size and on the scored panel that Stuart preferred. There is no stylistic reason to question the family history of the dating, but it is logical to speculate that Stuart may have finished Dearborn's picture after he returned to Roxbury. The uniform alone would have required more time with the sitter and his jacket.

Stuart's shrewd likeness captures the general's appearance, softens it at the edges, and brings it so far forward in the small picture plane that the subject seems monumental, grand, and important.[5] That Stuart may have glossed over two key features— Dearborn's imposing girth and his crooked nose—is revealed when the painting is compared with J. B. Binon's marble bust (fig. 168).[6] Like his comrade-in-arms Henry Knox (see cat. 80), Dearborn was large. The story is told that during the War of 1812, when the sixty-one-year-old Dearborn weighed an all-time high of two hundred fifty pounds and was unwell, his soldiers carted him from place to place in a small wheeled wagon of a type that was called a dearborn when later used by farmers.[7] Stuart's portrait is not idealized but rather aggrandized so that every aspect—from the deep crevice across the general's nose at the brow to his fleshy jowls—seems magnified. The full-frontal three-dimensionality of Binon's portrait provides a foil for the richly hued, painterly radiance of Stuart's. The similarity between the two is more provocative than the difference, however, and suggests that Stuart had some influence on the sculptor's work. Both portray Dearborn in the single-breasted, epauletted uniform of a senior major general with lavish leaf-and-acorn embroidery and a sash adorned with honors, including the small eagle denoting membership in the prestigious Society of the Cincinnati. In both portraits, Dearborn wears his hair in a close-cropped military style, while acknowledging fashion with the pyramidal combed-up pouf on top.

Perhaps Dearborn sought out the artist not only for his skills but also because of personal references from his friends, among them Sarah Bowdoin, who had sat for Stuart about 1805 (fig. 152). Recently widowed, Mrs. Bowdoin had become the object of Dearborn's affections, and his suit succeeded just about the time he sat for his portrait. The fact that Stuart did not paint Dearborn's portrait as a companion image, however, suggests that the picture was conceived before their marriage in the fall of 1813. It was a third marriage for Dearborn. Previously married first to Mary Bartlett and then to Dorcas Osgood Marble, he was twice widowed. The marriage was a second one for Mrs. Bowdoin. She moved to Roxbury with her new husband and traveled with him to Europe from 1822 to 1824, when he was appointed minister to Portugal by President James Monroe.

CRB

85. JOHN TRUMBULL

1818

Oil on wood, 26 x 21 ½ in. (66 x 54.6 cm)
Yale University Art Gallery, New Haven,
Connecticut; Bequest of Herbert L. Pratt (1945.238)

John Trumbull (1756–1843) was one of Stuart's closest friends.[1] They formed a lifelong bond based on shared experiences and the recognition of common temperament. Irascible and charming, these talented, goal-oriented painters often took on too much and did not suffer kindly the fools who tried to set them straight. As students together in Benjamin West's studio in 1780, they regularly cut up at their master's expense. They derided his methods and poked fun at his "*ten-acre* pictures," even as they were picking up their brushes to assist West or posing for him.[2] Trumbull's aspiration to history painting and Stuart's to portraiture kept their competitive natures at bay and raised each in the other's esteem. Trumbull generally dismissed portraiture as "little useful to Society, and unworthy of a man who has talents for more serious pursuits," but he allowed that "in that branch of the profession, the Name of Stuart, stands almost without a Rival, in this or any country or in any Age."[3] Stuart, in turn, disparaged Trumbull's rendering of human figures: "they look^d like they were painted with one eye"—a jibe, as Trumbull was blind in one eye. Despite his criticisms, however, Stuart thought quite highly of Trumbull's work.[4]

When Trumbull was imprisoned in London for treason in November 1780, Stuart visited him and entertained him with stories, gossip, and sketching. He also began a portrait of Trumbull (fig. 169), who later explained its unfinished state by saying that, after a week of sittings, Stuart "could make nothing of my damn'd sallow face."[5] When he was deported back to America, Trumbull left the picture in London, hoping perhaps that Stuart would finish it. In 1781 the *Public Advertiser* reported, "Mr. Trumbull, who during a long confinement of his person gave proofs that there is no imprisonment of his mind, sat for his own portrait in gaol, which is now arranged with a most elegant collection of paintings at the house of an artist near Piccadilly."[6] Trumbull finished the portrait himself sometime after he returned to London in 1784, but he always cherished it for Stuart's rendering of the visage. Later, looking at it with a friend, he commented, "I may not be a judge of the likeness—they say no one is of his own—but this I know, the face looks exactly as I felt then when Stuart used to come and greet me through the prison bars as 'Bridewell Jack.'"[7]

With the support of Benjamin West in London and Thomas Jefferson in Paris, Trumbull began his project to make paintings and engravings of the principal scenes of the American Revolution. He remained abroad until 1789, when he returned to the United States to make small portrait studies of the figures crucial to the accuracy of his historical tableaux. He also sought and was granted the same privilege that Stuart would request four years hence: sittings with George Washington. In 1794, he was back in London, this time in the diplomatic role of secretary to John Jay (see cat. 32), who was negotiating a new treaty between the United States and Great Britain. Trumbull fell in love with Sarah Hope Harvey and married her in London; they moved about 1804 to New York, where the clamor for portraits impelled him to give up historical work and paint faces for a while. His ambition and feeling that his work was not properly appreciated in New York drove him to try Boston; but, as he reminisced in his autobiography, "whenever I alluded to the idea of settling in Boston, and there pursuing my profession as a portrait painter, a cloud seemed to pass over and to chill the conversation. I could not, for a long time, account for this, but at length I learned that my old friend and fellow student, Stewart, who having pursued that branch of the profession for more than

1. On Trumbull, see Theodore Sizer, ed., *The Autobiography of Colonel John Trumbull, Patriot-Artist, 1756–1843* (New Haven: Yale University Press, 1953); Theodore Sizer, *The Works of Colonel John Trumbull, Artist of the American Revolution* (New Haven: Yale University Press, 1950); Irma B. Jaffe, *John Trumbull, Patriot-Artist of the American Revolution* (Boston: New York Graphic Society, 1975); Helen A. Cooper, *John Trumbull: The Hand and Spirit of a Painter*, exh. cat. (New Haven: Yale University Art Gallery, 1982). The largest collection of Trumbull manuscripts is the John Trumbull Papers, Manuscripts and Archives, Sterling Memorial Library, Yale University, New Haven.
2. Dunlap 1834, vol. 1, p. 178.
3. Trumbull, letter to Thomas Jefferson, June 11, 1789, quoted in *Autobiography of Colonel John Trumbull*, p. 159. Trumbull, letter to Edward Everett, January 12, 1827, enclosing a "list of painters who have attended to the historical branch of the profession now living in the U.S.," Trumbull Papers, Yale University.
4. Jouett 1816, p. 90.
5. Dunlap 1834, vol. 1, p. 23; Trumbull, letter to James Thacher, Librarian of the Pilgrim Society, Plymouth, Mass., March 14, 1840, Massachusetts Historical Society, Boston. See also "Pilgrim Society," *New England Historical and Genealogical Register* 1 (April 1847), p. 122, on Trumbull's gift of the portrait to the Pilgrim Society.
6. *Public Advertiser*, September 28, 1781.

Fig. 169. Gilbert Stuart and John Trumbull, *John Trumbull*, ca. 1780–84. Oil on canvas, 30 x 25 in. (76.2 x 63.5 cm). Pilgrim Hall Museum, Plymouth, Mass.

Fig. 170. Samuel Lovett Waldo and William Jewett, *John Trumbull*, ca. 1818. Oil on canvas, 33 x 26 in. (83.8 x 66 cm). Yale University Art Gallery, New Haven, Conn.; Gift of Alfred Wild Silliman and Benjamin Silliman, 4th, B.A. 1870, M.A. 1873

7. Whitley 1932, p. 27.
8. *Autobiography of Colonel John Trumbull*, p. 239.
9. See *Columbian Centinel*, November 28, December 2, 9, 16, 19, 1818, p. 2. John Trumbull, letter to Sarah Harvey Trumbull, November 30, 1818, Canning Collection of Papers Concerning John Trumbull, microfilm reel 3796, Archives of American Art, Smithsonian Institution, Washington, D.C.; Trumbull, letter to Sarah Harvey Trumbull, December 6 and 11, 1818, Trumbull Papers, series I, folder 32, Yale University.
10. *Columbian Centinel,* December 23, 1818, p. 2.
11. Trumbull, letter to Sarah Harvey Trumbull, December 9, 1818, Trumbull Papers, series I, folder 32, Yale University.
12. Trumbull, letter to Sarah Harvey Trumbull, December 11, 1818, Trumbull Papers, series I, folder 32, Yale University.
13. Allston, Boston, letter to James McMurtie, Philadelphia, December 24, 1818, Dana Family Papers I, box 55, Massachusetts Historical Society.
14. Jaffe, *John Trumbull,* p. 244.

twenty years, [and] established a very highly merited reputation, . . . [had chosen to] settle in Boston. This was enough. Boston was then a small town."[8] Instead, Trumbull took what he expected to be a short trip to England that lasted for the duration of the War of 1812. His return in 1815 coincided with the rebuilding of the Capitol in Washington, D.C., and, shrewdly seizing the opportunity to dust off his Revolutionary War project, he proposed to replicate his compositions on the interior of the large central chamber under the Capitol's dome. Congress selected four of his scenes. This was the first public commission to an artist in the United States.

In 1818 Trumbull set up a tour of one of his large paintings, *The Declaration of Independence, Philadelphia, 4 July 1776*. Its display in Boston reunited Trumbull and Stuart. The enormous picture was exhibited at Fanueil Hall from November 30 to December 19, and Trumbull remained in town to collect receipts and garner praise.[9] When he left Boston for Philadelphia just before Christmas to continue the tour, he had just over $1,700 from the door in his pocket and a portrait of himself by Stuart for his wife.[10] Sarah seems to have asked for the picture, for Trumbull wrote her, "I passed two hours of this morning with Stuart, in obedience to you. It was the second sitting and if it ends as it has begun, I shall have a right to say . . . 'It is a beautiful picture.' Joking aside, it promises all that you could wish."[11] That was on December 9, and two days later he sat again: "I have passed the morning with Stuart. His work advances rapidly and is very much like, I think you will be pleased."[12] According to Washington Allston (see cat. 88), the mutual friend of Stuart and Trumbull, the picture was finished by December 24, the day after Trumbull closed his show: "Stuart has painted an admirable portrait of Trumbull, who has had great success here with his picture."[13] Trumbull reportedly paid Stuart $150 for the picture, $50 more than he charged for the same size work in his own practice.[14]

After three or more sittings spread out over less than three weeks, Trumbull received a handsome portrait on a scored panel, all the more lovely for its limited palette and

85

15. The painting is listed in Mason 1879, p. 271; Park
1926, pp. 767–68, no. 854.

dearth of finicky detail, perhaps the result of fast brushwork.[15] Stuart painted the face
with precision and care, drawing the line of Trumbull's long nose down toward his
pointy chin and giving him the translucent skin and thin-lipped, beady-eyed gaze that
appear in Stuart's most captivating character studies. For the rest, Stuart worked quickly
in browns and grays. Trumbull's hair matches his coat not only in hue but also in texture, as the paint is dabbed and stroked by turns. The elegance of the work seems to
have escaped Trumbull, who cherished the earlier portrait, painted by Stuart in the
London prison. Stuart's daughter Jane reported that her sister Anne visited Trumbull in
New York about 1843 and found him staring at it: "He was sitting before his easel, with

16. Jane Stuart, quoted in Mason 1879, p. 64.
17. Trumbull, letter to Silliman, November 23, 1832, Trumbull Papers, Yale University.
18. On Trumbull and Hosack and their involvement in the American Academy of the Fine Arts (Trumbull was president 1817–36), see Carrie Rebora, "The American Academy of the Fine Arts, New York 1802–1842" (Ph.D. diss., City University of New York, 1990).

the picture before him, which my father had painted of him in London, but looking depressed and very much broken. The moment he recognized [Anne] he started from his seat, exclaiming: 'Good God! The spirit of your father has been hovering over me! I cannot tell what has possessed me, but I have been thinking about him all the morning, and of the many happy days of our early friendship. This it was that induced me to place this picture on the easel.'"[16] He may also have favored his contemporary portrait by Samuel Lovett Waldo and William Jewett, New York's popular painting team, which was high key in palette and featured flattering emblems of his painting and military exploits (fig. 170).

Of the later Stuart portrait, he confessed to his nephew Benjamin Silliman, "In truth, I never liked it. It had to my Eye something of a pert & methodistical look—which I am not conscious of possessing."[17] Trumbull liked it enough to give it to his wife, as promised, and after her death in 1824, he presented it to his friend and patron Dr. David Hosack, the prominent New York Hospital physician and professor at Columbia College.[18]

CRB

86. JAMES MONROE

1817
Oil on wood, 26⅝ x 21½ in. (67.6 x 54.6 cm)
Pennsylvania Academy of the Fine Arts,
Philadelphia; Pennsylvania Academy purchase
(1900.4)

James Monroe (1758–1831), a Virginian, served in the United States Senate from 1790 to 1794, when he was appointed minister to France (1794–96). Governor of Virginia from 1799 to 1802, minister to England from 1803 to 1807, and secretary of state during James Madison's presidency, he was elected fifth president of the United States in November 1816.[1] The following summer he made a tour of New England to smooth over tensions with the Federalists and encourage national unity. The visit introduced the "Era of Good Feelings," a phrase coined by the *Columbian Centinel*.[2] While in Boston he sat for this portrait. The *Newburyport Herald* reported the news: "A few days after the arrival of Mr. Monroe in Boston, he went out early one morning in his carriage, to sit for his portrait to Mr. Stuart. Not knowing his dwelling, he stopped a country man seated on his cart, and enquired for Mr. Stuart's house. The country man looked steadfastly at him. 'It is the President, I vow,' said he to himself, and, instinctively taking off his hat, he gave three loud and hearty cheers, and drove off, leaving the President unanswered and astonished."[3] According to the *Essex Register* for July 12, 1817, "Boston. July 10th. Early the three last mornings, previous to his departure, the President has had sittings at Mr. Stewart's room. This eminent painter will execute a portrait of the President to be sent to Virginia. The President has also bespoke, from the same pencil, a superb portrait of President Washington."[4] Additional details were reported in the *Columbian Centinel*: "[W]e are happy to learn, that, amidst the multiplicity of occupations and avocations, [the president] was able to afford four settings (while others slept) for one of the most celebrated Painters of the age to take a Likeness of him. This, we understand, was done at the instance of Mrs. Monroe, who was unwilling her husband should be in the neighborhood of such an inimitable master of the art without being gratified with a portrait from his pencil. . . . Connoisseurs . . . consider it one of the most felicitous efforts of the mighty powers of the Artist."[5]

Monroe's bust-size portrait is an image in black, gray, and white against a brown background. His hair is gray, and he wears a black coat, a gray waistcoat, and a white

Fig. 171. *James Monroe*, ca. 1817. Oil on wood, 25½ x 21⅝ in. (64.8 x 55 cm). National Gallery of Art, Washington, D.C.; Ailsa Mellon Bruce Fund (1979.4.3)

86

1. On Monroe, see *ANB*, vol. 15, pp. 681–84; Noble E. Cunningham Jr., *The Presidency of James Monroe* (Lawrence: University Press of Kansas, 1996).

2. Quoted in Cunningham, *Presidency of James Monroe*, pp. 37–38; and in David Meschutt, "Portraiture of James Monroe," in Lee A. Langston-Harrison, ed., *Images of a President: Portraits of James Monroe*, exh. cat. (Fredericksburg, Va.: James Monroe Museum and Memorial Library; Charlottesville, Va.: Ash Lawn-Highland, 1992), p. 17.

shirt with a cravat that is delineated with thick impasto. Stuart depicted soft lines in the flesh below the outer corners of Monroe's intensely blue eyes, and the lips appear slightly pursed. Monroe's expression, with arched eyebrows and a direct gaze, is very similar to that in portraits by John Vanderlyn (1816, Colonial Williamsburg Foundation; replica, National Portrait Gallery, Washington) and Charles Willson Peale (1818; Philipse Manor Hall, Yonkers, N.Y.), although Vanderlyn showed him looking to the side, and Peale gave his head a slight tilt and his mouth more of a smile. In 1819 Monroe was painted by Samuel F. B. Morse in a more dramatic portrait, a full-length showing him striding down some steps, looking to the right (City of Charleston, S.C.).[6]

3. *Newburyport Herald*, August 6, 1817, quoted in Park 1926, p. 528. The portrait is discussed in Mason 1879, p. 229; Park 1926, pp. 527–28, no. 553; Meschutt, "Portraiture of James Monroe," pp. 17–18, no. 11; Cunningham, *Presidency of James Monroe*, pp. 25–6, 37, 142–44; Evans 1999, p. 152 n. 8. Monroe gave the portrait to Lloyd Nicholas Rogers of Baltimore, who married his granddaughter Hortensia Hay. Rogers's daughter Eleanor Rogers Goldsborough sold the portrait to the Pennsylvania Academy of the Fine Arts in 1900. Rogers also owned Stuart's portrait of Bishop John Carroll (cat. 73).

4. Quoted in Park 1926, p. 528.

5. *Columbian Centinel*, July 19, 1817, quoted in Daniel Preston, ed., *The Papers of James Monroe*, vol. 1, *A Documentary History of the Presidential Tours of James Monroe, 1817, 1818, 1819* (Westport, Conn.: Greenwood Press, 2003), p. 230.

6. For these portraits, see Meschutt, "Portraiture of James Monroe," pp. 11–12 no. 7, 15–16 no. 10, 19–20 no. 12, 23–24 no. 14, and his checklist in *Images of a President*, reprinted as "The Iconography of James Monroe," in Harry Ammon, *James Monroe, a Bibliography* (Westport, Conn.: Meckler, 1991), pp. 101–4. On the individual portraits, see also Frederick S. Voss, *Portraits of the Presidents: The National Portrait Gallery* (Washington, D.C.: National Portrait Gallery, Smithsonian Institution in association with Rizzoli International Publications, 2000), pp. 32–33; Andrew J. Cosentino, *The Paintings of Charles Bird King (1785–1862)* (Washington, D.C.: Smithsonian Institution Press, 1977), pp. 33–35, fig. 18, p. 147 no. 169; Lillian B. Miller, ed., *The Selected Papers of Charles Willson Peale and His Family* (New Haven: Yale University Press, 1983–), vol. 3, pp. 619–23, fig. 53; William Kloss, *Samuel F. B. Morse* (New York: Harry N. Abrams, 1988), pp. 56–62; Paul J. Staiti, *Samuel F. B. Morse* (Cambridge: Cambridge University Press, 1989), pp. 57–58.

7. Horace Holley, letter to his wife, Mary, April 8, 1818, Horace Holley Papers, letter L40, William L. Clements Library, University of Michigan, Ann Arbor. The letter is partially quoted in Cunningham, *Presidency of James Monroe*, pp. 142–44.

8. Ibid.

9. On the replica in Gibbs's collection, see Miles 1995, pp. 277–79.

10. Morse, letter to Jedediah Morse, December 17, 1819, Samuel F. B. Morse Papers, Library of Congress, Washington, D.C., quoted in Kloss, *Samuel F. B. Morse*, pp. 60–61; cited in Staiti, *Samuel F. B. Morse*, p. 57.

11. Meschutt, "Portraiture of James Monroe," p. 23; William Kloss and Doreen Bolger, *Art in the White House: A Nation's Pride* (Washington, D.C.: White House Historical Association in cooperation with the National Geographic Society, 1992), pp. 82–83.

Monroe and his wife, Elizabeth Kortright Monroe, discussed Stuart and his portraits in 1818 with White House visitor Horace Holley, a Unitarian minister from Boston who was on his way to Kentucky to become president of Transylvania College. Holley wrote his wife a long letter indicating each speaker in the conversations.

There is a full length portrait of general Washington in the parlour, painted by Stewart. This led me to ask Mr. Monroe about the portrait of himself by Stewart. But I think I will give you the conversation as it happened. . . . [Holley] That is a painting by Stewart, I perceive. [Mrs. Monroe]. Yes, and it is a very good one. [Holley]. He is the best portrait painter in our country, and probably not inferior, in regard to the face, to any artist in the world. But he paints hands, limbs, and drapery badly. He spends the force of his genius on the characteristic expression of the countenance, and cares little for the other parts of the picture. [Monroe]. He ought to paint nothing but the head, and should leave the rest to such artists as Copley, who was said to be the painter of collars, cuffs, and button holes. [Holley]. Stewart is not ambitious of the distinction acquired in that way. His favorite expression in regard to his portraits, to show that he does as little as possible in the way of drapery, is "that picture has never been to the tailor's." . . . Have you ever received your portrait from Stewart yet? [Monroe]. No, Sir. It is not his habit to finish a picture and send it home. Have you ever seen it at his room? [Holley]. yes, Sir, several times. [Monroe] How far it is finished? [Holley]. Nothing but the head. [Mrs. Monroe]. Is it a good likeness? [Holley]. A remarkably good one. It is the general opinion that it is one of the artist's happiest efforts with his pencil. You will be pleased with it, but will observe immediately, when you see it, that your husband was sun-burnt as a traveller ought to be, and that the artist has been so long in the habit of copying faithfully what he sees that he has given this in the shading of the picture. [Mrs. Monroe]. I shall not like it the less for that. I think Stewart generally makes the color of the cheeks too brilliant, especially in the portraits of men, as in that of general Washington. [Holley]. The painting of Mr. Monroe then will meet your taste precisely.[7]

Monroe's daughter Elizabeth Kortright Monroe Hay suggested that Stuart should send the portrait of her father unfinished, to be completed by a different painter. The president, however, apparently preferred to wait.

[Monroe]. He promised to come on here this last winter, or during the session of congress, and to take a portrait of Mrs. Monroe. We are disappointed that he has not kept his word. He is a very sensible man, Mr. Holley, and appears to be well read. [Holley]. Yes, Sir, he tells a story extremely well, with great spirit, and with a striking talent of illustration. He must have studied books attentively at one period of life, and he retains his Latin very well. He has taken the portraits of so many of our distinguished men, & has been so much abroad, that he has an immense fund of anecdotes, and has learned characters very extensively. [Monroe]. When a gentleman sits three or four times for an artist, and each time one, two, or three hours, and is engaged in conversation, traits of character must be strongly exhibited, and much of biography and cast of mind will be furnished to the artist. [Holley]. Stewart sometimes gives his anecdotes concerning those who sit for him, but he always regards the limits of honorable treatment in his representations.[8]

Stuart probably delayed completion and delivery of the portrait in order to make a replica (fig. 171) for George Gibbs Jr. of New York, son of George Gibbs of Newport, Rhode Island, one-time business partner of Stuart's uncle Joseph Anthony.[9] The life portrait arrived in Washington sometime before December 1819, when Morse was painting his full-length of Monroe. Morse wrote his father on December 17, 1819, "I have succeeded to my satisfaction, and, what is better, to the satisfaction of himself and family; so much so that one of his daughters wishes me to copy the head for her. They all say that mine is the best that has been taken of him. The daughter told me (she said as a secret) that her father was delighted with it, and said it was the only one that in his opinion looked like him; and this, too, with Stuart's in the room."[10] The head-and-shoulders version that Morse painted for Monroe's daughter Elizabeth Hay is at the White House.[11]

EGM

87. JAMES MONROE

1821
Oil on canvas, 40¼ x 32 in. (102.2 x 81.3 cm.)
The Metropolitan Museum of Art, New York;
Bequest of Seth Low, 1916 (29.89)

This portrait of President James Monroe was painted in 1821 for Boston framer and gilder John Doggett, who had recently opened an art gallery, Doggett's Repository of Art, where he exhibited Rembrandt Peale's painting *The Court of Death* (1820; Detroit Institute of Arts) as one of his first ventures into the fine arts. Doggett commissioned Stuart to paint a series of portraits of the first five American presidents.[1] Only two survive, this of Monroe and the one of James Madison (fig. 154).[2] The paintings in this series were slightly smaller than standard half-length portraits and showed each president seated at a table with books and papers. In them Stuart replicated his own portraits of Washington (cat. 39) and Madison (cat. 76); he arranged a new sitting with Adams in 1821 (see cat. 59) and apparently finished and sold to Doggett the life portrait of Jefferson that he painted in 1805 (see cat. 77). To paint this portrait of Monroe, Stuart borrowed from George Gibbs Jr. his 1817 replica (fig. 171) of the original that was with Monroe in Virginia (cat. 86).[3] On May 19, 1821, Stuart wrote Gibbs, who lived in New York, to arrange for Doggett to borrow his portrait.[4]

In this portrait, Monroe is seated at a table draped with a red cloth, his right hand holding a document while his left hand rests on other papers. Also on the table are two books and an inkwell with a quill pen. The large red curtain draped behind him is pulled back to reveal a column and blue sky with both pink and black clouds. Gibbs's version of Monroe's portrait also has a dramatic sky, which is not in the life portrait. When lending his portrait to Doggett, Gibbs possibly exacted an agreement from Stuart that he would paint four portraits of the first presidents so that Gibbs, too, would have a series of five (figs. 103, 126, 154, 156, 171).[5] Although his series (known as the Gibbs-Coolidge portraits), which depicts each president in a head-and-shoulders composition, has traditionally been dated earlier, one indication of its late date is the fact that Stuart's first opportunity to copy the portrait of Madison at Bowdoin College did not occur until 1821. In addition, the coat in the Gibbs-Coolidge Adams is similar to the one depicted in the lithograph after Doggett's painting of Adams, now lost.

Doggett exhibited his set of five paintings at his Repository of Art from January 19 to March 2, 1822.[6] A writer in the *Boston Daily Advertiser* for June 20, 1822, said, "Had Mr. Stuart never painted any thing else, these alone would be sufficient to 'make his fame' with posterity. No one . . . has ever surpassed him in fixing the *very soul* on canvas;

1. On Doggett and the portraits by Stuart, see Mabel Munson Swan, "The 'American Kings,'" *Antiques* 19 (April 1931), pp. 278–81; Noble E. Cunningham Jr., *Popular Images of the Presidency: From Washington to Lincoln* (Columbia: University of Missouri Press, 1991), pp. 38–49; Sally Pierce and Catharina Slautterback, *Boston Lithography, 1825–1880: The Boston Athenaeum Collection* (Boston: Boston Athenaeum, 1991), pp. 3–4; Evans 1999, pp. 104–5, 153–54 n. 18.
2. On the portrait of Monroe, see Mason 1879, p. 229; Park 1926, p. 529, no. 555; John Caldwell and Oswaldo Rodriguez Roque, *American Paintings in The Metropolitan Museum of Art*, vol. 1, *A Catalogue of Works by Artists Born by 1815* (New York: Metropolitan Museum of Art, 1994), pp. 194–95.
3. On the replica painted for Gibbs, see Miles 1995, pp. 277–79.
4. Gilbert Stuart, letter to George Gibbs Jr., May 19, 1821, Papers of Oliver Wolcott Jr., Connecticut Historical Society, Hartford; quoted in Miles 1995, p. 266.
5. On the Gibbs-Coolidge series, see Miles 1995, pp. 265–79.
6. James L. Yarnall and William H. Gerdts, *The National Museum of American Art's Index to American Art Exhibition Catalogues: From the Beginning through the 1876 Centennial Year* (Boston: G. K. Hall, 1986), vol. 5, p. 3415, no. 87029; Pierce and Slautterback (*Boston Lithography*, p. 3) give the dates of the exhibition as January 19–March 22, 1822.

Fig. 172. Attributed to Nicholas-Eustache Maurin after Gilbert Stuart, *James Monroe*, 1828. Lithograph, 11 ½ x 9 ½ in. (29.1 x 24.2 cm). National Portrait Gallery, Smithsonian Institution, Washington, D.C. (NPG.87.58.5)

Fig. 173. Attributed to Nicholas-Eustache Maurin after Gilbert Stuart, *George Washington*, 1828. Lithograph, 11 ⅝ x 9 ¾ in. (29.6 x 24.7 cm). National Portrait Gallery, Smithsonian Institution, Washington, D.C. (NPG.79.83)

Fig. 174. Attributed to Nicholas-Eustache Maurin after Gilbert Stuart, *James Madison*, 1828. Lithograph, 12 ¹⁄₁₆ x 9 ¾ in. (30.7 x 24.7 cm). National Portrait Gallery, Smithsonian Institution, Washington, D.C. (NPG.87.58.4)

7. *Boston Daily Advertiser*, June 20, 1822, quoted in Cunningham, *Popular Images of the Presidency*, p. 41.

8. Allston, letter to Leslie, February 7, 1823, in Nathalia Wright, ed., *The Correspondence of Washington Allston* (Lexington: University Press of Kentucky, 1993), p. 202.

9. Ibid., p. 203.

10. On the Pendletons' lithographs, see Swan, "American Kings," pp. 279–80; Cunningham, *Popular Images of the Presidency*, pp. 42–49; Pierce and Slautterback, *Boston Lithography*, pp. 3–4, 20 pl. 3; Sally Pierce, "Early American Lithography: Images to 1830," in Sally Pierce with Catharine Slautterback and Georgia Brady Barnhill, *Early American Lithography: Images to 1830* (Boston: Boston Athenaeum, 1997), pp. 13–14, 56 nos. 33–37.

11. Quoted in Swan, "American Kings," p. 279; Cunningham, *Popular Images of the Presidency*, p. 48. While it is difficult to tell from this notice whether the paintings were actually sent to France, Swan ("American Kings," p. 281) quotes from an undated printed notice for subscribers of the series that the "original pictures . . . have lately been returned from France where they were correctly copied on stone by Monsieur Maurin, an eminent lithographer of Paris." The lithographs are attributed to French lithographer Nicholas-Eustache Maurin (1799–1850).

12. Adams, diary entry dated March 3, 1828, quoted in Cunningham, *Popular Images of the Presidency*, pp. 42, 48, from Charles Francis Adams, ed., *Memoirs of John Quincy Adams Comprising Portions of His Diary from 1795 to 1848* (1874–77; reprint, Freeport, N.Y.: Books for Libraries Press, 1969), vol. 7, p. 460.

but in the present instance he has done more; he has invested the individual of nature with the ideal of art."[7]

Doggett and Stuart also decided to have the portraits reproduced as prints for public sale. They first considered hiring an English engraver. American artist Washington Allston wrote to Charles Robert Leslie in London in 1823 for advice. "As they are amongst Stuarts best works, and in a manner (from their subjects) of national interest, it is Mr. Doggets wish to have them engraved in the best possible manner." According to Allston, "Stuart thinks the *line* [rather than stipple engraving] would be preferred, if the engraver unites fidelity with fine execution; so think I & it would besides give the greatest number of impressions."[8] Doggett stipulated the size of the paper and wanted to determine the expense, as well as "whether the Prints would be likely to sell in England. And whether the Pictures themselves would be likely to produce any profit if exhibited there."[9] When this plan failed, Doggett arranged with Boston copperplate engravers John and William S. Pendleton to have the paintings lithographed, a reproductive technique recently invented in Europe.[10] John Pendleton went to France in 1825 as purchasing agent for Doggett and returned with the lithographic stones bearing images of Stuart's portraits. He also brought with him a press and a French pressman to pull the prints. Doggett announced receipt of the lithographic stones in the *Columbian Centinel* for November 16, 1825, adding that during the visit of the marquis de Lafayette to Boston in 1824, Stuart's portraits "adorned the residence of the Nation's Guest."[11] The Pendletons were unsuccessful in printing these lithographs, and after John Pendleton made a second trip to France, they finally produced the series of lithographs in 1828. Titled the "American Kings," the prints were immediately popular and sold widely. John Quincy Adams did not like the lithographs, criticizing both the new medium and the paintings themselves, which he deemed "not in Stuart's best manner." He wrote that the lithographs "were made after copies taken by I know not whom, made in France, with a gloss of the mannerism of inferior French artists; and they have metamorphosed the five grave Presidents of the United States into five petits-maitres, courtiers of the old Court. All likeness and character and truth of nature have vanished in the process."[12]

87

13. Boston 1828, p. 2, nos. 27–31. The series belonging
    to Gibbs was apparently not well known.
14. For the history of these paintings, see Caldwell
    and Rodriquez Roque, *American Paintings*, p. 195;
    Theodore Bolton, "The Life Portraits of James
    Madison," *William and Mary Quarterly*, ser. 3, 8
    (January 1951), p. 43; Oliver 1967, p. 161.

The five paintings were included in the memorial exhibition of Stuart's work at the Boston Athenaeum in 1828; they were described in the catalogue as "the only uniform series of the Presidents in existence."[13] Sold in 1839 to Abel Phillips of Boston, the portraits were considered for acquisition by the federal government in a bill introduced in 1846 that was never passed. While they were on exhibition at the Library of Congress in 1851, a fire destroyed those of George Washington, John Adams, and Thomas Jefferson.[14]

EGM

88. WASHINGTON ALLSTON

ca. 1818

Oil on canvas, 24 x 21½ in. (61 x 54.6 cm)
The Metropolitan Museum of Art, New York; The
Alfred N. Punnett Endowment Fund, 1928 (28.118)

Washington Allston's disembodied face, floating just above the center of the canvas, seems to warrant more interrogation than would be demanded by an aborted picture. It shows that all the power of Stuart's portraits resides in the heads and not in the clothing, draperies, or attributes, no matter how finely rendered. He put his effort into technical and intellectual engagement with his sitter, and the result of this interaction, without exception, appears in the face. In the portrait of Allston, the passion of the painter is unmitigated: there is nothing mundane to temper the intensity of the floating face. As Allston's brother-in-law, the novelist Richard Henry Dana, put it: "It is the mere head, but such a head! and so like the man!"[1]

Study of the work gives clues to Stuart's process. The canvas is primed and ground color laid in; once the sitter's head is positioned, the face is delineated in sequences of color united by glazes, and minute touches capture the fine details of the lips, the nose, and especially the eyes, which are full of feeling. The hair is freely painted; Stuart would later have pulled the background up to the curls and then embellished the curls

Fig. 175. *Daniel Webster*, 1817–20. Oil on wood, 23 x 19 in. (58.4 x 48.3 cm). Hood Museum of Art, Dartmouth College, Hanover, N.H.; Presented in memory of Francis Parkman (1898–1990) by his sons—Henry, Francis Jr., Theodore B., and Samuel—and by Edward Connery Lathem in tribute to Elizabeth French Lathem (P.992.21)

Fig. 176. *Nathaniel Bowditch*, 1827–28. Oil on canvas, 29½ x 24½ in. (74.9 x 62.2 cm). Private collection

Fig. 177. *Jared Sparks*, ca. 1826. Oil on canvas, 25 x 20 in. (63.5 x 50.8 cm). New Britain Museum of American Art, New Britain, Conn.; Stephen B. Lawrence Fund and Charles F. Smith Fund (1955.6)

Fig. 178. *Edward Everett*, ca. 1820. Oil on canvas, 30 x 24 in. (76 x 61 cm). Massachusetts Historical Society, Boston

88

1. Mason 1879, p. 127. The painting is also listed in Park 1926, p. 98, no. 13; and John Caldwell and Oswaldo Rodriguez Roque, *American Paintings in The Metropolitan Museum of Art*, vol. 1, *A Catalogue of Works by Artists Born by 1815* (New York: Metropolitan Museum of Art, 1994), p. 195–96.
2. Quoted in Herbert 1836, p. 248.
3. Probate inventory of Gilbert Stuart, no. 28699, Massachusetts State Archives, Dorchester. See also Mary Tyler Peabody Mann, letter to Miss Rawlins Pickman, January 27, 1825, Horace Mann

again in still lighter strokes; this method is seen again and again in his portraits. The evident labor is fluid, even joyful. Stuart reveled in reading character in swift, controlled strokes. No wonder he so often failed to get beyond this point; upon leaving Dublin, Stuart left many canvases abandoned in this way, satisfied that "the artists of Dublin will get employed in finishing them. . . . The likeness is there, and the finishing may be better than I should have made it."[2] He even left one life portrait of George Washington unfinished (cat. 39).

Stuart's portrait of Allston was one of "8 unfinished sketches of Heads" recorded in the probate inventory of Stuart's home in 1828, just after his death.[3] The other heads

Papers, microfilm reel 37, Massachusetts Historical Society, Boston: "At Stewart's room I saw a portrait of Webster, Mr. Quincy, President Adams and lady, Bishop Griswold, Mr. Taylor & c. They were all unfinished."

4. Edward Everett's diary, June 1, 1838, and August 25, 1858, Edward Everett Papers, Massachusetts Historical Society. See also Mark Mitchell, Hood Museum of Art, Dartmouth College, Hanover, N.H., letter to Laura Mills, Metropolitan Museum, January 27, 2003, curatorial files, Department of American Paintings and Sculpture, The Metropolitan Museum of Art.

5. Mary Eliot Parkman, Beverly Farms, Mass., October 12, [1878/79], George Champlin Mason Papers, file A, Maunscripts Division, Rhode Island Historical Society, Providence.

6. Evans (1999, p. 155 n. 29) suggests that the Allston portrait may date from about 1818.

7. On Allston, see William H. Gerdts and Theodore E. Stebbins Jr., "A Man of Genius": The Art of Washington Allston (1779–1843), exh. cat. (Boston: Museum of Fine Arts, 1979); Nathalia Wright, ed., The Correspondence of Washington Allston (Lexington: University Press of Kentucky, 1993).

8. Allston, letter to William Dunlap, October 15, 1833, quoted in Dunlap 1834, vol. 1, p. 221, in which Allston says that he met Stuart on his return from Italy.

9. Quoted in William Ellery Channing, "Reminiscences of Washington Allston," Christian Register and Boston Observer, August 5, 1843, p. 124.

would have been of Daniel Webster (fig. 175), two of Edward Everett (fig. 178 and private collection), Nathaniel Bowditch (fig. 176), Jared Sparks (fig. 177), Joseph Story (Harvard University, Cambridge, Mass.), and John Quincy Adams (Harvard University, as finished by Thomas Sully). Stuart apparently had not worked on any of the portraits for a very long time. Those of Allston, Webster, and Everett were commissioned by their mutual friend Edward Dwight about 1818, and the interested parties must simply have given the painter the benefit of the doubt: someday he would finish them.[4] Webster's daughter had a childhood recollection that her father spoke of Stuart's death and then said, "I shall go to Stuart's room to-day & bring those pictures home in the carriage."[5] Webster came back with his own portrait and Allston's.

The logical dating for Allston's portrait seems to fall after October 1818, when he returned from a long sojourn abroad.[6] Dwight's commission probably brought Allston and Stuart together. The South Carolina-born and Harvard-educated Allston (1779–1843) had spent most of his nascent career in Europe.[7] Between 1801 and 1808, he studied at London's Royal Academy of Art under Benjamin West (by then its president), traveled in France and Italy, and then moved to New York, where he thought his interest in romantic landscape and religious scenes would play well. He spent the years from 1809 to 1811 in Boston and seems to have met Stuart, but he soon returned to London for another eight years.[8] He went back to Boston in October 1818, with what he hoped would be his masterpiece: a 12-by-16-foot rendition of the Old Testament story of Belshazzar's feast in which Daniel predicts the destruction of Babylon (Detroit Institute of Arts). The picture required more work, and Allston convinced a group of enthusiastic Bostonians to pool their support and create a $10,000 stipend. This financial backing provided freedom, but Allston lacked inspiration. It took him two years to unroll the canvas. He chose to do so in September 1820 in front of Stuart. Allston later recalled what Stuart had told him: "Mr. Allston's mind grows by, and beyond his work. What he does in one month, becomes imperfect in the next, by the very growth of his mind; so sir, it must be altered. He can never be satisfied with what is best done in one part of the picture, for it will cease to be so when he has finished another. The picture will never be finished, sir."[9]

Stuart probably had no bouts of conscience about quitting work on Allston's portrait, but Allston, who often visited Stuart's studio during the next decade, may have been taunted by the evidence that the older painter knew when to leave well enough alone. Allston, on the other hand, continued to wrestle with Belshazzar's Feast and never finished it—just as Stuart had predicted.

CRB

89. BISHOP JEAN-LOUIS ANNE MAGDELAINE LEFEBVRE DE CHEVERUS

1823
Oil on canvas, 36¼ x 28½ in. (92.1 x 72.4 cm)
Museum of Fine Arts, Boston; Bequest of Mrs.
Charlotte Gore Greenough Hervoches du Quilliou
(21.9)

When Bishop Jean-Louis Anne Magdelaine Lefebvre de Cheverus (1768–1836) left his parish in Boston for the episcopacy of Montauban, France, in the fall of 1823, a group of 226 gentlemen, including Harrison Gray Otis, Josiah Quincy (see cat. 91), John Lowell Jr., and Thomas Handysyd Perkins, petitioned Gustave-Maximilian-Just de Croy, grand almoner of France, to retract Cheverus's new assignment, pleading "it is impossible for us to make known to you by any words how entire, grateful and beneficent is the dominion of Bishop Cheverus over all to whom he ministers in his Apostolic Authority. We hold him to be a blessing and a treasure in our social community which we cannot part with and which, without injustice to any man we may affirm, if withdrawn from us can never be replaced."[1] That the petitioners were high-church Episcopalians underscores the extent to which Cheverus's charisma and eloquence made him a beloved Catholic in a city of Protestants.

Cheverus himself tried to refuse the appointment that would take him from New England. A native of Mayenne, France, and a graduate of the Jesuit College of Louis-le-Grand and the Saint-Magloire Seminary in Paris, Cheverus refused to swear to support the Civil Constitution of the Clergy, which was required of graduating seminarians by the French government.[2] In 1792 he fled to England, where he lived until his former professor Father Francis Matignon invited him to serve the Catholic Missionary in America. He arrived in Boston in 1796, and between missionary trips throughout New England, he oversaw the construction of a Roman Catholic church, the Cathedral of the Holy Cross, designed by Charles Bulfinch and built between 1799 and 1803. In 1810, he was consecrated the first Catholic bishop of Boston. During his long tenure in the city, he nearly doubled the population of his diocese. Cheverus was a mild-mannered, gentle disseminator of the faith, character traits that he no doubt honed in order not to incite hostility by his missionary activities. He seems never to have lost sight of the hatred held by some for his church. He worked hard for what he gained for Catholics in Boston and even three years after he had been called back to France, he wrote to Josiah Quincy, "I do not forget Boston so dear & familiar is the name of the beloved city that even in conversation I say Boston instead of Montauban."[3] His good work in France earned him appointment as archbishop of Bordeaux by July 1826, and ten years later the pope anointed him a cardinal.

In 1823 Cheverus's imminent departure from Boston caused a flurry of attentiveness. He wrote to a friend in France, "They want me painted, engraved, etc. The city wished to present me with an address, etc., etc. All the gazettes are concerned with me."[4] He sat for at least two artists before he left: Gilbert Stuart and the miniaturist Anson Dickinson. The Dickinson piece (unlocated), a small watercolor-on-ivory, would have been a private commission by one of the bishop's many followers, someone devoted enough to want to wear his face pinned close to the heart. The sittings with Stuart were for a portrait for the cathedral and another for a friend. The former seems not to have been finished by Stuart; the artist painted the head and another artist, perhaps much later, filled in the body and other details.[5] The latter picture was ordered from Stuart by Mary Babcock Gore, who desired a lasting likeness of the "dear little bishop."[6] Mrs. Gore sat for Stuart herself about 1815, after an extended trip to London where her husband, John, had sat for John Trumbull. The Stuart portrait of her (Museum of Fine Arts, Boston) works as a pendant image to Trumbull's painting of him (Gore Place, Waltham, Mass.).

1. Memorial to His Serene Highness the Prince of Croy, grand almoner of France and bishop of Strasbourg, transcribed in Samuel L. Knapp, "Memoir of Bishop Cheverus," *Boston Monthly Magazine* 1 (June 1825), p. 13.
2. Annabelle M. Melville, *Jean Lefebvre de Cheverus, 1768–1836* (Milwaukee, Wis.: Bruce Publishing Co., 1958); *ANB*, vol. 4, pp. 795–96.
3. Cheverus, letter to Quincy, April 8, 1826, Josiah Quincy Papers, Massachusetts Historical Society, Boston.
4. Cheverus, letter to Mme de Bonneuil, April 21, 1823, *Records of the American Catholic Historical Society* 15 (1904), p. 99, quoted in Melville, *Jean Lefebvre de Cheverus*, p. 256.
5. See Carol Troyen, letter to Richard Reardon for the archbishop of Boston, May 31, 1991, Museum of Fine Arts, Boston, archives: "the head, which compares favorably with ours [at the Museum of Fine Arts], may well have been executed by Stuart himself, while the rest of the painting—the Archbishop's body and hands, the swag of drapery in the backdrop, and the items he is holding—were probably done by a studio assistant or follower of Stuart's."
6. Quoted in Melville, *Jean Lefebvre de Cheverus*, p. 256. Stuart's portrait of Cheverus is listed in Mason 1879, p. 158; Park 1926, pp. 214–15, no. 155.

7. Swan (1938, p. 308) lists a visit from Mr. and Mrs. Gore on April 29, 1808. This could be the John Gores or their relatives Christopher Gore and his wife.

8. By 1824 Stuart apparently had given the portraits of Cheverus and Gardiner to his friend Isaac P. Davis, presumably for delivery to Davis's cousin Mrs. Gore; see Margaret Morton Quincy Greene (1806–82), Journal, July 18–October 16, 1824, Quincy Family Papers, QP 107, microfilm reel 7, Massachusetts Historical Society: "At 3 all being in readiness we drove to Cousin Isaacs, where we alighted and beheld the whole Davis and Jackson faction besides two superb portraits of Bishop Cheverus and Dr. Gardner, . . . and a variety of new productions which as usual Mr Davis continues to get before any other." Josiah Quincy (*Figures of the Past from the Leaves of Old Journals* [Boston: Roberts Brothers, 1883], p. 311) recalled seeing both portraits in the parlor of Mrs. Gore's high-style home at 5 Park Street, Boston.

9. Reverend J. S. J. Gardiner, D.D., *A Sermon Preached at Trinity Church, March 30, 1817. Being the Sunday after the Interment of John Gore, Esq.* (Boston: Munroe and Francis, 1817), p. 14.

10. Davis 2001, p. 107.

11. See *Boston Monthly Magazine* 1 (1825), frontispiece, "Rᵗ Rev.ᵈ John Cheverus / Bishop of Montauban / Formerly of Boston / Drawn & Engᵈ by D. C. Johnston from a Portrait by Stuart." An example of the original print is in the American Antiquarian Society Worcester, Mass.

12. "The Stuart Gallery," *Evening Gazette*, August 2, 1828, p. 2. See also Boston 1828.

In patronizing Stuart, Mrs. Gore carried on a family tradition: her parents, Adam and Martha Hubbard Babcock, had sat for him about 1806 (Museum of Fine Arts, Boston), shortly after Stuart arrived in Boston.[7]

When Mrs. Gore ordered Cheverus's portrait from Stuart, she apparently also commissioned a portrait of the minister of Trinity Church, the Reverend John S. Gardiner (unlocated), perhaps balancing her attachment to Cheverus with her regard for the leader of the church she actually attended (Mrs. Gore's husband held a pew at Trinity).[8] Reverend Gardiner delivered the eulogy for John Gore after his death in March 1817, and in it he charged Mrs. Gore never to forget that "favour is deceitful, and beauty is vain; but a woman that feareth the Lord, she shall be praised."[9] By commissioning portraits of clergymen, Mrs. Gore tended to a facet of her civic duties, extolling the virtues of two giants in Boston's religious circles and displaying the images in her home as proof of her respect for both Cheverus and Gardiner and for the two faiths they represented. Thus, she participated in what has recently been called "the wide-ranging antebellum phenomenon of Protestant audiences consuming images of Catholics."[10] Mrs. Gore allowed Stuart's portrait of Cheverus to be engraved and lithographed, published, and widely circulated.[11]

Mrs. Gore lent the portrait twice in the late 1820s to the Boston Athenaeum, first to the annual loan exhibition in 1827 and then to the memorial exhibition of Stuart's work in 1828. A reviewer of the 1828 show put the portrait at the top of a list of clergymen— "we have the heads of Bishop Cheverus, Doctors Kirkland, Gardiner, and Lathrop, Mr. Buckminster"—without distinction as to their denomination.[12] Those viewing the portrait at Mrs. Gore's home or at the Athenaeum could not mistake Cheverus's faith. Just as Stuart had painted Joseph Brant (cat. 17) with his large ceremonial gorget to make a visual connection between the exotic sitter and the English crown, in this instance the large gold cross marks Cheverus's Catholicism. Not just holding a Bible, as in so many portraits of religious figures from this era, Cheverus wears formal ecclesiastical garb pertinent to the ceremony of his church. The gold-embroidered cuffs of his gown show beneath his dark blue chasuble with crimson trim and detachable chevron collar. His right hand, on which he wears an episcopal ring, is poised in the act of benediction. For this sitter, the background drapery typical in the portrait tradition evokes a bishop's canopy. Stuart made a career of unambiguously presenting his sitters, but he rarely painted a portrait that made directness so alluring. Cheverus spent twenty-seven years inviting, but not pressing, Bostonian believers to join him in his faith, to explore their fascination with Catholicism. By Stuart's facile brush, he is an evangelist.

CRB

89

90. John Adams

1823–24

Oil on canvas, 30 x 25 in. (76.2 x 63.5 cm)

Museum of Fine Arts, Boston; Bequest of Charles Francis Adams (1999.590)

1. The portrait is discussed in Mason 1879, p. 125, as painted in 1825; Park 1926, p. 91, no. 4, as painted in 1823; Oliver 1967, pp. 188–201, 258–59, dated 1823; Evans 1999, pp. 100–103, 105–7. Laura Mills contributed to the research on this portrait.
2. John Quincy Adams, diary, August 25, 1823, Adams Papers, microfilm no. 37, Massachusetts Historical Society, Boston.
3. John Quincy Adams, diary, September 3, 1823, Adams Papers, microfilm no. 37, Massachusetts Historical Society, quoted in Oliver 1967, p. 188.
4. John Quincy Adams, diary, September 11, 1823, Adams Papers, microfilm no. 37, Massachusetts Historical Society, quoted in Oliver 1967, p. 188.
5. William Winston Seaton, unidentified 1823 letter, quoted in Whitley 1932, p. 172.
6. Charles Francis Adams, diary, September 9, 1824, in Aïda DiPace Donald and David Donald, eds., *Diary of Charles Francis Adams*, vol. 1, *January 1820–June 1825* (Cambridge, Mass.: Belknap Press of Harvard University Press, 1964), p. 318. He described Mrs. Thomas Lindall Winthrop (Elizabeth Bowdoin Temple) as "one of the Boston great ladies." Adams here referred to the portrait that Stuart painted of his father, John Quincy Adams, in 1818; see Andrew Oliver, *Portraits of John Quincy Adams and His Wife* (Cambridge, Mass.: Belknap Press of Harvard University Press, 1970), pp. 75–76. The portrait is now in the White House collection, Washington, D.C.
7. Charles Francis Adams, diary, September 22, 1824, in *Diary of Charles Francis Adams*, p. 331.
8. John Quincy Adams, diary, October 4, 1831, Adams Papers, microfilm no. 41, Massachusetts Historical Society, quoted in Oliver 1967, p. 201.
9. Quoted in Dunlap 1834, vol. 1, p. 165.
10. Charles Francis Adams, diary, September 22, 1824, in *Diary of Charles Francis Adams*, p. 331.
11. Josiah Quincy, *Figures of the Past from the Leaves of Old Journals* (Boston: Roberts Brothers, 1883), p. 83.

Stuart's last portrait of John Adams (1735–1826), second president of the United States, is one of his most memorable images.[1] When Adams's son John Quincy Adams commissioned the portrait, he was serving as President James Monroe's secretary of state in Washington, D.C. A visit with his father in Quincy, Massachusetts, at the end of August 1823, convinced him to commission the painting. Adams was "deeply affected" at meeting his father. "Within the two last years, since I had seen him, his eyesight has grown dim, and his limbs stiff and feeble. He is bowed with age, and scarcely can walk across a room without assistance."[2] Ten days later Adams "called . . . upon Stewart the Painter, and engaged him to go out to Quincy, and there paint a Portrait of my father—More than twenty years have passed since he painted the former portrait [cat. 59]; and time has wrought so much of change on his countenance that I wish to possess a likeness of him as he now is. Stewart started some objections, of trivial difficulties—The want of an Easel, of a room properly adapted to the light; but finally promised that he would go, and take with him his best brush, to paint a picture of Affection, and of curiosity for future times."[3] Adams went to his father's house again on September 11: "Stewart the Painter was there. My father had been sitting to him; and he told me that he would make a picture of it that should be admired as long as the materials would hold together."[4]

Completion of the portrait apparently took a full year. William Seaton, associate editor of the *National Intelligencer*, accompanied John Quincy Adams on the September 11, 1823, visit to Quincy and wrote that he found John Adams "sitting to the famous Stuart for his portrait, to be completed on his eighty-ninth birthday," that is, October 19, 1824.[5] John Quincy Adams's son Charles Francis Adams noted the final sitting in his diary in September 1824. On September 9, he recorded, "I was suddenly interrupted by Mrs. Winthrop and others who came in, to look at the portraits of my Grandfather and my father."[6] And on September 22, he wrote, "Mr. Stuart the painter came out here this morning for a final sitting for my Grandfather. I saw the portrait which is a remarkably fine one."[7] In 1831 John Quincy Adams recalled that the portrait "was painted at my special desire, about two years before my father's decease and when he was in his ninetieth year," which would have been 1824. "My purpose was to have a likeness of him in his last days by the first Painter in this Country. It has been a source of much gratification to me, that this was effected. The picture is an excellent likeness, and one of the best that Stewart ever painted."[8] Dr. Benjamin Waterhouse (see cat. 4) wrote in his memoirs that Stuart's "talents continued bright over three score years and ten: witness his portrait of the venerable President Adams, and that of his son John Quincy Adams, late President of these United States, in both of which Mr. Stuart far exceeded any other of his portraits. Vandyke himself might have been proud of either, especially that of the elder Adams."[9]

The portrait shows Adams seated in the corner of a sofa upholstered in red silk and edged with brass tacks. The curved arm and back of the sofa frame his frail body as he sits with crossed arms, his right hand on the top of a cane. While his face also shows his age in its softened features and wrinkled flesh, his rheumy blue eyes engage the viewer in a direct and intense exchange. Since he first painted Adams in 1800, Stuart's brushwork had softened, becoming less precise, and showing signs of a tremulous hand. However, he continued to use strong highlights and thin areas of shadow, with dark touches over light ones, as here, to convey volume and depth.

Fig. 179 *John Adams*, 1826. Oil on canvas, 30 x 25 in. (76.2 x 63.5 cm). Smithsonian American Art Museum, Washington, D.C.; Adams-Clement Collection, Gift of Mary Louisa Adams Clement in memory of her mother, Louisa Catherine Adams Clement

12. Ibid.
13. Washington Allston, "Obituary," *Columbian Centinel*, July 26, 1828, p. 1, dated July 17; reprinted from "The Late Mr. Stuart," *Boston Daily Advertiser*, July 22, 1828. Mason (1879, p. 33) reprinted the obituary (pp. 31–34), replacing the word "strength" with "thought."
14. John Quincy Adams, letter to his son George Washington Adams, November 19, 1826, Adams Papers, no. 478, Massachusetts Historical Society.
15. This portrait is described in Park 1926, p. 92, no. 6; Oliver 1967, pp. 192–93; Evans 1999, p. 107; Amy Pastan, *Young America: Treasures from the Smithsonian American Art Museum* (New York: Watson-Guptill Publications; Washington, D.C.: Smithsonian American Art Museum, 2000), pp. 94–95.

While Charles Francis Adams may have seen Stuart as "a singular man, a wag, but rather a disgusting object than otherwise,"[10] John Adams by contrast described the sittings to Josiah Quincy as a pleasant experience: "Speaking generally, . . . no penance is like having one's picture done. You must sit in a constrained and unnatural position, which is a trial to the temper. But I should like to sit to Stuart from the first of January to the last of December, for he lets me do just as I please and keeps me constantly amused by his conversation."[11] Quincy commented, "And this portrait is a remarkable work; for a faithful representation of the extreme age of the subject would have been painful in inferior hands. But Stuart caught a glimpse of the living spirit shining through the feeble and decrepit body. He saw the old man at one of those happy moments when the intelligence lights up the wasted envelope, and what he saw fixed upon his canvas."[12] American artist Washington Allston observed, "In his happier efforts, no one ever surpassed [Stuart] in embodying (if we may so speak) these transient apparitions of the soul. Of this not the least admirable instance is his Portrait (painted within the last four years) of the late President ADAMS whose then bodily tenement seemed rather to present the image of some dilapidated castle, than that of the habitation of the 'unbroken mind': but not such is the picture; called forth as from its crumbling recesses, the living tenant is there—still ennobling the ruin, and upholding it, as it were, by the strength of his own life. In this venerable ruin will the unbending Patriot and the gifted Artist speak to posterity of the first glorious century of our Republic."[13]

A few months after Adams's death on July 4, 1826, John Quincy Adams, now sixth president of the United States, commissioned Stuart to paint a "copy of that of my father," asking his son George Washington Adams to "send the copy of my father's Portrait, packed in the manner that Mr Stewart shall direct," to him in Washington.[14] The second version (fig. 179) is less searching and more emphatic, with some changes in the curve of the sofa, less texture in the upholstery, and less detail in the depiction of Adams's right hand. In 1829 John Quincy Adams gave the original to Charles Francis Adams, from whom it descended in the family to the last owner, also Charles Francis Adams, who bequeathed it to the Museum of Fine Arts, Boston, in 1999. The second version has belonged to the Smithsonian Institution since 1950, bequeathed by John Adams's descendant Mary Louisa Adams Clement.[15]

EGM

91. JOSIAH QUINCY

1824–25
Oil on canvas, 36⅛ x 28⅛ in. (91.8 x 71.4 cm)
Museum of Fine Arts, Boston; Gift of Miss Eliza Susan Quincy (76.347)

1. Robert A. McCaughey, *Josiah Quincy, 1772–1864: The Last Federalist* (Cambridge, Mass.: Harvard University Press, 1974); *ANB*, vol. 18, pp. 37–39; Matthew H. Crocker, *The Magic of the Many: Josiah Quincy and the Rise of Mass Politics in Boston, 1800–1830* (Amherst: University of Massachusetts Press, 1999); Michele M. Hilden, "The Mayors Josiah Quincy of Boston" (Ph.D. diss., Clark University, 1970).
2. See Stuart's portraits of William Phillips Jr. (Massachusetts General Hospital, Boston) and Quincy's relatives Philip J. Schuyler and his wife, Mary Ann Sawyer (both, New-York Historical Society).
3. Anna Cabot Lowell, letter to Eliza Susan Quincy, January 24, 1807, Anna Cabot Lowell Papers, Massachusetts Historical Society, Boston.
4. Josiah Quincy, *Figures of the Past from the Leaves of Old Journals* (Boston: Roberts Brothers, 1883), p. 83.
5. Eliza Susan Quincy, letter to Jane Stuart, September 20, 1876, George Champlin Mason Papers, file of Eliza Quincy's letters, Manuscripts Division, Rhode Island Historical Society, Providence. See also Eliza Susan Quincy's letters to George Champlin Mason (Mason Papers, Rhode Island Historical Society), August 10, September 9, 16, 1876, in which she also states this information; and Eliza Susan Quincy, letter to the trustees of the Museum of Fine Arts, Boston, June 2, 1876, Museum of Fine Arts archives, in which she donates the portrait to the museum and describes some of its history. Evans (1999, p. 42) draws the conclusion from Miss Quincy's description of Stuart's method of drawing in chalk that the artist prepared for Quincy's sitting by doing preliminary work from a cast. Depending upon how one interprets Miss Quincy's letter of September 20, 1876, Stuart either had the chalk drawing on the canvas before Quincy arrived, or he began it during the first sitting. There is no mention of use of a cast and no evidence that a cast of Quincy ever existed.

Born into a distinguished familiy of Bostonians, Josiah Quincy (1772–1864) lost his father in 1775 and was raised by his mother, Abigail Phillips Quincy, and his grandfathers, Colonel Josiah Quincy and William Phillips Sr.[1] Quincy studied law at Harvard College and was admitted to the Massachusetts bar in 1793 before entering politics as a Federalist. Narrowly defeated in his bids for a congressional seat in 1800 and 1802, he was elected in 1804 and remained in Washington for two terms. He next served as state senator, pushing agricultural progress and urban renewal, and then as a judge in the Municipal Court of Boston during the period of the city's incorporation. He was elected the second mayor of Boston in 1823 and served for five years, during which time he actively pursued such civic improvements as regular trash removal, establishing a fire department, developing the House of Industry, Correction, and Juvenile Reform, and cracking down on prostitution. In 1829, Quincy became one of a long line of distinguished presidents of Harvard; he remained there—cherished by the administration if not by the students, who found his methods severe—until he retired in 1845 at the age of seventy-three. By then Boston's new major was his son Josiah Quincy Jr.

Quincy and his wife, Eliza Susan Morton, sat for Stuart in Boston during the 1806 congressional recess, and they were followed in rapid succession by several relations.[2] The handsome pendant portraits of Quincy and his wife (figs. 180, 181) remained in Boston while Quincy shuttled back and forth to Washington. Anna Cabot Lowell wrote to Eliza Quincy in January 1807, "Your picture . . . has been a most interesting companion to us all for some weeks, my mother is delighted with it, and thinks the likeness incomparable. Every body who comes in is struck with it."[3] Quincy, who enjoyed the company of artists and had some knowledge of art history, liked Stuart's method of engaging his sitter: "[B]y his wonderful powers of conversation, he would call up different emotions in the face he was studying. He chose the best, or that which he thought most characteristic, and with the skill of genius used it to animate the picture."[4] At some point, Quincy purchased a portrait of George Washington that Stuart had in his studio (Museum of Fine Arts, Boston).

In late 1824 Quincy sat for Stuart again for a new portrait as a gift for his daughter, Eliza Susan Quincy, who later recalled, "The rest of Mr. Quincy's family were satisfied with the portrait . . . painted by Mr. Stuart in 1806, but I thought there ought to be another at the age of fifty-two years. He complied with my request . . . & in November 1824 I accompanied him to the house of Mr. Stuart in Essex Street Boston. He was gratified that Mr. Quincy in the midst of his engagements as Mayor, was willing to give him time for a portrait. His canvas was ready on his easel a bold outline was sketched in chalk & while conversing rapidly Mr. Stuart began to put on his colors, apparently at random, but of course every touch told."[5] Stuart worked on the portrait into the following year and possibly the next, with Quincy repeatedly in the studio and Stuart in his home as a guest. At the time, Quincy was preoccupied with a project to revitalize the area between Long Wharf and the town dock. With the help of architect Alexander Parris, Quincy planned to fill in much of the site and build new streets and three new market buildings, the center one a templelike structure. The complex, which would open in the summer of 1826, was called Quincy Market. According to Quincy's daughter, Stuart understood her father's passion for the project and decided to feature it in the portrait. She recalled that Stuart told her, "Mr Quincy likes to be in the open air, I am

91

Fig. 180. *Eliza Susan Morton Quincy*, 1806. Oil on wood, 30⅞ x 24¾ in. (78.4 x 62.9 cm). Milwaukee Art Museum, Milwaukee, Wis.; Layton Art Collection (L1990.9) (photo: Larry Saunders)

Fig. 181. *Josiah Quincy*, 1806. Oil on wood, 30¼ x 24½ in. (76.8 x 62.2 cm). Fine Arts Museums of San Francisco; Memorial Gift from Dr. T. Edward and Tullah Hanley, Bradford, Pa. (69.30.195)

not going to shut him up in a room.—I chuse to have a view of the market he is building in the background of the picture & his hand across the door, to show he has a hand in it."[6] The mayor sits against a blue sky as though near a window in Fanueil Hall overlooking the west facade of the central market building; he holds a plan of the complex. For the background of the portrait, Stuart could have used a print source or may have had someone draw the building for him, as he had done in his portrait of William Smith (cat. 61). This would explain the difference in handling between the softy focused, loose treatment of Quincy's head and the tight delineation of the building facade.

Mary Tyler Peabody Mann, who spent a day in late January visiting artist's studios in Boston, reported to her friend Rawlins Pickman that she had seen the unfinished portrait of Quincy at Stuart's.[7] Washington Allston saw the portrait in Stuart's studio about May 1825 and remarked that "the head was worthy of the old masters," eliciting from Stuart a quip, "And am not I an old master?"[8] John Neagle recalled that he studied the portrait of Quincy in July and August 1825 to guide him in his own efforts to paint a picture of Stuart (see fig. 4). Stuart walked in on Neagle with the two portraits side by side and scolded him. Neagle thought Stuart was bothered that he had not asked permission to move the picture of Quincy for his own purposes, but Stuart was annoyed that Neagle was copying in order to learn. "Does my face look like Mr. Quincy's?" Stuart asked. Neagle responded that he "was in hope of catching something from the work of the master without imitating it," which prompted the master to advise Neagle to "paint what you see, and look with your own eyes."[9]

CRB

6. Eliza Susan Quincy, letter to George Champlin Mason, September 25, 1878, Mason Papers, file of Eliza Quincy's letters, Rhode Island Historical Society.
7. Mary Tyler Peabody Mann, letter to Rawlins Pickman, January 27, 1825, Horace Mann Papers, microfilm reel 37, Massachusetts Historical Society.
8. Eliza Susan Quincy, letter to Jane Stuart, September 20, 1876, Mason Papers, file of Eliza Quincy's letters, Rhode Island Historical Society.
9. Neagle, quoted in Dunlap 1834, vol. 1, p. 216.

92. Lydia Pickering Williams

1824

Oil on canvas, 36 x 28 in. (91.4 x 71.1 cm)

Collection of Mary Elizabeth Sears Baring-Gould

1. "Died . . . on Thursday morning . . . Mrs. Lydia Williams, 89," *Boston Daily Advertiser*, October 25, 1824. Her portrait is listed in Mason 1879, p. 278; Park 1926, pp. 816–17, no. 913.
2. "Deaths: At Salem—George Williams, Esq. AEt. 65," *Boston Gazette and Weekly Republican Journal*, June 19, 1797.
3. Their children were Samuel, Henry, Lydia (m. Theodore Lyman), Timothy, Mary (m. William Pratt), John, Stephen (m. Alice Orne), Elizabeth (m. Moses Litle), Francis, Anna (m. Loammi Baldwin), and Charles. See Harrison Ellery and Charles P. Bowditch, *The Pickering Genealogy: Being an account of the first three generations of the Pickering family of Salem, Mass. and of the descendants of John and Sarah (Burrill) Pickering of the third generation* (Cambridge: University Press, 1897), pp. 119–21.
4. Evelyn Sears (great-great-granddaughter of the sitter), letter to Sarah Bullock, January 15, 1864, curatorial files, Museum of Fine Arts, Boston: "I have the letter of Mrs. Williams written to her 2

In 1824, at the eminent age of eighty-nine, Lydia Pickering Williams (1736–1824) sat for Stuart. She was the painter's oldest female client, and he captured her likeness just in time, for she died that October.[1] The daughter of Timothy and Mary Wingate Pickering of Salem, she married George Williams, a Baltimore shipmaster and merchant to whom the traits of prudence, economy, perseverance, and enterprise were ascribed.[2] They raised a family of eleven children before his death in 1797; she then moved to Boston.[3]

According to family history, her sons Samuel and Charles prevailed upon her to have Stuart paint her portrait in the interest of posterity.[4] They both resided in London and knew Stuart from their earlier years in Boston and through their friendships with Washington Allston (see cat. 88) and Stuart's nephew the painter Gilbert Stuart Newton. Samuel Williams had purchased Stuart's full-length portrait of George Washington at the Marquis of Lansdowne's estate sale in 1806, and in 1823 Stuart sent the new owner a letter he had from Washington agreeing to an appointment for a sitting (see "The Portraits of George Washington" and cat. 45). The Williams sons apparently had the portrait of their mother shipped to them right after it was finished. The artist Chester Harding, also in London, wrote to his wife about seeing Stuart's portrait of Mrs. Williams in December 1824 and January 1825.[5]

Mrs. Williams's younger brother Timothy Pickering had sat for Stuart in 1808 (fig. 182). His son Henry established a cordial relationship with Stuart, and he interviewed the artist in 1810 and several times in 1817,[6] when he also persuaded his own mother, Rebecca White Pickering (fig. 183), to sit for Stuart. Rebecca Pickering had not sat with her husband in 1808, objecting "that she was too old, & that in a few years, the portrait would be transferred by her grand children to the garret," but her son prevailed. Stuart promised to enchant her by saying, "Madame, do you imagine that every year

Fig. 182. *Timothy Pickering*, September 1808. Oil on canvas, 28 x 22½ in. (71.1 x 57.2 cm). Peabody Essex Museum, Salem, Mass.

Fig. 183. *Rebecca White Pickering*, 1817. Oil on wood, 31¼ x 24½ in. (79.4 x 62.2 cm). Carnegie Museum of Art, Pittsburgh; private collection: lent by Mrs. Richard Y. Fitzgerald and Mrs. Walter D. Pederson (79.1)

92

sons in London, who had asked for her portrait. It is in Waltham or I should like to have shown that to you also." The letter from Mrs. Williams to her sons is now unlocated.

5. Park (1926, p. 815) records that the portrait Harding saw was of Mrs. Cumberland D. Williams.

6. Pickering 1810 and 1817.

7. Pickering 1817 (October 20).

8. The unfinished portraits are in the New Orleans Museum of Art and the Museum of Fine Arts, Boston. M. C. Otis, letter to George Champlin Mason, November 16, no year given, and Mary Pratt, letter to Mason, July 29, no year, George Champlin Mason Papers, file P, Manuscripts Division, Rhode Island Historical Society, Providence.

9. *American Paintings in the Museum of Fine Arts, Boston* (Boston: Distributed by New York Graphic Society, Greenwich, Conn., 1969), p. 257. See also notes from Dorinda Evans, May 30, 1989, curatorial files, Museum of Fine Arts, Boston.

which is added to your life, diminishes my affection for you? And that because you have not now the bloom of youth, I must cease to love you?"[7] For Lydia Williams, Stuart painted a respectfully candid image, as he had for her sister-in-law. The soft focus on Mrs. Williams's face is countered by the extraordinary crispness of her lace cap and sheer muslin fichu. Hers is an image of modest serenity, with piercing dark eyes that seem to have witnessed much.

Stuart began three portraits of Mrs. Williams, two of which were left unfinished on her death. He was not averse to replicating his own work on commission—there are numerous instances of this. The two unfinished portraits bolster the notion that he quickly sent the completed portrait to Samuel and Charles Williams in London. Family members collected the other two versions, for all three portraits have family provenances into the twentieth century.[8] In one, Stuart finished the face, blocked in the background drapery as an outline for the figure, and sketched in oil the salient features of the composition. The other was probably finished to a similar degree, and the costume and background were completed by another artist. Stuart's daughter Jane produced a copy of this image for yet another member of the Williams family.[9]

CRB

Selected Bibliography and Frequently Cited Sources

ANB
American National Biography. General editors, John A. Garraty, Mark C. Carnes. New York: Oxford University Press, 1999–.

Boston 1828
Catalogue of an Exhibition of Portraits, Painted by the Late Gilbert Stuart, Esq. Exh. cat., Boston Athenaeum. Boston: Eastburn, 1828.

Boston 1880
Exhibition of Portraits Painted by Gilbert Stuart. Exh. cat., Museum of Fine Arts, Boston. Boston: Alfred Mudge and Son, printers, 1880.

Boston 1965
The Copley Society Loan Exhibition 1965: A New Look at Gilbert Stuart. Exh. brochure. Boston, 1965.

Boston 1976
Copley, Stuart, West in America and England. Exh. cat. Boston: Museum of Fine Arts, 1976.

Crean 1990
Crean, Hugh R. "Gilbert Stuart and the Politics of Fine Arts Patronage in Ireland, 1787–1793: A Social and Cultural Study." Ph.D. diss., City University of New York, 1990.

DAB
Dictionary of American Biography. Edited by Allen Johnson, Dumas Malone, et al. New York: Charles Scribner's Sons, 1928–.

Davis 2001
Davis, John. "Catholic Envy: The Visual Culture of Protestant Desire." In David Morgan and Sally M. Promey, eds. *The Visual Culture of American Religions*, pp. 105–28. Berkeley: University of California Press, 2001.

DeLorme 1979a
DeLorme, Eleanor Pearson. "Gilbert Stuart: Portrait of an Artist." *Winterthur Portfolio* 14 (winter 1979), pp. 339–60.

DeLorme 1979b
DeLorme, Eleanor Pearson. "The Swan Commissions: Four Portraits by Gilbert Stuart." *Winterthur Portfolio* 14 (winter 1979), pp. 361–95.

DNB
Dictionary of National Biography. Edited by Leslie Stephen and Sidney Lee, 1921–22; reprint, London: Oxford University Press, 1963–65.

Downes 1929
Downes, William Howe. "The Gilbert Stuart Exhibition in Boston." *American Magazine of Art* 20 (January 1929), p. 16.

Dunlap 1831
Dunlap, William. "Biographical Sketch of Gilbert Stewart." *Euterpeiad: An Album of Music, Poetry, and Prose* 2 (March 15, 1831), p. 223.

Dunlap 1834
Dunlap, William. *History of the Rise and Progress of the Arts of Design in the United States.* 2 vols. New York: George C. Scott and Co., printers, 1834.

Eisen 1932
Eisen, Gustavus A., assisted by C. J. Dearden. *Portraits of Washington.* Vol. 1, *Portraits in Oil Painted by Gilbert Stuart.* New York: R. Hamilton, 1932.

Evans 1984
Evans, Dorinda. "Gilbert Stuart: Two Recent Discoveries." *American Art Journal* 16 (summer 1984), pp. 84–99.

Evans 1999
Evans, Dorinda. *The Genius of Gilbert Stuart.* Princeton, N.J.: Princeton University Press, 1999.

Evans 2004
Evans, Dorinda. "Gilbert Stuart and Manic Depression: Redefining His Artistic Range." *American Art* 18 (spring 2004), pp. 10–31.

Fielding 1914
Fielding, Mantle. "Paintings by Gilbert Stuart Not Mentioned in Mason's Life of Stuart." *Pennsylvania Magazine of History and Biography* 38 (July 1914), pp. 311–34.

Fielding 1920
Fielding, Mantle. "Addenda and Corrections to Paintings by Gilbert Stuart Not Noted in Mason's Life of Stuart." *Pennsylvania Magazine of History and Biography* 44 (January 1920), pp. 88–91.

Fielding 1923
Fielding, Mantle. *Gilbert Stuart's Portraits of George Washington.* Philadelphia: Printed for the subscribers, 1923.

Fielding 1929
Fielding, Mantle. "Portraits by Gilbert Stuart Not Included in Previous Catalogues of His Works." *Pennsylvania Magazine of History and Biography* 53 (April 1929), pp. 132–36.

Flexner 1955a
Flexner, James Thomas. *Gilbert Stuart: A Great Life in Brief.* New York: Alfred A. Knopf, 1955.

Flexner 1955b
Flexner, James Thomas. "Gilbert Stuart, 'Primitive.'" *Antiques* 67 (March 1955), pp. 223–35.

George Washington 2002
George Washington: A National Treasure. Foreword by Marc Pachter; introduction by Richard Brookhiser; essays by Margaret C. S. Christman and Ellen G. Miles. Washington, D.C.: National Portrait Gallery, Smithsonian Institution, in association with the University of Washington Press, Seattle, 2002.

Harris 1964
Harris, Paul S. "Gilbert Stuart and a Portrait of Mrs. Sarah Apthorp Morton." *Winterthur Portfolio* 1 (1964), pp. 198–220.

Hart 1880
Hart, Charles Henry. "The Stuart Exhibition at the Museum of Fine Arts, Boston." *American Art Review* 1, no. 2 (1880), pp. 484–87.

Herbert 1836
Herbert, John Dowling. *Irish Varieties, for the Last Fifty Years: Written from Recollections.* London: William Joy, 1836.

Indianapolis 1941
Retrospective Exhibition of Portraits by Gilbert Stuart, 1755–1828. Exh. cat. Indianapolis: John Herron Art Museum, Art Association of Indianapolis, 1941.

Jouett 1816
"Notes Taken by M. H. Jouett while in Boston from Conve[r]sations on painting with Gilbert Stuart Esqr." In Morgan 1939, pp. 81–93.

Mason 1879
Mason, George C[hamplin]. *The Life and Works of Gilbert Stuart.* New York: Charles Scribner's Sons, 1879.

McLanathan 1986
McLanathan, Richard. *Gilbert Stuart.* New York: Harry N. Abrams with the National Museum of American Art, Smithsonian Institution, Washington, D.C., 1986.

Meschutt 1981
Meschutt, David. "Gilbert Stuart's Portraits of Thomas Jefferson." *American Art Journal* 13 (winter 1981), pp. 2–16.

Meschutt 1999
Meschutt, David. "Gilbert Stuart." In *ANB*, vol. 21, pp. 69–72.

Miles 1995
Miles, Ellen G., with contributions by Patricia Burda, Cynthia J. Mills, and Leslie K. Reinhardt. *American Paintings of the Eighteenth Century.* The Collections of the National Gallery of Art: Systematic Catalogue. Washington, D.C.: National Gallery of Art, 1995.

Miles 1999
Miles, Ellen G. *George and Martha Washington: Portraits from the Presidential Years.* Exh. cat. Washington, D.C.: Smithsonian Institution, National Portrait Gallery, in association with the University Press of Virginia, Charlottesville, 1999.

Morgan 1934
Morgan, John Hill. "The Date of Stuart's Death, the Place of His Burial, and the Inventory of His Estate." *Antiques* 25 (March 1934), pp. 90–92.

Morgan 1939
Morgan, John Hill. *Gilbert Stuart and His Pupils: Together with the Complete Notes on Painting by Matthew Harris Jouett from Conversations with Gilbert Stuart in 1816.* New York: New-York Historical Society, 1939.

Morgan and Fielding 1931
Morgan, John Hill, and Mantle Fielding. *The Life Portraits of Washington and Their Replicas.* Philadelphia: Printed for the subscribers, 1931.

Mount 1963
Mount, Charles Merrill. "The Irish Career of Gilbert Stuart." *Quarterly Bulletin of the Irish Georgian Society* 6 (January–March 1963), pp. 6–28.

Mount 1964
Mount, Charles Merrill. *Gilbert Stuart: A Biography.* New York: W. W. Norton and Co., 1964.

Mount 1971–72
Mount, Charles Merrill. "Gilbert Stuart in Washington: With a Catalogue of His Portraits Painted between December 1803 and July 1805." *Records of the Columbia Historical Society of Washington, D.C.* 48 (1971–72), pp. 81–127.

Novak 1967
Novak O'Doherty, Barbara. "Philosopher of the Face." *Art News* 66 (summer 1967), pp. 43–45.

Oliver 1967
Oliver, Andrew. *Portraits of John and Abigail Adams.* The Adams Papers, L. H. Butterfield, ed.; ser. 4, Portraits. Cambridge, Mass.: Belknap Press of Harvard University Press, 1967.

Park 1926
Park, Lawrence. *Gilbert Stuart: An Illustrated Descriptive List of His Works, with an Account of His Life by John Hill Morgan and an Appreciation by Royal Cortissoz.* 4 vols. New York: William Edwin Rudge, 1926.

Payne 1948
Payne, Elizabeth H. "An Early Portrait by Gilbert Stuart." *Bulletin of the Detroit Institute of Arts* 28, no. 1 (1948), pp. 19–23.

Pickering 1810, 1817
Pickering, Henry. "Account of an Interview with Mr. Stuart: Interview with Mr. Stuart, November 17, 1810"; "Conversations with Mr. Stuart the Painter: August 19th, 1817—Interview with Mr. Stuart"; "October 4, 1817"; "October 20, 1817"; "Wednesday October 29, 1817"; "Nov. 4, 1817"; "Nov. 10, 1817"; "Dec. 8, 1817." Manuscript, Henry Pickering Papers, Pickering Foundation, Salem, Mass.; on deposit at the Phillips Library, Peabody Essex Museum, Salem, Mass. (Ms. 0.608)

Powel 1920
Powel, Mary E. "Miss Jane Stuart, 1812–1888: Her Grandparents and Parents." *Bulletin of the Newport Historical Society* 31 (January 1920), pp. 1–16.

Pressly 1986
Pressly, William L. "Gilbert Stuart's 'The Skater': An Essay in Romantic Melancholy." *American Art Journal* 18, no. 1 (1986), pp. 43–51.

Rather 1993
Rather, Susan. "Stuart and Reynolds: A Portrait of Challenge." *Eighteenth-Century Studies* 27 (fall 1993), pp. 61–84.

Richardson 1970
Richardson, E[dgar] P. "China Trade Portraits of Washington after Stuart." *Pennsylvania Magazine of History and Biography* 94 (January 1970), pp. 95–100.

Saunders and Miles 1987
Saunders, Richard H., and Ellen G. Miles. *American Colonial Portraits 1700–1776.* Exh. cat., National Portrait Gallery. Washington, D.C.: Smithsonian Institution Press, 1987.

Sawitzky 1932–33
Sawitzky, William. "Some Unrecorded Portraits by Gilbert Stuart." *Art in America* 21 (1932–33). "Part One: Portraits Painted in England" (December 1932), pp. 15–27; "Part Two: Portraits Painted in Ireland" (March 1933), pp. 38–48; "Part Three: Portraits Painted in America" (June 1933), pp. 81–93.

"Stuart" 1931
"The Editor's Attic: Stuart, Doggett, and Some Others." *Antiques* 20 (July 1931), pp. 11–13.

G. Stuart 1861
"Remarks on Art: By Gilbert Stuart, 1816." *The Crayon* 8 (March 1861), pp. 49–50.

J. Stuart 1876
Stuart, Jane. "The Stuart Portraits of Washington." *Scribner's Monthly* 12 (July 1876), pp. 367–74.

J. Stuart 1877a
Stuart, Jane. "The Youth of Gilbert Stuart." *Scribner's Monthly* 13 (March 1877), pp. 640–46.

J. Stuart 1877b
Stuart, Jane. "Anecdotes of Gilbert Stuart." *Scribner's Monthly* 14 (July 1877), pp. 376–82.

Swan 1936
Swan, Mabel Munson. "Gilbert Stuart in Boston." *Antiques* 29 (February 1936), pp. 65–67.

Swan 1938
Swan, Mabel Munson. "Paging Gilbert Stuart in Boston." *Antiques* 34 (December 1938), pp. 308–9.

Swan 1953
Swan, Mabel Munson. "'Scraps'—The Missing Waterhouse Biography of Gilbert Stuart." *Art in America* 41 (spring 1953), pp. 88–91.

Tuckerman 1870
Tuckerman, Henry T. *Book of the Artists: American Artist Life Comprising Biographical and Critical Sketches of American Artists, Preceded by an Historical Account of the Rise and Progress of Art in America.* 1867; 2nd ed., New York: G. P. Putnam and Son, 1870.

Verheyen 1989
Verheyen, Egon. "'The most exact representation of the Original': Remarks on Portraits of George Washington by Gilbert Stuart and Rembrandt Peale." *Retaining the Original: Multiple Originals, Copies, and Reproductions*, pp. 127–39. Center for Advanced Study in the Visual Arts, Symposium Papers VII, Studies in the History of Art 20. Washington, D.C.: National Gallery of Art, 1989.

Von Erffa and Staley 1986
Von Erffa, Helmut, and Allen Staley. *The Paintings of Benjamin West.* New Haven: Yale University Press, 1986.

Washington, Providence 1967
Gilbert Stuart: Portraitist of the Young Republic, 1755–1828. Exh. cat., essay by E. P. Richardson. Washington, D.C.: National Gallery of Art; Providence: Rhode Island School of Design, 1967.

Waterhouse "Autobiography"
Waterhouse, Benjamin. "Autobiography," n.d. Ms. HMS c.17.5. Rare Books and Special Collections, Francis A. Countway Library of Medicine, Harvard Medical School, Boston.

Whitley 1932
Whitley, William T. *Gilbert Stuart.* Cambridge, Mass.: Harvard University Press, 1932.

Wick 1982
Wick (Reaves), Wendy C. *George Washington, an American Icon: The Eighteenth-Century Graphic Portraits.* Exh. cat. Washington, D.C.: Smithsonian Institution Traveling Exhibition Service; National Portrait Gallery, Smithsonian Institution, 1982.

Index

Page references to illustrations are in *italics*.